THE LAW OF KINSHIP

THE LAW
OF KINSHIP

ANTHROPOLOGY, PSYCHOANALYSIS,
AND THE FAMILY IN FRANCE

CAMILLE ROBCIS

CORNELL UNIVERSITY PRESS
Ithaca and London

This book has been published with the aid of a grant from the Hull Memorial Publication Fund of Cornell University.

Copyright © 2013 by Cornell University

All rights reserved. Except for brief quotations in a review, this book, or parts thereof, must not be reproduced in any form without permission in writing from the publisher. For information, address Cornell University Press, Sage House, 512 East State Street, Ithaca, New York 14850.

First published 2013 by Cornell University Press
First printing, Cornell Paperbacks, 2013

Printed in the United States of America

Library of Congress Cataloging-in-Publication Data

Robcis, Camille.
   The law of kinship : anthropology, psychoanalysis, and the family in France / Camille Robcis.
       p. cm.
   Includes bibliographical references and index.
   ISBN 978-0-8014-5129-4 (cloth : alk. paper) —
   ISBN 978-0-8014-7877-2 (pbk. : alk. paper)
   1. Family policy—France.   2. Sex role—Government policy—France.   3. Families—France—Philosophy.
   4. Domestic relations—France—Philosophy.
   5. Psychoanalysis and anthropology—France.
   6. Lévi-Strauss, Claude—Influence.   7. Lacan, Jacques, 1901–1981—Influence.   I. Title.
   HQ624.R63 2013
   306.850944—dc23
                                                      2012039150

Cornell University Press strives to use environmentally responsible suppliers and materials to the fullest extent possible in the publishing of its books. Such materials include vegetable-based, low-VOC inks and acid-free papers that are recycled, totally chlorine-free, or partly composed of nonwood fibers. For further information, visit our website at www.cornellpress.cornell.edu.

Cloth printing   10 9 8 7 6 5 4 3 2 1
Paperback printing   10 9 8 7 6 5 4 3 2 1

For Milena

It has become common—and even encouraged—to present kinship as the dinosaur of the social sciences. Those who make this claim are clueless. Kinship is indeed a dinosaur within the social sciences, but not in the sense that it belongs to the past! It is a dinosaur in the sense that "it is here," in an instrumental way, that it poses authentic problems. Until we understand how kinship figures at the heart of the social bond, it is difficult to see how we can access the intelligibility of the political or the economic, to mention only these two domains.

Françoise Héritier, "Regards au loin et alentour, entretien avec Georges Guille-Escuret."

☙ CONTENTS

Acknowledgments	*ix*
List of Abbreviations	*xiii*
Introduction	1
PART ONE: THE RISE OF FAMILIALISM	15
1. Familialism and the Republican Social Contract	17
2. Kinship and the Structuralist Social Contract	61
3. The Circulation of Structuralism in the French Public Sphere	102
PART TWO: THE CRITIQUE OF FAMILIALISM	141
4. The "Quiet Revolution" in Family Policy and Family Law	143
5. Fatherless Societies and Anti-Oedipal Philosophies	168
PART THREE: THE RETURN OF FAMILIALISM	211
6. Alternative Kinships and Republican Structuralism	213
Epilogue: Kinship, Ethics, and the Nation	262
Bibliography	*267*
Index	*287*

✒ ACKNOWLEDGMENTS

This project began as a reflection on alternative models of kinship, on the possibilities and limits of choosing one's kin, and imagining new modes of social, political, and intellectual belonging that could accommodate change and critique. The greatest reward of finishing this book is to realize how the community that has accompanied me in this process exemplifies the kind of kinship model that I was originally interested in. I am grateful to my mentors, colleagues, friends, and students, who have consistently pushed me to question all assumptions, think harder, and be clearer. This book is the product of long-standing conversations with each of them.

Several people were essential in shepherding this project in its early stages: Dominick LaCapra, whose generosity, dedication, and ethical and intellectual rigor never cease to amaze me; Steve Kaplan, who taught me so much about French history; and Tracy McNulty who guided me through Lacan's writings and who remained an incredible advocate despite disagreeing with me on so many occasions. Carolyn Dean got me thinking about French universalism and difference in the first place and inspired me to become a historian. Len Tennenhouse, Nancy Armstrong, Mary Ann Doane, Elizabeth Weed, and Neil Lazarus taught me how to think critically. So many of the ideas in this book emerged from discussions I had with Éric Fassin, Michel Feher, and Michel Tort. Beth Povinelli and Lou Roberts were critical in helping me reconceptualize the book manuscript. Joan Scott agreed to read my work when she barely knew me and she has since then consistently pushed me to refine and attune my arguments.

Cornell was an amazing school to attend as a graduate student and has been an even more amazing place to work. The history department has provided me with endless encouragement, support, and engagement. For their friendship and their feedback on these chapters, I am especially grateful to Vicki Caron, Holly Case, Duane Corpis, Durba Ghosh, Sandra Greene, Itsie Hull, Dan Magaziner, Mary-Beth Norton, Barry Strauss, Eric Tagliacozzo, Robert Travers, Claudia Verhoeven, and Rachel Weil. Outside the history department, several colleagues and friends have been absolutely essential

x   **ACKNOWLEDGMENTS**

in making daily life in Ithaca stimulating and delightful: Jeremy Braddock, Jason Frank, Becky Givan, Jerry Johnson, Rayna Kalas, Jenny Mann, Judith Peraino, Lucinda Ramberg, Masha Raskolnikov, and Amy Villarejo.

I was lucky to spend a year at the University of Pennsylvania Humanities Forum as a postdoctoral fellow and another at Princeton University as a fellow in the Program in Law and Public Affairs (LAPA). The year at Penn allowed me to distill the main argument for the book, and I could not have done this without the help of a wonderful group of people who happened to convene in Philadelphia that year: Emma Bianchi, Warren Breckman, Judith Brown, Virginia Chang, and David Kazanjian. David Eng deserves a special thank you for working through most of these ideas with me, for giving me the title for the book, and most importantly for being such a generous and brilliant friend. The LAPA fellowship provided me with a much needed leave to finish the book. I am grateful to Kim Scheppele, Leslie Gerwin, the LAPA staff, and my fellow fellows for making that year so great. Also at Princeton, I thank John Borneman, Peter Brooks, and Philip Nord for their sustained engagement with my work. Once again, I benefited from geography and was fortunate to coincide with Elizabeth Bernstein, Wendy Chun, Ruben Gallo, Terence Gower, Dagmar Herzog, Amy Kaplan, Karuna Mantena, Gayle Salamon, and Judith Surkis in Princeton that year.

Preliminary versions of these chapters were presented at various institutions. I am thankful to my hosts and to the audiences who urged me to clarify several key points: Cornell's European History Colloquium, the Society for French Historical Studies, the Penn Humanities Forum, the Gender and Sexuality Works in Progress Seminar, New York University's Institute of French Studies, the Law & Humanities Colloquium at the Cornell Law School, Williams College, the New York Group in European Intellectual and Cultural History, the New School, and Princeton's LAPA seminar and its Modern European Workshop. Thank you especially to the organizers of these events: David Bell, Ed Berenson, Federico Finchelstein, Stefanos Geroulanos, Heather Love, Bernie Meyler, Sam Moyn, Joel Revill, Jerry Seigel, and Frédéric Viguier.

This book would not have been possible without the financial support of the following institutions: the Institute for European Studies Luigi Einaudi Research Fellowship; the Social Science Research Council (SSRC) International Dissertation Field Research Fellowship; the Society for French Historical Studies John B. and Theta H. Wolf Travel Fellowship; and the Phi Beta Kappa Society Mary Isabel Sibley Research Fellowship. I am equally grateful to the libraries and archives that opened their doors to me: the Bibliothèque nationale de France, the Archives Nationales, the Archives

ACKNOWLEDGMENTS   xi

Françoise Dolto, the Institut mémoires de l'édition contemporaine (IMEC), the Archives contemporaines d'Indre-et-Loire, the Union nationale des associations familiales, the Centre de documentation at Sciences-Po, the Bibliothèque du Cedias at the Musée social, and the libraries of Cornell University, Columbia University, New York University, the University of Pennsylvania, and Princeton University.

John Ackerman at Cornell University Press has endorsed this project from the beginning and was able to see how the various parts of the book fit together even before I did. I am also extremely grateful to the two anonymous reviewers solicited by the press and for their thorough, generous, and engaged reports. Thank you to Anna Maria Maiolino for allowing me to use her beautiful piece for the cover of this book. Portions of Chapter 6 were published as "French Sexual Politics from Human Rights to the Anthropological Function of the Law," in *French Historical Studies* 33, no. 1 (Winter 2010): 129–56, and as "How the Symbolic Became French: Kinship and Republicanism in the PACS Debates," in *Discourse* 26, no. 3 (Fall 2004): 110–35. I thank Duke University Press and Wayne State University Press for allowing me to republish these materials.

Finally, I would like to acknowledge my family and my friends from Brown, Cornell, Paris, New York, and beyond who have enriched my life in more ways than I can explain: Alexis Agathocleous, Tanya Agathocleous, Anton Aparin, Tarek el-Ariss, Will Bishop, Xochitl Calderón, Julie Coe, Charly Coleman, Gloria Deitcher, Rossana Fuentes-Berain, Marcela Fuentes-Berain, Ben Kafka, Rachel Kleinman, Rose-Ellen Lessy, Amy McFarlane, Mark Miller, Thierry Nazzi, Maria Ospina, Simon Parra, Stephanie Pope, Patricia Reyes Spíndola, Sebastien Robcis, Beatriz Saucedo, Ruti Talmor, Caterina Toscano, Karen Tongson, Francesca Trivalleto, Heidi Voskhul, and Althea Wasow. Judith Surkis and Todd Shepard have read every page of this book, multiple times. My thanks also to David Lichtenstein for showing me the limits of theory and for always knowing what to say and what to not say. My parents, Henri Robcis and Sandra Fuentes-Berain, tracked down obscure books, collected newspaper clippings on family-related issues, and engaged me in endless debates. Their enduring trust, love, and support are the greatest gifts. Yael Kropsky has lived with this book as long as I have, and I am so grateful for her love and for the joy of imagining and practicing kinship otherwise.

⌘ ABBREVIATIONS

ANCD	Alliance nationale contre la dépopulation
ANIAS	Association nationale de l'insémination artificielle par substitution
CAPR	Comité d'action pédérastique révolutionnaire
CCNE	Comité consultatif national d'éthique
CDP	Centre démocratie et progrès
CECOS	Centres d'étude et de conservation des œufs et du sperme humains
CERFI	Centre d'études, de recherches et de formation institutionnelle
CFLN	Comité français de la Libération nationale
CFTC	Confédération française des travailleurs chrétiens
CGF	Commissariat général à la famille
CGT-FO	Confédération générale du travail-force ouvrière
CNAF	Caisse nationale des allocations familiales
CNR	Conseil national de la Résistance
CNRS	Centre national de la recherche scientifique
CUC	Contrat d'union civile
CUS	Contrat d'union sociale
EFP	École freudienne de Paris
ENA	École nationale d'administration
ENS	École normale supérieure
FFEPH	Fondation française pour l'étude des problèmes humains
FGERI	Fédération des groupes d'études et de recherches institutionnelles
FHAR	Front homosexuel d'action révolutionnaire
FLN	Front de libération nationale
GP	Gauche prolétarienne
HCCPF	Haut comité consultatif de la population et de la famille (1945–1970)
HCP	Haut comité de la population (1939)
INED	Institut national d'études démographiques

LIST OF ABBREVIATIONS

INRA	Institut national de la recherche agronomique
IPA	International Psychoanalytic Association
ISERM	Institut national de la santé et de la recherche médicale
JOC	Jeunesse ouvrière chrétienne
LOC	Ligue ouvrière chrétienne
LPGF	La plus grande famille
MCP	Mouvement de la condition paternelle
MLF	Mouvement de libération des femmes
MPF	Mouvement populaire des famille
MRP	Mouvement républicain populaire
OG	Opposition de gauche
PACS	Pacte civil de solidarité
PMA	Procréation médicalement assistée
PSU	Parti socialite unifié
RPF	Rassemblement du peuple français
SFIO	Section française de l'internationale ouvrière
SFP	Société française de psychanalyse
SPP	Société psychanalytique de Paris
UNAF	Union nationale des associations familiales
UNCAF	Union nationale des caisses d'allocations familiales
VLR	Vive la révolution

THE LAW OF KINSHIP

Introduction

In recent years, the family has emerged as a particularly controversial topic in French politics. The debates around the legislation of bioethics, same-sex unions, single-parent households, family names, surrogacy, transsexuality, and gay adoption have been furious. They have torn through party lines, generated heated parliamentary sessions, persevered in the courts, and inspired many scholars to intervene. France, of course, is not the only country where the political and social organization of sexuality and reproduction has triggered intense passions, but the particular arguments and vocabulary that were mobilized during these discussions were symptomatic of a distinctly French polemic. Indeed, as politicians elsewhere were turning to religion, morality, tradition, or nature to ground their objections against gay marriage and medically assisted reproduction, French judges and legislators found solace in structuralist anthropology and psychoanalysis, and more specifically, in the works of Claude Lévi-Strauss and Jacques Lacan. Deputies cited *The Elementary Structures of Kinship* in parliament to argue that heterosexual marriage was the foundation of all societies and, consequently, that gay marriage was not naturally but socially unacceptable. Others invoked Lacan to suggest that children raised by lesbians or single mothers would be lacking the "Name-of-the-Father" and were thus more likely to be psychotic. Others, still, insisted on the importance of the incest prohibition as they highlighted the "symbolic" nature of kinship relations and the "anthropological function

2   **INTRODUCTION**

of the Law." As elected officials referenced some of the most difficult and abstract anthropological and psychoanalytic concepts, scholars and intellectuals continued the discussion in academic publications and in the general media where they argued about the meaning of the symbolic order, the Oedipus complex, castration, psychosis, the Law, exogamy, and the anthropological invariables of society.

In an attempt to settle these debates, the French parliament passed a series of laws, most importantly the "bioethics laws" in 1994 and the Civil Pact of Solidarity (PACS) in 1999. With the bioethics laws, the government outlawed surrogacy and restricted assisted reproductive technologies to married or cohabiting heterosexual couples of procreative age. With the PACS, it offered various rights and benefits such as tax breaks, health insurance, housing, and inheritance rights to cohabiting couples, independent of their sexual orientation. Unlike marriage, the PACS did not include any parenting rights. Through both of these laws, the French government reinforced its commitment to the normative heterosexual family, a commitment that was equally shared by the Left and the Right. The PACS was celebrated as a step forward in the fight for equal rights for gays and lesbians, but the fact that the final law did not mention parenting was key. Homosexuals could now be recognized by the state as individuals and even as couples, but not as families. Similarly, single individuals wishing to conceive a child though medically assisted reproduction were explicitly forbidden to do so by the bioethics laws. It was this commitment to the normative heterosexual family—what I call here familialism—that was defended in abstract, scientific, and normative terms through the theoretical framework of structuralist anthropology and psychoanalysis. In particular, the concept of the symbolic derived from the works of Lévi-Strauss and Lacan proved particularly useful: kinship in the form of the normative heterosexual family was said to be symbolic, and, as such, any law that recognized alternative familial configurations breached the symbolic order and needed to be opposed.

Thus, on the right, representative Renaud Dutreil referred to Lévi-Strauss's *Elementary Structures of Kinship* in parliament to oppose the PACS: "all human societies have produced a certain number of norms: exogamy, the prohibition of incest, and heterosexuality . . . Society enriches itself in otherness. Today, the other is the other sex. Homosexuality is the fear of the other."[1] Another deputy, Jacques Myard, also cited Lévi-Strauss to argue

---

1. Clarisse Fabre, "Des députés proposent d'étendre le pacte civil de solidarité aux fratries," *Le Monde,* October 2, 1998, 6. Unless otherwise indicated, all translations from the French are my own.

INTRODUCTION   3

that the "anthropological foundations of our society are constituted by two pillars: sexual difference and generational difference, which, together, uphold the family. All anthropologists, all ethnologists, have brought to light this fundamental structure which constitutes the family."[2] Representative Jacques Kossowski turned to psychoanalysis to posit that "the Oedipal situation remains a model essential to the process of elaboration of the individual," and that it was "important that a child learn to be confronted with the other sex. This dialectic is necessary for him to forge an identity and become a subject as such. It is necessary to conserve, within the family, the two ancestral pillars of humanity which are femininity and masculinity." To say this, Kossowski added, was "in no way 'homophobic.'" It simply showed that the PACS "gravely threatens the millennial edifice that the family is."[3] Similar arguments were made on the left, with Elisabeth Guigou, the former Minister of Justice, who explained that while she strongly supported the PACS, she rejected the idea of gay parenting: "like many psychoanalysts and psychiatrists, I believe that for his psychic, social, and relational structuring, a child needs to be faced throughout childhood with . . . a model of sexual difference, a referent man and a referent woman."[4] Irène Théry, a sociologist hired by the socialist government to evaluate the civil union bill, deplored its "desymbolizing passion" because it refused to distinguish heterosexual and homosexual couples.[5] The psychoanalyst Jean-Pierre Winter warned against the dangers of producing "symbolically modified children."[6]

This book tells the story of how some of the most obscure and complex notions put forward by Lévi-Strauss and Lacan came to provide a theoretical justification for familialism. How did structuralism circulate with such apparent fluidity across the political spectrum? How did the family become the privileged site for reasserting a particular kind of social and psychic normativity, for rethinking the law, and for ultimately anchoring a new concept of the political in France? My aim is neither to write the history of familialism nor structuralism but rather to explain their entanglement and their success in French political culture. This project straddles intellectual history and political/legal history because there are textual and contextual explanations

---

2. Débats parlementaires, Assemblée nationale, November 7, 1998.

3. Ibid.

4. Débats parlementaires, Assemblée nationale, March 30, 1999.

5. Irène Théry, "Le contrat d'union sociale en question," *Esprit* 236 (1997): 159–87.

6. Jean-Pierre Winter, "Gare aux enfants symboliquement modifiés," *Le Monde des Débats,* March 2000, 18. Winter later developed this argument in Jean-Pierre Winter, *Homoparenté* (Albin Michel, 2010).

4   **INTRODUCTION**

for why anthropology, psychoanalysis, and family law came together in this puzzling way. Without considering the two together, we can only get a partial understanding of why this language proved to be so politically effective for both the Left and the Right. Thus, on a textual level, I argue that the early and more explicitly structuralist texts of Lévi-Strauss and Lacan were appealing to familialists for two main reasons. First, both authors constructed the heterosexual family as a trope for social and psychic integration. Sexual difference (figured in the incest prohibition and in the Oedipus complex) served as the catalyst for the transition from nature to society for Lévi-Strauss and as the anchoring of the symbolic for Lacan. Second, they treated the emergence of kinship, of the social, and of subjectivity as *structural* phenomena. Structuralism offered these thinkers a way to bypass what was historical, geographical, political, and even empirical in sexuality and in kinship and to define them instead as abstract, universal, and normative categories. I refer to the "structuralist social contract" of Lévi-Strauss and Lacan to describe this process through which both authors established a causal relation between kinship and socialization (particularly through the concept of the symbolic), posited sexual difference as the necessary condition for all social and psychic organization, and presented the transition to sociality as a logical and necessary outcome.

In a second step, I argue that this vision of kinship at the root of intersubjectivity coincides in surprising ways with the role that the family has played in modern French law and public policy. Both the 1804 Napoleonic Code and the 1939 Family Code, the foundational texts for French civil law and for family policy, respectively, are examples of political familialism in that they set up the family as the best unit to organize solidarity and build political consensus, the most universal and most abstractable mode of social representation, and the purest expression of the general will. Both documents insist on the idea that the family is never simply private: as the foundation of the social order, it is intimately connected to the public. I suggest, in other words, that the family is the condition of sociality in both the structuralist and the political social contracts. My contention here is not simply that the family was important for the formation of the social or that it operated as a microcosm of the social. Rather, the argument in these texts, political and philosophical, was more specific: the heterosexual family was *constitutive* of the social. There could be no social contract without the heterosexual family.

In light of this reading of structuralism and of French familialism, two problems remain: how did these concepts actually enter the political world and how were they ultimately translated into concrete laws and policies? Indeed, the politicization of Lévi-Strauss's and Lacan's thought is perplex-

INTRODUCTION   5

ing, given how removed from political life both authors were, particularly in a time when the figure of the "engaged intellectual" was so central to the French political landscape. Lévi-Strauss claimed again and again to have lost all interest in politics after 1945, when he returned to France from his years of exile in New York.[7] Similarly, he explained that he had chosen to stay away from politics because he "did not believe that they could be the object of a theoretical reflection,"[8] and that he saw "absolutely no link between structuralism and any political system."[9] Lacan was just as suspicious of organized politics, to the chagrin of many of his students who were actively involved in left-wing causes during the 1960s.

Furthermore, even though Lévi-Strauss and Lacan wrote extensively on kinship, they ultimately had little to say about real families. In fact, as I have indicated, their embrace of structuralism represented a move away from the concrete, the empirical, and the historical toward the abstract and the normative. Lacan, for instance, created his concept of the Name-of-the-Father to expand the role of the biological father in Freud's Oedipus complex and to include larger structures of authority. Although they were not always successful, both authors were quite explicitly invested in maintaining a tension between the prescriptive and the descriptive, between the normative and the heteronormative. It is this abstraction in the works of Lévi-Strauss and Lacan that has led many commentators to simply dismiss the references to structuralism during the recent family law debates as misunderstandings or misreadings. Especially in the case of Lacan, psychoanalysts have pointed to his deconstructive style and his aporetic concepts, which he specifically designed to defy appropriations and flat interpretations, as evidence that "if Lacan were alive" he would never abide by these positions.

One of my aims here is to pay attention to these linguistic and philosophical concerns, to examine the tensions inherent in Lacan's and Lévi-Strauss's writings while considering also how certain of their concepts might at times at least appear to invite certain "misreadings" or "misappropriations." Indeed, I am interested in how the meaning of these highly abstract concepts has changed as they have traveled from the social sciences to the political field, and how they were ultimately reworked into laws and policy.

---

7. Didier Eribon and Claude Lévi-Strauss, *De près et de loin* (Odile Jacob, 1988), 80; Alexandre Pajon, *Claude Lévi-Strauss politique: De la SFIO à l'UNESCO* (Privat, 2011), 9.

8. Claude Lévi-Strauss interview with André Burguière and Jean-Paul Enthoven, *Le Nouvel Observateur,* July 5, 1980, 18.

9. Cited in Bob Scholte, "The Structural Anthropology of Claude Lévi-Strauss," in *Handbook of Social and Cultural Anthropology,* ed. John Joseph Honigmann (Rand McNally, 1973), 648.

6   **INTRODUCTION**

Thus, the second, more contextual argument that I make in this book is that Lévi-Strauss's and Lacan's understanding of kinship, the social, and sexual difference—their structuralist social contract—was popularized and politicized through a series of "bridge figures." These were anthropologists and psychoanalysts who borrowed the conceptual frameworks of Lévi-Strauss and Lacan and "translated" them for popular culture and for the political world. By maintaining close relationships with decision makers and occupying key roles in governmental committees pertaining to family policy, they ensured that their ideas had a direct impact on the actual legislation of the family. It is through these bridge figures that the empty signifiers in Lévi-Strauss's and Lacan's work got "filled" with real fathers, real mothers, and real children. As such, the distinction between the normative and the heteronormative, still central for Lévi-Strauss and Lacan, collapsed by the time the bridge figures had filtered their theories into the political sphere. The bridge figures that interest me here did not simply exercise a vague and diffuse influence on government officials. Rather, their exchanges were rooted in very concrete networks through which we can map various points of convergence between politics and ideas.

Much has been written on the role of gender and sexuality in the works of Lévi-Strauss and Lacan, and on the history and sociology of the family in nineteenth- and twentieth-century France. This book builds upon these fields, but its originality is to bridge the two, to analyze how academic discourses on kinship have intersected and overlapped with political discourses on the family. I am interested in how both sets of discourses have positioned subjects in similar ways, naturalized certain assumptions, mobilized particular sets of norms, and presupposed a series of inclusions and exclusions around these norms. By bringing to light these mechanisms, my hope is that the recent debates around the family will contribute to three larger historical, theoretical, and methodological discussions: on the particularities of French political culture, on the nature of sexual difference, and on the relationship between texts and contexts in intellectual history.

The recent French polemics around the family did not arise in a historical or geographical vacuum. The international context, particularly that of the United States and Western Europe, was instrumental in pushing judges and elected officials to adapt French family law to "modern times." Legal cases involving surrogacy and adoption disputes, such as the famous 1988 case of "Baby M." in the United States, were cited as models for both the critics and the advocates of assisted reproductive technology. In 1994, the European Parliament adopted a resolution in favor of equal rights for gays and

INTRODUCTION 7

lesbians and encouraged the members of the European Union to open marriage to same-sex couples or to set up equivalent juridical measures—civil unions or registered partnerships. By the late 1990s, Denmark, Norway, Sweden, Iceland, the Netherlands, and Belgium had complied with this measure. Similarly, in the United States, several cities began offering domestic partner benefits to their municipal employees as early as the 1980s. In 1989, the New York State Court of Appeals affirmed that a gay couple was a family for the purposes of rent-control laws, and the California Bar Association came out in favor of gay marriage. In 1993, the Hawaii Supreme Court declared that the state had no compelling reason to deny marriage licenses to same-sex couples, a decision followed by the legalization of same-sex civil unions in Vermont in 1999. The promoters of the PACS relied extensively on these examples to argue for the importance of recognizable same-sex unions in France. In response, those opposed to the bill did so in the name of republicanism. Republicanism, a synonym here for French political culture, was characterized, they argued, by abstract universalism. Abstract universalism—to be able to speak and govern in the name of the general interest, of everyone—was the guarantee of equality before the law and preserved the unity, cohesion, and integration of the French nation. Same-sex unions were deemed anti-republican because they were perceived be to be catering to the particular—and hence nonuniversal—interests of homosexuals. They were, to cite one of the terms that recurred most often, *communitarian,* the opposite of *republican.*

The limits and possibilities of French universalism, as an ideal type and as a reality, were tested and debated throughout the 1990s, most notably with the citizenship reform that affected primarily France's large community of North African descent and with the *parité* law that sought to provide gender equality in politics. Both cases highlighted the difficulty for republicanism to accommodate difference, particularly that of race and gender.[10] The discussions around the family that I examine here were part of this conversation, which was gendered and raced. Those opposed to the recognition of alternative familial models emphasized the French *republican* understanding of the family, which, according to both the familialist and the structuralist

---

10. Joan Scott and Éric Fassin have provided extremely useful analyses of these debates around universalism. See for example Joan Wallach Scott, "French Universalism in the Nineties," *Differences* 15, no. 2 (2004) and *Parité! Sexual Equality and the Crisis of French Universalism* (University of Chicago Press, 2005). On the question of *communautarisme,* see John Bowen, *Why the French Don't Like Headscarves: Islam, the State, and Public Space* (Princeton University Press, 2006); Laurent Lévy, *Le spectre du communautarisme* (Amsterdam, 2005).

8   **INTRODUCTION**

social contracts they were invoking, was universal and heterosexual. They contrasted this French republican model to two other extremes, both communitarian and "differentialist": "Anglo-Saxon liberalism" on the one hand, and totalitarianism—whether in the form of communism, Nazism, or Islamism—on the other. Unlike these two poles, the French republican model of the family and of the social (which were connected) stood as the perfect balance of freedom and cohesion, able to avoid the extreme individualism, anomie, and market dependence of liberalism, and the excessive homogenization of totalitarianism. The heterosexual family, rhetorically assimilated to the French social, needed to be defended if France wanted to retain its political culture and if it wanted to be shielded from the globalizing forces of the twenty-first century.

If the transnational dimension of these French discussions on the family was key, the role of "French theory"—particularly of Lévi-Strauss and Lacan—was also critical in Anglo-Saxon discussions of kinship, gender, and sexuality. In her 1975 groundbreaking essay, "The Traffic in Women: Notes on the 'Political Economy' of Sex," the anthropologist Gayle Rubin singled out Lévi-Strauss and Lacan for having elaborated a "sex/gender system" responsible for legitimating the exchange of women and the institution of heterosexuality.[11] Because marriage and kinship, according to Rubin, required the division of the sexes and the subordination of women, feminism needed to call for a "revolution in kinship" and for a genderless society. In *Gender Trouble,* Judith Butler pursued this reflection around Lévi-Strauss, Lacan, and the "heterosexual matrix," and moved toward a theory of gender as a performative and signifying practice, a theory that she has been revising and refining since then. In her more recent work, particularly *Antigone's Claim* and *Undoing Gender,* Butler has returned to Lévi-Strauss and Lacan to wonder whether kinship is "always already heterosexual" and to ask whether it might be possible to rethink kinship outside of the foundational structures of the incest taboo and the Oedipal myth.[12]

But if Lévi-Strauss and Lacan were instrumental in the development of the theory of gender in the United States, they were also essential figures in one of the most trenchant and serious critiques of this theory of gender. Indeed, in recent years, psychoanalytically-inclined scholars such as Leo

---

11. Gayle Rubin, "The Traffic in Women: Notes on the 'Political Economy' of Sex," in *Toward an Anthropology of Women,* ed. Rayna R. Reiter, 157–210 (Monthly Review Press, 1975).

12. Judith Butler, *Antigone's Claim: Kinship between Life and Death* (Columbia University Press, 2000); *Gender Trouble: Feminism and the Subversion of Identity* (Routledge, 1990); and *Undoing Gender* (Routledge, 2004).

INTRODUCTION   9

Bersani, Joan Copjec, Tim Dean, Charles Shepherdson, Lee Edelman, Tracy McNulty, and Slavoj Žižek, have criticized Butler's understanding of gender for failing to capture the specificity of sexual difference, for misunderstanding the problem of embodiment and the unpredictable ways in which desire fixes itself on particular subjects.[13] Sexual difference, they have argued, is not just another historically developed human convention or norm that can be subverted: it is primary, originating, and foundational. It is neither socially constructed (as gender) nor biologically grounded (as sex), but it is nonetheless related to both. Most importantly, it is coextensive with language. In this context, Lévi-Strauss, Freud, and particularly Lacan have reemerged as useful figures to resist the so-called historicist impulse in the field of sexuality studies. As Charles Shepherdson has put it, "to think sexual difference is to think the end of historicism," or in the terms of Joan Copjec, "sex does not budge, and it is not heterosexist to say so."[14] Sexual difference, these thinkers have argued, cannot be deconstructed, nor can it be studied by social scientists or historians, because it is neither quantifiable nor representational. As the psychoanalyst Jacques-Alain Miller once told Michel Foucault in an interview, one cannot write the history of sexuality in the way that one would write the history of bread.[15] Much of the impetus behind this book comes from these debates around the nature of sexual difference. What happens to the abstraction, the universalism, the ahistoricity of structuralist concepts (such as castration, the incest prohibition, or sexual difference) when they literally move through history and when they absorb specific content? One of the goals of this book is to address these philosophical questions through historical analysis, as I consider what models of social, political, and cultural intelligibility can arise from the transcendental and foundationalist definitions of sexual difference that we find in the works of Lévi-Strauss, Lacan, and many of these contemporary psychoanalytic thinkers.

Finally, this book is engaged in a methodological conversation around the problems of reading and interpretation in history. One of the challenges

---

13. See, among others, Leo Bersani, *Homos* (Harvard University Press, 1995); Leo Bersani, *Intimacies* (University of Chicago Press, 2008); Judith Butler, Ernesto Laclau, and Slavoj Žižek, *Contingency, Hegemony, Universality: Contemporary Dialogues on the Left* (Verso, 2000); Joan Copjec, *Read My Desire: Lacan against the Historicists* (MIT Press, 1994); Lee Edelman, *No Future: Queer Theory and the Death Drive* (Duke University Press, 2004); Tracy McNulty, *Wrestling with the Angel: Experiments in Symbolic Life* (Columbia University Press, 2013); Charles Shepherdson, *Vital Signs: Nature, Culture, Psychoanalysis* (Routledge, 2000).

14. Copjec, *Read My Desire,* 211; Shepherdson, *Vital Signs,* 93.

15. Michel Foucault and Colin Gordon, *Power/Knowledge: Selected Interviews and Other Writings, 1972–1977* (Pantheon Books, 1980), 213.

10   **INTRODUCTION**

of intellectual history is to articulate the relationship between a text and its pertinent contexts, to expose how the context of a text might shape our reading of it but also to engage the text actively and refuse to treat it as a simple document or symptom of a particular time and place. Lévi-Strauss's and Lacan's unequivocal rejection of history and their explicit political disengagement make their thinking particularly interesting from the perspective of intellectual history. Indeed, most of the scholars who have commented on the use of their theories in recent family law decisions have contended that politicians were either "misreading" the original texts, or on the contrary, that they were expressing their "truth"—bringing out their latent homophobia or misogyny. Similarly, they have interpreted their works symptomatically as "signs of their times," as desperate defenses of a patriarchal order in a time of crisis of masculinity and authority. Alternatively, they have argued that the context in which these two figures were writing should not matter at all, that reading these figures historically refuses to engage with the radical ahistoricity of the theories.[16] My aim here is to avoid all of these positions and to consider instead how texts might ask certain questions of their contexts and vice versa. The structure of this book attempts to reflect this "dialogical approach" in the sense that the intellectual history chapters are neither illustrations, symptoms, or effects of the political history ones.[17] My argument is thus *not* that Lévi-Strauss and Lacan read the founding fathers of French familialism or vice versa but rather that they made *analogous* arguments. The familialist and the structuralist social contracts did meet up through the bridge figures, but they are not connected by cause and effect.

The Law of Kinship is divided into three parts that are organized chronologically and that interweave political/legal analysis, and intellectual/cultural history. The first section, consisting of the first three chapters, traces the roots

---

16. Michel Tort, for instance, emphasizes Lacan's Catholicism—personal and intellectual—to criticize the role of authority and transcendence in Lacanian psychoanalysis (particularly in the notion of the symbolic). Against Lacan, Tort calls for a "secularization of psychoanalysis," by which he means the historicization of its foundational concepts; see *Fin du dogme paternel* (Aubier, 2005). Didier Eribon also reads Lacan historically as responding to anxieties around masculinity and the "decline of the father" but to advocate for the rejection of psychoanalysis altogether; see *Une morale du minoritaire: Variations sur un thème de Jean Genet* (Fayard, 2001) and *Échapper à la psychanalyse* (Léo Scheer, 2005). Elisabeth Roudinesco's recent work provides a good example of the opposite move, to "save" Lacan from such conservative misreadings; see *La famille en désordre* (Fayard, 2002) and *Lacan, envers et contre tout* (Seuil, 2011).

17. I am indebted to the work of Dominick LaCapra for this "dialogical" approach to intellectual history. See for example Dominick LaCapra, *Rethinking Intellectual History: Texts, Contexts, Language* (Cornell University Press, 1983).

INTRODUCTION 11

of this theory of familialism postulating that the family is the categorical imperative behind all sociality and the enactor of universality. Chapter 1 provides a genealogy of familialism in French law and social policy. It centers on the Civil Code and the Family Code, which both consider the family essential to structure the social and the individual. The writers of the Civil Code hoped that the family would stabilize social bonds and individual passions in the aftermath of the Terror. The promoters of the Family Code postulated that the family would resolve the "depopulation crisis" that had plagued France since the end of the nineteenth century and that had become a keyword for many of the problems associated with modernity: nationalism, feminism, and the social question, among others. Chapter 2 offers a close analysis of Lévi-Strauss's and Lacan's early texts on kinship, which I read as social contract theories, as a "structuralist social contract." While Lévi-Strauss was primarily interested in the transition from nature to culture and in the overarching organization of society, Lacan focused on the effects of these social structures on the psyche. In both cases, I interpret their work as a "transcendental anthroposociology," to use the expression of Marcel Gauchet: anthroposociology in the sense that they sought to diagnose what was specifically human and link it to the social, and transcendental in terms of its normative ambitions.[18] The concept of the symbolic more specifically allowed them to triangulate the sexual, the subjective, and the social. Chapter 3 examines how this "structuralist social contract" came to circulate in the political sphere and in popular culture through three bridge figures: Georges Mauco, André Berge, and Françoise Dolto. All three were psychoanalysts who actively participated in the shaping of family policy in the second half of the twentieth century.

The second section of the book encompasses Chapters 4 and 5 and examines how this model of familialism came into crisis—politically and intellectually—during the 1960s and 1970s. Chapter 4 focuses on family law and family policy, which from 1964 to 1975 underwent what one legal scholar described as a "quiet revolution." Because of the new demographic context of the baby boom, the impact of May 1968, the end of the Gaullist regime, and the emergence of a new political culture with shifting priorities, family policy no longer served as a political rallying point. As postwar family activists grew less influential within the Fifth Republic, it became harder for them to uphold the most basic principles of familialism that had undergirded family policy, particularly the idea that the heterosexual family

---

18. Marcel Gauchet, *La condition historique* (Stock, 2003), 13.

12   **INTRODUCTION**

was absolutely essential to sociality. Moreover, during this period, family law—which had remained almost intact since the promulgation of the 1804 Civil Code—was radically revised. Rather than drawing on universal and transhistorical abstract principles to legislate issues such as parental authority, filiation, marriage, and divorce, the new set of laws sought to reflect the evolution of social mores and to adapt the French family to the "tide of history."

In the same section, Chapter 5 traces how the heterosexual family—or more precisely, the vision of sexual difference as the single conduit for sociality—became one of the targets of post-'68 French thought. The chapter focuses on Gilles Deleuze and Félix Guattari's *Anti-Oedipus* and on Luce Irigaray's early work, more specifically on their critiques of Lévi-Strauss and Lacan. I show how, by turning away from structuralism, Deleuze, Guattari, and Irigaray sought to reframe the social contract by positing alternative conceptions of the family and the symbolic, ones no longer anchored in sexual difference. For these thinkers and their followers, being "anti-Oedipal" was not only a theoretical position but, as Michel Foucault put it, "a lifestyle, a way of thinking and living." After exploring how "Oedipus" served as a trope to articulate the sexual, the theoretical, and the political during these years, I turn to two figures who attempted to enact this "anti-Oedipal lifestyle" in their lives and in their works: Guy Hocquenghem, one of the founders of the Front homosexuel d'action révolutionnaire (FHAR), and Antoinette Fouque, the coordinator of the feminist group Psychanalyse et politique.

Finally, in the last section of the book, which corresponds to Chapter 6, I offer a hypothesis for why, starting in the 1980s, many scholars and politicians found it useful to return to the structuralist social contract of Lévi-Strauss and Lacan. Around this time, lawyers, activists, social scientists, and politicians—some inspired by the new legal and political possibilities around the family described in Chapter 4, others by the kinds of theoretical critiques of structuralism described in Chapter 5—began to employ a discourse of rights, or *droits de l'homme*. They argued for their right to raise children outside of the context of the heterosexual nuclear family, their right to marry and to make different forms of private life publicly relevant, their right to choose a child's last name, or their right to choose a different gender. For those troubled by these claims, particularly for those on the left, the works of Lévi-Strauss and Lacan provided a counterargument to this discourse of rights, one in perfect accordance with the secular and erudite values celebrated in French political life. Family law, they contended, did not simply exist to satisfy individual demands or to confer random "rights" on individuals. Rather, its primary purpose was to ensure the proper integra-

INTRODUCTION 13

tion of individuals into the social world and to guarantee their psychic well-being. Gender, sexuality, and kinship did not simply pertain to the private: they were the universal and transhistorical structures upholding the public, the *état de droit*. Like abstract universalism, heterosexuality had now become one of the defining traits of the French Republic. The normative hetero-sexual family needed to be defended because it provided a basis to reart-iculate republicanism, to reassert a universalism that appeared increasingly threatened by postcolonialism, globalization, the European Union, and the ever-expanding American "way of life."

PART ONE

The Rise of Familialism

✦ CHAPTER 1

Familialism and the Republican Social Contract

Since 1789, politicians and intellectuals in France have worried about the question of "the social." The problem of how to reconcile social solidarity and individual liberty—one of the central paradoxes of the Revolution—has haunted French political theory from the Left to the Right since the eighteenth century. Is the social body constituted by particular interests that merely coexist (as in liberalism), or does it have a more general and mystical quality that transcends the sum of these parts (as in Rousseau's notion of the general will)? Throughout the nineteenth and twentieth centuries, this French "social question" was defined and redefined. It was a pressing concern for the Thermidorians and for Napoleon in the aftermath of the Terror, for the leaders of the July Monarchy who had to contend with the effects of industrialization and the new phenomenon of urban poverty, for Napoleon III who urbanized Paris from that perspective, and, of course, for the Republicans. "Thinking the social" became an imperative after 1848, as the republican ideal was confronted with democratic reality for the first time, and after the constitutional laws of 1875. The experiences of the Second Empire and of the Paris Commune had taught Republicans that winning elections was not enough. In addition, they needed to provide a model of social integration that could both reassure the more conservative parts of the population who were nostalgic for the empire and the monarchy

17

18   **CHAPTER 1**

and draw in the more radical groups increasingly seduced by the ideals of socialism.[1]

For the Republicans, one answer to this dilemma of the social contract was abstract universalism: the nation was the expression of the people's will, and elected representatives needed to transcend their particularities to speak in the name of the general interest, for the nation as a whole.[2] This French political model—which I am loosely calling republicanism—was, as Pierre Rosanvallon has characterized it, a "political culture of generality." It had a social expression in the celebration of the nation, a political expression in the rejection of intermediary bodies, and a procedural dimension through the emphasis on law.[3] This chapter suggests that a second answer to this specifically French version of the social question was the family. Family policy was particularly successful in France because the family had been, since the Revolution, intimately linked to the social question. Family activists presented the family as constitutive of the social, as the most universal and most abstractable mode of representation. The family, they insisted, was the secular institution that would lead to social cohesion and bring about solidarity. As such, no political party could have exclusive rights over family politics. The family was beyond politics: it was of universal interest and thus offered a particularly productive platform on which to build political consensus. Just like abstract universalism, the family became, throughout the nineteenth and twentieth centuries, one of the most the distinctive traits of French political culture.

This chapter traces a genealogy of familialism as a political culture and as an ideology. Familialism was an organized political movement with a legal

---

1. For more on how this social question was articulated historically, see Robert Castel, *Les métamorphoses de la question sociale: Une chronique du salariat* (Fayard, 1995); Jacques Donzelot, *L'invention du social: Essai sur le déclin des passions politiques* (Fayard, 1984); Janet R. Horne, *A Social Laboratory for Modern France: The Musée Social and the Rise of the Welfare State* (Duke University Press, 2001); Isabelle Lespinet-Moret, "La question sociale," in *Dictionnaire critique de la République*, ed. Vincent Duclert and Christophe Prochasson (Flammarion, 2002); Giovanna Procacci, *Gouverner la misère: La question sociale en France, 1789–1848* (Seuil, 1993); Paul Rabinow, *French Modern: Norms and Forms of the Social Environment* (MIT Press, 1989); Judith F. Stone, *The Search for Social Peace: Reform Legislation in France, 1890–1914* (State University of New York Press, 1985), chap. 1; Christian Topalov, ed., *Laboratoires du nouveau siècle: La nébuleuse réformatrice et ses réseaux en France, 1880–1914* (Ecole des hautes études en sciences sociales, 1999).

2. See Joan Wallach Scott, "French Universalism in the Nineties," *Differences: A Journal of Feminist Cultural Studies* 15, no. 2 (2004); Joan Wallach Scott, *Parité! Sexual Equality and the Crisis of French Universalism* (University of Chicago Press, 2005).

3. Pierre Rosanvallon, *Le modèle politique français: La société civile contre le jacobinisme de 1789 à nos jours* (Seuil, 2004), 13.

FAMILIALISM AND THE REPUBLICAN SOCIAL CONTRACT 19

infrastructure, administrative bodies, representatives, and lobbyists who maintained close relationships with decision makers and occupied key governmental posts. It should also, however, be understood as an *ideology*, as a system of representations in which the family operated as the enactor of the social contract, as the purest expression of the general will, as a structure essential for both the social and the individual. This vision of the family was inscribed at the heart of French political culture with two documents in particular: the 1804 Civil Code and the 1939 Family Code. While the former anchored the familial system in law, the latter made the family one of the principal vectors of social policy.

My goal here is not to provide a comprehensive account of these two legal frameworks but rather to account for their significance and their longevity. Indeed, although certain clauses pertaining to the family were modified throughout the nineteenth and twentieth centuries, the general framework of the Civil Code remained unchanged until the 1960s. The Civil Code can thus be considered, as the legal scholar Jean Carbonnier has suggested, France's "most authentic constitution" in the sense that it "encompassed the ideas around which French society was constituted in the wake of the Revolution and around which it continues to be constituted today."[4] Similarly, the measures put forth in the Family Code, which was voted into law at the end of the Third Republic, lasted throughout the Vichy Regime, the postwar reconstruction, and the Fourth Republic. From the 1880s to the 1960s, French family policy developed and grew, supported and enhanced by governments on both the right and the left.

The family has, of course, played an important political role in other countries, but two elements have distinguished French familialism: on an ideological level, the rhetorical conflation between the family and universalism, and on a structural level, the degree of commitment to family policy. France was indeed the first country to adopt an extensive system of family allowances, followed only by three fascist states—Germany, Italy, and Spain—who modeled their own family policies on the French example.[5] The historian of fascist Italy Victoria de Grazia has even suggested that fascist law never proposed to meddle in family affairs to the same degree as France's

---

4. Jean Carbonnier, "Le Code Civil," in *Les lieux de mémoire,* ed. Pierre Nora (Gallimard, 1984), 2:309.

5. See Gisela Bock and Pat Thane, *Maternity and Gender Policies: Women and the Rise of the European Welfare States, 1880s–1950s* (Routledge, 1991); John Macnicol, "Welfare, Wages, and the Family: Child Endowment in Comparative Perspective, 1900–50," in *In the Name of the Child: Health and Welfare, 1880–1940,* ed. Roger Cooter (Routledge, 1992).

20   CHAPTER 1

1939 Code de la famille.[6] Furthermore, by the time other European countries had implemented family allowances after World War II, France still had the most generous set of benefits, which were by then incorporated into the Social Security Plan.[7]

My argument here is that the success and singularity of French family policy can be attributed to two main factors. First, this *longue durée* construction of the family as the solution to the social question was key in convincing elected officials across the political spectrum to endorse a strong family policy. Second, the particularly dramatic French demographic context at the end of the nineteenth century and, more importantly, the all-encompassing discourse around "depopulation" were instrumental in pushing the 1939 Family Code into existence and in explaining the continued interest in the family after World War II.

⤙ The Civil Code and the Familial System of Law

The problem of the "social bond" framed the composition of the 1804 Civil Code. Writing only a few years after the end of the Terror, Jean-Étienne-Marie Portalis, one of the four jurists appointed by Napoleon in August 1800 to establish the foundations of a new civil legislation, explained in his Preliminary Discourse to the Conseil d'État that with the Revolution "all abuses had been attacked, all institutions questioned. With the simple voice of a gifted orator, the establishments that appeared most unshakeable, had crumbled. They were no longer rooted in mores or in public opinion." This appetite for destruction had "broken old habits, weakened all bonds . . . We no longer cared about the private relations that men held with one another. We only saw the political and general object." The revolutionary spirit had "violently sacrificed all rights for a political goal, and admitted no other consideration but that of the mysterious and variable interest of the state."[8]

Portalis, in line with Napoleon, viewed the Revolution as an overall "conquest," as a necessary break from centuries of arbitrary and unjust absolutist rule. However, as the previous passage makes clear, by privileging de-

---

6. Victoria De Grazia, *How Fascism Ruled Women: Italy, 1922–1945* (University of California Press, 1992), 89.

7. See Pierre Laroque, "Famille et Sécurité sociale," in *Niveaux de vie des familles: Travaux du Congrès mondial de la famille et de la population* (UNAF, 1947), 172.

8. P. A. Fenet and François Ewald, eds., *Naissance du Code civil: La raison du législateur* (Flammarion, 1989), 36–37.

FAMILIALISM AND THE REPUBLICAN SOCIAL CONTRACT   21

mocracy and abstract individualism, the Jacobins had forgotten the social, or
rather they had homogenized it into the nebulous and problematic concept
of the general will. The Terror in particular, Portalis believed, had highlighted
the limits of a political system based on nature and on the assumption of man's
original goodness. The Revolution had granted individual human rights as
natural rights, but in the course of doing so, it had torn apart an entire social
body based on orders, corporations, and other intermediary bodies designed
to "frame" the individual, whose emotions were ultimately unstable and volatile. It was this social that the authors of the Civil Code—and Napoleon's
regime more generally—hoped to reconstruct and strengthen, not by returning to a discredited feudal order, but by imagining new ways—new laws—to
link individuals to one another. For the writers of the Civil Code, civil laws
could uphold both the state and the citizen. Civil laws were, as Portalis put
it, "the source of mores, the palladium of property, and the guaranty of all
public and individual peace."[9]

To guarantee this "collective integration" of individuals, the Civil Code
was structured along two axes that were closely tied to one another: the family and private property. The family, which the writers of the Code described
as the "nursery of the State [*pépinière de l'État*],"[10] provided the best mechanism to manage and stabilize relations of sociability. Unlike other legisla-
tions such as the Prussian Code which attributed a series of abstract rights
to the individual, French civil law postulated that the "civil state" (*état civil*)
was a familial state. As Portalis famously concluded his Preliminary Discourse, "Our goal has been to tie mores to laws and to propagate the spirit
of the family which is so favorable . . . to the civil spirit [*esprit de cité*] . . .
Private virtues alone can guarantee public virtues and it is through the small
homeland [*patrie*], the family, that we tie ourselves to the great one. Only
good fathers, good husbands, and good sons make good citizens. The role
of civil institutions is to sanction and protect all the honest affections of
nature."[11] The new social contract envisioned by Napoleon—and France's

---

9. Ibid., 38. For a helpful introduction to the philosophy guiding the authors of the Civil Code, see
André-Jean Arnaud, *Les origines doctrinales du Code civil français* (Librairie générale de droit et de jurisprudence, 1969); Suzanne Desan, *The Family on Trial in Revolutionary France* (University of California
Press, 2004), 286–91; Jean-Louis Halpérin, *Le Code civil* (Dalloz, 2003). For a more general analysis
of these fundamental political questions in the aftermath of the Terror, see Andrew Jainchill, *Reimagining Politics after the Terror: The Republican Origins of French Liberalism* (Cornell University Press,
2008); Pierre Rosanvallon, *Le peuple introuvable: Histoire de la représentation démocratique en France*
(Gallimard, 1998).

10. Fenet and Ewald, *Naissance du Code civil,* 68.

11. Ibid., 90.

22   **CHAPTER 1**

postrevolutionary constitution, if we follow Jean Carbonnier—was one mediated by the family, and more specifically the patriarchal family.

As Suzanne Desan has argued, throughout the 1790s, family law served as a forum to explore and evaluate the practical meaning of the fundamental questions raised by the Revolution around the notions of freedom, equality, and social and individual rights. Thus, if family law was subject to numerous reforms and innovations during the early years of the Revolution, it also served to channel much of the popular discontent with the Revolution after the Terror. In a strong reaction against the revolutionaries' attempts to introduce individual rights and equality into the home, the Thermidorians, profoundly concerned with the reconstruction of the social, tightened the contours of the family and emphasized domesticity and patriarchy. Although the Civil Code preserved some of the revolutionary experiments in family law, it mainly consolidated the Thermidorian reforms that consecrated the legitimate and patriarchal family as the greatest source of social stability. In practical terms, this meant focusing on legitimate marriage and filiation. Both were, in the eyes of the writers of the Code, legal constructions that needed to be privileged over biological or empirical facts for the ultimate purpose of preserving the social peace. The "laws of nature" that had guided so many of the revolutionaries' initiatives were replaced by legal fictions that could provide the kind of consensus and normativity needed in a stable society.[12]

According to the architects of the Civil Code, marriage had little to do with the simple "attraction of the two sexes."[13] To be sure, men and women were naturally drawn to one another, but desire belonged to the "physical order of nature," the animal domain, whereas humans were subject to another kind of law, natural law defined as "the principles that govern man as a moral being, that is to say, as an intelligent and free being, destined to live with other intelligent and free beings like himself."[14] What characterized men *qua* men was thus this social and symbolic capacity. Animals mated

---

12. For more on the construction of gender and sexuality in the Civil Code, see Christian Biet and Irène Théry, *La famille, la loi, l'État de la Révolution au Code civil* (Imprimerie nationale Centre Georges Pompidou, 1989); Desan, *Family on Trial;* Rachel Ginnis Fuchs, *Contested Paternity: Constructing Families in Modern France* (Johns Hopkins University Press, 2008); Jennifer Ngaire Heuer, *The Family and the Nation: Gender and Citizenship in Revolutionary France, 1789–1830* (Cornell University Press, 2005); Patricia Mainardi, *Husbands, Wives, and Lovers: Marriage and Its Discontents in Nineteenth-Century France* (Yale University Press, 2003); Sylvia Schafer, *Children in Moral Danger and the Problem of Government in Third Republic France* (Princeton University Press, 1997).

13. Fenet and Ewald, *Naissance du Code civil,* 55 and 170.

14. Ibid., 170.

FAMILIALISM AND THE REPUBLICAN SOCIAL CONTRACT 23

because they were governed by instinct. Men married because they were social and subject to law. Marriage in this sense was a contract, one grounded in the natural complementarity of the sexes but far more powerful, a union "derived not from nature but from society and mores" in the words of Napoleon.[15] Marriage thus had a social capital, and, conversely, the government had an interest in marriage. While the revolutionaries had insisted on the contractual liberty of the individual in marriage, the Civil Code presented marriage as a vector of social solidarity, as a matter of state. As Portalis argued, marriage was unlike all other contracts in which individuals "stipulate for themselves, for their obscure and private interests." In marriage, "we stipulate not only for ourselves but for the other . . . for the State, for the general society of mankind."[16]

Despite the pressures from conservative Catholics to reinstate a religious definition of marriage, the writers of the Code chose to retain its secular nature precisely because marriage was so deeply connected to the *res publica*. In addition, they affirmed it as a marker of French modern civilization, which they opposed to primitive or nomadic populations whose marital customs reflected their less advanced governmental practices.[17] This essential publicness of marriage also explains why the Civil Code significantly complicated the possibility of divorce. No longer considered a right as it had been under the Revolution, divorce became an extreme remedy for a bad marriage. Marriages needed to subsist "not only for the spouses but for society, for the children, for the institution of the family."[18]

This particular understanding of conjugality was key for the Civil Code's definition of legitimate filiation, which was, like marriage, a legal construction with a particular social and public utility. If marriage could not be grounded in nature, filiation could be even less so. As Bigot de Préameneu, one of the writers of the Code, put it, "nature cannot serve as a guide" to determine paternity: sentiments were too capricious to establish general rules, and "nature had covered the transmission of our existence with an impenetrable veil." Yet it was fundamental that paternity not remain uncertain "because it is through paternity that families perpetuate and distinguish themselves from one another. As one of the bases of the social order, we

---

15. Jean-Louis Halpérin, *Histoire du droit privé français depuis 1804* (Presses universitaires de France, 1996), 26.

16. Fenet and Ewald, *Naissance du Code civil,* 65.

17. Ibid., 177.

18. Ibid., 186.

24   **CHAPTER 1**

must support it and strengthen it."[19] While maternity could be defined biologically because "the mother was always certain" (*mater semper certa est*), paternity was constructed exclusively in terms of marriage. Drawing heavily from Roman law, the Civil Code posited that a child was considered legitimate if his father and mother were married at the time of conception: "a child conceived during marriage has the husband as a father" or in its Latin version, *pater est quem nuptiae demonstrant* (literally, the father is the one that marriage designates as such).

If this legal construction of paternity favored the social order, it was also believed to favor fathers, who needed to be protected from women and from their illegitimate children. With paternity came the great responsibility of name, inheritance, and citizenship. The Civil Code chose to retain one of the most controversial measures of the Revolution, the *partage égal,* which mandated a more or less equal distribution of property among all heirs, male and female. The *partage égal* put an end to the *droit d'aînesse,* one of the pillars of the Old Regime, which postulated that the eldest son inherit the large majority of the family's estate. Although the Code envisioned certain mechanisms to allow fathers to favor one heir over another, fathers could no longer disinherit their children. This system of inheritance and property transmission thus depended on a tightly defined notion of descendancy. The Revolution had tried to allow certain rights and protections for "natural children"—the legal term that replaced the previous designation of "bastards"—but the Civil Code limited paternal obligation to the legitimate offspring. Just as society had, in the words of Napoleon, no interest in recognizing concubines, it had no interest in recognizing bastards.

The Civil Code's definitions of marriage and filiation were surprisingly uncontested. Even Benjamin Constant, often regarded as one of the founding fathers of liberalism, objected to the possibility of mothers naming the putative father of their child on the birth certificate on the grounds that it was immoral (because it could be used by immoral women, i.e., prostitutes), useless (because the child still had no rights), and dangerous (because it could imply that men were free to do as they pleased).[20] To protect fathers and support this legal construction of paternity—and consequently of the social—the Civil Code abolished paternity searches and reinforced paternal authority. Adoption was permitted, but it served primarily as a conduit for inheritance and was thus restricted to childless parents over fifty years old

---

19. Ibid., 222–23.

20. Ibid., 239–40.

FAMILIALISM AND THE REPUBLICAN SOCIAL CONTRACT   25

and to children over age twenty-five. Far from consecrating liberal individualism as many Marxist critics have argued, the Napoleonic Code sought first
and foremost to reinscribe the individual within the social. To be sure, this
was a patriarchal and bourgeois social, but to participate in this social meant to
be anchored in the family. Family in this context had nothing to do with nature or sex but rather with civil ties—fictive and voluntary ties—that linked
individuals to one another. After 1804, the civil state was a familial state.

⌖ Frédéric Le Play, the Family, and the Social Question

If the Civil Code was an attempt to solve the social question through the
family in the wake of the Revolution, new problems came to the foreground
in the nineteenth century with the rise of industrialism. As the sociologist
Frédéric Le Play wrote in his 1864 book *Social Reform in France,* the two
greatest "social vices" that had plagued France since 1789 were social division and political instability. Le Play blamed the upper classes for the social
division that affected even the smallest subdivisions of the social body: the
village, the workshop, and the family. As he put it, "the superior classes,
instead of acting together to lead society into a better path, mutually neu-
tralize one another by attempting to make contrary political principles pre-
vail by force at the risk of destroying the social order." The second vice, "an
even more evident symptom of the decline of a nation," was France's inability to prevent revolutions, "even amidst prosperity."[21]

Revolutions had indeed haunted Le Play's life and career. Born in 1806
in a small conservative Catholic Norman village, Le Play attended the prestigious Parisian engineering schools, the École polytechnique and the École
des mines. There, he was exposed to the various sociological debates of the
time, notably to the ideas of Auguste Comte and Saint-Simon. During the
1820s, he undertook an extensive walking tour around Germany with his
friend Jean Reynaud, a disciple of Saint-Simon, to study the mining industry. Speaking to workers, employers, and managers about their everyday life,
Le Play became aware of the social tensions generated by the booming
economy of the early Industrial Revolution. The new division of labor, he
noticed, had commodified personal relationships and radically transformed

---

21. Christopher Olaf Blum, *Critics of the Enlightenment: Readings in the French Counter-Revolutionary
Tradition* (ISI Books, 2004), 198–99. For the French versions, see Frédéric Le Play, *La réforme sociale
en France déduite de l'observation comparée des peuples européens* (Slatkine, 1982), 1:2–3.

26   **CHAPTER 1**

previous bonds of solidarity.[22] Unlike Comte, whose methodology tended to encourage speculative and deductive claims, Le Play insisted on grounding his analysis in the empirical data he collected and on combining economic and sociological analysis. The "science of society," Le Play believed, was an applied science that could be modeled on metallurgy. Grounded in field research, its main task was to rediscover "the secret of happiness" of societies.[23] Scientific work, in other words, implied a commitment to social reform.

Le Play was indeed able to exercise this social commitment through his teaching and throughout his career. He served in the Ministry of Public Works during the July Monarchy, in the cabinet of Prime Minister François Arago during the Second Republic, and as Napoleon's advisor on social questions during the Second Empire. He remained active even during the Third Republic, as the founder and director of the Unions for Social Peace, an organization designed to heal social divisions.[24] Through the Unions' journal, *La Réforme Sociale,* Le Play and his disciples succeeded in diffusing their ideas to wider circles. Furthermore, several of Le Play's students were involved in the Musée social, founded in 1896 to reflect on social questions and advise policymakers.[25] This was, for instance, the case of Emile Cheysson, one of the most active pro-family activists during the Third Republic.

Social instability, according to Le Play, could only be treated through reform, "a slow and regular improvement," which he defined in opposition to both revolutions and laissez-faire British-style "wild liberalism."[26]

---

22. In this way and many others, Le Play's project was similar to Durkheim's, even through the Durkheimian school spent much effort criticizing and dismissing Le Play's sociology. On this reception of Le Play, see Bernard Kalaora and Antoine Savoye, *Les inventeurs oubliés: Le Play et ses continuateurs aux origines des sciences sociales* (Champ Vallon, 1989); Antoine Savoye and Frédéric Audren, *Naissance de l'ingénieur social: Les ingénieurs des mines et la science sociale au XIXe siècle* (Presses de l'École des mines, 2008). Durkheim and Le Play both believed that sociology should be based on empirical observation and that the study of morality should be central. Similarly, both were concerned by the degradation of social relations in modernity, and both focused on the family as a way to revive these social bonds. One important difference is that while both thinkers rejected utilitarian and idealistic conceptions of society, Le Play never believed that it was possible to grasp the "social whole," or society in its totality. For more on this comparison, see Catherine Bodard Silver, ed., *Frédéric Le Play on Family, Work, and Social Change* (University of Chicago Press, 1982), 126.

23. I am borrowing here from Silver's introduction (ibid.).

24. Blum, *Critics of the Enlightenment,* xxxviii; Bernard Kalaora and Antoine Savoye, "Frédéric Le Play, un sociologue engagé," in *Ouvriers des deux mondes: Études publiées par la Société d'économie sociale à partir de 1856* (À l'enseigne de l'arbre verdoyant, 1983).

25. See Sanford Elwitt, "Social Reform and Social Order in Late Nineteenth-Century France: The Musée Social and Its Friends," *French Historical Studies* 11, no. 3 (1980); Horne, *Social Laboratory.*

26. Blum, *Critics of the Enlightenment,* 198. For a history of "reformism" during the nineteenth century, see Topalov, *Laboratoires du nouveau siècle.*

FAMILIALISM AND THE REPUBLICAN SOCIAL CONTRACT 27

As he explained to an English colleague, the British political economy had failed to resolve "such delicate problems as wages, competition, and international exchange . . . by leaving the greatest possible freedom to private interest."[27] These questions could be settled more "suitably for humanity" by organizing labor, industry, and exchange and making these institutions less alienating. More specifically, Le Play's understanding of reform, the key to the social question, "the secret of happiness" of societies, rested on two pillars: family policy and paternalism.

Le Play was one of the most important theorizers of French familialism as I am defining it here. First, on an ideological level, he conceived of the family as the solution to the social division and revolutionary instability paralyzing France. Second, he navigated academic and political circles with similar ease, thus ensuring that his ideas of reform had a real impact on society. Finally, he presented his program of reform as beyond left and right, as grounded in scientific empirical research rather than politics. Although he shared with Burke, Bonald, and de Maistre a suspicion of "grand historical theories," including those of Rousseau and other Enlightenment "sophists," Le Play was hardly a conservative in their sense. He never advocated a return to the Old Regime, which, he believed, was forever tainted by the "corruption of the upper classes."[28] Similarly, although he remained a practicing Catholic throughout his life, he never advocated clericalism. He participated both in the authoritative regime of Napoleon III and in the most democratic initiatives of the Second Republic such as the Luxembourg Commission, which was headed by the socialist Louis Blanc. Le Play described himself as "resolutely socialist"[29] in the sense that the unity, the strength, and the coherence of society were his primary preoccupations.

For Le Play, social instability was a product of modern individualism. Thus, social reform needed to begin by reinscribing individuals within larger wholes, the first of which was the family: "When individualism becomes the dominant form of social relations, men rapidly descend towards barbarism. Whenever, on the contrary, society is progressing, individuals eagerly seek the bonds of the family and unhesitantly renounce the independence that law and nature of things allow them."[30] Although the writers

---

27. Cited in Silver, *Frédéric Le Play,* 21.

28. Le Play, *La réforme sociale en France,* 1:27. Some of the key passages of *Réforme sociale* are translated in Blum, *Critics of the Enlightenment,* 197–223.

29. Cited in Françoise Arnault, *Frédéric Le Play: De la métallurgie à la science sociale* (Presses universitaires de Nancy, 1993).

30. Blum, *Critics of the Enlightenment,* 226.

28   **CHAPTER 1**

of the Civil Code had wrestled with this problem of individualism, they had, according to Le Play, ultimately failed to provide the necessary structures to truly uphold the family, and, consequently, the social more generally. More specifically, Le Play contended that by legalizing divorce, weakening paternal authority, and limiting testamentary freedom, the Civil Code had encouraged smaller families.[31] Familialism—and reform more generally— thus needed to focus on two main areas: amending the Civil Code in order to encourage the development of larger families and convincing the "social elites" to adopt these measures within the workplace.

In opposition to the modern shrinking family (the "unstable family") but also to the excessively authoritarian family structures of feudal Russia and eastern Europe (the "patriarchal family"), Le Play advocated the "stem family" (*famille souche*) as the best solution for France. In stem families, the father selected one child to remain close to the parental home, to work on the farm, and to eventually inherit, thus perpetuating the familial line. The stem family would "conciliate, in a just measure, the authority of the father and the liberty of the children, the inclination to innovate and the respect for tradition." The stem family, however, could only develop when there was "liberty of testament balanced by a strong custom of handing on the inheritance whole and entire."[32] This meant, in other words, reforming the Civil Code.

If individualism ravaged the family, it had also destroyed the social bonds of the workplace: "commercial competition has become a struggle for existence and rages unchecked by the traditions of former years. Only the strongest can resist its assaults; the others succumb. Outstanding individuals advance to the front rank: they rise higher and higher and reject the troublesome obligations which the old regime imposed in them with regard to the weak; the feeble, left to their own resources, sink lower and lower. Thus, social inequality develops, dragging after it a cortege of selfishness, suffering, hatred, and envy."[33] According to Le Play, paternalism was the other solution to the social tensions brought about by modernity. In his ideal society, employers would be responsible for the economic and social welfare of their workers. They would act as moral economists, encouraging private property while at the same time fostering networks of solidarity among the workers, advocating freedom and security at once. For Le Play and for familialism in

---

31. For the details of these reforms, see Margaret H. Darrow, *Revolution in the House: Family, Class, and Inheritance in Southern France, 1775–1825* (Princeton University Press, 1989); Desan, *Family on Trial*. For a discussion of paternal authority, see chap. 1 in Schafer, *Children in Moral Danger.*

32. Blum, *Critics of the Enlightenment,* 229.

33. Cited in Silver, *Frédéric Le Play,* 31.

the years that followed, social reform, whether at the level of state or of the factory, took a familial shape.

❧ The First Familialists: Pro-natalists, Social Catholics, and Paternalists

If Le Play established the theoretical foundations for much of the familialist movement in France, it was not until the 1890s that familialists were able to organize in order to make a series of political demands. The key factor in this familialist mobilization was France's demographic context, and more specifically the declining birthrate. Although the French birthrate had been on a steady decline since the 1850s, it was not until the 1880s that a series of alarming and highly publicized census reports revealed the extent of France's population crisis. France was not the only European country in which a falling birthrate was a source of political anxiety, but France had unquestionably experienced an idiosyncratic demographic transition. At the end of the eighteenth century, many European countries witnessed a decline in their death rate as people tended to live longer. This process was generally followed by a decline in the birthrate, as these same populations chose to restrict their family size. France, however, for reasons that demographers have yet to fully explain, saw its fertility and mortality decline simultaneously at the end of the eighteenth century, bringing about an extremely slow population growth.[34] France's demographic situation worsened from 1890 to 1939 as the number of deaths exceeded the number of births—or, to quote a famous expression of the time, as "the coffins outnumbered the cribs." This meant that the population was no longer renewing itself.[35]

During those years, "depopulation" emerged as one of the most powerful key words in both domestic and foreign policy. As one observer remarked in

---

34. See Joshua Cole, *The Power of Large Numbers: Population, Politics, and Gender in Nineteenth-Century France* (Cornell University Press, 2000), 2; Angus McLaren, *Sexuality and Social Order: The Debate over the Fertility of Women and Workers in France, 1770–1920* (Holmes & Meier, 1983); Jacques Vallin, *La population française* (La découverte, 1992), 22–35.

35. For empirical analyses of this phenomenon, see Yves Charbit, *Du malthusianisme au populationnisme: Les économistes français et la population, 1840–1870* (Presses universitaires de France, 1981); Jacques Dupâquier, ed., *Histoire de la population française,* vol. 3, *De 1789 à 1914* (Presses universitaires de France, 1988); John C. Hunter, "The Problem of the French Birth Rate on the Eve of World War I," *French Historical Studies* 2, no. 4 (1962); Joseph John Spengler, *France Faces Depopulation* (Duke University Press, 1979); Michael S. Teitelbaum and Jay M. Winter, *The Fear of Population Decline* (Academic Press, 1985); Richard Tomlinson, "The Disappearance of France, 1896–1940: French Politics and the Birth Rate," *Historical Journal* 28, no. 2 (1985).

30   **CHAPTER 1**

1910, "One can hardly open a newspaper or a review without finding an article on depopulation, on its causes and its effects, and on the remedies which must be implemented."[36] In the field of foreign policy, depopulation justified France's colonial missions. Similarly, it offered an attractive explanation for the military humiliation in the 1870 war against Prussia, which had resulted in the loss of Alsace-Lorraine. In fact, until World War II, most discussions of the "German threat" involved a reminder of the numerical superiority of the German population and army. As the minister of war Adolphe Messiny lamented in 1913, "a country can only have the army of its birth rate."[37] But France's "depopulation crisis" was not simply a problem of numbers. As many historians have suggested, depopulation served as an umbrella term to cover many of the most pressing political, social, and cultural questions of the Third Republic: nationalism, feminism, the "woman question," neo-Malthusianism and the spread of contraceptive technologies, the promotion of a new republican morality, the ideological war against the church, and the emergence of a new professional class of "experts" trained to interpret these numbers.[38] Thus, while the familialist movement in France claimed that family policy and paternalism were solutions to the depopulation problem, it also offered the family as the answer to these various social questions subsumed under this label of demographic crisis.

The most important and influential actors in early French familialism can be divided into three groups. The first were the *natalistes,* or pro-natalists, for whom the prime political battle was to stop depopulation by increasing the birthrate and fighting contraception, abortion, and all other methods designed to limit births. The most prominent pro-natalist group was the Alliance nationale pour l'accroissement de la population française founded in 1896 by an eminent demographer and statistician Jacques Bertillon, Émile Javal (a doctor and a mining engineer), Charles Richet (a member of the

---

36. Robert Hertz, *Socialisme et dépopulation* (1910), 3, cited in Cole, *Power of Large Numbers,* 181.

37. Cited in Hunter, "Problem of the French Birth Rate," 492.

38. See Elisa Camiscioli, *Reproducing the French Race: Immigration, Intimacy, and Embodiment in the Early Twentieth Century* (Duke University Press, 2009); Cole, *Power of Large Numbers;* Marie-Monique Huss, "Pronatalism in the Inter-War Period in France," *Journal of Contemporary History* 25, no. 1 (1990); McLaren, *Sexuality and Social Order;* Karen Offen, "Depopulation, Nationalism, and Feminism in Fin-de-Siecle France," *American Historical Review* 89, no. 3 (1984); Jean Elisabeth Pedersen, *Legislating the French Family: Feminism, Theater, and Republican Politics, 1870–1920* (Rutgers University Press, 2003); Mary Louise Roberts, *Civilization without Sexes: Reconstructing Gender in Postwar France, 1917–1927* (University of Chicago Press, 1994); Francis Ronsin, *La grève des ventres: Propagande néo-malthusienne et baisse de la natalité française, XIXe–XXe siècles* (Aubier Montaigne, 1980). See also the excellent issue of *French Historical Studies* 19, no. 3 (1996) on "Population and the State in the Third Republic."

FAMILIALISM AND THE REPUBLICAN SOCIAL CONTRACT   31

Paris Medicine Academy and Nobel Prize winner in 1913), and André Honnorat (who worked for the Navy Ministry and was later to become Minister of Public Instruction).

According to the Alliance, no scientific study had ever been able to establish a direct correlation between the fall of the birthrate and the number of marriages in society, the *recherche de paternité* laws, women's emancipation, socialist reforms, or even secularization.[39] Rather, all evidence indicated that parents chose to limit the size of their families for purely financial reasons: "the decrease of births is due to the aspirations of a father for his child."[40] As such, the only effective way to increase population was to promote legal measures—"tax equality of all families"—that would remove some of this financial burden from larger families.[41] Very much influenced by Le Play's writings, the Alliance proposed a set of legal reforms, such as entirely exempting families with more than three children from paying taxes while raising them for smaller families ("selfish families," as Bertillon referred to them) as compensation for the state. Similarly, it called for testamentary freedom and suggested increasing the taxes on the inheritance left to one or two children while creating a special fund with extra capital for fathers of more than three children. Indeed, according to Bertillon, "raising a child must be considered a form of taxation."[42] Children, and the family more generally, were what linked scattered individuals to the collectivity, and reproduction in this context was a social duty.

While some pro-natalist groups made the promotion of morality—chastity, fidelity, and spiritual life—a central component of their activism, the Alliance insisted on the neutral, scientific, and secular nature of its mission.[43] For Bertillon, the definitive way to raise the birthrate was not through moral reeducation but through legislative change. As such, Bertillon presented the Alliance as an organization beyond religious affiliations or political opinions, beyond any particularisms, in the service of the republican *laïc* state.

---

39. Jacques Bertillon, *Le problème de la dépopulation* (Armand Colin, 1897), 35.

40. Ibid., 23.

41. Procès verbaux de l'Alliance nationale, May 12, 1896, cited in Robert Talmy, *Histoire du mouvement familial en France (1896–1939)* (Union nationale des caisses d'allocations familiales, 1962), 1:67.

42. Bertillon, *Le problème de la dépopulation,* 46.

43. The Alliance liked to distinguish itself from more explicitly moral and "intransigent" groups such as Paul Bureau's Comité pour le relèvement de la natalité, which later became the Ligue pour la vie. For more on this, see Kristen Stromberg Childers, *Fathers, Families, and the State in France, 1914–1945* (Cornell University Press, 2003), 46–48; Martine Sevegrand, *Les enfants du bon Dieu: Les catholiques français et la procréation au XXe siècle* (Albin Michel, 1995), 43.

32   **CHAPTER 1**

Because of this pretense of ideological neutrality, the Alliance was able to attract several important political and intellectual figures of the republican elite such as Jean-Louis de Lanessan, Paul Strauss (both Freemasons), Émile Zola (whose 1899 novel *Fécondité* is another example of his interest in depopulation), Le Play's disciple Émile Cheysson, the Chief Rabbi of France, and powerful industrialists such as the Rothschild brothers. Of course, as several historians have pointed out, the claims of scientificity and ideological detachment did not mean that the legislative changes advocated by Bertillon were actually politically neutral.[44] By the interwar years, under the presidency of the indefatigable Fernand Boverat, the discourse of the Alliance (which had switched its name to the Alliance nationale contre la dépopulation) was explicitly sexist and racist.[45]

The second main current within French familialism was known as the *familiaux*. Unlike the pro-natalists, the *familiaux* inscribed their endeavors within Catholicism, or rather, within a particular vision of Social Catholicism.[46] The first generation of the Alliance believed that the best mechanism to fight depopulation was to increase the average birthrate of the overall population—that is, to encourage *all* families to have more babies. The Catholic *familiaux,* however, defended the specific rights of the *familles nombreuses* (a term that today refers to families with more than three children, but this number varied at the time) and insisted on the importance of raising families according to the precepts of the church. Like the Alliance, the *familles nombreuses* organizations lobbied for legislative changes such as tax breaks for larger families. The first association of *familiaux* activists was the Ligue populaire des pères et mères de familles nombreuses founded in 1908 by Captain Simon Maire, a low-ranking army officer and father of ten children. His league became the first real mass movement in family politics, with 600,000 members spread throughout France on the eve of World War I.[47] Little by little, other leagues began to emerge, such as the Ligue des fonctionnaires

---

44. On Bertillon's politics, see Cole, *Power of Large Numbers;* Offen, "Depopulation."

45. For more on Boverat's views on race and gender, see Camiscioli, *Reproducing the French Race;* Cheryl A. Koos, "Gender, Anti-Individualism, and Nationalism: The Alliance Nationale and the Pronatalist Backlash against the Femme Moderne, 1933–1940," *French Historical Studies* 19, no. 3 (1996); Roberts, *Civilization without Sexes,* chap. 4.

46. On Social Catholicism during the nineteenth century, see Jean Baptiste Duroselle, *Les débuts du catholicisme social en France (1822–1870)* (Presses universitaires de France, 1951); Katherine A. Lynch, *Family, Class, and Ideology in Early Industrial France: Social Policy and the Working-Class Family, 1825–1848* (University of Wisconsin Press, 1988); Jean-Marie Mayeur, *Catholicisme social et démocratie chretienne: Principes romains, experiences françaises* (Cerf, 1986).

47. Talmy, *Histoire du mouvement familial,* 1:150.

FAMILIALISM AND THE REPUBLICAN SOCIAL CONTRACT   33

pères de familles nombreuses for state officials in 1911, and in 1916 the most famous, La plus grande famille or "The Bigger Family."

La plus grande famille was created by a group of wealthy industrialists from the Roubaix-Tourcoing region in northern France (themselves fathers of *familles nombreuses*[48]) who felt uneasy with the popular aspect of the Capitaine Maire leagues which gathered, indiscriminately, workers, peasants, and members of the bourgeoisie. Coming from a strong Catholic and elitist background, and very much influenced by Le Play's theories circulating at the congresses of the Société d'économie sociale which many of these industrialists attended, the founders of La plus grande famille appealed to the "social authorities: industry leaders, merchants, bankers, lawyers, doctors, professors, engineers, etc, who had the privilege of having a large family." These "authorities" had a particular social responsibility:

> You who have proved that you understand the national value of a populated household, you who by your intelligence, your courage, your work, hold a high rank within the country's hierarchy, keep yourself from remaining isolated, absorbed by too many personal worries. Use your influence towards a collective goal and coordinate your efforts for a common success: it is time for you to unite in order to put an end to the denial of justice that is losing France by depopulating it.[49]

The purpose of this *association* was double. In practical terms, it was meant to gather these powerful industrialists to give them greater power to lobby for legislative changes similar to the ones proposed by the Alliance and to ensure their political representation and influence.[50] On a more indirect level, their second function was to comply with Le Play's plea to business leaders to "set an example" for the working classes, to stir moral and Catholic sentiments in them, but also to "help them help themselves" financially and spiritually:

> We will not feel secure, we will not be satisfied, we will not end our propaganda until the families of the leading classes will have understood

---

48. Achille Glorieux (1883–1965), one of the founders of the movement, had ten children, and Pierre Lestienne (1872–1947), his cofounder and brother-in-law, had sixteen. To participate in La plus grande famille, members needed to have at least five children. In Rémi Lenoir, *Généalogie de la morale familiale* (Seuil, 2003), 245.

49. Manifesto of La plus grande famille, October 1915, cited in Talmy, *Histoire du mouvement familial,* 1:181.

50. Yves de la Brière, "Pour la plus grande France par la plus grande famille," July 5, 1916, 9, Archives du Musée social.

34   **CHAPTER 1**

that their duty is to set an example. We will not stop until the families of workers and peasants, the great reservoir of men in France, will cease to be doomed, because of their fertility, to an undeserved misery and until they are guaranteed that minimum of comfort without which it is impossible for parents to raise a large family.[51]

This is where the program of these Social Catholic *familiaux* met or at least complemented the vision of the third kind of family activism: entrepreneurial paternalism, which was at the source of the first *caisses de compensation* (or welfare funds) for family allowances, the *caisses de famille*. Paternalism, modeled on Le Play's ideas that industrialists could be the most reliable guarantors of social peace, found a particular resonance in the Œuvre des cercles catholiques d'ouvriers (Work of the Catholic Working-Men's Circles) founded after the 1870 war by René La Tour du Pin and Albert de Mun.[52] Like Le Play, the members of the Œuvre des cercles took liberalism and socialism as two extremes within which the church could play a privileged socializing role, particularly through the family.[53] As the Œuvre des cercles wrote in their 1892 proceedings, "In order to ensure social peace, authorities need to safeguard . . . the worker's right to a wage sufficient for his normal maintenance as well as that of his family's." Furthermore, the text continued, "raising wages to a level that is sufficient for the worker's family to live is a question of justice and not of charity."[54]

---

51. Archives Achille Glorieux, cited in Talmy, *Histoire du mouvement familial,* 1:185.

52. For more on La Tour du Pin and de Mun, see Blum, *Critics of the Enlightenment;* Matthew H. Elbow, *French Corporative Theory, 1789–1948: A Chapter in the History of Ideas* (Columbia University Press, 1953); Benjamin F. Martin, *Count Albert de Mun, Paladin of the Third Republic* (University of North Carolina Press, 1978); Robert Talmy, *Aux sources du catholicisme social: L'école de La Tour du Pin* (Desclée, 1963).

53. The political ambiguity that we find in Le Play is more difficult to support in the cases of La Tour du Pin and de Mun, who explicitly opposed the Revolution and human rights and who called for a religiously grounded counterrevolution. Many commentators (e.g., Jean Baptiste Duroselle) have pointed to the continuity between legitimist and Social Catholic thinkers. Charles Maurras and others at the Action française later claimed to be working in the footsteps of La Tour du Pin, who never accepted the *ralliement* to the Republic (see note 70 of this chapter), was an anti-Dreyfusard, and was an admirer of Edouard Drumont and a convinced monarchist. That said, Social Catholicism eventually became, as Mayeur rightly points out, an umbrella term for many different political tendencies, including, for example, Marc Sangnier's Le Sillon, which was much closer to socialism than to royalist support. After World War II, even the Mouvement républicain populaire (MRP), the party of Georges Bidault and Maurice Schumann, both *résistants* to the Vichy regime, could be seen as adhering to the principles of Social Catholicism.

54. Both cited in Talmy, *Histoire du mouvement familial,* 1:53.

FAMILIALISM AND THE REPUBLICAN SOCIAL CONTRACT   35

These were almost the exact terms that Pope Leo XIII had used in his encyclical *Rerum Novarum,* published the previous year in 1891. The Vatican letter, which began with a condemnation of the social alienation brought about by industrialism, referred to socialism as a "false solution" because it "would rob the lawful possessor, distort the functions of the State, and create utter confusion in the community."[55] The church, according to the pope, could capitalize on this social disarray—and indirectly regain some of its prestige lost during the nineteenth century—by encouraging employers to protect workers, prevent conflicts, defend their employees' interests, improve the working conditions of women and children, and give their workers a *juste salaire* or "just wage." The *juste salaire,* which was at the immediate origin of family allowances, stipulated that despite any specific contract between workers and employers, "wages ought to be sufficient to support a frugal and well-behaved wage-earner."[56]

In the industrial regions of northern France, several *grands patrons,* many of whom were also *familiaux* activists, had by 1891 already set up elementary systems of family allowances. In Roubaix, a *caisse de maternité* was set up in 1888 to give 10 francs for a third child and 15 francs for each child thereafter. In Tourcoing, unionized workers with more than five children got an extra 5 francs each month.[57] In the Val des Bois, close to Reims, Léon Harmel, a textile manufacturer who had participated in the creation of the Œuvre des cercles catholiques with de Mun and La Tour du Pin, organized a fund in 1891 to complement the wages of worker families whose capital did not amount to what Harmel had calculated was necessary for them to live decently. Harmel also provided free medical care for workers and low-cost housing, and he actively encouraged his workers to turn to Catholicism.[58] Émile Romanet, another disciple of de Mun and La Tour du Pin, systematized this practice after concluding from a survey conducted within his steel factory near Grenoble that unmarried workers were less stable (and hence less desirable for the company) than *pères de famille,* but that the latter

---

55. *Rerum Novarum: Encyclical of Pope Leo XIII on Capital and Labor,* available from http://www.vatican.va/holy_father/leo_xiii/encyclicals/documents/hf_l-xiii_enc_15051891_rerum-novarum_en.html.

56. Ibid.

57. Talmy, *Histoire du mouvement familial,* 1:91.

58. For more on Harmel, see Joan L. Coffey, *Léon Harmel: Entrepreneur as Catholic Social Reformer* University of Notre Dame Press, 2003); Adrien Dansette, *Histoire religieuse de la France contemporaine* (Flammarion, 1952); Georges Guitton, *La vie ardente et féconde de Léon Harmel* (Éditions Spes, 1930); Pierre Trimouille, *Léon Harmel et l'usine chrétienne du Val des Bois: 1840–1914, fécondité d'une expérience sociale* (Centre d'histoire du catholicisme, 1974).

36   **CHAPTER 1**

had a difficult time making ends meet. In 1915, he decided to give fathers 0.20 francs per day per child under thirteen.[59]

For employers, of course, these allowances served other purposes than simply promoting Catholic ideals of the family. As Susan Pedersen has persuasively shown, the acute interest in family policy was intimately tied to a particular business strategy: inculcating habits of regularity and docility in workers, giving them a financial disincentive to strike, and undermining the appeal of trade unions.[60] Gérard Noiriel has described this form of entrepreneurial paternalism at the end of the nineteenth century as a "neo-liberal compromise."[61] The point was not to encourage *more* state intervention, but rather, from a sort of behavioral economics perspective, to shift the social question into the hands of the employers. In fact, many *grand patrons* were hostile to the 1932 law making family benefits mandatory. As Susan Pedersen has suggested, these employers did not just wish to influence the state, they sought to replace it: "their *caisses* would extract voluntary contributions from businessmen that the Ministry of Finance could only dream of. Operating 'independently,' they forced the logic of family-based redistribution outside the restricted sphere of industries sheltered by state control. By so doing, however, they created a financial system that made a comprehensive national policy—and their own ultimate supersession—possible."[62]

In more popular milieux, the ideas of Social Catholicism concerning the family were also pervasive through the activism of a number of priests known as the *abbés démocrates*. In 1902, the abbé Viollet founded in the fourteenth arrondissement in Paris the Société du logement ouvrier, which later

---

59. See Paul Dreyfus, *Émile Romanet, père des allocations familiales* (Arthaud, 1965).

60. Susan Pedersen, *Family, Dependence, and the Origins of the Welfare State: Britain and France, 1914– 1945* (Cambridge University Press, 1993), 285.

61. Gérard Noiriel, *Les ouvriers dans la société française: XIXe–XXe siècle* (Seuil, 1986), 77–78.

62. Pedersen, *Family, Dependence,* 15. The term "neoliberal" seems particularly adequate here in light of Michel Foucault's writings on neoliberal modes of governmentality. Contrary to the common belief that neoliberalism advocated the state's disengagement from social policy, Foucault argued that the central preoccupation of neoliberalism was the "conduct of conducts." Neoliberalism in this sense has been coexistent with biopolitics, the set of techniques designed to regulate life in the wide sense of the term. In the case of these Social Catholic businessmen, we can talk about a form of entrepreneurial governmentality that sought to turn workers into *homo œconomicus*: workers would believe that having children, remaining sober, or going to church was in their best interests. See Graham Burchell, Colin Gordon, and Peter Miller, eds., *The Foucault Effect: Studies in Governmentality* (Harvester Wheatsheaf, 1991); Michel Foucault, *The Birth of Biopolitics: Lectures at the Collège de France, 1978–79,* trans. Graham Burchell (Palgrave Macmillan, 2008); Martin Hewitt, "Bio-politics and Social Policy: Foucault's Account of Welfare," *Theory, Culture, and Society* 2, no. 1 (1983). On paternalism and liberalism, see François Ewald, *L'État providence* (Grasset, 1986), chap. 3.

FAMILIALISM AND THE REPUBLICAN SOCIAL CONTRACT   37

became the Fondation des œuvres du moulin vert. Initially designed to help
workers pay their rent, this association eventually became a forum for all
kinds social actions geared toward helping working-class families "help
themselves." As Viollet put it, "If we have the right to demand that the state
improve the fate of large families, we should not forget that families must
help themselves. They must not content themselves with political action.
They must become an economic power that will, by its own means, answer
to the many needs of the family."[63] Viollet's idea was to set up community
health centers, libraries, day-care centers, summer camps, and conference
rooms for working-class families in order to "save" the family from the
control of the state or the professional world. In Viollet's writings, we see
again this oscillation between socialism (absolute state control) and liberalism (absolute control by employers) in which the church can provide a
middle ground. Viollet, whose project of family *mutualité* (the earlier term
for social security) was the model for the types of *associations familiales* that
later proliferated, did not hesitate to use social action to spread Christian
ideals, particularly in the fields of marriage and reproduction. Thus, he
published and promoted books with titles such as *L'éducation de la pureté et
du sentiment* (1927), *La bonne entente conjugale* (1932), and *Petit traité du marriage:
Les lois du véritable amour* (1938) through his 1918 Association du mariage
chrétien.

Another of these priests was the abbé Lemire, who, in 1896, founded the
Ligue française du coin de terre et du foyer, which he presided over for
thirty years.[64] The association sought to consolidate the family around its
"natural bases," the earth and the hearth. In practical terms, this meant allowing workers to cultivate small land parcels for exclusive use by their
families. As an elected representative in 1894, Lemire was able to pass various laws to improve employees' working conditions, promote retirement
funds and family benefits, and transmit other measures inspired by Social
Catholicism. In 1899, with the help of other elected representatives—many
of whom were close to the Alliance nationale—Lemire succeeded in guar-
anteeing postal workers a monthly salary supplement of 50 francs if they
had at least three children. This represented a major development in the
history of the familial movement in France because postal employees were
civil servants and agreeing to give them family benefits indicated that the

---

63. Cited in Michel Messu, *Les politiques familiales: Du natalisme à la solidarité* (Éditions Ouvrières,
1992), 22. See also Sevegrand, *Les enfants du bon Dieu,* 47.

64. Jean-Marie Mayeur, *Un prêtre démocrate: L'abbé Lemire 1853–1928* (Castermann, 1968).

38   CHAPTER 1

state was now directly involved in family affairs. Indeed, soon after the postal workers, other public-sector employees began demanding family benefits. By 1900, the Alliance nationale estimated that 84,000 civil servants received these benefits. By the eve of World War I, the system of family funds, which was later consolidated under the Code de la famille, had already strong political and social roots.

ᴖ The Family Vote

Historians such as Jean-Marie Mayeur and Paul-André Rosental have pointed to the discrepancy between the vast literature deploring depopulation in France and the actual measures adopted by the authorities, which remained meager in comparison.[65] Aside from two extraparliamentary commissions set up to fight depopulation, concrete changes in family legislation were indeed few and scattered until the 1930s. However, I want to suggest that the work of these early familialists was central to explaining the importance of family policy within the French welfare state. First, from a structural perspective, these early familialists built an infrastructure for family policy that the state simply tapped into in the late 1930s. Second, from an ideological perspective, the rhetoric deployed by these early family activists came to form a *theory* of familialism, which posited that the family was the solution to the social question because it was universal and beyond any particular political affiliations. This construction of the family as synonymous with universalism was particularly apparent in the familialists' attempt to promote a family vote (or *suffrage familial*), an endeavor that ultimately failed but is nevertheless indicative of how familialism operated as an ideology.

The family vote consisted of giving each male head of the household— the *père de famille*—the number of votes corresponding to his number of children plus that of his wife. As early as 1848, Lamartine had claimed that "the day would come when the father will have as many votes as there are elderly, women, and children in his home, because in a better made society, it is not the individual but the family that is the permanent unit."[66] After the 1871 elections and the return of the *notables* on the political scene, the Baron de Jouvenel proposed a family vote to restore what he called

---

65. Jean-Marie Mayeur, *Les débuts de la Troisième République, 1871–1898* (Seuil, 1973), 57, Paul-André Rosental, *L'intelligence démographique: Sciences et politiques des populations en France, 1930–1960* (Odile Jacob, 2003), 77.

66. Cited in Joseph Landrieu, "Le vote familial" (thesis, Université de Lille, 1923), 13.

FAMILIALISM AND THE REPUBLICAN SOCIAL CONTRACT   39

the "principle of authority": "To not give fathers faced with the ballot
more rights than those given to a twenty-one-year-old child who has just
reached civil and political adulthood is to seriously undermine the most
respectable, most eminently protective principles of all societies: property,
work, the family."[67] The Assembly overwhelmingly rejected the measure as
a conservative scam to jeopardize universal suffrage.

Still, despite the bad reputation it acquired after this episode, familialists,
especially the Alliance nationale, continued to push for the family vote. In
July 1911, the abbé Lemire brought the idea up again at the Chamber of
Deputies, during a debate on electoral reform. According to Lemire, fran-
chise was "both a right and a function . . . It is not merely a right inherent
to a person that the law should grant to all; it is also a function, given to the
individual in view of the general good." And the general good, Lemire continued, demanded that women and children be represented: "A state is not
composed of juxtaposed individuals. The true social cell is the family. And
in a civilized country, the family is the legally recognized union between a
man and a woman."[68] The family vote was ultimately defeated, but the idea
that sovereignty belonged neither to the individual nor to the state but to the
family seduced many deputies who were already receptive to pro-natalist or
familialist opinions.

In his account of the family vote, Pierre Rosanvallon writes that Lemire's
proposal was impregnated with "Bonaldian principles."[69] As with Le Play,
however, this genealogy of familialism to a counterrevolutionary tradition
is difficult to sustain. To be sure, the promoters of the family vote shared
Bonald's attack on individualism and considered the family the primary
social unit, but familialism was neither external nor tangential to the Third
Republic. The theorizers of familialism were intellectuals, scientists, and
engineers in close proximity to political power, if they were not elected
officials themselves. Even within the more openly religious strand of familialism, very few activists were actual *ultras* or supporters of a monarchical
restoration. This was especially true of Social Catholics, even the ones believed to be more "intransigent." Paul Bureau, the head of Pour la vie, and the
abbé Viollet were both Dreyfusards, friends of Marc Sangnier, and close to
the *Sillon* movement. Both participated in the Semaines sociales, the "social

---

67. Cited in Talmy, *Histoire du mouvement familial,* 1:39. On this history of the family vote, see
Childers, *Fathers, Families,* 49–57.

68. Talmy, *Histoire du mouvement familial,* 1:120–21.

69. Pierre Rosanvallon, *Le sacre du citoyen: Histoire du suffrage universel en France* (Gallimard, 1992), 403.

40   **CHAPTER 1**

weeks" founded in 1904 by *laïc* Catholics to promote the church's social thought and apply it to the issues of the time, in particular to the problem of the working class, following Pope Leo XIII's 1891 encyclical. Lemire had a similar background, as a priest *"rallié"* to the republic who ran in the 1893 elections as a "Christian socialist."[70] Resolutely *laïcs,* these familialists found spirituality and secularism to be perfectly compatible. As such, they operated within the confines set up by republican law: they sought to reform the Civil Code, to modify tax and labor legislation, and to run for office, but never to overturn the Republic in favor of a monarchy or a theocracy. As such, they succeeded in inscribing familialist policy at the very heart of republicanism.

The universalization of the family in the familial vote is especially interesting in light of the women's vote, which became a recurring question at the end of the nineteenth century. Pierre Rosanvallon, who treats the question of the women's suffrage in the same chapter in which he addresses the family vote, has urged us to look beyond the three classic explanations for the famous French "lag" in granting women the right to vote. Instead of focusing on the cultural weight of Catholicism, the political fears of Republicans, and the institutional blockage of the Senate, Rosanvallon contends that the woman vote presented a fundamental philosophical and political problem for French political culture.[71] While women in Britain and the United States were given the right to vote because of their specificity (as women), France always insisted on political equality among individuals: "French-style universalism constituted . . . an obstacle to women's suffrage: women were denied the right to vote because of their particularity, because they were not true abstract individuals, because they remained too marked by the determinations of their sex."[72]

In much of her recent work, Joan Scott has addressed this question of women's "abstractability" within French universalism. According to Scott, within French republicanism, "the difference of sex was not considered to be susceptible to abstraction; it was irreducible, symbolic of a fundamental

---

70. The *"ralliement"* is the name given to Pope Leo XIII's incitation, around the 1890s, for French Catholics to abandon their hopes of a monarchical restoration and accept the French Republic and laïcité. In his monograph on Lemire, Jean-Marie Mayeur points to the political fluidity of Social Catholicism, of which Lemire is representative, and argues that Lemire's political ideals were very much in line with the political program of the République des députés. See Mayeur, *Un prêtre démocrate.* On the Semaines sociales, see Jean-Dominique Durand, ed., *Les semaines sociales de France: Cent ans d'engagement social des catholiques français 1904–2004* (Parole et silence, 2006).

71. Rosanvallon, *Le sacre du citoyen,* 393.

72. Ibid., 396.

FAMILIALISM AND THE REPUBLICAN SOCIAL CONTRACT   41

division or antagonism that could not be reconciled with the notion of an indivisible nation."[73] It is thus not a coincidence that the familial vote became popular around the end of the mid-nineteenth century, as women were becoming a more pressing political stake for Republicans. As historian Anne Verjus has argued, the claim in favor of a familial vote emerged as women were exiting the space of neutrality and invisibility of the early nineteenth century and as the electoral system demanded to be reorganized in light of this "woman question."[74] Women could not operate as abstract citizens not so much because of their sex but because of "their socio-natural status as wives and mothers of citizens, that is to say, as *members of a family,* like children and servants."[75] In contrast to this unsurpassable particularity of women, the family represented the most general of interests, the most abstract form of universalism, the true universalism that would include men, women, and children.

And indeed, family vote advocates consistently relied on this rhetoric of family universalism and women particularism. As the deputy Roulleaux-Dugage campaigned for the *vote familial* in parliament in 1920, "If universal suffrage is indeed founded on the absolute principle of equality among citizens . . . we must logically grant to all French people, of whatever age and sex, the equal right to be represented in parliament, as well as in the communal and departmental assemblies."[76] Women should indeed demand the right to vote, many familialists contended, but *only* as members of the family and not as "selfish" individualistic feminists. As one familialist lobbyer André Toulemon exclaimed, "French women, claim your stake in national sovereignty! You have the right to it in the name of the principles of our modern democracies founded on equality and on the absolute respect of the rights of the human person! But do not make this claim selfish: demand suffrage for all! . . . For your children and for the country, never be feminists without being familial."[77]

---

73. Scott, "French Universalism in the Nineties," 34–35. See also Joan Wallach Scott, *Only Paradoxes to Offer: French Feminists and the Rights of Man* (Harvard University Press, 1996); Scott, *Parité!*

74. Anne Verjus, "Vote familialiste et vote familial: Contribution à l'étude du processus d'individualisation des femmes dans la première partie du XIXe siècle," *Genèses: Sciences Sociales et Histoire,* no. 31 (1998): 31. See also Virginie de Luca, "Les femmes et les enfants aussi, ou le droit d'être représenté par le vote familial," in Michel Chauvière, ed., *Les mouvements familiaux et leur institution en France: Anthologie historique et sociale* (Comité d'histoire de la Sécurité sociale, 2006), 448–60.

75. Verjus, "Vote familialiste et vote familial," 35.

76. Cited in Landrieu, "Le vote familial," 34.

77. André Toulemon, *Le Suffrage familial et le vote des femmes* (Recueil Sirey, 1933), 232. Susan Pedersen points to this tension between feminism and familialism in Pedersen, *Family, Dependence,* 77 and 364.

42   CHAPTER 1

State Familialism: The Haut comité de la population and the Code de la famille

Because of these structural and ideological efforts of pro-family lobbyists at the turn of the century, the French state became very much involved in family affairs by the 1930s. World War I, and particularly the 1.4 million deaths, intensified the rhetoric of depopulation, persuading elected representatives to make family policy a national priority. In the bellicose climate of the interwar years, with the "German threat" accentuated by Hitler's rise to power and the enduring economic crisis, population questions gained a sense of political urgency. Moreover, France's cultural and social changes during this period, which produced a general anxiety around gender and sexuality, legitimated a familialist discourse that proposed to revalorize the family and traditional gender roles.[78] Family activists decided to organize national meetings, the Congrès de la natalité, where *familiaux* and *natalistes* could gather to plan their political strategy. During the first of these congresses, held in Nancy in 1919, the participants outlined six main tasks for family policy: the moral battle against pornography, abortion, and neo-Malthusian propaganda; the fight against slums and housing construction projects; the *vote familial;* the expansion of family benefits; subsidies for *familles nombreuses;* and a "moral reform of intelligences and wills."[79] Congress members also called for the creation of a permanent governmental committee for *natalité,* whose role would be to promote these measures. With the 1919 victory of the rightist coalition, the Bloc national and their Chambre bleu-horizon, this request was satisfied.

In 1920, the président du conseil, Alexandre Millerand, who had already invited three members of the Congrès de Nancy steering committee to participate in his government as ministers (Auguste Isaac as minister of commerce, Joseph-Honoré Ricard of agriculture, and Jules-Louis Breton of hygiene, assistance, and social planning), inaugurated a Conseil superieur de la natalité. Familial activists were thus able to pass a series of laws in the following years, including birth premiums for families with more than three children (*primes à la natalité*), military benefits for larger families, a tax increase for non-married citizens, and subsidized housing, discounts on train tickets, and student scholarships for *familles nombreuses.* During this period,

---

78. Among others, see Carolyn J. Dean, *The Frail Social Body: Pornography, Homosexuality, and Other Fantasies in Interwar France* (University of California Press, 2000); Roberts, *Civilization without Sexes.*

79. Talmy, *Histoire du mouvement familial,* 1:210.

FAMILIALISM AND THE REPUBLICAN SOCIAL CONTRACT   43

the state also promoted a "Medal for French Families" for mothers of five, eight, and ten children and it instituted an official Mother's Day.[80]

By 1928, more than half of the National Assembly had joined the "Family and Birthrate Group" (Groupe de la famille et de la natalité) and the Alliance nationale counted 40,000 members.[81] Even the communists, who were enthusiastic about neo-Malthusianism in the early twentieth century, were eventually swayed towards pro-natalism, such that by July 1936 all seventy-two French Communist Party deputies in the chamber had joined this Family and Birthrate Group.[82] Moreover, by 1937, Maurice Thorez, who claimed to be worried about the "birth rate crisis consuming our people," was calling in his speeches for a "national policy for the protection of children, mothers, and the family."[83] During those years, the pro-natalist bloc's most important accomplishment was the March 11, 1932, law that forced all employers in the industrial sector to become affiliated with a *caisse de compensation,* or welfare fund, for family benefits, thus making it mandatory for workers to receive *allocations familiales.*[84] Family benefits were no longer an extra incentive that employers could decide to offer; they became a worker's right, and thus part of "social security" more generally.[85]

One of the turning points in the history of familialism, marking the explicit intervention of the state in family policy, was a speech delivered by Senator Georges Pernot, also president of the Fédération nationale des associations de familles nombreuses, in February 1938. Citing statistics of births and deaths, Pernot deplored the German and Italian "numerical advantage" as well as the "moral sickness" of his country. France, Pernot contended,

---

80. Ibid., see vol. 2, chap. 9.

81. Miranda Pollard, *Reign of Virtue: Mobilizing Gender in Vichy France* (University of Chicago Press, 1998), 11.

82. Chrisitine Bard and Jean-Louis Robert, "The French Communist Party and Women, 1920–1939: From 'Feminism' to 'Familialism,'" in *Women and Socialism/Socialism and Women: Europe between the Two World Wars,* ed. Pamela Graves and Helmut Gruber (Berghahn Books, 1998); François Delpa, "Les communistes français et la sexualité (1932–1938)," *Le Mouvement Social* 91, April–June (1975); Pollard, *Reign of Virtue,* 18.

83. Delpa, "Les communistes français," 141.

84. For more on the logistics of the law, see Dominique Ceccaldi, *Histoire des prestations familiales en France* (Union nationale des caisses d'allocations familiales, 1957).

85. We can also note that family benefits represented an important financial help for working-class families. To give one example, in 1944 a Parisian family with three children and only the father working would receive 1,350 francs each month, which meant approximately US$250. Because the hourly salary for workers was of about 15 francs—2,900 francs a month—family benefits represented a financial complement of almost half of the salary. Bruno Valat, *Histoire de la Sécurité sociale (1945–1967): L'état, l'institution et la santé* (Economica, 2001), 18.

44   **CHAPTER 1**

needed a *real* family policy in the form of a legal document that would structure and solidify the dispersed measures already in place, as well as an official body of administrators whose task would be to devise and promote these laws: "We must create a policy that will restore this country's faith, soul, ideal, as well as its trust and confidence in the future."[86] The idea of a "family code" had come up during the 1930 Congrès de la natalité in Lille. Similarly, during the 1914 Semaines sociales in Grenoble, several familialists had reiterated their desire to create a Ministry of Population that would coordinate all issues related to the population within the different ministerial branches. In the years preceding the Family Code, the office of the président du conseil was flooded with letters from all kinds of family *associations* requesting an official committee on population. As Pernot and Boverat put it in a 1938 letter to the président du conseil, Édouard Daladier: "We address you with trust . . . and respectfully beg you as a matter of urgency to finalize the family policy and demographic program for which the entire country has understood the necessity." Referring to the various familialist initiatives already in place, the letter asked Daladier to set up a committee in charge of drafting a legal proposition to "coordinate all efforts and ensure the prompt realization of the appropriate reforms."[87]

Daladier, having just returned from Munich, accepted. On February 24, 1939, he created the Haut comité de la population, an organization designed to focus on the problems of birthrate and immigration. France, as Daladier put it, was "surrounded by nations in full demographic effervescence" which constituted a true threat for the present and the future. The existing legislative and regulative measures had proved too diverse and dispersed, and they lacked a "directive idea." Thus, Daladier explained, "It has become crucial in these condition to create an organization within the Présidence du conseil whose role will precisely be to develop a general program destined to remedy the current demographic situation, as it has been repeatedly demanded both within parliament and by general assemblies."[88] The Haut comité, which depended on the Secrétariat général de la présidence du conseil,[89] was composed of five permanent members: Senator Georges

---

86. Pernot's speech was republished in the journal *Pour la Vie* 68, March 1957, 88–104. See also Talmy, *Histoire du mouvement familial,* 2:224.

87. Letter from October 4, 1938, AN F 60 495.

88. *Journal Officiel,* February 24, 1939, AN F 60 495.

89. The Présidence du conseil was itself a rather new institution; it was created in March 1935 with the aim of balancing political powers in the midst of the 1930s parliamentary instability and giving more agency to the executive branch. It is in this context that these new "commissions," such as the

FAMILIALISM AND THE REPUBLICAN SOCIAL CONTRACT 45

Pernot; député and former minister Adolphe Landry; Philippe Serre, another député and former state under-secretary; Fernand Boverat, president of the Alliance nationale contre la dépopulation; Frédéric Roujou, the maître de requêtes at the Conseil d'état; and Jacques Doublet, an auditeur at the Conseil d'état, who was named secrétaire général of the Haut comité.[90] Eventually, the Comité grew as each ministry concerned with issues of population (justice, interior, public health, labor, finances, and foreign affairs) delegated their representatives. Several "experts," such as the statistician demographer and future president of the Institut national d'études démographiques (INED) Alfred Sauvy and the psychoanalyst Georges Mauco, who were at first invited as speakers, became permanent participants in the Haut comité meetings.

The fact that the Haut comité was in charge not only of promoting births but also of handling immigration was significant. For one, it confirmed the ideological direction toward which the familialist movement had already been leaning since World War I, one increasingly preoccupied with morality, hygiene, and racial purity. The point was no longer to raise the birthrate at whatever cost but to encourage French families to have more French babies. This was particularly evident in the language deployed by Boverat, who participated in many of the initial Haut comité meetings. In his interventions, Boverat repeatedly pleaded for the penalization of abortion, pointing to Germany and Italy as reference points for successful pro-natalist policies: "Today, nobody contests the need to fight abortion: the falling birth rate and depopulation which is its consequence will finally lead France to its ruin and to war if these factors are not curbed, and all the more rapidly since our country has as its neighbors peoples who each year register a considerable excess in births . . . The example of what has been achieved in Germany proves that it is perfectly possible."[91] Similarly, Georges Mauco argued that French authorities needed to limit Jewish immigration since the "Israelites," who had a difficult time "integrating" into French society, "fed

---

Haut comité but also the Conseil national économique in 1925, began to emerge. Pierre Rosanvallon describes these interwar consulting bodies as a form of "corporative state"—not as a precursor to Vichy and not as a replacement for universal suffrage, but rather as another model of social representation (*Le peuple introuvable,* 357–58). For more on the particular context of the Third Republic's political history within which the Comité was created, see also Rosental, *L'intelligence démographique,* 32–33.

90. For more on the personal and political background of these figures, see Rosental, *L'intelligence démographique,* 22–27.

91. Report by Fernand Boverat, "La lutte contre l'avortement," presented on April 22, 1939, AN F 60 494. We can also find in the Haut comité correspondence several letters denouncing midwives and doctors who performed abortions.

46   CHAPTER 1

the anti-Semitic movement."[92] The Haut comité, as Antoine Prost has suggested, inaugurated France's first real "*politique familiale*," a *politique* that was also a biopolitics: "The State knew which families it wanted and it adopted a coherent set of measures to favor these families and to penalize the others: it was an authentic *politique familiale*."[93] More broadly, the Haut comité's double mission also confirms the mutual imbrication of family and citizenship, a connection that historians such as Jennifer Ngaire Heuer, Karen Adler, and Elisa Camiscioli have highlighted in their works.[94]

In the sector on family law, the Haut comité's most important accomplishment was undoubtedly the Code de la famille, voted into law on July 29, 1939. The Family Code reflected the ideas of its redactors, the members of the Haut Comité, and more generally the ideas of much of the familialist movement. As one editorialist for a pro-family journal put it, "The Code de la famille . . . will remain in history as the greatest act ever accomplished in favor of the French family. After so many years of individualism, selfishness (single or in couples), Malthusianism, voluntary sterility, the wasting away of family institutions, and general lack of concern for the future, France gets a hold of herself and shows the world that she, too, wants to live and survive."[95] The Code was divided into four main sections: "help for the family," protection of the family, fiscal measures, and a fourth part on "diverse dispositions." The purpose of the first section was to unify family benefits and extend them to all professions. A new *prime à la première naissance* was added for the first child of French nationality born within two years after a legitimate marriage, as well as an *allocation de la mère de foyer* for stay-at-home mothers. Under the second section on protection, the Code claimed to protect maternity, children, *bonnes mœurs,* as well as the French "race."[96] This clause ranged from the fight against drugs and alcohol to the criminalization of abortion. "Abortionists" could get up to ten years in prison and a fine between 5,000 to 10,000 francs, and women who tried to have abortions

92. Séance du 28 mars 1939, AN F 60 494.

93. Antoine Prost, "L'évolution de la politique familiale en France de 1938 à 1981," *Le Mouvement Social* 129 (1984): 10.

94. Karen H. Adler, *Jews and Gender in Liberation France* (Cambridge University Press, 2003); Camiscioli, *Reproducing the French Race;* Heuer, *Family and the Nation.*

95. Revue de *La Famille,* organe des Caisses de compensation pour allocations familiales (founded in 1928) no. 196, August 15, 1939, 3, AN F 60 495.

96. As Carolyn Dean has shown in *The Frail Social Body, bonnes mœurs* was a keyword used to condemn all kinds of gender or sexual "deviances" that appeared to threaten the cohesion of the social body, especially pornography and homosexuality.

FAMILIALISM AND THE REPUBLICAN SOCIAL CONTRACT   47

risked up to two years of jail time and 100 to 2,000 francs in fines. Finally, in its last section, the Code enacted several of the familialist theories concerning taxes and inheritance, essentially forcing unmarried individuals to pay more and *familles nombreuses* to pay less.

Rather than canceling the various family legislative and regulative measures of the previous years, the Code chose to expand and solidify them into one legal document, into a "solid armature which would allow the family to flourish."[97] For many familialist activists, the Code's main achievement was thus not so much legal as it was psychological. The state was now definitely involved in family policy, and the Code appeared as a reward for their relentless activism. After "a century of individualism," a new era was beginning, "one in which the family would become the foundation for an entire social edifice."[98] The Code and the Haut comité inscribed familialism as both theory and practice at the very heart of the Republican order. The Vichy regime, which made the family one of the cornerstones of its National Revolution, was able to tap into this existing infrastructure (the Family Code and the Haut comité) and ideology (the family as the basic social cell) in order to give familialist causes their full legal, political, and administrative expressions.

⌁ Familialism under Vichy

Many historians of the Vichy period have singled out family policy as particularly indicative of the continuities between the Third Republic and the État français.[99] As Rémi Lenoir has written, the Vichy regime constituted a "sort of laboratory of what a familialist regime would look like had the various propositions elaborated since the end of the nineteenth century been applied literally and according to the spirit of their theorizers."[100] Although it is crucial to stress the important differences between a family policy conceived under a democratic regime, as consensual as it may have been on these issues, and one set up under a dictatorship, the similarities remain

---

97. Exposé des motifs précédant le Code, cited in Talmy, *Histoire du mouvement familial,* 2:234.

98. Ibid., 2:241. This is also the conclusion reached by Alain Drouard, "Le haut comité de la population et la politique de population de la France (1939–1966)," *Annales de Demographie Historique* 2 (1999): 172. On the particular history of the Code, see Chauvière, *Les mouvements familiaux,* 78–117.

99. See, for example, Robert O. Paxton, *Vichy France: Old Guard and New Order, 1940–1944* (Knopf, 1972), 166; Pollard, *Reign of Virtue,* 200.

100. Lenoir, *Généalogie,* 352.

48   **CHAPTER 1**

nonetheless striking on both ideological and institutional levels.[101] I would suggest that these continuities can be explained by two factors: first, the extensive and deeply rooted administrative network set up by the familialist actors of the Third Republic, and second, the particular ideology that posited the family as a remedy for depopulation and as the enactor for the social, a specifically French social that would avoid political partisanship—or, more precisely here, the extremes of communism and liberalism.

The social was indeed a central preoccupation for Maréchal Pétain. "To be national," declared Pétain in 1942, "our revolution must be social. I do not want my country to have either Marxism or liberal capitalism."[102] Liberalism, capitalism, and collectivism were "foreign products imported into France, which France, left to her true self, quite naturally rejects." Within this context, the family was the primary corporation, the foundation of the social and consequently, of the political order. "The right of families," Pétain argued, "is anterior and superior to that of the state and to that of the individuals. The family is the essential cell; it is the very base of the social edifice. It is that upon which we must build."[103] This understanding of the family as the "glue" to the social was inscribed in Vichy's July 1941 Constitution, which declared that "the State considers first and foremost the individual in relation to the groups to which he belongs . . . These groups are the organic elements of the Nation and of the State" (Article 52). Among these social groups, "the family is the basic social group. It ensures the material continuity of the Nation and develops the moral feelings necessary to its greatness" (Article 53).[104]

The continuities between the type of family policy proposed by familialists and the one implemented by Vichy were not only ideological. On a practical level, familialism penetrated various state infrastructures, particularly in three fields: the administrative branches pertaining to family policy, family law, and the official representative bodies of families. Only in this last

---

101. Francine Muel-Dreyfus, for example, warns us against the "continuity thesis" of family policy between the Third Republic and Vichy, in *Vichy et l'éternel féminin: Contribution à une sociologie politique de l'ordre des corps* (Seuil, 1996), 95.

102. Maréchal Pétain, 1942 speech, cited in Elbow, *French Corporative Theory,* 172.

103. "La Politique sociale de l'avenir," in *Revue des Deux Mondes* (September 15, 1940), cited ibid., 177. For more on Vichy corporatism, see Steven L. Kaplan, "Un laboratoire de la doctrine corporatiste sous le régime de Vichy: L'Institut d'études corporatives et sociales," *Le Mouvement Social* 195, April–June (2001).

104. For more on Vichy's family policy, see Michèle Bordeaux, *La victoire de la famille dans la France défaite: Vichy 1940–1944* (Flammarion, 2002); Childers, *Fathers, Families;* Muel-Dreyfus, *Vichy et l'éternel féminin;* Pollard, *Reign of Virtue.*

FAMILIALISM AND THE REPUBLICAN SOCIAL CONTRACT 49

field did Vichy innovate in the domain of family policy. In June 1940, in the midst of the French military defeat, the président du conseil Paul Reynaud decided to create, as planned by the Code de la famille, a Ministry of the Family.[105] Headed by Georges Pernot, the new ministry was meant to coordinate the help to families displaced by the war. After the proclamation of the new Vichy regime on July 10, 1940, this ministry underwent a series of name changes; the Secrétariat d'état à la famille et à la jeunesse in July 1940 finally became, on September 7, 1941, the Commissariat général à la famille, directed by Philippe Renaudin. Renaudin, a *maître de requêtes* at the Conseil d'état, was to become the main architect of Vichy's family policy.

Like Pétain, Renaudin denounced, in terms reminiscent of Le Play's, the "one hundred and fifty years of legal individualism, an economy of production and competition, industrial work that makes the family explode, a regime of goods and transmissions that pulverizes our heritage, the dissolution of mores, the generalization of a spirit contemptuous of all hierarchy . . . The familial foundation, built on authority, discipline, solidarity, and future life, has given way."[106] Although Renaudin praised the creation of the Haut comité and the Code de la famille, they were only a "belated effort of a nation beginning, with anguish, to discover its weaknesses."[107] The family was not simply important for the nation, it was *necessary* for the very existence of the social. As he argued, "For the state, to say that the family is essential is not enough; it is constitutive. As the basic cell, it blossoms in the commune, a coming together of hearths, and from generation to generation in the nation of which it is the living substance. Between state and family, the reactions are direct; the greatness of the one leads to the greatness of the other; the weakening or deficiency of families determines the decline of the state."[108] The purpose of the Commissariat was double: to reform and expand legislation pertaining to the family along the guidelines set up by the Code, and to "moralize" families through its national office for propaganda. With the slogan "coordinate, control, lead," the Commissariat sought to harmonize the different ministries, to ensure the rightful application of the laws, and to

---

105. *Journal Officiel,* November 1940, 5619. For more on the creation of this ministry, see Rosental, *L'intelligence démographique,* 55.

106. Philippe Renaudin, "La famille dans la nation" (L'office de propagande générale, June 16, 1943), 9, Archives du Musée social.

107. Ibid., 4.

108. Ibid., 6.

50   CHAPTER 1

spread familialist ideas.[109] Although the main office was located in Paris, the Commissariat sent out regional representatives (the Délégués régionaux à la famille, or DRF) to oversee this project on a local level.[110]

In parallel, several advisory boards were created around the Commissariat to rethink family policy. The Comité consultatif de la famille française, which had more or less the same function as the Haut comité, was founded in 1941 to deliberate on "all questions relating to the material and moral interests of the family." Its role was to take up the attributions previously granted to the Conseil supérieur de la natalité and to the Haut comité de la population.[111] Not only were their archives directly transferred to the new organization, but most members of the Conseil had been important interwar family activists: Georges Pernot, Jacques Doublet, Alfred Sauvy, and the abbé Viollet.[112] The Comité set up seven research teams focusing on legislation, housing, food rationing, financial help for families, education, childhood, and moral protection of the family.[113] In June 1943, the Comité was replaced by the Conseil supérieur de la famille, which acquired greater responsibilities but remained similar in its role and composition.

Another family-centered think tank was the Fondation française pour l'étude des problèmes humains, also known as the Fondation Carrel, founded in November 1941, whose role was to "collect statistics and gather information on 'human questions,' set up research centers, find practical solutions, and proceed to all demonstrations seeking to improve the psychological, mental, and social state of the population."[114] The members of

---

109. For more on the structure and composition of the Commissariat, see Bordeaux, *La victoire de la famille,* chap. 1.

110. On the DRFs, see ibid., 34.

111. *Journal Officiel,* June 7, 1941.

112. For the full list of the members of the Conseil, see Bordeaux, *La victoire de la famille,* 309–16.

113. Ibid., 41.

114. Article 2, cited ibid., 44. The Fondation Carrel was also seen as a potential counterpart to the Centre national de recherche scientifique (CNRS), thought to be "too red and too Republican" for Vichy. The regent of the Fondation, Alexis Carrel, was a Catholic physiologist (and Nobel laureate) and adherent of Jacques Doriot's pro-Nazi Parti populaire français (PPF). He was one of the most important eugenicists of his time, and his legacy has been the subject of much controversy in France (with some seeing him as a scientific pioneer and others as one of the most dangerous Nazi sympathizers). For more on this, see Lucien Bonnafé and Patrick Tort, *L'homme, cet inconnu? Alexis Carrel, Jean-Marie Le Pen et les chambres à gaz* (Syllepse, 1992); Alain Drouard, *Une inconnue des sciences sociales: La fondation Alexis Carrel, 1941–1945* (Maison des sciences de l'homme, 1992); Annick Ohayon, *Psychologie et psychanalyse en France: L'impossible rencontre, 1919–1969* (La découverte, 2006), chap. 8; Andrés Horacio Reggiani, *God's Eugenicist: Alexis Carrel and the Sociology of Decline* (Berghahn Books, 2006); Rosental, *L'intelligence démographique.*

FAMILIALISM AND THE REPUBLICAN SOCIAL CONTRACT   51

the Fondation Carrel included Fernand Boverat, who was in charge of the Équipe natalité (while he still ran the Alliance nationale), and Jacques Doublet, one of the principal redactors of the Code de la famille. According to one observer, Robert Aron, Doublet was the one to suggest including "family" in Vichy's motto "Famille, Travail, Patrie."[115] The Commissariat's office of propaganda, relying on the radio, the press, and the cinema, accomplished what the most "intransigent" familialists like Boverat had only dreamed of a few years earlier.[116]

In the legal field, the Vichy government essentially pursued the family policy initiated by the Code de la famille, generalizing and expanding the system of family allowances, increasing help for *familles nombreuses,* multiplying patriotic recognitions (such as family prizes), shifting the tax burden from larger families to unmarried citizens, and even implementing the controversial *vote familial.* But the most important changes under Vichy were not so much the organizations funded directly by the state, such as the Comité consultatif de la famille française or the Fondation Carrel, but those with partial state subsidies: the *associations familiales.* If the family was to replace the individual as the primary political unit, it needed to exist as a full entity within the political sphere. Thus, families needed to be organized. As Paul Renaudin put it, "Once restored, the family will complete the influence it has upon our institutions and will penetrate the political terrain. As a social cell, it is naturally called to become a political cell, the intermediary between the individual and the State."[117] Or as another family activist of the time, Pierre Sauvage, wrote,

If the "National Revolution" wants to truly be familial, the family needs to have the place it deserves within the organizations created by the government of the French state, and not only the place, but also the ability to speak . . . The family must become the kingpin of the nation and for that, it must be linked to the government of the state. Representation for heads of family must exist at the different levels of the nation (counties, departments, etc.), and within the different orga-

---

115. See Rosental, *L'intelligence démographique,* 301, and also Aline Coutrot, "La politique familiale," in *Le gouvernement de Vichy: 1940–1944,* ed. René Rémond (Presses de Sciences Po, 1972), 261.

116. In January 1940, for example, the general director of the Administration de la radiodiffusion nationale wrote to Pernot to inform him that he agreed to broadcast a show encouraging soldiers in the army to have more children (AN F 60 494). See also Pollard, *Reign of Virtue,* 114–16.

117. Renaudin, "La famille dans la nation," 25.

52   **CHAPTER 1**

nizations, councils, and committees that deal with problems directly or indirectly related to the family.[118]

This was indeed the idea behind the Conseil national des familles—an umbrella organization for all the different family associations—and the Maison de la famille, created in May 1942 at the place Saint-Georges in Paris to house the Centre national de coordination, the Féderation des familles nombreuses de France, the Confédération générale des familles, and the Alliance nationale.[119] Most importantly, this concern for familial representation motivated the December 29, 1942, law known as the "loi Gounot." The latter—also called the Charte de la famille, and modeled on Vichy's Charte du travail—was designed to institutionalize "familial corporatism" by planning a pyramidal organization of family associations. The associations at the base, implanted in urban neighborhoods, would gather in departmental associations, themselves regulated by the Fédération nationale des familles. The goals of the loi Gounot were to allow families to:

> give their opinion on family-related matters and propose measures that appear to conform to the moral and material interests of families; to serve as the official representatives of families with the authorities and to provide mandated representatives for official occasions; to develop family spirit (through propaganda, teaching, and education); to collaborate with professional organizations, for instance through the family delegates; to take and promote all initiatives that seek to defend, encourage, and help the family, and to fight against immorality and social scourges; to bring moral and material support to various groups whose goal is familial.[120]

Although the loi Gounot did not manage to achieve much in its short existence, it was crucial in generating what Miranda Pollard has described as a "structural alliance between government and grass roots that incorporated 'family' officially into the public agenda."[121] Renaudin was clearly aware of this when he presented the loi Gounot as the outcome of a long familialist movement that "for many years had served the family and claimed a greater place for it within our institutions." The law allowed heads of families to

---

118. Pierre Sauvage, *La politique familiale de l'État français* (Action populaire/Éditions Spes, 1941), 63.

119. Bordeaux, *La victoire de la famille,* 68–69.

120. *Journal Officiel,* December 31, 1941, 4246–4247. See also Annex 5, ibid., 321. On the history of the loi Gounot, see Chauvière, *Les mouvements familiaux,* 118–46.

121. Pollard, *Reign of Virtue,* 112.

serve as "consultants within the administration, to manage family services directly and even other public services, and to promote the education and the protection of the family. It granted them the responsibilities due to them and allowed them to act rather than to ask for help."[122] With Vichy, and especially with the loi Gounot, the family—or, more precisely, the kind of family envisioned by familialist activists—became a full political actor.

Given the centrality of the family in the rhetoric of the Vichy government, historians such as Paul-André Rosental and Miranda Pollard have pointed to the relatively modest budget actually allocated for family policy and to the little power that many pro-family structures such as the Haut comité actually had during the Vichy year. But as Pollard suggests, "family politics is not just about discrete policies or budgets, it is the official discursive shifts and realignments around 'Family' that count . . . If we see family policy in these terms, then Vichy was, arguably, very successful."[123] And indeed, despite the fact that France did not institute a solid and lasting familialist policy until the Liberation, these "discursive shifts and realignments around 'Family'" are crucial indicators of how familialism as an ideology and as a infrastructure filtered through the political sphere. Masking their claims as universal and nonpartisan, familialists from the Third Republic to Vichy paved the way for the absorption of family policy into the French social security system.

✒ Postwar Family Policy and "National Reconciliation"

As it became increasingly clear that Germany was losing the war, and as the members of the Resistance began to organize the new government that would supplant the Vichy state, the topic of family policy resurfaced. The question, however, was no longer "should France have a family policy?" as it had been formulated throughout the Third Republic, but rather "what kind of family policy should France have?" Given the war's economic ravages, the upheaval of the national infrastructure, and the general discredit of the Right, a strong social policy was not merely an option but a prerequisite for any viable reconstruction government. Although France already had, apart from family allowances, an elaborate network of welfare and social

---

122. Renaudin, "La famille dans la nation," 26.

123. Pollard, *Reign of Virtue,* 119.

54   **CHAPTER 1**

benefits progressively acquired throughout the Third Republic and classified under the rubric of *droit social,* these were mostly composed of semiprivate and occupational funds. As such, they tended to remain incomplete, insufficient, or disorganized.[124]

Thus, in September 1944, only a few weeks after the Liberation of France, the minister of labor, Alexandre Parodi, entrusted Pierre Laroque, a member of the Resistance and a jurist who had previously served on the Conseil d'état, with the task of setting up a single, comprehensive, and universal plan of social security. In line with the ambition of the Conseil national de la résistance (CNR) for a strong, centralized, and unified state, the new social security was to "guarantee that in any circumstances, each individual would have the means necessary to ensure his subsistence as well as his family's, in decent conditions."[125] Most importantly, social security represented for the Resistance the possibility of a new social contract for France, one that would heal the wounds of the Vichy years, restore Republican legality, and rebuild networks of solidarity. This was evident in Laroque's presentation of the plan in 1945: "Our social security plan is part of the larger common effort to build a new social order. We conceive of this new social order as emerging from ideas that break with the past, as erasing the flaws of a now revolved regime, as resting on entirely new principles."[126] As the historian Paul Dutton has characterized it, social security as it materialized in the decades after World War II was "an intrinsic part of French democracy. It is simultaneously both the agent and evidence of national solidarity. It is 'the

---

124. Because generalized social insurance was not set up until 1945, France is often referred to as a "late bloomer" in terms of social reform, particularly in comparison with many of its European neighbors who had already secured strong welfare states by the end of the nineteenth century. In Germany, for instance, Bismarck's *Soziale Sicherheit,* which encompassed health, accident, and old-age insurance and was intended to ease social tensions, was already fully functional by the 1880s. In recent years, historians have revised the historiographical tendency to treat nineteenth-century France as a "laggard" in social reform, arguing that France did not "lag" behind its German or British counterparts but that it simply had a different organization of social distribution, one that, as we have seen, privileged family benefits (e.g., see Pedersen, *Family, Dependence,* 17). On the broader history of welfare in France before 1945, see Paul V. Dutton, *Origins of the French Welfare State: The Struggle for Social Reform in France, 1914–1947* (Cambridge University Press, 2002); Ewald, *L'État providence;* Philip Nord, "The Welfare State in France, 1870–1914," *French Historical Studies* 18, no. 3 (1994); Procacci, *Gouverner la misère: La question sociale en France, 1789–1848;* Comité d'histoire de la Sécurité sociale, *La Sécurité sociale: Son histoire à travers les textes* (Association pour l'étude de l'histoire de la Sécurité sociale, 1994), vols. 1 and 2; Topalov, *Laboratoires du nouveau siècle;* John H. Weiss, "Origins of the French Welfare State: Poor Relief in the Third Republic, 1871–1914," *French Historical Studies* 13, no. 1 (1983).

125. Cited in Valat, *Histoire de la Sécurité sociale,* 4.

126. *Journal Officiel,* January 8, 1944, cited ibid., 10.

FAMILIALISM AND THE REPUBLICAN SOCIAL CONTRACT　　55

social' in French social democracy and France's society and politics are un-intelligible without an understanding of it."[127]

From its inception, however, this plan presented its founders with an important theoretical problem. By 1939, family benefits constituted France's most important modality of social welfare. Thus, the dilemma facing La-roque and the CNR ministers in 1944 was figuring out how to preserve the majority of these highly popular family rights formalized through the Code de la famille without appearing to support and continue a crucial Vichy policy. This ambivalence was apparent in the speech by Adrien Tixier (later to become the minister of the interior) to the provisionary consultative As-sembly in Alger in January 1944: "These last several days, I have reread the Code de la famille. It is a monument. All subjects are broached." But, he added, "this vast edifice does not reveal a firm will to protect the family. I think we will need to trim, concentrate, and revise. To this code, we will need to add a budget for the defense of the family."[128] This desire to retain the fundamental principles and structures of the Code de la famille while at the same time marking a rupture with the Vichy regime permeated most discussions of postwar family policy. As the members of the Comité français de la Libération nationale (CFLN) put it in a January 1944 *Note sur l'orientation future de la politique familiale,* it was a delicate matter to defend a notion such as the family that, because of Vichy, was now imbued with a "patriarchal, reactionary, and religious resonance."[129] Similarly, Robert Debré, a promi-nent pediatrician and important familialist of the interwar years, wrote, in the context of a piece on de Gaulle and natalism, that after the Family Code, "it was a debacle. The Vichy government eliminated the Haut comité de la population et de la famille." Only at the Liberation was de Gaulle "able to reestablish it. To demonstrate the gravity of the French population prob-lem, he decided (an exceptional decision) to preside personally over the first sessions of this Haut comité."[130] While it is true that Vichy dismantled the Haut comité, this move was primarily formal, and, as we have seen, most of its members were reshuffled in the various administrative bodies linked to family policy. Much of the Haut comité's work persisted, in the Comité consultatif de la famille française, for instance.

---

127. Dutton, *Origins of the French Welfare State,* 11.

128. Cited in Valat, *Histoire de la Sécurité sociale,* 32.

129. Cited in Rosental, *L'intelligence démographique,* 79.

130. Robert Debré, "Le général de Gaulle et la natalité française," *Espoir* 21, December 1977, 13, AN 577 AP.

56   **CHAPTER 1**

The continuities in family policy—both in terms of the structures and of the individual decision makers—among Vichy, the Liberation, and the Fourth Republic are remarkable. According to a December 1944 decree, the provisional government attributed to the Ministry of Public Health the task of setting up the government's family policy. This was done through three organizations created in March 1945: the Secrétariat général à la famille et à la population, presided over by Alfred Sauvy (also the director of the Institut national d'études démographiques and a former member of both the 1939 Haut comité and Vichy's Conseil supérieur de la famille); the Conseil consultatif de la population et de la famille; and the Comité inter-ministériel de la population et de la famille, designed to bring together the representatives from the different ministries concerned with population questions. Finally, in April 1945, the government reinstated the Haut comité consultatif de la population et de la famille under the direct leadership of Charles de Gaulle who attended most meetings and who was greatly preoc-cupied by demographic questions. The Haut comité was to be "consulted by the government on all measures concerning the protection of the family, the development of natality, rural population, urban deconcentration, the establishment of foreigners on French soil and their integration into the French population."[131]

The composition of this Haut comité, chosen by de Gaulle himself, is revealing of the many continuities in family policy personnel and also gives us a good sense of the kinds of measures advocated by the Haut comité: Maxime Blocq-Mascart, a right-wing corporatist critic of the Third Re-public with anti-Semitic sympathies, who later became a member of the Resistance; Fernand Boverat, director of the *natalité* sector at the Fondation Carrel; Robert Debré, as previously mentioned; Simone Collet, president of La plus grande famille; Jeanne Marcelle Delabit, the only left-wing member of the committee, who was nonetheless opposed to communism, as a found-ing member of the Confédération générale du travail-force ouvrière (CGT-FO) trade union bloc; Adolphe Landry, one of the Code de la famille's principal authors, who participated in Vichy's Conseil supérieur de la famille; Maurice Monsaigeon, vice president of La plus grande famille, who had also sat in Vichy's Conseil supérieur de la famille and who had presided over the Centre national de coordination des activités familiales, the focal point for Vichy's familial corporatism; Robert Prigent, another familialist emanat-ing from the Social Catholicism milieu, active in both the Jeunesse ouvrière

---

131. Charles de Gaulle cited in Adler, *Jews and Gender,* 73.

FAMILIALISM AND THE REPUBLICAN SOCIAL CONTRACT   57

chrétienne (JOC) and the Ligue ouvrière chrétienne (LOC); and finally, Georges Mauco, the Comité's secretary, a psychoanalyst and population expert (to whom I will return in Chapter 3).[132] As this list suggests, the Liberation was particularly lenient vis-à-vis family activists, even those who were directly involved in the Vichy regime. Philippe Renaudin, the mastermind behind Vichy's family policy, was pardoned by a purge committee and eventually reintegrated into the Conseil d'état. Furthermore, the collaboration between explicit right-wingers, ex-Vichy officials, socialists, Gaullists, Social Catholics (who were by then mostly gathered around the Mouvement républicain populaire, or MRP), and Résistants is notable, especially given the acute political divisions of the postwar years. Once again, family policy appeared to be the subject of a widespread consensus.

To coordinate these different organizations, the provisional government set up in December 1945 the Ministry of Population headed by Robert Prigent. The ministry's tasks included overseeing the distribution of family benefits, planning tax reductions, studying demography, promoting medical and hygienic legislation, and consulting with the justice department on family-related issues. The Institut national d'études démographiques (INED), created in October 1945 and headed by Alfred Sauvy, replaced the Fondation Carrel as the center for the study of demography. It retained its old offices and many of its members.[133] Populationist concerns also found a forum in a section of the first Plan, called the Commission de la consommation et de la modernisation sociale, created in April 1946. Just as the production and consumption of energy or steel could be "planified," so could demography. During a September 1947 meeting, we can note the presence of Pierre Laroque ("father" of the social security plan) as vice president, Robert Debré, as head of the Natalité et enfance subcommittee, and Alfred Sauvy as head of "demography." According to the proceedings of this meeting, the goal of the committee was to increase the size of the French population by 10 to 25 million in the next 25 years, in hopes of reaching a total population of 50 to 60 million inhabitants. To attain this goal, the committee proposed three main paths, sounding once again remarkably close to the Haut comité's predictions before the war: increasing immigration, through

---

132. *Journal Officiel,* April 19, 1945: Décret du 3 avril 1945 portant création d'un Comité interministériel et d'un haut comité consultatif de la population et de la famille (AN 577 AP). See also Procès verbaux des réunions du Haut comité de la population et de la famille (AN 577 AP). For more biographical information on each of these figures, see Adler, *Jews and Gender,* 75–82; Drouard, "Le Haut comite de la population"; Lenoir, *Généalogie.*

133. On the genesis and history of the INED, see Rosental, *L'intelligence démographique.*

58   **CHAPTER 1**

a tightly controlled selection process, decreasing the mortality rate, and increasing the birthrate.[134] Other familialist unofficial measures from the 1930s such as the Medal of the French Family or Mother's Day, which were enthusiastically supported by the Vichy regime, were not only maintained at the Liberation but were expanded and legalized in 1947 and 1950, respectively.[135]

One of the most notable carryovers from the Vichy years was the loi Gounot, which was "republicanized" on March 3, 1945, as the Union nationale des associations familiales (UNAF).[136] According to Roger Burnel, a former president of the UNAF, it was de Gaulle himself who, while in exile, encouraged "families to participate in the moral, psychological, social, economic, and civic reconstruction of the country after the liberation."[137] For Burnel, there was a "major difference between the aspirations of the Vichy regime and the accomplishments of the provisional government" because "the latter respected the freedom of association while the former contended that there be only one association, by county or by *département*."[138] In other words, according to Burnel, the main difference between Vichy's loi Gounot and the UNAF resided in the form and mode of association; the *purpose* of family associations was the same. As stated in its founding charter, the role of the UNAF was to "advise the authorities on all questions pertaining to the family; to represent the entirety of French families; to manage all services of familial interest that the authorities deem their responsibility; to legally defend the moral and material interests of the family."[139] The justifications for the existence of the UNAF were directly in line with the familialist rhetoric of the late nineteenth and early twentieth centuries and with Vichy's, as exemplified in Maurice Monsaingeon's opening speech at a preliminary meeting: "We hope that the day will come when the family, the essential and vital organ of the nation, will have . . . its place within the

---

134. Premier rapport de la Commission de la consommation et de la modernisation sociale, September 1947, AN 80 AJ 10.

135. Lenoir, *Généalogie,* 383. For more on Mother's Day during Vichy, see Muel-Dreyfus, *Vichy et l'éternel féminin,* 135.

136. "Republicanized" is the term used by Michel Chauvière, "Les mouvements familiaux," in François de Singly, *La famille, l'état des savoirs* (La découverte, 1991). See also Chauvière, *Les mouvements familiaux,* 161–79.

137. Interview with Roger Burnel, *Familles Rurales,* Jan–Fev. 1995, 18, Archives UNAF.

138. Ibid.

139. Ordonnance du 3 mars 1945, Archives UNAF.

FAMILIALISM AND THE REPUBLICAN SOCIAL CONTRACT   59

framework of the state . . . Good families make good nations."[140] Or as
Robert Prigent put it, following a diatribe against abortion and prostitution:
"we familialists say to the government officials of the French administration: the family is not a Vichy issue. The family is a French issue."[141] The
UNAF was housed (and remains to this day) at the Place Saint-Georges in
Paris's ninth arrondissement, where Vichy's féderation des familles nombreuses de France had had its headquarters.

As for family benefits, most of the Code de la famille's dispositions either
remained intact or were increased.[142] During the preparatory discussions
around the social security plan, the MRP, heavily represented within the
UNAF (and, by June 1946, the first party in France), worried that if family
benefits were subsumed under a general unified and centralized fund or
caisse, they might be managed by more secular administrators who were less
open to familialist ideas. Thus, on October 4, 1945, the UNAF succeeded
in keeping local caisses autonomous. On August 22, 1946, all systems of
family benefits were integrated into the general structure of social security,
making them dependant on a caisse nationale. The August law added two
new benefits to the previous allocations familiales: a maternity premium
(replacing Vichy's birth premiums) and an allocation prénatale to encourage
sanitary surveillance for future mothers.[143] One important advantage of this
centralized national caisse was to rally the communists to family policy.
Indeed, the Communist Party, which had the largest number of elected
deputies right after the war, had been hesitant to support the previous caisses
for family benefits because they were most often controlled by employers.[144]
In 1948, a housing subsidy (allocation logement) was added to the list of family
benefits.[145] Finally, the finance reform law of December 31, 1945, instituted
the quotient familial, which divided the taxable income of a family according

---

140. "La création de l'UNAF," Familles Rurales, Jan–Fev. 1995, 21, Archives UNAF. It might be interesting in this context to think of Matthew Elbow's analysis of de Gaulle as someone "close in spirit to
French corporatism" (Elbow, French Corporative Theory, 202–3) and of Jean-Marie Mayeur's study of
the similarities between Gaullism and Social Catholicism (Mayeur, Catholicisme social, chap. 8).

141. Ibid.

142. On June 19, 1945, a law increased family benefits by 15 percent for the second child and 25
percent for the third. See Drouard, "Le Haut comite de la population," 180.

143. Ceccaldi, Histoire des prestations familiales; Drouard, "Le Haut comite de la population," 180;
Messu, Les politiques familiales, 72–73.

144. Prost, "L'évolution de la politique familiale," 10–11.

145. Susanna Magri, Logement et reproduction de l'exploitation: Les politiques étatiques du logement en
France (1947–1972) (Centre de sociologie urbaine, 1977), 312.

60   **CHAPTER 1**

to the number of children. The idea was to "make income taxes as neutral as possible in relation to the purchasing power of families, taking into account the differing number of dependents [*charges inégales*]."[146]

In the postwar years, everybody seemed to agree that it was crucial for France to have a vigorous pronatalist policy. According to a 1947 poll, 73 percent of French citizens believed that it was important to increase France's population.[147] But the incorporation of family benefits into the Sécurité sociale also had a larger significance. Family policy was not on the agenda of a specific political party or religious group but rather constituted a key component of French social policy, just like health insurance or pension funds. It had become a unit to organize social distribution and for thinking about solidarity. In the fall of 1946, the constitution of the Fourth Republic mirrored this consecration of the family by stating that "the nation will provide the family with the means necessary for its development." The family was at the heart of the Republican social contract.

---

146. Prost, "L'évolution de la politique familiale," 13.

147. Ibid., 11.

✎ CHAPTER 2

Kinship and the Structuralist Social Contract

Law and social policy were not the only fields in France concerned with the relationship between the familial and the social. In the social sciences, kinship—which by definition straddled the social and the familial—had always been an important object of study, especially for anthropology and psychoanalysis. As these two disciplines were redefined in the aftermath of World War II, so was the study of kinship. More specifically, Claude Lévi-Strauss and Jacques Lacan radically reconfigured the study of kinship by adopting structuralism as a mode of analysis. This chapter offers a reading of Lévi-Strauss's and Lacan's early texts on kinship which, I argue, shared a number of features with the familialist discourse described in the previous chapter. First, familialism and structuralism both posited a direct and necessary relation between the familial and the social. Just as familialists stressed the foundational role of the family for the republican social contract, Lévi-Strauss and Lacan insisted on the importance of the heterosexual family for all social and psychic organization, whether it be in the passage from nature to culture for Lévi-Strauss or in the emergence of the symbolic for Lacan. I propose to read their writings on kinship as social contract theories, as treatises on the social bond, on social and psychic integration, and on "the political" understood, as Claude Lefort has defined it, as the "principle or set of principles generative of the relationships that men hold amongst each

62   CHAPTER 2

other and with the world."[1] Within this framework, the political, what gives
society its foundation, unity, and basic coherence, is sexual difference. This
took the form of the incest prohibition for Lévi-Strauss and the form of
castration for Lacan.

A second element linking these structuralist analyses of kinship to familialism has to do with the role of politics, or rather the explicit erasure of
politics and history. Familialists, we saw, insisted that the family was universal and as such that it transcended political divisions. Similarly, by turning to
structuralism and more specifically, through their concept of the symbolic,
Lévi-Strauss and Lacan evacuated history and politics from the study of kinship. The structuralist social contract of Lévi-Strauss and Lacan thus depended
on this double clause: sexual difference as the condition for sociality, and the
heterosexual family as a logical necessity, a universal and transhistorical normative structure, rather than a temporally and geographically specific formation. Although Lévi-Strauss and Lacan were disciplinary radicals and
even though the problem of the political figured prominently in their studies of kinship, politics were significantly absent from their works.

Lévi-Strauss's Disciplinary Break

In 1949, having recently returned from New York where he had spent the
war in exile at the New School for Social Research, Claude Lévi-Strauss
published *The Elementary Structures of Kinship.* His book caused an immediate sensation on the French intellectual scene. Simone de Beauvoir, who
reviewed it for *Les Temps Modernes,* praised it for dragging French sociology
"out of its sleep."[2] In theoretical terms, Lévi-Strauss's project appeared immensely ambitious. As he stated in his introduction, the goal of *The Elementary Structures* was to propose a definitive theory of how the social related to
the biological, to determine once and for all where "nature end[ed] and
culture beg[an]."[3] This was, as Georges Bataille remarked in another early
review of the work, one of philosophy's fundamental—and fundamentally
unsolved—problems.[4] Moreover, Lévi-Strauss's contemporaries were struck

---

1. Claude Lefort, *Essais sur le politique: XIXe–XXe siècles* (Seuil, 1986), 8.

2. Simone de Beauvoir, "L'être et la parenté," *Les Temps Modernes* 491 (1949): 943.

3. Claude Lévi-Strauss, *The Elementary Structures of Kinship,* trans. James Harle Bell and John Richard von Sturmer (Beacon Press, 1969), 4.

4. Georges Bataille, "L'inceste et le passage de l'animal à l'homme," *Critique,* no. 44 (1951).

KINSHIP AND THE STRUCTURALIST SOCIAL CONTRACT 63

by the exhaustiveness of his research, the range of the scholarship he engaged with, and the amount of ethnographic data he had assembled. Lévi-Strauss, who had written much of *The Elementary Structures* during his exile years in the United States, had benefited from the rich collection of English-language sources at the New York Public Library. In addition, he was able to establish close ties with some of the most prominent American anthropologists of the time, in particular Franz Boas at Columbia University and many of his students, including Ralph Linton, Ruth Benedict, Alfred Kroeber, and Robert Lowie.[5] Lévi-Strauss, in fact, dedicated *The Elementary Structures* to the memory of Lewis Henry Morgan—one of the pioneers of American ethnography and one of the first scholars to systematically study kinship systems—partly to acknowledge his debt toward this "American school of anthropology" that had so deeply shaped his work.

Lévi-Strauss's contact with Boasian anthropology was particularly formative because France, unlike Great Britain and the United States, did not have a strong tradition of social and cultural anthropology. Nineteenth-century French anthropology had been vibrant with the Société d'anthropologie and the École d'anthropologie, founded by the doctor and anatomist Pierre Broca in 1859 and 1875, respectively, and with the Musée d'histoire de l'homme and the Musée d'ethnographie completed in 1879 in the Palais du Trocadéro in Paris. However, most of these early anthropologists were physicians and natural scientists who were interested primarily in archeology and the study of human "races." Although the École aspired to study the human races in all their forms, its investigations quickly became restricted to the study of physical type and to the demonstration of a supposed correlation between physical type and the degree of development of a specific race.[6] At the turn of the century, many of the anthropologists affiliated with the École—Louis Marin, for example—lamented the effects of "depopulation," the demise of the family and religion, and the looming "German menace." By 1940, several anthropologists of the École d'anthropologie

---

5. Lévi-Strauss's life in New York is well documented in Denis Bertholet, *Claude Lévi-Strauss* (Plon, 2003); Vincent Debaene, "'Like Alice through the Looking Glass': Claude Lévi-Strauss in New York," *French Politics, Culture and Society* 28, no. 1 (2010); Vincent Debaene and Frédéric Keck, *Claude Lévi-Strauss: L'homme au regard éloigné* (Gallimard, 2009); Didier Eribon and Claude Lévi-Strauss, *De près et de loin* (Odile Jacob, 1988). For more on Boas and his students during this time, see Franz Boas and George W. Stocking, *A Franz Boas Reader: The Shaping of American Anthropology, 1883–1911* (University of Chicago Press, 1982).

6. Donald Bender, "The Development of French Anthropology," *Journal of the History of Behavioral Science* 1 (1965): 142. See also Elizabeth A. Williams, "The Science of Man: Anthropological Thought and Institutions in Nineteenth-Century France" (Ph.D. diss., Indiana University, 1983).

64   **CHAPTER 2**

found in Pétain's government the possibility of putting into practice some of their intellectual hypotheses. Both the École's principal publication, the *Revue Anthropologique,* and the Société de géographie commerciale officially proclaimed their allegiance to the National Revolution. Henri Briand, the director of the *Revue* and a professor of heredity at the École, praised the Vichy regime for introducing physical education into French schools to "preserve the race." Georges Montandon, another professor at the École, who had occupied the chair of ethnology since 1935, was named "technical director" of the Institut d'étude des questions juives et ethno-raciales set up by the Commissariat général aux questions juives in 1941. Montandon, who had served as director of the journal *L'Ethnie Française,* had devoted his research to proving the existence of a Jewish and Negroid "ethnic type."[7]

As anthropology in France became increasing synonymous with physical anthropology by the end of the nineteenth century, sociology emerged as the privileged discipline for social and cultural analysis. In particular, sociology found a new impetus with the work of Émile Durkheim and his students. For Durkheim, the goal of sociology was to discern the specificity of "the social," its totalizing and *sui generis* nature, the whole that was irreducible to the sum of its parts. Marcel Mauss, Durkheim's nephew and disciple, encouraged sociologists to study "total social facts": facts involving the totality or near totality of society and institutions, facts that were universal, "at the same time juridical, economic, religious, and even aesthetic and morphological . . . political and domestic."[8] Moreover, to distinguish himself from the École d'anthropologie's increasingly conservative positions, Mauss who was a member of the French Socialist Party (the Section française de l'internationale ouvrière, or SFIO), and who wrote for the communist paper *L'Humanité,* preferred to describe his work as "ethnology" rather than "anthropology."[9] Strongly affiliated with the Left, Mauss, along with Paul Rivet and Lucien Lévy-Bruhl, founded the Institut d'ethnologie in 1925 under the patronage

---

7. Herman Lebovics, *True France: The Wars over Cultural Identity, 1900–1945* (Cornell University Press, 1992), chap. 1. For more on Montandon, see Daniel Fabre, "L'ethnologie française à la croisée des engagements (1940–1945)," in *Résistants et résistance,* ed. Jean-Yves Boursier (L'Harmattan, 1997); Marc Knobel, "L'ethnologue à la dérive: Montandon et l'ethnoracisme," *Ethnologie Française* 18 (1988); William H. Schneider, *Quality and Quantity: The Quest for Biological Regeneration in Twentieth Century France* (Cambridge University Press, 1990), 257–60. On the conservative strand of French anthropology, see Jean Jamin, "L'anthropologie et ses acteurs," in *Les enjeux philosophiques des années 50* (Éditions du Centre Pompidou, 1989); Herman Lebovics, "Le conservatisme en anthropologie et la fin de la Troisième République," *Gradhiva* 4 (1988).

8. Marcel Mauss, *The Gift: The Form and Reason for Exchange in Archaic Societies* (Norton, 1990), 79.

9. See Marcel Fournier, *Marcel Mauss* (Fayard, 1994).

KINSHIP AND THE STRUCTURALIST SOCIAL CONTRACT   65

of the Cartel des Gauches.[10] Similarly, in 1937 he participated in the reno-
vation of the Musée d'ethnographie du Trocadéro, which would become
the Musée de l'homme. Funded by the Popular Front government, the new
museum was meant to play a role in the democratization of knowledge that
Mauss and his colleagues advocated.[11]

Before his departure for New York in 1941, Lévi-Strauss had been active
in leftist politics, especially in his student days. Reading Marx, which he
claims was essential for his intellectual awakening, led him to other socialist
authors such as Proudhon and the revolutionary hero Gracchus Babeuf,
about whom he wrote a series of articles.[12] As a philosophy student at university, Lévi-Strauss was elected secretary of a student socialist group, the
Groupe d'études socialistes des cinq écoles normales supérieures. He maintained close ties with the Parti ouvrier belge (led at the time by Henri de
Man), wrote for the newspaper *L'Étudiant Socialiste,* and was a member of
the SFIO for many years.[13] After the German occupation, Lévi-Strauss,
who was of Jewish descent, was sent to teach high school in the *zone libre*
of the south of France. He was unable to continue after the promulgation of
the 1940 racial laws.[14] Finally, Lévi-Strauss decided to accept the New
School's invitation to move to New York City.

By the time he had returned to France at the end of the war, Lévi-Strauss
claimed to have lost all interest in politics.[15] Indeed, with *The Elementary*

---

10. See Bender, "Development of French Anthropology," 145. For an in-depth analysis of Mauss's
politics, see Sylvain Dzimira, *Marcel Mauss, savant et politique* (La découverte, 2007).

11. Régis Meyran, "Races et racismes: Les ambiguïtés de l'antiracisme chez les anthropologues de
l'entre-deux-guerres," *Gradhiva* 27 (2000): 65. See also Alice L. Conklin, "L'ethnologie combattante de l'entre-deux-guerres," in *Le siècle de Germaine Tillion,* ed. Tzvetan Todorov (Seuil, 2007).

12. See Eribon and Lévi-Strauss, *De près et de loin,* 16.

13. On Lévi-Strauss's youthful political activism, see Stéphane Clouet, *De la rénovation à l'utopie socialistes: Révolution constructive, un groupe d'intellectuels socialistes des années 1930* (Presses universitaires
de Nancy, 1991); Debaene and Keck, *Claude Lévi-Strauss;* Alexandre Pajon, "Claude Lévi-Strauss:
D'une métaphysique socialiste à l'éthnologie (1ère partie)," *Gradhiva,* no. 28 (2000); Alexandre
Pajon, "Claude Lévi-Strauss: D'une métaphysique socialiste à l'éthnologie (2ème partie)," *Gradhiva,*
no. 29 (2001); Alexandre Pajon, *Claude Lévi-Strauss politique: De la SFIO à l'UNESCO* (Privat,
2011). See also the chronology established by Vincent Dabaene in the Pléiade edition of Claude
Lévi-Strauss, *Œuvres* (Gallimard, 2008).

14. Eribon and Lévi-Strauss, *De près et de loin,* 43. The racial laws also forced Marcel Mauss to resign
from his chair at the Collège de France in 1942. See Brigitte Mazon, *Aux origines de l'École des hautes
études en sciences sociales: Le rôle du mécénat américain, 1920–1960* (Cerf, 1988), 71.

15. Eribon and Lévi-Strauss, *De près et de loin,* 68, 80. Vincent Debaene disputes Lévi-Strauss's
chronology concerning his "departure from politics" by pointing to various of his texts on foreign
relations written in the postwar period, and to his involvement in the UNESCO until the early
1950s. See Vincent Debaene, "A propos de 'La politique étrangère d'une société primitive,'"

66   **CHAPTER 2**

Structures of Kinship, Lévi-Strauss appeared to suddenly break with the tradition of politically engaged social sciences. Reclaiming the category of "anthropology," Lévi-Strauss positioned his work at the crossroads of French sociology and American anthropology. In the latter, Lévi-Strauss found a model of "scientificity," fieldwork, and ethnographic analysis that the French sociological school was missing. Conversely, Durkheimian sociology provided Lévi-Strauss the totalizing theoretical model that the American school of anthropology, from his perspective, lacked. *The Elementary Structures* was thus not simply another interpretation of kinship formation: it was a fundamental philosophical intervention, a theoretical manifesto for a new explicitly scientific discipline, one that would later be known as "structuralist anthropology."

↝ The Passage from Nature to Culture and the Emergence of the Family

On the most general level, *The Elementary Structures of Kinship* is concerned with the distinction between nature and culture, or as we tend to refer to it today, with the nature/nurture debate. Is human identity (physical and behavioral) determined by biological innate and instinctual attributes, or is it the product of a complex interaction of our social, educational, and familial contexts? This question, Lévi-Strauss tells us, has puzzled sociologists, biologists, and anthropologists for years. Given the inherent difficulty in isolating humans from any social interaction (even in the case of newborns or the so-called wolf-children), many social scientists have opted for a functionalist model that simply juxtaposes culture to biology or vice versa, or else they have abandoned the question altogether. Similarly, social scientists have attempted to discern traces of culture in animal life, particularly among great apes. Chimpanzees, for instance, can "articulate several monosyllables and

---

Ethnies, no. 33–34 (2009); Laurent Jeanpierre, "La politique culturelle française aux États-Unis de 1940 à 1947," in *Entre rayonnement et réciprocité: Contributions à l'histoire de la diplomatie culturelle* (Publications de la Sorbonne, 2002); Laurent Jeanpierre, "Les structures d'une pensée d'exilé: La formation du structuralisme de Claude Lévi-Strauss," *French Politics, Culture and Society* 28, no. 1 (2010); Emmanuelle Loyer, *Paris à New York: Intellectuels et artistes français en exil (1940–1947)* (Grasset, 2005). For more on the role of anthropology during this period, see Todd Shepard, "Algeria, France, Mexico, UNESCO: A Transnational History of Antiracism and Decolonization, 1932–1962," *Journal of Global History* 6 (2011); Wiktor Stoczkowski, *Anthropologies rédemptrices: Le monde selon Lévi-Strauss* (Hermann, 2008).

KINSHIP AND THE STRUCTURALIST SOCIAL CONTRACT   67

disyllables but they never attach any meaning to them."[16] Although monkeys can utter sounds, these are never *signs* in the sense that a particular signified is attached to a particular signifier. To use one of Lévi-Strauss's most important concepts, animals are incapable of "symbolic thought." Most significantly, Lévi-Strauss argues, "the social life of monkeys does not lend itself to the formulation of any norm . . . Not only is the behavior of the single subject inconsistent, but there is no regular pattern to be discerned in collective behavior."[17] This lack of norms and regularity is particularly striking in the chimps' sexual activity, where "monogamy and polygamy exist side by side."[18] Thus, Lévi-Strauss claims, it is "this absence of rules [that] seems to provide the surest criterion for distinguishing a natural from a cultural process."[19] "Let us suppose," Lévi-Strauss famously posits, "that everything universal in man relates to the natural order, and is characterized by spontaneity, and that everything subject to a norm is cultural and is both relative and particular."[20]

Within the overall structure of Lévi-Strauss's argument, this passage is key. Indeed, it comes as *the* answer, the only answer to this "insoluble question" of where nature stops and culture begins, a question that, as Lévi-Strauss has told us, has haunted both philosophy and the social sciences. Without a proper understanding of nature and culture, any "understanding of social phenomena" is precluded.[21] Yet as Lévi-Strauss makes clear in his examples of newborns and the wolf-children, a "pure state of nature" is a hypothetical construction; it is by definition, foreclosed. If a nondomesticated animal might be able to return to a form of natural behavior, "such cannot be expected of man, since the species has no natural behavior to which an isolated individual might retrogress."[22] Whereas "wild children may be cultural monstrosities . . . under no circumstances can they provide reliable evidence of an earlier state."[23] From birth, because of their capacity to symbolize, men are always already "in society." The state of nature, in

---

16. Lévi-Strauss, *Elementary Structures of Kinship,* 6.

17. Ibid.

18. Ibid., 7.

19. Ibid., 8.

20. Ibid.

21. Ibid., 4.

22. Ibid., 5.

23. Ibid.

68   **CHAPTER 2**

other words, is neither an event nor a place but rather an empty structure necessary to Lévi-Strauss's argument. As Lévi-Strauss puts it in the beginning of his book, "this distinction between nature and society, while of no historical significance, does contain a logic, fully justifying its use by modern sociology as a methodological tool."[24] It is in this sense that we should understand Lévi-Strauss's assertion that "no empirical analysis . . . can determine the point of transition between natural and cultural facts, nor how they are connected."[25] Thus, Lévi-Strauss refers to his definitions of nature and culture (or society, as Lévi-Strauss uses these terms interchangeably) according to norm and universality as proceeding from an "ideal analysis" as opposed to what he calls a "real analysis."[26] By "ideal," Lévi-Strauss appears to indicate that he is relying on a priori concepts that need to be posited abstractly because they cannot be deduced from experience. It is this ideal analysis that guides the remainder of *The Elementary Structures*.

If *The Elementary Structures* claims to address the difference between nature and culture, it also concerned with the elementary structures of kinship, marriage rules, nomenclature, and the system of rights and prohibitions set up by these systems. What links the discussion of the nature/culture dichotomy to that of kinship structures is the prohibition of incest. Indeed, as Lévi-Strauss writes, if we define nature by universality and culture by the existence of relative and particular norms,

> we are then confronted with a fact, or rather a group of facts, which in light of the previous definitions, are not far removed from a scandal: we refer to that complex group of beliefs, customs, conditions and institutions described succinctly as the prohibition of incest, which presents, without the slightest ambiguity, and inseparably combines, the two characteristics in which we recognize the conflicting features of two mutually exclusive orders. It constitutes a rule, but a rule which alone among all the social rules, possesses at the same time a universal character.[27]

The prohibition of incest, Lévi-Strauss argues, is the only phenomenon with "the distinctive characteristics both of nature and of its theoretical contradiction, culture. [It] has the universality of bent and instinct, and the coercive

---

24. Ibid., 3.

25. Ibid., 8.

26. Ibid.

27. Ibid., 8–9.

KINSHIP AND THE STRUCTURALIST SOCIAL CONTRACT   69

character of law and institution . . . [and, as such] presents a formidable mystery to sociological thought."[28] According to Lévi-Strauss, sociologists have not only failed to give a definitive explanation of the distinction between nature and culture, they also have been unable to determine the precise origin of this incest prohibition and account for the sacredness of this prohibition, in all times and all cultures. More specifically, Lévi-Strauss contends, sociologists who have tried to explain the incest taboo have fallen into one of three methodological "traps," resulting from an inadequate conceptualization of nature and culture and of the relationship that binds these two terms.

The first type of explanation was advanced, among others, by Lewis Henry Morgan and Henry Maine. It claims that incest being a *natural* phenomenon, the prohibition was imposed by societies who had become aware of the hazardous biological (that is, natural) effects of consanguinity. In this case, "the incest prohibition is taken to be a protective measure, shielding the species from the disastrous results of consanguineous marriage."[29] "This theory," Lévi-Strauss contends, "is remarkable in that it is required by its very statement to extend to all human societies, even to the most primitive, which in other matters give no indication of such eugenic second-sight, the sensational privilege of knowing the alleged consequences of endogamous unions. This justification for the prohibition of incest is of recent origin, appearing nowhere in our society before the sixteenth century."[30] Genetic foreshadowing thus cannot justify the existence of the incest taboo because the medical ramifications of incest have been only recently fully grasped and because biology alone cannot account for the arbitrariness of which unions are considered incestuous and which are not. In this context, Lévi-Strauss adds, "it is in the field of biological concepts that we find the last traces of transcendence still prevalent in modern thought."[31] With this clarification, Lévi-Strauss indicates that he is situating his project outside of biology, outside of the natural sciences, but also outside of transcendence.

The second type of explanation, advocated by Edward Westermarck and Havelock Ellis, "tends to do away with one of the terms of the antinomy between the natural and social characteristics of this institution . . . The prohibition of incest is no more than the social projection or reflection of

---

28. Ibid., 10.

29. Ibid., 13.

30. Ibid.

31. Ibid., 14 (translation modified).

70   CHAPTER 2

natural feelings or tendencies which can be entirely explained by human nature."[32] In other words, people would have a *natural* repugnance toward incest (triggered, as Ellis argued, by domesticity and the "negative effects of daily habit upon erotic excitability"), and the prohibition would merely be the formal expression of this universal deep-rooted instinct. However, Lévi-Strauss tells us, not only do incestuous relations exist—thus dispelling this idea of a "universal sentiment" of disgust—but psychoanalysis has taken great care to show that the only universal feeling when it comes to incest is an unconscious desire for it, as evidenced by the Oedipus complex. Moreover, this theory of the "natural horror" produced by incest can hardly account for the aura of sacredness that the prohibition bears in most societies. As Lévi-Strauss contends, one would not need to forbid something so explicitly if it did not correspond to some widespread wish or longing.[33]

Finally, according to a third type of explanation, the prohibition would be a purely *social* phenomenon, "a rule whose origin is purely social, its expression in biological terms being accidental and of minor importance."[34] This is the perspective we find (with some variations) in the writings of James Frazer, John McLennan, Herbert Spencer, John Lubbock, or Émile Durkheim. For Lévi-Strauss, these authors share the same "methodological vice": they treat the prohibition as a historical event, as a remnant from the distant past.[35] As such, they rely on elaborate models of past societies (like Lubbock's references to old warrior tribal customs or the fear of menstrual blood in Durkheim), which not only appear historically improbable but also present a larger and more critical logical issue:

> They attempt to establish a universal phenomenon on an historical sequence, which is by no means inconceivable in some particular case but whose episodes are so contingent that the possibility of this sequence being repeated unchanged in every human society must be wholly excluded . . . It is possible to imagine that, in a given society, the origin of some particular institution is to be explained by some highly arbitrary transformations. History provides examples. But history also shows that, according to the society considered, such processes

---

32. Ibid., 16.

33. Ibid., 18.

34. Ibid., 19.

35. Ibid., 20.

KINSHIP AND THE STRUCTURALIST SOCIAL CONTRACT   71

may result in widely differing institutions, and that where analogous institutions have found independent origins in various parts of the world, the historical sequences leading up to their appearances are themselves highly dissimilar. This is what is termed convergence.[36]

Furthermore, Lévi-Strauss continues, "if the whole institution is no more than a survival, how can the universality and vitality of the rule be understood, when only occasional formless traces of it might conceivably be brought to light, or does the prohibition of incest correspond in modern society to new and different functions? . . . The historical explanation does not exhaust the problem."[37] Thus, to summarize, we could say that for Lévi-Strauss natural explanations of the incest taboo can account for universality but not the rule, whereas historical/sociological accounts can account for the rule but not its universality.

It is in opposition to these two options that Lévi-Strauss sets up his own model of interpretation of the incest prohibition, which he suggests, moves beyond the biological/historical accounts. "The problem of the incest prohibition," Lévi-Strauss writes, "is not so much to seek the different historical configurations for each group as to explain the particular form of the institution in each particular society. The problem is to discover what profound and omnipresent causes could account for the regulation of the relationships between the sexes *in every society and age*."[38] To pinpoint this problem of regulation, Lévi-Strauss argues that we must understand the incest prohibition as situated at the *transition* from nature to culture, and that as such it is, by definition, both nature *and* culture: "The prohibition of incest is in its origin neither purely cultural nor purely natural, nor is it a composite mixture of elements from both nature and culture. It is the fundamental step [*démarche*] because of which, by which, but above all in which, the transition from nature to culture is accomplished."[39]

The prohibition of incest, Lévi-Strauss concludes, is the link between man's biological existence and his social existence.[40] It is, we could say, the

---

36. Ibid., 22.

37. Ibid., 23.

38. Ibid. (emphasis mine).

39. Ibid., 24. The term *démarche* here is interesting because it refers not only to the physical action of "stepping" but also to the intellectual activity of "moving forward" as in *démarche intellectuelle* or *démarche de pensée*.

40. Ibid., 24–5.

72   **CHAPTER 2**

necessary condition for the social contract, the structure that brings men from the scattered state of nature into a integrated "social":

Nature		**Culture/Society**
Universality	**Incest Prohibition**	Norms, regularity
Spontaneous	$\longrightarrow$	Relative, particular

In this diagram, the arrow—the incest prohibition—goes in one direction only because the state of nature, as Lévi-Strauss makes clear, is always already foreclosed. Lévi-Strauss confirms this idea when, describing the prohibition of incest as the link between nature and culture, he writes:

> This union is neither static nor arbitrary, and as soon as it comes into being, the whole situation [*la situation totale*] is completely changed. Indeed, it is less a union than a transformation or transition. Before it, culture is still non-existent; with it, nature's sovereignty over man is ended. The prohibition of incest is where nature transcends itself. It sparks the formation of a new and more complex type of structure and is superimposed upon the simpler structures of physical life through integration, just as these themselves are superimposed upon the simpler structures of animal life. It brings about and is in itself the advent of a new order.[41]

As this passage suggests, the incest prohibition and culture become at some point rhetorically synonymous. This "new order" is premised on the existence of the incest prohibition, but also on the dichotomy between nature and culture, one in which nature exists as a purely hypothetical construct that is nonetheless necessary for the logic of the argument to work.

If Lévi-Strauss consecrates the prohibition of incest as the "rule of rules" of his "new order," he is primarily interested in the positive effects of his prohibition. Indeed, if men cannot marry the women in their own family or clan, they must look for the women in other families, and thus establish connections—social bonds—with them: "The prohibition of incest is less a rule prohibiting marriage with the mother, sister or daughter, than a rule obliging the mother, sister or daughter to be given to others. It is the supreme rule of the gift."[42] From this perspective, marriage (as opposed to sex) is thus not so much an erotic arrangement as it is an economic phenomenon,

---

41. Ibid., 25.

42. Ibid., 480.

KINSHIP AND THE STRUCTURALIST SOCIAL CONTRACT 73

with "economic" referring here to the relation or articulation of the different parts of a system.[43] Lévi-Strauss's construction of marriage as a gift exchange testifies to his intellectual debt to the French sociological tradition, and particularly to the work of Marcel Mauss. As Mauss suggested in his 1924 "Essay on the Gift," the act of giving, which is never free, pure, or disinterested, is generally followed by a counter-gift from the receiver of the initial gift. What matters most, Mauss argues, is that the gift be reciprocated within the right amount of time, neither too quickly nor too late. This was the conclusion that Bronislaw Malinowski had arrived at, a decade earlier, based on his own fieldwork in New Guinea and on his observation of the *kula* system of exchange. For Mauss (and, for that matter, for Lévi-Strauss), Malinowski was never able to move beyond a functionalist interpretation of this schema or to generalize the individual exchanges in order to explore its full social and cultural ramifications.

Mauss indeed argued that "it is not individuals but collectivities that impose obligations of exchange and contract upon each other."[44] Furthermore, the exchange of gifts is not limited to material objects but to social obligations more generally. This led Mauss to label the system of exchange a "total social fact": "What they exchange is not solely property and wealth, movable and immovable goods, and things economically useful. In particular, such exchanges are acts of politeness: banquets, rituals, military services, women, children, dances, festivals, and fairs, in which economic transaction is only one element, and in which the passing on of wealth is only one feature of a much more general and enduring contract."[45] One of the main consequences of this system of exchange of *prestations* (or services) is the development of a certain moral system in which giving, owing, and reciprocating opens individuals to one another: "If one gives things and returns them, it is because one is giving and returning 'respects' . . . Yet it is also because by giving one is giving *oneself,* and if one gives *oneself,* it is because one 'owes' *oneself*—one's person and one's goods—to others."[46] Therefore, the exchange can only have meaning—or *signify*—in relation to

---

43. Ibid., 38.

44. Mauss, *The Gift,* 5. For an excellent analysis of how this model of exchange influenced Lévi-Strauss, see Christopher Johnson, *Claude Lévi-Strauss: The Formative Years* (Cambridge University Press, 2003). See also Marcel Hénaff, *Claude Lévi-Strauss and the Making of Structural Anthropology* (University of Minnesota Press, 1998); Frédéric Keck, *Claude Lévi-Strauss: Une introduction* (Pocket/ La découverte, 2005).

45. Mauss, *The Gift,* 5.

46. Ibid., 46.

74   **CHAPTER 2**

other signifiers in that same system: "It is by considering the whole entity that we could perceive what is essential, the way everything moves, the living aspect, the fleeting moment when society, or men, become sentimentally aware of themselves and of their situation in relation to others."[47]

According to Mauss, giving is not only a mode of expressing trust and generosity vis–à–vis the other, but can also be an act of overt aggression, destined to highlight the power of the giver over the recipient, as in the example of the potlatch. In all cases, however, giving is a way of establishing a relationship (whether it be positive or negative) with an other. It is in this sense that Mauss calls the exchange of gifts *symbolic:* "Durkheim and I have been teaching for a long time that men can only enter into communion and communicate through symbols, signs that are common, permanent, and exterior to the individual states of mind . . . For a long time we have thought that one of the characteristics of the social fact is precisely its symbolic aspect."[48] In other words, individuals are linked to the collectivity, to the social world, through this process of exchange, or more specifically in *The Elementary Structures of Kinship,* through the exchange of women.[49]

Kinship as Symbolic

Mauss's analysis of this "symbolic" aspect of social relations was in many ways a continuation of the work that his uncle, Émile Durkheim, had undertaken during the Third Republic. Writing in a time of great industrial and social change, Durkheim, like Le Play, was preoccupied with the "social question" and with the erosion of the traditional normative frameworks provided by the church and the family, which Durkheim referred to as vectors of "mechanical solidarity." As a sociologist, Durkheim devoted much of his work to the understanding and promotion of a new kind of solidarity—other devices for social cohesion, better adapted to the secular modern

---

47. Ibid., 80.

48. Marcel Mauss, *Sociologie et anthropologie* (Presses universitaires de France, 1950), 294.

49. Many feminist critics have pointed to the role of women in the process of exchange, in particular Judith Butler, *Gender Trouble: Feminism and the Subversion of Identity* (Routledge, 1990); Luce Irigaray, *This Sex Which Is Not One,* trans. Catherine Porter (Cornell University Press, 1985); Gayle Rubin, "The Traffic in Women: Notes on the 'Political Economy' of Sex," in *Toward an Anthropology of Women,* ed. Rayna R. Reiter (Monthly Review Press, 1975); Monique Wittig, *The Straight Mind and Other Essays* (Beacon Press, 1992). As Rubin puts it, "Since Lévi-Strauss argues that the incest taboo and the results of its application constitute the origin of culture, it can be deduced that the world historical defeat of women occurred with the origin of culture, and is a prerequisite of culture" (176).

KINSHIP AND THE STRUCTURALIST SOCIAL CONTRACT 75

world. He called it "organic solidarity," referring to the kinds of social relations that are not inherited but rather acquired—through professional associations or through marriage, for example. In his last book, *The Elementary Forms of Religious Life,* published in 1912, Durkheim pursued his study of the social bond and devised the term "effervescence" to describe those moments in which particular individuals experienced their shared existence, their social bond, together.

In the totalizing models of Durkheim, Mauss, and Lévi-Strauss, the social is never simply an agglomeration of its individual components—rather, the very essence of the social is to be found in the articulation, the bond that links scattered individuals to the group, a bond that, moreover, appears to have an affective dimension.[50] In *The Elementary Structures of Kinship,* the primary function of this symbolic exchange is the formation and consolidation of social bonds. As Lévi-Strauss puts it, "Exchange—and consequently the rule of exogamy which expresses it—has in itself a social value. It provides the means of binding men together, and of superimposing upon the natural links of kinship the henceforth artificial links—artificial in the sense that they are removed from chance encounters or the promiscuity of family life—of alliance governed by rule."[51] Similarly, Lévi-Strauss emphasizes the "social benefit" of exogamous marriage, which asserts the social existence of other people [*autrui*].[52] Marriage, Lévi-Strauss contends, is the road to solidarity, to social integration. In this context, he refers to Durkheim's distinction between mechanical solidarity (the example he gives is the relationship between brothers) and organic solidarity (brothers-in-law, for example), to privilege the latter as the true social bond: "The first form of solidarity adds nothing and unites nothing; it is based upon a cultural limit, satisfied by [*qui se satisfait par*] the reproduction of a type of connection the model for which is provided by nature. The other brings about an integration of the group on a new plane."[53] Hence, in the scope of Lévi-Strauss's argument, incest is not so much morally or biologically objectionable as it is

---

50. For more general accounts of Durkheim's concept of solidarity, see Dominick LaCapra, *Émile Durkheim: Sociologist and Philosopher* (Cornell University Press, 1972); Steven Lukes, *Emile Durkheim, His Life and Work: A Historical and Critical Study* (Allen Lane, 1973); Judith Surkis, *Sexing the Citizen: Morality and Masculinity in France, 1870–1920* (Cornell University Press, 2006). For an interesting analysis of the affective quality of effervescence, see Michèle H. Richman, *Sacred Revolutions: Durkheim and the Collège de Sociologie* (University of Minnesota Press, 2002).

51. Lévi-Strauss, *Elementary Structures of Kinship,* 480.

52. Ibid.

53. Ibid., 484.

76   CHAPTER 2

fundamentally selfish and antisocial: "incest, in the broadest sense of the word, consists in obtaining by oneself, and for oneself, instead of by another, and for another."[54] It is in that sense that Lévi-Strauss asserts that "incest is socially absurd before it is morally culpable."[55] Incest means the refusal to participate in the social contract—a refusal that is theoretically impossible because man, as we have seen, is always already social.

In her important essay "The Traffic in Women: Notes on the 'Political Economy' of Sex," Gayle Rubin suggested that the incest taboo as Lévi-Strauss constructs it in *The Elementary Structures of Kinship* presupposes a prior taboo, one on homosexuality: "A prohibition against *some* heterosexual unions assumes a taboo against *non*-heterosexual unions. Gender is not only an identification with one sex; it also entails that sexual desire be directed toward the other sex."[56] Judith Butler developed this point in *Gender Trouble* and in many of her subsequent writings, arguing that "for heterosexuality to remain intact as a distinct social form, it *requires* an intelligible conception of homosexuality and also requires the prohibition of that conception in rendering it culturally unintelligible."[57] Commenting on these readings, Sharon Marcus has noted that while homosexuality does indeed haunt Claude Lévi-Strauss's *Elementary Structures of Kinship*, "Lévi-Strauss does not associate homosexuality with incest or with the precultural."[58] In particular, Marcus observes that Lévi-Strauss refers to homosexuality and to fraternal polyandry as "solutions" to the scarcity of wives, thus concluding that Lévi-Strauss *does* recognize homosexuality but "only to the extent that he could subsume it within heterosexuality . . . The universality of the incest taboo means not that homosexuality is equally taboo, but rather that even homosexuality is ultimately governed by the prohibition on incest and the imperative to exogamy."[59]

If Lévi-Strauss does indeed find a way to figure homosexuality within the confines of his social contract (but only to the extent that it is subdued under the universality of the exchange), the single unmarried individual is

---

54. Ibid., 489.

55. Ibid., 485.

56. Rubin, "Traffic in Women," 180.

57. Butler, *Gender Trouble*, 104.

58. Sharon Marcus, *Between Women: Friendship, Desire, and Marriage in Victorian England* (Princeton University Press, 2007), 196.

59. Ibid., 196.

KINSHIP AND THE STRUCTURALIST SOCIAL CONTRACT   77

much more problematic within his framework. As an illustration of this nonsocialized subject who remains outside the system of exchange, Lévi-Strauss gives the example of a bachelor he met in Brazil who "rarely went out, except to go hunting by himself, and when the family meals began around the fires, he would as often as not have gone without if a female relative had not occasionally set a little food at his side, which he ate in silence."[60] From Lévi-Strauss's description of this bachelor, we can conclude that the exclusion from the social contract is not only social, it also is psychological. Portrayed as "anxious," "wretched," and ill-looking, the bachelor testifies to the fact that "marriage is of vital importance for every individual, being, as he is, doubly concerned, not only to find a wife for himself but also to prevent those two calamities of primitive society from occurring in his group, namely, the bachelor and the orphan."[61] Marriage, in other words, has both a social and an individual benefit.

Kinship is thus symbolic according to Lévi-Strauss not because of its content but because of its structure. As Lévi-Strauss explains in his introduction to the 1950 collection of Mauss's essays *Sociologie et anthropologie,* "Any culture can be considered a set of symbolic systems among which figure predominantly language, matrimonial rules, economic relations, art, science, religion. All these systems seek to express certain aspects of physical reality and of social reality, and even more, *the relations that these two types of reality have with one another,* and that the symbolic systems themselves have with one another."[62] What is symbolic here is not something intrinsic to particular things, people, or events, but rather the articulation between the "physical reality" that we could call nature, and the "social reality" that we could call culture. In this context, although Lévi-Strauss praises Mauss for attempting to think the link between the individual and the social in innovative ways, he criticizes him for not pushing his interpretation far enough: "Mauss still believes it is possible to elaborate a sociological theory of symbolism, when we clearly should be looking for the symbolic origin of society."[63] In an article on the French sociological tradition published in a 1947 collection edited by Georges Gurvitch, Lévi-Strauss made a similar point about Durkheim:

---

60. Lévi-Strauss, *Elementary Structures of Kinship,* 39.

61. Ibid.

62. Claude Lévi-Strauss, "Introduction à l'œuvre de Marcel Mauss," in Marcel Mauss, *Sociologie et anthropologie* (Presses universitaires de France, 1950), xix (emphasis mine).

63. Ibid., xxii.

78   **CHAPTER 2**

We cannot explain the social phenomenon, the existence of the state of culture is in itself unintelligible if symbolism is not treated by sociological thought as an a priori condition . . . sociology cannot explain the genesis of symbolic thought, *it must take it as a given* . . . Society cannot exist without symbolism but instead of showing how the appearance of symbolic thought makes social life both possible and necessary, Durkheim sought to do the opposite, which is to say, to make symbolism spring from the state of society.[64]

The Elementary Structures of Kinship can be read, I have suggested, as an answer to this methodological impasse facing, according to Lévi-Strauss, the French sociological school. Indeed, since Lévi-Strauss posits nature and culture as a priori categories and since the incest prohibition is defined as the link between the two, we could say that the incest prohibition also needs to be taken as an a priori condition to understand social relations, culture, or the *pensée symbolique*. As such, Lévi-Strauss is able to answer his critiques of Durkheim ("sociology cannot explain the genesis of symbolic thought, it must take it as a given") and of Mauss (who wanted to "elaborate a sociological theory of symbolism" instead of finding "a symbolic origin of society").

☛ Beyond History

Lévi-Strauss's passages on the hypothetical state of nature are strikingly resonant with Rousseau's political writings. The connection with Rousseau is noteworthy because Lévi-Strauss consistently acknowledged his intellectual influence. As Lévi-Strauss suggested in a 1962 lecture, Rousseau "did not restrict himself to anticipating ethnology: he founded it . . . in a practical way, by writing the *Discourse on the Origin and Foundations of Inequality*, which poses the problem of the relation between nature and culture and in which we can see the first treatise of general ethnology."[65] Indeed, the distinction between a state of nature and a state of culture informs all of the *Second Discourse*, which Rousseau wrote to account for the origins of social institutions.

---

64. Claude Lévi-Strauss, "La sociologie française," in *La sociologie au XXe siècle*, ed. Georges Gurvitch (Presses universitaires de France, 1947), 526–27. For more on Lévi-Strauss's relation to Durkheim, see vol. 2, chap. 3 of *Structural Anthropology*, "Ce que l'ethnologie doit à Durkheim."

65. Claude Lévi-Strauss, *Structural Anthropology*, trans. Claire Jacobson and Brooke Grundfest Schoepf (Basic Books, 1963), 2:35. Rousseau also holds a crucial place in *Triste Tropique* (Plon, 1955), Lévi-Strauss's autobiographical account of his fieldwork in Brazil.

KINSHIP AND THE STRUCTURALIST SOCIAL CONTRACT   79

As Rousseau writes: "For it is by no means a light undertaking to distinguish properly between what is original and what is artificial in the actual nature of man, or to form a true idea of a state which no longer exists, perhaps never did exist, and probably never will exist; and of which it is nevertheless, necessary to have true ideas, in order to form a proper judgment of our present time."[66] Rousseau appears to join Lévi-Strauss in this double idea according to which the state of nature has no historical basis but is nonetheless conceptually necessary to be able to have "proper judgment" or, we could say, philosophical thought.

According to Ernst Cassirer, Rousseau like Hobbes and other contract theorists who relied on this division between nature and culture to build their ideal system of governance operated according to a "new Renaissance logic" in which "the object of a definition . . . is not merely to analyze and describe a given conceptual content; it is to be a means for constructing conceptual content and for establishing it by virtue of this constructive activity."[67] As such, Cassirer argues: "They observe rather the inner law according to which the whole either originated or at least can be conceived as originating. And they clarify within this law of becoming the real nature and behavior of this whole; they not only show *what* this whole is, but *why* it is."[68] This observation is similar to Jacques Derrida's famous critique of Lévi-Strauss first developed in his essay "Structure, Sign, and Play in the Discourse of the Human Sciences" and expanded in *Of Grammatology*. For Derrida, who calls the opposition between nature and culture "in spite of all its rejuvenations and its disguises, . . . congenital to philosophy," Lévi-Strauss "felt at one and the same time the necessity of utilizing this opposition and the impossibility of making it acceptable."[69] Obviously, Derrida writes,

> there is no scandal except in the *interior* of a system of concepts sanctioning the difference between nature and culture. In beginning his work with the *factum* of the incest-prohibition, Lévi-Strauss thus puts himself in a position entailing that this difference, which has always

---

66. Jean-Jacques Rousseau, *The Social Contract and Discourses,* trans. G. D. H. Cole (Everyman, 1973), 44.

67. Ernst Cassirer, *The Philosophy of the Enlightenment* (Princeton University Press, 1951), 253.

68. Ibid., 253–54 (emphases in original). For another interesting interpretation of the state of nature as a "conceptual shorthand" in political theory (this time in the case of Hobbes), see Sheldon S. Wolin, *Politics and Vision: Continuity and Innovation in Western Political Thought* (Princeton University Press, 2004), 235–37.

69. Jacques Derrida, *Writing and Difference,* trans. Alan Bass (University of Chicago Press, 1978), 282–83.

80   **CHAPTER 2**

been assumed to be self-evident, becomes obliterated or disputed. For, from the moment that the incest-prohibition can no longer be conceived within the nature/culture opposition, it can no longer be said that it is a scandalous fact, a nucleus of opacity within a network of transparent significations. The incest-prohibition is no longer a scandal one meets with or comes up against in the domain of traditional concepts; it is something which escapes these concepts and certainly precedes them—probably as the condition of their possibility. It could perhaps be said that the whole of philosophical conceptualization, systematically relating itself to the nature/culture opposition, is designed to leave in the domain of the unthinkable the very thing that makes this conceptualization possible: the origin of the prohibition of incest.[70]

In *The Elementary Structures*, Lévi-Strauss appears to be acutely aware of the arbitrariness not only of the category of nature but also of the social. As he writes toward the end of his book, kinship and the prohibition of incest "become clear as soon as one grants that society must exist. *But society might not have been.* Have we therefore resolved one problem, as we thought, only to see its whole importance shifted to another problem, the solution to which appears even more hypothetical than that to which we have devoted all our attention?"[71] No, answers Lévi-Strauss:

If our proposed interpretation is correct, the rules of kinship and marriage are not made necessary by the social state. They are the social state itself, reshaping biological relationships and natural sentiments, forcing them into structures implying them as well as others, and compelling them to rise above their original characteristics. The natural state recognizes only indivision and appropriation, and their chance admixture [*hasardeux mélange*] . . . What is this world unless it is that to which social life ceaselessly bends itself in a never wholly successful attempt to construct and reconstruct an approximate image of it, that world of reciprocity which the laws of kinship and marriage, in their own sphere of interest, laboriously derive from relationships which are otherwise condemned to remain either sterile or immoderate [*abusives*]?[72]

---

70. Ibid., 283. See also Jacques Derrida, *Of Grammatology*, trans. Gayatri Chakravorty Spivak (Johns Hopkins University Press, 1997), 104 (emphasis in original).

71. Lévi-Strauss, *Elementary Structures of Kinship*, 490 (emphasis mine).

72. Ibid.

KINSHIP AND THE STRUCTURALIST SOCIAL CONTRACT   81

Furthermore, Lévi-Strauss continues, to posit the existence of nature, the social, and the incest prohibition is not merely an "act of faith": "the progress of contemporary social anthropology would be of small account if we had to be content with an act of faith—fruitful no doubt, and in its time, legitimate—in the dialectic process ineluctably giving rise to the world of reciprocity."[73] The incest prohibition, in other words, is more than a simple random or arbitrary justification.

To clarify this claim, Lévi-Strauss turns to Freud's *Totem and Taboo*. The choice of *Totem and Taboo* is significant because this work represents one of Freud's most elaborate attempts to link the social to the sexual.[74] In Freud's narrative, the brothers' murder of the father and the sacrificial meal that follows mark the institution of the superego. Out of the brothers' guilt emerges the rule of law, morality, religion, and also exogamy, because the father can no longer keep all the women for himself. The prohibition of incest marks the birth of culture, of the symbolic as such. As Freud puts it, "the beginnings of religion, morals, society, and art converge in the Oedipus complex. This is in complete agreement with the psycho-analytic finding that the same complex constitutes the nucleus of all neuroses."[75] For Freud, the structural equivalence between culture, morality, society, and psychic adjustment has a series of consequences. In particular, Freud suggests that being outside this social contract has not only social but also psychic consequences. As he explains, "the asocial nature of neuroses has its genetic origin in their most fundamental purpose, which is to take flight from an unsatisfying reality into a more pleasurable world of phantasy. The real world, which is avoided in this way by neurotics, is under the sway of human society and of the institutions collectively created by it. To turn away from reality is at the same time to withdraw from the community of man."[76]

---

73. Ibid.

74. Freud says so explicitly in his preface: *Totem and Taboo* represents "a first attempt on my part at applying the point of view and the findings of psychoanalysis to some unsolved problems of social psychology." In Sigmund Freud, *Totem and Taboo: Some Points of Agreement between the Mental Lives of Savages and Neurotics* (Norton, 1989), xxvii. For an interesting reading of *Totem and Taboo* focusing on the parallel construction of social and sexual orders, see Eugène Enriquez, *De la horde à l'État: Essai de psychanalyse du lien social* (Gallimard, 1983). See also chap. 11, "Sur les origines et les fondements de la prohibition de l'inceste: Freud et Lévi-Strauss," in Maurice Godelier, *Métamorphoses de la parenté* (Fayard, 2004). Along similar lines, Elisabeth Roudinesco calls *Totem and Taboo* a "political book of Kantian inspiration . . . it proposes a theory of democratic power centered on three necessities: the necessity of a foundational act, the necessity of the law, the necessity to renounce despotism" ("De près et de loin: Claude Lévi-Strauss et la psychanalyse," *Critique* 55, no. 620–21 (1999): 172).

75. Freud, *Totem and Taboo*, 194.

76. Ibid., 93.

82   CHAPTER 2

Lévi-Strauss focuses on Freud's analogy between individual psyche and social formations to maintain the uniqueness and specificity of the incest taboo. As he writes,

> Freud's work is an example and a lesson. The moment the claim was made that certain extant features of the human mind could be explained by an historically certain and logically necessary event, it was permissible, and even prescribed, to attempt a scrupulous restoration of the sequence. The failure of *Totem and Taboo,* far from being inherent to the author's proposed design, results rather from his hesitation to avail himself to the ultimate consequences implied in his premises. He ought to have seen that phenomena involving the most fundamental structure of the human mind could not have appeared once and for all. They are repeated in their entirety within each consciousness, and the relevant explanation falls within an order which transcends both historical successions and contemporary correlations.[77]

In other words, although Lévi-Strauss credits Freud for thinking the individual and the social together through this "social contract model," he criticizes him for remaining caught in historical explanations that Freud himself constantly put into question.[78] Freud's methodological "timidity," Lévi-Strauss continues, leads him to a "strange and double paradox":

> Freud successfully accounts, not for the beginning of civilization but for its present state; and setting out to explain the origin of a prohibition, he succeeds in explaining, certainly not why incest is consciously condemned, but how it happens to be unconsciously desired. It has been stated and restated that what makes *Totem and Taboo* unacceptable, as an interpretation of the prohibition of incest and its origins, is the gratuitousness of the hypothesis of the male horde and of primitive murder, a vicious circle deriving the social state from the events which presuppose it . . . The desire for the mother or the sister, the murder of the father and the sons' repentance, undoubtedly do not correspond to any fact or group of facts occupying a single place in history. But perhaps they symbolically express an ancient and lasting dream. The power of this dream, its power to mould men's thoughts unbeknown

---

77. Lévi-Strauss, *Elementary Structures of Kinship,* 491.

78. Freud, for example, calls his story "a hypothesis which may seem fantastic but which offers the advantage of establishing an unsuspected correlation between groups of phenomena that have hitherto been disconnected" (*Totem and Taboo,* 175).

KINSHIP AND THE STRUCTURALIST SOCIAL CONTRACT   83

to them, arises precisely from the fact that the acts it evokes have never been committed, because culture has opposed them at all times and in all places.[79]

The main problem with *Totem and Taboo* according to Lévi-Strauss is thus not the actual event that Freud focuses on (the killing of the father), but rather the fact that Freud attempts to think this prohibition *historically*. Freud's inability to rid himself of history is particularly paradoxical, according to Lévi-Strauss, because in his other writings Freud has often suggested that "certain basic phenomena" such as anxiety and sublimation "find their explanation in the permanent structure of the human mind, rather than in its history."[80] Thus, Lévi-Strauss concludes, Freud's "hesitations" in *Totem and Taboo* are revealing: "They show a social science like psychoanalysis—for it is one—still wavering between the tradition of an historical sociology . . . and a more modern and scientifically more solid attitude, which expects a knowledge of its future and past from an analysis of the present."[81] This "more modern and scientifically more solid attitude" will be structuralism.

Indeed, the last pages of *The Elementary Structures* can be read as a theoretical manifesto for Lévi-Strauss's new discipline of structural anthropology. Avoiding the methodological impasses of biology and history, of the natural sciences and the social sciences, structural anthropology would also avoid the political polarization of anthropology and ethnology prior to the war. Indeed, as Lévi-Strauss puts it, "only one science has reached the point at which synchronic and diachronic explanation have merged . . . This social science is linguistics . . . When we consider its methods, and even more its object, we may ask ourselves whether the sociology of the family, as conceived of in this work, involves as different a reality as might be believed, and consequently whether it has not the same possibilities at its disposal."[82] Lévi-Strauss's interest in linguistics dated from his years in New York, particularly from his friendship with Roman Jakobson who was also exiled at the École libre des hautes études during the war.[83] Besides Jakobson, the works of Saussure, Troubetzkoy, and Benveniste were all foundational for Lévi-Strauss's introduction to structural linguistic theory. For Lévi-Strauss, structural linguistics offered an alternative to history and historical sociology

---

79. Lévi-Strauss, *Elementary Structures of Kinship,* 491.

80. Ibid.

81. Ibid., 492.

82. Ibid., 492–93.

83. For more on Lévi-Strauss and Jakobson, see Eribon and Lévi-Strauss, *De près et de loin,* 63–65.

84   **CHAPTER 2**

by providing a universal, logical, and relational model particularly well adapted to the study of "total facts." This model was not only descriptive in its nature but was also explanatory. As such, it allowed him to posit a set of general rules.

The analogy between kinship and linguistics that Lévi-Strauss sets up at the end of his book has a series of crucial consequences. First, if we return to the previous graph, language can be added on the side of culture as another effect of the incest prohibition (in the opposite camp of nature). Language, kinship, culture, symbolic thought, sociality, and psychic adjustment are now structurally equivalent, whereas sounds (with no signifier attached to them), mating, nature, selfishness, isolation (like the bachelor), and psychic damage are on the other side. Another way to say this is that the structuralist social contract is also a linguistic contract: it assumes that signifiers and signified are attached to one another in a particular way. Consequently, being outside the social contract means not being able to "signify" to others:

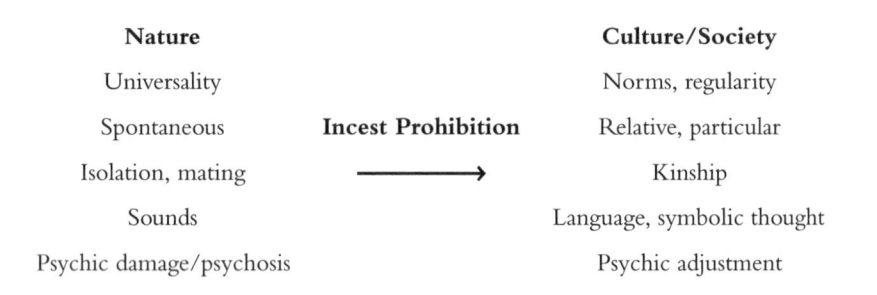

Nature		**Culture/Society**
Universality		Norms, regularity
Spontaneous	**Incest Prohibition**	Relative, particular
Isolation, mating	$\longrightarrow$	Kinship
Sounds		Language, symbolic thought
Psychic damage/psychosis		Psychic adjustment

It is in this sense that we should understand Lévi-Strauss's assertions that "the relations between the sexes can be conceived as one of the modalities of a great 'communication function' which also includes language," and that "language and exogamy represent two solutions to one and the same situation," namely, the situation of social exchange.[84] In opposition to the tower of Babel "when words were still the essential property of each particular group"—in the state of nature for example—words have now "become common property," and as such they function as vehicles of solidarity:

> If the incest prohibition and exogamy have an essentially positive function, if the reason for their existence is to establish a tie between men which the latter cannot do without if they are to raise themselves

---

84. Lévi-Strauss, *Elementary Structures of Kinship,* 494, 496.

KINSHIP AND THE STRUCTURALIST SOCIAL CONTRACT   85

from a biological to a social organization, it must be recognized that linguists and sociologists do not merely apply the same methods but are studying the same thing. Indeed, from this point of view, "exogamy and language . . . have fundamentally the same function—communication and integration with others" . . . The incest prohibition is universal like language.[85]

Lévi-Strauss's embrace of structuralism at the end of his book is thus— intellectually and disciplinarily—strategic. Faced with the theoretical difficulty presented by his concepts of nature and society (and, if we follow Derrida, by the need to rely on this opposition without being able to justify it), Lévi-Strauss contends that the incest taboo is neither cultural nor social, but rather structural, and, like language, it is universal and somehow inevitable. As Maurice Merleau-Ponty has suggested in his analysis of *The Elementary Structures,* exchange is taken for granted—it is presented as *allant de soi:* "Subjects who live in a society are not necessarily aware of the principle of exchange that regulates them, just as the speaking subject does not need a linguistic analysis of his language in order to speak. Rather, the structure is used as if it were obvious."[86] The *structure* of this social contract might not be obvious (and in fact, according to Lévi-Strauss, it is not), but its *practice,* its *performance* is. In this sense, Lévi-Strauss can argue that it is neither "symbolic thought" nor culture that produces the prohibition of incest. This would be a sociohistorical explanation. Rather, the prohibition and its correlation of exogamy and the family are coextensive with the symbolic: they are the "general condition of culture."[87]

↝ Lacan and the Principle of Double Differentiation

Jacques Lacan was one of the early enthusiastic readers of *The Elementary Structures of Kinship.* Lacan and Lévi-Strauss knew each other personally, and in the years after Lévi-Strauss's return from New York, they navigated similar intellectual circles, had amicable relations, and occasionally attended each other's seminars. By the time Lacan came across Lévi-Strauss's work, he had already been using the term "structure" in relation to subjectivity in much

---

85. Ibid., 493.

86. "De Mauss à Claude Lévi-Strauss" in Maurice Merleau-Ponty, *Éloge de la philosophie et autres essais* (Gallimard, 1967), 128.

87. Lévi-Strauss, *Elementary Structures of Kinship,* 24.

86   **CHAPTER 2**

of his work. In his 1932 doctoral thesis, *On Paranoid Psychosis and Its Relations to the Personality,* Lacan maintained that psychosis was not the outcome of a specific malfunctioning of the brain as many neuroscientists believed. Rather, he suggested that many factors—some biological and some cultural—intervened.[88] For Lacan, the subject was never isolated as many psychiatrists assumed. It was neither the autonomous reflexive Cartesian self nor the transcendental Kantian actor. Instead, the philosophical model that appeared to best translate Lacan's psychoanalytic understanding of the self was Hegel's.

Lacan became particularly engaged with Hegel's thought through Alexandre Kojève's popular seminar on the *Phenomenology of Spirit,* which Lacan attended in the thirties. There, he met other thinkers interested in the relationship between the individual and the social, including Georges Bataille, Pierre Klossowski, Roger Caillois, and the other members of the Collège de sociologie.[89] For many of these French readers of the *Phenomenology,* Hegel provided a model of subjectivity in which the Other (who is desired but who is also the agent of desire and consequently of recognition) is essential for the self-certain subject to come into being. Hegel offered a way to bypass the divide between the individual and the social by suggesting that the two were neither autonomous nor overdetermined by one or the other, but rather that they were mutually constitutive. Lacan's early work was deeply influenced by Hegel's notion of desire and by his understanding of subjectivity. This was particularly evident in Lacan's model of the "mirror stage," which sought to provide a visual model to account for the formation of the ego, caught in this process or recognition and misrecognition between self and other.[90]

In 1938, the editors of the *Encyclopédie française* asked Lacan to contribute an entry on the family. In this text, Lacan continued to explore the parallels

---

88. Jacques Lacan, *De la psychose paranoïaque dans ses rapports avec la personnalité suivi de Premiers écrits sur la paranoïa* (Seuil, 1975), 346.

89. On the importance of Hegel for the French academic landscape of the thirties, see Mikkel Borch-Jacobsen, *Lacan: The Absolute Master* (Stanford University Press, 1991); Judith Butler, *Subjects of Desire: Hegelian Reflections in Twentieth-Century France* (Columbia University Press, 1999); Carolyn J. Dean, *The Self and Its Pleasures: Bataille, Lacan, and the History of the Decentered Subject* (Cornell University Press, 1992); Michael S. Roth, *Knowing and History: Appropriations of Hegel in Twentieth-Century France* (Cornell University Press, 1988). On the Collège more specifically, see the introduction to Denis Hollier, ed., *Le Collège de sociologie: 1937–1939* (Gallimard, 1979).

90. For a more general introduction to Lacan's construction of subjectivity, see Bruce Fink, *The Lacanian Subject: Between Language and Jouissance* (Princeton University Press, 1995); Kaja Silverman, *The Subject of Semiotics* (Oxford University Press, 1983), chap. 4.

KINSHIP AND THE STRUCTURALIST SOCIAL CONTRACT   87

between the psychic and the social. Lacan's construction of the family in this 1938 piece was strikingly similar to Lévi-Strauss's in *The Elementary Structures.* Indeed, according to Lacan, one of the family's most distinctive features was that it was anchored in both nature (as evidenced, for instance, by the "maternal instinct") and culture (the example he gives is paternity).[91] Thus, he argued, psychoanalysis "must adapt to this complex structure and has no use for philosophical theories that reduce the human family either to a biological fact, or to a theoretical element of society."[92] The family, Lacan explained, was of particular interest to psychoanalysis because it played a primordial role in the transmission not only of genes but more importantly of culture. As he put it, it "presides over the fundamental processes of psychic development . . . more generally, it transmits the structures of behavior and representation that go beyond the conscious. Between generations, it establishes a psychic continuity whose causality is of a mental order."[93]

In order to elucidate this theoretical specificity of the family, Lacan turned to two concepts, both popular within the psychoanalytic literature of the 1930s: the *imago* and the *complex*. The former (etymologically linked to the "image") describes one's "unconscious representations."[94] The latter refers to the interaction of the different *imagos*. Unlike the *instinct,* which pertains solely to nature and biology, the *complex* has two distinctive features: it operates at the level of culture while still remaining grounded in biology, and it describes *ideal* relations, which might not correspond to any empirical fact but can be conceptually useful:

> By opposing the complex to the instinct, we are not denying all biological foundation to the complex. In defining it through certain ideal relations, we still link it to its material foundation. This foundation is the function it fulfills in the social group; and this biological basis can be seen in the individual's vital dependence on the group. While the instinct has an organic prop and is nothing other than the regulation of this prop in a biological function, the complex only occasionally

---

91. Jacques Lacan, *Autres écrits* (Seuil, 2001), 24. The family essay was partially translated into English in a special issue of *Semiotext(e)* (1981) called "Polysexuality," trans. Andrea Kahn, 190–200; and in *Critical Texts* 5, no. 3 (1988), 12–29, trans. Carolyn Asp. I also consulted Cormac Gallagher's translation, *Family Complexes in the Formation of the Individual* (Atony Rowe, 2003).

92. Lacan, *Autres écrits,* 24.

93. Ibid., 25.

94. Ibid. The adjective "unconscious" is important here because it differentiates the *imago* from the "real" representation.

88   CHAPTER 2

has an organic relation, when it compensates for a biological deficiency by the regulation of a social function.[95]

Lacan proceeded to single out three particularly important "family complexes": the weaning complex (or *complexe de servrage*), connected to the
imago of the maternal breast; the intrusion complex (or *complexe d'intrusion*),
when the child realizes he has siblings (also known as the *imago of the counterpart*); and finally the Oedipus complex, related to the paternal imago.[96]
Although the first two complexes eventually disappeared from Lacan's work,
the Oedipus complex gained greater prominence. In very simplified terms,
in Freud's version of the Oedipus complex, the child desires the parent of
the opposite sex, perceives the other parent as a rival and resents that parent,
but eventually learns to repress that desire. For the subject, this process leads
to sexual differentiation. The boy will metaphorize his desire by choosing
women who are "like" the mother. The girl, upset by her anatomical "deficiency," will eventually have a baby of her own in an attempt to compensate for her lack of and desire for a penis. The father, in this sense, has a
double function: "The parent of the same sex appears to the child both as
the agent of sexual prohibition and the example of its transgression . . . This
double process has a fundamental genetic importance, because it remains
inscribed in the psyche in two permanent instances: the repressive instance,
called the superego, and the sublimating instance called the ego-ideal. They
represent the completion of the Oedipal crisis."[97]

Freud, as we saw before, was equally interested in the social consequences of the Oedipus complex. *Totem and Taboo* revolves around this issue.
Just as the child can reach maturity by renouncing the mother and obeying
the father's law, in the primal horde, the brothers' guilt triggered by the killing
of their father forces them to turn toward exogamy, morality, and religion. At
both the micro and the macro levels (the subject and the social), the post-
Oedipal phase is the phase of the law, identification, and normativity. Lacan's
objection to *Totem and Taboo* is similar to the one that Lévi-Strauss develops
in *The Elementary Structures of Kinship,* namely, that Freud remains too historical in his attempt to locate the origin of the prohibition. According to
Lacan, the "evolution of sexuality" and the "constitution of reality" require

---

95. Ibid., 34. This notion of an "ideal rapport" is interesting in relation to Lévi-Strauss's own pro-
pensity toward ideal analyses in the study of kinship.

96. For an extended analysis of these three complexes, see Markos Zafiropoulos, *Lacan et les sciences
sociales: Le déclin du père (1938–1953)* (Presses universitaires de France, 2001), chap. 1.

97. Lacan, *Autres écrits,* 46.

KINSHIP AND THE STRUCTURALIST SOCIAL CONTRACT 89

a "more rigorous conception of the *structural* relations" linking the two.[98] Lacan's first observation is that the figure of authority within the family is not necessarily the biological father. Citing Malinowski, whose fieldwork attested to the possibility of a maternal uncle holding this position of authority, Lacan challenges the universality of the Oedipus presupposed by Freud (and by "Western culture" more generally), claiming instead that "the Oedipus complex is relative to a social structure."[99] If the societies studied by Malinowski failed to present the same sorts of neuroses that exist in the Western world, they also lacked the great cultural artifacts brought about by the process of sublimation and the repression of the paternal imago. The second main point argued by Lacan is that psychosis and neurosis have a familial origin. This does not mean that they are hereditary but rather that they are causally related to these familial *imagos* or unconscious family representations.[100] Although these causal relations operate differently in psychosis and in neurosis, Lacan concludes that

> the Oedipus complex presupposes a certain typicality [*typicité*] in the psychological relation between the parents. We have particularly insisted on the twofold role played by the father in representing authority and being at the center of the revelation of sexuality. It is to this very ambiguity of his imago, as the incarnation of repression and as the catalyst of an essential access to reality, that we have related the twofold progress typical to a culture, of a certain tempering of the superego and of a highly evolutionary orientation of the personality.[101]

While these early texts revealed Lacan's interest in the structural, especially for the analysis of the family, it was not until later that Lacan came to fully embrace structuralism for psychoanalysis. It was in 1953 that Lacan, in his own words, "took [his] stand in psychoanalysis."[102] Nineteen fifty-three was, first of all, a year of great changes within the psychoanalytic international community. Since 1934, Lacan had been a member of the Société psychanalytique de Paris (SPP), founded in 1926 by René Laforgue and Marie Bonaparte, two of Freud's closest collaborators in France. Many of Lacan's early ideas (his theory of the mirror stage, for example) were first presented at

---

98. Ibid., 49.

99. Ibid., 56.

100. Ibid., 62.

101. Ibid., 79.

102. Marcelle Marini, *Jacques Lacan: The French Context* (Rutgers University Press, 1992), 152.

90   **CHAPTER 2**

the SPP. As the group reorganized after the war, several important theoretical and institutional points of contention divided the society's members. Among these, the most recurrent was the question of psychoanalytic training. For analysts like Sacha Nacht and Serge Lebovici, psychoanalysis needed to be rooted in neurobiology; consequently, a medical background was a prerequisite for all future analysts. For others such as Daniel Lagache, Françoise Dolto, Juliette Favez-Boutonier, and Lacan, the only requirement for becoming an analyst was to undergo an analysis of one's own, complemented by some kind of supervision. The analysts also disagreed on the length of the sessions, the potential affiliation of psychoanalysis with the university (which would be responsible for delivering diplomas and such), and other similar considerations. As institutional tensions rose, Lacan's group decided to split from the SPP to found the Société française de psychanalyse (SFP) on June 18, 1953. Because of the unorthodox practices of many of its members, most notably Lacan, the SFP was excluded from the International Psychoanalytic Association (IPA). It took ten years, arduous negotiations, and the eventual expulsion of Lacan for the SFP to eventually be accepted by the IPA.[103]

The SFP's first meeting was held at the Hôpital Sainte-Anne on July 8, 1953. Lacan gave a presentation entitled "The Symbolic, the Imaginary, and the Real."[104] This was the first time that Lacan invoked his famous triad which was to become the springboard for much of his thinking to come. While the imaginary referred to a thematic Lacan had been involved with for some time (as evidenced in the concept of the *imago*), both the real and the symbolic marked a new step in his work, one in which language held a central role. Lacan's concept of the symbolic also testified to his intellectual debt to Lévi-Strauss, a debt that he often acknowledged.[105] The Sainte-Anne 1953 conference served as a preview to one of Lacan's best-known texts, "The Function and Field of Speech and Language in Psychoanalysis." Also known as "the Rome Discourse," Lacan delivered this text on September 26, 1953, at an international psychoanalysis meeting in Italy. Playing on

---

103. For more on the 1953 *scission,* see ibid., 117; Elisabeth Roudinesco, *Jacques Lacan: Esquisse d'une vie, histoire d'un système de pensée* (Fayard, 1993); Elisabeth Roudinesco, *La bataille de cent ans: Histoire de la psychanalyse en France,* 2 vols. (Ramsay, 1982, 1986), 2:260; Sherry Turkle, *Psychoanalytic Politics: Freud's French Revolution* (Basic Books, 1978), 105. See also Jacques-Alain Miller, ed., *La Scission de 1953: La communauté psychanalytique en France* (Navrin, 1990), originally published as a special issue of *Ornicar.*

104. This text was republished as Jacques Lacan, *Des noms-du-père* (Seuil, 2005).

105. In a 1956 interview, he claims for instance to have been particularly influenced by Lévi-Strauss's emphasis on the "function of the signifier, with the meaning that the term has in linguistics: a signifier, not only because of its laws, but because it prevails over the signified on which it imposes them"; cited in Roudinesco, *Jacques Lacan,* 282.

KINSHIP AND THE STRUCTURALIST SOCIAL CONTRACT   91

the theme of "excommunication" and addressing most of the thorny issues that had alienated Lacan and his colleagues from the IPA, the Rome Discourse was received as a theoretical manifesto for the new SFP, confirming Lacan's move toward language analysis and structuralism.

Language was the starting point of Lacan's "return to Freud" because language, the patient's word or rather *parole* was, according to Lacan, the only medium available to psychoanalysis.[106] Lacan opposed his notion of language to that of the ego-psychologists or the behaviorist school interested in establishing "communication" with the patient.[107] Psychoanalysis, he argued, ought to focus on the gaps in language, the silences, the paradoxes, the symptoms, the *actes manqués,* "even if it communicates nothing."[108] It should focus, in other words, on the discourse of the unconscious defined as "that part of the concrete discourse qua transindividual, which is not at the subject's disposal in reestablishing the continuity of his conscious discourse."[109] Psychoanalytic technique could not be "understood nor therefore correctly applied," Lacan continued, "if one misunderstands the concepts on which it is based."[110] More specifically, according to Lacan, contemporary psychoanalysts had overlooked the two most important concepts invented by Freud, whose importance was consistently confirmed by the analytic experience: the unconscious and sexuality. Both of these took on "their full meaning only when oriented in a field of language and ordered in relation to the function of speech."[111]

To link the unconscious, sexuality, and language, Lacan opposes humans to animals. Just as Lévi-Strauss contended that what distinguished chimpanzees from humans was the former's inability to symbolize, Lacan writes that language (which is human as opposed to animal "communication") is characterized by the distinction between the signifier and the signified. Freud's genius discovery, according to Lacan, was "that of the field of the effects, in man's nature, of his relations to the symbolic order and the fact that their meaning goes all the way back to the most radical instances of symbolization in being. To ignore the symbolic order is to condemn Freud's discovery to forgetting and analytic experience to ruin."[112] The symbolic nature of man's

---

106. Jacques Lacan, *Écrits: A Selection,* trans. Bruce Fink (Norton, 2002), 40.

107. Ibid., 38.

108. Ibid., 44.

109. Ibid., 50.

110. Ibid., 39.

111. Ibid.

112. Ibid., 63.

92   **CHAPTER 2**

exchanges can be witnessed, Lacan tells us, in the exchange of gifts. Turning to the pacific Argonauts (who had been studied by both Malinowski and Mauss), Lacan establishes an equivalence between language and the law, "because the law of man has been the law of language:" "These gifts, the act of giving them and the objects given, their transmutation into signs, and even their fabrication, were so closely intertwined with speech . . . For these gifts are already symbols, in the sense that symbol means pact, and they are first and foremost signifiers of the pact they constitute as the signified."[113] Gift-giving, in other words, is not only social—it is also linguistic.

Among the laws of gift-giving and socialization more generally, the most important are the rules of matrimonial alliance: "marriage ties are governed by an order of preference whose law concerning kinship names is, like language, imperative for the group in its forms, but unconscious in its structure."[114] Lacan thus posits an analogy among language, the law, kinship, and the unconscious. He articulates this most explicitly in the following passage:

> This is precisely where the Oedipus complex—insofar as we still acknowledge that it covers the whole field of our experience with its signification—will be said, in my remarks here, to mark the limits our discipline assigns to subjectivity: namely, what the subject can know of his unconscious participation in the movement of the complex structures of marriage ties, by verifying the symbolic effect in his individual existence of the tangential movement towards incest that has manifested itself ever since the coming of a universal community. The primordial Law is therefore the law which, in regulating marriage ties, superimposes the reign of culture over the reign of nature, the latter being subject to the law of mating. The prohibition of incest is merely the subjective pivot of that Law, laid bare by the modern tendency to reduce the objects the subject is forbidden to choose to the mother and sisters, full license, moreover, not yet being entirely granted beyond them. *This law, then, reveals itself clearly enough as identical to a language order.* For without names for kinship relations, no power can institute the order of preferences and taboos that knot and braid the thread of lineage through the generations.[115]

---

113. Ibid., 61.

114. Ibid., 65.

115. Ibid., 65–66 (emphasis mine).

KINSHIP AND THE STRUCTURALIST SOCIAL CONTRACT 93

In underscoring the subjective consequence of the incest prohibition, Lacan appears to complete Lévi-Strauss's project where it ended, with Freud and language. Lacan in fact highlights this continuity between psychoanalysts (described as "practitioners of the symbolic function"[116]), anthropologists, and linguists. In this context, he also reemphasizes the importance of Lévi-Strauss, who "in suggesting the involvement in myths of language structures and of those social laws that regulate marriage ties and kinship, is already conquering the very terrain in which Freud situates the unconscious."[117]

Thus, we could revise the diagram of *Elementary Structures* as follows:

Nature		Culture/Society
Universality	**Incest Prohibition**	Norms, regularity
Spontaneous	⟶	Relative, particular
Mating	**Oedipus Complex**	Matrimonial rules/law
Communication		Language/signification

Once again, the arrow can only go from left to right because man is always already subject to this symbolic order: "man thus speaks, but it is because the symbol has made him man."[118] In the remainder of his text, Lacan makes clear that a dysfunction in the Oedipus complex also entails a dysfunction in language and in socialization. For instance, he writes that "it is the confusion of generations which, in the Bible as in all traditional laws, is cursed as being the abomination of the Word and the desolation of the sinner."[119] As an example of this "confusion of generations," Lacan mentions the case of a "falsified filiation" that can be responsible for "dissociating the subject's personality." Similarly, he cites the (apparently "not invented") case of a "man marrying the mother of the woman with whom he has had a son."[120] Along these lines, signaling that any violation of this social/Oedipal contract has a linguistic manifestation, Lacan defines madness (a synonym here for psychosis) as "a discourse in which the subject . . . is spoken instead of

---

116. Ibid., 71.

117. Ibid., 72.

118. Ibid., 65.

119. Ibid., 66.

120. Ibid.

94   CHAPTER 2

speaking."[121] In neurosis, Lacan tells us, the "speech is driven out of the concrete discourse that orders consciousness, but it finds its medium either in the subject's natural functions . . . or in the images that, at the border between the *Umwelt* and the *Innenwelt,* organize their relational structuring. A symptom here is the signifier of a signified that has been repressed from the subject's consciousness."[122] Just as the role of the psychoanalyst is to introduce the signifier (and in the third section of his text Lacan shows just how Freud did so in some of his most famous case studies), the father is this "third" who is necessary for the "generations" not to be "confused." More specifically, Lacan introduces here his concept of the Name-of-the-Father or *Nom-du-père,* based on the homophony *nom* as name and *non* as no, to expand the role of the biological father in the Oedipus complex—as the one who breaks the dual identificatory relation between mother and child—to other structures of authority: "It is in the *name of the father* that we must recognize the basis of the symbolic function which, since the dawn of historical time, has identified his person with the figure of the law."[123]

The Rome Discourse set up the theoretical agenda for Lacanian psychoanalysis and for much of French psychoanalysis in the years to come. In his 1954–1955 seminar *The Ego in Freud's Theory and in the Technique of Psychoanalysis,* Lacan continued to elaborate on this notion of a "symbolic function," which would eventually give rise to a symbolic *order:*

> What is original in Lévi-Strauss's notion of the elementary structure? Throughout he emphasizes the fact that nothing is understood about the facts now collected for some considerable time concerning kinship and the family, if one tries to deduce them from any natural or naturalizing dynamic. Incest as such doesn't elicit any natural feeling of horror . . . There is no biological reason, and in particular no genetic one, to account for exogamy . . . And what does he base this on? On the fact that, in the human order, we are dealing with the complete emergence of a new function, encompassing the whole order in its entirety . . . The human order is characterized by the fact that the symbolic function intervenes at every moment and at every stage of its existence. In other words, the whole thing holds together [*tout se tient*] . . . In order to conceive what happens in the domain proper to the human order, we must start with the idea that this order consti-

---

121. Ibid., 68.

122. Ibid.

123. Ibid., 66 (emphasis in original).

KINSHIP AND THE STRUCTURALIST SOCIAL CONTRACT 95

tutes a totality. In the symbolic order the totality is called a universe. The symbolic order from the first takes on its universal character.[124]

Lacan's symbolic is thus not only independent of nature, but, like a Maussian total social fact, it is universal, ordered, and formal in the sense that it is regulated by mathematical logic.[125] The symbolic does not in any way refer to a "collective unconscious," which would translate some fundamental "human nature," but rather it undercuts the division between the individual and the social because "if the symbolic function functions, we are inside it. And I would even say—we are so far into it that we can't get out of it."[126] It is in this context that Lacan can state that "the Oedipus complex is both universal and contingent, because it is uniquely and purely symbolic."[127] By universal, Lacan is not referring here to the empirical everywhere, or to the sum of the individual parts. In fact, Lacan defines psychosis as the foreclosure of the signifier, as a "hole" in the symbolic due to the absence of the Name-of-the-Father. Rather, he appears to be designating a deeper structural understanding of "the whole," which we have already seen in the work of Lévi-Strauss:

> The value of the distinction between nature and culture which Lévi-Strauss introduces in his *Elementary Structures of Kinship* is that it allows us to distinguish the universal from the generic. There's absolutely no need for the symbolic universal to spread over the entire surface of the world for it to be universal. Besides, as far as I know, there's nothing which entails the world unity of human beings. There's nothing which is concretely realized as universal. And yet, as soon as any symbolic system is formed, straightaway it is, *de jure,* a universal as such.[128]

Lacan's explicit distancing vis-à-vis the empirical and the historical is reminiscent of Lévi-Strauss's positions in the *Elementary Structures.* Just as Lévi-Strauss repeatedly indicated that although the state of nature did not correspond to a real fact it remained conceptually necessary, Lacan adopted a similar position when he claimed that the Oedipus complex needed not

---

124. Jacques Lacan, *The Ego in Freud's Theory and in the Technique of Psychoanalysis, 1954–1955,* trans. Sylvana Tomaselli (Norton, 1988), 29.

125. Lacan defines mathematic formalization as such: "When one speaks of mathematical formalization, we are dealing with a set of conventions from which you can generate a whole series of consequences, of theorems which follow on from one another, and establish certain structural relations, a law, in the strict sense of a law, within a set" (ibid., 34).

126. Ibid., 31.

127. Ibid., 33.

128. Ibid.

96   CHAPTER 2

be "present on the surface of the entire earth" to still be universal. Rather, Lévi-Strauss's point is that man will never be able to return to a state of nature, which is, by definition, always already foreclosed. Similarly, for Lacan, man will never lead a purely instinctual existence: no object (even the mother or the child) will ever be able to fully satisfy desire, just as language will never be full, transparent, or immediate. Thus, in Lacan's work, the Oedipus complex appears to function primarily as a *normative* framework. Lacan develops this idea in his later seminars, particularly in the 1956–1957 seminar *Object Relations and Freudian Structures*. The Oedipus complex, he tells us, refers not only to heterosexuality (for instance, Lacan calls the Oedipus the "path to integrating the heterosexual position"[129]) but also to one's position in relation to the Name-of-the-Father (which in his work eventually becomes capitalized). In other words, the Oedipus complex regulates the family, the psyche, and the social world, all at once:

> If psychoanalytic theory assigns a normative function to the Oedipus complex, let us remember that experience has taught us that it is not enough for it to lead the subject to a choice of object: this choice of object must moreover be heterosexual. Experience has also taught us that there are all sorts of forms of apparent heterosexuality. The decidedly heterosexual relation can occasionally hide a non-typical position, one that analytic investigation will show to be derived from a decidedly homosexualized position. It is hence not enough for the subject to reach heterosexuality after the Oedipus complex. The subject, whether a girl or a boy, must reach it so that he situates himself correctly in relation to the father function. This is the heart of the *problématique* of the Oedipus complex.[130]

To the extent that the Oedipus complex is indeed normative, Lacan claims that it operates in the realm of the symbolic: "The end of the Oedipus complex correlates with the establishment of the law as repressed yet permanent in the unconscious. It is to this extent that there is something that answers in the symbolic. The law is not simply, in effect, that of which we ask why. After all, it is there that the community of men is introduced and implied."[131] Once again, Lacan complicates the notion of empiricism and

---

129. Jacques Lacan, *La relation d'objet: Le séminaire, Livre IV, 1956–1957* (Seuil, 1994), 203.

130. Ibid., 201.

131. Ibid., 211.

KINSHIP AND THE STRUCTURALIST SOCIAL CONTRACT   97

necessity when he explains that the Oedipus complex (and consequently the symbolic order) is necessary: "I am not speaking of biological necessity, nor of an internal necessity, but of a necessity at least empirical, since it is in experience that we discovered it."[132]

While the Name-of-the-Father allows Lacan to distinguish the empirical from the normative, we can nonetheless detect a certain ambivalence in his work around this relationship between the real father and the Name-of-the-Father, a certain desire to distinguish normativity from normalization. At times, Lacan seems to imply that the Name-of-the-Father is merely performative. Yet this performance appears necessary for achieving some kind of psychic normalcy, if by normalcy we mean non-psychosis. As he writes about *Totem and Taboo,*

> The symbolic father is the name of the father. It is the mediating element essential to the symbolic world and its structuring. It is necessary to this weaning, more essential than the primitive weaning through which the child comes out of his pure and simple coupling with maternal omnipotence. The *name of the father* is essential to every articulation of human language . . . For the castration complex to be truly lived by the subject, the father really has to play along. He has to assume his function as the castrating father, the father function under its concrete, empirical, and I was about to say degenerated form, with a mind to the figure of the primordial father and the tyrannical and more or less horrifying form in which the Freudian myth presented him. It is to this extent that the father, as he exists, fulfills his imaginary function in what within it is empirically intolerable, and even revolting, when he makes his incidence felt as castrating. Only under this angle is the castration complex lived.[133]

In his 1957–1958 seminar, Lacan returned to the normative function of the Oedipus complex. Describing the Oedipus complex as having a "normalizing function," Lacan also characterized it as having a "normative function, not only in the moral structure of the subject, or in his relation to reality, but in the assumption of his sex."[134] Similarly, he pointed to the ambiguity

---

132. Ibid., 363.

133. Ibid., 364 (emphasis in original).

134. In Jacques Lacan, *Les formations de l'inconscient: Le séminaire, Livre V, 1957–1958* (Seuil, 1998), 162, 165.

98   **CHAPTER 2**

between the actual and the symbolic father: "Even in cases where the father is not there, where the child has been left alone with the mother, Oedipal complexes that are perfectly normal—normal in the two senses, normal insofar as they are normalizing on one hand, and also normal insofar as they denormalize, I mean through the neurotic effect, for example—are established in a way that is exactly homogenous with other cases."[135] Or again:

> What is the father? I do not mean within the family—because within the family, he is anything he wants to be. He is a shadow, a banker, he is everything he has to be, he is or he isn't, and this is sometimes important, but sometimes not at all. The real question is to know what he is within the Oedipus complex. Well, there the father is not a real object, even if he must intervene as a real object to embody castration. If he is not a real object, what is he then? He is also not a purely ideal object because, when that is the case, there can only be accidents. Yet, the Oedipus complex is certainly not merely a catastrophe, since it is the foundation of our relationship to culture, as they say . . . The father is the symbolic father . . . The father is a metaphor.[136]

In a way, these excerpts can be read as evidence that the father for Lacan remains a purely formal category where the content may vary: an empty signifier. The father, he suggests, is neither exclusively biological nor ideal, but rather symbolic. Similarly, Lacan hints at times that the Oedipus complex need not be equated with heteronormativity and with sexed fatherhood. In his 1959–1960 seminar *The Ethics of Psychoanalysis,* for example, Lacan cautions against the conflation of ethics and normativity. The goal of psychoanalysis should never be to "restore a normative balance with the world . . . One sometimes sees such a gospel preached in the form of the genital relation that I have more than once referred to here with a great deal of reservation and even with a pronounced skepticism."[137] These passages, however, are generally vague, and Lacan remains inconclusive on this question, to say the least. What appears more standard in his work is the slippage from the universality and normativity of authority structures to heteronormativity and the authority of the sexed father.

---

135. Ibid., 168.

136. Ibid., 174.

137. Jacques Lacan, *The Ethics of Psychoanalysis, 1959–1960,* trans. Dennis Porter (Norton, 1992), 88.

↳ The Symbolic, Normativity, and Ethics

In his seminar on the ethics on psychoanalysis, Lacan returned to Lévi-Strauss and the problem of the incest prohibition. Reiterating Lévi-Strauss's assertion that the prohibition has little to do with nature, Lacan pushed this idea further to argue that the prohibition would not exist if men did not unconsciously desire incest, or more precisely if they did not desire to break the taboo against incest. This desire, Lacan contended, could never be fulfilled because as Freud had previously shown in his study of the pleasure principle, desire and lack were coextensive with human subjectivity. In Lacan's words,

> The desire for the mother cannot be satisfied because it is the end, the terminal point, the abolition of the whole structure of demand, which is the one that at its deepest level structures man's unconscious. It is to the extent that the function of the pleasure principle is to make man always search for what he has to find again, but which he will never attain, that one reaches the essence, namely, that sphere or relationship which is known as the law of the prohibition of incest.[138]

It is in relation to this lack—a lack brought about by castration and coextensive with human subjectivity—that Lacan develops his paradoxical notion of ethics:

> Ethics is not simply concerned with the fact that there are obligations, that there is a bond that binds, orders, and makes social law. There is also something that we have frequently referred to here by the term "the elementary structures of kinship"—the elementary structures of property and of the exchange of goods as well. And it is as a result of these structures that man transforms himself into a sign, unit, or object of a regulated exchange in a way that Claude Lévi-Strauss has shown to be fixed in its relative unconsciousness. That which over generations has presided over this new supernatural order of the structures is exactly that which has brought about the submission of man to the law of the unconscious. But ethics begins beyond that point. It begins at the moment when the subject poses the question of that good he had unconsciously sought in the social structures. And it is at that mo-

---

138. Ibid., 68.

100   **CHAPTER 2**

ment, too, that he is led to discover the deep relationship as a result of which that which presents itself as a law is closely tied to the very structure of desire. If he doesn't discover right away the final desire that Freudian inquiry has discovered as the desire of incest, he discovers that which articulates his conduct so that the object of his desire is always maintained at a certain distance.[139]

Far from having anything to do with "goodness" or "happiness," Lacan's ethics respond to the subject's constitutive lack. As we can see in this passage, ethics also begin with the elementary structures of kinship. Kinship (or more specifically, heterosexual exchange) is thus not only at the root of the social and of the subjective, it is also at the basis of ethics. This "distance" of desire, metaphorized in the Oedipus complex and the incest taboo, appears to be essential not only on a psychic level but also on a social level. The prohibition of incest is not made necessary by any empirical reality, nor does it translate an ideal type of moral conduct, a manifestation of the general "good." Rather, it is ethical because it is psychically *and* socially necessary. As Slavoj Žižek has suggested, the symbolic for Lacan appears as a "forced choice":

> What is the entire psychoanalytic theory of "socialization," of the emergence of the subject from the encounter of a presymbolic life substance of "enjoyment" and the symbolic order, if not the description of a sacrificial situation which, far from being exceptional, is the story of everyone and as such *constitutive?* This constitutive character means that the "social contract," the inclusion of the subject in the symbolic community, has the structure of a *forced choice:* the subject supposed to choose freely his community (since only a free choice is morally binding) does not exist prior to this choice, he is constituted by means of it. The choice of community, the "social contract," is a paradoxical choice where I maintain the freedom of choice only if I "make the right choice": if I choose the "other" of the community, I stand to lose the very freedom, the very possibility of choice (in clinical terms: I choose psychosis).[140]

The structuralist social contract, as I have argued, was also constructed as a "forced choice," or as Merleau-Ponty puts it, as *allant de soi*. Although the

---

139. Ibid., 75–76.

140. Slavoj Žižek, *Enjoy Your Symptom! Jacques Lacan in Hollywood and Out* (Routledge, 1992), 74–75 (emphases in original).

KINSHIP AND THE STRUCTURALIST SOCIAL CONTRACT

concept of the symbolic functioned somewhat differently in the works of Lévi-Strauss and Lacan, in both cases it served as a conceptual device to establish a direct correlation between kinship and socialization, as a trope for social and psychic integration. While it seems clear that Lévi-Strauss and especially Lacan refused to simply assimilate the symbolic to the social, the relationship between the two terms was never fully articulated. Moreover, by linking sexual difference to language and to subjectivity, both authors presented the symbolic as a *structural* category, as a universal outside of history. Lévi-Strauss's and Lacan's "political," one in which, as both authors have told us, "*tout se tient,*" depends on sexual difference. The heterosexual family not only makes the social congeal and cohere, it is the universal and transhistorical "forced choice" that makes ethics possible.

CHAPTER 3

The Circulation of Structuralism in the French Public Sphere

As discourses, familialism and structuralism shared a number of features. Both insisted on the direct correlation between the family and socialization, and both treated kinship as a nonhistorical and universal structure with a normative function. Familialism, however, was not simply an ideology; it was a concrete movement anchored in a wide legal and administrative infrastructure. By the 1960s, structuralism was also solidly implanted in the social science disciplines. In 1959, Lévi-Strauss was elected to the prestigious Collège de France. In 1960, he founded the Laboratoire d'anthropologie sociale, a research center affiliated with the École des hautes études in which many contemporary French anthropologists were trained. Furthermore, he coordinated the publication of the widely circulated anthropological journal *L'Homme,* which had been launched in 1961 as a counterpart to the U.S.-based *American Anthropologist* and the British *Man.*[1]

Lacan's career during those years was somewhat more turbulent. The 1953 scission of the Société française de psychanalyse (SFP) from the Société psychanalytique de Paris (SPP) was followed by Lacan's own dissolution of the SFP in 1964 to found the École freudienne de Paris (EFP). In 1964, Lacan accepted Louis Althusser's invitation to teach at one of the

---

1. Didier Eribon and Claude Lévi-Strauss, *De près et de loin* (Odile Jacob, 1988), 93–94.

THE CIRCULATION OF STRUCTURALISM   103

main Parisian centers of academic excellence, the École normale supérieure (ENS). Whereas his lectures at the Hôpital Sainte-Anne had been primarily attended by physicians, psychologists, and fellow psychoanalysts, Lacan's students at the ENS were young, enthusiastic about structuralism, and destined to become some of France's most important thinkers in the humanities, the social sciences, and politics. It was at the ENS that Lacan acquired some of his most loyal disciples, including his successor and future son-in-law, Jacques-Alain Miller. It was also at the ENS that he was exposed to some of his harshest critics, who disapproved of his tremendous popularity, cryptic style, and extravagant ways. These included Robert Flacelière, the ENS director at the time, who finally forced Lacan to leave the École in 1969.[2] Later that year, Lacan managed to obtain a new location for his seminar within the Faculté de droit where he drew even larger crowds. Although his ideas failed to attract the kind of disciplinary consensus generated by Lévi-Strauss in anthropology, Lacan remained a necessary reference in French psychoanalysis, whether others argued with, for, or against him.[3]

Despite the fact that structuralism was blooming within the fields of anthropology and psychoanalysis, the question remains of how this vocabulary and this understanding of kinship came to circulate in the French public sphere. More specifically, how did the construction of the family as a trope for social and psychic integration—what I have been calling the structuralist social contract—come to be adopted in the world of politics? Indeed, most of the pro-family activists mentioned in the first chapter never actually read or studied Lacan or Lévi-Strauss—especially since many of the theorists of familialism preceded them. Similarly, it seems unlikely that either Lacan or Lévi-Strauss had any direct contact with family policymakers, given how removed both figures were from the world of politics. In this chapter, I am less concerned with the disciplinary history of anthropology and psychoanalysis in France (which has been, at least for the latter, well documented).[4]

---

2. Lacan's expulsion from the ENS also marked, incidentally, the end of his friendship with Lévi-Strauss, who refused to sign a petition circulated by François Wahl asking for Lacan's reinstatement at the ENS. See Denis Bertholet, *Claude Lévi-Strauss* (Plon, 2003), 316; Elisabeth Roudinesco, *Jacques Lacan: Esquisse d'une vie, histoire d'un système de pensée* (Fayard, 1993), 445.

3. For a study of how Lacan shaped the French psychoanalytic scene, see Sherry Turkle, *Psychoanalytic Politics: Freud's French Revolution* (Basic Books, 1978). As Jean-François de Sauverzac has put it, psychoanalysis in France did not begin with Lacan, but "its history cannot be understood without the reinterpretation [*l'interprétation après coup*] allowed by his work"; *Françoise Dolto, itinéraire d'une psychanalyste* (Aubier, 1993), 194.

4. See François Dosse, *Histoire du structuralisme* (La découverte, 1991); Gérald Gaillard, *The Routledge Dictionary of Anthropologists* (Routledge, 2003); Roudinesco, *Jacques Lacan*.

104   **CHAPTER 3**

Rather my aim is to trace the genealogy of this structuralist social contract in the French public sphere more widely, particularly in political and popular culture.[5]

This chapter argues that the structuralist social contract became a reference for French family law through a series of "bridge figures." These were mostly psychoanalysts who appropriated the terminology devised by Lacan and who were directly involved in formulating family policy in the second half of the twentieth century. Most of these bridge figures can hardly be called "Lacanian" in the sense that they would follow Lacan's writings *à la lettre*. My intention is not to correct their misreadings or to defend a certain "purity" in Lacanian thought, but rather to explore how these figures *literalized* certain Lacanian key concepts pertaining to kinship. Indeed, as we saw, both Lévi-Strauss and Lacan attempted to maintain a tension between the descriptive and the prescriptive, between the normative and the heteronormative. These distinctions, however, collapsed once their theories were filtered into the public sphere. Inasmuch as this chapter seeks to map out the various political and popular networks in which these ideas circulated, it is also interested in the effect of this "translation" on the original works themselves.[6] By focusing on three bridge figures—Georges Mauco, André Berge, and Françoise Dolto—we can return to the original and ask what happens to a universal, transhistorical, and structural definition of kinship once it is translated, applied, and once it literally "goes through history." In other words, what happened to the structuralist social contract once it stopped operating a discourse and became a practice?

✒ Family Policy at the Haut comité de la population et de la famille: 1945–1970

The goals of the Haut comité de la population when it was created in 1939 were to raise the birthrate and to promote carefully selected immigration,

---

5. Structuralism created a *public* in Michael Warner's definition of the term as "an ongoing space of encounter for discourse. Not texts themselves create publics, but the concatenation of texts through time." *Publics and Counterpublics* (Zone Books, 2002), 90.

6. I am thinking of translation here as a mode, following Walter Benjamin: "Translation is a mode. To comprehend it as a mode one must go back to the original, for that contains the law governing the translation: its translatability. The question of whether a work is translatable has a dual meaning. Either: Will an adequate translator ever be found among the totality of its readers? Or, more pertinently: Does its nature lend itself to translation and, therefore, in view of the significance of the mode, call for it?" *Illuminations* (Harcourt Brace & World, 1968), 70.

THE CIRCULATION OF STRUCTURALISM   105

all in the hope of solving France's long-lasting "depopulation problem." After a series of structural changes and reshuffling of personnel during the Vichy years resulting in the Comité consultatif de la famille française in 1941 and later the Conseil supérieur de la famille in 1943, the Haut comité was revived by General de Gaulle in April 1945 under the official title of Haut comité consultatif de la population et de la famille.[7] While de Gaulle and his associates in the field of family policy repeatedly manifested their desire to distinguish themselves from their Vichy predecessors, much of the staff of the new organization was composed of important interwar family activists, several of whom, as mentioned in the first chapter, had held official positions in the Vichy administration. Among these figures who shaped both interwar and postwar family policy was Georges Mauco, who was also a particularly good example of a bridge figure who brought psychoanalysis to the political world.

Born in Paris in 1899, Mauco was first noticed by public officials for his work as a geographer trained in the school of Vidal de la Blanche, and more specifically for his 1932 doctoral thesis on immigration in France. Through his thesis, which compared the degree of potential "assimilability" of various immigrant groups, Mauco acquired wide recognition from both the Left and the Right. The Left welcomed Mauco's supposed "humanitarian" approach to immigration and his appeals for better conditions to assist new immigrants. The Right, and especially the anti-Semitic Right, also embraced Mauco for having meticulously linked particular social behaviors such as criminality to ethnic background. In their eyes, Mauco was an ally in the pervasive condemnation of immigration during the interwar years, particularly that of eastern European origin.[8] Mauco's first contact with the political world was thus as a population expert. It was in that capacity that former minister Henri de

---

7. Procès verbaux de réunions du Haut comité de la population et de la famille, April 30, 1945. AN 577 AP.

8. See Olivier Roux's presentation of the Fonds Mauco at the Archives nationales. Mauco's work on immigration has been the subject of much attention in recent years, particularly in relation to the various administrative overlaps between Vichy, the Third Republic, and the post-Liberation context. See Karen H. Adler, *Jews and Gender in Liberation France* (Cambridge University Press, 2003); Rémi Lenoir, *Généalogie de la morale familiale* (Seuil, 2003); Paul-André Rosental, *L'intelligence démographique: Sciences et politiques des populations en France, 1930–1960* (Odile Jacob, 2003); Elisabeth Roudinesco, "Georges Mauco (1899–1988): Un psychanalyste au service de Vichy. De l'antisémitisme à la psychopédagogie," *L'Infini* 51 (1995); Alexis Spire, *Étrangers à la carte: L'administration de l'immigration en France, 1945–1975* (Grasset, 2005); Patrick Weil, *La France et ses étrangers: L'aventure d'une politique de l'immigration, 1938–1991* (Calmann-Lévy, 1991); Patrick Weil, *Liberté, égalité, discriminations: De l'"identité nationale" au regard de l'histoire* (Grasset, 2008).

106   **CHAPTER 3**

Jouvenel asked him in 1935 to head the Comité d'études du problème des étrangers.[9] Frustrated with the lack of resources for this particular committee, Mauco decided to join instead the demographer Adolphe Landry in his newly established Haut comité de la population, which became a hub for family activists like Fernand Boverat, president of the Alliance contre la dépopulation, to meet demographers and other population experts in the hope of solving France's depopulation problem.[10]

Parallel to his career in social policy, Mauco discovered psychoanalysis. He began reading Freud in the 1920s while he was working as a schoolteacher after attending the École normale d'instituteurs. There, Mauco writes, he was confronted with the "the importance of affective relations between young people and their educators."[11] In 1924, through one of his students, he met the wife of René Laforgue. Laforgue was one of the founders of the SPP with Pichon, Codet, Hesnard, Allendy, and Freud's close friend, Marie Bonaparte. Soon after, Mauco embarked on analysis with Laforgue, joined the SPP, and began attending psychoanalytic conferences. By 1939, Mauco was well established within the SPP and had published numerous articles on children and education.[12] It was also during those formative years that Mauco developed professional relationships—and in some cases friendships—with other French psychoanalysts, including Juliette Boutonnier, André Berge, and Françoise Dolto, all of whom were also in analysis with Laforgue. This common experience had led the four of them to refer to themselves as a "club": the *club des piqués*.[13]

Mauco's career peaked after the Liberation, as de Gaulle and the Fourth Republic allocated more power and funds to pro-natalist groups. In his memoirs, Mauco recalls being summoned by Gaston Palewski, de Gaulle's chief of staff, as early as September 1940 to "present his demographic projects, especially those relating to the creation of an Haut comité de la population et de la famille."[14] At the end of the war, Mauco met de Gaulle with Landry and Louis Joxe, the government's secretary general, and together they elaborated the decree that set up the structure and organization of the new Haut comi-

---

9. Georges Mauco, *Vécu: 1899–1982* (Émile-Paul, 1982), 89, AN 577 AP.

10. Ibid., 90.

11. Ibid., 58, 75.

12. Ibid., 83.

13. For more on this, see Alain de Mijolla, *Freud et la France: 1885–1945* (Presses universitaires de France, 2010), 685–87, 817; Alain de Mijolla, ed., *Dictionnaire international de la psychanalyse: Concepts, notions, biographies, œuvres, événements, institutions* (Calmann-Lévy, 2002), 903.

14. Mauco, *Vécu*, 113.

THE CIRCULATION OF STRUCTURALISM   107

té.[15] According to Mauco, de Gaulle, who was haunted by France's demographic "decline," had a personal investment in the Haut comité. He insisted on presiding over the meetings and on setting the daily agenda.[16] In a typical session, the members of the Haut comité would offer presentations on topics pertaining to the family or to immigration, and they would set different policy goals. On April 3, 1945, for example, Mauco recounts submitting to de Gaulle some graphs illustrating the "non-replacement of generations for almost a century and the decline of France which, from the first rank of European powers, had fallen to the last rank."[17] According to Mauco, de Gaulle agreed that the general public and young people especially needed to be informed of the "seriousness of this problem" through a little manual to be produced by the Alliance contre la dépopulation, one of the most important (and increasingly right-wing) pro-natalist lobby groups in France.

By April 1945, the Haut comité had set up a new Family Code largely based on the 1939 version, and it had defined an action plan for family policy and immigration for the years to come.[18] For the next twenty years, the agenda of the Haut comité included promoting the Family Code, advising the Office national d'immigration (ONI), creating support networks to welcome foreigners, fostering the creation of psycho-pedagogical centers, supporting the demographic plan requested by parliament in 1950, studying the demographics of France's colonies, counseling the Plannification Committee to determine how many new jobs were needed by region, and devising a new code to "truly help the elderly."[19]

---

15. Georges Mauco, "Le général de Gaulle et le Haut comité de la population et de la famille" in *Espoir,* no. 21, December 1977, 22, AN 577 AP.

16. Ibid. De Gaulle's presence in the Haut comité is confirmed by a series of memos signed by de Gaulle in Mauco's private papers. One document (in AN 577 AP, box 3) shows a table seating plan organized as follows (the biographies of most of these individuals can be found in Chapter 1): Sauvy, Mauco, Boverat, Mme. Collet, de Gaulle, Mme. Delabit, Monsaingeon, Joxe, Prigent, Debré, Landry, Blocq-Mascart, and Doublet.

17. Ibid. This journal *Espoir* also has a reproduction of a typed memo written by Mauco, dated September 10, 1945, on which de Gaulle has scribbled some comments, asking for further clarification on the expenses attached to the proposal, and concluding "after seeing this note, I will be sure to make it happen" (20). Robert Debré also offers an account of de Gaulle's involvement in these meeting in that same journal: "La Général de Gaulle et la natalité française" by Robert Debré in *Espoir,* no. 21, December 1977, 13. It is interesting to note, in this context, the close relationship between the Alliance nationale, government officials, and psychoanalysts such as Mauco. In browsing through the UNAF's journal *Pour la Vie: Études Démographiques et Familiales* during those years, we can see numerous advertisements and articles promoting the books of Mauco and André Berge.

18. Mauco, *Vécu,* 119.

19. Letter by Georges Mauco to Monsieur Donnedieu de Vabres, February 7, 1965, AN 577 AP, box 3.

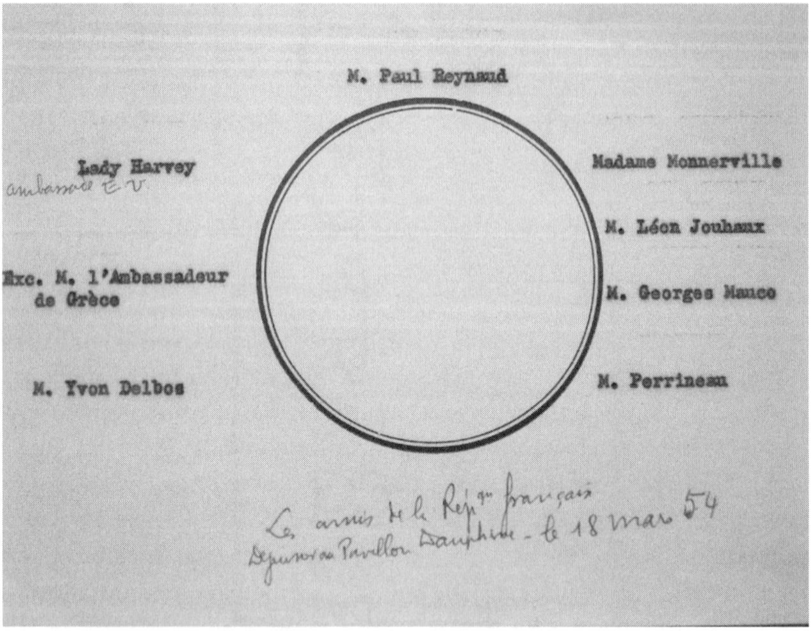

108   CHAPTER 3

M. Paul Reynaud

Lady Harvey   Madame Monnerville

Exc. M. l'Ambassadeur   M. Léon Jouhaux
de Grèce
                               M. Georges Mauco

M. Yvon Delbos   M. Perrineau

FIGURE 1.   Seating plan from 1954 that shows Mauco next to various governmental figures, including Paul Reynaud from the Commissariat du plan. (AN 577 AP, box 2)

Even after de Gaulle's temporary retreat from politics between 1946 and 1958, Mauco continued to enjoy a similar prestige among the leaders of the Fourth Republic. He was in frequent contact with Pierre Mendès-France, whom he called "the *président du conseil* who gave most attention to the problems of population," and with Edgar Faure, who according to Mauco not only "admitted the utility of psychoanalytic knowledge" but also encouraged him, while he was the minister of education, to find ways for educators to benefit from it.[20] During his time at the Haut comité, Mauco traveled with ease within the highest political circles, as shown by the various dinner and cocktail party invitations and seating charts in his private papers (Figures 1 and 2). He was also engaged in an extensive correspondence with various ministers and high-powered officials, among them Georges Pompidou, Michel Debré (in the Ministry of Defense and the Ministry of the Economy), Joseph Fontanet (in the Ministry of Labor, Employment, and Population), Albin Chalandon (in the Ministry of Housing), Jean-Marcel Jeanneney (in the Ministry of Social Affairs), Georges Galichon (de Gaulle's

20. Mauco, *Vécu*, 122–23.

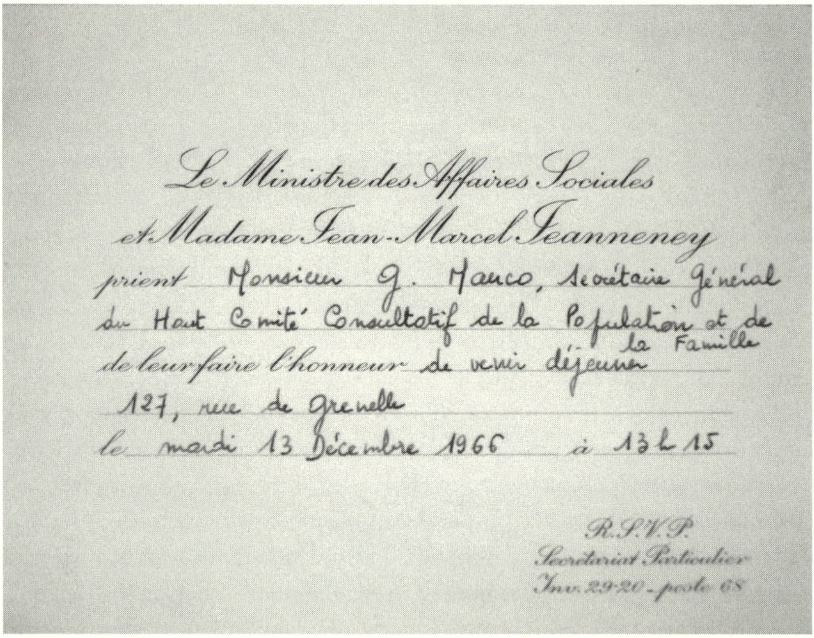

THE CIRCULATION OF STRUCTURALISM 109

FIGURE 2. Invitation to a lunch with Minister of Social Affairs Jean-Marcel Jeanneney. (AN 577 AP, box 2)

private secretary), and Paul Reynaud (at the Commission des finances de l'économie générale et du plan).[21] Mauco's exchanges with these political figures were not limited to administrative details but were actual substantive dialogues, often about psychoanalysis. Edgar Faure, for instance, the sitting minister of education, thanked Mauco in a letter dated December 8, 1968, for bringing to his attention "the anguish and even the trauma that certain students could experience" as a result of the 1968 events.[22] Similarly, in 1975, Michel Poniatowski, the minister of the interior at the time, expressed his gratitude to Mauco for sending him his book *Éducation et sexualité*. "I am very interested in questions pertaining to education, and as such I read [your book] with great interest," Poniatowski wrote. "The theses that you develop provide many answers for those of us preoccupied with reforming pedagogy, and consequently, with changing society."[23] Through these various

---

21. AN 577 AP, box 3.

22. AN 577 AP, box 2.

23. Letter from July 21, 1975, AN 577 AP, box 3.

110   **CHAPTER 3**

contacts with public officials, Mauco helped bring psychoanalysis, little by little, to the political scene.

According to Mauco, his greatest intellectual debt was to his analyst, René Laforgue.[24] Laforgue was primarily known for his popularization of psychoanalysis through his literary analyses and psychoanalytically inflected studies of Robespierre, Rousseau, Talleyrand, and Baudelaire. Mauco played a somewhat similar role in the sense that he was less interested in conceptual innovation than in making psychoanalytic principles accessible to the public, something he often acknowledged: "Some might blame me for altering the scientific rigor of psychoanalysis by vulgarizing certain of its tenets. I am among those who believe that the psychoanalytic contribution should remain neither the privilege of a rich clientele nor the commercial monopoly of medicine. And neither should it be a 'cursed attempt and a secret science' (Merleau-Ponty) jealously guarded by sects of initiates."[25] As such, Mauco's writings present an eclectic set of references, mostly drawn from a Freudian register, but also from Lacan. Although there is evidence that Mauco attended Lacan's seminar, he describes himself in his memoirs as having a rather ambivalent relationship with Lacan.[26] On the one hand, Mauco praised Lacan's theoretical genius and rigor; on the other, he remained highly critical of his style and of the mystique associated with his personality, which Mauco repeatedly describes as "theatrical" in his memoirs.[27] During the 1953 split, Mauco refused to follow Lacan to the SFP, choosing instead to stay at the SPP with Juliette Favez-Boutonier, Daniel Lagache, André Berge, and Angelo Hesnard. Affirming that he was not a doctor, he claimed to prefer to "stay out these rivalries" and remain an "objective observer."[28] Most important for our purposes here, Mauco appropriated much of Lacan's vocabulary, particularly the concepts of the symbolic, the phallus, and the Name-of-the-

---

24. Mauco, *Vécu*, 159. For more on Laforgue's biography, see Mijolla, *Freud et la France;* Annick Ohayon, *Psychologie et psychanalyse en France: L'impossible rencontre, 1919–1969* (La découverte, 2006), 73–77; Elisabeth Roudinesco, *La bataille de cent ans: Histoire de la psychanalyse en France*, 2 vols. (Ramsay, 1982, 1986); Sauverzac, *Françoise Dolto*, 93–105. According to Agnès Desmazières, Laforgue was one of the founding fathers of a "French-style psychoanalysis" that was especially hospitable to Catholic ideas; see *L'inconscient au paradis: Comment les catholiques ont reçu la psychanalyse* (Payot, 2011).

25. Georges Mauco, *Psychanalyse et éducation* (Aubier-Montaigne, 1979), 16.

26. In Lacan's 1953 lecture on "The Symbolic, the Real, and the Imaginary," Mauco asked Lacan a series of questions on, interestingly enough, the problem of the symbolic. See Jacques Lacan, *Des noms-du-père* (Seuil, 2005), 54–56.

27. Mauco, *Vécu*, 78, 164.

28. Ibid., 162.

THE CIRCULATION OF STRUCTURALISM   111

Father, which, as I have argued, were important tools for linking the psychic to the social, and for positioning sexual difference as the foundation of culture and society.

Like Lacan, Mauco places desire at the center of subjectivity and hence at the center of the psychoanalytic project. In that sense, psychoanalysis is neither aimed at providing "moral support" nor at curing, but rather at "deciphering unconscious desires . . . unveiling the deep sentiments which weigh upon the subject and determine his relations to the other, particularly those to whom he is closest affectively: parents, husband or wife, children, grand-parents, teachers."[29] Unlike animals, for whom desire exists primarily to satisfy a particular need, human desire, Mauco argues (once again following Lacan who referred to Hegel on this point), is primarily the desire for recognition by an other: "what human sensibility demands, is not indeed the satisfaction of a need, *it is a relation with an other:* that is to say, a dialogue, an exchange."[30] Exchange is thus at the root of sociability, and Mauco contends, once again in the tradition of Lévi-Strauss and Lacan, at the root of language: "The difference between desire and need, is the tendency and the aptitude of desire to be said to an other, to be received by an other, to be expressed and verbalized. It is through desire that man acquires language."[31] From this link between desire and sociability, Mauco sets up the incest prohibition, or Oedipus complex, as the fundamental step in the development of the child's subjectivity. Most importantly, he is able to locate the father as the most significant agent in this double process of identification and prohibition.[32]

It is in his discussion of the Oedipus complex and the father that Mauco's importation of Lacan's vocabulary into his work is perhaps most visible. Mauco defines the father as "the one who gives his name." The father's function is essentially social because "he must be experienced as the authority who imposes the rules necessary to regulate relationships in collective life . . . He must be capable of making [the child] accept the feelings of prohibition without triggering an anxious aggression."[33] Similarly, Mauco writes that "the father symbolizes the prohibition and the disciplining force

---

29. Mauco, *Psychanalyse et éducation,* 13.

30. Ibid., 33 (emphasis in original).

31. Ibid., 34.

32. Ibid., 36.

33. Ibid., 54.

112   **CHAPTER 3**

which permits, through the mastery of his desires, the psychic construction of the human being." In this context, Mauco describes the child as the "product of the paternal phallus."[34] "To deal with the father," Mauco argues, "is to deal with the very principle of human society." The father symbolizes "power and authority" and "he is the one who, from the dawn of human life, has concretized the incest prohibition, that is to say the social law. Without this prohibition, the child would not be able to structure himself psychically and man would be unable to access culture. This is because humans can only structure themselves psychically in relation to a law, that is to say, in relation to a given order."[35] In this context also, Mauco refers to a "paternal imago" that "is inscribed in each of us, in a profound and indelible way" and which he defines as the "symbol of the prohibition that allows us to pass from animality to humanity though the ascesis of the drives."[36] For Mauco, in other words, social and sexual laws are strictly parallel, and in both cases the father is the necessary conduit:

> Paternity engages man in the totality of his being. It is the achievement of his personality. But most importantly, it allows him to gain access to an essential function in human culture, that of representing the law. By symbolizing the prohibition of desire, he contributes in breaking the dual relationship between mother and child. Though this essential function, the father represents an order which allows the child to situate himself and to structure himself in relation to others.[37]

Lacan, as we saw, was concerned with distinguishing the symbolic father from the biological father, with differentiating psychic sexuation, gender, and sexuality, even though he did not always achieve this consistently in his work. Mauco, however, appeared far less interested in distinguishing the two. If the father had to behave in a "manly" fashion for the Oedipus to be resolved "normally," the mother had to remain "feminine." Mauco writes, for example, that it is extremely important that the "father be able to affirm his virile nature and that the mother and the children accept him in his sym-

---

34. Ibid., 53.

35. Georges Mauco, *La paternité: Sa fonction éducative dans la famille et à l'école* (Éditions universitaires, 1971), 9.

36. Ibid., 10.

37. Ibid., 173.

THE CIRCULATION OF STRUCTURALISM 113

bolic function of disciplining force without which there are no renunciations and no mastery."[38] Similarly, Mauco refers to paternity as the "consecration of the virile personality."[39] If the father represents culture, the law, and the social, the mother represents nature, the fusional relationship with the child, and the instinctual. Mauco calls her first and foremost "body": she is "nourishment (suction and taste), hearing (sound), smell, and movement, caress, sight, holding, security, satisfaction and dissatisfaction."[40] Mauco, in that sense, *literalized* Lacan's theories and filled the abstract signifiers of the structuralist social contract with real sexed figures:

> While the mother nourishes a dual relationship, lived in fusion, the father naturally has a power of symbolization that we do not find in the mother. The father belongs to culture, the mother more to nature . . . It is through the Oedipus complex that the father's symbolic value takes all of its magical power of pre-genital desire. It is through the Oedipus complex that the child is able to leave pure subjectivity and gain access to objectivity. The father thus allows the passing from the biological to the cultural though speech.[41]

Because Mauco collapses sex, gender, and psychic position, the system of equivalences linking the family to psychic and social adjustment—the structuralist social contract—takes on a new twist. Thus, Mauco can argue that if "the mother takes over the role of the father, the dynamic of the whole family is disturbed."[42] Similarly, he posits that an absent father often leads to juvenile delinquency.[43] After a series of case studies of "badly socialized" children (who reject all authority, who are dyslexic, anorexic, shy, homosexual, and so on), Mauco concludes that most behavioral trouble has to do "with deficiencies of the paternal image. Deficiencies that psychoanalysis has brought to light in what it has called the 'Oedipus complex.' For it is within this triangular situation of the child and the parental couple that a resolution must be found for the anguish of desire in its conflict with the requirements of collective reality and with the ancestral prohibition of

---

38. Mauco, *Psychanalyse et éducation,* 55.

39. Ibid., 57.

40. Ibid., 68.

41. Mauco, *La paternité,* 47.

42. Mauco, *Psychanalyse et éducation,* 55.

43. Ibid., 66.

114   CHAPTER 3

incest."[44] Or, as he puts it perhaps most clearly in a lecture on pedagogy where he was asked what exactly the Oedipus complex meant for educators and pedagogues, "It means social insertion, it means happiness in the relation to the other, it means sublimation, it means socialization, access to culture, it means mental growth."[45]

✂ The École des parents, the Centre Claude Bernard, and the Emergence of Psycho-Pedagogy

One of Mauco's greatest accomplishments during his time at the Haut comité was the creation of the first psycho-pedagogical center, the Centre Claude Bernard, on May 1, 1946. The philosophy behind the center was very much in line with Mauco's views on psychoanalysis, and more spe-cifically, with his understanding of desire and the role of the other in the construction of individual subjectivity. According to Mauco, parents and teachers were among the most important "others" for a child's affective development. Thus, many of the child's social difficulties could be traced back to some dysfunction of the triangular relationship between the child and the parents, as illustrated by the Oedipus complex. As a result, these social problems could also be remedied if the dynamics were corrected, with the assistance of psychoanalytically trained professionals. In exchange for the small sum of 25 francs (which could be negotiated for families of fewer means, and which eventually came to be covered by social secu-rity[46]), parents could schedule an appointment at the center if their child exhibited signs of "character and behavior trouble" such as "shyness, emotionality, enuresis, tics, nervousness, shoplifting, sexual anomalies."[47] As Mauco put it, what distinguished a consultation at the Centre Claude Bernard from a general medical consultation was the psychoanalytic train-ing of the doctors, who could "use the immediate action [of psychoanaly-sis] on the child and his parents." In this context, symptoms would tend to

---

44. Ibid., 65–66.

45. *Pratique des mots,* December 8, 1971, 13: Journées de Septembre 1971 sur la PRL (Pédagogie relationnelle du langage), AN 577 AP, box 10.

46. "Le Centre psycho-pédagogique du lycée Claude Bernard pour l'enseignement secondaire." IMEC BER 3.13.

47. *L'Éducation Nationale,* jeudi 27 juin 1946, no. 31,13, AN 577 AP, box 8.

THE CIRCULATION OF STRUCTURALISM

FIGURE 3. Photograph of a "psychodrama" at the Centre Claude Bernard (AN 577 AP, box 8)

disappear faster and more effectively than in a traditional medical procedure.[48]

Among the most popular techniques used at the Centre Claude Bernard were "psychodramas," a style of group therapy developed by the American psychologist Jacob Moreno. When the psychodrama technique was imported to France through psychoanalysts such as Kestemberg, Lebovici, Gravel, Anzieu, Testemale, and Dubuisson, it was simultaneously revised to give it a more Freudian orientation. The idea was to reenact certain structures and dynamics around the child through a process of improvisation guided by psychoanalysts, usually a man and a woman, intended to "symbolically represent the parental couple"[49] (Figures 3, 4, 5, and 6). In one of the case reports, for example, Mauco recounts a session with a six-year-old

---

48. AN 577 AP, box 8. See also Roudinesco, *La bataille de cent ans,* 2:222. For a detailed explanation of the logistics of the Centre, see Georges Mauco, ed., *L'inadaptation scolaire et sociale et ses remèdes: Cahiers de pédagogie moderne* (Armand Colin, 1959).

49. Mauco, *Psychanalyse et éducation,* 248.

116   **CHAPTER 3**

FIGURE 4.   Photograph of a "psychodrama" at the Centre Claude Bernard (AN 577 AP, box 8)

boy named Jacques, who had been brought in by his parents because of his nervousness, violence, bad manners, and general misbehavior. Mauco writes that after only five sessions "there was a rapid affective transference, the child exteriorized his aggression, especially with regard to the father who was not very understanding."[50] The parents consequently sent a letter thanking Mauco and the center for making Jacques more docile and easier to interact with. Only two weeks after its opening, the center had already assisted sixty patients; between October 1947 and July 1948, this number rose to 585.[51] In 1948, a second psycho-pedagogical center opened, this time in Strasbourg.

The Centre Claude Bernard provided a forum for politicians to interact with psychoanalysts and for psychoanalytic ideas to circulate. As the child psychoanalyst and friend of Mauco's, Maud Mannoni, put it in the preface to one of her books, "by bringing psychoanalysis into the public sector in

---

50. AN 577 AP, box 8.

51. Letter from Mauco to Wallon, June 6, 1946, AN 577 AP, box 8.

THE CIRCULATION OF STRUCTURALISM   117

FIGURE 5.   Photograph of a "psychodrama" at the Centre Claude Bernard (AN 577 AP, box 8)

1945, Georges Mauco imagined that he would, like Freud, bring them the plague and lead public authorities to doubt themselves. The authorities have digested the plague. Even better, they have turned it into a parallel education tool."[52] The steering committee of the center was indeed composed of psychologists, teachers, and public officials from the ministries of education and of health.[53] Through the center, they interacted with the staff, most of

---

52. Mauco, *Vécu,* 150. According to Alain de Mijolla, Mauco recounted in an interview with him that it was Freud himself who, upon meeting Mauco, had insisted on the fact that the "future of psychoanalysis was in education. It is better to prevent than to cure" (*Freud et la France,* 565).

53. AN 577 AP, box 8. Among the members of the steering committee, we can list Henri Wallon (professor at the Collège de France), Roussy (rector of the Paris Academy), Monod (Director of Secondary Teaching), Douary (Director of School and University Hygene), Le Guilan (representa-

118   CHAPTER 3

FIGURE 6. Photograph of a "psychodrama" at the Centre Claude Bernard (AN 577 AP, box 8)

whom had some form of psychoanalytic training.[54] As André Berge and Maurice Debesse put it, "the psychoanalytic perspective" was what distinguished the work of the center, the general action of the team.[55]

Among the psychoanalysts most involved in the center were Juliette Favez-Boutonier (who was a professor of philosophy at the Lycée Fénelon

---

tive from the Ministry of Health), Mauco, Voisin (president of the Parents Association), Heuyer (child neuropsychiatrist), Pugibet (*inspecteur général* for the Department of Education), and Peyssard (professor *agrégé* and general inspector at the Ministry of Public Health and Population).

54. A series of curricula vitae collected in AN 577 AP, boxes 7 and 8, indicate that while most of the Center's personnel had a psychology degree, many also had a "personal psychoanalytic experience" or belonged to one of the psychoanalytic societies of the time (see in particular the report by Mmes. Anzieu and Barrau). See also Mauco, ed., *L'inadaptation scolaire*, 194–98.

55. André Berge and Maurice Debesse, "Contre l'inadaptation," *L'Éducation*, October 21, 1971, 12, AN 577 AP, box 8.

THE CIRCULATION OF STRUCTURALISM 119

and a practicing doctor at the Hôpital Sainte-Anne), André Berge, and Françoise Dolto.[56] All three had strong ties to both the world of institutional psychoanalysis and the political world. All three had also been active in education policy for some time, notably through the École des parents. Founded in 1929 by Hélène Vérine, who at the time was serving on the Comité consultatif de la famille française, the École des parents et des éducateurs was a project dear to interwar family lobbying groups such as the Alliance nationale. In its first years, the École served primarily as a locale in which young parents, supposedly more conscientious than their own parents about their marriage and their children's education (including their sexual education), could gather and discuss various educational "techniques" and receive marriage counseling, all for the purpose of having happier, more fulfilled families.

Created in part to counterbalance the Third Republic's efforts to control and secularize public education, the École's founding principles involved social and moral education and the "renewal of the family spirit in France."[57] Among the founding members, the École counted General Borie, head of the Alliance nationale pour l'accroissement de la population française. The École's secretary, Mme. Jean Camus, was a mother of twelve children. The board of the organization was composed of parents, Social Catholics, educators, and priests, including the abbé Viollet.[58] Vérine invited various psychoanalysts, and in particular Mauco, Boutonnier, Berge, and Dolto, to participate in conferences and to deliver papers on the family, so that political representatives could be exposed to psychoanalytic ideas.[59] During the Occupation, many of the École's leaders actively participated in the Vichy regime: Georges Bertier, the abbé Viollet, Georges Lamirand, and Hélène Vérine whose contribution to the National Revolution's manifesto, *France 1941: La revolution nationale, un bilan, un programme,* praised the family, the natural order, and the *éternel féminin.*[60]

---

56. Letter by Mauco to the Dr. Douary, the Director of School and University Hygiene, January 28, 1946, AN 577 AP, box 8. See also Mauco, *Psychanalyse et éducation,* 263.

57. Jacques Donzelot, *La police des familles* (Éditions de minuit, 1977), 172.

58. Ohayon, *Psychologie et psychanalyse,* 185. Ohayon describes the École's mission as the systematic "reduction of the social to the psychological."

59. Lenoir calls the École des parents "a spot for liberal Catholics to meet and diffuse psychoanalytic theories and new pedagogical methods which aimed to reconcile the principles of parental authority with the ideas of personal autonomy, notably that of the child" (*Généalogie,* 408).

60. Francine Muel-Dreyfus, *Vichy et l'éternel féminin: Contribution à une sociologie politique de l'ordre des corps* (Seuil, 1996), 181–84; Ohayon, *Psychologie et psychanalyse,* 188.

120   CHAPTER 3

In many ways, the ethos behind the École des parents was comparable to the one guiding the Centre Claude Bernard. Mauco underlined this similarity when he wrote, in the context of the center: "The collectivity has vested interest in this parental training. Society is worth what parents are worth. The adaptability and social efficiency of the individual depend on his familial apprenticeship." Only strong fathers, Mauco contended, could raise "vigorous children who will be able to achieve self-control." One way to reach this goal was through education, and in this context, the École des parents had "already shown what it is possible to do in this domain. Through its lectures, through radio, through its journal and publications, it has exposed educators to the recent developments in relational psychology."[61] André Berge also commented on these parallels when he explained that both the Centre Claude Bernard and the École des parents served as mechanisms to "popularize psychoanalysis."[62] As its directors emphasized, the École had a clear moral mission, but it never "distributed recipes, sermons, or advice." As Berge explained, "the Écoles des parents have never claimed to propagate a normative teaching, but only to open perspectives that could perhaps lead to an ethic, to the extent that they increase mutual understanding between different ages, different beings, and different groups of beings."[63]

Like Mauco, Berge's ideas on psychoanalysis and on the family did not remain confined to scientific circles. By virtue of his position both at the Centre Claude Bernard and at the École des parents, Berge was able to establish strong ties with the public administration, a relationship that is evidenced by his numerous letters to and from public officials. As such, the minister of education in July 1976 wrote to Berge to thank him for sending him a copy of his book *Aujourd'hui l'enfant:* "I was particularly touched by your gesture and your dedication which I take as precious encouragement for my work. I have indeed long been aware of the considerable role you have played in educating the government, the concerned professionals, and parents, to take a better approach to the problems of childhood. I am also impressed by your personal involvement in finding solutions to many often desperate individual cases."[64]

---

61. Mauco, *Psychanalyse et éducation*, 243.

62. André Berge, *De l'écriture à la psychanalyse: Entretiens avec Michel Mathieu* (Clancier Guénaud, 1988), 102.

63. "Les écoles des parents autrefois et demain." IMEC BER 3.23.

64. Ministère de l'Éducation Nationale à André Berge, July 5, 1976. IMEC BER 8.131.

THE CIRCULATION OF STRUCTURALISM   121

What exactly was this "ethical behavior" preached at the Centre Claude Bernard and at the École des parents? André Berge, who was appointed director of the Centre Claude Bernard in 1947, is another interesting figure to explore this question and to trace the circulation of psychoanalytic ideas within the political sphere. Berge was born in 1902 into a powerful Catholic bourgeois Parisian family. His father was a civil engineer and a member of the Académie d'agriculture, and his mother was the daughter of the former president Félix Faure.[65] He studied literature and philosophy before undertaking a medical career with an emphasis on psychiatry. In 1939, Berge began to undergo analysis with Laforgue, whom he had met through Marc Schlumberger. It was through Laforgue that Berge met Laforgue's other patients: Juliette Favez-Boutonier, Françoise Dolto, and Georges Mauco.[66] Like Mauco, Berge maintained an ambivalent relationship to Lacan, sometimes disavowing him publicly, and other times quoting him and relying on his work.[67] What is evident in Berge's psychoanalytic work, however, is his conception of the family as a structural entity with particular rules and with ties to the social world.

In a 1959 conference, for example, Berge explained that the family constituted a "heterogeneous group." Such groups had an organic unity and were essentially structured: "The elements that compose them are differentiated and therefore not interchangeable. Any modification of their order risks breaking the equilibrium of the entire edifice. These heterogeneous groups are generally oriented toward creative and constructive action . . . I speak of 'familial structuring' [because] the term structure presupposes the existence of a conscious or unconscious plan according to which the roles are distributed among the members of the community."[68] Not only was the family, according to Berge, quintessentially structured, but it was also positioned in between nature (which Berge refers to as a "biological imperative") and culture (which Berge claims can vary according to socioeconomic and cultural contexts). Although the family transcends the purely social or cultural, it re-

---

65. Berge, *De l'écriture à la psychanalyse,* 13.

66. During the Occupation, Boutonnier, Dolto, Schlumberger, and Berge often met to discuss psychoanalysis at Boutonnier's apartment in Paris on the rue de la Montagne-Sainte-Geneviève, which inspired them to take on the name of the "quartor Sainte-Geneviève" (ibid., 69). Apparently, Laforgue used to invite his patients on weekends to his country house in Roquebrussanne (ibid., 57).

67. Ibid., 48, 97.

68. "La prise de conscience des rôles dans le structuration familiale." Extrait de la *Revue de neuropsychiatrie infantile et d'hygiène mentale de l'enfance,* 7ᵉ année, March–April 1959, no. 3–4; signed A. Berge, Directeur du Centre Claude Bernard, Administrateur de l'École des parents, 1. IMEC BER 4.7.

122   **CHAPTER 3**

mains linked to social structure in fundamental ways. As Berge writes, "from a social point of view, the family offers the child a constellation of characters who play certain roles that prefigure the roles that he will play himself or that he will see played around him when he finds himself among adults."[69] While these roles used to be understood spontaneously and unconsciously, Berge argues that with modernity—essentially because of feminism and because of man's greater interest in the functioning of his own mind—the process needs to be spelled out in more obvious terms.

By referring to the various "roles" within the family, Berge, once again, points to the fundamental function of sexual difference during this Oedipal phase. Like Mauco, Berge uses gender, sex, and psychic structure interchangeably: "The day that the child discovers sexual difference and realizes that society is composed of masculine and feminine individuals, a new phase begins: the boy and the girl must begin to learn what their position in life is. We say that they are 'polarized' between the father and the mother who represent, by definition, the masculine and feminine poles."[70] Or again, "At the end of this Oedipal phase, the child, having learned to identify with the parent of the same sex, realizes that there are two ways of loving, depending on whether the one to be loved appears as an object of love (to be seduced or conquered) or as a model to imitate."[71]

Also similar to Mauco, Berge presents the Oedipal stage as a trope for social and psychic cohesion. As he writes, "Despite all the nuances one needs to bring to this general schema, experience shows that [the Oedipal model] cannot be upset without this resulting in problems and disequilibrium. If the father and the mother no longer know how to play their roles of husband and wife, they can no longer play as needed their roles vis-à-vis the child, during the Oedipal period."[72] These problems are evidenced at the clinical level where "the child who confusingly perceives that there is something wrong in the familial structure protests and reacts in his own way. He can lie, steal, be aggressive and fussy, or on the contrary, passive, inhibited. His personal structure reflects the familial structure."[73] Finally, Berge concludes, "When the understanding of the roles of each member of the family progresses, we can deduce, not 'a priori' but 'a posteriori,' some norms that

---

69. Ibid, 2.

70. Ibid, 3.

71. Ibid, 5.

72. Ibid, 6.

73. Ibid.

THE CIRCULATION OF STRUCTURALISM   123

might belong to a moment in history but others which can be considered universal. The discovery of these norms takes on a scientific value and becomes suitable for teaching."[74] Understanding and teaching these universal norms could also be called, it would appear, psychoanalysis, at least as these promoters of psycho-pedagogy understood it.

❧ Psychoanalysis and the Media

The Haut comité de la population et de la famille, the Centre Claude Bernard, and the École des parents offer three different examples of institutions pertaining to the family in which psychoanalysts and public officials interacted, both on a practical and intellectual level. They can also help us examine more closely how psychoanalytic ideas about the family, and particularly the structuralist social contract anchored in sexual difference and on the Oedipus complex, reached a larger public that was not necessarily aware of psychoanalytic theory as such. After the 1950s, psychoanalysis found an even more important vector of circulation within the public sphere: popular culture, and more specifically radio and television.

The idea of relying on the media to promote a particular conception of the family and of the social was not new. Familialist activists had suggested turning to the media since the 1930s. And it was not *any* thought on the family that needed to be advanced. Although Vichy represented the culmination of government control over what could and could not be said about the family, familialists managed to influence governmental censors for years after the end of the war. As late as 1968, Mauco, as head of the Haut comité de la population et de la famille, urged the minister of social affairs, Jean-Marcel Jeanneney, to cancel a television show on sexual education that foregrounded the issue of contraception: "As the government is worrying about maintaining the French birthrate, it is unfortunate that a public service should contribute to the diffusion of Malthusian ideas, and that it should present sexual education in a way that profoundly deforms nature and affection."[75] Similarly, the Alliance nationale often relied on the radio and press in the interwar years and during the war.

---

74. Ibid. Several of these ideas were taken up and developed in the collection of essays: André Berge, *Écrivain, psychanalyste, éducateur* (Desclée de Brouwer, 1995).

75. Letter, February 26, 1968, AN 577 AP, box 3.

124   **CHAPTER 3**

Among the psychoanalysts examined in this chapter, both Berge and Mauco made frequent appearances on the radio and pleaded with public officials to follow their example. When, for instance, Berge was invited to discuss the question of parental authority in January 1954, he used some of his usual terms and concepts to develop his train of thought:

> It is not always the mothers who take on maternal attitudes and the fathers paternal attitudes. In principle, however, we define as maternal the very natural anguish that mothers experience when they see their children getting away from them, detaching themselves, in some sense dissociating themselves from their personality by repeating on the psychological level what has happened a first time on a physical level when the child was born and the umbilical cord cut."[76]

Similarly, Mauco relied on the basic premises of the structuralist social contract when asked to explain what the psychoanalytic treatment at the Centre Claude Bernard involved in an interview with the popular magazine the *Nouvel Observateur*. In the case of a neurotic child, Mauco explained, "Our work consists in understanding the expressions he gives to his desires—desires that he cannot manifest—his imaginary realm, and the fantasies that inhabit him. We try to understand where he is in relation to the acceptance of his sex and in relation to the acceptance of his triangular family situation, that is to say his relation to his father and to his mother, the Oedipal relation." In this context, Mauco continued, "All of Freudian psychoanalysis is centered on the Oedipus complex: for the small child, for whom the Oedipus complex is still to come, and for the child beyond eight or nine who, by that age, should have resolved his Oedipus complex if he is to be a socialized being."[77] The problem with alienated children, according to Mauco, was the absence of this "triangular situation," a situation that relegated them to the dominion of the imaginary and that manifested itself in linguistic anomalies.[78] Pressed to account for the increasing number of children with social difficulties, Mauco cited as an essential factor the "abdication of fathers" [*la démission des pères*]: "The child, in this symbolic structuring trinity, needs very differentiated roles between father and mother. He needs for each of them to have their own particular domain, without eclipsing the

---

76. L'autorité et les parents (textes pour radio 1953–1954). January 6, 1954, DA 7 343-7. IMEC BER 7.21.

77. "Ces enfants normaux qui ne peuvent pas vivre," *Nouvel Observateur,* December 2, 1968, 5–14, p. 5, AN 577 AP, box 10.

78. Ibid., 7.

THE CIRCULATION OF STRUCTURALISM 125

other."[79] The "healing method" at the Centre Claude Bernard was, Mauco concluded, "the psychoanalytic method." Explicitly aligning himself with Lacan, Mauco explained that "in our school, the École freudienne, which was founded and directed by Jacques Lacan, we have found that it was beneficial, when dealing with a child, to have a close relationship with the parents. This is, we could say, our distinguishing feature."[80]

Of the various psychoanalysts mentioned in this chapter, none was as active in the media—and, we could even say, in the public sphere more largely—as Françoise Dolto. Dolto, née Marette, was born in 1908 to a large and well-to-do family.[81] After a childhood immersed in the world of the Parisian bourgeoisie, she decided to attend medical school. Dolto had acquired an early interest in Freud and psychoanalysis, and medicine seemed like the best career to further explore these topics. Moreover, the fact that Dolto's brother was himself enrolled in medical school was a determining factor for her parents to allow her to study at the same institution, at a time when the presence of women in higher education was still the exception. It was during her first years in university that Dolto and her brother Philippe befriended Marc Schlumberger. Schlumberger, who had begun to undergo analysis in Vienna with Hermann Nunberg, suggested that Dolto meet René Laforgue, who agreed to become Dolto's psychoanalyst in 1934. In the following years, Dolto became acquainted with other young analysts-in-training, particularly with Boutonnier, Berge, and Mauco, all students of Laforgue, with whom she formed the *club des piqués*. In 1938, she joined the SPP, to which other young analysts such as Lacan and Lagache were attached.

In addition to psychoanalysis, Dolto specialized in pediatrics. During her residency, she met the child psychoanalyst Sophie Morgenstern, who was developing a new technique that she characterized as "in between Anna Freud and Melanie Klein" for treating children.[82] Dolto also worked extensively with Georges Heuyer and Édouard Pichon, both very interested in child psychoanalysis. In 1939, she defended her thesis "Psychanalyse et pé-

---

79. Ibid.

80. Ibid., 9.

81. For more on Dolto's life, see Françoise Dolto, *Autoportrait d'une psychanalyste: 1934–1988* (Seuil, 1989); *Correspondance* (Hatier, 1991); and *Une vie de correspondances: 1938–1988* (Gallimard, 2005). Also see Michel H. Ledoux, *Introduction à l'œuvre de Françoise Dolto* (Rivages, 1990); Yann Potin, ed., *Françoise Dolto: Archives de l'intime* (Gallimard, 2008); Roudinesco, *La bataille de cent ans,* vol. 2; Sauverzac, *Françoise Dolto.*

82. Claudine Geissmann and Pierre Geissmann, *Histoire de la psychanalyse de l'enfant: Mouvements, idées, perspectives* (Bayard, 1992), 92; Sauverzac, *Françoise Dolto,* 115.

126   **CHAPTER 3**

diatrie," which carried the seeds of many of her future arguments. One of the most prominent themes of "Psychanalyse et pédiatrie" was the analysis of the Oedipus complex. According to Dolto, the primary function of the psychoanalyst was to help, or rather to accompany, the subject through the fundamental process of castration. Like Lacan, Dolto linked this process to language.[83] Another recurrent idea in Dolto's first book was her insistence on distinguishing psychoanalysis from morality, in ways that were reminiscent of Mauco or Berge. Psychoanalysis had nothing to with morality, but it had, nonetheless, "an educational value for sure."[84]

In the years following the war, Dolto gained increasing public notoriety, initially through her frequent talks at the École des parents and at the Centre Claude Bernard.[85] At the École des parents, she delivered a lecture in March 1950 for parents who were separated; in April 1950, one on the situation of only children; in December 1950, one on the role of grandparents; in February 1954, one entitled "The Age of the Parents"; and another in December 1979 trying to help parents broach the issue of domestic finances. In her paper on only children, Dolto contended that being an only child "did not make one sick," but it nonetheless posed a series of psychic and most importantly social difficulties for the child: "Attached to his mother who is indispensable to him, the child, who lacks society, thinks that this is what society is."[86] In this context, a sibling could "allow intercomprehension." Through a sibling, the child can feel like "an other, he can project himself into the other and establish a real contact. He can leave behind the narcissism which had conditioned his behavior until then and which had prevented him—because he only had himself to understand—from understanding the other by going outside himself."[87] In order to account for the only child's social malaise, Dolto resorts to the vocabulary of the *imago,* which, as we saw before, was a crucial concept in Lacan's early work on the family:

---

83. Françoise Dolto, *Psychanalyse et pédiatrie: Les grandes notions de la psychanalyse, seize observations d'enfants* (Seuil, 1971), 141.

84. Ibid., 161.

85. We can find evidence of André Berge writing to Dolto to schedule her conferences at the Centre Claude Bernard in Dolto, *Une vie de correspondances,* 559. Many of her lectures for the École des parents were republished in the collection edited by Claude Halmos: Françoise Dolto, *Les chemins de l'éducation* (Gallimard, 1994). The manuscripts can also be found at the Archives Françoise Dolto.

86. Dolto, *Les chemins de l'éducation,* 103, 105.

87. Compte rendu de la Conférence prononcée le 3 mars 1950 à l'École des parents sur l'enfant unique. Archives Françoise Dolto.

THE CIRCULATION OF STRUCTURALISM   127

The imago is for each of us an interiorized image. Each of us carries
within ourselves . . . an "imago" of the father and of the mother,
an ideal image of an adult self who answers to our need for self-
development, an ideal image of a "self at a later stage." The realization
of this "imago" is very difficult for the only child because he sees
himself as a given (he didn't see himself be born and didn't see any
sister or brother be born) . . . He conceives of his father and mother
as an "imago" that is sterile and mutilated in relation to the image that
we carry within us; indeed he intuitively feels that growth leads to reproduction. Then, the "imago" of his father and his mother becomes
anxious because it is incomplete.[88]

Among the symptoms displayed by only children, Dolto cites anorexia as
being one of the most common.[89] In Dolto's discussion of only children,
we see the same back and forth between the sexual and the social that Lacan
exhibited in his 1938 text on the family. As Dolto explains in this essay, "Because the only child does not experience any sensorial exchanges with other
children, he cannot participate in any exchanges on the level of sexuality."[90]

The École des parents and the Centre Claude Bernard provided receptive audiences for Dolto's first ideas on the family and also allowed her to
branch out to other organizations interested in questions of kinship and
sexuality. In 1962, Dolto delivered a lecture entitled "Situation actuelle de
la famille" to two women's groups, Jeunes femmes and Cercles féminins,
where she continued to develop the idea of symbolic parenting regulated
through social and psychic laws and anchored in sexual difference: "There
need to be three people for a child to be conceived: the father, the mother,
and the subject that is incarnated in the first cell produced by the conjunc-
tion of the two initial cells. We may forget that there are three of us but the
child never will. If there is parenting without these three, there is the seed
of psychosis."[91] And like Lacan, Dolto distinguished the biological father
from the symbolic father who "gives the law" by "giving his name": "Each

---

88. Dolto, *Les chemins de l'éducation*, 108–9. In her March 16, 1950, École des parents conference on
separated parents, Dolto also touched on this issue of identification with the parental imago. Children who lived with only one parent could no longer identify with both and thus could not develop
properly. Manuscript, p. 24, at the Archives Françoise Dolto.

89. Ibid., 111.

90. Ibid., 114.

91. Conférence "Situation Actuelle de la Famille," *Jeunes Femmes* (Bulletin de l'Association des
groupes "Jeunes femmes et Cercles féminins"), August–September–October, no. 63, (1962): "Soli-
daires d'un monde en transformation," 43, Archives Françoise Dolto.

128   **CHAPTER 3**

human has an internal idea of what a mother and what a father are, even if one of the two was not 'really' there. The father is the one who introduces you into the laws of exchange of society, exchanges of behavior and exchanges of power . . . He is also the one who gives (or does not give) his name to the subject and thus grants him (or does not grant him) recognition."[92] In this context, Dolto associates paternity and authority, which she claims is essential in education: "Let us make sure when we assert the law to a child that it is indeed a real law, a supra-familial law that rules over the civic group to which he belongs."[93] Law and paternity, in other words, are never simply private or arbitrary: they carry a universal power in their very essence.

As these last three passages reveal, Dolto shared Lacan's interest in a structuralist refiguring of castration, sexual difference, and the Name-of-the-Father. She also sought to elucidate the relationship between language and castration and between the law and psychosis. Of the various "bridge figures" discussed in this chapter, Dolto had by far the closest and most direct relationship with Lacan, but also perhaps the most complicated. In personal terms, the two were close. Dolto often mentioned, for example, that they *tutoied* or used the informal *tu* with each other. Both were members of the SPP until the 1953 split, after which Dolto chose to follow Lacan to the SFP, mainly because she disapproved of the increasing pressure to systematize and normalize psychoanalysis.[94]

Intellectually speaking, however, Dolto often distanced herself from Lacan's theories, claiming that she did not understand them, particularly after the seventies when Lacan was increasingly drawn to mathematical formulas

---

92. Ibid.

93. Ibid., 45.

94. As Dolto said in a letter to Lacan from May 19, 1953, "I am very eager to give my trust, my allegiance, my support to whoever will lead the destinies of this French group in a human and non robotic manner . . ." (Archives Françoise Dolto). Some excerpts were republished in Jacques-Alain Miller, ed., *La scission de 1953: La communauté psychanalytique en France* (Navarin, 1990). The relationship between Lacan and Dolto grew sour toward the end of their lives, especially as Dolto became increasingly involved in the media and in the study of Christianity. Two of Lacan's closest disciples, Jacques-Alain Miller and Charles Melman, supposedly referred to Dolto as "lice in Lacan's head" and the "*bondieu sarde,*" and as "giving advice to parents" and seeking power. Dolto expressed her dismay in a letter to Lacan on January 14, 1980, in which she further explained that "my work and my person have always been in accord with yours . . . If I am a 'pro Lacan' analyst and not a 'Lacanian,' this fashionable word, it is because your teaching upholds—for me and for those with whom I work—the search for the truth which speaks since Freud, through his suffering and that of others" (Archives Françoise Dolto).

THE CIRCULATION OF STRUCTURALISM   129

and began to privilege the study of the Real over the Symbolic.[95] Most importantly, while Dolto and Lacan shared a vocabulary and both emphasized the notion of castration as the defining trait of the human, what they meant by the term was radically different. In both cases, castration was a process brought about by the incest prohibition that required an internalization, a confrontation with, or a disregard of the law (depending on the structure of neurosis, perversion, or psychosis). And in both cases, castration was intimately linked to language and signification. For Lacan, however, castration pointed to the essential alienation of humans, to the foundational absence and lack that marked subjectivity and language: if the Other was the necessary mediator of recognition, this was always a form of *misrecognition*.[96] Dolto, on the contrary, discussed castration in terms of presence and wholeness.[97] When she argued, for example, that "we exist only because we are linked to others through speech," she explained that communication "allows the suffering person to be reunified, to regain cohesion, to regain the sense of self-worth that was disintegrated in the animal suffering that beings can sometimes bear."[98]

As Jean-François de Sauverzac has suggested, Lacan's theories provided the "theoretical foundation" for Dolto's work: both focused on "the primacy of language and of the Symbolic," and both emphasized "the essential role of desire which is constitutive of the subject and which provides the springboard for the analytic treatment."[99] Or as Michel Ledoux writes, the main intellectual connection between Lacan and Dolto "has to do with the valorization of language as the specificity of the human being, the primacy granted to language and to the symbolic function."[100] More specifically, I would argue that Dolto appropriated the structuralist contract of

---

95. In an interview, "Françoise Dolto défend Lacan," *Lire,* no. 111, December 1984, 86, Dolto claimed, "I often confessed to him: 'I never understand what you write.' Lacan would sometimes be interested in my clinical work. But when I gave him my reports, he would say 'I have nothing to add. You have said what needs to be said.'"

96. For an analysis of this process of "failed interpellation" in Lacan's work, see Slavoj Žižek, *The Sublime Object of Ideology* (Verso, 1989).

97. Ledoux, *Introduction à l'œuvre de Françoise Dolto,* 51–52.

98. Françoise Dolto and Danielle Marie Lévy, *Parler juste aux enfants: Entretiens* (Mercure de France, 2002), 13.

99. Sauverzac, *Françoise Dolto,* 282; for more on Sauverzac's comparison between Dolto and Lacan, see his introduction (11–20).

100. Ledoux, *Introduction à l'œuvre de Françoise Dolto,* 233.

130   **CHAPTER 3**

Lacan to tie the Oedipus complex to language, the unconscious, castration, and the social more generally.

In 1969, Lucien Maurice, the director of the radio station Europe 1, invited Dolto (under the nickname of "Doctor X") to speak on the radio and answer questions from children and teenagers. Due to the success of her show, Dolto was recruited in 1976 by another radio station, France-Inter, to respond to written questions from parents who were anxious about their children's education.[101] These conversations were eventually published in a three-volume collection entitled *Lorsque l'enfant paraît*. Although Dolto was initially reluctant to ground her responses on her psychoanalytic "expertise," she eventually agreed. First, she explained, the fact that people were compelled to write down their concerns forced them in a way to explicitly formulate a demand. Second, she argued, the radio could serve as a mechanism to channel transference.[102] In this context, Dolto believed that it was advisable to have a man and a woman interact on the radio in the responses so that they could represent (in a way that was similar to the psychodramas at the Centre Claude Bernard) the father and the mother, because "education always involves a mother and a father."[103] Finally, the idea was not to provide individual consultations, but rather to select the questions that could be of interest to everyone, because "children interest everyone."[104] As Dolto explained in her first radio show on France-Inter, her goal was to help fathers and mothers who found it difficult to cope with their children but not difficult enough to involve a doctor or psychoanalyst.[105] According to Dolto, her radio shows did not constitute a "psychoanalytic treatment" because this label only designates the "contract between a patient and an ana-

---

101. For Dolto's account of how she was recruited to work on the radio, see "Françoise Dolto et la radio," *Psychiatrie Française*, no. 2 (1984), 159, Archives Françoise Dolto. We could note, in passing, that Dolto was not the first psychoanalyst to appear on the radio. In Great Britain, Donald Winnicott gave a series of talks on the BBC about children. See D. W. Winnicott, *Winnicott on the Child* (Perseus, 2002). In France, another station, RTL, had begun the trend of discussing sexuality on the radio with Ménie Grégoire, a sexologist who had, interestingly enough, also been analyzed by René Laforgue. For more on Grégoire, see Guy Robert, "Un état dans l'état RTL: Le divan radiophonique de Menie Grégoire," *Cahiers du Comité d'Histoire de la Radiodiffusion* 55, January–February (1998). By 1970, Grégoire's show counted more than 2.5 million listeners.

102. "Françoise Dolto et la radio," *Psychiatrie Française*, no. 2 (1984), 160–63. See also Dolto's interview "Lorsque l'enfant paraît," in *Diététique Aujourd'hui*, January 1978, 16, in which she claims that she "discovered radio, its power and the role it can play" and that "the fact of writing already compels people to articulate a problem" (Archives Françoise Dolto).

103. Dolto, "Françoise Dolto et la radio," 161.

104. Ibid, 159.

105. Manuscript transcript of *Lorsque l'enfant paraît*, Archives Françoise Dolto.

THE CIRCULATION OF STRUCTURALISM   131

lyst, which bears on the transference of what takes place with this person."[106] Rather, her shows were *public* psychoanalysis.

It would be an understatement to say that Dolto's books and radio shows were very popular. By 1990, *Lorsque l'enfant paraît* had sold 300,000 copies, *La cause des enfants* 130,000 copies, and Dolto's autobiographical work, *Autoportrait d'une psychanalyse,* more than 80,000.[107] Throughout the 1980s, Dolto also appeared regularly on television. She was often invited, for example, to Bernard Pivot's much-watched cultural show *Apostrophes.*[108] By the 1980s, France seemed to be experiencing a real "Doltomania."[109] In her responses on the radio, Dolto not only relied on difficult psychoanalytic terms and notions, but she also based many of her answers on the theoretical premises of the structuralist social contract and insisted in particular on the foundational role of the father. Thus, she argued, babies needed to hear the voice of both their mother and their father because "everything that is spoken becomes human, the rest is traumatic." Fathers needed to play soccer with their boys to socialize them, but parents ought not to be too physically affectionate with their children because, for the incest prohibition to "go well," it was necessary to maintain a safe distance between parent and child. If children did not have their father's family name, they might be forced to wrestle with a "completely de-structuring significance."[110]

Elsewhere, Dolto provided the conceptual justification for her positions. Sexual difference, she explained, "is the first thing to say, to express . . . In fact sexuation and sexuality are what roots the identity of a being in his body. That is why it is so important."[111] Sexual difference, Dolto argued, was intrinsically linked to the "symbolic function": "It exists in all human beings, it is an internal language. The human being has speech, which does not mean a verbal language. He has speech, that is to say the possibility to represent that which makes him live."[112] Similarly, Dolto claimed that it was fundamental to tell the child his "place in kinship," because it was the only

---

106. "Radio S.O.S.," *Psychologies,* June 1977, 11.

107. "Dolto parle encore à nos enfants," *L'Express,* January 12, 1990, 56.

108. The show (now available on DVD), aired on Antenne 2 on December 24, 1984. For an analysis of the impact of *Apostrophes* on French culture, see Tamara Chaplin, *Turning on the Mind: French Philosophers on Television* (University of Chicago Press, 2007), 132–38.

109. For more on Dolto's popularization of psychoanalysis, see the first part of Dominique Mehl, *La bonne parole: Quand les psys plaident dans les médias* (Martinière, 2003).

110. Françoise Dolto, *Lorsque l'enfant paraît* (Seuil, 1977).

111. Dolto and Lévy, *Parler juste aux enfants,* 28–29.

112. Ibid., 92.

132   **CHAPTER 3**

way to teach him about the incest prohibition: "If he does not know who is his father is and who his mother is, everyone is mom and dad, and that is not possible! There is only one father and one mother."[113] Like Lévi-Strauss and Lacan, the incest prohibition has for Dolto a positive and productive effect in the sense that it allows the child to enter and participate in society. Unlike Lacan who describes castration as a fundamentally traumatic process, Dolto sees it as essentially reassuring: "Because of the prohibition of incest, the desire of the child is open to others who are outside the limited sphere [*société*] of the family. This is what guarantees that the child will have social relations of great value, both affective and real, and also relations of symbolic friendship with beings whom he will be able to love."[114] Similarly, Dolto constructs incest as primarily asocial, as a refusal of the social contract: "Incest means: 'not separated.' . . . Incest is deathly on all levels. On the contrary, we need to go toward new beings who are not related to us, who are not rooted in our same origins. An exchange through speech, through language, through creation . . . The more we extend the relations beyond our own parents, the more we live like human beings and the more we take responsibility for ourselves."[115]

Within this scenario of the incest prohibition, the parents (who are presumably the show's target audience) occupy a key position. Dolto does not argue that paternity and maternity are exclusively biological, but it remains unclear in her work how exactly the relationship between the symbolic and the biological is theorized. Dolto's slippage between gender, sex, and psychic position is particularly evident in a televised interview with the journalist Jean-Louis Servan-Schreiber, titled "The Work of Parenting." According to Schreiber, Dolto's theories on the radio and in her writings give "an extraordinarily traditional image of the relationship between the mother and the father . . . The father is the authority, the mother is at home and somewhat overwhelmed"—by the 1970s, was not "all this becoming obsolete? Does it not apply precisely to a previous generation?" Her schema, Dolto answered, would never become obsolete because "we will never be able to change biology. We will never be able to graft fetuses in a man's peritoneum." The mother is the first adult representation for the child, but according to Dolto this necessarily entails the presence of a father, if not real, at least imaginary: "There is an unconscious triangulation in the child which

---

113. Ibid., 33.

114. Ibid., 36.

115. Ibid., 44.

THE CIRCULATION OF STRUCTURALISM   133

means that, when he says the mother, it implies the father . . . even if he exists only in the mother's imaginary and even if the child does not know him. There is a triangular situation because at the origin, the human being is born of a triangular situation."[116] Given the rigidity of this structural paradigm, Servan-Schreiber continues, what happens when women decide to raise children on their own, without a male partner? "The child will encounter serious problems if the mother does not have men in her private life. The child will need a man as a projection of his birth father," she says. "We have to understand," Dolto continues, that "children, male or female, need adults of both sexes to construct themselves, to personify them, as they become adults." If this construction does not happen during childhood, there is a good chance that the child "will have a lag: a verbal lag, a motor lag."[117] Although Dolto acknowledges that a child raised by a single mother can eventually "structure himself" if he is surrounded by other "male referents," there is a greater risk if the mother's immediate surrounding is composed of women only:

> There is a higher risk if the mother sees only women, or if the triangular relation is constructed by two women, that something will be delayed in the genital emotional language. Of course the genitalia will mature, but they will mature as genitalia without language, that is to say, an upright animal, an anonymous human species, because the mother's loved being, the chosen being for sexual relations, is a being who is not of the child's sex, or if he or she is of the child's sex, it is an unbearably strong rival. For example, a little girl whose mother has homosexual relations with a woman is in a situation of dereliction in relation to her sex . . . [That is to say] a situation of despair, and the little girl will never emerge from it. Because the affection that a woman gives another woman is as much an affection of the filial, maternal, sisterly type, as it is conjugal. Hence, the child, the girl-child has no space within it. As for the boy-child, he projects what we call the Phallus—the value for his mother—on a woman, and this damages him [le fausse] . . . He identifies with a woman to become a man . . . He is a lesbian man.[118]

---

116. Dolto, *Les chemins de l'éducation,* 34. The original manuscript of the show can be found at the Archives Françoise Dolto in a somewhat modified version: "Entretien avec Jean-Louis Servan-Schreiber sur TF1: Le métier de parents," aired on December 4, 1977.

117. Ibid., 39–40.

118. Ibid., 40–41.

134   **CHAPTER 3**

Finally, Servan-Schreiber, who observes that there is ultimately little free-dom in Dolto's world for those parents who choose to operate outside of a "classical framework," asks Dolto what it means in practical terms to have this "unstructured" child. According to Dolto, saying that a child is "unstruc-tured" is "not a critique" in terms of good or bad. Rather, Dolto's point is that the parental couple will necessarily structure the child's adult life: "There is a certain determinism that is played out. But everything can be lived through and this does not mean that people will be unhappy. It is difficult to say these things in psychoanalysis, because we never have a value judgment. It is neither good nor bad, it is an energetic judgment, it is a structure being developed."[119] With this last statement, Dolto points once again to the distinc-tion between morality and ethics, a distinction that, we have seen, equally in-forms Lévi-Strauss's and Lacan's works. If psychoanalysis is not here to judge, it is here to offer an ethics. If this particular "determinism" is indeed premised on a strict division of gender roles, Dolto fails to account for how exactly this "psychically different" form of structuring relates to its social characteristics.

The media were not, however, the only vector through which Doltoma-nia entered the public sphere. Like Mauco and Berge, Dolto was also in-volved in several governmental structures pertaining to the family. As such, she was frequently consulted in family policy decisions, particularly in four domains: sexual education, divorce and custody laws, adoption, and bioeth-ics. In all of these areas, Dolto relied on psychoanalytic terms and concepts to draw a set of prescriptive measures for the government to implement. In the field of sexual education, we can mention an interview with Dolto re-published in a July 1973 memorandum from the Ministry of Education addressed to all school directors. Dolto began the interview by asserting that "in the domain of sexuality, there are two basic notions for the formation of the human being: difference, which constitutes attraction and generates dyna-mism, and the prohibition of incest, which is the basis for the law. Both must be taught to children, starting in kindergarten."[120] The prohibition of incest, according to Dolto, was fundamentally tied to the social. Children needed to "integrate the law of society" and the "most basic law" was the prohibition of incest. The attractions toward a sibling or a parent

---

119. Ibid., 42.

120. Reprinted in *Parents et maîtres,* no. 81, Novembre 1973: circulaire no. 73–299 du 23 juillet 1973 aux Recteurs, aux Inspecteurs d'académie, aux Chefs d'établissement, aux Inspecteurs départemen-taux de l'éducation nationale. Objet: Information et éducation sexuelles (Cabinet du Ministre), 366, Archives Françoise Dolto.

THE CIRCULATION OF STRUCTURALISM   135

[are] natural attractions but attractions that culture forbids. Our sex is the part of our bodies that carries the charnel fruit, but the human being carries the fruit through all sensible exchange with an other. And we "symbolize" our relations with others through language. The human being is made in such a way that, if he has not gone through castration, he cannot symbolize. The child who only partakes in a communication destined to sterility will never discover the pleasure of a creative communication.[121]

It is unclear how Dolto thought schools needed to "teach kinship" in practical terms, but in one memo she suggests that teachers should establish, in the clearest possible way, that although sexual relations with others was permissible, they could never involve members of one's family. Boundaries needed to be explicit and clearly demarcated. Or, as she put it in another 1979 text entitled "Father and Mother," it is imperative that schools teach children the basic notions of kinship because "if the vocabulary of kinship is either uncertain or ignored, children can experience a deep sense of confusion in their familial and social relations. They need to be structurally rooted—consciously and unconsciously—in the law of incest prohibition."[122]

In the next chapters, I will return in more detail to the specifics of the divorce, adoption, and bioethics legislation that Dolto influenced. For now, I would only like to map some of the networks through which this structuralist psychoanalytic vocabulary on the family circulated in governmental circles. In 1980, Monique Pelletier, the Ministre délégué chargé de la famille et de la condition féminine, invited Dolto to participate in a reflection group on the issues of divorce and the custody of children after a separation. Pelletier, a lawyer by training who had worked many years in Paris's juvenile courts, had joined the government in 1978 as the right hand to the minister of justice Alain Peyrefitte in Valéry Giscard d'Estaing's government. A mother of seven children, Pelletier had, throughout the 1970s, been involved with the École des parents, which she directed in 1971. In 1978, she was appointed to the Ministry of the Condition of Women, which in 1980 became the Ministry of Family and the Condition of Women.[123] Under the umbrella of Pelletier's ministry, Dolto participated in a series of governmental

---

121. Ibid, 367.

122. Reprinted in Dolto, *Les chemins de l'éducation*, 58.

123. For an overview of Monique Pelletier's career, see the series of interviews on France Culture on *À voix nue* on March 1–5, 2010.

136   **CHAPTER 3**

advisory committees where she collaborated with various other family "experts," including lawyers and judges.[124]

Just as with Mauco and Berge, it is important to stress that these collaborative efforts did not just involve administrative discussions but also substantial intellectual exchanges between psychoanalysts such as Dolto and political figures such as Pelletier. We see Dolto's influence on Pelletier's thought, for instance, in an interview in which Pelletier referred to Dolto when she was asked to give her opinion on the sharing of children's custody after divorces. According to Pelletier, judges needed to consider not only the practical aspects of shared custody but the psychological impact on the child: "If Françoise Dolto says . . . after thirty years of experience, I notice that such and such solutions have serious drawbacks, it is important that the judges know that. Judges are not psychologists, and they do not have to be, but they need to be informed on these questions."[125]

Throughout her work on divorce legislation in the seventies and early eighties, Dolto was particularly adamant about one point: the need for the father to be present in the child's life, as the repository of the symbolic function. As she explained, the child's psyche was determined by the triangular relationship in which he was born: "For the child, at the beginning of his life, the roles of the two parents are non-dissociable because there is a triangular situation at birth. The child is born from the encounter of two people, and we can say that from his origin, he has always heard these two people. It is really a triangular situation, and that is why we see certain difficulties emerge when fathers, according to the discourse of mothers, 'abdicate.'"[126] In the context of this triangle, Dolto insists on the symbolic position of the father, which she contrasts with the mother's biological definition: "A mother is a mother from the moment she knows she is preg-

---

124. In an interview, "Penser aux enfants en cas de divorce," propos recueillis par Yves de Gentil-Baichis, Pelletier mentions a study group that included Dolto and judges Jacqueline Maguin and Henri Molines. Dolto also collaborated with the psychologist Nicole Alby and with the sociologist Jacques Commaille, who was involved in many family policy decisions in the 1980s and 1990s. These three "experts" were sent by Pelletier to a high school in the suburbs of Paris (the Lycée d'enseignement pratique Eugénie Cotton de Montreuil) in December 1980 to interview teenagers whose parents had divorced. The point, Dolto explained, was to "help the Law [*rendre service à la Justice*], and in some sense, to better help the children of future divorced couples" (Archives Françoise Dolto).

125. Ibid.

126. Dolto et Claude Chassagny, psychanalyste, "Le père, aujourd'hui et demain," *Pratique des Mots*, 6 juin 1971: extrait de l'enregistrement effectué au Centre de pédagogie relationnelle du langage (sur les ondes le 13 mai 1971), 24, Archives Françoise Dolto.

THE CIRCULATION OF STRUCTURALISM   137

nant. A father is primarily a father in speech."[127] Or again: "It is the father's voice that welcomes the child: the voice of the father joined to that of the mother. Thus, a human being that is born is already entirely within the symbolic function."[128]

Once more, Dolto's resistance to history, and more particularly to the historicization of the father's role, is striking. When asked by a member of the audience about the relationship between sociology and the family, or more specifically, about how the "global transformations of society" had intervened at the level of this basic triangle, Dolto responded: "The basic triangle will never change. It is given by biology itself. However, is seems to me that in certain cases, parents forget the necessity of a triangular life for the child." As she concludes further in her talk, "As far as I am concerned, I do not think that there is a possibility today of conceiving a radical modification of the father's role, given the nature of this role."[129] Dolto's theoretical support for "strong fathers" also manifested itself in her participation in the early "father's movement," particularly through the group Mouvement de la condition paternelle (MCP), which sought equal parental responsibility in cases of divorce. Dolto gave a series of talks to the group, engaged in an extensive correspondence with some of its leaders, and promised to intervene with judges and lawyers in certain cases.[130]

Dolto's involvement was also substantial in other domains of family policy. To get a sense of the kind of vocabulary and the conceptual framework that informed Dolto's contributions, we can examine the proceedings of a lecture that she delivered in 1984 to social workers involved in adoption cases. The role of psychoanalysis, she claimed, was to "'uphold' what we refer to in the psychoanalytic jargon as 'castrations.' This means knowing clearly what is possible and what is impossible, and accepting that what is impossible is impossible because it is the law. It might remain desirable, but it is not possible, and it must be accepted as such."[131] Similarly, Dolto insisted on the fact that "the only true and lasting prohibition remaining is that of incest . . .

---

127. Ibid.

128. Ibid., 25.

129. Ibid., 27.

130. See MCP (Mouvement de la condition paternelle: pour une responsabilité parentale égale en cas de divorce). Programme du colloque international: l'enfant du divorce et son père. Paris: 31 mars/1 avril 1978, Archives Françoise Dolto.

131. Françoise Dolto and Nazir Hamad, *Destins d'enfants: Adoption, familles d'accueil, travail social* (Broché, 1995), 11.

138   **CHAPTER 3**

It is the only absolute prohibition that a human being is bound to respect to be able to continue developing."[132] Social workers in this context have a responsibility to make children aware of this prohibition, to forbid, for instance, sexual games between brothers and sisters that seek to reenact the "primal scene": "the brother and the sister try to represent the initial coitus of the parents of which the child is the fruit. To sleep with the fruit of the two parents when one is oneself the fruit of these two parents is the meeting *in utero* of a child with another, as if they were twins, but also with their parents."[133] Or again: "children born of incest will not be able to establish relationships with others. Parents cannot tell them that they are brothers and sisters, and they are thus forced to lie. But children know the truth. They are destined to social sterility, and then to human sterility. By the third generation, they will probably become schizophrenics."[134]

Here again, Dolto fluctuates between a biologistic and a culturalist perspective. On the one hand, she is resolute in her characterization of biology as "destiny." On the other hand, she highlights the limits of a purely biologistic understanding of incest and of human life more generally. For example, she argues that incest "is not against nature, it is against culture."[135] Similarly, she criticizes the *loi du sang,* according to which a child's legal parents are always his biological parents, as opposed to, say, his adoptive parents: "If we believe that blood counts more than structure, then human beings become simple mammals, as if physical traces determined that we were someone's child. Humans are not reducible to their biological ties. It is through culture and through language that relationships become structuring."[136] Structure, in other words, trumps both biology and culture. As such, Dolto proved to be receptive to the legislative changes concerning adoption, especially the 1972 law that placed "legitimate children" on the same level as "natural children," which I examine in the next chapter. Dolto was contacted notably by the director of the Aide sociale à l'enfance of the Départment des Hauts-de-Seine to participate in several reflection groups with the adoption services personnel.[137]

---

132. Ibid., 18.

133. Ibid., 19.

134. Ibid.

135. Ibid., 57.

136. Ibid., 73.

137. Ibid., 145. For an analysis of how psychoanalysis informs adoption agencies today, see Bruno Perreau, *Penser l'adoption: La gouvernance pastorale du genre* (Presses universitaires de France, 2012).

THE CIRCULATION OF STRUCTURALISM   139

In the eighties, when bioethics became a hotly debated topic, Dolto was also asked to sit on several panels designed to reflect on the best ways to regulate medically assisted procreation. In this context, she interacted with several important political figures such as Robert Badinter, the minister of justice from 1981 to 1986, and other prominent intellectuals such as the anthropologist Françoise Héritier. Dolto's approach to medically assisted procreation was similar to her views on adoption: she supported it as long as the child was told the truth about his origins.[138] Interestingly enough, the rhetorical connection between medically assisted procreation and incest, which, as we will see, recurred so frequently throughout the 1980s and 1990s, was already apparent in Dolto's early consideration on medically assisted procreation. Asked in an interview whether she agreed with Claude Lévi-Strauss that the incest taboo was universal, Dolto replied, "Absolutely. The desire for incest is a necessity. It is what constitutes the human: the joy of fantasizing, but also the prohibition of realizing it. The desire to sleep with one's mother or one's father is indispensable to the affective and intellectual development of the child, it is what allows him to become himself. The fact that it is forbidden to enact it generates an economy of extraordinary suffering. If the incest prohibition did not exist, there would no longer be creativity. If incest were realized, there would be none either. It is the foundation of the human."[139]

Though their texts and their public interventions, Mauco, Berge, and Dolto provided a "translation" of the structuralist social contract for French political and popular culture. Sexual difference, they insisted, was at the root of all psychic, familial, and social organization, and this phenomenon was structural: universal, ahistorical, and logical. By occupying key posts in government committees and by using the media in innovative ways, Mauco, Berge, and Dolto were all able to ensure that their theoretical considerations had real and direct influence on the legislation of gender and sexuality. Although their translations were often "unfaithful" to the original, all three emphasized the foundational role of the prohibition of incest for both humans and the social. They also collapsed the abstraction and theoretical openness that Lévi-Strauss and Lacan attempted to uphold by "filling" the empty signifiers that structuralism posited with real people, real mothers, fathers, and children. As the universal and transhistorical model

---

138. *L'Express,* March 18–24, 1988, 121, Archives Françoise Dolto.

139. Ibid, 122.

140   CHAPTER 3

of kinship devised by Lévi-Strauss and Lacan went through history, sexual difference was literalized. The structuralist social contract could no longer be called descriptive: it was a prescriptive discourse, a model of ethical behavior that needed to be followed to guarantee psychic and social well-being.

PART TWO

The Critique of Familialism

CHAPTER 4

The "Quiet Revolution" in Family Policy and Family Law

By 1945, familialism appeared to have triumphed in France. Pro-family activists had succeeded in implementing the two main issues on their political agenda which they had been pushing since the interwar years: family benefits—universalized and standardized under the Sécurité sociale banner—and a system of political representation for family interests in the Union nationale des associations familiales (UNAF). A series of governmental advisory bodies had flourished during the Liberation years, such as the Haut comité consultatif de la population et de la famille, the Ministry of Population, the Institut national d'études démographiques (INED), and the Conseil économique et social. The "family vote," although eventually rejected, was thoroughly debated and seriously considered in the preliminary discussion of the 1946 Constitution.[1] The interwar familialists who had collaborated with the Vichy regime had not only been pardoned by the provisional government, but most of them had been reintegrated into the new official government structures. De Gaulle was particularly attached to a natalist

---

1. See Sylvie Chaperon, *Les années Beauvoir (1945–1970)* (Fayard, 2000), 39; Jean-Yves Le Naour and Catherine Valenti, *La famille doit voter: Le suffrage familial contre le vote individuel* (Hachette littératures, 2005), chap. 7. For the Haut comité's position on the family vote, see Alain Drouard, "Le Haut comité de la population et la politique de population de la France (1939–1966)," *Annales de Demographie Historique* 2 (1999): 180.

144   **CHAPTER 4**

program, but it was also the electoral success of the Mouvement républicain populaire (MRP), the most important political party by 1946, that was responsible for the consecration of familialist causes.[2]

By the 1970s, however, the glory days of French familialism appeared to be long gone. Institutions such as the UNAF seemed more and more anachronistic and detached from the concerns of young couples.[3] In 1966, the Haut comité, which had been attached to the prime minister's office so that it could oversee the different ministries dealing with issues pertaining to the family and to immigration, was transferred to the Ministry of Social Affairs. This move affected its power and agency. After the Ministry of Social Affairs split in 1970 into the Ministry of Labor and Employment and the Ministry of Public Health and Social Security, the funds allocated for family affairs were also divided. From 1974 to 1978, the Haut comité stopped meeting altogether.[4]

Most importantly, from 1964 to 1975, French family law was profoundly transformed. It underwent what one legal scholar has described as a "quiet revolution" [*une révolution tranquille*] that challenged many of the foundations established by the 1804 Civil Code.[5] In 1979, the natalist lobby at the National Assembly (which included Michel Debré) attempted to pass a series of amendments to the new family laws reforms, particularly those concerning reproduction. Each one of them was overturned.[6] The family, it seemed, was no longer the political rallying point it had once been. From serving as a focal point for the articulation of social policy after the war, the family came to exemplify what needed to be reformed in what Prime Minister Jacques Chaban-Delmas, in 1969, called the "new society" [*nouvelle société*].

This chapter traces the changes that occurred in family law and family policy from approximately 1964 to 1975. As I suggested in the first chapter,

---

2. Because the MRP welcomed so many Vichy collaborators after the war, it acquired the nickname "Machine à recycler les pétainistes" (Recycling Machine for Pétain Supporters), "Mouvement des réverends pères" (Movement of the Reverend Fathers), and "Mensonge, réaction, perfidie" (Lies, Reaction, Perfidy). Cited in Le Naour and Valenti, *La famille doit voter,* 216.

3. See, for example, the article "L'UNAF est vivement critiquée par des jeunes ménages," *Le Monde,* December 3, 1969.

4. Drouard, "Le Haut comité de la population," 178–79. The Haut conseil was briefly relived in 1978 under the umbrella of the Ministry of Labor and Participation, but it was not until 1985, under President Mitterrand, that it regained its postwar prestige under the new name of Haut comité de la population et de la famille.

5. Gérard Cornu, *Droit civil: Introduction, les personnes, les biens* (Montchrestien, 2001).

6. Janine Mossuz-Lavau, *Les lois de l'amour: Les politiques de la sexualité en France, 1950–2002* (Payot & Rivages, 2002), 144.

THE "QUIET REVOLUTION" IN FAMILY POLICY LAW   145

the success of familialism as a movement and as an ideology was due to its capacity to infiltrate various governmental structures by presenting the family as a universal, nonpartisan entity that would ensure social cohesion and solidarity. By the 1960s, however, this ahistorical vision of the family was more difficult to maintain. For one, the demographic context and the political situation of France had changed, and familialist actors were increasingly marginalized. Moreover, the family, like everything else, suddenly seemed subject to the "tide of history" of the sixties. Instead of reflecting abstract normative and universal principles, family policy and family law needed to adapt to history, to the profound changes undergone by French society during that decade.

✒ A New Demographic Panorama

Although the architects of French family policy saw in the family the possibility of instituting a new social model, they claimed to be motivated, first and foremost, by the French "depopulation crisis." Similarly, the elected officials who approved the Code de la famille in 1939, as well as de Gaulle in 1945, used the pretext of demography to promote their government's family policy. By the 1970s, however, familialists could no longer rely on demographic numbers and statistics to advance their cause. From 1946 to 1962, the French population had increased from 40 to 46 million, and to 52 million by 1975: it had grown by 12 million in the span of thirty years. The birthrate in France had been 15 per 1,000 from 1935 to 1939, but it had climbed to 21 per 1,000 in 1946, and exceeded 18 per 1,000 throughout the 1960s.[7] France, like several other countries in the post–World War II era, was experiencing a baby boom. This phenomenon was linked to demographic trends common to several Western countries in the years after World War II, but the French case was also a product of the economic prosperity of the *trente glorieuses.* To a large extent, this demographic expansion also testified to the considerable success of the various postwar family policies previously discussed. As demographer Louis Henry put it in 1948, the French demographic boom was unquestionably linked to the family benefits that had "enhanced the prestige of the family" during a time when the family "had become suspect for many progressive minds." "Given the mentality of the French," Henry added, "it would not surprise me if some had just enough children

---

7. Jacques Vallin, *La population française* (La découverte, 1992).

146   CHAPTER 4

to access the same rights as others. In the same way some people, who subscribe to social security, would be glad to get sick in order to get their contributions back in the form of medical care."[8]

Besides raising the birthrate, the second mission of the post–World
War II "population policy" had been to promote immigration as a means
for population growth. Family benefits and immigration were considered
two sides of the same coin by institutions such as the Haut comité and the
Ministry of Population. As de Gaulle put it in a speech before the National
Assembly in March 1945, "We have devised a great plan in order to call to
life the twelve million beautiful babies that France needs in the next ten years.
This will reduce our absurd rates of mortality and of infant and juvenile mor-
bidity. Furthermore, we will introduce in the course of the coming years,
with rigor and intelligence, good immigrants into the French collective."[9]
France had always been a "country of immigration,"[10] but it was only during
the second half of the nineteenth century that politicians, social scientists,
and intellectuals began to discuss immigration as a "problem" that required a
specific set of rational policies to regulate it. The family, as we have seen,
became an object of scientific study around the same time.[11] As such, when
the Haut comité was set up in 1939, it developed not only the Family Code,
but also a series of immigration plans, inspired notably by Georges Mauco's
work on the potential "assimilability" of different types of foreigners, and on
a set of "ethnic quotas" derived from these numbers.

Most of the legislation restricting immigration was passed during the last
years of the Third Republic, triggered in part by the economic crisis and the
rise of xenophobia and anti-Semitism during the thirties.[12] The Vichy regime, however, systematized and institutionalized these measures, adopting

---

8. Cited in Paul-André Rosental, *L'intelligence démographique: Sciences et politiques des populations en France, 1930–1960* (Odile Jacob, 2003), 202.

9. Cited in Patrick Weil, *La France et ses étrangers: L'aventure d'une politique de l'immigration, 1938–1991* (Calmann-Lévy, 1991), 69.

10. See, for example, Peter Sahlins, *Unnaturally French: Foreign Citizens in the Old Regime and After* (Cornell University Press, 2004).

11. On the parallels between family and immigration policies during the post–World War II years, see Karen H. Adler, *Jews and Gender in Liberation France* (Cambridge University Press, 2003). According to Patrick Weil, the year 1938 marks the shift in which the French State embraced a coherent immigration policy (*La France et ses étrangers,* 21).

12. For more on this, see Vicki Caron, *Uneasy Asylum: France and the Jewish Refugee Crisis, 1933–1942* (Stanford University Press, 1999), 91; Mary Dewhurst Lewis, *The Boundaries of the Republic: Migrant Rights and the Limits of Universalism in France, 1918–1940* (Stanford University Press, 2007); Gérard Noiriel, *Le creuset français: Histoire de l'immigration, XIXe–XXe siècles* (Seuil, 1988).

THE "QUIET REVOLUTION" IN FAMILY POLICY LAW 147

an unambiguously racist immigration policy premised on an ethnic hierarchy. At the Liberation, de Gaulle was torn between two positions. On the one hand, Mauco and other prominent familialists such as Alfred Sauvy and Robert Debré urged him to retain the Vichy system of ethnic quotas. On the other hand, several of his ministers (particularly Alexandre Parodi, the minister of labor, Adrien Tixier, the minister of the interior, and André Pelabon, the director of national security), advocated that he clearly demarcate his government's policy from that of Vichy in all fields, including immigration, in order to restore republican legality and revive the ideals of *égalité* and *fraternité*. In the end, the provisional government, opting for the "republican solution," promulgated two laws: one on October 19, 1945, that defined the requirements for French nationality, and another on November 2, 1945, that delineated the conditions of entry into the country for those seeking permanent residency.[13] As a result of these laws, from 1945 to 1975 (a period Alexis Spire refers to as the "*trente glorieuses* of immigration administration") the number of foreigners residing in France more than doubled, climbing from 1.6 to 4.2 million.[14] This wave of immigration contributed substantially to France's population increase during that time.

A New Political Culture

Besides the demographic evolution from 1945 to 1975, a second important factor in the decline of familialism during that period was the progressive waning of the MRP party. Founded clandestinely during the war in January 1944, the MRP sought to incarnate the ideals of Social Catholicism. In that capacity, it served as an umbrella organization for many familialists to advance their vision of the family as integral to the social. As Germaine Poinso-Chapuis, an MRP deputy who served as the minister of public health and population in the Robert Schuman cabinet from 1947 to 1948,

---

13. See Alexis Spire, *Étrangers à la carte: L'administration de l'immigration en France, 1945–1975* (Grasset, 2005); Georges Tapinos, *L'immigration étrangère en France: 1946–1973* (Presses universitaires de France, 1975), 18–19; Weil, *La France et ses étrangers*, 79. It is interesting in this context to compare the history of immigration as presented by Weil and Spire. The former appears particularly eager to mark this break between Vichy and the Liberation and to stress the formal liberalism of the 1945 codes, which did not impose any quotas. Spire, however, seems much more interested in the practical applications of these laws, which, he argues, were very often implemented along informal ethnic lines. For a more detailed account of the debates on immigration after the Liberation, see Patrick Weil, *Liberté, égalité, discriminations: L'"identité nationale" au regard de l'histoire* (Grasset, 2008), chap. 1.

14. See the statistics in Spire, *Étrangers à la carte,* 364, 372.

148   CHAPTER 4

put it in 1950, "The family should not exist in itself; it is not an end, it is a means: the means for each of its members to access their full development and to realize their purpose."[15] The 1945 legislative elections represented a great victory for the MRP, a success that was partly due to its centrist political positions and to its affiliation with de Gaulle. The newly formed party joined the Communists and the Socialists in a government that came to be known as the *tripartisme*. By June 1946, the MRP had become the leading party in France.[16]

By 1951, however, the MRP had lost half its voters. First, it had severed its ties with de Gaulle over his January 1946 departure and his constitutional project later that year. Second, governing with the SFIO and the Communist Party had proved increasingly difficult. The MRP's downfall was accelerated by the emergence of de Gaulle's new party, the Rassemblement du peuple français (RPF), in 1947. Many MRP voters gravitated toward de Gaulle, especially after the series of political crises that shook the Fourth Republic. Finally, the Fifth Republic, with its strong executive branch and its system of runoff voting, dismantled what was left of the MRP. By 1962, the MRP garnered only 5.3 percent of the votes; after 1964, it stopped having its annual meeting. Its remaining members chose to rally to the majority government, to adhere to the new centrist party, the Centre démocratie et progrès (CDP), to join the opposition in the Centre démocrate (CD), or else to move to a new socialist party founded in 1960, the Parti socialite unifié (PSU), which attracted some of the more left-leaning members of the MRP. Familialism did not disappear with the MRP, but it did lose a powerful political platform. As Rémi Lenoir has argued, after the decline of the MRP, familialism lost its "status as an officially recognized great national cause," to be reduced, politically and intellectually, to "the defense of a form of ideological corporatism."[17]

The fraying of familialism throughout the sixties and seventies was not only due to the weakening of the MRP; it also reflected the changes in the presidency from de Gaulle to Georges Pompidou, who was in power from 1969 to 1974. Unlike de Gaulle, who had been haunted by the specter of "depopulation" and who, as a result, had placed family policy atop his

---

15. Cited in Pierre Laroque and Rémi Lenoir, *La politique familiale en France depuis 1945: Rapport du groupe de travail sur la politique familiale en France depuis 1945, présidé par Pierre Laroque* (Documentation française, 1985), 14.

16. For more on the political trajectory of the MRP, see Jean-Pierre Rioux, *La France de la IVe République* (Seuil, 1980), vol. 1, chap. 7.

17. Rémi Lenoir, *Généalogie de la morale familiale* (Seuil, 2003), 457.

THE "QUIET REVOLUTION" IN FAMILY POLICY LAW 149

political agenda, Pompidou appeared far less interested in the topic. Mauco, for instance, repeatedly complained in his memoirs about Pompidou's lack of involvement in the Haut comité. Apparently, Pompidou only presided over it twice in the course of three years, as opposed to de Gaulle who had taken an acute interest in these meetings.[18] Pompidou's indifference toward institutions such as the Haut comité was probably partly a function of his personality.[19] Most importantly, it symbolized the change of political priorities from 1945 to 1970. De Gaulle's main concern at the Liberation had been reconstruction (and hence also *demographic* reconstruction), but Pompidou's was industrialization and modernization. As May '68 had brought to light with particular acerbity, French schools and universities had not been able to keep up with the population increase of the baby boom. Similarly, the housing crisis in urban areas was becoming a more pressing issue by the day.[20] Before the government could encourage couples to have more children, it needed to address these shortages. Finally, it was during Pompidou's presidency that the first effects of the 1973 oil crisis were felt, both economically and socially. The Sécurité sociale budget was increasingly strained from escalating medical costs, the aging of the population, and the rise in unemployment. As a result, family benefit funds were often transferred to other domains.

Finally, the problems of familialism during this time were also a function of what Lenoir has referred to as the Fifth Republic's "new definition of administrative and political work." In this context, a new generation of École nationale d'administration (ENA) or polytechnique-trained civil servants were given key positions in the various "social affairs" organizations and ministries. For many of them, the family was to be administered like any other social matter, along technocratic, rational, and systematic management methods similar to those applied to the world of finances.[21] The UNAF and the Caisse nationale des allocations familiales (CNAF), for instance, which had traditionally recruited personnel from the Conseil d'état, one of the last bastions of familialism, were beginning to hire administrators from

---

18. For Mauco's impressions of Pompidou, see *Espoir*, no. 21, December 1977, 26, AN 577 AP; Georges Mauco, *Vécu 1899–1982* (Émile-Paul, 1982), 128, 166. Mauco's narrative is confirmed by Drouard, "Le Haut comité," 189.

19. Mauco suggests, for instance, that Pompidou disapproved of the Haut comité's reliance on child psychoanalysis: Pompidou "gave the image of an *agrégé* professor, a brilliant intellectual imbued in traditional classical culture, whose Cartesian rigor excluded everything that did not enter into his scholastic knowledge, notably the existence of an affective unconscious life in the child" (*Vécu*, 128).

20. See, for example, Kristin Ross, *Fast Cars, Clean Bodies: Decolonization and the Reordering of French Culture* (MIT Press, 1995), 151–56.

21. Lenoir, *Généalogie*, 457. See also Laroque and Lenoir, *La politique familiale,* chap. 2.

150   **CHAPTER 4**

other sectors such as the Cour des comptes or the Inspection des finances. Many of these civil servants were less sympathetic—or at least less committed—to the kind of familialism that had inspired the birth of these organizations.[22]

To examine more closely this changing conception of the family I want to look briefly at the career of Jacques Delors, who is particularly interesting because of his background as a Social Catholic activist. During his youth, Delors had been involved in the Jeunesse ouvrière chrétienne (JOC) and in Christian syndicalism (through the Confédération française des travailleurs chrétiens, or CFTC). In 1953, he and his wife joined Vie Nouvelle, a political and intellectual group for left-wing Christians inspired by the philosophy of Emmanuel Mounier.[23] At least on paper, Delors appeared to share the profile of many of the early familialists, the Social Catholics who had developed French family policy at the end of the nineteenth century. In 1962, Delors left the Banque de France, where he had worked after graduating, to join the social affairs division of the Commissariat general au plan. As we saw in the first chapter, the Plan was one of the organizations most active in designing family policy after the war. During his time at the Plan from 1962 to 1969, Delors also began teaching at the ENA, one of the most prestigious graduate schools of administration. In the context of a 1967 seminar at the ENA, Delors conducted, with the help of his students, an extensive empirical analysis of what he called "social indicators." According to Delors, these indicators "highlight[ed] the explicit but often implicit choices that the collectivity or individuals make, without measuring all the consequences of such decisions."[24] Through this study, Delors and his students hoped to measure "through a series of quantifiable data, the state of the nation in different domains of economic and social activity" in order to guide governmental social policy decisions according to "rational budget choices."[25]

On the one hand, Delors's commitment to the ideals of Social Catholicism are evident in the very concept of "social indicator," which is premised on the assumption that the economic and the social are intimately connected. As

---

22. See Lenoir, *Généalogie,* 462.

23. In his memoirs, Delors discusses the intellectual impact that *Rerum novarum* had on him and his adhesion to Vie nouvelle. See Jacques Delors, *Mémoires* (Plon, 2004), 34–40. Vie Nouvelle also helped create later groups like Citoyen 60 and the Club Jean-Moulin. See Claire Andrieu, *Pour l'amour de la République: Le Club Jean Moulin, 1958–1970* (Fayard, 2002).

24. Jacques Delors, *Contribution à une recherche sur les indicateurs sociaux* (S.É.D.É.I.S., 1971), 8.

25. Ibid. For more on the methodology behind the "indicateurs sociaux," see Delors's introduction (7–12).

THE "QUIET REVOLUTION" IN FAMILY POLICY LAW   151

he put it, there is "no economic without the social, no social without the economic, and no economic without modernization."[26] On the other hand, we can highlight at least two important differences between Delors's vision of the family and that of the early Social Catholic familialists. First, as the Delors-directed ENA study concluded, the family was not the only locus of solidarity; it was just one among many "social indicators." As Delors and his collaborators suggested in the section on the family, "the renewal of generations is a particularly important aspect of social development. The family is not the only way to contribute to this renewal: a number of births occur outside marriage."[27] Consequently, those children born outside of marriage also deserved governmental aid, to "give individuals a certain equality." Thus, the state, Delors's study concluded, needed to focus more on the individual and less on groups such as the family in order to promote solidarity and social cohesion. Moreover, the list of "social indicators" included categories that would have been entirely unfathomable for the nineteenth-century *familiaux*. Not only did it mention children born out of wedlock, but it also addressed contraception, divorce, and single-parent households. The elderly and the handicapped were also cited as target groups to consider.[28]

This diversification of appropriate "conduit groups" for solidarity obviously reflected the social changes that had occurred over the past fifty years. More significantly, however, it denoted a changing perception on the part of the state of what the family was or ought to be. A few years after the ENA study, Delors was recruited by Jacques Chaban-Delmas, Georges Pompidou's prime minister from 1969 to 1972, to serve as his personal advisor on social issues. This was a particularly important post because Chaban-Delmas had inherited the social turmoil of May '68 and was resolved to build what he famously—and controversially—labeled the *nouvelle société* or "new society." According to Chaban-Delmas, this new society aimed to be "more just, more fraternal and more able to give young people the means to realize their full potential."[29] Family policy was one way to achieve this goal. Delors's

---

26. Delors, *Mémoires*, 78.

27. Delors, *Contribution*, 46. See also Delors, *Mémoires*, 64; Lenoir, *Généalogie*, 460.

28. Delors, *Contribution*, 12.

29. Chaban-Delmas cited in Delors, *Mémoires*, 74. The discourse on youth and fraternity was prevalent throughout this entire period. See Richard Ivan Jobs, *Riding the New Wave: Youth and the Rejuvenation of France after the Second World War* (Stanford University Press, 2007); Susan Weiner, *Enfants Terribles: Youth and Femininity in the Mass Media in France, 1945–1968* (Johns Hopkins University Press, 2001).

152   CHAPTER 4

career, we could say, reflected the evolution of familialism from its inception to the mid-seventies. From serving as the central category for thinking the social in Social Catholicism, the family had become just another subdivision of economic and social policy that could be studied and debated "scientifically." In other words, the family had become historicizable.

This changing notion of the family and of family policy was reflected in the many debates around family benefits during the sixties and seventies. For instance, one of the most cherished principles of early familialist advocates was that family benefits should remain independent of family income. According to this logic, a low-income family with four children should receive the same amount of help as a high-earning family with the same number of children. Familialists had been particularly attached to this tenet. Robert Prigent, one of the most vocal interwar family activists, who presided over the Committee for the Study of the Problems of the Family, instituted in 1960 by the Ministry of Public Health and Population, had insisted that the financial help given to families was "not a measure of welfare [*assistance*]: it is a measure of social redistribution of incomes, it is a step toward tax equality [*l'égalité des charges*]."[30] If family benefits were just another mechanism—like welfare—to help lower-income citizens, familialists feared that the family would lose all of its theoretical specificity. By the late sixties, however, fixed family benefits appeared less and less politically tenable. The *allocation logement* (or housing subsidy), which fluctuated according to family income, had already been reformed in 1961 to favor more destitute families.[31] In 1969, a study conducted by Pierre Laroque in the context of the Plan recommended the implementation of a sliding scale for family benefits adjusted according to family income. Chaban-Delmas endorsed this idea in his initial address before the National Assembly on September 16, 1969.[32] During these years, the family became one among many criteria for the redistribution of resources among social classes.[33]

The evolution of family policy during this period can also be apprehended through the new types of family benefits set up at that time. On December 23, 1970, for example, the government implemented an *allocation d'orphelin,* which, as its name indicates, was meant to help parents

---

30. In *Le Monde,* April 3, 1960. This report was also published in the journal *Pour la Vie* (March 1962).

31. Susanna Magri, *Logement et reproduction de l'exploitation: Les politiques étatiques du logement en France (1947–1972)* (Centre de sociologie urbaine, 1977).

32. Laroque and Lenoir, *La politique familiale,* 23; Antoine Prost, "L'évolution de la politique familiale en France de 1938 à 1981," *Le Mouvement Social* 129 (1984), 20.

33. Lenoir develops this argument in *Généalogie,* 460.

THE "QUIET REVOLUTION" IN FAMILY POLICY LAW   153

raising orphaned children. More to the point, the allocation targeted single parents—divorced, widowed, or simply unmarried—who had become more prominent and visible throughout French society.[34] This was a long step away from the kind of family that the nineteenth-century familialists had had in mind when they defended the interests of the *familles nombreuses.* Similarly, a benefit for handicapped children was passed on July 13, 1971, indicating that physical handicaps were considered a legitimate category for wealth redistribution, and also highlighting the shift from a family policy to a policy of child support. Along similar lines, the most crucial reform, passed on January 3, 1972, concerned the *allocation de salaire unique* or single salary subsidy. Originally, this was a benefit set up to help families in which the mother chose to stay at home; the amount attributed to this particular benefit had been on a steady decline since its creation, but the 1972 law abolished it altogether.[35] It was replaced by an *allocation pour frais de garde,* which could be translated as a "childcare benefit," for families and working mothers. This benefit was reserved for families earning less than a specific threshold. The government, it seemed, had switched its focus from the ideal of the housewife or *femme au foyer,* championed by the early familialists and by Vichy, to the figure of the working mother in the new social, political, and economic landscape.

A New Legal Paradigm

The new demographic and political contexts in France contributed to redefining family policy in the sixties and seventies, but it was the various social changes occurring during those years that affected the family in the most profound ways, in particular the so-called sexual revolution. The legalization of contraception in 1967 (the loi Neuwirth) and abortion in 1975 (the loi Veil) significantly contributed to the dissociation of sexuality from reproduction.[36] So did feminism. The Mouvement de libération des femmes

---

34. In 1975, for example, the French census counted more around 706,000 women raising children on their own. In Laroque and Lenoir, *La politique familiale,* 27. On July 9, 1976, the *allocation d'orphelin* became the *allocation de parent isolé,* a name that reflected its true purpose more adequately.

35. See Prost, "L'évolution de la politique familiale," 19.

36. The loi Neuwirth was named after Lucien Neuwirth, the representative who proposed the contraception bill. The loi Veil referred to the minister of health at the time, Simone Veil, who endorsed the decriminalization of abortion. The bibliography on both topics is extensive. See for example Chaperon, *Les années Beauvoir;* Gisèle Halimi, *La cause des femmes* (Grasset, 1973); Jean-Yves Le Naour and Catherine Valenti, *Histoire de l'avortement: XIXe–XXe siècle* (Seuil, 2003); Mossuz-

154   **CHAPTER 4**

(MLF), born in 1970, presented contraception and abortion as strategies for achieving equality between men and women. In their public protests and publications, the theme of nonreproductive sexuality was prominent.[37] As we will see in the next chapter, the Front homosexuel d'action révolution-naire (FHAR) created in 1971 also contributed to the critique of the nu-clear family. On a more general level, May '68 (which had inspired both the MLF and the FHAR) brought "sexual liberation" to the forefront of public life, by presenting it as one of the key components of the revolution.[38] Re-lationships between children and adults were also changing during this time. In challenging de Gaulle and the "fascistic" structures of power, the students involved in May '68 claimed to be challenging their fathers and authority more generally. Young people were having sex earlier, and the family was no longer the only model to encompass sexual relations.[39] Furthermore, more children were born out of wedlock. The "couple"—celebrated in litera-ture, the press, and the cinema of the time, as Kristin Ross has persuasively shown—was slowly replacing the "family" as the privileged unit of the French modernized middle class.[40]

As this sexual revolution was changing practices and mores, the law ap-peared antiquated in many domains, particularly in the field of family law, still governed by the 1804 Civil Code. Several administrations—particularly during the Third Republic—debated reforming the more outdated clauses of the Civil Code, but none really did. Among the most important changes in the field of family law was the 1884 loi Naquet legalizing divorce, which had been outlawed in 1816 as part of the Restoration's desire to overturn the

---

Lavau, *Les lois de l'amour;* Françoise Picq, *Libération des femmes: Les années-mouvement* (Seuil, 1993); Evelyne Sullerot, *Le grand remue-ménage: La crise de la famille* (Fayard, 1997).

37. In her memoirs/history of the MLF, Françoise Picq recounts an amusing song that the MLF sang, supposedly for Michel Debré, the minister of war at the time and, as we have seen, a very im-portant figure within French familialism: "Debré, nous n'te ferons plus d'enfants. Non, non, non, non . . . Pour faire de la chair à canon, Non, non, non . . . S'abrutir à la production, Oh non! Et vive la contraception . . . Plus jamais ne nous marions, Non, non, non, non . . . Ne restons plus à la maison, Non, non, non, non . . . Leur amour c'est comme une prison, Oh non! Faisons des fêtes et des chansons . . ." The main MLF journal, *Le Torchon Brûle,* also offers numerous examples of car-toons, artwork, and articles urging women to choose not to have children.

38. We can note the sexual nature of some of the students' most famous slogans, for example: "The more I make love, the more I want to make the revolution"; "Invent new sexual perversions"; "My desires are reality," or else "I come in the cobblestones [*je jouis dans les pavés*]."

39. On the youth and sex, see Mossuz-Lavau, *Les lois de l'amour,* chap. 3. See also Jobs, *Riding the New Wave;* Weiner, *Enfants Terribles.*

40. See Ross, *Fast Cars,* part 3.

THE "QUIET REVOLUTION" IN FAMILY POLICY LAW   155

revolution's heritage.[41] A series of scattered reforms followed, including one on marriage in 1907, on paternity in 1912, and on adoption in 1923, but none of these were particularly consequential.[42] Moreover, several laws were passed outside the Civil Code's contours, often resulting in immediate contradictions with some of the premises of the Code. Even the crucial 1939 Family Code was only partly integrated into the Civil Code. As a result, many jurists and elected representatives insisted on the need to conduct an in-depth revision of the Napoleonic Code. In 1901, the Société d'études legislatives began such a project, but it was never finalized. After the Liberation, a committee of twelve jurists headed by Léon Julliot de la Morandière tried to take over the task, but with no success.[43]

It was not until the Fifth Republic that the Civil Code was considerably modified, under the impetus of the minister of justice Jean Foyer, who claimed to want to "rejuvenate the law and family law,"[44] and Jean Carbonnier, a professor of law and dean at the Sorbonne from 1955 to 1976. Legal historians have attributed the success of these reforms to two main factors. On a methodological level, the legal changes were incorporated into the existing structure of the Code, following what jurists called a "grafting method," hence without affecting the Code's foundational form. On a theoretical level, the fact that Carbonnier oversaw all these reforms gave them a conceptual unity, an overall coherence that they might not have had otherwise.

In this sense, a closer look at Carbonnier's legal philosophy can shed some light on the family law reforms that took place between 1964 and 1975. One of the most important and persuasive arguments for modifying family law by the 1960s was the increasingly pronounced discrepancy between the Code's formal legal paradigm and the social practices in the wake of the sexual revolution. As Senator Jean Conedera expressed it in 1959, "The Napoleonic Code, which has lasted one hundred and fifty years, is no longer in harmony with the mores of modern economy."[45] Carbonnier appeared to share this point of view. As he explained in an retrospective interview, "in

---

41. For more on the loi Naquet, see Edward Berenson, "The Politics of Divorce in France of the Belle Epoque: The Case of Joseph and Henriette Caillaux," *American Historical Review* 93, no. 1 (1988).

42. For the details of these reforms, see Rachel Ginnis Fuchs, *Contested Paternity: Constructing Families in Modern France* (Johns Hopkins University Press, 2008).

43. For a summary of the proposed reforms, see the newspaper *Combat,* April 12, 1960.

44. Jean Carbonnier, *Droit et passion du droit: Sous la Ve République* (Flammarion, 1996), 196.

45. Cited in the newspaper *L'Aurore,* October 23, 1959.

156   **CHAPTER 4**

the field of civil law . . . [and] more specifically in the field of family law, it seemed to me that a certain evolution of mores had occurred and that our legislation needed to account for it."[46] Similarly, in his *Essais sur les lois* published in 1978, Carbonnier wrote that "the family law reforms only adapted civil law to the change of mores" and that "the new mores [were] reflected in the new law"—or, in his famous maxim, "to each his family, to each his law [*à chacun sa famille, à chacun son droit*]."[47] In order to best account for and incorporate this "evolution of mores" into the law, Carbonnier and his team conducted a series of surveys, polls, and data-gathering initiatives to orient their analyses and recommendations before submitting them to the executive branch.[48] As the legal historian Jacqueline Rubellin-Devichi confirms, "All the [family law] reforms, except the one concerning adoption, were preceded by surveys which revealed how much people's opinions had changed."[49]

Carbonnier's interest in sociological fieldwork appeared to fit particularly well with his legal philosophy, commonly referred to as "juridical sociology."[50] In very broad terms, juridical sociology proposed to use the methodological tools provided by sociology to analyze legal principles. Laws varied according to time and place; they were, in other words, historical and historicizable.[51] In a collection of interviews published in the 1990s, Carbonnier explained that he began to think about the relation between the law and history very early on while he was still in law school, particularly after reading Lévy-Bruhl and Durkheim who inspired him to ponder the relation

---

46. Simona Andrini and André-Jean Arnaud, *Jean Carbonnier, Renato Treves et la sociologie du droit: Archéologie d'une discipline* (LGDJ, 1995), 34.

47. Jean Carbonnier, *Essais sur les lois* (Répertoire du notariat defrénois, 1978), 169, 170, 262, 167.

48. Andrini and Arnaud, *Jean Carbonnier,* 34–35.

49. Jacqueline Rubellin-Devichi, *L'évolution du statut civil de la famille depuis 1945* (Éditions du Centre national de la recherche scientifique, 1983), 20. In 1968, Carbonnier created a new center, the Laboratoire de sociologie juridique, over which he presided and which supervised these sociological surveys and polls. For a historical analysis of opinion polls during this period, see Jon Cowans, "Wielding the People: Opinion Polls and the Problem of Legitimacy in France since 1944" (Ph.D. diss., Stanford University, 1994).

50. See Jean Carbonnier, *Sociologie juridique* (Presses universitaires de France, 1978). For more on Carbonnier's legal philosophy, see Carbonnier, *Essais sur les lois,* and *Flexible droit: Textes pour une sociologie du droit sans rigueur* (Librairie générale de droit et de jurisprudence, 1969). See also the introductions to Carbonnier's *Écrits* (Presses universitaires de France, 2008), and Association Henri Capitant, ed., *Hommage à Jean Carbonnier* (Dalloz, 2007).

51. Although it may seem a large historical and geographical stretch, it might be interesting to compare Carbonnier's *Sociologie juridique* with the American Legal Realism movement, which attempted to reorient the law toward empiricism and the social sciences. See, for instance, John Henry Schlegel, *American Legal Realism and Empirical Social Science* (University of North Carolina Press, 1995).

THE "QUIET REVOLUTION" IN FAMILY POLICY LAW   157

between abstract universal norms and sociologically specific evidence.[52] These theoretical concerns drove Carbonnier to specialize in civil law, which, he claimed, could "only be understood by legal scholars."[53] It was in this context that Carbonnier turned to family law, particularly in his doctoral thesis which focused on matrimonial regimes. His thesis, Carbonnier claimed, "had a very important historical dimension. I was very interested in history, and after all, history is an aspect of sociology."[54]

Carbonnier's legal vision has been the subject of some debate in recent years. Many understood his enigmatic formulas as arguing for the fundamental relativity of the law, a relativity that would prevent it from making any transhistorical or universal pronouncements. Others, however, including sociologist Irène Théry and legal scholar Catherine Labrusse-Riou, have sought to "rescue" his thought, claiming instead that Carbonnier was careful to preserve the delicate balance between "legal pluralism" and "the fundamental principles of the law."[55] According to Théry, it was the legislators who misinterpreted Carbonnier's thought and pushed his reforms toward "legal pluralism," of which both Théry and Labrusse-Riou are critical. In Théry's terms, despite what many believe, Carbonnier never "renounced the law." Based on Carbonnier's writings and interviews, however, it seems fair to suggest that he ascribed a rather limited role to the law as a discipline and to the legal scholar as a political figure, especially compared with other legal thinkers who have, since then, intervened in family law.

In contrast to the legal experts examined in Chapter 6, Carbonnier never proposed a "global theory of society."[56] In his mind, the jurist's responsibility was "not to extract a norm suspended in the social environment, but rather to guarantee that the norm, wherever it comes from, is not a foreign body within the social environment."[57] As one of Carbonnier's interviewers summarized it, "The sociological jurist [like Carbonnier] seems to be . . . the one who tries to best integrate the contemporary facts of social, political, and economic life of the system in which he participates into the science of law. He does not present himself as a technician of law, but as an artisan of

---

52. Andrini and Arnaud, *Jean Carbonnier,* 27. This is confirmed in Carbonnier's autobiographical essay in Carbonnier, *Écrits.*

53. Andrini and Arnaud, *Jean Carbonnier,* 31.

54. Ibid., 29.

55. Irène Théry, *Le démariage: Justice et vie privée* (Odile Jacob, 1993), 116. Her analysis of Carbonnier is pp. 97–117. For Labrusse-Riou's position, see her introduction in Carbonnier, *Écrits,* 41–43.

56. Andrini and Arnaud, *Jean Carbonnier,* 33.

57. Ibid., 72.

158   **CHAPTER 4**

pragmatism."[58] According to the legal scholar Catherine Labrusse-Riou, Carbonnier's approach to the family marked a decisive step in the history of French law because it "profoundly modified the classical principles of legal interpretation. The law was no longer satisfied by strict and sole exegesis. It required more imagination and intelligence in order to allow it to constantly adapt to the social and ideological evolution of contemporary families."[59]

The first major family law reform undertaken by Carbonnier concerned Title X of the Civil Code's First Book, on guardianship: "*De la tutelle.*" Enacted on December 14, 1964, the law established the conditions of guardianship for a child whose parents had died while he was still a minor or a child whose parents had abused him or failed to provide for him adequately. His well-being but also the administration of his patrimony would be entrusted to a guardian (if the parents had previously designated one) or to a family council composed of four or five family members appointed by a judge. The entire process would be overseen by a judge.[60] A few years later, on January 3, 1968, the government added another clause to the section on guardianship, this time concerning adults (the legal age of majority was, at the time, twenty-one) lacking capacity. The 1964 law was important because it sought to correct some of the historical injustices of the previous guardianship laws in favor of children and women, who had often suffered under the prior system.[61] The 1964 reform had, however, another consequence, which might have been tangential but which had a crucial significance: for the first time, the law recognized the existence of a "natural family" as opposed to the "legitimate family."[62] As such, it presented the first breach in the Republican social/sexual order established with the Civil Code, which, as we saw in the first chapter, rested on the notion of legitimacy.

---

58. Ibid., 12. In this context, it is interesting to note that the author of this book attributes Carbonnier's "pragmatism" to his Protestantism (ibid., 90). Of course, pragmatism is also a form of political intervention but one that is sometimes seen as more "neutral." On Carbonnier's complicated relationship to religion, see Judith Surkis, "Hymenal Politics: Marriage, Secularism, and French Sovereignty," *Public Culture* 22, no. 3 (2010): 548–50.

59. Catherine Labrusse-Riou, *Droit de la famille; 1. Les personnes* (Masson, 1984), 30–31.

60. See ibid., 407–11.

61. For an example of how the system of guardianship could work to the detriment of women in the late nineteenth century, see Sylvia Schafer, "Between Paternal Right and the Dangerous Mother: Reading Parental Responsibility in Nineteenth-Century French Civil Justice," *Journal of Family History* 23, no. 2 (1998): 178.

62. Carbonnier, *Droit et passion du droit,* 201.

THE "QUIET REVOLUTION" IN FAMILY POLICY LAW   159

In 1966, legislators tackled the laws on adoption that had been obsolete for many decades.[63] In 1804 and throughout the nineteenth century, adoption served primarily as a conduit for inheritance. It offered childless individuals the possibility of arranging the transmission of their estate to the person of their choice. As a result, adoption was an extremely long and convoluted process, subject to all kinds of restrictions, and ultimately remained quite uncommon. Adoptees had to be over twenty-one (the age of majority), and adopters over fifty. Adopters could not have previous children or legitimate heirs. In the 1920s, partly in reaction to World War I which had left thousands of children orphaned, the law was changed to permit the adoption of minors. In 1939, in the context of the Code de la famille, the *légitimation adoptive,* which allowed children born out of wedlock to become legitimate, was set in place, but the adoptive parents had to be married.[64] Finally, on July 11, 1966, a new adoption law was passed. It was designed to liberalize the adoption process by expanding the categories of those legally allowed to adopt children, adding to married couples, single individuals, and married individuals who had received the consent of their spouse. The law also replaced the *légitimation adoptive* with two types of adoption: *adoption plénière,* which gave adopted children the same rights as legitimate children and erased all legal ties between the child and the birthparents; and *adoption simple,* which "added" the filiation of the adoptive parents to that of the birthparents and transferred parental authority to the adoptive couple.[65] The 1966 law constituted yet another strike against the system of legitimacy, which appeared increasingly outdated in both the legal and the social realms.

The parliamentary debates around the 1966 law also reveal the importance of history for the legal reforms. For instance, elected representatives regularly referred to the controversy surrounding the *affaire Novack,* which

---

63. Unlike the other laws of the period, the adoption law was not actually redacted by Carbonnier despite the fact that it was conceived in the "same spirit" as the other laws. See Jacques Commaille and Marie-Pierre Marmier-Champenois, "Sociologie de la création de la norme: L'exemple de changements législatifs intervenus en droit de la famille," in *La création du droit: Aspects sociaux* (Éditions du Centre national de la recherche scientifique, 1981), 143.

64. For a short history of the adoption law reform, see ibid., 147; Labrusse-Riou, *Droit de la famille,* 169–70. For more on the longer history of adoption legislation in France, see Marcela Iacub, *L'empire du ventre: Pour une autre histoire de la maternité* (Fayard, 2004), 132; Bruno Perreau, *Penser l'adoption: La gouvernance pastorale du genre* (Presses universitaires de France, 2012), 20–24.

65. See Perreau, *Penser l'adoption,* 192; Janine Revel, *La filiation* (Presses universitaires de France, 1998), chap. 3.

160   CHAPTER 4

captivated the media, the courts, and many political figures for over a decade. The case involved a dispute between the biological parents of Didier Novack, who had been given up for adoption at birth in 1954, and his adoptive parents. Novack's biological mother was unmarried at the time she put up her son for adoption The biological father did recognize the child but his "recognition" did not carry any legal weight because he was not married to the child's mother. The biological parents eventually married and sought to regain custody of their child who had, by then, been placed with an adoptive family. The case bounced from court to court—and the child from family to family—until the *cour de cassation*—France's highest court for civil disputes—awarded custody of Didier to his adoptive family in 1964. Several politicians—including the prime minister Edgar Faure—intervened in the *affaire Novack* in favor of the "natural parents" and deplored the unfairness of the legal system of legitimation.[66] Family law, they contended, appeared increasingly incongruous with the realities of the time.

It was the 1972 "law on filiation," however, that constituted the final blow to the Napoleonic Code's concept of legitimacy and the sexual regime it had inaugurated. The January 3, 1972, *réforme de la filiation* was designed to put an end to all legal distinctions between legitimate and natural children.[67] The point of the reform was not only to "allow truth to triumph," as Jean Foyer claimed, but also to put an end to the inequalities and legal discrimination that children born out of wedlock had historically faced. The 1972 law was very much in line with the other Carbonnier reforms. It was also the culmination of the gradual integration of "natural children" into legality. On March 25, 1896, for instance, a decree raised a natural child's inheritance from a third to a half. Another statute on July 2, 1907, allowed a natural child's birthparents to exercise their authority—or *puissance paternelle*—on their child, a privilege that had been limited to legitimate parents until then. Similarly, when family benefits were discussed in the Code de la famille, it was decided that natural children should receive the same state benefits as legitimate children. According to Marcela Iacub, the 1972 law was particularly important because it "put an end to the empire of matrimonial appearances" by favoring biology and truth

---

66. Perreau, *Penser l'adoption*, 22–24.

67. For a detailed analysis of the 1972 law, see Claude Colombet, *La filiation légitime et naturelle: Étude de la loi du 3 janvier 1972 et de son interprétation* (Dalloz, 1977); Fuchs, *Contested Paternity*, 260–64. And for a summary of the kinds of theoretical questions that the law inspired, see Labrusse-Riou, *Droit de la famille*, 88–89.

THE "QUIET REVOLUTION" IN FAMILY POLICY LAW   161

over marriage and contract.[68] The 1972 law, Iacub argues, inaugurated the shift from the *mariage-ventre* system (or marriage-belly) to the *ventre-chair* (or flesh-belly) paradigm.[69] Another way to put this would be to suggest that with the 1972 law the biological, the empirical, and the historical began to trump the normative, the universal, and the symbolic in the field of family law.

This tension between the normative and the historical was particularly evident in the parliamentary debates that preceded the 1972 law.[70] When the advocates of the new law defended their bill, most of them began by emphasizing the contradictions between the state of the law and the state of society. As Jean Foyer put it, "The prodigious evolution of ideas and customs sweeping our time have made these legislative antiquities and old-fashioned juridical procedures seem intolerable were we to continue to enforce them. If we were to choose to maintain their validity without being able to use them because of their desuetude, they are derisory."[71] Similarly, René Pleven asserted,

> Much too often, the ideas of the Civil Code led to a valorization of the legal family at the expense of the real family, and to the juridical attachment of the child to people who were not his real parents or the ones who raised him. No one, I think, would deny that we have here a source of confusion for the child and for the parents, a cause for maladjustment, and all in all, a danger for society. Our project, more humane and more realistic, will prevent the crystallization of a number of pathological situations that have resulted from the defense of a family which no longer exists.[72]

---

68. Iacub, *L'empire du ventre*, 151.

69. Ibid., 191. Iacub's book is a polemic against feminism, which she blames for introducing these notions of truth, biology, and nature into the law. In this context, Iacub turns to the Civil Code's notion of filiation, which she argues was truly "constructionist" (the term she uses is "political") because it allowed women to raise children that they had not given birth to (women who "supposed" a child, for example). More generally, her goal is to promote what she calls a positivistic or liberal understanding of the law, one in which the individual will and freedom can play a central role. Her book is also a response to the recent legal thinkers in France who have insisted on the "anthropological function of the law," particularly in the domain of family law. On this, see Camille Robcis, "French Sexual Politics from Human Rights to the Anthropological Function of the Law," *French Historical Studies* 33, no. 1 (2010).

70. Débats parlementaires, October 5, 1971, esp. 4281.

71. Jean Foyer in Débats parlementaires, October 5, 1971, 4272.

72. René Pleven in Débats parlementaires, October 5, 1971, 4282.

162   **CHAPTER 4**

In the words of the minister of justice, the 1972 laws were "a text of social justice" to "promote a new society, more humane, and more just."[73] Or, as Jean Foyer had declared in 1965, "We should return to the idea, both sensible and simple, that filiation is first and foremost a fact, a physiological reality. Is it not somewhat abusive to let this fact depend exclusively on the will, either of the parents, or even of the child?"[74]

Carbonnier also redacted a series of laws that revolutionized the field of marriage law. The first, enacted on July 13, 1965, specified the respective rights and duties of spouses within marriage. This reform was designed to grant more independence to each spouse, especially to women who depended on their husbands for many of the most common everyday activities such as opening a bank account, signing a contract, or appearing in court. The law insisted on the equality of the spouses in the administration of their joint patrimony and put forward the notion of "family interests" as the guiding principle behind marriage.[75] As the minister of justice Jean Foyer summarized it, "In practice, and especially in cases where the wife has a separate profession, the matter is in actuality very close to a jointly acquired property regime. In effect, community ownership (or usufruct) rights over movable goods are suspended. Each spouse can administer and dispose of their own goods, and the wife can administer and dispose of her immovable property."[76] In the case of a separation, each spouse would keep his or her own property and divide the goods acquired during the marriage, in a legal arrangement called a *séparation des biens avec société d'acquêts* as opposed to *séparation des biens avec communauté*. As the parliamentary debates around this marriage reform made clear, and as the press echoed, the 1965 law responded primarily to practical necessities affecting women's lives. This explains why being able to open a bank account became such a highly symbolic act. As Jean Foyer contended, the 1965 marriage law sought to "decolonize the married woman."[77]

---

73. René Pleven, Garde des sceaux, in Débats parlementaires, October 5, 1971, 4293.

74. Jean Foyer, "Notre République," Septembre 24, 1965, cited in Iacub, *L'empire du ventre*, 21.

75. Labrusse-Riou, *Droit de la famille*, 230. See also Denis Périer-Daville, "En France, à partir du 1er février, la femme devient juridiquement l'égale de son mari," *Le Figaro*, January 29, 1966; and Claire Barsal's interview of Jean Foyer, "Consacrer l'égalité de l'homme et de la femme dans le mariage," *Notre République*, March 19, 1965.

76. Débats parlementaires, cited in André Colomer, "Le nouveau régime matrimonial légal en France," *Revue Internationale de Droit Comparé* 18, no. 1 (1966), 62.

77. Much can be said about this expression. It is interesting, for instance, to compare it with the catchphrase popularized by Henri Lefebvre and the Situationists in the 1960s: "the colonization of everyday life." Kristin Ross mentions this as an example of the "various ways in which the practice

THE "QUIET REVOLUTION" IN FAMILY POLICY LAW   163

This "decolonization of the married woman" continued with the June 4, 1970, reform of the Civil Code's First Book's Title IX, replacing the concept of "paternal power" by that of "parental authority."[78] The law attributed the legal authority over children to both parents, conferring it solely to the mother if she was not married. In addition, the revised notion of parental authority was exclusively defined around the interests of the child: "The authority belongs to the father and the mother to protect the child in his security, his health, and his morality" (Article 371–2). The 1970 law reinforced the 1889 disposition on the *déchéance de l'autorité* (or loss of authority) by allowing the courts to intervene if a parent abused his or her power.[79] Once again, this reform was presented as being in accordance with the times and as the logical evolution of the campaign for women's rights since 1945. As André Tisserand affirmed in his presentation of the law before the General Assembly, after women had been granted the right to vote in 1945 and been given the right to administer their property within marriage in 1965, this 1970 law represented a logical step in the struggle of women to gain full political equality: "It is good to write down and to say to young couples about to get married, standing at dawn in front of a state official, that the woman is now equal to her husband and that it will be her task to find, with him, the conditions under which she can exercise this right."[80]

Once again, the main justifications put forward by promoters of the law relied on sociological facts that highlighted the flagrant contradictions between law and social reality. One deputy pointed to the fact that women were as important as men in society, citing the example of the most recent *major à l'ENA* (the number-one ranked student graduating from the ENA)

---

of colonialism outlived its history" and in which France "brought home" colonialism. For Ross, this expression typifies the interconnectedness of modernization and decolonization, a process that Ross's book wants to bring to light (see *Fast Cars,* 7). The fact that Jean Foyer would use the rhetoric of decolonization to address sexual modernization could be seen as further evidence for Ross's thesis. We might also think here of Todd Shepard's critique of the discourse that presented decolonization as an effect of the "tide of history," which served as a tool to depoliticize colonialism and colonial racism. Similarly, the "decolonization of the married woman" would offer a way to avoid addressing the specific nature of the Civil Code's sexism. See Todd Shepard, *The Invention of Decolonization: The Algerian War and the Remaking of France* (Cornell University Press, 2006).

78. For the history of paternal authority, see Jean Delumeau and Daniel Roche, *Histoire des pères et de la paternité* (Larousse, 2000), 382–83. The shift from *power* to *authority* was also significant in light of the May '68 contestation of power.

79. For the details of the law, see Labrusse-Riou, *Droit de la famille,* 266–98.

80. *Débats parlementaires,* April 7–8, 1970, 808–809. A summary of these debates can also be found in *Le Monde,* April 10, 1970, 6.

164   CHAPTER 4

being a woman.[81] Another deputy argued that "there [was] a discordance between the evolution of ideas and lifestyles and the texts that regulated family law."[82] Similarly, René Pleven claimed that once the law was passed, the sharing of parental authority would be "immediate, since, for almost all parents, the fact has preceded the law."[83] It is also interesting in this context to pause over the objections put forward by the law's opposing side, as most of them emphasized the difference between the "fundamental principles of the law" (presented as fixed, transcendent, and derived from Christian values) and mores or "legal pluralism." As one deputy, Pierre Mazeaud, claimed,

> By replacing paternal power by parental authority . . . we want to fundamentally change the organization of the family as it has been established by our positive law imbued with the Christian idea that the wife, in association with her husband, allows the latter to exercise authority in regard to children . . . Do not accuse me of anti-feminism. It would be a mistake. But realize that this project risks aggravating the dissolution of the family which is still the basic cell of all of society . . . The family must have a direction, a leader capable of taking all decisions that impose themselves in the common interest of its members . . . The notion of paternal power, as it results from the laws currently active, answers to this necessary organization of the family.[84]

Likewise, for Michel de Grailly, another representative challenging the law, "the function of the law is not to enunciate doctrinal affirmations but to fix norms of positive law."[85]

This debate around the function of the law, its political applications, and its relation to norms, social customs, and history was prolonged a few years later in the context of the last of Carbonnier's family law revisions: the July 11, 1975, reform of divorce. Carbonnier had begun revising the law in 1973, at the request of Pompidou's last minister of justice, Jean Taittinger. Pompidou's unexpected death in 1974 delayed the project, which then passed on to the next president, Valéry Giscard d'Estaing. The main accomplishment of the 1975 law was to simplify divorce procedures and to introduce the notion of no-fault divorce. In place of the *divorce pour faute,* which until 1975

---

81. Débats parlementaires, April 7–8, 1970, 816.

82. Ibid., 811. Thome-Patrenôtre also cites "sociological studies" to make her case.

83. Ibid., 849.

84. Ibid., 813.

85. Ibid., 858.

THE "QUIET REVOLUTION" IN FAMILY POLICY LAW   165

had been the only legally valid way to obtain a marriage annulment, the new law instituted three categories of divorce: by mutual consent (*sur demande conjointe*); demanded by one party and accepted by the other, and for "a break in common life" (*rupture de la vie commune*). The *divorce pour faute,* applicable in cases of adultery, for example, was retained after considerable debate. The Left in particular objected to the "hypocrisy" of such a provision.[86]

Once again, it was the discrepancy between social practices and the active legal texts that appeared to be at the origin of the legal reform. As representative Georges Donnez claimed in his presentation of the bill, "In the last couple of years, countries whose traditions and cultures are similar to ours have already reformed their divorce laws. As such, we needed to ask ourselves whether our laws were in harmony with the customs and aspirations of the country."[87] Similarly, a representative from the Left, André Chandernagor stated, "The project comes to recognize belatedly but positively what the evolution of customs and the good will of jurisprudence have recognized for a long time."[88] Finally, the minister of justice, Jean Lecanuet, relied on statistics and sociological evidence to defend the law.[89] And, like the other Carbonnier family law reforms, the divorce proposition was preceded by much data gathering. In particular, the government relied on a survey run by the INED that indicated that 89 percent of the French population favored a simplification of divorce procedures.[90]

On the right, opponents of the law such as Jean Fontaine lamented the "ruin of society" that would ensue from this "de-dramatization" of divorce: it would constitute a "new step toward a generalized moral mediocrity, under the excuse of adapting legislation to the demands of our time, in the view that law should follow fact."[91] Jean Foyer, who paradoxically enough had, a few years earlier, orchestrated the filiation reform, was among the most vocal opponents of the new law, which he described as an effect of the "unbridled liberalism" plaguing French society:

Its avowed ambition to adapt the law to customs—to customs that are thankfully only those of a minority of French people—testifies to a

---

86. For the different types of divorce, see Labrusse-Riou, *Droit de la famille,* 327–54.

87. Cited in Théry, *Le démariage,* 83.

88. Cited ibid., 88.

89. Ibid., 86.

90. For more on the sociological data gathering around divorce, see Commaille and Marmier-Champenois, "Sociologie."

91. Cited in Théry, *Le démariage,* 93.

166   **CHAPTER 4**

curious evolution of legislative philosophy. In matters of divorce, as in many other domains, is the legislator's mission no longer to declare legal what ought to be, but simply to declare just what is? From the law as a more or less imperfect, awkward, or inexact translation of natural law, we are asked to move to this notion of a law-assessment that legitimizes the practices revealed by juridical sociology . . . It is not my confessional convictions that urge me to say this at the podium, it is my conscience as a legislator: the unbridled liberalism that our recent laws have made even freer is starting to lead us to the suicide of the French nation through depopulation. As statistics will soon show, the weakening of the institution of marriage can only accelerate this movement. We will therefore have no reason to take pride in voting a text which, like divorce itself, will only be the statement of a failure.[92]

In the end, the law that was passed constituted a compromise. As Jean Lecanuet described it, it offered "a balance between the principles to which the majority of French people remain attached and the evolution of opinion and customs, an evolution upon which we can pronounce a value judgment but which is a fact the legislator must confront."[93]

According to the contemporary sociologist Irène Théry, the 1960s and 1970s marked a transition from a "normative logic to a social logic."[94] As we saw in Chapter 1, the architects of the 1804 Civil Code were indeed deeply invested in a normative framing of the family as the transhistorical and universal root of the social. By historicizing the Civil Code and adapting it to the "new social mores," the family as an institution could suddenly be historicized. As Théry argues, the 1975 divorce law highlighted the normative impasse facing French politics after the sixties, and especially, after 1968. The Right, Théry tells us, opposed the law because of its obstinate refusal to even consider the impact that history and social evolution had on legal norms. The response of the Left, however, was equally disappointing in Théry's eyes. Because the Left could only understand the law in negative terms, as

---

92. Cited ibid., 94. It is interesting in this context to compare the recurrent references to Carbonnier's Protestant background to Foyer's fervent Catholicism (he is, for instance, a member of the Vatican-sponsored antiabortion group Pro Vita), which clearly informs his politics and his legal thinking. In an interview with *Le Figaro*, Foyer claimed that in modern law "the Catholic tradition has given way to the Protestant one" (*Le Figaro*, August 9, 1988, cited ibid.). As Judith Surkis has shown, Carbonnier's divorce reform was in fact the product of a complex negotiation with religion and canon law. See Surkis, "Hymenal Politics," 548–50.

93. Cited in Théry, *Le démariage*, 95.

94. Ibid., 91.

THE "QUIET REVOLUTION" IN FAMILY POLICY LAW

an instrument of domination, it chose to "abandon the law" altogether. Thus, Théry suggests, neither camp was able to offer an adequate "third way" to think about the foundations of legal and social norms, and by extension, to think the foundations of the social.[95] Hence, according to Théry: "The aspiration toward more freedom and authenticity which were at the origin of the privatization of marriage did not in any way lead to the development of new symbolic reference points, to greater equality, freedom, and justice, or to a heightened sense of human existence. Instead, they appear to have dissolved into the grey wash of the increasingly administrative normalization of private life."[96] Finally, Théry concludes, "One of the most profound paradoxes of this era of *unmarriage [démariage]*, which began producing its full effects at the turning point of the 1970s–1980s, is that it demands a reconstruction in other terms of symbolic and legal reference, at the very moment when we are turning away from the law."[97] It is precisely the search for this "alternative symbolic and legal reference" to regulate public and private life, both the family and the social, that the next two chapters seek to elucidate.

---

95. Ibid., 119–21.

96. Ibid., 125.

97. Ibid. Théry uses the expression *démariage* (as opposed to divorce) to insist on the symbolic importance of marriage for the structure of society. The *démariage* is not the end of marriage but its new social configuration (ibid., 15).

❧ CHAPTER 5

Fatherless Societies and Anti-Oedipal Philosophies

During the 1960s and 1970s, the law was not the only domain that questioned the legal fiction of paternity or used the family to rethink social norms. The idea that a critique of the nuclear heterosexual family would lead to a more forceful *social* critique was certainly not specific to France. In West Germany, the New Left embraced the "sexual revolution," which they argued would protect their country against the resurgence of fascism.[1] For these German '68ers, there was no doubt that sexuality and politics were intimately and causally connected. Around this time, in the United States, several women who had grown increasingly dissatisfied with both the sexual conservatism of the New Left and the limited demands of second-wave feminism organized in groups under the banner of "radical feminism." The oppression of women, they argued, was not merely a symptom of capitalist exploitation that would naturally disappear with the advent of a socialist revolution, nor would it be solved by giving women full access to the public sphere as second-wave feminists such as Betty Friedan had contended. Instead, feminism needed to better understand the construction of gender

---

1. For an excellent analysis of the complicated ways in which the Left in Germany negotiated sexuality and the memory of fascism in the 1960s and 1970s, see Dagmar Herzog, *Sex after Fascism: Memory and Morality in Twentieth-Century Germany* (Princeton University Press, 2005), esp. chap. 4. See also Klaus Theweleit, *Male Fantasies* (University of Minnesota Press, 1987).

168

FATHERLESS SOCIETIES AND ANTI-OEDIPAL PHILOSOPHIES   169

(although they tended to use the term "sexual function" instead) and the operation of social and sexual norms in order to dismantle them. In this context, the family appeared to provide a particularly fruitful terrain. In her 1970 *Dialectic of Sex,* for example, the radical feminist Shulamith Firestone called for the elimination of the family structure, "the vinculum through which the psychology of power can be smuggled."[2]

In France, the intellectual critique of the family in the seventies also came from the Left and from feminism, but it was articulated somewhat differently than in Germany or the United States. Indeed, I would argue that many French thinkers of the time elaborated their critique of the family and of the prevailing social order through a critique of structuralism, and more specifically, a critique of what I have been calling the "structuralist social contract" of Lévi-Strauss and Lacan. As I have suggested so far, the concept of the symbolic—which Lacan had inherited and adapted from Lévi-Strauss— offered structuralism a new way of tying together the subjective, the sexual, and the social, defining all three terms universally, transhistorically, and in relation to a particular ethical and normative framework. As such, a critique of the Lacanian symbolic could theoretically also bring about a critique of the three terms structuring the symbolic: the subjective, the sexual, and the social. This was precisely the point made by several French philosophers of the 1970s, including the three figures I focus on in this chapter: Gilles Deleuze and Félix Guattari, whose collaborative work, *Anti-Oedipus,* appeared in 1972; and Luce Irigaray, who developed this analysis in two of her first published works, *Speculum of the Other Woman* in 1974 and *This Sex Which Is Not One* in 1977. For these thinkers, the critique of the structuralist social contract rooted in the heterosexual family was the condition for producing freer subjects and less authoritarian societies, for developing a new ethics no longer premised on the exchange of women.

The critiques of the symbolic presented by Irigaray, Deleuze, and Guattari were, in many ways, in line with a wider reassessment of structuralism in French philosophy. In 1967, Jacques Derrida published *Of Grammatology,* in which he conducted a meticulous reading of Lévi-Strauss's *Elementary Structures,* particularly of the passage concerning the nature/culture divide. According to Derrida, Lévi-Strauss remained caught within the Western "metaphysics of presence" and "logocentrism," a term Derrida coined to describe this understanding of writing as a mere representation of speech.

---

2. Shulamith Firestone, *The Dialectic of Sex: The Case for Feminist Revolution* (Morrow, 1970). For more on this, see Alice Echols, *Daring to Be Bad: Radical Feminism in America, 1967–1975* (University of Minnesota Press, 1989).

170   **CHAPTER 5**

Moreover, Lévi-Strauss's structuralist system of exchange, anchored on the opposition between nature and culture, and on its corollary, "the Law" or prohibition of incest, provided Derrida with a springboard to critique the inclusions and exclusions central to this philosophical tradition and to introduce his concept of deconstruction. The Lévi-Straussian system of exchange, Derrida concluded, required a transcendental referent, a center, and the series of binary oppositions set up around this center. A year before, in 1966, Michel Foucault had made a similar claim against psychoanalysis and ethnology in *The Order of Things,* accusing these disciplines of relying on a particular historical narrative with a particular causality and humanistic presuppositions. Foucault characterized it as the "a priori of all the sciences of man—those great caesuras, furrows, and dividing-lines which traced man's outline in the Western episteme and made him a possible area of knowledge."[3]

Foucault perfected his critique of the structuralist social and sexual contract in 1976 in the first volume of *The History of Sexuality.* There, he argued that the primary function of the family was to channel sexuality—which, he claimed, naturally operated along "mobile, polymorphous, and contingent techniques of power"—into a system of alliance, "a system of marriage, of fixation and development of kinship ties, of transmission of names and possessions."[4] The family thus "conveys the law and the juridical dimension in the deployment of sexuality; and it conveys the economy of pleasure and the intensity of sensations in the regime of alliance."[5] This premise, Foucault continued, explains a number of conventions and taboos set up around the family, and among them, the obsession with the prohibition of incest:

> If for more than a century the West has displayed such a strong interest in the prohibition of incest, if more or less by common accord it has been seen as a social universal and one of the points through which every society is obliged to pass on the way to becoming a culture, perhaps this is because it was found to be a means of self-defense, not against an incestuous desire, but against the expansion and the implications of this deployment of sexuality which has been set up, but which, among its many benefits, had the disadvantage of ignoring the laws and juridical forms of alliance. By asserting that all societies without exception, and consequently our own, were subject to this rule of rules, one

---

3. Michel Foucault, *The Order of Things: An Archaeology of the Human Sciences,* trans. Alan Sheridan (Vintage Books, 1973), 378.

4. Michel Foucault, *The History of Sexuality,* trans. Robert Hurley (Vintage Books, 1980), 1:106.

5. Ibid., 1:108.

FATHERLESS SOCIETIES AND ANTI-OEDIPAL PHILOSOPHIES 171

guaranteed that this deployment of sexuality . . . would not be able to escape from the grand and ancient system of alliance. Thus the law would be secure, even in the new mechanics of power . . . If one considers the threshold of all culture to be prohibited incest, then sexuality has been, from the dawn of time, under the sway of law and right. By devoting so much effort to an endless reworking of the transcultural theory of the incest taboo, anthropology has proved worthy of the whole modern deployment of sexuality and the theoretical discourses it generates.[6]

After his discussion of anthropology, Foucault turned to psychoanalysis, which he located in the long history of power/knowledge around sex. Despite Freud's original intention to demarcate his new science from neurology and psychiatry, psychoanalysis remained entangled with a similar set of limitations, a continuity that Foucault had already hinted at in his 1961 *Madness and Civilization*. Indeed, psychoanalysis

> rediscovered the law of alliance, the involved workings of marriage and kinship, and incest at the heart of this sexuality, as the principle of its formation and the key to its intelligibility. The guarantee that one would find the parents-children relationship at the root of everyone's sexuality made it possible—even when everything seemed to point to the reverse process—to keep the deployment of sexuality coupled to the system of alliance. There was no risk that sexuality would appear to be by nature, alien to the law: it was constituted only though the law. Parents, do not be afraid to bring your children to analysis: it will teach them that in any case it is you whom they love. Children, you really shouldn't complain that you are not orphans, that you always rediscover in your innermost selves your Object-Mother or the sovereign sign of your Father: it is through them that you gain access to desire.[7]

---

6. Ibid., 1:109. Foucault is referencing Lévi-Strauss directly when he uses expressions such as the "rule of rules" or the "threshold of culture."

7. Ibid., 1:113. Foucault's language would seem to indicate that he is referring to Lacan, especially by insisting on the role of desire, the law, and the sign, even though he never mentions him directly and even though Foucault was often quite close to Lacan intellectually, particularly in his conception of the law as productive. This is confirmed by Jacques-Alain Miller, who claimed that "we cannot understand anything about the *History of Sexuality* if we do not recognize in Foucault not an explanation of Lacan, but an explanation with Lacan." *Michel Foucault, philosophe: Rencontre internationale, Paris, 9, 10, 11 janvier 1988* (Seuil, 1989), 81.

172   **CHAPTER 5**

Louis Althusser had been one of the most enthusiastic supporters of Lacan and of his theories, inviting him to conduct a seminar at the École normale supérieure, and reappropriating many of Lacan's key concepts—particularly around the question of interpellation and subject formation—for his own work.[8] Yet even Althusser was pointing to the limits of the structuralist grid, which could not, according to Althusser, address the problem of ideology. As he asked in a 1969 essay on "Freud and Lacan,"

> How can we rigorously formulate the relation between the formal structure of language, the absolute precondition for the existence and intelligibility of the unconscious, on the one hand, the concrete kinship structures on the other, and finally the concrete ideological formations in which the specific functions implied by the kinship structures (paternity, maternity, childhood) are lived? Is it conceivable that the historical variation of these latter structures (kinship, ideology) might materially affect some or other aspect of the instances isolated by Freud? . . . What relations are there between analytic theory and 1. the historical preconditions of its appearance, and 2. the social preconditions of its application?[9]

For Althusser, "a mass of research remains to be done on these ideological formations" such as paternity, maternity, conjugality, and childhood. This, however, was "a task for historical materialism" and not for psychoanalysis.[10]

Finally, to give one last example, we could mention Robert Castel's 1973 book *Le psychanalysme*. Castel, who was trained as a sociologist and had been very much influenced by Foucault and Bourdieu, coined the term *psychanalysme* to describe the complicity between psychoanalysis and "dominant ideology." More specifically, Castel denounced the political and social uses (or abuses) of psychoanalysis, especially in light of psychoanalysis's explicit and persistent position of social and political neutrality.[11] Among other things, Castel criticized French psychoanalysis for its esoteric language, its

---

8. Althusser noted for instance that "the most original aspect of Lacan's work, his discovery" was to have shown "that this transition from (ultimately purely) biological existence to human existence (the human child) is achieved within the Law of Order, the law I shall call the Law of Culture, and that this Law of Order is confounded in its *formal* essence with the order of language" (emphasis in original). Louis Althusser, *Lenin and Philosophy, and Other Essays* (New Left Books, 1971), 209.

9. Ibid., 217.

10. Ibid., 211.

11. Robert Castel, *Le psychanalysme* (Maspero, 1973), 10.

FATHERLESS SOCIETIES AND ANTI-OEDIPAL PHILOSOPHIES   173

blindness to ideology, its commodification, its narcissism, its "social extra-territoriality."[12] Castel's book was broadly disseminated and thoroughly debated. The psychoanalyst Octave Mannoni, a close colleague of Lacan's, published a twenty-page article refuting Castel's argument point by point: it concluded that Castel ought to undergo analysis himself. Castel's work was even discussed within the confines of the École freudienne where, supposedly, other young psychoanalysts unhappy with the ruling Lacanian orthodoxy had organized a clandestine seminar devoted to this problem of *psychanalysme*.[13] In 1972, the journal *Esprit* published a special issue around *Anti-Oedipus* entitled "The Death of Oedipus and Anti-Psychoanalysis." As Jacqueline Rousseau-Dujardin described these years in an article on Lacan in the journal *L'Arc*, "For the last two years, in France at least, the tone of the writings *on* psychoanalysis has changed. Until recently, in so-called intellectual milieux, people sang its praises; now, its death knell is rung [*on lui sonne les cloches*]: the first strike was given on the Left, with much fanfare, by *Anti-Oedipus* which, even though it rang false, rang loudly; *Le psychanalysme* responded from a neighboring bell tower, less striking but better founded."[14]

This chapter aims to elucidate the specificity of the French intellectual critique of the structuralist symbolic by focusing on the early works of Deleuze, Guattari, and Irigaray. While all the figures listed previously were, like Deleuze, Guattari, and Irigaray, deeply aware of the interconnectedness of the symbolic and the social, these three authors offer a slightly different perspective in their interrogation of the Oedipal economy, to the extent that they not only critique its foundation but also offer an alternative vision of a social order premised on an alternative concept of the symbolic. In their works, the critique of structuralism is the starting point for a larger critique of normative subjectivities, families, and social formations, whether it be capitalism, colonialism, or patriarchy. After exposing the main lines of their arguments and their programs for implanting an alternative social order, I turn to the activists of the Front homosexuel d'action révolutionnaire (FHAR) and of the feminist group Psychanalyse et politique (known as Psych et Po) who attempted to incorporate and "apply" the theories of *Anti-Oedipus* and of Irigaray, respectively, to their political action in order to promote "anti-Oedipal lifestyles."

---

12. Ibid., introduction.

13. Interview with Robert Castel by Edouard Gardella and Julien Souloumiac in *Revue Tracés,* no. 8.

14. Jacqueline Rousseau-Dujardin, "Du temps, qu'entends-je?" *L'Arc,* no. 58, 1974, 31.

174   **CHAPTER 5**

Deleuze and Guattari's *Anti-Oedipus*

Gilles Deleuze and Félix Guattari met in 1969. Deleuze, an *agrégé* philosophy professor who had previously written monographs on Hume, Nietzsche, Kant, Bergson, Proust, Sacher-Masoch, and Spinoza, had, earlier that year, accepted a teaching position at the new University of Paris VIII known as Vincennes. Vincennes, which opened its doors in December 1969, was created in response to the May '68 student uprising. The minister of education at the time, Edgar Faure, proposed a law in November 1968 to reform higher education, taking into account some of the student demands. The law promised, among other things, a greater degree of curricular flexibility and student participation in the university's administrative committees. Vincennes was conceived as an "experimental center" to test out liberal pedagogical theories. Students could be accepted without the *baccalauréat,* the high school diploma mandatory for enrollment in all other universities. They were encouraged to take classes in various disciplines and were only required to choose a "major" in a particular field, a decentralization unprecedented in the French curriculum. Courses were organized around a system of *unités de valeur* (or "value units") that students could choose among. But Vincennes's innovation was not only administrative. On a theoretical level, the university sought to challenge the authoritarianism of student-teacher relationships and, more generally, to question structures of power, hierarchy, and subjection.[15]

For Deleuze and his colleagues—who, in the philosophy department, included Michel Foucault and François Châtelet—Vincennes appeared as a perfect forum to reflect on the practical ramifications of their philosophical theories of power. The problem of power was also at the heart of Guattari's work, although his medium for approaching this question was different from Deleuze's. Deleuze once described his personality as "more like a hill: I don't move much, I can't manage two projects at once, I obsess over my ideas, and the few movements I do have are internal." Guattari, in the words of Deleuze, was more like "an 'intersection' of groups, like a star. Or perhaps I should compare him to the sea: he always seems to be in motion, sparkling with light. He can jump from one activity to another. He doesn't sleep

---

15. For more on Vincennes, see the collection of archival documents and testimonies in Jean-Michel Djian, ed., *Vincennes: Une aventure de la pensée critique* (Flammarion, 2009). There is some scattered information about the management of the university in Elisabeth Roudinesco, *La bataille de cent ans: Histoire de la psychanalyse en France* (Ramsay, 1986), 2:558–59, and in Sherry Turkle, *Psychoanalytic Politics: Freud's French Revolution* (Basic Books, 1978), 175–80.

FATHERLESS SOCIETIES AND ANTI-OEDIPAL PHILOSOPHIES   175

much, he travels, he never stops. He never ceases. He has extraordinary speeds."[16] By the time Deleuze met him, Guattari was involved in a number of political and intellectual activities, which could be grouped under three main categories, intersecting indeed "like a star": psychiatry, psychoanalysis, and politics.

Guattari's interest in psychiatry began in the 1950s, and was triggered partly by one of his high school teachers, Fernand Oury. Oury, who had been following Lacan's career and the development of psychoanalysis in France more generally, was one of the first promoters of "institutional pedagogy," an approach to education that took into account the child's un-conscious and the psychic dynamics of the classroom. Oury suggested that Guattari—who was at the time frustrated with his studies to become a pharmacist—meet his brother Jean, who in 1953 had founded La Borde, a private psychiatric clinic at Cour-Cheverny in the Loire region. Prior to La Borde, Jean Oury had been involved in several other psychiatric institu-tions that had been experimenting with alternative treatments for psychotic patients. These institutions were part of a movement that came to be known as "institutional psychotherapy." As its name indicates, institutional psycho-therapy responded to a double demand: first, to the increasing awareness of the deplorable conditions in many public mental health institutions, and second, to the gradual incorporation of psychoanalysis (particularly the theories of Freud and Lacan) into psychiatric care. Unlike the British or Italian anti-psychiatry movements promoted by figures such as Ronald Laing, David Cooper, Franco Basaglia, and Giovanni Jervis (all of whom Oury and Guattari had read extensively), the point of institutional psycho-therapy was never to abolish the asylum as an institution, but to radically reconceive its practical and intellectual foundations.

Although the term "institutional psychotherapy" was only devised in 1952, the practice emerged in the 1940s at the Saint-Alban hospital in a small town in central France. During World War II, Saint-Alban, like much of the French population, suffered from food restrictions under the Occu-pation. Hospitals, however, were particularly affected, and by the end of the war, 40,000 French inpatients died of hunger.[17] Alerted by this disaster, the personnel at Saint-Alban had made it its mission to hoard enough food with the help of the local population to subsist and feed its patients. During those

---

16. Gilles Deleuze, *Two Regimes of Madness: Texts and Interviews 1975–1995,* trans. Ames Hodges and Mike Taormina (Semiotext(e), 2006), 237.

17. See Isabelle von Bueltzingsloewen, *L'hécatombe des fous: La famine dans les hôpitaux psychiatriques français sous l'Occupation* (Aubier, 2007).

176   **CHAPTER 5**

years, Saint-Alban also provided a shelter for many artists and intellectuals who were fleeing fascism and the Vichy regime. Surrealist artists such as Paul Éluard and Tristan Tzara and the historian of science Georges Canghuilhem all transited through Saint-Alban. The hospital soon became famous as a center in which artists, intellectuals, avant-garde doctors—such as François Tosquelles, a Spanish refugee who had escaped the Franco regime— and left-wing militants—such as the communist Lucien Bonnafé—cohabited with psychotic patients, exchanged ideas, and attempted to reconcile Marx and Freud, while pondering the topic of madness. This peculiar environment drew Jean Oury, who from 1947 to 1949 interned at the Saint-Alban hospital, collaborating with other promising young doctors, including Frantz Fanon, the Martinique-born psychiatrist and Algerian freedom fighter.[18]

One of the main goals of institutional psychotherapy was to challenge the nineteenth-century asylum structure, which, according to the founders of institutional psychotherapy, functioned more like a prison than a caregiving facility. In particular, institutional psychotherapy objected to the asylum's "pyramidal hierarchy" and to its "fixed roles" with detached, unquestionable, and supposedly omniscient doctors who lacked empathy with their patients.[19] For institutional psychotherapy, this model had become untenable, particularly after the experience of the war had highlighted the dangers of what they called *institutions concentrationnaires* or concentration-camp-like institutions. Instead of confining patients to isolation, solitary treatments, or one-on-one analyses with their doctor, institutional psychotherapy encouraged collective work, group activities, clubs, artistic creation, and the "explosion of fixed roles" within the medical team.

Institutional psychotherapy was built on the theoretical premise, put forth by both Freud and Lacan, that transferential relationships were difficult—if not impossible—with psychotic subjects. Thus, the promoters of institutional psychotherapy argued, rethinking the transferential process and the doctor/ patient relationship was the starting point for any potential treatment of

---

18. For more information on the history of institutional psychotherapy, see Jean Aymé, "Essai sur l'histoire de la psychothérapie institutionnelle," in *Actualités de la psychothérapie institutionnelle* (Matrices, 1985); Julian Bourg, *From Revolution to Ethics: May 1968 and Contemporary French Thought* (McGill-Queen's University Press, 2007), chap. 10; Pierre Chanoit, *La psychothérapie institutionnelle* (Presses universitaires de France, 1995); Patrick Faugeras, ed., *L'ombre portée de François Tosquelles* (Érès, 2007); Félix Guattari, *Psychanalyse et transversalité: Essais d'analyse institutionnelle* (La découverte, 2003); Joseph Mornet, *Psychothérapie institutionnelle: Histoire & actualité* (Champ Social, 2007).

19. See the dialogue between Jean Oury and Féliz Guattari, "Sur les rapports infirmiers-médecins," in Guattari, *Psychanalyse et transversalité,* 7–17.

FATHERLESS SOCIETIES AND ANTI-OEDIPAL PHILOSOPHIES 177

psychosis. Guattari proposed to replace transference, which he described as a "stuck, insoluble mechanism . . . predetermined, 'territorialized' on a role" with a new concept that he called "transversality."[20] Opposed to both "verticality" and "horizontality," transversality could give a new expression to the psychotic unconscious, which, he argued, was a group unconscious.[21] Along similar lines, the daily activities at La Borde were organized around a double-entry chart called *la grille*, which tracked the daily chores of the staff and the patients as well as their reactions or feelings toward the particular tasks. As Guattari described it, the *grille* sought to "deregulate the 'normal' order of things."[22] Guattari began practicing at La Borde full time in 1955. As an academic extension of his work there, he founded in 1964 the interdisciplinary research group Fédération des groupes d'études et de recherches institutionnelles (FGERI), which, in 1967 merged into the Centre d'études, de recherches et de formation institutionnelle (CERFI). In 1966, the center began publishing its own journal, *Recherches,* on which various intellectuals of the time, including Foucault, collaborated, and which addressed social issues such as psychiatry, psychoanalysis, urbanism, homosexuality, women, and the family.

The relationship between institutional psychotherapy and psychoanalysis was complicated, as was that between Guattari and psychoanalysis. Most of the promoters of institutional psychotherapy insisted on their intellectual debt to Freud and Lacan. When Tosquelles fled the Franco regime during the Spanish Civil War, he was supposedly only able to carry two books with him, one of which was Lacan's thesis on paranoia (the other was Hermann Simon's work on the Gütersloh asylum). In his writings, Oury constantly acknowledged the influence of Lacan, whom he had met in 1947.[23] By the 1970s, however, Oury became increasingly critical of Lacan's heuristic style

---

20. Ibid., 79.

21. Ibid.

22. Félix Guattari, "La grille," 1987 (IMEC, GTR2.Aa-10.27). For more on La Borde, see Éric Favereau, "Portrait de Jean Oury," *Libération,* June 27, 1998. See also François Dosse, *Gilles Deleuze et Félix Guattari: Biographie croisée* (La découverte, 2007), chap. 3; Anne-Marie Norgeu, *La Borde: Le château des chercheurs de sens* (Érès, 2006); Jean Oury, *Onze heures du soir à La Borde* (Gallilée, 1995); Jean Claude Polack and Danielle Sivadon-Sabourin, *La Borde: Ou, Le droit à la folie* (Calmann-Levy, 1976). See also the clinic's website: http://www.cliniquedelaborde.com. For a different approach, also highly informative about the day-to-day activities and operation of La Borde, see the documentary by Nicolas Philibert, *La moindre des choses* (Éditions Montparnasse, 1996), which follows the production of a Witold Gombrowicz play at La Borde. For more on Guattari's life and work at La Borde, see the special issue of *Libération,* August 31, 1992.

23. See, for example, Oury, *Onze heures,* 20.

178   CHAPTER 5

and of his growing remoteness from actual clinical work. Guattari's relation to Lacan was equally ambivalent (for reasons that I will elucidate later in this chapter). Throughout the 1950s, however, he faithfully attended Lacan's seminar, and in 1962, he began an analysis with Lacan, which lasted seven years. At the end of it, in 1969, just as Guattari was refining his critique of Lacan in what would become *Anti-Oedipus*, he still decided to join Lacan's group, the École freudienne.[24]

Finally, if Guattari's political engagements were as varied as his intellectual interests, they nonetheless shared a defining feature: the relentless critique of all forms of fixed power, hierarchy, or authoritarianism. As a student, Guattari was active in the Jeunesses communistes, and like many of his peers he joined the French Communist Party. Throughout the early fifties, he became disillusioned with the party's subservience to Moscow, particularly after the Hungarian Revolution in 1956. Likewise, he condemned the party's stance on Algeria, and became vociferously critical of its official position, leaving it in 1956. Guattari channeled his political activism into alternative groups such as the leftist Voie communiste, which he ran from 1955 to 1965, the Opposition de gauche (OG), which he established in 1966, the Mouvement du 22 mars, or the Porteurs de valises ("luggage carriers"), a clandestine support group for the Front de libération nationale (FLN) of Algeria. In parallel, Guattari championed various Latin American revolutionary movements, defended the French students and the workers in 1968, signed petitions to help the Vietnamese resistance, endorsed the early French gay liberation movement, and was later involved in the nascent environmental activism.[25]

Anti-Oedipus was the product of the intellectual encounter between Deleuze and Guattari, an almost perfect combination of each author's background and personality. The actual writing of the book was done collaboratively with a particular style designed to mimic the multiple, rhizomatic, and flowing "modes of assemblage" that the book advocated. The idea was to imitate the unconscious and to avoid the stable, immutable, and ultimately "Oedipal" style of writing of the ego. Thus, during their collaboration, Deleuze and Guattari would meet, take notes when the other was talking, and eventually continue the conversation through letters and texts

---

24. Dosse, *Gilles Deleuze,* 91; Félix Guattari, *Chaosophy,* trans. David L. Sweet, Jarred Becker, and Taylor Adkins (Semiotext(e), 1995), 10.

25. See Jean-Baptiste Marongiu and Marc Ragon, "Un militant tout-terrain," *Libération,* 31 August 1992, 33; Gilles Deleuze, *Pourparlers, 1972–1990* (Éditions de minuit, 1990), 26. For a detailed account of Guattari's life, see Dosse, *Gilles Deleuze.*

FATHERLESS SOCIETIES AND ANTI-OEDIPAL PHILOSOPHIES 179

that they would, in turn, annotate.[26] *Anti-Oedipus*, however, was also the product of the very particular context of May '68 and its aftermath. As Guattari explained in 1972,

> This collaboration is not the product of a simple meeting of two individuals. Aside from a variety of circumstances, there was a whole political context that led up to it. Initially, it was less a question of pooling our knowledge than an accumulation of our uncertainties; we were confused about the turn of events after May '68. We both belong to that generation whose political consciousness awoke during the Liberation, in the enthusiasm and naiveté and the conspiring myths of fascism that came with it. Also, the questions left unanswered by the aborted revolution of May '68 developed in a counter-point that we found troubling: we were worried, like many others, about the future being prepared for us by those singing hymns of a newly made-over fascism that would make you wish for the Nazis of the old days. Our starting point was to consider how during these crucial periods, something along the order of desire was manifested throughout the society as a whole, and then was repressed, liquidated, as much by the government and police as by the parties and so-called workers unions and, to a certain extent, the leftist organizations as well.[27]

For Deleuze, Guattari, and much of the French intellectual Left, the failure of May '68 to bring about revolution could not be understood within a traditional socioeconomic paradigm: it was clear that a communist revolution was "in the interest" of the working class in social and economic terms, yet workers systematically voted *against* their interests, sabotaging their own potential emancipation. The explanation for this phenomenon, these thinkers argued, had to lie somewhere else, namely, at the level of subjectivity. Subjects had been conditioned to think and act a certain way through a particularly insidious process. Althusser called this ideology. Deleuze and Guattari designated it as Oedipalization, the repression of man's innate desire.[28]

---

26. See Stéphane Nadaud's introduction to Félix Guattari, *The Anti-Oedipus Papers,* trans. Kélina Gotman (Semiotext(e), 2006), and "Letter to Uno: How Félix and I Worked Together," in Deleuze, *Two Regimes of Madness,* 237–40.

27. Gilles Deleuze, *Desert Islands and Other Texts, 1953–1974,* trans. Michael Taormina (Semiotext(e), 2004), 216. See also Manola Antonioli, Frédéric Astier, and Olivier Fressard, *Gilles Deleuze et Félix Guattari: Une rencontre dans l'après Mai 68* (L'Harmattan, 2009).

28. I am drawing here on Michel Feher's analysis in "Mai 68 dans la pensée," in *Histoire des gauches en France,* vol. 2, ed. Jean-Jacques Becker and Gilles Candar (La découverte, 2004), esp. 2:608.

180   **CHAPTER 5**

The theory of desire in *Anti-Oedipus* can be traced back to Deleuze's prior philosophical work, and more specifically to his interest in Spinoza, to whom he devoted two books, one in 1968 (*Spinoza et le problème de l'expression*) and another in 1970 (*Spinoza: Philosophie pratique*). Drawing on Spinoza's definition of desire as the essence of man, and of nature as an infinite and all-encompassing reality assimilated to God, Deleuze and Guattari, in the first pages of *Anti-Oedipus,* establish an identity between production and consumption on one hand, and between man and nature on the other. Man, they tell us, is a "desiring machine": "*Social production is purely and simply desiring-production itself under determinate conditions.* We maintain that the social field is immediately invested by desire, that it is the historically determined product of desire, and that libido has no need of any mediation or sublimation, any psychic operation, any transformation, in order to invade and invest the productive forces and the relations of production. *There is only desire and the social and nothing else.*"[29] From this passage alone, we can already detect a series of crucial differences from a thinker such as Lacan, but also from Hegel, for whom desire is, by definition, lacking, negative, and dependent on an exterior object, an "other."[30]

Once these preliminary hypotheses are set up, the authors of *Anti-Oedipus* ask a question which in many ways serves as the guiding thread for the book: "Does the recording of desire go by way of the various stages in the formation of the Oedipus complex? Disjunctions are the form that the genealogy of desire assumes; but is this genealogy Oedipal, is it recorded in the Oedipal triangulation? Is it not more likely that Oedipus is a requirement or a consequence of social reproduction, insofar as this latter aims at domesticating a genealogical form and content that are in every way intractable?"[31] Can desire, in other words, be captured within the framework of the Oedipus complex? According to its authors, the goal of *Anti-Oedipus* is neither to question the significance of the parents for the child's emotional development nor to "deny the vital importance of parents, of love attachments of children to their mothers and father." Rather, it is to understand "what the place and the function of parents are within desiring-production, rather than doing the opposite and forcing the entire interplay

---

29. Gilles Deleuze and Félix Guattari, *Anti-Oedipus: Capitalism and Schizophrenia,* trans. Robert Hurley, Mark Seem, and Helen R. Lane (University of Minnesota Press, 1983), 29 (emphases in original).

30. For more on this, see Judith Butler, *Subjects of Desire: Hegelian Reflections in Twentieth-Century France* (Columbia University Press, 1999), 205–17.

31. Deleuze and Guattari, *Anti-Oedipus,* 13.

FATHERLESS SOCIETIES AND ANTI-OEDIPAL PHILOSOPHIES   181

of desiring-machines to fit within the restricted code of the Oedipus."[32] Another way to put this would be to say that *Anti-Oedipus* investigates whether the child's parents occupy a particular *structural* position within the child's subject formation, or whether Freud and especially Lacan were right in assigning such importance to the Oedipal regulatory mechanism. The point is not to question the existence of an Oedipus complex, or even its universality, but rather the fact that it is naturalized, depoliticized, and presented as the necessary condition for all social and subject formations:

> We even believe what we are told when Oedipus is presented as a kind of invariant. But the question is altogether different: is there an equivalence between the productions of the unconscious and this invariant—between desiring-machines and the Oedipal structure? Or rather, does not the invariant merely express the history of a long mistake, throughout all its variations and modalities; the strain of an endless repression? What we are calling into question is the frantic Oedipalization to which psychoanalysis devotes itself, practically and theoretically, with the combined resources of image and structure.[33]

Deleuze and Guattari's objections to the structuralist version of the Oedipus complex are multiple. First, Freud's Oedipus structure depends on a definition of the subject as lacking whereas defining the subject as desire implies a constitutive plenitude: "Such is always the case with Freud. Something common to the two sexes is required, but something that will be lacking in both, and that will distribute the lack in two nonsymmetrical series, establishing the exclusive use of the disjunctions: you are girl or boy!"[34] Lacan emphasizes this constitutive lack in his concept of castration:

> Castration is at once the common lot—that is, the prevalent and transcendent Phallus, and the exclusive distribution that presents itself in girls as desire for the penis, and in boys as fear of losing it or refusal of a passive attitude. This something in common must lay the foundation for the exclusive use of the disjunctions of the unconscious—and teach us resignation. Resignation to Oedipus, to castration: for girls, renunciation of their desire for the penis; for boys, renunciation of male protest—in short "assumption of one's sex." This something in common, the great Phallus, the Lack with two nonsuperimposable

---

32. Ibid., 47.

33. Ibid., 53.

34. Ibid., 59.

182   **CHAPTER 5**

sides, is purely mythical; it is like the One in negative theology, it introduces lack into desire and causes exclusive series to emanate, to which it attributes a goal, an origin, and a path of resignation.[35]

By relying on concepts such as "the great Phallus" or "the Lack," psychoanalysis is intrinsically metaphysical. Like Kant, who "intended to discover criteria immanent to understanding so as to distinguish the legitimate and illegitimate uses of the syntheses of consciousness" and who "in the name of *transcendental* philosophy (immanence of criteria) . . . denounced the transcendental use of syntheses such as appeared in metaphysics," Deleuze and Guattari claim that "in like fashion [they] are compelled to say that psychoanalysis has its metaphysics—its name is Oedipus."[36] All of the fundamental concepts of psychoanalysis have to be posited transcendentally, just like God in metaphysics. In that sense, "the question of the father is like that of God: born of an abstraction, it assumes the link to be already broken between man and nature, man and the world, so that man must be produced by something exterior to nature and to man."[37]

According to Deleuze and Guattari, the Oedipus complex is also problematic from a logical perspective. It is anchored on what the authors call a "double bind" in the sense that it is at the same time the problem and the solution of one and the same question. "Why," they ask, "does psychoanalysis reinforce the transcendent use that introduces exclusions and restrictions everywhere in the disjunctive network, and that makes the unconscious swing over into Oedipus? And why is Oedipalization precisely that?" "It is because," they argue, "the exclusive relation introduced by Oedipus comes into play not only between the various disjunctions conceived as differentiations, *but between the whole of the differentiations that it imposes and an undifferentiated [un indifférencié] that it presupposes.* Oedipus informs us: if you don't follow the lines of differentiation daddy-mommy-me, and the exclusive alternatives that delineate them, you will fall into the black night of the undifferentiated."[38] But, Deleuze and Guattari continue, "Oedipus creates both the differentiations that it orders and the undifferentiated with which it threatens us. With the same movement the Oedipus complex inserts desire into triangulation, and prohibits desire from satisfying itself with the terms

---

35. Ibid., 59–60.

36. Ibid., 75.

37. Ibid., 107.

38. Ibid., 78 (emphasis in original).

FATHERLESS SOCIETIES AND ANTI-OEDIPAL PHILOSOPHIES   183

of the triangulation."[39] This process, which Deleuze and Guattari call the "Freudian blackmail," is designed so that "everything is made to begin with Oedipus, by means of explanation, with all the more certainty as one has reduced everything to Oedipus by means of application."[40] However, "only in appearance is Oedipus a beginning, either as a historical or prehistorical origin, or as a structural foundation. In reality it is a completely ideological beginning, for the sake of ideology."[41]

Finally, and most importantly for our purposes here, Oedipus functions, according to Deleuze and Guattari, as a normative regulator through which certain subjects and behaviors are judged normal and integrated, and others deviant, both psychically (with the schizophrenic, for instance) and socially: "Oedipus is a means of integration into the group, in . . . the adaptive form of its own reproduction that makes it pass from one generation to the next."[42] Incest is conceptually necessary to set up the prohibition but also, according to the logic of the structuralist social contract and as Deleuze and Guattari highlight here, to define the symbolic, the system of exchanges, and consequently, the social: "By placing the distorting mirror of incest before desire (that's what you wanted, isn't it?) desire is shamed, stupefied, it is placed in a situation without exit, it is easily persuaded to deny 'itself' in the name of more important interest of civilization (what if everyone did the same, what if everyone married his mother or kept his sister for himself? There would no longer be any differentiation, any exchanges possible). We must act quickly and soon. Incest, a slandered shallow stream."[43]

The obsession with incest is equally prevalent, Deleuze and Guattari tell us, in modern anthropology, and particularly in the work of Lévi-Strauss. Just as psychoanalysis needs the pervert and the psychotic for the neurotic to feel normal, anthropology requires the savage and the barbarian for the civilized man to impose his ruling. Citing the anthropologist Edmund Leach, Deleuze and Guattari reproach anthropology for disregarding all elements that fall outside the "declension of alliance and filiation:" "Every time one interprets kinship relations in the primitive commune in terms of a structure unfolding in the mind, one relapses into an ideology of large segments that makes alliance depend on the major filiations, and that finds itself contradicted by

---

39. Ibid., 78–79.

40. Ibid., 101.

41. Ibid.

42. Ibid., 103.

43. Ibid., 120.

184   **CHAPTER 5**

practice."[44] Moreover, "ethnologists are constantly saying that kinship rules are neither applied nor applicable to real marriages: not because these rules are ideal but rather because they determine critical points where the apparatus starts up again—provided it is blocked, and where it necessarily places itself in a negative relation to the group. Here it becomes apparent that the social machine is identical with the desiring-machine."[45]

In this context, Deleuze and Guattari mention the work of Edmond Ortigues, a psychoanalyst close to Lacan who in 1966 published *L'Œdipe africain* based on his fieldwork in Senegal, which led him to argue for the prevalence of an Oedipus complex in traditional African societies. For Deleuze and Guattari, this is yet another act of colonial violence. "How are we to understand those who claim to have discovered an Indian Oedipus or an African Oedipus?" they ask: "They are the first to admit that they re-encounter none of these mechanisms or attitudes that constitute our own Oedipus (our own presumed Oedipus). No matter, they say that the structure is there, although it has no existence whatever that is 'accessible to clinical practice'; or that the problem, the point of departure, is indeed Oedipal, although the developments and the solutions are completely different from ours."[46] All ethnological or psychoanalytic debates around the universality of the Oedipus complex are beside the point since "Oedipus-as-universal recommences the old metaphysical operation that consists in interpreting negation as a deprivation, as a lack: the symbolic lack of the dead father, or the Great Signifier."[47]

If Deleuze and Guattari engage with a series of anthropologists and psychoanalysts in *Anti-Oedipus,* their primary interlocutor appears to be Jacques Lacan. Lacan is mentioned several times but always with ambivalence, unlike Freud who is subjected to a much more vigorous critique. Thus, Deleuze and Guattari write that they "owe to Jacques Lacan the discovery of this fertile domain of a code of the unconscious, incorporating the entire chain—or several chains—of meaning: a discovery thus totally transforming analysis." But immediately after, they add: "But how very strange this domain seems, simply because of its multiplicity—a multiplicity so complex that we can scarcely speak of one chain or even of one code of desire."[48] Similarly, they cite Lacan's 1970 seminar in which he claimed to have never

---

44. Ibid., 147 (emphasis in original).

45. Ibid., 151.

46. Ibid., 169–70.

47. Ibid., 171.

48. Ibid., 38.

FATHERLESS SOCIETIES AND ANTI-OEDIPAL PHILOSOPHIES   185

spoken of an Oedipus complex but rather of a "paternal metaphor."[49] Consequently, the authors of *Anti-Oedipus* blame Lacan's disciples for their "overtly or secretly pious" interpretation of Lacanism, and for their "less and less sensitive [attitude] to the false problems of Oedipus."[50]

Yet although Lacan's name does not figure prominently in *Anti-Oedipus,* the book remains, from start to finish, one long dialogue with Lacanian structuralist psychoanalysis, and more specifically an engagement with his structuralist social contract, as evidenced by the notions of "the Great Signifier," the Phallus, lack, and the Signifier, which recur throughout the book. Lacan might have changed the terms of psychoanalysis, but for Deleuze and Guattari the concepts remained the same. Psychoanalysis still sought to break the "production of desire" and to channel language into fixed restrictive codes. As Deleuze explained in a 1977 interview, in the context of Freud's clinical essays,

> It is said that there is no longer any of this today: significance has replaced interpretation, the signifier has replaced the signified, the analyst's silence has replaced the commentaries, castration is revealed more certain than Oedipus, structural functions have replaced parental images, the name of the Father has replaced my daddy. We see no important practical changes . . . It's all very well to say to us: you understand nothing, Oedipus, it's not daddy-mommy, it's the symbolic, the law, the arrival of culture, it's the effect of the signifier, it's the finitude of the subject, it has the 'lack-to-be which is life.' And if it's not Oedipus, it will be castration, and the supposed death drives. Psychoanalysts teach infinite resignation, they are the last priests.[51]

Much has been written in recent years about the relationship among Deleuze, Guattari, and Lacan. On the one hand, authors such as Slavoj Žižek, Alain Badiou, and Tim Dean have attempted to recuperate Deleuze as a "Lacanian" thinker.[52] Others such as Didier Eribon have focused on Deleuze's *Anti-Oedipus* as the paradigmatic anti-psychoanalytic text to which

---

49. Ibid., 53.

50. Ibid., 83.

51. Gilles Deleuze and Claire Parnet, *Dialogues,* trans. Hugh Tomlinson and Barbara Habberjam (Columbia University Press, 1987), 82.

52. Alain Badiou, *Deleuze: La clameur de l'être* (Hachette, 1997); Tim Dean, *Beyond Sexuality* (University of Chicago Press, 2000); Slavoj Žižek, *Organs without Bodies: Deleuze and Consequences* (Routledge, 2004). For an interesting critique of Žižek's book, see Daniel W. Smith, "The Inverse Side of the Structure: Žižek on Deleuze on Lacan," *Criticism* 46, no. 4 (2004).

186 **CHAPTER 5**

we can return for today's critique of psychoanalysis.[53] What is indisputable in any case, judging from Deleuze and Guattari's correspondence, from their subsequent interviews, and especially from Guattari's diaries from the *Anti-Oedipus* period (published under the title *The Anti-Oedipus Papers*), is that Lacan was a fundamental interlocutor—if not the main one—for both authors. In August 1971, for example, Guattari recorded the following dream:

> Another dream about Lacan! This is insane! I can hear them, from here, saying: "badly eliminated transference," etc. In a sense, it's true if transference is Oedipal reterritorialization artificially woven onto the space of the couch. I have Oedipal rot sticking to my skin. Not passively, but with all the will to power of the death drive. The more I become disengaged—the more I try to become disengaged—from twenty years of Lacano-Labordian comfort, the more this familialist carcass enfolds me secretly. I would rather admit anything else.[54]

According to Guattari, Lacan was curious about the production of *Anti-Oedipus,* and he had attempted to get a hold of a manuscript from both Deleuze and Guattari before its publication. When Guattari was asked about his book, he answered, "I told him that I still consider myself to be a front-line Lacanian, but I've chosen to scout out areas that have not been explored much, instead of trailing in the wake . . ."[55] Guattari also recounts in detail a dinner with Lacan on October 6, 1971, which began with Lacan asking him to explain schizoanalysis: "'So what is schizo-analysis?' The beginning of the meeting was very hard. I messed up a reference to a sacred Lacanian formula, and tried to redeem myself as well as I could. Unbelievable authoritarianism with the maître d'. I was hot and not very hungry. I laid it all out. The *'a'* is a desiring machine; deterritorialization, history. I expounded on everything that I could think of in anthropology and political economy." And while Guattari spent the entire evening trying to convince Lacan that he remained deeply committed to psychoanalysis, he observed, "It's too late! Something had already been broken. Maybe things had always been broken between the two of us. But also, has he ever accessed anyone, has he ever talked to anyone? I wonder! He sets himself up as a despotic signifier. Hasn't he condemned himself to this kind of solitude with no respite?"[56] Similarly, a few

---

53. Didier Eribon, *Echapper à la psychanalyse* (Léo Scheer, 2005).

54. Guattari, *Anti-Oedipus Papers,* 305 (translation modified).

55. Ibid., 343.

56. Ibid., 344.

FATHERLESS SOCIETIES AND ANTI-OEDIPAL PHILOSOPHIES   187

months later, Guattari recounted a conversation with Jean Oury to whom he confessed, "Conflict with Lacan can be avoided. It will depend on his attitude. There's no turning back now. At first, there was no hostility toward Lacanism. It was the logic of our development that led us to emphasize the dangers of an a-historic interpretation of the signifier that promotes a dualist subjectivity and an unconscious level of representation."[57]

Psychoanalysis, Deleuze and Guattari conclude, is not responsible for inventing the Oedipus complex or for repressing desire. Society itself is. Psychoanalysis, however, legitimizes and encourages this process of repression. It seeks, in other words, to preserve the status quo and to block the production of progressive artistic or political productions:

> No, psychoanalysts invent nothing, though they have invented much in another way, and have legislated a lot, reinforced a lot, injected a lot. All that psychoanalysts do is to reinforce the movement; they add a last burst of energy to the displacement of the entire unconscious. What they do is merely to make the unconscious speak according to the transcendent uses of synthesis imposed on it by other forces: Global Persons, the Complete Object, the Great Phallus, the Terrible Undifferentiated of the Imaginary, Symbolic Differentiations, Segregations. What psychoanalysts invent is only the transference, a transference Oedipus, a consulting-room Oedipus of Oedipus, especially noxious and virulent, but where the subject finally has what he wants, and sucks away at his Oedipus on the full body of the analyst. And that's already too much.[58]

And, finally,

> The Oedipal uses of synthesis, Oedipalization, triangulation, castration, all refer to forces a bit more powerful, a bit more subterranean, than the family, than ideology, even joined together. There we have all the forces of social production, reproduction, and repression. This can be explained by the simple truth that very powerful forces are required to defeat the forces of desire, lead them to resignation, and substitute everywhere reactions of the daddy-mommy type for what is essentially active, aggressive, artistic, productive, and triumphant in the unconscious itself.[59]

---

57. Ibid., 349.

58. Deleuze and Guattari, *Anti-Oedipus,* 121.

59. Ibid., 122.

188   **CHAPTER 5**

According to Deleuze and Guattari, the main goal of their project was not to dismiss psychoanalysis per se: "We refuse to play 'take it or leave it,' under the pretext that theory justifies practice, or that one cannot challenge the process of 'cure' except by starting from elements drawn from this very cure."[60] Rather, it was to bring to light its complicity with authoritarian and normalizing structures of power. Thus, they argue, "psychoanalysis cannot become a rigorous discipline unless it accepts putting belief in parenthesis, which is to say a materialist reduction of Oedipus as an ideological form."[61] This is precisely what *schizoanalysis* hoped to achieve. "The psychoanalyst," Deleuze and Guattari tell us, "reterritorializes on the couch, in the representation of Oedipus and castration. Schizoanalysis on the contrary must disengage the deterritorialized flows of desire, in the molecular elements of desiring-production."[62] In this context, "the schizoanalytic argument is simple: desire is a machine, a synthesis of machines, a machinic arrangement— desiring machines. The order of desire is the order of production; all production is at once desiring-production and social production."[63]

Although schizoanalysis is never defined much more explicitly than this, one could argue that in clinical terms it would probably look like the kind of work undertaken at institutions such as Saint-Alban or La Borde. Because one of the main premises of *Anti-Oedipus* is that the psychic and the social are always mutually dependent, schizoanalysis is not only a psychic procedure, it is also a political gesture seeking to bring about real and profound social change, revolutionary change. It is in this sense that Deleuze and Guattari call desire revolutionary because the proliferation of what they call "uncoded desire" would necessarily bring down the established social order. Thus, when Deleuze and Guattari write that "in certain respects it is correct to question all social formations starting from Oedipus,"[64] it is not because the Oedipal structure reveals the "truth" of the unconscious, but rather because it is intimately tied to capitalism and because capitalism, in a Marxist vision, is universal. It is in this sense and in this sense only that Deleuze and Guattari argue that Oedipus is indeed universal: "In reality, it is universal because it is the displacement of the limit that haunts all societies, the displaced represented [*le représenté déplacé*] that disfigures what all societies

---

60. Ibid., 117.

61. Ibid., 107.

62. Ibid., 314.

63. Ibid., 296.

64. Ibid., 175.

FATHERLESS SOCIETIES AND ANTI-OEDIPAL PHILOSOPHIES   189

dread absolutely as their most profound negative: namely, the decoded flows of desire."[65]

Any leftist political program must thus be rooted in a critique of the structuralist social contract, of the Oedipal model in its symbolic and structural configuration: "the family has become the locus of retention and resonance of all social determinations. It falls to the reactionary investment of the capitalist field to apply all the social images to the simulacra of the restricted family, with the result that, wherever one turns, one no longer finds anything but father-mother—this Oedipal filth that sticks to our skin."[66] Or again: "In the territorial or even despotic machine, social economic reproduction is never independent of human reproduction, of the social form of this reproduction . . . The reproduction process is not directly economic, but passes by way of the noneconomic factors of kinship."[67] Ultimately, *Anti-Oedipus* suggests, the critique of Oedipus is the prerequisite to any critique of capitalism, of society, of organized exchanges. Oedipus, the authors claim, "is always colonization pursued by other means, it is the interior colony, and . . . where we Europeans are concerned, it is our intimate colonial education."[68] In order to shed this "colonial yoke," to end the "colonization of everyday life," it is not so much the conditions of *production* that must be destroyed as the means of *reproduction*—that is to say, the family, or more precisely familialism in its current form.

⤳ Luce Irigaray's Feminine Symbolic

In January 1975, Deleuze along with Jean-François Lyotard published a letter in the important journal *Les Temps Modernes* protesting the sudden dismissal of seven faculty members of the psychoanalysis department at the University of Vincennes. Comparing this move to the "Stalinist purges," Deleuze and Lyotard accused the École freudienne, and Lacan more directly, of "intellectual and emotional terrorism" and of "unconscious-washing . . . no less authoritarian and frightening than brainwashing." "The question," they claimed, "is not one of doctrine but concerns the organization of

---

65. Ibid., 177.

66. Ibid., 269.

67. Ibid., 262.

68. Ibid., 170. Deleuze and Guattari refer to Oedipus as "our intimate colonial formation that corresponds to the form of social sovereignty. We are all little colonies and it is Oedipus that colonizes us" (265).

190   **CHAPTER 5**

power." And, referring to Lacan, they added, "It is the first time a private individual of any stature has granted himself the right to intervene in a university in a sovereign manner in order to carry out, or have carried out, a reorganization involving dismissals and nominations of teaching personnel."[69] Among the different academic divisions at Vincennes, the Department of Psychoanalysis occupied a privileged position. It had gathered some of the most famous French psychoanalysts of the time (including Michèle Montrelay, Jean Clavreul, Michel de Certeau, and Jacques-Alain Miller). Furthermore, for the first time, psychoanalysis was officially recognized by the university and was able to grant students diplomas and operate as an autonomous academic discipline.

Although Lacan had always voiced his resistance to grounding psychoanalysis in an academic setting, he had originally supported the Vincennes experiment. In January 1969, he appointed his friend and colleague Serge Leclaire as chair of the psychoanalysis department. By the end of that same year, Leclaire's Vincennes seminar, which dealt with issues such as the paternal function, incest, and the relation between psychoanalysis and other disciplines (and which was eventually published under the title *Œdipe à Vincennes*), had been transcribed by one of his students and published without the authorization of the École freudienne. This strongly displeased Lacan. Also in 1969, Lacan was relieved of his teaching position at the École normale supérieure. In the course of his seminar that year, he developed his famous "four discourses," which included the "discourse of the master" and the "discourse of the university." In addition, Lacan criticized the traditional university structure, Vincennes's free-flowing *unités de valeur*, and his Maoist students who were, he believed, desperately seeking a master and a totalizing system of knowledge.[70] Vincennes appeared to have failed to live up to Lacan's expectations, and Lacan made his position increasingly clear between 1969 and 1974. More and more apprehensive about Leclaire's role, Lacan eventually persuaded him to resign, leave his post to Jean Clavreul, and transfer more power to his son-in-law Jacques-Alain Miller.

Between October and November 1974, seven of the Vincennes faculty members—five of whom were women—were inexplicably fired from their

---

69. Letter republished in Deleuze, *Desert Islands*, 61–62. For more details on the dismissal, see the article by M. Nguyen in the same issue of *Temps Modernes*, no. 342, January 1975, 858–61. See also Dosse, *Gilles Deleuze*, 412–13; Roudinesco, *La bataille de cent ans*, 2:560.

70. See Jacques Lacan, *L'envers de la psychanalyse: Le séminaire, Livre XVII, 1969–1970* (Seuil, 1991). For the details of the Vincennes crisis, see Elisabeth Roudinesco's preface to Serge Leclaire, *Œdipe à Vincennes: Séminaire 69* (Fayard, 1999), 7–15.

FATHERLESS SOCIETIES AND ANTI-OEDIPAL PHILOSOPHIES 191

teaching positions. The list included Luce Irigaray, who in October 1974 had just published a major work, *Speculum of the Other Woman,* in which she conducted a forceful critique of Freud's writings on women, femininity, and sexual difference.[71] Between 1973 and 1976, Irigaray sharpened this critique in a series of essays appearing in various academic journals, which were eventually grouped in 1977 under the title *This Sex Which Is Not One.* Before the publication of *Speculum,* however, Irigaray's work and career could hardly be described as "heretical" in relation to Lacanian psychoanalysis. Trained in linguistics, philosophy, and psychoanalysis, Irigaray had worked at the Hôpital Sainte-Anne, the same institution where Lacan had begun his career. She underwent analysis with Serge Leclaire, attended Lacan's seminar at the École normale supérieure, and belonged to the École freudienne (from which she was eventually expelled). Her first book, *Le langage des déments,* challenged the misconception that schizophrenic discourse was not subject to any linguistic rules or structures. Drawing on her double background in linguistics and psychoanalysis, Irigaray brought to light a particular logic and set of formal features that she referred to as a "demential grammar."[72]

In both *Speculum of the Other Woman* and *This Sex Which Is Not One,* Irigaray's relationship to Freudian and Lacanian psychoanalysis is complex, ambivalent, and in certain ways comparable to Deleuze and Guattari's. While the main goal of *Anti-Oedipus* was to critique the symbolic order as the ultimate repressive version of Freud's Oedipus complex, Deleuze and Guattari never denied the *existence* of this symbolic order, or of the two other terms of the Lacanian triad, the imaginary and the real. On the contrary, their focus and privileging of the real and the schizophrenic testify the extent to which both authors continued to operate within a certain

---

71. Irigaray later referred to her expulsion from Vincennes as an attempt to "quarantine her from the analytic world." In Elaine Hoffman Baruch and Lucienne J. Serrano, eds., *Women Analyze Women: In France, England, and the United States* (New York University Press, 1988), 163–64. See also Alice Jardine and Anne M. Menke, eds., *Shifting Scenes: Interviews on Women, Writing, and Politics in Post-68 France* (Columbia University Press, 1991), 98; Stuart Schneiderman, *Jacques Lacan: The Death of an Intellectual Hero* (Harvard University Press, 1983), 42–43. Luce Irigaray reproduced her teaching proposal for the 1975 spring term at Vincennes: "A commission of three members named by Jacques Lacan wrote me without further explanation that my proposal 'could not be accepted.'" It turns out, Irigaray tells us, that this proposal concerned the figure of Antigone in the work of Sophocles, Hölderlin, Hegel, and Brecht, and more specifically Antigone's attempt to confront "the law." In Luce Irigaray, *This Sex Which Is Not One,* trans. Catherine Porter (Cornell University Press, 1985), 167. It is interesting to notice how Judith Butler, years later, also focused on the figure of Antigone to explore the problem of kinship in psychoanalysis and the possibility of constructing an alternative to the Oedipal economy; *Antigone's Claim: Kinship between Life and Death* (Columbia University Press, 2000).

72. Luce Irigaray, *Le langage des déments* (Mouton, 1973).

192   **CHAPTER 5**

psychoanalytic paradigm.[73] Similarly, I would argue, Irigaray's critique of the social order envisioned by Freudian and Lacanian psychoanalysis—of the structuralist social contract more specifically—is one articulated "from the inside." In that sense, Irigaray's relation to Freud differs from other feminist critics such as Simone de Beauvoir in significant ways. Irigaray might have agreed with certain elements of Beauvoir's critique, in particular with the objection to Freud's reliance on a transcendent, deterministic, and male-centered model to study women and the consequent interpretation of women as "lacking" and their role as "objects" within the male economy of exchange. Yet she would never subscribe to Beauvoir's existentialist philosophy with its stress on consciousness, choice, and freedom.

According to Irigaray, one of the major impediments of psychoanalysis is that "female sexuality has always been conceptualized on the basis of masculine parameters."[74] In biological terms, Freud describes the woman's clitoris as a "small penis," which, in psychic terms, leads him to define femininity entirely in relation to masculinity: "[Female] sexuality is never defined with respect to any sex but the masculine. Freud does not see two sexes whose differences are articulated in the act of intercourse, and more generally speaking, in the imaginary and symbolic processes that regulate the workings of a society and a culture. The 'feminine' is always described in terms of deficiency or atrophy, as the other side of the sex that alone holds a monopoly on value: the male sex."[75] Thus, Irigaray argues, for Freud "'sexual difference' is a derivation of the problematics of sameness, it is, now and forever, determined within the project, the projection, the sphere of representation, of the same."[76] Moreover, although Freud's ambition was to absolutely distinguish the psychic from the biological and the social, his notions of sexuality remain, in Irigaray's eyes, linked to reproduction: "The anatomical references Freud uses to justify the development of sexuality are almost all tied . . . to the issue of reproduction."[77]

---

73. For a comparison of Deleuze and Irigaray and their "stated desire to move beyond Lacanianism," see Rosi Braidotti, "Of Bugs and Women: Irigaray and Deleuze on the Becoming-Woman," in Carolyn Burke, Naomi Schor, and Margaret Whitford, eds., *Engaging with Irigaray: Feminist Philosophy and Modern European Thought* (Columbia University Press, 1994), 111–37.

74. Irigaray, *This Sex Which Is Not One,* 23.

75. Ibid., 69.

76. Luce Irigaray, *Speculum of the Other Woman,* trans. Gillian G. Gill (Cornell University Press, 1985), 26.

77. Irigaray, *This Sex Which Is Not One,* 71.

FATHERLESS SOCIETIES AND ANTI-OEDIPAL PHILOSOPHIES   193

Freud was Irigaray's primary target in *Speculum,* but by the time *This Sex Which Is Not One* appeared she was taking on Lacan with the same vigor. In an essay entitled "Così Fan Tutti" (a play on the Mozart title that replaced the feminine plural *tutte* with the masculine plural *tutti*), Irigaray focused on Lacan's 1972–1973 seminar *Encore,* which centered on the problem of femininity.[78] Sexual difference, as Lacan famously argued, did not concern anatomical difference but rather one's position vis-à-vis the phallus. By shifting the focus from the body to language, Lacan, according to Irigaray, hoped to present us with the "truth of the truth about female sexuality."[79] Ultimately, however, women could never be *subjects* within the "phallic circulation," only "others," powerless and yet necessary.

Language, according to Irigaray, is the symptom of the woman's psychic structural frustration, which leaves her to function "as a hole" in the elaboration of imaginary and symbolic processes:

> But this fault, this deficiency, this "hole," inevitably affords women too few figurations, images, or representations by which to represent herself. It is not that she lacks some "master signifier" or that none is imposed upon her, but rather that access to a signifying economy, to the coining of signifiers, is difficult, even impossible for her because she remains an outsider, herself (a) subject to their norms. She borrows signifiers but cannot make her mark, or re-mark upon them. Which all surely keeps her deficient, empty, lacking, in a way that could be labeled "psychotic": a latent but not actual psychosis, for want of a practical signifying system.[80]

Within this order, which Irigaray deems "phallogocentric," hysteria is all that the woman has left. When the hysteric speaks, she is only retransmitting the language that she has been taught within the family, the school, and society.[81] Psychoanalysis in this context is not responsible for women's oppression—

---

78. For a wonderful reading of the mimetic relation between Irigaray and Lacan in "Cosi Fan Tutti," see Elizabeth Weed, "The Question of Style," in Burke, Schor, and Whitford, *Engaging with Irigaray,* 79–109.

79. Irigaray, *This Sex Which Is Not One,* 87.

80. Irigaray, *Speculum of the Other Woman,* 71.

81. Irigaray, *This Sex Which Is Not One,* 136. "Phallogocentric" is a neologism based on Derrida's concept of "logocentrism" (itself derived from ethnocentrism), which Derrida used to describe the metaphysical investment of having writing "represent" speech, thus conveying some sort of truth, and from "phallocentric" in relation to the Lacanian phallus, the universal signifier.

194   **CHAPTER 5**

society and, more precisely, the structures of power, are. Nevertheless, Irigaray blames psychoanalysis for being complicit with this normative social model: "Psychoanalysis, unfortunately, does not bring, or no longer brings, the 'plague,' but it conforms too closely to a social order."[82]

One modality of this complicity is psychoanalysis's refusal to question its own historical positions and limitations. As Irigaray puts it, directly quoting Lacan, "Psychoanalytic theory thus utters the truth about the status of female sexuality, and about the sexual relation. But it stops there. Refusing to interpret the historical determinants of its discourse—'. . . that thing I detest for the best of reasons, that is, History'—and in particular what is implied by the up to now exclusively masculine sexualization of the application of its laws, it remains caught up in phallocentrism, which it claims to make into a universal and eternal value."[83] Or again:

> The insufficient questioning of historical determinations is part and parcel, obviously, of political and material history. So long as psychoanalysis does not interpret its entrapment within a certain type of regime of property, within a certain type of discourse (to simplify, let us say that of metaphysics), within a certain type of religious mythology, it cannot raise the question of female sexuality. This latter cannot in fact be reduced to one among other isolated questions within the theoretical and practical field of psychoanalysis; rather, it requires the interpretation of the cultural capital and the general economy underlying that field.[84]

"Metaphysical," we will remember, was also the adjective used by Deleuze and Guattari to describe psychoanalysis. In fact, Irigaray also compares Freud to Kant for relying on transcendental hypotheses.[85] In this context, Irigaray calls psychoanalysis a "negative theology"[86] based on a notion of desire as lack, but also as trapped in idealism, particularly with the concept of the phallus.[87] Given this framework, the point is not to reject psychoanalysis as a whole: this would be the "anti-analyst" position, which would simply

---

82. Ibid., 146.

83. Ibid., 102–3.

84. Ibid., 125.

85. On Kant, see Irigaray, *Speculum of the Other Woman,* 44. On Freud's metaphysical a priori, see Irigaray, *This Sex Which Is Not One,* 73, 123.

86. Irigaray, *This Sex Which Is Not One,* 89.

87. Ibid., 110.

FATHERLESS SOCIETIES AND ANTI-OEDIPAL PHILOSOPHIES   195

reverse the terms of the debate without fundamentally changing them. Instead, Irigaray describes her mission as follows: "I am trying to interpret the traditional operation of the analytic institution starting from what it fails to grasp of female sexuality, and from the masculine homosexual ideology that subtends it. And in particular from its relation to power."[88] In this context, "homosexual" does not refer to the sexual orientation but rather is to be taken literally as "of the same sex." As we will see, Irigaray's political position will be based on *difference* as opposed to this *sameness*.[89]

As for Deleuze and Guattari, Irigaray's primary objection to the symbolic order is that it introduces a particular social order. For Irigaray, it is one defined by men's exchange of women.[90] Irigaray juxtaposes structuralist anthropology (in particular, Lévi-Strauss's *Elementary Structures*) to structuralist psychoanalysis to argue:

> The society we know, our own culture, is based upon the exchange of women. Without the exchange of women, we are told, we would fall back into the anarchy (?) of the natural world, the randomness (?) of the animal kingdom. The passage into the social order, into the symbolic order, into order as such, is assured by the fact that men, or groups of men, circulate women among themselves, according to a rule known as the incest taboo. Whatever familial form this prohibition may take in a given state of society, its signification has a much broader impact. It assures the foundation of the economic, social, and cultural order that has been ours for centuries.[91]

Within this model of exchange, women can only be commodities (the recurring term is *marchandises*), with use-values and exchange-values for men.[92] Moreover, "the use, consumption, and circulation of their sexualized bodies underwrite the organization and the reproduction of the social order, in which they never have taken part as 'subjects.'"[93] As fetish-objects "in ex-

---

88. Ibid., 145.

89. For an interesting analysis of Irigaray's use of the hetero and homo, see Elizabeth Grosz, "The Hetero and the Homo: The Sexual Ethics of Luce Irigaray," in Burke, Schor, and Whitford, *Engaging with Irigaray,* 335–50.

90. Gayle Rubin came to remarkably similar conclusions in "The Traffic in Women: Notes on the 'Political Economy' of Sex," in *Toward an Anthropology of Women*, ed. Rayna R. Reiter (Monthly Review Press, 1975).

91. Irigaray, *This Sex Which Is Not One,* 170.

92. Ibid., 31.

93. Ibid., 84.

196   **CHAPTER 5**

changes, [women] are the manifestation and the circulation of a power of the Phallus, establishing relationships of men with each other."[94] In this system, described by Irigaray as a "socio-cultural endogamy," women can never actually participate in the exchange, and yet they remain necessary for the exchange to take place: it "forbid[s] commerce with women. Men make commerce of them, but they do not enter into any exchanges with them."[95] Within this structuralist social contract, women can only occupy certain prototypical social roles, just as psychoanalysis limits them to certain proto-typical psychic structures, in the case of the hysteric, for example. Thus, the mother, protected by the incest taboo, exists only to guarantee the repro-duction of the system, to preserve the social order without intervening or changing it. Conversely, the virgin serves as pure exchange value, while the prostitute is "tolerated" as "usage that is exchanged."[96]

According to Irigaray, psychoanalysis relies on the family to ascribe par-ticular psychic traits through the Oedipus complex. Similarly, the social/ economic order needs the family to perpetuate its existence: "the family has always been the privileged locus of women's exploitation . . . In the patriar-chal family, man is the proprietor of woman and children. Not to recognize this is to deny all historical determinism."[97] Within this framework, Irigaray describes heterosexuality as "nothing but the assignment of economic roles: there are producer subjects and agents of exchange (male) on the one hand, productive earth and commodities (female) on the other." Although this model is *homosexual* in the sense that it is run and established by men and for men only, it necessitates heterosexuality. Moreover, it requires the explicit condemnation of homosexuality "because the 'incest' involved in homo-sexuality has to remain in the realm of pretense." Indeed, Irigaray suggests that real homosexual relations (as in same-sex sexual acts)

> openly interpret the law according to which society operates, they threaten in fact to shift the horizon of that law. Besides, they challenge the nature, status, and "exogamic" necessity of the product of ex-change. By short-circuiting the mechanisms of commerce, might they also expose what is really at stake? Furthermore, they might lower the sublime value of the standard, the yardstick. Once the penis itself be-comes merely a means to pleasure, pleasure among men, the phallus

---

94. Ibid., 183.

95. Ibid., 172.

96. Ibid., 186.

97. Ibid., 142.

FATHERLESS SOCIETIES AND ANTI-OEDIPAL PHILOSOPHIES   197

loses its power. Sexual pleasure, we are told, is best left to those crea-
tures who are ill-suited for the seriousness of symbolic rules, namely
women. Exchanges and relationships, always among men, would thus
be required and forbidden by law.[98]

Given these restrictions, what can women do? As Irigaray asks, "What
can be said of a feminine sexuality 'other' than the one prescribed in, and
by, phallocratism? How can its language be recovered, or invented? How,
for women, can the question of their sexual exploitation be articulated with
the question of their social exploitation? What position can women take,
today, with respect to politics?"[99] On these questions, Irigaray is perhaps
clearest on one point: the kind of political action she is advocating cannot
be constructed as a simple reversal of the existing order, one modeled along
the same political and philosophical presuppositions. In that sense, it seems
particularly surprising that so many of Irigaray's readers—especially those
coming from materialist feminism—have accused her of essentialism given
that her project wants to achieve precisely the opposite effect. By undermining the *two* terms of the woman-man binary and by refusing to simply
reverse the terms of the equation (or of the inequality), Irigaray's procedure
appears, if anything, closer to Derridian deconstruction than to essentialism
or reverse-essentialism.[100]

Thus, Irigaray wonders, "It would be interesting to know what might
become of psychoanalytic notions in a culture that did not repress the
feminine. Since the recognition of a 'specific' female sexuality would challenge the monopoly on value held by the masculine sex alone, in the final
analysis by the father, what meaning could the Oedipus complex have in a
symbolic system other than patriarchy?" But answering her own question,
she immediately asserts, "But that order is indeed the one that lays down the
law today. To fail to recognize this would be as naïve as to let it continue to
rule without questioning the conditions that make domination possible."[101]
Similarly, she suggests that "what is important is to disconcert the staging
of representation according to *exclusively* 'masculine' parameters, that is,

---

98. Ibid., 192–93.

99. Ibid., 119.

100. For an analysis of the debate surrounding Irigaray's "essentialism," see Naomi Schor, "The
Essentialism Which Is Not One," and Margaret Whitford, "Reading Irigaray in the Nineties," in
Burke, Schor, and Whitford, *Engaging with Irigaray*. See also Diana Fuss, *Essentially Speaking: Femi-
nism, Nature and Difference* (Routledge, 1989), chap. 4.

101. Irigaray, *This Sex Which Is Not One,* 73.

198   **CHAPTER 5**

according to a phallocratic order. It is not a matter of toppling that order so as to replace it—that amounts to the same thing in the end—but of disrupting and modifying it, starting from an 'outside' that is exempt, in part from phallocratic law."[102] Or, to give one last example,

> It clearly cannot be a matter of substituting feminine power for masculine power. Because this reversal would still be caught up in the economy of the same, in the same economy—in which, of course, what I am trying to designate as "feminine" would not emerge. There would be a phallic "seizure of power." Which, moreover, seems impossible: women may 'dream' of it, it may sometimes be accomplished marginally, in limited groups, but for society as a whole, such a substitution of power, such a reversal of power, is impossible.[103]

Irigaray's caution against a form of politics premised on the reversal of phallocratic order explains her ambivalence toward feminism as an organized political movement, and more specifically toward the Mouvement de libération des femmes (MLF). According to Irigaray, organized feminist movements have accomplished a number of things:

> liberalized contraception, abortion, and so on. These gains make it possible to raise again, differently, the question of what the social status of women might be—in particular through its differentiation from a simple reproductive-maternal function. But these contributions may always just as easily be turned against women. In other words, we cannot yet speak, in this connection, of a feminine politics, but only of certain conditions under which it may be possible. The first being an end to silence concerning the exploitation experienced by women: the systematic refusal to 'keep quiet' practiced by the liberation movements.[104]

Her fear, however, is that by focusing on "equality," feminist movements will simply struggle for women to have the same opportunities as men in the *public* sphere, without questioning and transforming the *private*—the subjective and the sexual. For Irigaray, demands for civil rights are "certainly indispensable stages in the escape from their proletarization on the exchange market. But if their aim were simply to reverse the order of things, even supposing this to be possible, history would repeat itself in the long run, would

---

102. Ibid., 68 (emphasis in original).

103. Ibid., 130.

104. Ibid., 128.

FATHERLESS SOCIETIES AND ANTI-OEDIPAL PHILOSOPHIES 199

revert to sameness: to phallocratism. It would leave room neither for women's sexuality, nor for women's imaginary, nor for women's language to take (their) place."[105] Similarly, she writes:

> when women's movements challenge the forms and nature of political life, the contemporary play of powers and power relations, they are in fact working toward a modification of women's status. On the other hand, when these same movements aim simply for a change in the distribution of power, leaving intact the power structure itself, then they are resubjecting themselves, deliberately or not, to a phallocratic order. This latter gesture must of course be denounced, and with determination, since it may constitute a more subtly concealed exploitation of women. Indeed, that gesture plays on a certain naiveté that suggests one need only be a woman to remain outside the phallic order.[106]

The MLF should thus not renounce its demands for equality in the sphere of civil rights. But it should also reflect on how to articulate "the double demand—for equality and difference."[107]

Irigaray's insistence on the interdependence of the political/social and the subjective/psychic makes sense in light of her extensive discussion of the symbolic order, which, as I have suggested, serves to structure the subjective, the sexual, and the social, all at once. Thus, the MLF has focused on transforming the social, but Irigaray wants to imagine other strategies to rethink the other two terms of the triad, the sexual and the subjective. It is in this context that she preaches masturbation—or "self-affection"—as a way to sidestep the male-centered phallic model of sexuality. Because self-affection falls *outside* the Oedipal economy, it is not surprising that psychoanalysis and society have taken such an interest in repressing the practice: "No effort is spared to prevent this touching, to prevent her from touching herself: the valorization of the masculine sex alone, the reign of the phallus and its logic of meaning and its system of representation, these are just some of the ways women's sex is cut off from itself and woman is deprived of her 'self-affection.' "[108]

Irigaray's reliance on psychoanalysis, and more specifically on Lacanian psychoanalysis, is evident in her attention to language, which, as we have

---

105. Ibid., 33.

106. Ibid., 81.

107. Ibid.

108. Ibid., 133.

200   **CHAPTER 5**

seen, is intimately tied to the symbolic. Language would provide a new system of representation for women: "In order to prevent the other—not the inversed *alter ego* of the 'masculine' subject or *its* complement, or *its* supplement, but that other, woman—from being caught up again in systems of representation whose goal of teleology is to reduce her within the same, it is of course necessary to interpret *any process of reversal, of overturning,* also as an *attempt to duplicate the exclusion of what exceeds representation*: the other, woman."[109] Irigaray calls this new system of representation of the feminine the *parler-femme,* or "speaking (as) woman," which, as Irigaray's English translators tell us, "would try to disrupt or alter the syntax of discursive logic, based on the requirements of univocity and masculine sameness, in order to express the plurality and mutuality of feminine difference and mime the relations of 'self-affection.'"[110] The last essay in *This Sex Which Is Not One,* "When Our Lips Speak Together," seeks precisely to put this *parler-femme* into application, with lips referring to both the sexual organ and the medium for language:

> If we don't invent a language, if we don't find our body's language, it will have too few gestures to accompany our story. We shall tire of the same ones, and leave our desires unexpressed, unrealized. Asleep again, unsatisfied, we shall fall back upon the words of men—who, for their part, have "known" for a long time. But *not our body.* Seduced, attracted, fascinated, ecstatic with our becoming, we shall remain paralyzed. Deprived of *our movements.* Rigid, whereas we are made for endless change. Without leaps or falls, and without repetitions.[111]

Anti-Oedipal Lifestyles: Psych et Po and the FHAR

For Deleuze, Guattari, and Irigaray, the critique of the structuralist symbolic was not simply a philosophical enterprise. Because kinship was intimately tied to the social and the individual, any revolutionary program required a revolution in kinship, a transformation of sexuality and "lifestyle." During the 1960s and 1970s, two groups attempted to "apply" the anti-Oedipal theories of Deleuze, Guattari, and Irigaray. The first was a branch of the women's movement calling itself Psychanalyse et politique, which

---

109. Ibid., 156 (emphasis in original).

110. Ibid., 222 (emphasis in original).

111. Ibid., 214.

FATHERLESS SOCIETIES AND ANTI-OEDIPAL PHILOSOPHIES 201

became known as Psych et Po. The second was the Front homosexuel d'action révolutionnaire (FHAR), led by the charismatic figure of Guy Hocquenghem.

Psych et Po began as a consciousness-raising group for women founded in the aftermath of May '68. The group met on Friday evenings at the home of Antoinette Fouque, who is often considered the leader of the movement. Fouque, a professor of literature writing a doctoral thesis with Roland Barthes, had worked as an editor at the Éditions du Seuil throughout the sixties. In particular, she had assisted François Wahl, Lacan's editor, in the laborious publication of the *Écrits*. Fouque's encounter with psychoanalysis, and more specifically with Lacan, was decisive. She attended his seminars on a regular basis and eventually decided to undergo analysis with Lacan himself from 1969 to 1974.[112] In 1970, she was asked to give a seminar at Vincennes where Psych et Po drew large crowds and became a social movement of its own. Fouque's Friday meetings were conceived as an extension of her theoretical work.

According to Fouque, Psych et Po grew out of a double disillusionment: with Marxism on the one hand, and with the kind of materialist feminism inspired by Simone de Beauvoir which guided much of the MLF on the other. As Fouque puts it, "nothing really suited us" in the doctrines of Marx, Engels, and Lenin: "We were eager to free ourselves from the constraints of our domestic, professional, and emotional lives. We wanted to expand the field of our subjectivity. We wanted to throw ourselves into the discovery of women through the discovery of each other, starting with ourselves. We were launched in Marxist-Leninist-Maoist causes but we swam against the current."[113] Moreover, Fouque continues, "I was hoping to understand what was unconscious in our political commitments. I wanted to bring out the power of psychoanalysis, not only in institutions and schools, but in the discovery of the unconscious and its theorization. To me, it seemed vital that one of us knew and questioned the other, and vice versa. In short, the unconscious existed in the political and the political in the unconscious."[114]

Psychoanalysis thus offered a double possibility, at the level of the subjective and of the political. The Friday meetings were structured like a group therapy session presided over by Fouque, in which the women would explore

---

112. See Antoinette Fouque, *Il y a deux sexes: Essais de féminologie* (Gallimard, 2004), 26–27. Elisabeth Roudinesco claims that Fouque's analyst was Irigaray, but this seems contradicted by Fouque's own account. See Roudinesco, *La bataille de cent ans*, 2:525.

113. Fouque, *Il y a deux sexes*, 32.

114. Ibid., 33.

202   **CHAPTER 5**

their fears, their fantasies, and their internalized misogyny. The goal was to reach a certain "erotic independence," to unearth the specificity of a feminine unconscious.[115] But psychoanalysis was not just a tool for self-exploration: it was considered, as thinkers such as Irigaray had suggested, the best mechanism to examine and understand the social and the political. As Psych et Po described itself in a 1972 issue of the feminist newspaper *Le Torchon Brûle,* its purpose was to analyze "our contradictions . . . the work we do using ourselves, our bodies, our unconscious, our sexuality as the starting point, always trying to link subjectivity to history and the political to the sexual."[116] Because "women's power is not legal, patriarchal, sadistic, pederastic, it is not concerned with representation, with leadership, with names, with rape, repression, hatred, avarice, knowledge, order, individualism, with abstractions. It is a non-power of the matrix, of birthings, giving, chaos, differences, of collective freedoms, of openings, of bodies, of recognitions, of lifting censorships, of pleasure, outside the law, it is a power-to, act-think-do, by/for all women, all."[117] The point of the movement was to think about equality and difference together, to place sexual difference as the "fourth principle" of society, alongside liberty, equality, and fraternity. All this was destined to trigger, in Fouque's words, a "revolution of the symbolic."[118]

Psych et Po left very few written traces, and by the 1980s its name was associated with many scandals and controversies that made it difficult to measure or adequately assess its legacy.[119] Yet if we consider Psych et Po in

---

115. For an amusing account of these sessions, see Anne Tristan and Annie de Pisan, *Histoires du M.L.F.* (Calmann-Lévy, 1977), 90, and Françoise Picq, *Libération des femmes: Les années-mouvement* (Seuil, 1993), 127.

116. Cited in Claire Duchen, *Women's Rights and Women's Lives in France, 1944–1968* (Routledge, 1994), 32.

117. *Le Torchon Brûle,* cited ibid., 36 (translation modified).

118. Fouque, *Il y a deux sexes,* 53.

119. In 1979, for instance, Psych et Po registered the name Mouvement de libération des femmes as an official *association* with the MLF logo. Many of the MLF members, especially those who disapproved of Psych and Po's strategies, which they deemed obscure, sectlike, and elitist, were furious. They circulated a petition denouncing Psych et Po for attempting to "monopolize the women's liberation movement—either to capture it or to destroy it." For more on this, see Duchen, *Women's Rights,* 32–39, and the text by Nadja Ringart in *Chroniques d'une imposture: Du mouvement de libération des femmes à une marque commerciale* (Association mouvement pour les luttes féministes, 1981). Another scandal emerged when, after the death of Simone de Beauvoir, Fouque wrote an obituary in *Libération* hoping that Beauvoir's death would "accelerate the entry of women in the Twenty-First Century" and condemning Beauvoir's "intolerant universalism, heinously assimilationist, sterilizing, reductive of all others." In opposition, she called for the need to be open to "pluralism, to fecund differences which, as each of us knows, take their sources, are informed by, and begin,

FATHERLESS SOCIETIES AND ANTI-OEDIPAL PHILOSOPHIES   203

light of Irigaray's theories, we can see how the "revolution of the symbolic" might lead to a kind of political action different from both the Marxism and existentialism that had dominated feminism at the time. Feminism, according to Psych et Po, needed to operate at a double level: on the subjective and on the social. Through psychoanalysis and consciousness-raising groups, women would be able to shed their Oedipal education. On a more collective level, the group launched a series of bookshops, magazines, and even a publishing company called the Édition des femmes, whose goal was precisely to enact the kind of *parler-femme* preached by Irigaray. Language, kinship, and society were intimately linked, and any true revolutionary action needed to "articulate history and the unconscious."[120]

The history of the Front homosexuel d'action révolutionnaire intersected with that of the MLF. Both were products of May '68, and both were born out of the generalized spirit of contestation and disenchantment with the traditional Marxist approach to questions of gender and sexuality. In May 1970, Antoinette Fouque, Monique Wittig, and other MLF feminists were booed by leftist students as they conducted their first official meeting at Vincennes. During the occupation of the Sorbonne in May 1968, a certain Comité d'action pédérastique révolutionnaire (CAPR) put up posters denouncing homophobia and celebrating sexual diversity—they were immediately taken down. On March 10, 1971, the famous radio "sex-therapist" Ménie Grégoire devoted one of her shows to "homosexuality, this painful problem." Several activists from the MLF who were interested in the idea of a "gay liberation" movement interrupted the show, screaming "It's not true, we are not suffering!" The FHAR was officially born that day. From 1971 to 1974, the same auditorium of the École des beaux-arts on the rue Bonaparte that had hosted the MLF meetings since 1968 became the formal headquarters of the FHAR gatherings. The members of both organizations interacted, several crossed over, and the FHAR joined the MLF in its first public march in the streets of Paris on November 20, 1971.

Prior to the creation of the FHAR, the only organization available to French homosexuals was Arcadie, a secretive association of self-described "homophiles" modeled on the Swiss Der Kreis, founded in 1954 by a philosophy teacher, André Baudry. Condemning effeminacy and promiscuity, Arcadie sought to promote a homosexual lifestyle inspired by the ancient

---

with sexual difference"; cited in Catherine Rodgers, "Elle et Elle: Antoinette Fouque et Simone de Beauvoir," *Modern Language Notes* 115 (2000): 741.

120. Picq, *Libération des femmes,* 126.

204   **CHAPTER 5**

Greeks. Above all, it sought to facilitate the normalization and integration of homosexuals in society.[121] Despite the visible discomfort of most left-wing groups around gay issues, a new form of activism was emerging in the seventies, inspired partly by the American examples of the civil rights movement, radical feminism, and the gay liberation movement that had been developing since the Stonewall protests in 1969. In 1970, the Maoist group Vive la révolution (VLR) reprinted in its journal *Tout* (the full title being *Tout: Ce Que Nous Voulons!* or "Everything: We Want!") a speech delivered by Huey Newton of the Black Panthers in support of the women's and gay liberation movements.[122] Less than a year after, *Tout* published another issue that featured a four-page article on homosexuality and included a manifesto entitled "We Are More Than 343 Sluts [*Salopes*]. We Have Been Buggered by Arabs. We Are Proud of It and We Will Do It Again."[123] Their intention was to parody the highly controversial manifesto published in *Le Nouvel Observateur* earlier that month signed by 343 women—many of whom were famous public figures such as Simone de Beauvoir, Catherine Deneuve, Jeanne Moreau, Gisèle Halimi—claiming that they had had an abortion.[124] The government banned that issue of *Tout* and managed to seize 10,000 copies. Jean-Paul Sartre, the great patron of the Left who was *Tout*'s nominal director of publication, was brought up on charges of obscenity (*outrage aux bonnes mœurs*).[125]

Among the principal contributors to this issue of *Tout* on homosexuality was Guy Hocquenghem, a 25-year-old writer, philosopher, and graduate of

---

121. The best account of Arcadie's history is Julian Jackson, *Living in Arcadia: Homosexuality, Politics, and Morality in France from the Liberation to AIDS* (University of Chicago Press, 2009). There is also some scattered information on the group in Scott Gunther, *The Elastic Closet: A History of Homosexuality in France, 1942–Present* (Palgrave Macmillan, 2009); Frédéric Martel, *Le rose et le noir: Les homosexuels en France depuis 1968* (Seuil, 1996); Janine Mossuz-Lavau, *Les lois de l'amour: Les politiques de la sexualité en France, 1950–2002* (Payot & Rivages, 2002).

122. For an analysis of how the different leftist groups of time reacted to the FHAR and for more on Hocquenghem, see Ron Haas, "Guy Hocquenghem and the Cultural Revolution in France after May 1968," in *After the Deluge: New Perspectives on the Intellectual and Cultural History of Postwar France,* ed. Julian Bourg (Lexington Books, 2004).

123. The centrality of race in this statement is of course significant given the memory of the Algerian war haunting France. For an excellent analysis of the complicated relations between race and sexuality during this period, see Todd Shepard, " 'Something Notably Erotic': Politics, 'Arab Men,' and Sexual Revolution in Post-Decolonization France, 1962–1974," *Journal of Modern History* 84, no. 1 (2012).

124. See Mossuz-Lavau, *Les lois de l'amour,* 97–98. The magazine *Charlie-Hebdo* referred to the women as the 343 *salopes* or "sluts," the same term that the FHAR had used in *Tout*.

125. Haas, "Guy Hocquenghem," 190. See also Michael Moon's introduction to the English edition of Guy Hocquenghem, *Homosexual Desire* (Duke University Press, 1993).

FATHERLESS SOCIETIES AND ANTI-OEDIPAL PHILOSOPHIES

the École normale supérieure, who was active in the VLR group. Before joining the Maoist association, Hocquenghem had belonged to a series of communist student organizations, to Trotskyite groups, and to various communes in the suburbs of Paris. He was also very active during the May '68 protests. Before entering the École normale supérieure, while he was at the prestigious Lycée Henri IV, Hocquenghem had been involved with his philosophy teacher, René Schérer, a close friend of Deleuze, Lyotard, and Foucault, who also taught at Vincennes. Schérer introduced Hocquenghem to some of the major philosophical figures of the time, including Deleuze and Guattari whose work made a profound impression on the young writer. During the FHAR meetings, Hocquenghem emerged as the sort of leader who could discern the theoretical underpinnings of the blooming gay liberation movement.[126] In January 1972, Hocquenghem gave a long interview to *Le Nouvel Observateur* for a special issue on "The Homosexual Revolution." Later that year, his most famous work *Le désir homosexuel* came out, only a few months after *Anti-Oedipus. Homosexual Desire* inaugurated the dialogue among Hocquenghem, Deleuze, and Guattari that was to continue for many years.[127]

From the introduction to *Homosexual Desire*, Hocquenghem's intellectual debt to *Anti-Oedipus* is evident. Because of society's fear of homosexuality, Hocquenghem writes, "homosexual desire is socially eliminated from childhood by means of a series of family and educational mechanisms."[128] To speak of a "homosexual desire" as such is meaningless, Hocquenghem tells us, because desire is not object-dependent; rather, it emerges as a multiple, uninterrupted, "unbroken and polyvocal flux."[129] Following Deleuze and Guattari on this understanding of desire, Hocquenghem argues that, since its inception, psychoanalysis has attempted to marginalize homosexuality, to shame it, to define it as a perversion, as narcissism, and ultimately to "Oedipalize it": "the Oedipus complex is the only effective means of controlling the libido. Stages need to be built, a pyramidal construction that will

---

126. For a peek at how these meetings were structured, see the documentary film by Carole Roussopolous on the FHAR from 1971, as well as Lionel Soukaz's 1979 *Raz d'Ep*, to which Hocquenghem contributed.

127. Deleuze, for instance, wrote the preface to Hocquenghem's 1974 book *L'après-mai des faunes,* translated into English in Deleuze, *Desert Islands,* 284–88. Hocquenghem also contributed to Guattari's journal *Recherches,* which in 1973 published an issue entitled "Three Million Perverts: The Great Encyclopedia of Homosexualities." Guattari was fined for this issue, as an *outrage aux bonnes mœurs.*

128. Hocquenghem, *Homosexual Desire,* 49.

129. Ibid., 50.

206   **CHAPTER 5**

enclose homosexual desire within the three sides of the triangle."[130] Similarly, Hocquenghem writes, "in the eyes of the psychoanalytic institution, [desire] must exist only as lack, or absence. It must always signify something, always relate to an object which will then become meaningful within the Oedipal triangulation."[131]

And like Deleuze and Guattari, Hocquenghem is as critical of Lacan's structuralist paradigm as he is of Freud: "The world of Oedipal sexuality is deprived of a free plugging in of organs, of the relations of direct pleasure. There is just one organ—a purely sexual organ—at the center of the Oedipal triangulation, the 'One' which determines the position of the three elements of the triangle. This is the organ which constructs absence; it is the 'despotic signifier,' in relation to which the situations of the whole person are created."[132] Because of the direct connection between the sexual and the social as articulated in the structuralist social contract, Hocquenghem refers to his society as "phallocratic," "inasmuch as social relationships as a whole are constructed according to a hierarchy which reveals the transcendence of the great signifier. The schoolmaster, the general and the departmental manager are the father-phallus; everything is organized according to the pyramidal mode, by which the Oedipal signifier allocates various levels and identifications."[133]

In *Homosexual Desire*, Hocquenghem's argument is indeed premised on the connection between the sexual, the psychic, and the social, as articulated by Lévi-Strauss, Lacan, Deleuze, Guattari, and Irigaray. For Hocquenghem, since the primary modality of social relations at the time he is writing is capitalism, the Oedipus complex and capitalism are also intrinsically linked. In fact, capitalism uses the Oedipus complex to control minds, to master the means of *re*production: "Capitalist ideology's strongest weapon is its transformation of the Oedipus complex into a social characteristic, an internalization of oppression which is left free to develop, whatever the political conditions."[134] Within this "control of minds," the family, Hocquenghem argues, plays a crucial role:

> The place of the family is now less in the institutions and more in the mind. The family is the place where sexual pleasure is legal, though

---

130. Ibid., 79.

131. Ibid., 77.

132. Ibid., 95.

133. Ibid., 96.

134. Ibid., 93.

FATHERLESS SOCIETIES AND ANTI-OEDIPAL PHILOSOPHIES 207

no longer in the sense that everybody has to marry in order to take their pleasure within the law; far from putting an end to the exclusive function of reproductive heterosexuality, the actual dissolution by capitalism of the functions of the family has turned the family into the rule inhabiting every individual under free competition. This individual does not replace the family, he prolongs its farcical games. The decoding of the fluxes of pleasure is accompanied by their axiomatisation, just as the disappearance of the journeyman's apprenticeship and the discovery of labor as value go hand in hand with the private ownership of the means of production.[135]

As this passage suggests, "the mind" should be the primary fighting terrain for the Left as opposed to the "institutions" which is what Marxism has traditionally focused on: "It is no longer sufficient to analyze society in terms of a conflict between conscious groups united by their interests (the classes). We must also recognize the existence, besides conscious (political) investments, of unconscious libidinal investments which sometimes conflict with the former."[136]

The fight against the Oedipal domination of the minds is thus also a revolutionary fight for a new society. Hocquenghem, however, distances himself from the revolutionary politics informing most leftist movements in the seventies: the driving force for social change is no longer class struggle, but desire. In his later work, Hocquenghem describes his strategy as one not destined for revolution but for *volutions*: "We must give up the dream of reconciling the official spokesmen of revolution with the expression of desire . . . Revolutionary demands must be derived from the very movement of desire; it isn't only a new revolutionary model that is needed, but a new questioning of the content traditionally associated with the term 'revolution,' particularly the notion of the seizure of power."[137] Moreover, Hocquenghem tells us, "revolutionary tradition maintains a clear division between the public and the private. The special characteristic of the homosexual intervention is to make what is private—sexuality's shameful little secret—intervene in public, in social organization."[138] Unlike Hirshfeld's

---

135. Ibid., 93–94.

136. Ibid., 72.

137. Ibid., 135. In his following work, *L'après-mai des faunes,* Hocquenghem explains that because revolutions can come so close to reactionary politics, "nous ne ferons plus en ré." In Guy Hocquenghem, *L'après-mai des faunes; volutions* (Grasset, 1974), 19.

138. Hocquenghem, *Homosexual Desire,* 136.

208   **CHAPTER 5**

Scientific Humanitarian Committee in Germany or Arcadie, the kind of homosexual struggle that Hocquenghem advocates is one where it is "no longer a matter of justifying, or vindicating, or even attempting a better integration of homosexuality within society."[139] Rather, the point is to explode society, to radically rethink the very terms of sociality.

Hocquenghem's new "social contract" privileges the figure of the anus, which Hocquenghem opposes to the phallus and which he defines with examples from the writings of Georges Bataille and Daniel Paul Schreber. In Freud's work, Hocquenghem contends, "the anus has no social desiring function left, because all its functions have become excremental: that is to say chiefly private."[140] Similarly, he writes, "whereas the phallus is essentially social, the anus is essentially private. If phallic transcendence and the organization of society around the great signifier are to be possible, the anus must be privatized in individualized and Oedipalized persons."[141] Whereas the phallic stage serves as an "identity stage," the anus "ignores sexual difference."[142] In contrast to the anus, the phallus "guarantees a social role."[143] This, in some ways, is exactly what Lacan and Lévi-Strauss argue. It is in this sense that Hocquenghem advocates "savagery" as opposed to "civilization" and that he refers to the homosexual movement as fundamentally uncivilized: "Civilization forms the interpretive grid through which desire becomes cohesive energy."[144] Against these grids, these pyramidal structures, these hierarchies, Hocquenghem defends a headless movement, an "unavowable community" that in his terms would have "no real center, no representatives."[145] His group would be a subject rather than subjected:

> The group which is composed of individuals, the phallic and hierarchical group, is subjected; it obeys civilized institutions whose values it adopts because the individual feels weaker than the institution, and because the individual's tempo is circumscribed by death while the institutions are apparently immortal. In the subject group, the opposition between the collective and the individual is transcended; the subject group is stronger than death because the institutions appear to

---

139. Ibid., 133.

140. Ibid., 96.

141. Ibid.

142. Ibid., 102.

143. Ibid., 97.

144. Ibid., 137.

145. Ibid., 146.

FATHERLESS SOCIETIES AND ANTI-OEDIPAL PHILOSOPHIES   209

it to be mortal. The homosexual subject group—circular and horizontal, annular and with no signifier—knows that civilization alone is
mortal.[146]

ᴖ Anti-Oedipal Ethics

In his preface to the English edition of *Anti-Oedipus*, Michel Foucault calls
Deleuze and Guattari's work, "a book of ethics, the first book of ethics to be
written in France in quite a long time."[147] *Anti-Oedipus*, Foucault suggests,
despite its "extraordinary profusion of new notions and surprise concepts,"
should not be understood as a new "philosophy." It is not "a flashy Hegel."
Rather, it should be read as an "art": "Questions are less concerned with
why this or that than with how to proceed. How does one introduce desire
into thought, into discourse, into action? How can and must desire deploy
its forces within the political domain and grow more intense in the process
of overturning the established order? *Ars erotica, ars theorica, ars politica*."[148]
Comparing *Anti-Oedipus* to Saint Francis de Sales's *Introduction to the Devout
Life*, Foucault argues that "being anti-Oedipal has become a life style, a way

---

146. Ibid., 147. We can mention in this context the similarities between Hocquenghem's work and
recent contributions to queer theory that rely on psychoanalysis to advocate selflessness, sublimation, and a new form of queer relationality. I am thinking in particular of the works of Tim Dean
(*Beyond Sexuality* and *Unlimited Intimacy*) and Leo Bersani (in particular *Homos* and *Intimacies*). In
their recent works on barebacking, "bug chasing," and "gift giving" within the gay male community, both authors imagine a new form of gay identity outside of normativity, a community based
on nonstructured intimacies, a new kind of non-ego-based identifications and ethics. What interests me in the comparison is how Dean, Bersani, and Hocquenghem can reach similar conclusions
through completely opposite means, as Dean and Bersani depend on psychoanalysis while Hocquenghem's argument is premised on the critique of the Oedipal model. Dean appears to want to
"save" Hocquenghem as well as Deleuze and Guattari from the "anti-Lacanian" label. As he puts it,
"in view of the tendency to read *Anti-Oedipus* as an unequivocal denunciation of the Freudo-
Lacanian tradition, it is also worth noting that Félix Guattari, who was gay, had been trained by
Lacan and remained both a member of his École freudienne de Paris (EFP) and a practicing analyst
even after the publication of *Anti-Oedipus*. Hocquenghem too, while composing *Homosexual Desire*,
was teaching philosophy at Vincennes, practically next door to Lacan's department of psychoanalysis, and therefore effectively he was working in a Lacanian milieu" (Dean, *Beyond Sexuality*, 243–
44). Although these biographical elements may or may not be true (in his diaries, Guattari talks
primarily about his relationship with women and not men), they hardly suffice to suggest that *Anti-
Oedipus* was not an "unequivocal denunciation of the Freudo-Lacanian tradition." As I have argued,
both Guattari and Deleuze had complicated personal relationships with Lacan, but *Anti-Oedipus*
itself is very much a critique of the Lacanian structuralist system, and in particular of the symbolic,
and so is Hocquenghem's *Homosexual Desire*.

147. Deleuze and Guattari, *Anti-Oedipus*, xiii.

148. Ibid., xii.

210   **CHAPTER 5**

of thinking and living."[149] Similarly, I would suggest that Irigaray's work proposes an *ethics of sexual difference*—the title of one of her later books: "A revolution in thought and ethics is needed if the work of sexual difference is to take place. We need to reinterpret everything concerning the relations between the subject and the discourse, the subject and the world, the subject and the cosmic, the microcosmic and the macrocosmic."[150] For Irigaray, the point was not to develop a new theory or "philosophy" of womanhood, but rather to indicate—and to invent if necessary—a set of practices that could open the self to the other.

As I have argued in this chapter, Deleuze, Guattari, Irigaray, Fouque, and Hocquenghem all sought in different ways to rework the structuralist social contract through alternative kinships. Deeply aware of the connections between the sexual, the social, the psychic, the linguistic, and the ethical, these authors sought to imagine new modes of subjectivities, socialities, and behaviors. As Foucault suggests, ethical work required "*ars erotica, ars theorica, ars politica*" all at once. And indeed, for these thinkers the philosophical critique of the structuralist symbolic, the refusal of normative kinship, and the social revolution were part of the same project: the possibility of theorizing and enacting anti-Oedipal ethics.

---

149. Ibid., xiii. The distinction between morality and ethics is crucial in Foucault's thought. Foucault highlights this difference at the end of *The Order of Things* and develops it more fully in volumes 2 and 3 of *The History of Sexuality*. See Michel Foucault, *Histoire de la sexualité* (Gallimard, 1976), 2:32–37; Foucault, *Order of Things,* 327–28.

150. Luce Irigaray, *An Ethics of Sexual Difference,* trans. Carolyn Burke and Gillian Gill (Cornell University Press, 1993), 6.

PART THREE

The Return of Familialism

✒ CHAPTER 6

Alternative Kinships and Republican Structuralism

During the last two decades of the twentieth century, the debate around the historicity of the family continued. Some politicians, lawyers, and scholars insisted on the need to adapt the family to modern society, to the "tide of history." Others, such as Irène Théry, deplored the legal "instrumentalization" of the family and called for the creation of new norms, for "alternative symbolic and legal references."[1] The most contentious family laws passed after the 1980s—and in particular, the two that interest me in this chapter, the 1994 bioethics laws designed to regulate medically assisted reproduction and the 1999 Pacte civil de solidarité (PACS) which gave a series of legal benefits to more loosely defined "couples," independent of their sexual orientation—were significantly different from the previous modifications of the Civil Code.

First, starting in the early 1980s, lawmakers had to contend with the development of biotechnologies and the popularization of assisted reproductive technologies. The invention of in vitro fertilization, the possibility of "freezing" sperm, the birth of the first "test tube babies," and medical experiments with surrogacy prompted a series of ethical questions. Legislators were not only concerned with the legality of each of these procedures.

---

1. Irène Théry, *Le démariage: Justice et vie privée* (Odile Jacob, 1993), 125.

213

214   CHAPTER 6

They were also expected to determine and define who could have access to them, whether they should be limited to heterosexual couples of reproductive age, or whether they should be open to individuals, unmarried couples, postmenopausal women, and homosexuals.

Second, the social actors involved in the debates had changed. The "quiet revolution" of the 1960s and 1970s was primarily geared toward married or no-longer-married mothers and fathers. In other words, the laws had been constructed for and around the heterosexual reproductive family. By the 1980s, however, new groups were coming to the forefront and asking for rights, in particular single parents (who came to be known as *famille monoparentales*) and homosexuals.

Third, the international context—and perhaps France's relation to this context—was different. Legal cases involving surrogacy and adoption disputes, such as the famous 1988 case of "Baby M." in the United States, were cited as models by both the critics and the advocates of assisted reproductive technology. Gay activists in France also relied on the examples of other European countries that had legalized same-sex unions, which by the 1990s included Denmark, Norway, Sweden, Iceland, the Netherlands, and Belgium as well as some states in the United States. The definition, the limits, and the stakes of the reproductive family were renegotiated, nationally and internationally, during the 1980s and 1990s.

The bioethics laws and the PACS were debated for almost ten years, through six changes of administration, before they were passed. Disputed in the legislature, the courts, and the media, these laws broke traditional alliances on the right and the left and sparked prolonged and heated controversies. My interest in these legislative decisions is twofold. First, both debates were characterized by the frequent intervention of "experts" who called for a return to what I have been referring to as the structuralist social contract. Anchoring their claims in the works of Lévi-Strauss and Lacan, these experts argued against medically assisted procreation and same-sex unions on the basis that that they violated the fundamental pillar of the social contract: the family, and more specifically sexual difference. Navigating between the intellectual and the political realms, these experts functioned as the kind of bridge figures that have interested me in the previous chapters.

Second, many of these experts perceived the demands for civil unions and for access to assisted reproductive technologies as the culmination of a general fascination with legal, social, and philosophical anti-normativity, a process that began in the 1960s with the political critique of familialism and the intellectual critique of structuralism. After the "turning point of the

ALTERNATIVE KINSHIPS AND REPUBLICAN STRUCTURALISM 215

1960s," to borrow Irène Théry's expression (both a legal and a philosophical turning point), the heterosexual reproductive family could no longer serve as the basis of "the political," as the transcendental structure holding the social in place. Moreover, because kinship, according to these experts, was structurally connected not only to the social but also to the psychic, the linguistic, and the ethical, same-sex unions and medically assisted procreation challenged all of these domains and left us in a world of "indifferentiation," of social confusion and psychic malaise. It is in this context that many of these experts pleaded for a return to Republican familialism *and* to structuralism. Interweaving these two discourses, they argued that the family should be reconceived as the transcendental and transhistorical normative structure grounding the social. Thus, family law should turn to the thought of Lévi-Strauss and of Lacan or, more specifically, to their structuralist social contract, to their theory of the symbolic, or, to use the term proposed by Marcel Gauchet, to their "transcendental anthroposociology."[2] Family law, they argued, did not exist to satisfy individual demands or to reflect social and historical reality. Rather, it had a fundamental "anthropological" or "symbolic" function that ensured the proper integration of individuals into the social world and guaranteed their psychic well-being.

The rhetorical and political force of this argument, I wish to suggest, lay in the conflation of this structuralist social contract and republican familialism. The symbolic as theorized by Lévi-Strauss and Lacan, became, throughout these debates, synonymous with republicanism more broadly, with the specifically French model of social organization, always defined in opposition to totalitarianism on one extreme (whether in the form of Communism, Nazism, or, more recently, Islamic fundamentalism) and the "Anglo-Saxon" liberal framework on the other extreme. In this context, the demands to liberalize bioethics and marriage were presented not only as an instrumentalization of the law ("legal positivism" was the most recurring term), but as an attack on France that would have pernicious effects on both the social and the psyche. Thus, when lawyers, activists, social scientists, and politicians—some inspired by the new legal and political possibilities around the family described in Chapter 4, others by the kind of theoretical critiques of structuralism described in Chapter 5—turned to the discourse of privacy and rights (or *droits humains*) to argue for their right to raise children outside of the context of the heterosexual nuclear family, these experts insisted that such demands violated the symbolic nature of the social and

---

2. Marcel Gauchet, *La condition historique* (Stock, 2003), 13, 18.

216   **CHAPTER 6**

the "anthropological function of the law." The only "right" to be had, the latter contended, was the right to be integrated into a symbolic order defined around a normative construction of the heterosexual reproductive family. Despite triggering an important public debate around the normative function of the family, both the 1994 bioethics laws and the 1999 PACS ultimately left the heterosexual reproductive family intact as the only structure able to uphold the social and the individual, and thus, as the only structure that the law ought to recognize.

Assisted Reproductive Technology in the 1980s

On February 24, 1982, the first French test tube baby, Amandine, was born in a maternity clinic outside of Paris. The medical team supervising Amandine's conception had followed the footsteps of their British colleagues who, in 1978, had performed the first successful in vitro fertilization procedure, which gave birth to Louise Brown. By 1982, artificial insemination was no longer a new technology, as it had become more common throughout the 1970s. The Centres d'étude et de conservation des œufs et du sperme humains (CECOS) had been operational since 1973, and ten years later it was estimated that 7,000 children had been born by artificial insemination. Amandine, however, was the first publicized case to be performed within a hospital facility; as a result, she was the first to receive extensive media coverage. In the years after Amandine's birth, the French press documented the evolution of reproductive technologies throughout the world, focusing particularly on cases that appeared to test the limits of ethics and the law. In 1985, a French woman, Corinne Parpalaix, requested to be inseminated with her deceased husband's sperm, which she had had frozen. In Great Britain, a white couple gave birth to a black baby because of a paperwork error by a sperm bank employee.

More importantly, artificial insemination presented a series of immediate problems for French filiation law, which began to recognize biological ties between father and child after 1972. Children born through sperm donation had logically two fathers, at the very least: one biological and one social. Thus, legislators and experts argued in the columns of the French press whether the biological father ought to retain any legal rights over the child; whether unmarried men ought to be allowed to donate their sperm, and whether the donation ought to be anonymous; whether sperm should be sold, and whether it should be frozen; and whether artificial insemination should be restricted to married couples, or whether it should be made

ALTERNATIVE KINSHIPS AND REPUBLICAN STRUCTURALISM   217

available to unmarried individuals, cohabiting heterosexual couples, divorced individuals, and homosexuals.

The new reproductive technologies of the 1980s threatened not only the coherence of paternity but also challenged the Civil Code's definition of maternity as *mater semper est*. Surrogacy, unregulated in France until the 1994 bioethics law, emerged as a particularly problematic issue. In 1983, France opened its first surrogacy association, the Association nationale de l'insémination artificielle par substitution (ANIAS). Unlike its British and American counterparts, which treated surrogacy like any other contractual transaction, ANIAS insisted that surrogacy arrangements remain "gratuitous gifts." In 1984, however, a young woman whom the media called "Patricia" agreed to carry the child of a couple in exchange for 50,000 francs. The press was similarly enthralled with the "first surrogate grandmother," a forty-eight-year old South African woman who, in 1987, gave birth to triplets who were genetically the children of her daughter and son-in-law.[3] In these cases, public commentators deplored the commodification of reproduction, the subjection of kinship to the "rules of market," the "enslavement" of women, and the violation of the incest taboo.

During these years, the press became particularly captivated by one doctor, Sacha Geller. In opposition to the ANIAS, Geller helped to create three associations through which surrogate mothers could receive financial compensation for their services: Alma mater and Les cigognes (the storks), geared toward the surrogate mothers, and Sainte Sarah (in reference to the biblical character), geared toward sterile women. Geller proposed to set the surrogacy "salary" at 50,000 francs, which by his calculations corresponded to 5,000 francs per month for nine months of pregnancy plus one postpartum month. This sum amounted to the minimum wage (salaire minimum interprofessionnel de croissance, or SMIC). In addition to their financial compensation, surrogate mothers were always given the option to keep the child if they changed their mind in the course of the pregnancy.

Legally speaking, Geller's plan was impeccable. Since the Revolution, France had a peculiar legal measure known as "*accouchement sous X*." A mother who did not want to keep her baby could anonymously—or "in secret," to use the terms of the Civil Code—give birth to the child, which would then be registered by the hospital as "born under X."[4] Thus, if an

---

3. *Le Monde*, June 7–8, 1987.

4. For a history and legal analysis of the *accouchement sous X*, see Cécile Ensellem, *Naître sans mère? Accouchement sous X et filiation* (Presses universitaires de Rennes, 2004).

218   **CHAPTER 6**

infertile couple requested a surrogate, Geller would impregnate the surrogate with the sperm of the intended father. The child would be "born under *X*" with no official mother but would be recognized by the father at birth. Eventually, his wife would also be able to adopt the child so that in legal terms, and in perfect accord with French filiation laws, the baby would have one father and one mother only. The French courts were less than enthusiastic about Geller's legal maneuvers. In the absence of an official law banning surrogacy, judges invented new legal concepts such as the "non-disposability" of human bodies, the "perversion [*détournement*]" of the adoption institution, the "precarious" filiation of a child born from a surrogate mother, and the "socially undesirable" effects of surrogacy.[5] After a long legal battle, the Cour de cassation dissolved Alma mater in 1989, putting an end to Geller's attempt to promote a paid and contractual form of surrogacy in France.[6]

Pressed with the growing concern around bioethics, President François Mitterrand set up in 1983 a national committee, the Comité consultatif national d'éthique pour les sciences de la vie et de la santé (CCNE), designed to advise legislators on how best to regulate these new technologies in the fields of biology, medicine, and public health.[7] The CCNE was asked to organize annual conferences on various topics pertaining to bioethics and to publish their deliberations in order to keep the public informed. Headed by Jean Bernard, a medical researcher appointed by the president of the Republic, the committee was composed of thirty-six members: four representing France's main philosophical and religious groups; fourteen chosen by various governmental bodies (the Assembly, the Senate, the courts, and various ministries) for "their competence and their interest in ethical problems"; and fourteen emanating from various research institutions such as the Académie des sciences, the Collège de France, the Centre national de la recherche scientifique (CNRS), the Institut national de la santé et de la recherche médicale (ISERM), the Institut Pasteur, the Institut national de la recherche agronomique (INRA), and the universities.[8]

---

5. For a full analysis, see Marcela Iacub, *L'empire du ventre: Pour une autre histoire de la maternité* (Fayard, 2004), 223. According to Ruwen Ogien, these concepts were based on metaphysics rather than on jurisprudence; see *La vie, la mort, l'État: Le débat bioéthique* (Grasset, 2009).

6. Sacha Geller recounts his involvement in the battle to legalize surrogacy in Sacha Geller, *Mères porteuses oui ou non?* (Frison-Roche, 1990). For more on Geller and this history, see Iacub, *L'Empire du ventre*, 216–36; Dominique Mehl, *Naître: La controverse bioéthique* (Bayard, 1999), 64–73.

7. *Journal Officiel,* February 23, 1983.

8. For an in-depth study of the various members of the CCNE and for more on its broader history, see Dominique Memmi, *Les gardiens du corps: Dix ans de magistère bioéthique* (Éditions de l'école des hautes études en sciences sociales, 1996). All of the CCNE's opinions (or *avis*) are compiled in

ALTERNATIVE KINSHIPS AND REPUBLICAN STRUCTURALISM   219

In May 1984, the first opinion published by the CCNE concerned the sampling of embryonic tissue and dead human fetuses for therapeutic, diagnostic, and scientific ends. Although the CCNE came out in favor of the legalization of research on embryos, it defined the latter as a "potential person." The third opinion, published on October 23, 1984, tackled, as its title indicated, "the ethical problems raised by artificial reproduction techniques." Even at this early stage of its existence, the CCNE's position was one of caution with regard to assisted reproduction, particularly surrogacy, which it condemned as a materially exploitative and psychologically dangerous procedure. In their words, "the *Mater semper certa est* adage has not only a juridical value, but also a psychological and social value which we should not unsettle without the greatest circumspection."[9] By dissociating reproduction from parenting, assisted reproduction, the CCNE suggested, "directly question[ed] the way in which French society conceives of the status of the family [*statut familial*]."[10]

Whereas this first report already wondered whether "having a child" was a right that everyone should have under any conditions or circumstances, the eighth opinion, published on December 15, 1986, specified that artificial insemination had to be limited to sterile couples composed of a man and a women living together in a "stable relationship."[11] Many of the terms and concepts that were to structure the bioethics debates in the years to come were already present in this opinion, imploring that "human dignity" be preserved and warning against modern society's "procreative relentlessness [*archarnement procreatif*]." France Quéré, a theologian and member of the CCNE, wrote, for example, in her conclusion to the scientific report attached to the opinion, that "a child is the work of our flesh, not of our calculations and of our hands. It is engendered and not fabricated."[12] Quéré's choice of words is significant because both *chair* and *engendré* have a spiritual, almost sacred connotation, which distinguishes them from the purely biological or materialistic, a nuance confirmed by her choice of the adjective "transcendent" to describe the child as a human being. This opposition

---

Didier Sicard, ed., *Travaux du comité consultatif national d'éthique* (Presses universitaires de France, 2003). Soon after the foundation of the CCNE, other European countries followed France's example in entrusting ethical issues to a body of experts: Sweden in 1985, Denmark in 1987, Luxembourg in 1988, the Netherlands in 1989, and Italy in 1990.

9. Sicard, *Travaux du comité consultatif*, 102.

10. Ibid., 81.

11. Ibid., 113.

12. Ibid., 134.

220   **CHAPTER 6**

between *engendrement* and *procreation,* which came up again and again, had crucial consequences for the policies adopted.

In January 1985, at the request of Mitterrand, the CCNE organized a two-day colloquium entitled "Genetics, Procreation, and the Law." This was one of the first instances where legal scholars, in reference to the supposedly disastrous social and psychic effects of surrogacy, anonymous sperm donation, and frozen embryos, and in reaction also to Geller's legal scheming, alluded to a particular "anthropological" or "symbolic" function of French civil law. Because the CCNE had invited a number of public officials, the colloquium also provided a forum for these legal scholars to interact with lawmakers, many of whom would later refer to the "symbolic function of the law" in the parliamentary debates and procedures that followed. The colloquium, in other words, served as a forum for the popularization of this structuralist social contract linking kinship to the social and the psychic. Among the colloquium participants were the jurists and family law experts Jean Carbonnier and Catherine Labrusse-Riou; the psychoanalyst Françoise Dolto; the anthropologist Françoise Héritier; Pierre Laroque who had been involved in family policy since the de Gaulle postwar days; the sociologist Bruno Latour; Roger Burnel, the president of the Union nationale des associations familiales (UNAF); the former minister of the "feminine condition," Madeleine Pelletier; numerous scientists, including artificial insemination pioneers such as Jacques Testart; and philosophers and various journalists, including Jean-Yves Nau, the correspondent for *Le Monde* for questions of sexuality and reproduction.

In his talk, Jean Carbonnier, the former dean of the Faculty of Law at the Sorbonne and one of the most important law professors in France (see chap.4), claimed that although French civil law gave a central role to the notion of "personal will [*volonté*]," the new modes of artificial reproduction rested on a "highly individualistic philosophy."[13] Carbonnier condemned the legal philosophy espoused by many advocates of assisted reproduction for whom the law appeared simply as a "cooperative of individual forms of happiness [*une coopérative de bonheurs individuels*]." Individual happiness was not "a properly legal notion in France, despite the fact that the term [was] inscribed in the U.S. Constitution." Instead, Carbonnier suggested, what was really at the heart of French law—particularly that of family law—was the "collective interest." "A more impalpable social interest is attached to

---

13. *Actes du colloque génétique, procréation et droit* (Actes Sud, 1985), 80–81.

ALTERNATIVE KINSHIPS AND REPUBLICAN STRUCTURALISM   221

filiation law: by linking children to their parents this law contributes to the cohesion, vertical and horizontal, of the entire social body."[14] Along similar lines, Catherine Labrusse-Riou invoked the law's "symbolic function" to argue against the possibility of unmarried individuals accessing artificial insemination.[15] Kinship, she argued, could not be entirely subsumed in the biological: "single-parent artificial procreation would force the jurist to found filiation, paternal most of the time, on a purely genetic element. This would not be opportune . . . A father and a mother are more than just genitors [*Un père et une mère sont autre chose que des géniteurs*]."[16]

Among the government representatives invited to the colloquium was Robert Badinter, at the time minister of justice. Although Badinter avoided taking a public stand on these questions of bioethics during the CCNE colloquium, he did so a few weeks later in a talk entitled "Human Rights in the Face of the Progress in Medicine, Biology, and Biochemistry" that he delivered at the Council of Europe, on March 18, 1985. Given the hesitation concerning medically assisted procreation that many of the legal scholars and social scientists had expressed at the CCNE colloquium, Badinter's speech appeared to be an unequivocal argument in favor of the liberalization of the new reproductive technologies. Indeed, for Badinter, medically assisted procreation for married couples was relatively straightforward, both in ethical and legal terms. In such cases, civil law would need to be only slightly adapted in order to permit one or both of the intended parents to adopt their child before the birth. A much more contentious issue in his mind was the possibility of allowing single women to have children on their own, through an anonymous sperm donor, for example. As he put it, "To give all human beings the freedom of using artificial procreation technologies is ultimately to expand a woman's capacity to engender. More to the point, it is underlining the fact that while a man needs a woman to procreate, the woman, herself, might no longer need a man!"[17] According to Badinter, it was this fear that one day a women might no longer need a man to have a baby (or, to use his terms, the fear of *un masculin déclinant et une liberté declinée au seul féminin*) that was really behind the opposition to artificial insemination.

---

14. Ibid., 81.

15. Ibid., 39.

16. Ibid., 41.

17. Robert Badinter, "Les droits de l'homme face au progrès de la médecine, de la biologie et de la biochimie," *Le Débat* 36 (1985): 7.

222   **CHAPTER 6**

A second argument often invoked to prevent unmarried individuals from accessing reproductive technologies was that it was in the child's best interest to have two parents. "To be sure," Badinter replied, "for the child, two parents are most likely better than one. But what value can this wise observation have in our societies where divorce is common, where a mother can choose to be single or to remain ignorant of everything about her partner, where we are not moved by the fate of children born of a syphilitic woman who has married an alcoholic man? There is surely some paradox in invoking the child's interest to forbid him from being born."[18] Thus, Badinter continued, legislators needed to find answers not in this fictive "right of a child not-yet-born" nor in sexist fears about women taking over society, but rather in "our philosophy of human rights"—the philosophy, he argued, that underlay French law and "European civilization" more broadly.[19]

To link human rights to the question of reproduction, Badinter singled out two rights in particular, both of which, he reminded us, were solidly inscribed in the European Convention on Human Rights. The first, corresponding to Article 2, was the right to life. For Badinter, this formulation implied not only the right to live but also the right to *give life* and, consequently, the right to choose the means by which to do so.[20] The second was Article 8, stipulating a right to *intimité,* which, in the English version of the Convention, is translated as a right to privacy. Thus, Badinter continued, if the French state were to limit reproductive technologies to only married couples, it would do so in violation of Article 8, because one's marital status ultimately concerns one's private life, and in one's private life "every adult is an absolute master in our society. Our laws give an adult the right to be chaste or not, heterosexual or homosexual, to live alone or in a couple. And our laws guarantee the right for each of us not only to lead the kind of private life we choose, but also to see that there is absolute respect for the intimacy of this private life."[21] Given this definition of privacy, which, Badinter underscored, was one of the cornerstones of French republicanism, banning single women from access to artificial insemination would not only block their paths to personal fulfillment or happiness (*épanouissement*), but it also was an act of explicit discrimination and thus unacceptable within French law: "The right to give life cannot be denied to a woman who wants

---

18. Ibid., 8.

19. Ibid., 6.

20. Ibid., 8.

21. Robert Badinter, "Lecture faite . . ." *Le Débat* 36 (1985): 38.

ALTERNATIVE KINSHIPS AND REPUBLICAN STRUCTURALISM   223

to have a child. We should thus not prohibit her means to do so. Unless we want to enter into a different type of society. And all discrimination in this regard, whether it has a theological, philosophical, or political foundation, can only be the source of human injustice."[22]

Badinter's declarations caused an uproar in the French political world. As the head of the UNAF put it, Badinter's speech was symptomatic of the "savage liberalism" sweeping France.[23] Marcel Gauchet, the editor of *Le Débat,* offered to publish Badinter's speech a few months later in a special edition of his journal on "law, medicine, and life." Gauchet also invited five "experts" on questions of reproduction, including a biologist, a theologian, a scientist, an anthropologist, and a sociologist, to respond. As Gauchet stated in his introductory editorial, what was at stake in these debates was the "definition of individual rights, which is to say the political articulation between the living and the social." Despite the differences in disciplines and methodologies among these five respondents, all converged on an essential point: Badinter's legal framework of human rights—which came not from republicanism but from liberalism—could not provide an adequate basis for thinking through the problems of reproduction, gender, and sexuality. An-thropology, or at least a particular version of structuralist anthropology, could. This vision of "legal anthropology" in which the law held a double structural function for the social and the psyche found its most compelling theoriza-tion in the work of Françoise Héritier.

A student of Claude Lévi-Strauss and one of the most important contem-porary anthropologists in France, Héritier—whose publications and public commentaries were cited extensively throughout the bioethics debates—responded to Badinter's argument in an essay entitled "The Individual, the Biological, and the Social."[24] Héritier's main objection to Badinter was that his argument rested on a fundamental confusion between *engendrement,* the

---

22. Ibid., 39.

23. "Pour ou contre les mères porteuses," *Le Quotidien de Paris,* March 29, 1985.

24. Héritier was elected at the Collège de France in 1982 as chair of the Comparative Study of African Societies. Before that, she taught at the École pratique des hautes études and was associated both with the CNRS and the Laboratoire d'anthropologie sociale created by Lévi-Strauss in 1960. Although her fieldwork focused on kinship structures in Western Africa, Héritier's seminars at the Collège de France and at the École des hautes études en sciences sociales (EHESS) became increas-ingly tied to contemporary social problems such as incest, violence, identity, and alterity. In several of her essays, Héritier addresses her position of anthropologist *as* expert in social matters. See, for example, Françoise Héritier, *Masculin/féminin* (Paris: Odile Jacob, 1996), 17. Among her many gov-ernmental positions, we can list the Conseil national du sida, the Conseil économique et social, the Haut conseil de la francophonie, the Haut conseil de la population et de la famille, the Conseil de l'association française des femmes, le Conseil national pour les personnes âgées, and of course the

224   **CHAPTER 6**

biological fact of reproduction, and *filiation,* the legal act through which paternity and maternity were inscribed into the social order. Speaking "as an anthropologist," she explained, "there are no societies, to my knowledge, that do not make a difference between the social roles of *Pater* and *Mater* that establish filiation and the physiological functions of *genitor/genitrix,* the difference, in a way, between filiation and engenderment."[25] Whereas *engendrement* could indeed be understood as a private choice, *filiation* was, by definition, public, because it was the legal translation of a norm previously defined by the community. And as a norm, filiation always linked back to a mother and a father. In other words, filiation was, by definition, premised on sexual difference:

> Filiation is by nature a social bond [*un lien social*], which society takes into account to mark a child's inscription into one or many groups. In the ways we use it, [*Dans notre usage*], it is undifferentiated [*indifférenciée*] and bilateral to the extent that through the individuals incarnating the social roles of Pater and Mater, it attaches the child in the same way to the different lines running through ancestors of both sexes as they have been designated also through filiation.[26]

According to Héritier, "the social [could] never be reduced to the biological."[27] This by no means implied, however, that all biological configurations could be or should be legally acceptable: "If filiation is cut from, or at least does not necessarily stem from engendering, it is nonetheless substantially linked to the idea of a bisexuated reproduction, which is to say that it necessarily refers to the paternal and maternal status as the supports of the affiliation to the group. The idea of the thing is more important than reality [*L'idée de la chose prime sur la réalité*]."[28] As this statement suggests, the crux of the problem for Héritier was not of an empirical nature. From a purely biological standpoint, all kinds of kinship formations were possible and imaginable; indeed, Héritier cited the growing number of single-parent households in the 1980s as an example. The main issue, however, concerned the normative, the "idea of the thing," which, for Héritier, was in-

---

CCNE. For a full biography, see Jean-Luc Jamard, Emmanuel Terray, and Margarita Xanthakou, eds., *En substances: Textes pour Françoise Héritier* (Paris: Fayard, 2000), 583–84.

25. Françoise Héritier-Augé, "L'individu, le biologique et le social," *Le Débat* 36 (1985): 28.

26. Ibid., 29.

27. Ibid.

28. Ibid.

ALTERNATIVE KINSHIPS AND REPUBLICAN STRUCTURALISM   225

evitably rooted in sexual difference. Thus, what differentiated a married couple unable to conceive and having to resort to medically assisted procreation from a single woman desiring to have a child on her own was that the former, by having committed to marriage, had also somehow committed to this normative imperative, to this "idea of the thing," to what Héritier designated as the "arbitrary or artifice of the social." As she explained, "the fundamental element that serves as the touchstone to make this distinction is the will [*volonté*] of the partners, previously expressed and inscribed in a matrimonial status, that is to say in the arbitrary or artifice of the social."[29] From this claim, we can deduce that the law is the mechanism responsible for institutionalizing this "arbitrary and artificial" nature of the social, a social made possible only through sexual difference, or more precisely here, through heterosexual marriage. Thus, according to Héritier's argument, unmarried women wanting to have children on their own posed a problem not at the level of nature or biology, but at the level of culture. In other words, *they were the ones imprisoned in biologism* for refusing to accept the "arbitrary and artificial" nature of the social.

The exchange between Héritier and Badinter brought to light two conflicting visions of kinship, and also two conflicting notions of social organization and of normativity. Badinter's argument was based on a definition of marriage as pertaining to "private life," but Héritier's response erected marriage and heterosexual kinship as the condition of sociality. Far from belonging to "one's private life," marriage and kinship constituted, in fact, the very essence of the social—they *were* the public. As such, privacy or human rights—which according to Héritier were closer to "individual rights" in Badinter's argument—could not possibly provide an adequate legal philosophy for thinking through sexuality and reproduction. As Héritier put it,

> The individual who benefits from human rights is an anonymous, abstract, asexual [*asexué*], non-temporal being: he is a pure bearer of rights, all alone. However, in the act of engendering, one has to admit that the abstract individual is both an active and passive participant: the one who procreates and the one who is procreated [*dans l'acte d'engendrer, il faut bien admettre que l'individu abstrait est à la fois partie prenante et partie prise: celui qui procrée et celui qui est procréé*]. This simple observation sends us back to a fundamental philosophy: it is impossible to think pure individuality, either intellectually or socially. The

---

29. Ibid.

226   **CHAPTER 6**

individual can only be thought of in relation to the Other, to others. Thinking the individual thus comes up against the relation, which immediately involves the very essence of the social [*La pensée de l'individu achoppe donc sur la relation, laquelle implique immédiatement l'essence même du social*].[30]

Although Héritier characterized Badinter's invocation of human rights as "generous," she warned against the terrible consequences of conducting social policy along these lines. On a psychic level, individuals would not be able to be "instituted"—or "integrated"—into the social. On a social level, it would result in chaos, in a fragmented world where "everything goes" and "everyone does as one can [*chacun fait son salut à sa manière*]."[31] As she concluded her essay,

> Robert Badinter's interpretation of human rights brings us freedom, and it is profoundly generous, but it makes the individual a self-enclosed monad, the unique reference for being in the world. As such, it is contrary to the goal we should strive for, of altruism and solidarity. His point of view is no doubt utopian to the extent that he misunderstands or incorrectly uses the very notion of the social. The individual can never be thought alone: he exists only in relation. There only needs to be a relation between two individuals for the social to exist. [The social] is never the simple sum of the rights of each of its members, but rather an arbitrary dimension constituted by rules, in which (social) filiation can never be reduced to the purely biological.[32]

The idea that the liberalization of medically assisted reproduction—or rather the legal recognition of nontraditional forms of kinship made possible by assisted reproduction—would be tantamount to the destruction of the social and to psychosis was one of the recurring themes in the other contributions to this issue of *Le Débat*. All the scholars asked to respond to Badinter insisted on the excessive "individualism" and "liberalism" of his legal approach, to which they opposed a more "anthropological" vision of the law, one that would ground the individual and the social at once. The biologist Antoine Danchin, also explicitly positioning himself on the side of culture, argued that the main object of the law should not be biology but

---

30. Ibid., 30.

31. Ibid., 31.

32. Ibid., 32.

ALTERNATIVE KINSHIPS AND REPUBLICAN STRUCTURALISM   227

culture, because "it is impossible to speak of man while making an abstraction of his culture."[33] While Danchin acknowledged that the scientist in him was interested in biological experimentation and possibilities, "as a man," he explained, "what really counts is cultural kinship, not biological kinship."[34] Indeed, he continued,

> What counts for the creation of a balanced, if not stable, social group, is the individual feeling of an *identity*. This feeling is constructed throughout childhood, through the assimilation of sociocultural markers [*repères*] which allow each of us to make choices. The possibility of making choices is the very foundation of freedom. But nobody can choose without rules. In our societies, written law is a sort of concrete explanation of these rules. As such, the law allows each of us to have an identity, and to belong to a defined social group.[35]

In an interesting passage echoing Héritier's assertion that the "idea of the thing" was more important than the thing itself—in other words, that the normative trumped the empirical—Danchin suggested that "we must be capable of admitting the arbitrariness of our laws, and their provisional nature. But that does not, in any way, dispense us from observing them."[36] Among these rules, arbitrary yet necessary to observe, Danchin mentioned one in particular: "the first rule that a society should put forward is the preservation of diversity . . . This would also mean, for man, the preservation of sexual difference."[37] It is this notion of the law rhetorically assimilated to the social and to sexual difference that Danchin opposed to Badinter's "positivism," which, he argued, overlooked crucial anthropological transcendentals:

> It is as the result of a profound positivist illusion, which tends to confuse our desires with reality by making us believe in a definitive and totally objectified knowledge, that we could choose to submit our ethics to scientific knowledge. It seems to me that a more healthy realism would show us how much our knowledge depends on one of our biological particularities, which is our capacity for language and for the formation of cultures.[38]

---

33. Antoine Danchin, "Nature ou culture?," *Le Débat* 36 (1985): 20.

34. Ibid.

35. Ibid., 21.

36. Ibid.

37. Ibid., 23.

38. Ibid., 21.

228   **CHAPTER 6**

Finally, Danchin concluded, Badinter's legal perspective announced "the concretization of a dangerously destructive individualism that little by little has brought about the disappearance of the idea of the public good [*bien public*] in its focus on individual well-being [*bien-être individuel*]."[39]

This opposition between individualism and sociality also underpinned the contribution of Olivier de Dinechin, a theologian who turned not to religion but to anthropology to refute Badinter. Filiation, according to de Dinechin, was the key issue here: "To engender, to postulate a son, a daughter, mother and father, is a foundational human reality. Its juridical manifestation is only a surface formality. It has psychological, relational, social, cultural, and spiritual dimensions that are the object of specialized studies that show its consistency. Like all great anthropological realities, however, it is enigmatic, that is to say it harbors aporias [*porteuse d'apories*] that constantly raise questions about it."[40] Like Héritier and Danchin, de Dinechin reproached Badinter for conceiving of the law as a simple "game of formalities," for "proposing to displace ethical norms under the robe of a juridical extension [*le déplacement de normes éthiques sous le vêtement d'une extension juridique*],"[41] for his "cultural relativism," and for his "accentuated individualism [which] leads to the logic of a certain liberal philosophy."[42] As he put it, "every person is, to be sure, an absolute, and a pole of inalienable rights. However, these rights are not unlimited; they are measured by the commitment [*engagement*] that the person must take in relation to the other."[43]

As the responses by Héritier, Danchin, and de Dinechin make clear, it was Badinter's appeal to human rights that they perceived as symptomatic of an "excessive liberalism" that encouraged them to turn to anthropology to argue for a different understanding of man, the law, and also society. Writing at the end of the 1980s, Catherine Labrusse-Riou emphasized the need for a new legal theory that would be able to account for the profound changes occurring in the fields of gender, sexuality, and reproduction: "What is missing, dramatically, in our thought, is the foundation of the limit. Human rights in their various manifestations cannot account for this . . . What we will need are new juridical categories that we will have to elaborate to

---

39. Ibid., 20.

40. Olivier de Dinechin, "Le fait et le droit," *Le Débat* 36 (1985): 26.

41. Ibid., 25.

42. Ibid., 26.

43. Ibid.

ALTERNATIVE KINSHIPS AND REPUBLICAN STRUCTURALISM   229

attempt to regulate this power over life."[44] Unless jurists can elaborate these "new legal categories," the law will remain purely "positivistic" in content:

> Contemporary legislative and regulatory law is perceived as a simple technical tool of social and bureaucratic management. It has lost its capacities of abstraction and interpretation . . . It has abandoned all notion of permanence to adhere to immediate reality and its constant changes. It no longer considers itself authorized to signify what is just from the point of view of the law. Thus, it no longer offers active resistances, and its complexity defies all possibility of deriving meaning. Human rights require a secular arm, institutions, and procedures that are clear enough, without which they are only a wordy ointment [*une pommade verbeuse*] of good intentions with no sanctions.[45]

Here again, Labrusse-Riou's argument assimilates human rights, legal positivism, social deregulation, and the psychic malaise of the subject caught in the "excessive individualism of Western societies."[46] Although this new legal philosophy inspired by structural anthropology and psychoanalysis did not necessarily emanate from a position of consensus, it would ultimately provide one. As she explained in another article on bioethics, in a language reminiscent of mysticism,

> Even if the origins or the foundations of legitimacy remain partly enigmatic, the principle of a normativity, articulated around values, implicit or not, and the requirement of a coherence among the elements composing the genealogic institution, gain their necessity, vital for the individuals as for society, from sources localizable by experience, knowledge, conviction, but not verifiable by experimental science. Their functions stem not only from their operative efficacy [*l'efficacité opératoire*], nor even from a positive demonstration of their grounding. In today's jargon, we speak of a symbolic order, a sort of normativity that is objective because it is exterior to the individual but protective of its person within a culture that cannot be completely relativistic.[47]

---

44. Catherine Labrusse-Riou, "L'homme à vif: Biotechnologies et droits de l'homme," *Esprit* 156 (1989): 64.

45. Ibid., 65.

46. Ibid.

47. Catherine Labrusse-Riou, "Sciences de la vie et légitimité," in *Droits des personnes et de la famille: Mélanges à la mémoire de Danièle Huet-Weiller* (Presses universitaires de Strasbourg, 1994), 284. Many

230   **CHAPTER 6**

The structuralist symbolic, in other words, could provide a new normative paradigm, as well as a new politics.

⏪ Structuralism between Liberalism and Totalitarianism

If anthropology provided a model of sociality attractive to many French scientists and legislators trying to think through medically assisted procreation, psychoanalysis also emerged as a privileged resource. Psychoanalysts were asked to intervene extensively in the bioethics debates to ponder the sudden revival of the *désir d'enfant* (the desire to have children), the effects anonymous donation would have on a child's psyche, the possibility of reproducing without the sexual act, or the medicalization of reproduction more generally. Psychoanalytic responses to these problems varied widely and ranged from the unyielding condemnation of *all* assisted procreation techniques, to their endorsement with reservations in certain key domains.

Françoise Dolto, who participated in the "Genetics, Procreation, and the Law" conference, and who was repeatedly consulted, claimed that, from a psychoanalytic point of view, she did not object to artificial insemination so long as the child was told the truth about his origins, because the "origin" had a decisive impact on social and psychic development.[48] As she put it during the colloquium, speaking as a psychoanalyst "confronted with the unconscious,"

> It is true that there are secrets that give a couple support, but when an act is felt as human, it is spoken. To keep a secret about the life of a child is to imply that something might hurt him, and telling him belatedly that he has been adopted might be traumatic. If the truth is told during the first days of his life, it provides pleasure [*cela fait jouissance*] and it will not leave any traces. It is what is not told that shocks the unconscious.[49]

---

of Labrusse-Riou's texts on bioethics were republished in the anthology Catherine Labrusse-Riou, *Écrits de bioéthique* (Presses universitaires de France, 2007). The introduction by Muriel Fabre-Magnan provides a good overview of Labrusse-Riou's theoretical concerns.

48. *L'Express,* March 18–24, 1988, 121.

49. *Actes du colloque génétique,* 45.

ALTERNATIVE KINSHIPS AND REPUBLICAN STRUCTURALISM   231

For Dolto, if the symbolic law of reproduction was "told" to the child born through artificial insemination, then it was important that the real law (that is, the legal establishment) protect him.

Dolto's position was taken up by Geneviève Delaisi de Parseval who began working with sterile couples referred to her by the CECOS sperm banks. Delaisi de Parseval relied on her double training in psychoanalysis and ethnology to condemn the purely biological approach to filiation and reproduction, to warn against the psychic effects of secrecy, especially around origins, and to plead for a more sustained form of psychoanalytic help for all couples requesting access to artificial procreation technologies.[50] For Delaisi de Parseval, children were primarily born "in the heads" of their parents.[51] The biological thus needed to be relativized, framed. As she put it in an interview with the newspaper *Le Figaro*, it was lamentable that in the bioethics bill "nobody took into consideration all the psychoanalytic work on the negative effects that secret origins have. These are questions that we understand quite well in the cases of adopted children, but that we should also consider for all those who have a 'hole' or something not told in their history."[52]

During the ten years that preceded the bioethics laws, psychoanalysts were constantly solicited by the media. Psychoanalyst Françoise Hurstel, for instance, was invited by the newspaper *Révolution* to debate with psychologist Yves Clot and the lawyer Paul Teyssonière on the question of filiation. For Hurstel, the 1972 filiation law called into question the legal foundation of parenting: "It seems to me that what has characterized French paternity since the Civil Code (and well before) . . . has to do with the fact that the three functions of the father were entirely linked: the function of genitor, the function of educator and caretaker, and the function of name-giver and anchoring point of alliance and filiation." For Hurstel, it was the dissociation of these three functions that posed the main psychic threat: "The paternal function cannot be defined in the biological order. This criterion must come in second after the social criterion." In response, Yves Clot called for a "new social bond" because the question of filiation was intimately tied to the "management of the social relations of reproduction.

---

50. For an extensive analysis of Geneviève Delaisi de Parseval's position and for more on the psychoanalytic intervention in the bioethics debate, see Dominique Mehl, *La bonne parole: Quand les psys plaident dans les médias* (Paris: La Martinière, 2003), 85–145.

51. Cited ibid., 96.

52. Interview with Genenviève Delaisi, "Face au secret de leur famille," *Le Figaro*, February 16, 1994.

232   **CHAPTER 6**

What seems to be in crisis today is the notion that the law would be a railing [*un garde-fou*] against what happens in civil society, that it would simply be the adaptation of law to fact, setting limits and prohibitions."[53]

Along similar lines, the psychoanalyst Marie-Magdeleine Chatel wrote in *Libération* against the violence of the *"tout biologique"* or the all-biological: "Thanks to medicine, we think that we will have a child because we want one. Well no! It doesn't work like that, on command. Desire cannot be ordered. It is even destroyed by the scientific voluntarist ideology whose naïve altruism is invading us."[54] Also in *Libération,* the psychologist Beatrice Koeppel appealed to crucial psychoanalytic notions to once again warn us against the "biologization" of reproduction:

> If we are interested in the history of subjects who have suffered because of their inability to have a child, and who enter, with their desire, their discourses, their libidinal investments, into the IVF [in vitro fertilization] cycle, we can turn to the works of psychoanalysts who have much to say about the parental couple. We are no longer in scientific register but in that of the symbolic, which throws the unconscious to the front of the scene.[55]

Finally, another psychoanalyst, Muriel Flis-Trèves, in an article for *Le Monde* entitled "Someone Always Knows," decried the law sanctioning donor anonymity. For Flis-Trèves, anonymity caused "holes of memory": "To forbid the right to know one's origins is to forbid the child from having the right to think."[56] All of these arguments appear premised on the logic of the structuralist social contract, establishing a necessary connection among sexual difference, sociality, and thought—"at the origins," at the moment of the incest prohibition and of castration.

During the bioethics debates, one of the psychoanalysts who insisted most forcefully on the centrality of the sexual difference for all social and psychic organization was Monette Vacquin, the author of a book titled *Frankenstein or the Deliriums of Reason,* who was also interviewed extensively in the media.[57] As Vacquin put it in the newspaper *Libération,* "Today, artificial

---

53. "Libérez les bébés," *Révolution,* July 17, 1986.

54. Marie-Magdeleine Chatel, "Une folie de l'infécondité," *Libération,* February 15, 1994.

55. Beatrice Koeppel, "Procréation médicalement assistée et désir d'enfant," *Libération,* July 31, 1992.

56. Muriel Flis-Trèves, "Toujours quelqu'un sait," *Le Monde,* November 26, 1992.

57. Monette Vacquin, *Frankenstein, ou, les délires de la raison* (François Bourin, 1989).

ALTERNATIVE KINSHIPS AND REPUBLICAN STRUCTURALISM   233

procreation, frozen embryos, genetic manipulations give science the powers
that Mary Shelley had anticipated." As she continued,

> We are forced to recognize that medically assisted procreation in the
> last decade has been the theater of a devilish experimentation. Every-
> thing that could be tried, given the current state of knowledge, was
> tried: egg donations and the dissociation of motherhood, the birth
> of twins a few years apart from one another, postmortem insemina-
> tion, surrogate grandmothers. Can we seriously consider the fact that
> man manipulates his reproduction—engenderment within sexuality
> and sexual difference—as if it were a simple medical progress exempt
> from the darkest forces?[58]

Similarly, in *Le Monde,* Vacquin declared that in our world of "desexualiza-
tion, biologization of paternity, and dissociation of parenting," we "no longer
need to look for Oedipus in Thebes, it is within techno-science that he
seems to have found a home."[59]

In the same article, Vacquin defended the bill on bioethics proposed by
Christine Boutin, a right-wing deputy close to the Vatican and one of very
few French political figures to publicly voice her opposition to abortion.[60]
Throughout the bioethics parliamentary debates, Boutin was one of the
most vocal adversaries of assisted procreation. Her claim to fame came a few
years later, however, when she rose to the forefront of the war against the
PACS. For Vacquin, Boutin's project contributed to the "emergence of a
truly democratic reflection, liberated from absurd Left-Right splits, especially
unwelcome in terrains that link us all, and rendered derisory by the menace
of scientific totalitarianism and the pulverization of our reference points."[61]
In this context, Vacquin claimed, ethics was different from "virtue." The

---

58. Monique Vacquin, "Frankenstein et l'enfantement du contemporain," *Libération,* May 9, 1990.

59. Monette Vacquin, "De la science au délire," *Le Monde,* Débats, May 10, 1990, 2. The references to Oedipus are abundant in Vacquin's book. She mentions, for example, the "modern Oedipus who thinks of himself as Prometheus" (196). Antigone and Jocasta also make several
appearances: "What we give to Science, we cannot take from Culture. Cry, Antigone" (210), and
"Then appears . . . another knowledge—a feminine knowledge? [*un savoir feminin*], an anxious
tension which inscribes Mary [Shelley] in the filiation of Antigone or Electra, these restless ques-
tioners of the laws of the past" (221).

60. In 1995, Boutin served as a consultant for the Pontifical Council for the Family created by Pope
John Paul II. Around the same time, she founded a group at the National Assembly called "Osons
la Famille!" or "Let's dare the family!" (i.e., let's dare to support the family).

61. Vacquin, "De la science au délire," 2.

234   CHAPTER 6

point was not to lay moral interdictions on scientific innovations, but rather "to preserve, within our psyches and those of our descendants, the differentiations derived from fundamental prohibitions that make culture and allow thought."[62] In another article for *Libération,* Vacquin demanded the "castration" of biology by other disciplines such as philosophy, law, psychoanalysis, and anthropology, because "nothing indicates that we are psychically equipped to resist such a disorganization, such a shattering of our most fundamental reference points."[63] Finally, to give one last example, in the popular weekly magazine *L'Évènement du Jeudi,* Vacquin implored legislators not to "confuse scientific work, which appropriates natural laws to master objects, with symbolic transgressions that destroy references." Artificial procreation, she continued, "denies our anchoring in the sexual." In these questions pertaining to procreation, "everyone refers to their desire as their only law. It is an infantile attitude, motivated by the least civilized forces, those which refuse the symbolic."[64] Vacquin cited the legal theorist and psychoanalyst Pierre Legendre, one of the most ardent defenders of the "anthropological function of the law" for whom prohibitions provided "a shelter for our species against self-destruction." Similar to other experts invoking the symbolic, Vacquin explained that "of course, there is no scientific foundation for the prohibition. But it is a cultural construction that all human societies need. There can be no possible collective life without points of reference that make sense for all of us."[65]

If anthropology served as a tool to dismiss scientific "positivism," psychoanalysis emerged as an alternative to biology. In both cases, structuralism offered a normative grid that could override empiricism. As I suggested in Chapter 2, normativity—more nuanced and complicated to be sure, but still a form of normativity—did indeed figure in the works of Lévi-Strauss and Lacan. Despite his disclaimers about the empirical nonexistence of the "state of nature," Lévi-Strauss indicated the importance of this always-already-foreclosed "nature" for construction of the incest taboo as the nec-

---

62. Ibid.

63. Monette Vacquin, "Quelles limites au délire biologique?" *Libération,* July 1, 1991.

64. "Un risque pour les médecins: Le désir de toute puissance: Interview avec Monette Vacquin," *L'Évènement du Jeudi,* January 13–19, 1994.

65. Ibid. For more on Legendre, see Peter Goodrich, *Law and the Unconscious: A Legendre Reader* (St. Martin's Press, 1997); Pierre Legendre, "Ce que nous appelons le droit: Entretien avec Pierre Legendre," *Le Débat* 74 (1993); Camille Robcis, "French Sexual Politics from Human Rights to the Anthropological Function of the Law," *French Historical Studies* 33, no. 1 (2010). See also Alain Supiot, *Homo Juridicus: On the Anthropological Function of the Law* (Verso, 2007).

ALTERNATIVE KINSHIPS AND REPUBLICAN STRUCTURALISM   235

essary limit, as the condition for society and collective life. The prohibition of incest and the "Law" marked the beginning of order, the transition from the state of chaos, violence, and non-differentiation, to the realm of sexual difference, culture, and thought.

For Vacquin, the symbolic also provided this effect of social regulator, preventing society from descending into the "extremes": on the one hand, the liberal, individualistic, free-for-all American model, and on the other, totalitarianism, whether it be in its communist or fascist variant. Totalitarianism emerged as a particularly important keyword during the bioethics debates. Vacquin, for instance, compared artificial procreation to the *Lebensborn,* the Nazi experimental camps for eugenics and "race improvement." Everything was linked, she argued:

> Frankenstein and the spontaneous horror of Mary [Shelley] for a laboratory creation. Its immediate echo in everyone's unconscious and its constitution as a modern myth. The relentless attempt to give an impossible scientific definition of man. Nazism and the usage of bodies taken as a sum of organs. The compulsive presence in Hitlerian discourses of signifiers, such as poison and breast. The *Lebensborn* and the fantasy of a birth that guarantees purity: there is nothing more obscene than this purity, whether we seek it in monstrous experimental breeding or in the asepsis of the laboratory.[66]

One may note, in passing, Vacquin's singling out of "bodies taken as a sum of organs," which we can compare to Héritier's refusal to consider the social as "the sum of its individual parts" or the law as the addition of individual rights. This "symbolic function," which supplements the sum of individual parts, is what can protect society against totalitarianism, against what Vacquin calls the "concentration camp of the soul":

> If science, in the hegemony of its pronouncements, tends to present itself and to be received as the only mode of rationality, then the totalitarian inscription can insidiously insert itself into the very heart of democratic societies, within the confines of each consciousness. The realization of fantasies where alterity would be eradicated would insinuate within everyone's psyche a particularly perverse totalitarianism: something like a concentration camp of the soul, from which we would be unable to exit for the very reason that we are unaware we are in it.[67]

---

66. Vacquin, *Frankenstein,* 199.

67. Ibid., 204–5.

236   CHAPTER 6

The references to "wild liberalism" and to "totalitarianism" were pervasive in both the bioethics and the PACS debates. The *Le Débat* forum in which Badinter's text was published was followed by two other sections, one on the "Opacity of the United States" and another titled "Faced with the Soviet Union." If liberalism and human rights came to serve as synonyms for the market, positivism, individualism, and "wild capitalism," totalitarianism came to signify violence and homogenization. Both liberalism and totalitarianism, however, appeared to result from a dysfunction in sexual difference, a dysfunction "at the origins" that has long-term effects on the social and on the individual caught between capitalist anomie on the one hand and Nazi or Communist oppression on the other. French republicanism—the real one, not Badinter's version, but one that properly understood the relationship between private and public and the necessary connection between sexual difference, sociality, and psychic adjustment— could offer an alternative to these two extremes.

⤞ The 1994 Bioethics Laws: The "Perfect Crime"

After much media discussion, expert advice, and amendments that went back and forth from the Assembly, the Senate, and the courts, the bioethics laws were finally passed on July 29, 1994.[68] Throughout the long parliamentary and senate deliberations around the law, it was obvious that the anthropological, psychoanalytic, and legal "experts" had had a crucial impact on legislators. Representative Christine Boutin opened her speech at the National Assembly in November 1992 by explaining that while political questions required political answers, assisted procreation was a matter of ethics and of social organization. Boutin cited both Catherine Labrusse-Riou and Monette Vacquin:

> It is certain, as Catherine Labrusse-Riou writes, that "the eviction of sexuality and anonymity lead to a series of contradictions in filiation law and to a destructuring of kinship relations." This is not negligible! To fully appreciate what this means, we can turn to the work of Monette Vacquin, a psychoanalyst and a doctor, who considers that if we consecrate this notion of anonymity, society will not only affect our way of reproducing, but also our way of thinking.[69]

---

68. For a detailed history of the parliamentary and senate debates, see Mehl, *Naître,* chap. 8.

69. Débats parlementaires (Assemblée nationale), November 19, 1992, 5746.

ALTERNATIVE KINSHIPS AND REPUBLICAN STRUCTURALISM   237

By refusing to state in clear terms the "non-disposability" of the human body, the law would lead, Boutin continued, still citing Labrusse-Riou, to a "bursting of the social body." Furthermore, it would be a testament to the law's inability to "found the social bond."[70]

Other senators and representatives also expressed opinions on the relationship between the social and the familial that were similar to those of the anthropologists, psychoanalysts, and jurists cited earlier. According to Senator Bernard Seillier, "the human person develops primarily by establishing conscious and responsible relationships with peers [*semblables*]. Can the deep cohesion of a society survive if we wound so fundamentally the relationship that is primordial amongst all, that of filiation?"[71] As Seillier continued,

> If an egg is fertilized outside of the maternal body, there is by definition a dissociation from natural procreation. I will note in passing that in human life dissociative phenomena are rarely synonymous with progress in humanization. We can think, for example, of the fragmentation of work—what we call "labor in pieces" [*travail en miettes*]. In natural procreation, the unity of the act of love and of its potential consequence, that is to say the conception of another human being, is not without value or signification.[72]

As we can see in this passage, Seillier links reproduction, sociality, and solidarity, a connection reinforced by a statement made a few days later:

> Where does the depressed state of our society, the growing solitude, and rise of exclusion, come from, if not primarily from our irresponsibility in the transmission of life, the transmission of love? Humanity is not a herd that can be managed as stables of free breeding. A society of solidarity can only be founded upon the free exercise of a responsibility that we personally assume toward our peers, and in the very first instance, within the familial framework. This is why all attacks against the family are attacks on the fundamental law of society.[73]

As the parliamentary and senate debates on the bioethics laws progressed, lawmakers were increasingly adamant about limiting access to medically assisted procreation to couples in "stable relationships," to those who could

---

70. Ibid., 5747.

71. Débats parlementaires (Sénat), January 13, 1994, 117.

72. Ibid.

73. Ibid., 119.

238   **CHAPTER 6**

potentially have had the child through "natural means." In other words, even if the "conditions of origin" were deficient, the law needed to pretend that they were not. As the legal scholar Marcela Iacub described them, the 1994 assisted procreation laws were designed as a "perfect crime": they carefully covered all traces of medically assisted procreation so that children could still believe that they were the product of their parents' sexual act, as if technology had never intervened.[74] And indeed, in its final version, the 1994 law claimed:

> The point of medically assisted procreation is to remedy an infertility whose pathological character has been medically diagnosed. It can have as its object to prevent the transmission to a child of an illness of particular seriousness. The man and the woman forming a couple must be alive, of an age to procreate, married or able to bring the proof of a common life of at least two years, and they must preliminarily agree to the transfer of embryos or to insemination.[75]

Since 1992, Christine Boutin had insisted on adding an amendment specifying that the couples mentioned in the law needed to be heterosexual: "This precision is of importance because it ensures that the child will have a father and a mother, and that both of them will be alive."[76] Bernard Bioulac, who introduced the law, responded that the commission had extensively debated, "as recently as yesterday, the notion of the couple. I understand the preoccupations of Madame Boutin, but all guarantees have been taken to exclude homosexuality from this matter . . . To specify that it is 'a man and a woman who constitute a couple' is a form of tautology."[77] Other senators such as Franck Sérusclat referred to the example of Spain, where legislators had opted for complete freedom in terms of access to artificial procreation, opening it to unmarried individuals, homosexual couples, postmortem insemination, and so on. This was probably due, Sérusclat suggested, to a counterreaction against so many years of Catholic oppression.[78] France, however, had a different ethics—one grounded, by all accounts, in sexual difference.

---

74. Marcela Iacub, *Le crime était presque sexuel et autres essais de casuistique juridique* (Epel, 2002), 147.

75. *Code de santé publique,* livre 6, chap. II, Art. L 152–2.

76. Débats parlementaires (Assemblée nationale), November 24, 1992, 5977.

77. Ibid.

78. Débats parlementaires (Sénat), January 13, 1994, 133.

⤳ Competing Republicanisms: The Long Road to the PACS

A few years after the bioethics furor began, in June 1990, the Socialist senator, Jean-Luc Mélenchon submitted the first version of the Contract for Civil Partnership (Contrat de partenariat civil), a bill designed to offer a series of rights to all cohabiting couples, whether heterosexual, homosexual, roommates, siblings (*fratries* was the legal term), or joined by any other bond. Although the bill did not focus on same-sex couples (for complicated reasons that I will return to), both the national and international context suggested that homosexual couples were the target audience for the new law.

In France, two cases in particular had highlighted the legal difficulties encountered by same-sex couples on a daily basis. The first concerned an Air France steward who sued the company for refusing to give his partner the discount travel rates that it provided to other domestic partners (*conjoints en union libre*). In November 1984, an industrial tribunal (*conseil prud'homme*) gave the right to the plaintiff, arguing that with the "evolution of mores," two men living together could indeed be considered *concubins,* the technical term that, until then, had designated heterosexual couples living together outside of marriage. One year later, however, Air France won its appeal to a Paris court, which ruled that according to a prominent legal dictionary, *concubinage* could be defined only in heterosexual terms. The same year, another highly publicized case involved a lesbian who tried to register her partner under her health insurance. The Rennes court of appeals declared that *concubinage* was still defined by "dictionaries and common opinion" as the "state of a man and a woman, living together as husband and wife, without being married."[79] Both decisions were confirmed in 1989 by the *cour de cassation*.

A few years later, a young man whose boyfriend had died of AIDS lost his legal battle to transfer the lease of their common apartment to his name and found himself evicted. In December 1997, the *cour de cassation* reiterated that *concubinage* "could result only from a stable and continuous relationship which had the appearance of marriage, hence between a man and a woman."[80] This case, which was taken up by several gay-rights organiza-

---

79. Cited in Daniel Borrillo and Pierre Lascoumes, *Amours égales: Le PACS, les homosexuels et la gauche* (La découverte, 2002), 26. See also *Le Monde,* July 13, 1989.

80. Cited ibid., 27: "Le concubinage ne peut résulter que d'une relation stable et continue ayant l'apparence du mariage, donc entre un homme et une femme." The wording of this decision sounds

240   **CHAPTER 6**

tions, appeared particularly unfair to many French citizens. France had been one of the countries most affected by the early stages of the AIDS epidemic, and, as in many other nations, political leaders had been slow and hesitant to get involved.[81] Transferring apartment leases was only one of the many legal and emotional trials encountered by gay couples during the first years of the AIDS crisis in France. They had also been routinely denied hospital visitations, prevented from acting as their partner's primary health proxies, and denied any symbolic recognition from the state.

The PACS promoters were also inspired by the international context. Indeed, during the 1990s, several European countries were setting up various forms of domestic partnerships for same-sex couples: Denmark in 1989, Norway in 1992, Sweden in 1994, Iceland in 1996, the Netherlands in 1998, and Belgium in 1999. Moreover, on February 8, 1994, the European Parliament adopted a resolution in favor of equal rights for gays and lesbians within the European Union. The Parliament encouraged its members to either open marriage to same-sex couples or to set up equivalent juridical measures—civil unions or registered partnerships—to guarantee them all the rights and obligations of marriage. In the United States also, several cities had begun offering domestic partner benefits to their municipal employees as early as the 1980s.

Although Senator Mélenchon's 1990 civil partnerships proposal generated some political and media attention, it was not until 1992 that the movement toward the recognition of same-sex couples gained full political steam. In October 1991, the Collectif pour le contrat d'union civil, a group composed of lawyers, gay activists, members of the Planning Familial, and politicians from socialist groups and from the Green Party, came together to draft a second bill, called this time the Contrat d'union civile (CUC). Two Socialist deputies belonging to the Collectif, Jean-Pierre Michel and Jean-Yves Autexier, presented the bill to the National Assembly in October 1992. Like Mélenchon's first proposal, the CUC focused strategically on "the

---

as cumbersome in French as it does in English, with the vague passive tense *ayant l'apparence*, and the logical articulator *donc,* which is here difficult to sustain given that marriages are clearly not always "stable and continuous relationships." For more on these cases and on the early history of the PACS, see Gérard Bach-Ignasse and Yves Roussel, *Le PACS juridique et pratique* (Denoël, 2000); Scott Eric Gunther, *The Elastic Closet: A History of Homosexuality in France, 1942–Present* (Palgrave Macmillan, 2009); Frédéric Martel, *Le rose et le noir: Les homosexuels en France depuis 1968* (Seuil, 1996), chap. 17; Janine Mossuz-Lavau, *Les lois de l'amour: Les politiques de la sexualité en France, 1950–2002* (Payot & Rivages, 2002), chap. 6.

81. For a history of France's AIDS crisis in the 1980s, see Gunther, *Elastic Closet,* chap. 3; Martel, *Le rose et le noir.*

ALTERNATIVE KINSHIPS AND REPUBLICAN STRUCTURALISM   241

couple" as opposed to the "homosexual couple," thus allowing any two individuals to form a CUC. This CUC would grant each member of the couple inheritance rights, social security benefits, tax benefits, and housing rights. The Collectif managed to gather great support for the bill, partly because of its savvy use of the media, mass mailings, and petitions.[82]

Most importantly, the CUC succeeded in forging key political alliances by tailoring the bill to France's particular political culture. Just as Badinter had anchored his defense of medically assisted procreation on human rights, the promoters of the CUC grounded themselves in universalism, which, they argued, was the distinguishing characteristic of French republicanism. The CUC was quintessentially universalist, they contended, because it refused to distinguish homosexual from heterosexual, or even sexual from nonsexual as siblings and roommates were also included as potential CUC beneficiaries. Thus, Elisabeth Badinter, wife of Robert Badinter and an important figure in the French intellectual world, brought her support to the CUC precisely because it was "universalistic." As she told the newspaper *Libération,* "I am convinced that we are now within the right to 'indifference': leave us alone, we are like everyone else. The right to difference is what gives rise to the ghettoization of minority communities, to the rejection of the majority community, and to oppression."[83]

In a 1992 poll, 72 percent of the French public declared itself in favor of the CUC. Although some of the individual clauses of the CUC (such as the possibility to transfer apartment leases) were immediately approved by the National Assembly, the CUC as a whole was cast aside in 1993 after the victory of the Right in the legislative elections and the appointment of Jacques Chirac as president in 1995. As Jacques Toubon, minister of justice in the Alain Juppé cabinet, put it in 1996—in terms that were reminiscent of the rhetoric of the Alliance nationale a century before: "Public order is opposed to [the CUC]. I will say it very clearly: there is no question of creating a civil union contract. On the contrary, our goal is to guarantee that in this country there be more marriages, more births, so that France can be stronger."[84]

During that time, however, the gay rights organization AIDES (founded in 1984 by Daniel Defert, Michel Foucault's lifelong companion) drafted

---

82. For more information on the early days of the CUC, see Bach-Ignasse and Roussel, *Le PACS juridique,* 131–37.

83. *Libération,* April 23, 1992.

84. *Le Monde,* June 22, 1996.

242   **CHAPTER 6**

another project, the Contrat de vie sociale (CVS), this time limited to couples involved in a *sexual* relationship. The CVS eventually merged with the CUC to become the Contrat d'union sociale (CUS). In September 1995, the mayor of the small town of Saint-Nazaire declared himself willing to deliver "certificates of marital life" to same-sex couples within his jurisdiction.[85] In March 1996, several intellectuals—including Pierre Bourdieu, Jacques Derrida, Didier Eribon, Michelle Perrot, Paul Veyne, and Pierre Vidal-Naquet—signed a petition published in *Le Monde* titled "For the Legal Recognition of the Homosexual Couple" that demanded that France follow the resolution of the European Parliament that called for equal rights for gay and lesbian couples.[86] A few months later, more than 200 French intellectuals, artists, and public figures added their names to the petition from *Le Monde,* which was reprinted in *Le Nouvel Observateur.*[87] In 1996, Gay Pride chose to focus on the CUC, and more than 100,000 people marched in the streets of Paris demanding the "right to indifference." As one of the Pride coordinators explained in an interview, "We are not within an Anglo-Saxon, communitarian logic, of 'ghettos.' It is exactly the opposite. This contract has a universal impact: it seeks to recognize the link between two persons who have a project of common life, whatever their sex may be."[88] Several figures from the Left had begun to show an interest in the petitions and the marches, and in 1996, the Socialist Party included the CUC in its electoral agenda. With the Left's sweeping victory in the 1997 elections and the rise of Lionel Jospin as prime minister, the CUC appeared to be well on its way. In reality, its problems were just beginning.

---

85. Danielle Rouard, "Saint-Nazaire reconnaît officiellement les couples homosexuels," *Le Monde,* September 6, 1995.

86. *Le Monde,* March 1, 1996.

87. "L'appel des 234: Pour une reconnaissance légale du couple homosexuel," *Le Nouvel Observateur,* September 9, 1996. For a list of the signatories, see www.france.qrd.org/.

88. Élisabeth Fleury, "Interview with Laurent Queige," *L'Humanité,* June 28, 1997. The terms used here are important and will recur throughout the debates. They are also difficult to translate because they refer to a particular set of French concepts that have no equivalent in the United States where multiculturalism is not considered necessarily socially divisive and where the idea of an "Anglo-Saxon logic" is essentially incoherent. Éric Fassin's work offers an excellent analysis of how the term *communautarisme* has been opposed to *républicanisme* for specific political aims. See "L'épouvantail américain," in Clarisse Fabre and Eric Fassin, *Liberté, égalité, sexualité: Actualité politique des questions sexuelles* (Belfond, 2003). See also Laurent Lévy, *Le spectre du communautarisme* (Amsterdam, 2005). For a historical explanation of how this "logic of universalism" was developed in France, see Enda McCaffrey, *The Gay Republic: Sexuality, Citizenship and Subversion in France* (Ashgate, 2005), chap. 1; Joan Wallach Scott, "French Universalism in the Nineties," *Differences: A Journal of Feminist Cultural Studies* 15, no. 2 (2004); Joan Wallach Scott, *Parité! Sexual Equality and the Crisis of French Universalism* (University of Chicago Press, 2005).

ALTERNATIVE KINSHIPS AND REPUBLICAN STRUCTURALISM 243

The opposition to the CUC (which was eventually renamed the Contrat d'union civile et sociale or CUCS, then the Pacte d'intérêt commun or PIC, and finally the Pacte civil de solidarité or PACS), just like the opposition to medically assisted procreation, was articulated along two intersecting axes: republicanism and structuralism. Because the promoters of the PACS insisted on the republican and universal character of their bill, it was difficult to attack it on the grounds that it was liberal. Similarly, neither religion, morality, nor even tradition appeared to be convincing arguments within the secular, modern, and inclusive self-presentation and self-understanding of French political culture. Thus, even the Right and the Catholic Church presented their opposition to PACS as a defense of republicanism, a true republicanism that recognized the very *social* nature of marriage and parenting. And once again, the opposition assimilated sexual difference with universalism.

In April 1998, more than 12,000 French mayors signed a petition asking for the rejection of the PACS. Claiming to be fighting for the "defense of republican marriage," the mayors referred to the PACS as "true homosexual marriage" in disguise.[89] As the mayor behind the petition, Michel Pinton, insisted, opposing the PACS was not a crude act of homophobia. "We are not homophobes!" he exclaimed in an interview with *Le Figaro*. Rather, he explained, homosexuality pertained to the private, but secular marriage [*le mariage laïc*] "was a French concept tied to the history of the Republic" and hence was intrinsically public.[90] The conservative politician Philippe de Villiers reiterated these concerns in *Le Figaro:* "Why am I resolutely opposed to anything that could be assimilated to a marriage of homosexuals? Because we see what is hiding behind this claim. Marriage presupposes the establishment of a stable frame to give birth to children. Yet we see appearing, even before the CUS is in place, a new demand by homosexual lobbies, that is to say the possibility of adopting children or having access to artificial insemination." As de Villiers continued, the state had a particular interest in marriage "because the state has a responsibility to favor those bonds that tend to ensure the continuity of society. Marriage, which brings the hope of new births, is of general interest for the state and for the nation."[91] Even Christine

---

89. For a complete dossier on these anti-PACS mayors, see "Campagne contre les Maires anti-PaCS," www.prochoix.org/mairesantipacs/antipacs.html. See also Caroline Fourest and Fiammetta Venner, *Les anti-PaCS, ou, la dernière croisade homophobe* (Prochoix, 1999).

90. Marie-Laure Germon, "L'instigateur de la pétition anti-Pacs reçu jeudi à Matignon," *Le Figaro,* September 1, 1998, 2.

91. Philippe de Villiers, "Contre le 'Contrat d'union sociale,'" *Le Figaro,* June 12, 1998.

244   **CHAPTER 6**

Boutin, who had never made a secret of her faith or her ties to the Vatican, objected to the PACS *as* a Republican. Reminding us of her "great affection for homosexuals," she explained that as an elected representative she "defended the Republic and that which founds its unity: the republican marriage is the great success of the Revolution. It is open to all, whatever their race, their intelligence, their wealth. I happen to be Catholic. There is, however, no contradiction between my private and my public life."[92] According to these deputies, their opposition to the PACS was not inspired by homophobia or an overt will to discriminate against gays and lesbians, nor was it a right-wing position. Rather, the opposition claimed to be inspired by the defense of republican marriage, of *laïcité,* of general interest, and ultimately of the Republic.[93]

But more surprising than the references to republicanism on the part of Catholics were the references to structuralism, and more specifically to the symbolic as a keyword for the structuralist social contract linking sexual difference, social, and psychic structures, and universalism. As the Catholic group Paroles wrote in an editorial for *Le Monde,* "Is the point to demonstrate the equivalence or the absence of difference between a homosexual union and a heterosexual one? We would be in total disagreement on purely anthropological grounds." The state, they continued, "had the duty to uphold the institutions of the social bond, beginning with the family."[94] Louis-Marie Billé, archbishop of Lyon, worried that the PACS might transform certain particular sexual tendencies into "social references through the symbolic weight of the law."[95] Other bishops invoked sexual difference and its link to the symbolic: "There is no equivalence between the relationship formed by two persons of the same sex and that formed by a man and a woman. Only the latter can be qualified as a couple because it involves

---

92. Blandine Grosjean, "Christine Boutin, l'ultracatholique qui défend le mariage républicain," *Libération,* September 30, 1998.

93. The fact that these various figures claimed to not be homophobic does not of course mean that homophobia was absent from the debates. In fact, several deputies, none of whom were considered particularly extreme, held some of the most violent discourses ever heard at the assembly. Pierre Lellouche, an RPR deputy (from President Chirac's party), suggested that homosexuals be sterilized to ensure that they would not decide to have children, while his colleague Jacques Myard joked that the proposal should also include zoophiles. For a list of these insults, see the annex, "*Best of* homophobe," in Borrillo and Lascoumes, *Amours égales,* 127–38. See also Fourest and Venner, *Les anti-PaCS.*

94. *Le Monde,* September 8, 1998.

95. "Mgr Billé s'en prend au Pacs. Tout en refusant de se placer sur le terrain politique, l'église catholique entend apporter des éléments de discernement dans ce débat," *La Croix,* September 12, 1998, 8.

ALTERNATIVE KINSHIPS AND REPUBLICAN STRUCTURALISM 245

sexual difference, the conjugal dimension, and the possibility of exercising paternity and maternity. Homosexuality cannot, evidently, represent this symbolic set."[96]

One of the most important advocates of this symbolic imperative within the Catholic community was Tony Anatrella, a priest and psychoanalyst who served as an advisor to French bishops on questions of sexuality and reproduction. Anatrella, author of a book titled *The Forbidden Difference: Sexuality, Education, Violence Thirty Years after May 1968,* tirelessly protested against the PACS in the newspapers, on the radio, and on television. According to Anatrella, "non-normative relations" had always existed. However, the PACS aimed to build "an equivalence between institutions that do not have the same psychological and social value." The PACS was, in his eyes, a "social relation of psychotic character" by which he meant, a social relation *outside* of the symbolic. As he put it, "to say that society is organized around the relation man/woman is in no way discriminatory and even less so, 'homophobic.' Homosexuality stems from a subjective experience and therefore belongs to the domain of the private. Socially it does not symbolize anything, except the conjuring away of the sexual real [*l'escamotage du réel sexuel*]."[97] As these statements suggest, sexual difference was rhetorically assimilated to the public so that the PACS, despite being conceived as universal and republican, could in fact be relegated to the realm of the private.

The Right and the Catholics, however, were not the only ones disturbed by the PACS. Although the term "homosexual" did not even appear in the bill presented in 1997 by the Socialist Party, many politicians on the left were less than enthusiastic about the law, especially Prime Minister Lionel Jospin, who feared that the PACS would have a negative political impact.[98]

---

96. *Le Monde,* September 18, 1998.

97. Tony Anatrella, "Ne pas brouiller les repères symboliques," *Le Figaro,* June 16, 1998. Anatrella's work is inscribed within the larger Vatican critique of gay rights and queer theory. For more on this, see Hélène Buisson-Fenet, *Un sexe problématique: L'église et l'homosexualité masculine en France (1971–2000)* (Presses universitaires de Vincennes, 2004); Mary Anne Case, "After Gender the Destruction of Man? The Vatican's Nightmare Vision of the 'Gender Agenda' for Law," *Pace Law Review* 31, no. 3 (2012); Éric Fassin, "Les 'forêts tropicales' du mariage hétérosexuel," *Revue d'Éthique et de Théologie Morale* 261 (2010); Danièle Hervieu-Léger, *Catholicisme, la fin d'un monde* (Bayard, 2003). See also Pope Benedict XVI's call for a "law that derives from nature"—that is, a natural law very close to a symbolic law—that would "act as a corrective to the positive law." In Jürgen Habermas and Joseph Ratzinger, *The Dialectics of Secularization: On Reason and Religion* (Ignatius Press, 2006).

98. For an analysis of the Left's uneasiness vis-à-vis the PACS, see Éric Fassin, "*PaCS Socialista*: La gauche et le 'juste milieu,'" *Le Banquet* 12–13 (1998); reprinted in Éric Fassin, *L'inversion de la question homosexuelle* (Amsterdam, 2005), 21–41. For a step-by-step account of the Left's relation to the PACS, see Borrillo and Lascoumes, *Amours égales.*

246   **CHAPTER 6**

Thus, the promoters of the PACS spent most of their energy refuting the two main arguments of the Right. They repeated to their adversaries that the PACS *was* indeed universalistic and republican, and they underlined the fact that it would have absolutely no impact on marriage or filiation. Marriage and parenting were, they claimed, two entirely separate matters. Representative Jean-Pierre Michel, for example, explained that the Collectif for the PACS had specifically wished "that the project not be confined to homosexuals alone as was the case in several northern European countries, because the group was opposed to the notion that the French republic could design a text for a particular community."[99] Moreover, the very concept of *concubinage,* Michel continued, was a republican idea, defended notably by one of the founding fathers of the French Socialist Party, Léon Blum. Similarly, Michel insisted, the PACS was not "an inferior marriage. Republican marriage remains strong, and as a mayor, I strongly support it . . . It is primarily through this institution that the social bond can reproduce itself. In comparison with marriage, the PACS is simply a legal status [*statut juridique*]."[100] Along similar lines, Catherine Tasca, the president of the legal commission at the National Assembly and a former minister of communication, explained that "it would not be a good idea, at this stage in the evolution of our society, to link the question of filiation" to the PACS.[101] The PACS, Tasca continued, must remain neutral in terms of "the status of children born of parents united by a PACS. Filiation rules must remain regulated by the Civil code."[102] According to Catherine Trautmann, the minister of culture and communications, the PACS was simply the best solution to respond to the legal difficulties encountered by "certain people," while at the same time "respecting the principles that founded our Republic."[103]

Finally, Elisabeth Guigou, Jospin's minister of justice, who, despite her original reticence, became one of the PACS's primary defenders once the Socialist Party had officially endorsed it, argued that the PACS was "in conformity with the responsibilities of a republican and secular state." In an interview with the sociologist Evelyne Sullerot, one of the staunchest PACS

---

99. Jean-Pierre Michel and Irène Théry, "Concubinage ou union sui generis: Le statut et les droits," *Le Banquet* 12–13 (1998): 2.

100. Ibid., 4.

101. Catherine Tasca, "Le pacte civil de solidarité: Une reconnaissance responsable de la diversité des unions," *Le Banquet* 12–13 (1998): 2.

102. Ibid.

103. *Réforme,* October 10, 1998.

ALTERNATIVE KINSHIPS AND REPUBLICAN STRUCTURALISM

opponents, Guigou contended that within the French context, it was "logical to not restrict [the PACS] to a community because communitarianism is not the tradition of our law." In response to Sullerot's accusation that Guigou was merely backing down under the "pressure of the homosexual lobby," Guigou emphasized the *universal* character of the law. First, she claimed, the aim of the law was not only to provide a solution to certain "unbearable situations" faced by homosexual couples (affected by AIDS, for example), but also to "unbearable" heterosexual situations, which she illustrated with the example of a divorced woman who, after living in a free union with a gentleman and buying an apartment with him, was evicted after his death. Second, Guigou argued, the PACS was not only an initiative of the Left since her predecessor at the Ministry of Justice, Jacques Toubon, had also solicited a legal report on domestic partnership during his term—a report that had, incidentally, come out against the institution of civil unions. Once again, Guigou told Sullerot that the PACS had "nothing to do" with homosexual parenting, adding that on a personal level she was strongly opposed to the idea of same-sex parenting because "to construct and structure his personality, the child needs a father and a mother."[104]

And yet the issue of homosexual parenting (or *homoparentalité,* as it began to be called[105]) returned again and again. As the Union pour un mouvement populaire (UMP) representative Dominique Dord put it,

> If the PACS were instituted in the name of equality among citizens, it would become quickly impossible, incoherent, and even illegal to refuse to PACS contractors the possibility of welcoming and raising children . . . We would sacrifice the right of the child in favor of the right to the child. Yet we are reminded every day of the damages that so many pre- and post-adolescents encounter because of the absence of a father image or because of the disintegration of families. In a century when everything is becoming possible, even the most unreasonable choices, let us not play sorcerer's apprentices. Let us not destabilize the fundamental principles of social development and the strongest symbols of our civilization.[106]

---

104. "Guigou-Sullerot: Le grand débat sur le Pacs," *Le Figaro Magazine,* October 17, 1998, 18–22.

105. According to Bruno Perreau, the notion of *parentalité* was invented around this time to designate the quality of "being a good parent"—as opposed to a simple breeder. *Homoparentalité* was thus the term promoted by gay rights organizations (such as the Association des parents et futurs parents gays et lesbiens [APGL]) fighting to legalize same-sex parenting. See Bruno Perreau, *Penser l'adoption: La gouvernance pastorale du genre* (Presses universitaires de France, 2012), 14.

106. Dominique Dord, "Pacs: Un mauvais projet," *Le Figaro,* September 10, 1998.

248   **CHAPTER 6**

Despite his apocalyptic language, Dord had, in fact, a point. Same-sex couples had two ways available to have children: through adoption or through assisted procreation.

By the late 1990s, adoption laws in France were still regulated by a 1966 statute that allowed married couples or single individuals over the age of 28 to adopt, without any reference to the adoption candidate's sexual orientation. In practical terms, however, adoption licenses had been almost systematically denied to single gay men or to single lesbians who refused to keep their sexual orientation secret. This was the case of Philippe Fretté, a 37-year-old gay single teacher in Paris who was refused an adoption license because of his "lifestyle" (*choix de vie* was the exact term) and because of the "absence of maternal references" in his daily existence. The decision was affirmed in 1995 by France's highest court of appeals in administrative matters, the Conseil d'état, and in 2001 by the European Court of Human Rights, which established it as a precedent.[107] Similarly, and as previously indicated, the 1994 bioethics laws were resolute about banning same-sex couples from medically assisted reproduction. The law did, however, allow cohabiting couples to benefit from artificial insemination if they were able to provide evidence of a "stable relationship of at least two years." These were exactly the kinds of relationships that the PACS sought to encompass. Thus, as Dominique Dord and others suggested, if the PACS were instituted, it would indeed become increasingly difficult, if not discriminatory, to allow certain *pacsé* couples to have children (heterosexuals) while banning others (homosexuals). This was especially true since in the eyes of the law heterosexual and homosexual *pacsé* couples were considered identical, to the point that the government is to this day prevented from collecting any statistics concerning the percentage of same-sex couples among *pacsés.*

The trepidations of the Left around the PACS came to a peak on Friday October 9, 1998, the day on which the bill was scheduled to be voted at the National Assembly. Many Socialists simply did not show up, making way for the Right—which was at the time the minority party—to rely on a particular legal measure, the *exception d'irrecevabilité,* to dismiss the bill in question as unconstitutional. Since the proclamation of the Fifth Republic in 1958, this motion had been used only once, in 1978 in a matter concerning the value added tax (taxe sur la valeur ajouté, or TVA) and the European Union.

For the Right, the defeat of the PACS represented its first great political victory over the Jospin administration. Although various Socialist deputies

---

107. See Perreau, *Penser l'adoption,* 90–101.

ALTERNATIVE KINSHIPS AND REPUBLICAN STRUCTURALISM   249

provided a series of excuses and justifications for their absence that day (including the fact that the vote was scheduled on a Friday and that many deputies return to their home constituencies over the weekend), it was obvious that the Left was clearly more uncomfortable about the PACS than gay activists wanted to believe. The following day, the cover of *Le Monde* read: "Socialist Deputies Were Ashamed of the PACS." The front page of *Libération* claimed: "The PACS Rejected at the Assembly. The Flight of the Socialist Party [*Le PS en fuite*]."[108]

☙ How the Symbolic Became French

Although the Right and the Catholic church invoked structuralism and republicanism to ground the family in sexual difference and object to the PACS, it was primarily left-wing intellectuals who theorized the link between the two. More specifically, it was a series of intellectuals—self-described "republicans"—who formalized this connection among heterosexuality, the social, the psychic, and "Frenchness" in the media, in academic publications, and within governmental structures. Throughout the PACS debates, the symbolic came to signify French political culture: republicanism. The symbolic, in other words, became French. As such, the defense of heterosexual marriage and filiation was not presented as a political choice or position, but rather as a fight for the social in its very essence. Moreover, just as with reproductive technologies, the empirical mattered less than the normative: with the PACS, what was at stake was psychic, social, political, and cultural unity—cohesion. Finally, just like in the bioethics discussions, the intellectuals who "applied" the structuralist social contract to the PACS had an important and direct influence on many of the political figures who debated and eventually passed the final version of the law.

One of these intellectuals was the philosopher Guy Coq, author of a book on *laïcité* and republicanism, and a frequent contributor to the journal of social Catholic inspiration *Esprit*. Coq was also the president of the Friends of Emmanuel Mounier Association, as well as one of the founders of the Fondation du 2 mars, formerly known as the Fondation Marc Bloch, a think tank created to defend the values of French republicanism, promote a

---

108. For an interesting overview of the debates at the National Assembly, see the ethnographic account of Marc Abélès, *Un ethnologue à l'Assemblée* (Odile Jacob, 2000). See also Martel, *Le rose et le noir*, chap. 18. The full version of the parliamentary debates is available at www.assemblee-nationale.fr/11/dossiers/pacs.asp.

250   CHAPTER 6

"strong democracy," and fight against the tyranny of the *pensée unique,* an expression that emerged around this time to refer to neoliberalism, Americanism, capitalism, and *communautarisme.* In an editorial in *Libération,* Coq highlighted the "contradictions" of the PACS. "The state," he explained,

> "has the urgent responsibility to favor those behaviors and interpersonal bonds that tend to ensure the perpetuity of society, despite the dying of individuals . . . If for the state and the law, all forms of couples are equal, how can we forbid [*comment fonder l'interdit*] a homosexual couple from adopting a child or having one by other means? Yet the child has a fundamental right to be raised in a privileged symbolic relation between a woman and a man. This cultural mechanism is probably one of the foundations that have brought about the civilization legitimizing democracy."[109]

Coq's piece was influential enough for Philippe de Villiers to cite it in his own column against the PACS. Republicanism, in other words, could provide a link between a Social Catholic left-leaning position and one more solidly inscribed in the French Right to oppose the PACS. Coq was also one of the "experts" invited to speak on the PACS before the Senate in January 1999.[110] In his public speeches, Coq insisted on this necessary connection between the State and heterosexual/symbolic relationships, a connection that was a *cultural* institution, as opposed to a *natural* one. Homosexual parenting would thus not be a deviation from nature as a religious or a homophobic argument would have it, but rather from culture, which in Coq's argument is rhetorically assimilated with civilization and democracy.

In January 1999, several renowned intellectuals published a manifesto in *Le Monde* titled "Let's Not Leave the Critique of the PACS to the Right!" The signatories of the manifesto claimed that they would not accept that "the parliamentary debates on the PACS be reduced to scheming, guilt trips, and threats of excommunication, when what [was] at stake [was] the fundamental upheaval of the imaginary and symbolic structures of an entire society." "Should it be normal," they asked, "that all differences be treated as discriminatory and that those who choose or accept to live a different

---

109. Guy Coq, "Le contresens du contrat d'union sociale," *Libération,* July 1, 1997.

110. "La commission des lois du Sénat a procédé à des auditions publiques sur la proposition de loi adoptée par l'Assemblée nationale relative au pacte civil de solidarité (PACS)," Sénat, Communiqué de presse, January 27, 1999.

ALTERNATIVE KINSHIPS AND REPUBLICAN STRUCTURALISM   251

lifestyle demand at the same time that it be neutralized in the name of equality?"[111]

Among the authors of the petition figured, once again, Françoise Héritier. A few months earlier, Héritier had argued in an interview with the Catholic newspaper *La Croix* that "No Society Admits Homosexual Parenting." According to Héritier, not only was sexual difference foundational to society, but gay parenting was "unthinkable":

> What I have tried to show [in my work] is that the anatomical, physiological, and functional difference of the sexes—by functional, I mean the fact that it is the woman who bears the children—is at the basis of the fundamental opposition that allows us to think. Because thinking is first of all classifying, classifying is essentially discriminating, and the fundamental discrimination is based on sexual difference. It is an irreducible fact: we cannot claim that these differences do not exist; they are the unsurpassable limits of thought [*butoirs indépassables de la pensée*], like the opposition between day and night. Our modes of thinking and our social organization are founded on the principal observation of the sexes. And we cannot reasonably maintain that this difference figures at the heart of the homosexual couple.[112]

For Héritier, sexual difference and thinking were intrinsically linked because of the logic of the structuralist social contract. This was, she insisted, a normative matter, not an empirical one. Thus, in response to anthropologists who had come out in favor of the PACS on the basis of their ethnographic work with same-sex families, Héritier noted, "We should not rely on anthropological precedents which in fact have nothing to do with the current situation, to legitimize the demand for homosexual parenting."[113] Even if gay parenting had proved empirically viable in the past or in the present—presumably socially and psychically—it remained fundamentally "unthinkable" in normative terms.

Perhaps due to her various political contacts, to the notoriety of her scholarship, to her chair at the Collège de France, to her proximity to Lévi-Strauss,

---

111. Caroline Eliacheff, Antoine Garapon, Nathalie Heinich, Françoise Héritier, Aldo Naouri, Paul Veyne, Heinz Wismann, "Ne laissons pas la critique du PACS à la droite!," *Le Monde,* January 27, 1999. This editorial was also republished in *La Croix,* February 23, 1999.

112. Marianne Gomez, "Interview with Françoise Héritier: Pacte civil de solidarité: 'Aucune société n'admet de parenté homosexuelle'," *La Croix,* November 9, 1998.

113. Ibid.

252   **CHAPTER 6**

or perhaps because she had so forcefully argued for the link between kinship and social structure, Héritier's views were quoted extensively during the PACS debates. The philosopher Sylviane Agacinski—who also happened to be married to Prime Minister Lionel Jospin—cited Héritier's work in her 1998 *Politique des Sexes,* to affirm the existence of a social order based on sexual difference that could not be reduced to the sum of its individual parts.[114] The primary purpose of Agacinski's book was to provide an intellectual justification for the 1999 *parité* law, a bill designed to give women equal representation in the political arena, which her husband Lionel Jospin was promoting. As Joan Scott, Éric Fassin, and Michel Feher have persuasively shown, the PACS ended up playing a crucial role in Agacinski's argument.[115] For Agacinski, sexual difference structured both our social order and our psyche and was intimately tied to democracy, republicanism, and Frenchness. Within the logic of her argument, the *parité* law was the only way to reach political equality between men and women *while* keeping this essential difference intact. In opposition to this sexual difference preserved in *parité,* Agacinski listed examples of negative "erasures of difference" including transsexuality, queer theory, and gay parenting. Thus, while Agacinski ultimately came out in favor of the PACS (and according to one source, was even the one responsible for Jospin's interest in same-sex domestic partnerships[116]), her support of the PACS was premised on the necessary banning of same-sex parenting. As she explained in the 2001 preface to her book's second edition, "Sexual orientation concerns sexualities, whereas sexual difference has always been defined in relation to procreation and filiation. With the PACS, the legalization of homosexuality has no direct connection to the family or to marriage because, contrary to what you may read here and there, marriage was not instituted to legalize heterosexuality, but to regulate filiation." Given this framework, Agacinski reiterated the need to "recognize the double origin of the child" and thus the importance of banning homosexual parenting. This, she added, was in no way discriminatory because "one can easily be parent *and* homosexual, and there are many homosexual parents, but it is not *as homosexual . . .* that one is mother

---

114. Sylviane Agacinski, *Politique des sexes: Précédé de mise au point sur la mixité* (Seuil, 2001), 43–44, 146; *Parity of the Sexes,* trans. Lisa Walsh (Columbia University Press, 2001).

115. See Éric Fassin and Michel Feher, "Parité et PACS: Anatomie politique d'un rapport," in Daniel Borrillo and Éric Fassin, eds., *Au-delà du PACS: L'expertise familiale à l'épreuve de l'homosexualité* (Presses universitaires de France, 2001), 13–43. See also Scott, *Parité!,* 100–23.

116. Martel, *Le rose et le noir,* 618.

ALTERNATIVE KINSHIPS AND REPUBLICAN STRUCTURALISM   253

or father: it is first of all as man or woman, and thus with a second parent of another sex."[117]

Héritier's writings on sexual difference also informed the viewpoint of the sociologist Irène Théry, one of the most important bridge figures in the PACS debates. Théry, who as we saw in Chapter 4, had written on marriage, divorce, and family law, was one of the key players in the PACS debates. Like Coq, Théry was called before the Senate to assess the PACS legislation. Moreover, she was solicited by Elisabeth Guigou and Martine Aubry (at the time, the minister of labor and solidarity) to produce a report on the state of the family—including an assessment of the CUS. In their letter to Théry dated February 3, 1998, Guigou and Aubry mobilized the rhetoric of republicanism and of the structuralist social contract, calling the family "a fundamental reference [repère]," "the birthplace of solidarity," "the central link [maillon] to social cohesion." Given this unique function of the family, "is the law adapted to the realities of today's families?" "What are the unavoidable [incontournables] rules?" What can be left to individual will?"[118] With this report, in other words, Théry was asked explicitly to take a position on this question of whether family law should embrace transcendental norms or whether it should reflect the "reality of the times." Although Théry addressed the question on same-sex partnerships in her report, her most sustained critique of the PACS (which at the time was called CUS) was published in October 1997 in the journal *Esprit* and also as a booklet for the Foundation Saint-Simon titled "Perspectives: Four Reforms and Not One."

Like the Fondation du 2 Mars, the Fondation Saint-Simon was a think tank for intellectuals and business leaders to gather and discuss various political, social, and economic questions. Founded in 1982 by the historians François Furet, Pierre Rosanvallon, Emmanuel Le Roy-Ladurie, and Pierre Nora, and the economists and business-world figures Alain Minc and Roger Fauroux, the Fondation Saint-Simon played a role comparable to that of the nineteenth-century Musée social, which had provided a space for intellectuals, business executives, and politicians to exchange ideas on the family and the social more generally. Just as the Musée social had inscribed itself ideologically as an alternative to liberalism and socialism, the Fondation

---

117. Agacinski, *Politique des sexes,* 13. Agacinski also published a summary of these ideas in an editorial for *Le Monde* titled "Contre l'effacement des sexes," in which she specifically names Judith Butler as one of the thinkers responsible for this "erasure of the sexes." *Le Monde,* February 6, 1999.

118. Irène Théry, *Couple, filiation et parenté aujourd'hui: Le droit face aux mutations de la famille et de la vie privée* (Odile Jacob/La documentation française, 1998), 9–10.

254   **CHAPTER 6**

Saint-Simon was created in opposition to totalitarianism—in its fascist, communist, or Islamic fundamentalist forms—and also to counter "Anglo-Saxon" liberalism, with its social implications of identity politics and *communautarisme.* As an alternative to these two "extremes," many at the Fondation Saint-Simon—especially those who had repudiated their communist past (Furet, for example) and those who came from the world of Christian syndicalism and trade unions (Rosanvallon, for example)—preached a return to republicanism. It was this form of republicanism that progressively became associated with sexual difference.

From 1982 to 1999, the Fondation held monthly lunches and seminars around the presentation of one of the members or an invited guest. Most of the leading French politicians in the eighties and nineties passed through the Fondation, including Robert Badinter, Jacques Chirac, Michel Rocard, and Laurent Fabius. The Fondation also published a series of works, most often in the form of booklets (*notes*), which it distributed to various political leaders, CEOs, administrators, and intellectuals.[119] This was the format in which Théry's piece on the PACS was originally circulated in political spheres. We can also remark, in passing, that this was not the first time that the Fondation had explored the question of homosexuality and politics. In April 1996, Frédéric Martel, author of a controversial history of homosexuality in France, *Le Rose et le Noir,* also published one of the concluding chapters to his book as a booklet for the Fondation. His piece was titled "The Communitarian Temptation: Homosexual Liberation and the Struggle against AIDS." Martel, who claimed Alain Finkielkraut and François Furet as his intellectual mentors, structured his argument around the opposition between a French republican, integrated, and politically moderate gay community versus one inspired by American-style radical and communitarian solutions as exemplified by the phenomenon of a gay pride march or the development of gay and lesbian studies.[120]

---

119. For more on the structure and operations of the Fondation Saint-Simon, see Vincent Laurent, "Enquête sur la Fondation Saint-Simon: Les architectes du social-libéralisme," *Le Monde Diplomatique,* September 1998; Christophe Prochasson, *Saint-Simon ou l'anti-Marx : Figures du saint-simonisme français XIXe- XXe siècles* (Perrin, 2005), 309–21. For more on Rosanvallon and Furet's trajectories, see Michael Scott Christofferson, "An Antitotalitarian History of the French Revolution: François Furet's *Penser la Révolution française* in the Intellectual Politics of the Late 1970s," *French Historical Studies* 22, no. 4 (1999); Andrew Jainchill and Samuel Moyn, "French Democracy between Totalitarianism and Solidarity: Pierre Rosanvallon and Revisionist Historiography," *Journal of Modern History* 76 (2004).

120. Martel's book generated much controversy and debate in France. See the response to his critics in the second edition of the *Rose et le noir* (688–718), previously published in *Esprit,* November 1996.

ALTERNATIVE KINSHIPS AND REPUBLICAN STRUCTURALISM 255

After a long and complex argument, Théry ended up opposing the CUS for three main reasons: because the CUS sought to encompass nonsexual relationships, because it refused to distinguish homosexual from heterosexual couples, and because it undermined the power of republican marriage. Ultimately Théry accused the CUS promoters of using the law for purely functional purposes, of endangering the symbolic foundations of society and the true republican values of France. The CUS had, according to Théry, an unstoppable "desymbolizing passion." As Théry argued, human culture was defined by two symbolic differences: one between the sexual and the nonsexual and another between the masculine and the feminine. The function of the law was to "institute" these differences and distinctions:

> The law is not a simple management or policing tool. It also has, maybe primarily, an instituting function, in the sense that it contributes to setting up, in the language of common law, a certain number of crucial anthropological distinctions. These distinctions delineate a *symbolic order* which is indispensable both to common life in human societies to which it gives signification, and to individuals whose construction as subjects depends upon their inscription within the universe of the institution. Within these major distinctions, among the most fundamental is the one that distinguishes the bond authorizing a sexual relation from the bond excluding or prohibiting it. This is why to imagine, as we can read in the presentation of the motivations behind the civil union contract, that the difference between a "couple" (a notion that implies a sexual dimension) and a "non-couple" (that doesn't imply it) would suddenly be obsolete, is both a sociological absurdity and an anthropological irresponsibility.[121]

Moreover, Théry continued, citing Héritier in a footnote:

> The attempt to define the couple as a "sexual preference" also stems from the desymbolizing passion described above. Indeed, the couple, whether it be homosexual or heterosexual, is never reducible to a sexual relationship. It is also a sexed bond [*lien sexué*], in the sense that it is inscribed in this symbolic order of sexual difference, which we call *gender difference* [*différence des genres*]. This symbolic of the genders, of the masculine and the feminine, exists in all human societies: it is that by which culture gives meaning to the sexed characteristic of the

---

121. Irène Théry, "Le contrat d'union sociale en question," *Esprit* 236 (1997): 174.

256   **CHAPTER 6**

living species that we are but to which we are not reduced. The de-symbolizing passion consists precisely in believing that we can do without this inscription of the couple within the symbolic order of gender, that the bond can be reduced to the relationship, the sexed to the sexual, and that we can forgo instituting the masculine and the feminine.[122]

Sexual difference was, according to Théry, a universal anthropological transcendent that the law merely formalized. Similarly, the symbolic was the sexual and gendered imperative for the existence of culture—and as such, was separate from nature. Once again following Héritier, Théry located marriage and filiation at the heart of this symbolic.[123] Gay couples could live together, they could have children, and these children could even be okay on a psychological level as the various empirical studies had suggested, but these are all *situations de fait* (facts) as opposed to *situations de droit* (law). Only the latter could be symbolic.[124]

If *concubinage* and same-sex parenting were not able to *symbolize* anything according to Théry, marriage—or more specifically, the 1792 republican marriage, "the greatest conquest of the republic,"—was intrinsically symbolic.[125] Unlike religious marriage, which Théry defined as belonging to the private sphere, republican marriage was associated with *laïcité,* with the Declaration of Human Rights, and with equality of all citizens before the law.[126] As Théry put it, republican marriage established a link between "democratic debate, the values of citizenship, and private life."[127] In other words, it was the only form of private life that could be simultaneously public, the only one associated with all the public values of France (human rights, equality, democracy). In this context, Théry called the CUS a "republican mirage": "This 'contract for all,' which reveals itself to be perfectly compatible with the harshest forms of separatism of culture and mores, has nothing

---

122. Ibid., 178. Théry later developed this distinction between the *sexué* and the *sexuel* in Irène Théry, *La distinction de sexe: Une nouvelle approche de l'égalité* (Odile Jacob, 2007).

123. Théry, "Le contrat d'union sociale," 180. Théry insists on this distinction between nature and culture by claiming that Western culture has always refused unisexed filiation (two mothers or two fathers) in order to preserve culture, not nature.

124. Ibid. For an interesting analysis of how this ideal versus empirical opposition structured the gay marriage debates in France and the United States differently, see Éric Fassin, "Same Sex, Different Politics: 'Gay Marriage' Debates in France and the United States," *Public Culture* 13, no. 2 (2001).

125. Théry, "Le contrat d'union sociale," 160, 170.

126. Ibid., 170.

127. Ibid., 171.

ALTERNATIVE KINSHIPS AND REPUBLICAN STRUCTURALISM 257

particularly 'republican' about it. It is unclear by what mystery such a watchword [*mot d'ordre*] has been able to become the emblem for the fight against the slippery slope of communitarianism, the Americanization of mores, and the *politically correct*."[128] By contesting the "republican" character of the CUS and relegating it to the realm of cultural "separatism" and American-style communitarianism, Théry was once again playing into the rhetoric of France as an equilibrium or middle ground between liberal and totalitarian politics.

Just as with the bioethics laws, this putative position between American and totalitarian alternatives proved to be one of the most powerful rhetorical devices in the PACS discussions. Political theorist Hugues Portelli called the socialist promoters of the PACS a "government of lobbies" and claimed that voting for the PACS would "bring France closer to an American model of decision-making." For him, the PACS was merely another "infringement upon the republican tradition."[129] Alain-Gérard Slama, another political scientist, wrote in his weekly *Figaro* column that the PACS would constitute "a decisive step in the process of the complete socialization of individuals which is currently sweeping democracies into its spiral."[130] And Pierre Legendre, a jurist and psychoanalyst who had been hired by the Left in the eighties to reflect on the problem of kinship as the director of the Laboratoire européen pour l'étude de la filiation, worried that "the little PACS episode [was] indicative of how the State [took] leave of its functions of guarantor of reason." "To institute homosexuality as a familial category [*statut familial*]," Legendre continued, was to "put the democratic principle at the service of fantasy." In this context, the law, "founded on a genealogical principle," would "give way to a hedonistic logic descended from Nazism."[131]

Michel Schneider, a psychoanalyst and public administrator who had graduated from the École nationale d'administration (ENA) and worked at the Ministry of Culture, provided perhaps one of the most striking uses of this rhetoric of political extremes to condemn the PACS in his work *Big Mother: Psychopathology of Political Life*. Schneider's argument was also premised on the existence of a symbolic order intimately tied to the social, which Schneider defined by citing both Lévi-Strauss and Lacan:

---

128. Ibid., 165.

129. Hugues Portelli, "Le gouvernement des lobbies," *La Croix,* November 20, 1998, 14.

130. Alain-Gérard Slama, "Pacs: L'irrésistible engrenage," *Le Figaro* Magazine, September 26, 1998, 36.

131. Antoine Spire, interview with Pierre Legendre, "Nous assistons à une escalade de l'obscurantisme," *Le Monde,* October 23, 2001, 21.

258 **CHAPTER 6**

We speak of the social bond, and we deplore its fracture but we don't think as much about its nature . . . The answer is simple: the symbolic system, the various representations that tell each one of us what he is and what he is not. Human actions and representations can be inserted within a pre-established and structuring order, distinct from both the real and the imaginary. According to the anthropologist Claude Lévi-Strauss, it encompasses "language, matrimonial rules, economic relations, science, art, religion." This bond of bonds ties psychic bonds and social bonds, real bonds and imaginary bonds.[132]

Psychoanalysts, Schneider continues, citing Lacan this time, were "practitioners of the symbolic function," and thus had a particular ability to reflect on social and political questions.[133] As Schneider explained, the notion of the symbolic as defined by Lacan was particularly useful to think through political topics:

Lacan's theory of the symbolic represents his main contribution to a psychopathology of the political bond. Following him and thanks to him, I give this word a very simple meaning: the part of the Other within us, the reminder that living is living together according to rules that are transmitted and not chosen. The symbolic is exactly the opposite of "I am authorized by myself alone." In a symbolic system, bonds do not result from the voluntary action of individuals; they precede the individual as a tradition and bring a constraint to bear upon themselves. What is symbolic is that which we cannot change, regardless of our likes or dislikes: names, kinship rules, language, grammar, sexual difference, the finitude of life. The symbolic is what is bigger and more powerful than us, more ancient and more lasting. What does not belong to us, what is not us, but that without which we could not be. If it restricts the freedom of choice, it also increases this real freedom which is desire. Things we do not choose have a great advantage: they protect us from our drives and from our most primitive thoughts. They survive aggression and guilt, and because of this, they limit them. Parents, because we have not chosen to be born nor to have them as parents, allow the role of construction that is not

---

132. Michel Schneider, *Big mother: Psychopathologie de la vie politique* (Odile Jacob, 2002), 185.

133. Ibid., 186.

ALTERNATIVE KINSHIPS AND REPUBLICAN STRUCTURALISM 259

dependent on oneself. If they were chosen, they would depend on us and we would depend on them limitlessly.[134]

According to Schneider, the "psychopathology of political life" was due precisely to the erosion of this symbolic order, to the fading of distinctions and prohibitions in favor of individual rights and freedoms, in favor of a "politics of recognition" which Schneider claimed, came from "the influence of Anglo-Saxons and from their fundamental moralism."[135] Within this symbolic order, sexual difference and filiation were two of the few untouchable foundations.[136] The PACS—and more specifically the door that it opened for legalizing gay parenting—violated those last two pillars of the symbolic order: "All homo- or autoparenting would topple procreation from the symbolic order and its universal law of incest prohibition, which Lévi-Strauss constructs as the 'threshold between nature to culture.' This rule does not so much prohibit one from marrying mother, sister or daughter, as it requires one to 'give mother, sister, or daughter to another.' All procreation liberated from the other opens a breach in the civilized order. The result would no longer be symbolic kinship, but narcissistic kinship, and would lead to pathologies generated by the lack of the paternal bond."[137]

A few lines below this quote, on the same page, Schneider turns to another example of destruction of sexual difference, almost, it would seem, to give us a frame of comparison: Islamic fundamentalism. As he writes, "Intolerable within certain individual phantasmatic structures, sexual difference is no less so for certain collective psychopathologies."[138] Among these, he cites the Algerian GIA (Groupe islamiste armé), the Afghan Taliban, and the perpetrators of the September 11th attacks:

It is in fact in reaction to our representation of sexual difference based on the equality of rights that Islamic culture radicalized in Islamic fundamentalism maintains and hardens its non-egalitarian views. The target of the terrorists was American power, but insofar as it seemed undermined by the rights (especially the sexual ones) progressively conquered by women. The unsustainable fantasy was not that the

---

134. Michel Schneider, "L'État comme semblant," *Cités: Philosophie, Politique, Histoire* 16 (2003): 48.

135. Schneider, *Big mother,* 215.

136. Ibid., 202–3.

137. Ibid., 231.

138. Ibid.

260   **CHAPTER 6**

feminine could spring from the exterior, but that it had contaminated phallic power from within.[139]

For Schneider, fundamentalists wanted "to destroy in us what they fear[ed] would spread within their countries: the non-differentiation between the sexes and a generalized symbolic indifference." Thus, to resist the threat of fundamentalism, France must remain "differentiated," and, consequently, it must prevent the legalization of the same-sex unions and gay parenting: "For us, the only way to reach equality is through nondifferentiation; for radical Islam, it remains unthinkable that an asymmetry is not necessarily an inequality."[140] According to this tautological construction, France must remain symbolic because the symbolic is the repository of republicanism and Frenchness.

In her critique of the CUS, Irène Théry proposed to replace the new law with a series of specific reforms. She advocated more rights (housing rights, tax breaks, and health insurance) for all cohabiting couples. She proposed a reform of marriage, divorce, and inheritance legislation to essentially make marriage more accessible and attractive for heterosexual couples. Parallel to this, Théry suggested that the government create a "contract of coupled life" restricted to same-sex couples, similar to the one that many Scandinavian nations had set up. "The proposition of a true, 'contract of coupled life,'" Théry argued, "is a way to engage much more clearly in the legal recognition of the homosexual couple, in the name of equality, while saying no to assimilation, in the name of difference."[141] This new contract, Théry specified, would grant same-sex couples exactly the same rights given by marriage *except* the right to adopt children or to conceive them through assisted procreation.

In 1996, while the Right was still in power and as demands for same-sex unions were gaining strength, the Minister of Justice Jacques Toubon, enlisted a family law specialist, Jean Hauser, to study the question of same-sex partnerships. In the spring of 1998, Hauser delivered his report, which proposed to replace the CUC with the PIC (Pacte d'intérêt commun). The PIC was designed to simply regulate the common possessions of couples without granting them any particular recognition by the state. The PIC could

---

139. Ibid., 233.

140. Ibid., 234. For more on Schneider's views on sexual difference and democracy, see Michel Schneider, *La confusion des sexes* (Flammarion, 2007).

141. Théry, "Le contrat d'union sociale," 185.

ALTERNATIVE KINSHIPS AND REPUBLICAN STRUCTURALISM   261

easily be added to the Civil Code's section on contracts without modifying any family law dispositions. As Hauser put it, "We immediately decided to work on a model that was simple but completely autonomous. It relied exclusively on the fact of common life and the bringing together of a certain number of means and of goods. The advantage (or the inconvenience) of the chosen method was to eliminate the ideological weight of the question."[142]

But "the ideological weight of the question" was precisely what was at stake in both the bioethics and the PACS debates. To be sure, both artificial insemination and the PACS were initially presented as problems of law and as demands for a set of specific rights. But in fact both posed a much larger question, one that touched on the pillars of the French public sphere: the family. What would it mean for heterosexuals and homosexuals to have equal access to publicness? In its most radical interpretation, when it was open to siblings and friends especially, the PACS even offered the possibility of constructing a public sphere no longer anchored on sexuality but rather on "common life," or on what the anthropologist John Borneman has called "units of care."[143] Assisted procreation and the PACS offered the possibility of imagining a new symbolic—one that could remain normative without being necessarily universalistic or transhistorical—but also, and perhaps most importantly, another concept of the social, of republicanism, and, ultimately, of France.

---

142. Cited in Borrillo and Fassin, *Au-delà du PACS*, 42.

143. John Borneman, "Caring and Being Cared For: Displacing Marriage, Kinship, Gender and Sexuality," *International Social Science Journal* 49, no. 4 (1997): 583. See also Will Bishop, "The Marriage Translation and the Contexts of Common Life: From the Pacs to Benjamin and Beyond," *Diacritics* 35, no. 4 (2005): 59–80; Janet Carsten, *After Kinship* (Cambridge University Press, 2004); Sarah Franklin and Susan McKinnon, *Relative Values: Reconfiguring Kinship Studies* (Duke University Press, 2001).

Epilogue
Kinship, Ethics, and the Nation

By the time it was voted in 1999, the PACS essentially encompassed the same rights and benefits as marriage, except for two: filiation and nationality. Unlike married couples, PACS contractors could neither acquire French citizenship nor have access to adoption and medically assisted procreation. The fact that reproduction and nationality were both excluded from the PACS was significant. As I have indicated in this book, discussions of kinship—whether it be in the fields of law, anthropology, or psychoanalysis—have always entailed a discussion of the social and of the "ethical order" in the Hegelian sense of *Sittlichkeit*. Kinship has served as a mechanism to define which modes of social belonging, political participation, and cultural intelligibility are allowed and which are banned. Kinship, in other words, has been intimately tied to the nation. The fact that family planning and immigration were often controlled by the same agencies (such as the Haut comité de la population) and the fact that the rhetoric of republicanism surfaced again and again in the bioethics and PACS debates point to the fundamental interrelation of kinship and nation.

The foundational role of the family in the process of "imagining communities" is, of course, neither specific to France nor to the twentieth century, and many historians and political theorists have persuasively shown how social contracts have always involved specific sexual contracts. Furthermore, in many other countries, "experts" from all disciplines have regularly

EPILOGUE   263

intervened in the field of family law, and conservative critics have also posited a direct connection between familial and social structures. In the United States, for example, Justice Antonin Scalia's dissent in the 2003 case of *Lawrence v. Texas* emphasized the "massive disruption of the current social order" that would ensue if the laws banning sodomy were declared unconstitutional. Similarly, juvenile delinquency, drug and alcohol abuse, teenage pregnancy, or welfare dependency have all frequently been attributed to some kind of dysfunction within the family—generally divorce, unmarried mothers, or absent fathers.

Yet, the genealogy that I have traced here does seem specific to France in at least one way: the centrality of history in these debates around the family. The politicians, legal thinkers, and intellectuals featured in this book all took for granted the link between kinship and the social. However, they presented this link either as an immutable, universal, and transhistorical bond or as the product of a particular time and place, a bond that could potentially be transformed, philosophically and politically. The debates around the family in France were thus debates about the historical or transhistorical nature of norms—and thus about the ethical at its core. Structuralist anthropology and psychoanalysis were appealing in the legal and political spheres precisely because they provided a model of kinship that appeared to evacuate all historicity. Within the legal world, the question was framed as struggle between a sociological/positivist/liberal vision of the law versus one that sought first and foremost to protect and promote its anthropological or symbolic function. Within psychoanalysis and anthropology, it was articulated as a dispute around the notion of the symbolic and the possibility of imagining new modes of psychic and social relationality, such as the anti-Oedipal for Deleuze and Guattari, the anal for Hocquenghem, or the feminine for Irigaray.

Other countries wrestling with complicated questions around the family did not turn to structuralism, partly because they had other effective discourses available, whether it be religion or the social sciences. It is interesting, for example, to notice how in the United States many of the conservative sociologists who have emphasized the socially devastating effects of "broken homes"—David Popenoe, David Blankenhorn, or Linda Waite, for example—have grounded their arguments in empiricism. From their perspective, the battle was one of numbers and statistics: a battle against other social scientists who also used numbers and statistics to argue that children conceived or raised by same-sex, divorced, nonbiological, or single parents were just as likely to be socially adapted or troubled as those raised in traditional nuclear families. The stakes were, of course, normative, but

264   **EPILOGUE**

the tools were empirical. In the case of France, however, the matter was never presented in terms of facts, pragmatics, or realities. Historians and social scientists who had actually studied differently configured families were hardly consulted by the media or the administration. Foreign studies were very rarely cited. Rather, what was at stake was *the* symbolic as the ahistorical normative structure regulating all social and psychic life.

Within the recent French family debates, neither the symbolic nor republicanism were actually defined or explained. Instead, these concepts were invoked tautologically: the symbolic was what was republican; the republican was symbolic. Both were universal and provided social cohesion and psychic support. As I have tried to show, this notion of the symbolic did indeed derive from the works of Lévi-Strauss and Lacan, but its political uses were very much removed from the authors' original intentions. In fact, many contemporary critics—Tracy McNulty, Lee Edelman, and Tim Dean, for example—have highlighted the fact that Lacan constructed the symbolic as a fantasy, as a *fiction,* one necessary for the subject's desire but always potentially challengeable and malleable. Similarly, the republicanism invoked by the opponents to the PACS and to medically assisted procreation had little to do with the historical reality of French republicanism as it was theorized and practiced in 1789, 1792, 1848, 1870, 1905, or 1945. In this case as well, many historians of modern France have convincingly shown that in all of these instances republicanism was never a monolithic entity, that in fact it was far less unified, cohesive, and centralized than the post-1980s proponents of the republican model have maintained. Just to give one example, *laïcité* as it was redefined in 2004 by the Conseil d'état was quite a departure from its 1905 definition. As it was invoked after the 1980s, republicanism appeared to be the self-evident reality of France, one that was sexed, gendered, and raced in very specific ways.

Thus, I am interested in the notions of the symbolic and republicanism not so much because of their failure to correspond to a more truthful reading of Lévi-Strauss and Lacan or to an authentic historical reality, but rather because of their fantasmatic power, because of the immense political weight that both concepts carry today. These notions appear to have resurfaced since the 1980s to *resist* history, to reinscribe French political culture, anthropology, and psychoanalysis in a historical and social rigidity that it never actually had. In this sense, these family debates must be understood within the larger context of French political culture after the 1980s, which was increasingly anxious about immigration and globalization. More specifically, with the rise of the National Front, many of these self-declared republican thinkers were haunted by the following dilemma: if we retain the double

EPILOGUE 265

possibility of acquiring French nationality through *jus soli* (right of soil, which remained in place despite the various immigration reforms that have made this process significantly more complicated) and through *jus sanguinis* (filiation), who should be allowed to reproduce? If homosexuals or single parents are allowed to reproduce, who will be produced through this process? What will the nation look like? And most importantly, what new norms will govern life in common?

❧ BIBLIOGRAPHY

Archival Sources

Archives contemporaines d'Indre-et-Loire

Fonds Ménie Grégoire: 66J de 1 à 451

Archives nationales (AN)

Comité français de la libération nationale
  F 60 1677: Commissariat aux affaires sociales
  F 60 1723: Projets d'organisation de la politique familiale
Commissariat général du plan de modernisation et d'équipement
  AJ 80 10: Rapport de la Commission de la consommation et de la moderni-
  sation sociale, Septembre 1947
Fonds de la Société psychanalytique de Paris (SPP)
  101 AS I 61: Section psychanalyse d'enfants
Fonds Georges Mauco
  577 AP 1 to 577 AP 2: Papiers personnels
  577 AP 3 to 577 AP 7: Population et immigration
  577 AP 8 to 577 AP 13: Psychanalyse et pédagogie
Ministère de l'Intérieur
  F1 A 3252: Population, santé, Sécurité sociale, réfugiés, secrétariat général
  du gouvernement et services du premier ministre
  F 60 494 to F 60 497: Haut comité de la population (1939–1940)
  F 60 605: Natalité
  F 60 649: Allocations familiales
  F 60 1021: Documentation

Archives Françoise Dolto

31: Lacan
32: Éducation, la famille (divorce, mariage, adoption)
42: Radio

Centre des archives contemporaines

760136: INED/Fondation française pour l'étude des problèmes humains
860269: Direction de la population et des migrations et Haut comité de la
  population et de la famille, 1945–1975
990046: Commissariat général au plan

268 BIBLIOGRAPHY

Centre de documentation de l'union nationale des associations familiales (UNAF)

Institut mémoires de l'édition contemporaine (IMEC)

Collection Collège de France, Marcel Mauss
Fonds André Berge
Fonds Félix Guattari

Fondation nationale des sciences politiques (dossiers de documentation)

PACS (408/3; 3 volumes)
Politique familiale de la France (Boîte 1149; 17 volumes)
Procréation médicalement assistée (Boîte 474/31; 2 volumes)

Musée Social (Bibliothèque)

Selected Newspapers and Journals

Journal Officiel
La Croix
Le Figaro
Le Monde
Le Nouvel Observateur
Libération
Population & Avenir (Journal de l'Alliance nationale)
Pour la Vie: Revue d'Études Familiales

Books and Articles

Abélès, Marc. *Un ethnologue à l'Assemblée.* Paris: Odile Jacob, 2000.
Actes du colloque génétique, procréation et droit. Arles: Actes Sud, 1985.
Adler, Karen H. *Jews and Gender in Liberation France.* Cambridge: Cambridge
        University Press, 2003.
Agacinski, Sylviane. *Parity of the Sexes.* Translated by Lisa Walsh. New York:
        Columbia University Press, 2001.
————. *Politique des sexes: Précédé de mise au point sur la mixité.* Paris: Seuil, 2001.
Althusser, Louis. *Lenin and Philosophy, and Other Essays.* London: New Left Books,
        1971.
Anatrella, Tony. *La différence interdite: Sexualité, éducation, violence trente ans après mai
        68.* Paris: Flammarion, 1998.
————. "Ne pas brouiller les repères symboliques." *Le Figaro,* June 16, 1998.
Andrieu, Claire. *Pour l'amour de la République: Le Club Jean Moulin, 1958–1970.*
        Paris: Fayard, 2002.
Andrini, Simona, and André-Jean Arnaud. *Jean Carbonnier, Renato Treves et la sociolo-
        gie du droit: Archéologie d'une discipline.* Paris: LGDJ, 1995.
Antonioli, Manola, Frédéric Astier, and Olivier Fressard. *Gilles Deleuze et Félix
        Guattari: Une rencontre dans l'après Mai 68.* Paris: L'Harmattan, 2009.
Arnaud, André-Jean. *Les origines doctrinales du Code civil français.* Paris: Librairie
        générale de droit et de jurisprudence, 1969.
Arnault, Françoise. *Frédéric Le Play: De la métallurgie à la science sociale.* Nancy:
        Presses universitaires de Nancy, 1993.

BIBLIOGRAPHY 269

Association Henri Capitant, ed. *Hommage à Jean Carbonnier.* Paris: Dalloz, 2007.

Aymé, Jean. "Essai sur l'histoire de la psychothérapie institutionnelle." In *Actualités de la psychothérapie institutionnelle,* 32–69. Vigneux: Matrices, 1985.

Bach-Ignasse, Gérard, and Yves Roussel. *Le PACS juridique et pratique.* Paris: Denoël, 2000.

Badinter, Robert. "Lecture faite . . ." *Le Débat* 36 (1985): 37–39.

———. "Les droits de l'homme face au progrès de la médecine, de la biologie et de la biochimie," *Le Débat* 36 (1985): 4–14.

Badiou, Alain. *Deleuze: La clameur de l'être.* Paris: Hachette, 1997.

Bard, Chrisitine, and Jean-Louis Robert. "The French Communist Party and Women, 1920–1939: from 'Feminism' to 'Familialism.'" Translated by Nicole Dombrowski. In *Women and Socialism/Socialism and Women: Europe between the Two World Wars,* edited by Pamela Graves and Helmut Gruber, 321–47. Providence: Berghahn Books, 1998.

Baruch, Elaine Hoffman, and Lucienne J. Serrano, eds. *Women Analyze Women: In France, England, and the United States.* New York: New York University Press, 1988.

Bataille, Georges. "L'inceste et le passage de l'animal à l'homme." *Critique,* no. 44 (1951): 43–61.

Beauvoir, Simone de. "L'être et la parenté." *Les Temps Modernes* 491 (1949): 943–49.

Bender, Donald. "The Development of French Anthropology." *Journal of the History of Behavioral Science* 1 (1965): 139–51.

Benjamin, Walter. *Illuminations.* New York: Harcourt Brace & World, 1968.

Berenson, Edward. "The Politics of Divorce in France of the Belle Epoque: The Case of Joseph and Henriette Caillaux." *American Historical Review* 93, no. 1 (1988): 31–55.

Berge, André. *De l'écriture à la psychanalyse: entretiens avec Michel Mathieu.* Paris: Clancier Guénaud, 1988.

———. *Écrivain, psychanalyste, éducateur.* Paris: Desclée de Brouwer, 1995.

Bersani, Leo. *Homos.* Cambridge: Harvard University Press, 1995.

———. *Intimacies.* Chicago: University of Chicago Press, 2008.

Bertholet, Denis. *Claude Lévi-Strauss.* Paris: Plon, 2003.

Bertillon, Jacques. *Le problème de la dépopulation.* Paris: Armand Colin, 1897.

Biet, Christian, and Irène Théry. *La famille, la loi, l'État de la Révolution au Code civil.* Paris: Imprimerie nationale Centre Georges Pompidou, 1989.

Bishop, Will. "The Marriage Translation and the Contexts of Common Life: From the Pacs to Benjamin and Beyond," *Diacritics* 35, no. 4 (2005): 59–80.

Blum, Christopher Olaf. *Critics of the Enlightenment: Readings in the French Counter-Revolutionary Tradition.* Wilmington: ISI Books, 2004.

Boas, Franz, and George W. Stocking. *A Franz Boas Reader: The Shaping of American Anthropology, 1883–1911.* Chicago: University of Chicago Press, 1982.

Bock, Gisela, and Pat Thane. *Maternity and Gender Policies: Women and the Rise of the European Welfare States, 1880s–1950s.* London: Routledge, 1991.

270 BIBLIOGRAPHY

Bonnafé, Lucien, and Patrick Tort. *L'homme, cet inconnu? Alexis Carrel, Jean-Marie Le Pen et les chambres à gaz.* Paris: Syllepse, 1992.

Borch-Jacobsen, Mikkel. *Lacan: The Absolute Master.* Stanford, Calif.: Stanford University Press, 1991.

Bordeaux, Michèle. *La victoire de la famille dans la France défaite: Vichy 1940–1944.* Paris: Flammarion, 2002.

Borneman, John. "Caring and Being Cared for: Displacing Marriage, Kinship, Gender and Sexuality." *International Social Science Journal* 49, no. 4 (1997): 573–85.

Borrillo, Daniel. *Bioéthique.* Paris: Dalloz, 2011.

———. *Le droit des sexualités.* Paris: Presses universitaires de France, 2009.

Borrillo, Daniel, and Eric Fassin. *Au-delà du PACS: L'expertise familiale à l'épreuve de l'homosexualité.* Paris: Presses universitaires de France, 2001.

Borrillo, Daniel, and Pierre Lascoumes. *Amours égales: Le PACS, les homosexuels et la gauche.* Paris: La découverte, 2002.

Bourg, Julian. *From Revolution to Ethics: May 1968 and Contemporary French Thought.* Montreal: McGill-Queen's University Press, 2007.

Bowen, John Richard. *Why the French Don't Like Headscarves: Islam, the State, and Public Space.* Princeton, N.J.: Princeton University Press, 2006.

Bueltzingsloewen, Isabelle von. *L'hécatombe des fous: La famine dans les hôpitaux psychiatriques français sous l'Occupation.* Paris: Aubier, 2007.

Buisson-Fenet, Hélène. *Un sexe problématique: L'église et l'homosexualité masculine en France (1971–2000).* Paris: Presses universitaires de Vincennes, 2004.

Burchell, Graham, Colin Gordon, and Peter Miller, eds. *The Foucault Effect: Studies in Governmentality.* London: Harvester Wheatsheaf, 1991.

Burke, Carolyn, Naomi Schor, and Margaret Whitford, eds. *Engaging with Irigaray: Feminist Philosophy and Modern European Thought.* New York: Columbia University Press, 1994.

Butler, Judith. *Antigone's Claim: Kinship between Life and Death.* New York: Columbia University Press, 2000.

———. *Gender Trouble: Feminism and the Subversion of Identity.* New York: Routledge, 1990.

———. *Subjects of Desire: Hegelian Reflections in Twentieth-Century France.* New York: Columbia University Press, 1999.

———. *Undoing Gender.* New York: Routledge, 2004.

Butler, Judith, Ernesto Laclau, and Slavoj Žižek. *Contingency, Hegemony, Universality: Contemporary Dialogues on the Left.* London: Verso, 2000.

Camiscioli, Elisa. *Reproducing the French Race: Immigration, Intimacy, and Embodiment in the Early Twentieth Century.* Durham, N.C.: Duke University Press, 2009.

Carbonnier, Jean. *Droit et passion du droit: Sous la Ve République.* Paris: Flammarion, 1996.

———. *Écrits.* Paris: Presses universitaires de France, 2008.

———. *Essais sur les lois.* Paris: Répertoire du notariat defrénois, 1978.

———. *Flexible droit: Textes pour une sociologie du droit sans rigueur.* Paris: Librairie générale de droit et de jurisprudence, 1969.

———. "Le Code civil." In *Les lieux de mémoire.* Vol. 2. Edited by Pierre Nora, 293–315. Paris: Gallimard, 1984.

BIBLIOGRAPHY 271

————. *Sociologie juridique.* Paris: Presses universitaires de France, 1978.

Caron, Vicki. *Uneasy Asylum: France and the Jewish Refugee Crisis, 1933–1942.* Stanford, Calif.: Stanford University Press, 1999.

Carsten, Janet. *After Kinship.* Cambridge: Cambridge University Press, 2004.

Case, Mary Anne. "After Gender the Destruction of Man? The Vatican's Nightmare Vision of the 'Gender Agenda' for Law." *Pace Law Review* 31, no. 3 (2012): 802–17.

Cassirer, Ernst. *The Philosophy of the Enlightenment.* Princeton, N.J.: Princeton University Press, 1951.

Castel, Robert. *Le psychanalysme.* Paris: Maspero, 1973.

————. *Les métamorphoses de la question sociale: Une chronique du salariat.* Paris: Fayard, 1995.

Ceccaldi, Dominique. *Histoire des prestations familiales en France.* Paris: Union nationale des caisses d'allocations familiales, 1957.

Chanoit, Pierre. *La psychothérapie institutionnelle.* Paris: Presses universitaires de France, 1995.

Chaperon, Sylvie. *Les années Beauvoir (1945–1970).* Paris: Fayard, 2000.

Chaplin, Tamara. *Turning on the Mind: French Philosophers on Television.* Chicago: University of Chicago Press, 2007.

Charbit, Yves. *Du malthusianisme au populationnisme: Les économistes français et la population, 1840–1870.* Paris: Presses universitaires de France, 1981.

Chauvière, Michel, ed. *Les mouvements familiaux et leur institution en France: Anthologie historique et sociale.* Paris: Comité d'histoire de la Sécurité sociale, 2006.

Childers, Kristen Stromberg. *Fathers, Families, and the State in France, 1914–1945.* Ithaca, N.Y.: Cornell University Press, 2003.

Christofferson, Michael Scott. "An Antitotalitarian History of the French Revolution: François Furet's *Penser la Révolution française* in the Intellectual Politics of the Late 1970s." *French Historical Studies* 22, no. 4 (1999): 557–611.

————. *French Intellectuals against the Left: The Antitotalitarian Moment of the 1970s.* New York: Berghahn Books, 2004.

Chroniques d'une imposture: Du mouvement de libération des femmes à une marque commerciale. Paris: Association mouvement pour les luttes féministes, 1981.

Clouet, Stéphane. *De la rénovation à l'utopie socialistes: Révolution constructive, un groupe d'intellectuels socialistes des années 1930.* Nancy: Presses universitaires de Nancy, 1991.

Coffey, Joan L. *Léon Harmel: Entrepreneur as Catholic Social Reformer.* Notre Dame, Ind.: University of Notre Dame Press, 2003.

Cole, Joshua. *The Power of Large Numbers: Population, Politics, and Gender in Nineteenth-Century France.* Ithaca, N.Y.: Cornell University Press, 2000.

Colombet, Claude. *La filiation légitime et naturelle: Étude de la loi du 3 janvier 1972 et de son interprétation.* Paris: Dalloz, 1977.

Colomer, André. "Le nouveau régime matrimonial légal en France." *Revue Internationale de Droit Comparé* 18, no. 1 (1966): 61–78.

Comité d'histoire de la sécurité sociale. *La sécurité sociale: Son histoire à travers les textes.* Paris: Association pour l'étude de l'histoire de la sécurité sociale, 1994.

272   BIBLIOGRAPHY

Commaille, Jacques, and Marie-Pierre Marmier-Champenois. "Sociologie de la création de la norme: L'exemple de changements législatifs intervenus en droit de la famille." In *La création du droit: Aspects sociaux,* 135–205. Paris: Éditions du Centre national de la recherche scientifique, 1981.

Conklin, Alice L. "L'ethnologie combattante de l'entre-deux-guerres." In *Le siècle de Germaine Tillion,* edited by Tzvetan Todorov, 39–60. Paris: Seuil, 2007.

Copjec, Joan. *Read My Desire: Lacan against the Historicists.* Cambridge, Mass.: MIT Press, 1994.

Cornu, Gérard. *Droit civil, introduction, les personnes, les biens.* Paris: Montchrestien, 2001.

Coutrot, Aline. "La politique familiale." In *Le gouvernement de Vichy: 1940–1944,* edited by René Rémond, 245–63. Paris: Presses de Sciences Po, 1972.

Cowans, Jon. "Wielding the People: Opinion Polls and the Problem of Legitimacy in France since 1944." Ph.D. diss., Stanford University, 1994.

Danchin, Antoine. "Nature ou culture?" *Le Débat* 36 (1985): 20–24.

Dansette, Adrien. *Histoire religieuse de la France contemporaine.* Paris: Flammarion, 1952.

Darrow, Margaret H. *Revolution in the House: Family, Class, and Inheritance in Southern France, 1775–1825.* Princeton, N.J.: Princeton University Press, 1989.

Dean, Carolyn J. *The Frail Social Body: Pornography, Homosexuality, and Other Fantasies in Interwar France.* Berkeley: University of California Press, 2000.

———. *The Self and Its Pleasures: Bataille, Lacan, and the History of the Decentered Subject.* Ithaca, N.Y.: Cornell University Press, 1992.

Dean, Tim. *Beyond Sexuality.* Chicago: University of Chicago Press, 2000.

———. *Unlimited Intimacy: Reflections on the Subculture of Barebacking.* Chicago: University of Chicago press, 2009.

Debaene, Vincent. "'Like Alice through the Looking Glass': Claude Lévi-Strauss in New York." *French Politics, Culture and Society* 28, no. 1 (2010): 46–57.

———. "A propos de 'La politique étrangère d'une société primitive.'" *Ethnies,* no. 33–34 (2009): 132–38.

Debaene, Vincent, and Frédéric Keck. *Claude Lévi-Strauss: L'homme au regard éloigné.* Paris: Gallimard, 2009.

De Grazia, Victoria. *How Fascism Ruled Women: Italy, 1922–1945.* Berkeley: University of California Press, 1992.

Deleuze, Gilles. *Desert Islands and Other Texts, 1953–1974.* Translated by Michael Taormina. Los Angeles: Semiotext(e), 2004.

———. *Pourparlers, 1972–1990.* Paris: Éditions de minuit, 1990.

———. *Two Regimes of Madness: Texts and Interviews 1975–1995.* Translated by translated by Ames Hodges and Mike Taormina. Los Angeles: Semiotext(e), 2006.

Deleuze, Gilles, and Félix Guattari. *Anti-Oedipus: Capitalism and Schizophrenia.* Translated by Robert Hurley, Mark Seem, and Helen R. Lane. Minneapolis: University of Minnesota Press, 1983.

Deleuze, Gilles, and Claire Parnet. *Dialogues.* Translated by Hugh Tomlinson and Barbara Habberjam. New York: Columbia University Press, 1987.

BIBLIOGRAPHY 273

Delors, Jacques. *Contribution à une recherche sur les indicateurs sociaux*. Paris: S.É.D.É.I.S., 1971.

———. *Mémoires*. Paris: Plon, 2004.

Delpa, François. "Les communistes français et la sexualité (1932–1938)." *Le Mouvement Social* 91, April–June (1975): 121–52.

Delumeau, Jean, and Daniel Roche. *Histoire des pères et de la paternité*. Paris: Larousse, 2000.

Derrida, Jacques. *Of Grammatology*. Translated by Gayatri Chakravorty Spivak. Baltimore: Johns Hopkins University Press, 1997.

———. *Writing and Difference*. Translated by Alan Bass. Chicago: University of Chicago Press, 1978.

Desan, Suzanne. *The Family on Trial in Revolutionary France*. Berkeley: University of California Press, 2004.

Desmazières, Agnès. *L'inconscient au paradis: Comment les catholiques ont reçu la psychanalyse*. Paris: Payot, 2011.

Dinechin, Olivier de. "Le fait et le droit." *Le Débat* 36 (1985): 24–17.

Djian, Jean-Michel, ed. *Vincennes: Une aventure de la pensée critique*. Paris: Flammarion, 2009.

Dolto, Françoise. *Autoportrait d'une psychanalyste: 1934–1988*. Paris: Seuil, 1989.

———. *Correspondance*. Paris: Hatier, 1991.

———. "Françoise Dolto et la radio." *Psychiatrie Française*, no. 2 (1984): 27–32.

———. *La cause des enfants*. Paris: Robert Laffont, 1994.

———. *Les chemins de l'éducation*. Paris: Gallimard, 1994.

———. *Lorsque l'enfant paraît*. Paris: Seuil, 1977.

———. *Psychanalyse et pédiatrie: Les grandes notions de la psychanalyse, seize observations d'enfants*. Paris: Seuil, 1971.

———. *Une vie de correspondances: 1938–1988*. Paris: Gallimard, 2005.

Dolto, Françoise, and Nazir Hamad. *Destins d'enfants: Adoption, familles d'accueil, travail social*. Paris: Broché, 1995.

Dolto, Françoise, and Danielle Marie Lévy. *Parler juste aux enfants: Entretiens*. Paris: Mercure de France, 2002.

Donzelot, Jacques. *La police des familles*. Paris: Éditions de minuit, 1977.

———. *L'invention du social: Essai sur le déclin des passions politiques*. Paris: Fayard, 1984.

Dosse, François. *Gilles Deleuze et Félix Guattari: Biographie croisée*. Paris: La découverte, 2007.

———. *Histoire du structuralisme*. Paris: La découverte, 1991.

Dreyfus, Paul. *Émile Romanet, père des allocations familiales*. Paris: Arthaud, 1965.

Drouard, Alain. "Le Haut comite de la population et la politique de population de la France (1939–1966)." *Annales de Demographie Historique* 2 (1999): 171–97.

———. *Une inconnue des sciences sociales: La Fondation Alexis Carrel, 1941–1945*. Paris: Maison des sciences de l'homme, 1992.

Duchen, Claire. *Women's Rights and Women's Lives in France, 1944–1968*. London: Routledge, 1994.

Dupâquier, Jacques, ed. *Histoire de la population française*. Vol. 3, *De 1789 à 1914*. Paris: Presses universitaires de France, 1988.

274 BIBLIOGRAPHY

Durand, Jean-Dominique, ed. *Les semaines sociales de France: Cent ans d'engagement social des catholiques français 1904–2004.* Paris: Parole et silence, 2006.

Duroselle, Jean Baptiste. *Les débuts du catholicisme social en France (1822–1870).* Paris: Presses universitaires de France, 1951.

Dutton, Paul V. *Origins of the French Welfare State: The Struggle for Social Reform in France, 1914–1947.* Cambridge: Cambridge University Press, 2002.

Dzimira, Sylvain. *Marcel Mauss, savant et politique.* Paris: La découverte, 2007.

Echols, Alice. *Daring to Be Bad: Radical Feminism in America, 1967–1975.* Minneapolis: University of Minnesota Press, 1989.

Edelman, Lee. *No Future: Queer Theory and the Death Drive.* Durham, N.C.: Duke University Press, 2004.

Elbow, Matthew H. *French Corporative Theory, 1789–1948: A Chapter in the History of Ideas.* New York: Columbia University Press, 1953.

Elwitt, Sanford. "Social Reform and Social Order in Late Nineteenth-Century France: The Musée Social and Its Friends." *French Historical Studies* 11, no. 3 (1980): 431–51.

Enriquez, Eugène. *De la horde à l'État: Essai de psychanalyse du lien social.* Paris: Gallimard, 1983.

Eribon, Didier. *Echapper à la psychanalyse.* Paris: Léo Scheer, 2005.

———. *Sur cet instant fragile: Carnets, janvier-août' 2004.* Paris: Fayard, 2004.

———. *Une morale du minoritaire: Variations sur un thème de Jean Genet.* Paris: Fayard, 2001.

Eribon, Didier, and Claude Lévi-Strauss. *De près et de loin.* Paris: Odile Jacob, 1988.

Ewald, François. *L'État providence.* Paris: Grasset, 1986.

Fabre, Clarisse, and Eric Fassin. *Liberté, égalité, sexualité: Actualité politique des questions sexuelles.* Paris: Belfond, 2003.

Fabre, Daniel. "L'ethnologie française à la croisée des engagements (1940–1945)." In *Résistants et Résistance,* edited by Jean-Yves Boursier, 319–400. Paris: L'Harmattan, 1997.

Fassin, Éric. "Les 'forêts tropicales' du mariage hétérosexuel." *Revue d'Éthique et de Théologie Morale* 261 (2010): 201–22.

———. *L'inversion de la question homosexuelle.* Paris: Amsterdam, 2005.

———. "*PaCS Socialista*: La gauche et le 'juste milieu.'" *Le Banquet* 12–13 (1998): 147–59.

———. "Same Sex, Different Politics: 'Gay Marriage' Debates in France and the United States." *Public Culture* 13, no. 2 (2001): 215–32.

Faugeras, Patrick, ed. *L'ombre portée de François Tosquelles.* Ramonville Saint-Agne: Érès, 2007.

Favereau, Éric. "Portrait de Jean Oury." *Libération,* June 27, 1998.

Feher, Michel. "Mai 68 dans la pensée." In *Histoire des gauches en France.* Vol. 2. Edited by Jean-Jacques Becker and Gilles Candar, 599–623. Paris: La découverte, 2004.

Fenet, P. A., and François Ewald, eds. *Naissance du Code civil: La raison du législateur.* Paris: Flammarion, 1989.

Fink, Bruce. *The Lacanian Subject: Between Language and Jouissance.* Princeton, N.J.: Princeton University Press, 1995.

BIBLIOGRAPHY 275

Firestone, Shulamith. *The Dialectic of Sex: The Case for Feminist Revolution.* New York: Morrow, 1970.

Foucault, Michel. *The Birth of Biopolitics: Lectures at the Collège de France, 1978–79.* Translated by Graham Burchell. New York: Palgrave Macmillan, 2008.

———. *The History of Sexuality.* Vol. 1. Translated by Robert Hurley. New York: Vintage Books, 1980.

———. *The History of Sexuality.* Vol. 2. Translated by Robert Hurley. New York: Vintage Books, 1990.

———. *Histoire de la sexualité.* 3 vols. (Gallimard, 1976).

———. *The Order of Things: An Archaeology of the Human Sciences.* Translated by Alan Sheridan. New York: Vintage Books, 1973.

Foucault, Michel, and Colin Gordon. *Power/Knowledge: Selected Interviews and Other Writings, 1972–1977.* New York: Pantheon Books, 1980.

Fouque, Antoinette. *Il y a deux sexes: Essais de féminologie.* Paris: Gallimard, 2004.

Fourest, Caroline, and Fiammetta Venner. *Les anti-PaCS, ou, la dernière croisade homophobe.* Paris: Prochoix, 1999.

Fournier, Marcel. *Marcel Mauss.* Paris: Fayard, 1994.

Franklin, Sarah, and Susan McKinnon. *Relative Values: Reconfiguring Kinship Studies.* Durham, N.C.: Duke University Press, 2001.

Freud, Sigmund. *Totem and Taboo: Some Points of Agreement between the Mental Lives of Savages and Neurotics.* New York: Norton, 1989.

Fuchs, Rachel Ginnis. *Contested Paternity: Constructing Families in Modern France.* Baltimore: Johns Hopkins University Press, 2008.

Fuss, Diana. *Essentially Speaking: Feminism, Nature and Difference.* New York: Routledge, 1989.

Gaillard, Gérald. *The Routledge Dictionary of Anthropologists.* London: Routledge, 2003.

Garréta, Anne F. "Re-Enchanting the Republic: 'Pacs,' Parité and le Symbolique." *Yale French Studies* 100 (2001): 145–66.

Gauchet, Marcel. *La condition historique.* Paris: Stock, 2003.

Geissmann, Claudine, and Pierre Geissmann. *Histoire de la psychanalyse de l'enfant: Mouvements, idées, perspectives.* Paris: Bayard, 1992.

Geller, Sacha. *Mères porteuses oui ou non?* Paris: Frison-Roche, 1990.

Godelier, Maurice. *Métamorphoses de la parenté.* Paris: Fayard, 2004.

Goodrich, Peter. *Law and the Unconscious: A Legendre Reader.* New York: St. Martin's Press, 1997.

Guattari, Félix. *The Anti-Oedipus Papers.* Translated by Kélina Gotman. New York: Semiotext(e), 2006.

———. *Chaosophy.* Translated by David L. Sweet, Jarred Becker, and Taylor Adkins. New York: Semiotext(e), 1995.

———. *Psychanalyse et transversalité: Essais d'analyse institutionnelle.* Paris: La découverte, 2003.

Guitton, Georges. *La vie ardente et féconde de Léon Harmel.* Paris: Éditions Spes, 1930.

Gunther, Scott Eric. *The Elastic Closet: A History of Homosexuality in France, 1942–Present.* New York: Palgrave Macmillan, 2009.

276   BIBLIOGRAPHY

Haas, Ron. "Guy Hocquenghem and the Cultural Revolution in France after
   May 1968." In *After the Deluge: New Perspectives on the Intellectual and Cultural
   History of Postwar France*, edited by Julian Bourg, 175–99. Lanham, Md.:
   Lexington Books, 2004.

Habermas, Jürgen, and Joseph Ratzinger. *The Dialectics of Secularization: On Reason
   and Religion*. San Francisco: Ignatius Press, 2006.

Halimi, Gisèle. *La cause des femmes*. Paris: Grasset, 1973.

Halpérin, Jean-Louis. *Histoire du droit privé français depuis 1804*. Paris: Presses
   universitaires de France, 1996.

———. *Le Code civil*. Paris: Dalloz, 2003.

Hénaff, Marcel. *Claude Lévi-Strauss and the Making of Structural Anthropology*.
   Minneapolis: University of Minnesota Press, 1998.

Héritier, Françoise. *Masculin/féminin*. Paris: Odile Jacob, 1996.

———. "Regards au loin et alentour: Entretien avec Georges Guille-Escuret."
   Journal des Anthropologues 76 (1999): 7–23.

Héritier-Augé, Françoise. "L'individu, le biologique et le social." *Le Débat* 36
   (1985): 27–32.

Hervieu-Léger, Danièle. *Catholicisme, la fin d'un monde*. Bayard, 2003.

Herzog, Dagmar. *Sex after Fascism: Memory and Morality in Twentieth-Century
   Germany*. Princeton, N.J.: Princeton University Press, 2005.

Heuer, Jennifer Ngaire. *The Family and the Nation: Gender and Citizenship in Revolutionary France, 1789–1830*. Ithaca, N.Y.: Cornell University Press, 2005.

Hewitt, Martin. "Bio-politics and Social Policy: Foucault's Account of Welfare."
   Theory, Culture, and Society 2, no. 1 (1983): 67–84.

Hocquenghem, Guy. *Homosexual Desire*. Durham, N.C.: Duke University Press,
   1993.

———. *L'après-mai des faunes; volutions*. Paris: Grasset, 1974.

Hollier, Denis, ed. *Le Collège de sociologie: 1937–1939*. Paris: Gallimard, 1979.

Horne, Janet R. *A Social Laboratory for Modern France: The Musée Social and the Rise
   of the Welfare State*. Durham, N.C.: Duke University Press, 2001.

Hunter, John C. "The Problem of the French Birth Rate on the Eve of World
   War I." *French Historical Studies* 2, no. 4 (1962): 489–503.

Huss, Marie-Monique. "Pronatalism in the Inter-War Period in France." *Journal of
   Contemporary History* 25, no. 1 (1990): 39–68.

Iacub, Marcela. *Le crime était presque sexuel et autres essais de casuistique juridique*.
   Paris: Éditions Epel, 2002.

———. *L'empire du ventre: Pour une autre histoire de la maternité*. Paris: Fayard, 2004.

Irigaray, Luce. *An Ethics of Sexual Difference*. Translated by Carolyn Burke and
   Gillian Gill. Ithaca, N.Y.: Cornell University Press, 1993.

———. *Le langage des déments*. The Hague: Mouton, 1973.

———. *Speculum of the Other Woman*. Translated by Gillian Gill. Ithaca, N.Y.:
   Cornell University Press, 1985.

———. *This Sex Which Is Not One*. Translated by Catherine Porter. Ithaca, N.Y.:
   Cornell University Press, 1985.

Jackson, Julian. *Living in Arcadia: Homosexuality, Politics, and Morality in France from
   the Liberation to AIDS*. Chicago: University of Chicago Press, 2009.

BIBLIOGRAPHY 277

Jainchill, Andrew. *Reimagining Politics after the Terror: The Republican Origins of French Liberalism*. Ithaca, N.Y.: Cornell University Press, 2008.

Jainchill, Andrew, and Samuel Moyn. "French Democracy between Totalitarianism and Solidarity: Pierre Rosanvallon and Revisionist Historiography." *Journal of Modern History* 76, March (2004): 107–54.

Jamin, Jean. "L'anthropologie et ses acteurs." In *Les enjeux philosophiques des années 50,* edited by Christian Descamps, 99–115. Paris: Éditions du Centre Pompidou, 1989.

Jardine, Alice, and Anne M. Menke, eds. *Shifting Scenes: Interviews on Women, Writing, and Politics in Post-68 France*. New York: Columbia University Press, 1991.

Jeanpierre, Laurent. "La politique culturelle française aux États-Unis de 1940 à 1947." In *Entre rayonnement et réciprocité: contributions à l'histoire de la diplomatie culturelle,* 85–116. Paris: Publications de la Sorbonne, 2002.

———. "Les structures d'une pensée d'exilé: La formation du structuralisme de Claude Lévi-Strauss." *French Politics, Culture and Society* 28, no. 1 (2010): 58–76.

Jobs, Richard Ivan. *Riding the New Wave: Youth and the Rejuvenation of France after the Second World War.* Stanford, Calif.: Stanford University Press, 2007.

Johnson, Christopher. *Claude Lévi-Strauss: The Formative Years*. Cambridge: Cambridge University Press, 2003.

Kalaora, Bernard, and Antoine Savoye. "Frédéric Le Play, un sociologue engagé." In *Ouvriers des deux mondes: Études publiées par la Société d'Economie Sociale à partir de 1856,* 320–33. Thomery: À l'enseigne de l'arbre verdoyant, 1983.

———. *Les inventeurs oubliés: Le Play et ses continuateurs aux origines des sciences sociales.* Seyssel: Champ Vallon, 1989.

Kaplan, Steven L. "Un laboratoire de la doctrine corporatiste sous le régime de Vichy: L'Institut d'études corporatives et sociales." *Le Mouvement Social* 195, April–June (2001): 35–77.

Keck, Frédéric. *Claude Lévi-Strauss: Une introduction*. Paris: Pocket/La découverte, 2005.

Knobel, Marc. "L'ethnologue à la dérive: Montandon et l'ethnoracisme." *Ethnologie Française* 18 (1988): 107–13.

Koos, Cheryl A. "Gender, Anti-Individualism, and Nationalism: The Alliance Nationale and the Pronatalist Backlash against the Femme Moderne, 1933–1940." *French Historical Studies* 19, no. 3 (1996): 699–723.

Labrusse-Riou, Catherine. *Droit de la famille; 1. Les personnes.* Paris: Masson, 1984.

———. *Écrits de bioéthique.* Presses universitaires de France, 2007.

———. "L'homme à vif: Biotechnologies et droits de l'homme," *Esprit* 156 (1989): 60–70.

———. "Sciences de la vie et légitimité." In *Droits des personnes et de la famille: Mélanges à la mémoire de Danièle Huet-Weiller,* 283–303 (Strasbourg: Presses universitaires de Strasbourg, 1994).

Lacan, Jacques. *Autres écrits.* Paris: Seuil, 2001.

———. *De la psychose paranoïaque dans ses rapports avec la personnalité suivi de Premiers écrits sur la paranoïa.* Paris: Seuil, 1975.

278   BIBLIOGRAPHY

————. *Des noms-du-père.* Paris: Seuil, 2005.

————. *Écrits: A Selection.* Translated by Bruce Fink. New York: Norton, 2002.

————. *The Ego in Freud's Theory and in the Technique of Psychoanalysis, 1954–1955.* Translated by Sylvana Tomaselli. New York: Norton, 1988.

————. *The Ethics of Psychoanalysis, 1959–1960.* Translated by Dennis Porter. New York: Norton, 1992.

————. *La relation d'objet: Le séminaire, Livre IV, 1956–1957.* Paris: Seuil, 1994.

————. *L'envers de la psychanalyse: Le séminaire, Livre XVII, 1969–1970.* Paris: Seuil, 1991.

————. *Les formations de l'inconscient: Le séminaire, Livre V, 1957–1958.* Paris: Seuil, 1998.

LaCapra, Dominick. *Émile Durkheim: Sociologist and Philosopher.* Ithaca, N.Y.: Cornell University Press, 1972.

————. *Rethinking Intellectual History: Texts, Contexts, Language.* Ithaca, N.Y.: Cornell University Press, 1983.

Landrieu, Joseph. "Le vote familial." Thesis, Université de Lille, 1923.

Laroque, Pierre. "Famille et Sécurité sociale." In *Niveaux de vie des familles: Travaux du Congrès mondial de la famille et de la population* (Paris: UNAF, 1947).

Laroque, Pierre, and Rémi Lenoir. *La politique familiale en France depuis 1945. Rapport du groupe de travail sur la politique familiale en France depuis 1945, présidé par Pierre Laroque.* Paris: Documentation française, 1985.

Laurent, Vincent. "Enquête sur la Fondation Saint-Simon: Les architectes du social-libéralisme." *Le Monde Diplomatique,* September (1998).

Lebovics, Herman. "Le conservatisme en anthropologie et la fin de la Troisième République." *Gradhiva* 4 (1988): 3–17.

————. *True France: The Wars over Cultural Identity, 1900–1945.* Ithaca, N.Y.: Cornell University Press, 1992.

Leclaire, Serge. *Œdipe à Vincennes: Séminaire 69.* Paris: Fayard, 1999.

Ledoux, Michel H. *Introduction à l'œuvre de Françoise Dolto.* Paris: Rivages, 1990.

Lefort, Claude. *Essais sur le politique: XIXe–XXe siècles.* Paris: Seuil, 1986.

Legendre, Pierre. "Ce que nous appelons le droit: Entretien avec Pierre Legendre." *Le Débat* 74 (1993): 107–22.

Le Naour, Jean-Yves, and Catherine Valenti. *Histoire de l'avortement: XIXe–XXe siècle.* Paris: Seuil, 2003.

————. *La famille doit voter: Le suffrage familial contre le vote individuel.* Paris: Hachette littératures, 2005.

Lenoir, Rémi. *Généalogie de la morale familiale.* Paris: Seuil, 2003.

Le Play, Frédéric. *La réforme sociale en France déduite de l'observation comparée des peuples européens.* Geneva: Slatkine, 1982.

Lespinet-Moret, Isabelle. "La question sociale." In *Dictionnaire critique de la République,* edited by Vincent Duclert and Christophe Prochasson. Paris: Flammarion, 2002.

Lévi-Strauss, Claude. *The Elementary Structures of Kinship.* Translated by James Harle Bell and John Richard von Sturmer. Boston: Beacon Press, 1969.

————. "Introduction à l'œuvre de Marcel Mauss." In *Sociologie et anthropologie,* ix–lii. Paris: Presses universitaires de France, 1950.

———. "La sociologie française." In *La sociologie au XXe siècle*, edited by Georges Gurvitch, 523–45. Paris: Presses universitaires de France, 1947.

———. *Œuvres*. Paris: Gallimard, 2008.

———. *Structural Anthropology*. Translated by Claire Jacobson and Brooke Grundfest Schoepf. New York: Basic Books, 1963.

———. *Tristes tropiques*. Paris: Plon, 1955.

Lévy, Laurent. *Le spectre du communautarisme*. Paris: Amsterdam, 2005.

Lewis, Mary Dewhurst. *The Boundaries of the Republic: Migrant Rights and the Limits of Universalism in France, 1918–1940*. Stanford, Calif.: Stanford University Press, 2007.

Loyer, Emmanuelle. *Paris à New York: Intellectuels et artistes français en exil (1940–1947)*. Paris: Grasset, 2005.

Lucey, Michael. *The Misfit of the Family: Balzac and the Social Forms of Sexuality*. Durham, N.C.: Duke University Press, 2003.

Lukes, Steven. *Emile Durkheim, His Life and Work: A Historical and Critical Study*. London: Allen Lane, 1973.

Lynch, Katherine A. *Family, Class, and Ideology in Early Industrial France: Social Policy and the Working-Class Family, 1825–1848*. Madison: University of Wisconsin Press, 1988.

Macnicol, John. "Welfare, Wages, and the Family: Child Endowment in Comparative Perspective, 1900–50." In *In the Name of the Child: Health and Welfare, 1880–1940*, edited by Roger Cooter, 244–75. London: Routledge, 1992.

Magri, Susanna. *Logement et reproduction de l'exploitation: Les politiques étatiques du logement en France (1947–1972)*. Paris: Centre de sociologie urbaine, 1977.

Mainardi, Patricia. *Husbands, Wives, and Lovers: Marriage and Its Discontents in Nineteenth-Century France*. New Haven, Conn.: Yale University Press, 2003.

Marcus, Sharon. *Between Women: Friendship, Desire, and Marriage in Victorian England*. Princeton, N.J.: Princeton University Press, 2007.

Marini, Marcelle. *Jacques Lacan: The French context*. New Brunswick, N.J.: Rutgers University Press, 1992.

Martel, Frédéric. *Le rose et le noir: Les homosexuels en France depuis 1968*. Paris: Seuil, 1996.

Martin, Benjamin F. *Count Albert de Mun, Paladin of the Third Republic*. Chapel Hill: University of North Carolina Press, 1978.

Mauco, Georges. *La paternité; sa fonction éducative dans la famille et à l'école*. Paris: Éditions universitaires, 1971.

———, ed. *L'inadaptation scolaire et sociale et ses remèdes: Cahiers de pédagogie moderne*. Paris: Armand Colin, 1959.

———. *Psychanalyse et éducation*. Paris: Aubier-Montaigne, 1979.

———. *Vécu 1899–1982*. Paris: Émile-Paul, 1982.

Mauss, Marcel. *The Gift: The Form and Reason for Exchange in Archaic Societies*. New York: Norton, 1990.

———. *Sociologie et anthropologie*. Paris: Presses universitaires de France, 1950.

Mayeur, Jean-Marie. *Catholicisme social et démocratie chretienne: Principes romains, experiences francaises* Paris: Cerf, 1986.

BIBLIOGRAPHY

————. *Les débuts de la Troisième République, 1871–1898*. Paris: Seuil, 1973.

————. *Un prêtre démocrate: L'abbé Lemire 1853–1928*. Paris: Castermann, 1968.

Mazon, Brigitte. *Aux origines de l'École des hautes études en sciences sociales: Le rôle du mécénat américain, 1920–1960*. Paris: Cerf, 1988.

McCaffrey, Enda. *The Gay Republic: Sexuality, Citizenship and Subversion in France*. Burlington, Vt.: Ashgate, 2005.

McLaren, Angus. *Sexuality and Social Order: The Debate over the Fertility of Women and Workers in France, 1770–1920*. New York: Holmes & Meier, 1983.

McNulty, Tracy. *Wrestling with the Angel: Experiments in Symbolic Life*. New York: Columbia University Press, 2013.

Mehl, Dominique. *La bonne parole: Quand les psys plaident dans les médias*. Paris: La Martinière, 2003.

————. *Les lois de l'enfantement: Procréation et politique en France (1982 – 2011)*. Paris: Presses de Science Po, 2011.

————. *Naître: La controverse bioéthique*. Bayard, 1999.

Memmi, Dominique. *Les gardiens du corps: Dix ans de magistère bioéthique*. Paris: Éditions de l'École des hautes études en sciences sociales, 1996.

Merleau-Ponty, Maurice. *Éloge de la philosophie et autres essais*. Paris: Gallimard, 1967.

Messu, Michel. *Les politiques familiales: Du natalisme à la solidarité*. Paris: Éditions ouvrières, 1992.

Meyran, Régis. "Races et racismes: Les ambiguïtés de l'antiracisme chez les anthropologues de l'entre-deux-guerres." *Gradhiva* 27 (2000): 63–76.

Michel, Jean-Pierre, and Irène Théry. "Concubinage ou union sui generis: Le statut et les droits." *Le Banquet* 12–13 (1998).

Michel Foucault, philosophe: Rencontre internationale, Paris, 9, 10, 11 janvier 1988. Paris: Seuil, 1989.

Mijolla, Alain de, ed. *Dictionnaire international de la psychanalyse: Concepts, notions, biographies, œuvres, événements, institutions*. Paris: Calmann-Lévy, 2002.

————. *Freud et la France: 1885–1945*. Paris: Presses universitaires de France, 2010.

Miller, Jacques-Alain, ed. *La Scission de 1953: La communauté psychanalytique en France*. Paris: Navarin, 1990.

Mornet, Joseph. *Psychothérapie institutionnelle: Histoire & actualité*. Nîmes: Champ social, 2007.

Mossuz-Lavau, Janine. *Les lois de l'amour: Les politiques de la sexualité en France, 1950–2002*. Paris: Payot & Rivages, 2002.

Muel-Dreyfus, Francine. *Vichy et l'éternel féminin: Contribution à une sociologie politique de l'ordre des corps*. Paris: Seuil, 1996.

Noiriel, Gérard. *Le creuset français: Histoire de l'immigration, XIXe–XXe siècles*. Paris: Seuil, 1988.

————. *Les ouvriers dans la société française: XIXe–XXe siècle*. Paris: Seuil, 1986.

Nord, Philip. *France's New Deal: From the Thirties to the Postwar Era*. Princeton, N.J.: Princeton University Press, 2010.

————. "The Welfare State in France, 1870–1914." *French Historical Studies* 18, no. 3 (1994): 821–38.

Norgeu, Anne-Marie. *La Borde: Le château des chercheurs de sens. La vie quotidienne à la clinique psychiatrique de La Borde*. Toulouse: Érès, 2006.

Offen, Karen. "Depopulation, Nationalism, and Feminism in Fin-de-Siecle France." *American Historical Review* 89, no. 3 (1984): 648–76.

Ogien, Ruwen. *La vie, la mort, l'État: Le débat bioéthique.* Paris: Grasset, 2009.

Ohayon, Annick. *Psychologie et psychanalyse en France: L'impossible rencontre, 1919–1969.* Paris: La découverte, 2006.

Oury, Jean. *Onze heures du soir à La Borde.* Paris: Gallilée, 1995.

Pajon, Alexandre. "Claude Lévi-Strauss: D'une métaphysique socialiste à l'éthnologie (1ère partie)." *Gradhiva*, no. 28 (2000): 33–45.

———. "Claude Lévi-Strauss: D'une métaphysique socialiste à l'éthnologie (2ème partie)." *Gradhiva*, no. 29 (2001): 1–24.

———. *Claude Lévi-Strauss politique: De la SFIO à l'UNESCO.* Toulouse: Privat, 2011.

Paxton, Robert O. *Vichy France: Old Guard and New Order, 1940–1944.* New York: Knopf, 1972.

Pedersen, Jean Elisabeth. *Legislating the French Family: Feminism, Theater, and Republican Politics, 1870–1920.* New Brunswick, N.J.: Rutgers University Press, 2003.

Pedersen, Susan. *Family, Dependence, and the Origins of the Welfare State: Britain and France, 1914–1945.* New York: Cambridge University Press, 1993.

Perreau, Bruno. *Penser l'adoption: La gouvernance pastorale du genre.* Paris: Presses universitaires de France, 2012.

Philibert, Nicolas. *La moindre des choses.* DVD. Paris: Éditions Montparnasse, 1996.

Picq, Françoise. *Libération des femmes: Les années-mouvement.* Paris: Seuil, 1993.

Polack, Jean Claude, and Danielle Sivadon-Sabourin. *La Borde: Ou, le droit à la folie.* Paris: Calmann-Levy, 1976.

Pollard, Miranda. *Reign of Virtue: Mobilizing Gender in Vichy France.* Chicago: University of Chicago Press, 1998.

Potin, Yann, ed. *Françoise Dolto: Archives de l'intime.* Paris: Gallimard, 2008.

Procacci, Giovanna. *Gouverner la misère: La question sociale en France, 1789–1848.* Paris: Seuil, 1993.

Prochasson, Christophe. *Saint-Simon ou l'anti-Marx: Figures du saint-simonisme français XIXe- XXe siècles.* Paris: Perrin, 2005.

Prokhoris, Sabine. *Le sexe prescrit: La différence sexuelle en question.* Paris: Flammarion, 2002.

Prost, Antoine. "L'évolution de la politique familiale en France de 1938 à 1981." *Le Mouvement Social* 129 (1984): 7–28.

Rabinow, Paul. *French Modern: Norms and Forms of the Social Environment.* Cambridge: MIT Press, 1989.

Reggiani, Andrés Horacio. *God's Eugenicist: Alexis Carrel and the Sociology of Decline.* New York: Berghahn Books, 2006.

Renaudin, Philippe. "La famille dans la nation." L'Office de propagande générale, June 16, 1943.

Revel, Janine. *La filiation.* Paris: Presses universitaires de France, 1998.

Richman, Michèle H. *Sacred Revolutions: Durkheim and the Collège de sociologie.* Minneapolis: University of Minnesota Press, 2002.

Rioux, Jean-Pierre. *La France de la IVe République.* 2 vols. Paris: Seuil, 1980.

BIBLIOGRAPHY

Robcis, Camille. "French Sexual Politics from Human Rights to the Anthropological Function of the Law." *French Historical Studies* 33, no. 1 (2010): 129–56.

Robert, Guy. "Un état dans l'état RTL: Le divan radiophonique de Menie Grégoire." *Cahiers du Comité d'Histoire de la Radiodiffusion* 55, January–February (1998): 88–154.

Roberts, Mary Louise. *Civilization without Sexes: Reconstructing Gender in Postwar France, 1917–1927.* Chicago: University of Chicago Press, 1994.

Rodgers, Catherine. "Elle et Elle: Antoinette Fouque et Simone de Beauvoir." *Modern Language Notes* 115 (2000): 741–60.

Ronsin, Francis. *La grève des ventres: Propagande néo-malthusienne et baisse de la natalité française, XIXe–XXe siècles.* Paris: Aubier Montaigne, 1980.

Rosanvallon, Pierre. *Le modèle politique français: La société civile contre le jacobinisme de 1789 à nos jours.* Paris: Seuil, 2004.

———. *Le peuple introuvable: Histoire de la représentation démocratique en France.* Paris: Gallimard, 1998.

———. *Le sacre du citoyen: Histoire du suffrage universel en France.* Paris: Gallimard, 1992.

Rosental, Paul-André. *L'intelligence démographique: Sciences et politiques des populations en France, 1930–1960.* Paris: Odile Jacob, 2003.

Ross, Kristin. *Fast Cars, Clean Bodies: Decolonization and the Reordering of French Culture.* Cambridge, Mass.: MIT Press, 1995.

Roth, Michael S. *Knowing and History: Appropriations of Hegel in Twentieth-Century France.* Ithaca, N.Y.: Cornell University Press, 1988.

Roudinesco, Elisabeth. "De près et de loin: Claude Lévi-Strauss et la psychanalyse." *Critique* 55, no. 620–621 (1999): 169–85.

———. "Georges Mauco (1899–1988): Un psychanalyste au service de Vichy. De l'antisémitisme à la psychopédagogie." *L'Infini* 51 (1995): 67–84.

———. *Jacques Lacan: Esquisse d'une vie, histoire d'un système de pensée.* Paris: Fayard, 1993.

———. *La bataille de cent ans: Histoire de la psychanalyse en France.* 2 vols. Paris: Ramsay, 1982, 1986.

———. *Lacan, envers et contre tout.* Paris: Seuil, 2011.

———. *La famille en désordre.* Paris: Fayard, 2002.

Rousseau, Jean-Jacques. *The Social Contract and Discourses.* Translated by G. D. H. Cole. London: Everyman, 1973.

Rousseau-Dujardin, Jacqueline. "Du temps, qu'entends-je?" *L'Arc,* no. 58 (1974): 31.

Rubellin-Devichi, Jacqueline. *L'évolution du statut civil de la famille depuis 1945.* Paris: Éditions du Centre national de la recherche scientifique, 1983.

Rubin, Gayle. "The Traffic in Women: Notes on the 'Political Economy' of Sex." In *Toward an Anthropology of Women,* edited by Rayna R. Reiter, 157–210. New York: Monthly Review Press, 1975.

Sahlins, Peter. *Unnaturally French: Foreign Citizens in the Old Regime and After.* Ithaca, N.Y.: Cornell University Press, 2004.

Sauvage, Pierre. *La politique familiale de l'état français.* Paris: Action populaire/ Éditions Spes, 1941.

Sauverzac, Jean-François de. *Françoise Dolto, itinéraire d'une psychanalyste.* Paris: Aubier, 1993.

Savoye, Antoine and Frédéric Audren, eds. *Naissance de l'ingénieur social: Les ingénieurs des mines et la science sociale au XIXe siècle.* Paris: Presses de l'Ecole des mines, 2008.

Schafer, Sylvia. "Between Paternal Right and the Dangerous Mother: Reading Parental Responsibility in Nineteenth-Century French Civil Justice." *Journal of Family History* 23, no. 2 (1998): 173–89.

———. *Children in Moral Danger and the Problem of Government in Third Republic France.* Princeton, N.J.: Princeton University Press, 1997.

Schlegel, John Henry. *American Legal Realism and Empirical Social Science.* Chapel Hill: University of North Carolina Press, 1995.

Schneider, Michel. *Big mother: Psychopathologie de la vie politique.* Paris: Odile Jacob, 2002.

———. *La confusion des sexes.* Paris: Flammarion, 2007.

———. "L'État comme semblant." *Cités: Philosophie, Politique, Histoire,* no.16 (2003): 43–54.

Schneider, William H. *Quality and Quantity: The Quest for Biological Regeneration in Twentieth Century France.* Cambridge: Cambridge University Press, 1990.

Schneiderman, Stuart. *Jacques Lacan: The Death of an Intellectual Hero.* Cambridge, Mass.: Harvard University Press, 1983.

Scholte, Bob. "The Structural Anthropology of Claude Lévi-Strauss." In *Handbook of Social and Cultural Anthropology,* edited by John Joseph Honigmann, 637–746. Chicago: Rand McNally College, 1973.

Scott, Joan Wallach. "French Universalism in the Nineties." *Differences: A Journal of Feminist Cultural Studies* 15, no. 2 (2004): 32–53.

———. *Only Paradoxes to Offer: French Feminists and the Rights of Man.* Cambridge, Mass.: Harvard University Press, 1996.

———. *Parité! Sexual Equality and the Crisis of French Universalism.* Chicago: University of Chicago Press, 2005.

Sevegrand, Martine. *Les enfants du bon Dieu: Les catholiques français et la procréation au XXe siècle.* Paris: Albin Michel, 1995.

Shepard, Todd. "Algeria, France, Mexico, UNESCO: A Transnational History of Antiracism and Decolonization, 1932–1962." *Journal of Global History* 6 (2011): 273–97.

———. *The Invention of Decolonization: The Algerian War and the Remaking of France.* Ithaca, N.Y.: Cornell University Press, 2006.

———. " 'Something Notably Erotic': Politics, 'Arab Men,' and Sexual Revolution in Post-Decolonization France, 1962–1974." *Journal of Modern History* 84, no. 1 (2012).

Shepherdson, Charles. *Vital Signs: Nature, Culture, Psychoanalysis.* New York: Routledge, 2000.

Sicard, Didier, ed. *Travaux du comité consultatif national d'éthique.* Paris: Presses universitaires de France, 2003.

Silver, Catherine Bodard, ed. *Frédéric Le Play on Family, Work, and Social Change.* Chicago: University of Chicago Press, 1982.

Silverman, Kaja. *The Subject of Semiotics*. New York: Oxford University Press, 1983.

Singly, François de. *La famille, l'état des savoirs*. Paris: La découverte, 1991.

Smith, Daniel W. "The Inverse Side of the Structure: Žižek on Deleuze on Lacan." *Criticism* 46, no. 4 (2004): 635–50.

Spengler, Joseph John. *France Faces Depopulation*. Durham, N.C.: Duke University Press, 1979.

Spire, Alexis. *Étrangers à la carte: L'administration de l'immigration en France, 1945–1975*. Paris: Grasset, 2005.

Stoczkowski, Wiktor. *Anthropologies rédemptrices: Le monde selon Lévi-Strauss*. Paris: Hermann, 2008.

Stone, Judith F. *The Search for Social Peace: Reform Legislation in France, 1890–1914*. Albany: State University of New York Press, 1985.

Sullerot, Evelyne. *Le grand remue-ménage: La crise de la famille*. Paris: Fayard, 1997.

Supiot, Alain. *Homo Juridicus: On the Anthropological Function of the Law*. London: Verso, 2007.

Surkis, Judith. "Hymenal Politics: Marriage, Secularism, and French Sovereignty." *Public Culture* 22, no. 3 (2010): 531–56.

———. *Sexing the Citizen: Morality and Masculinity in France, 1870–1920*. Ithaca, N.Y.: Cornell University Press, 2006.

Talmy, Robert. *Aux sources du catholicisme social: L'école de La Tour du Pin*. Tournai: Desclée, 1963.

———. *Histoire du mouvement familial en France (1896–1939)*. Aubenas: Union nationale des caisses d'allocations familiales, 1962.

Tapinos, Georges. *L'immigration étrangère en France: 1946–1973*. Paris: Presses universitaires de France, 1975.

Tasca, Catherine. "Le pacte civil de solidarité: Une reconnaissance responsable de la diversité des unions." *Le Banquet* 12–13 (1998): 1–7.

Teitelbaum, Michael S., and Jay M. Winter. *The Fear of Population Decline*. Orlando, Fla.: Academic Press, 1985.

Théry, Irène. *Couple, filiation et parenté aujourd'hui: Le droit face aux mutations de la famille et de la vie privée: Rapport à la Ministre de l'emploi et de la solidarité et au garde des sceaux, Ministre de la justice*. Paris: Odile Jacob/La documentation française, 1998.

———. *La distinction de sexe: Une nouvelle approche de l'égalité*. Paris: Odile Jacob, 2007.

———. "Le contrat d'union sociale en question." *Esprit* 236 (1997): 159–87.

———. *Le démariage: Justice et vie privée*. Paris: Odile Jacob, 1993.

Theweleit, Klaus. *Male Fantasies*. Minneapolis: University of Minnesota Press, 1987.

Tomlinson, Richard. "The Disappearance of France, 1896–1940: French Politics and the Birth Rate." *Historical Journal* 28, no. 2 (1985): 405–15.

Topalov, Christian, ed. *Laboratoires du nouveau siècle: La nébuleuse réformatrice et ses réseaux en France, 1880–1914*. Paris: École des hautes études en sciences sociales, 1999.

Tort, Michel. *Fin du dogme paternel*. Paris: Aubier, 2005.

Toulemon, André. *Le suffrage familial et le vote des femmes*. Paris: Recueil Sirey, 1933.

BIBLIOGRAPHY   285

Trimouille, Pierre. *Léon Harmel et l'usine chrétienne du Val des Bois: 1840–1914, fécondité d'une expérience sociale.* Lyon: Centre d'histoire du catholicisme, 1974.

Tristan, Anne, and Annie de Pisan. *Histoires du M.L.F.* Paris: Calmann-Lévy, 1977.

Turkle, Sherry. *Psychoanalytic Politics: Freud's French Revolution.* New York: Basic Books, 1978.

Vacquin, Monette. *Frankenstein, ou, les délires de la raison.* Paris: François Bourin, 1989.

Valat, Bruno. *Histoire de la Sécurité sociale (1945–1967): L'état, l'institution et la santé.* Paris: Economica, 2001.

Vallin, Jacques. *La population française.* Paris: La découverte, 1992.

Verjus, Anne. "Vote familialiste et vote familial: Contribution à l'étude du processus d'individualisation des femmes dans la première partie du XIXe siècle." *Genèses: Sciences Sociales et Histoire,* no. 31 (1998): 29–47.

Warner, Michael. *Publics and Counterpublics.* New York: Zone Books, 2002.

Weil, Patrick. *La France et ses étrangers: L'aventure d'une politique de l'immigration, 1938–1991.* Paris: Calmann-Lévy, 1991.

———. *Liberté, égalité, discriminations: L'"identité nationale" au regard de l'histoire.* Paris: Grasset, 2008.

Weiner, Susan. *Enfants Terribles: Youth and Femininity in the Mass Media in France, 1945–1968.* Baltimore: Johns Hopkins University Press, 2001.

Weiss, John H. "Origins of the French Welfare State: Poor Relief in the Third Republic, 1871–1914." *French Historical Studies* 13, no. 1 (1983): 47–78.

Williams, Elizabeth A. "The Science of Man: Anthropological Thought and Institutions in Nineteenth-Century France." Ph.D. diss., Indiana University, 1983.

Winnicott, D. W. *Winnicott on the Child.* Cambridge, Mass.: Perseus, 2002.

Winter, Jean-Pierre. "Gare aux enfants symboliquement modifiés." *Le Monde des Débats,* March 2000, 18.

———. *Homoparenté.* Paris: Albin Michel, 2010.

Wittig, Monique. *The Straight Mind and Other Essays.* Boston: Beacon Press, 1992.

Wolin, Sheldon S. *Politics and Vision: Continuity and Innovation in Western Political Thought.* Princeton, N.J.: Princeton University Press, 2004.

Zafiropoulos, Markos. *Lacan et les sciences sociales: Le déclin du père (1938–1953).* Paris: Presses universitaires de France, 2001.

———. *Lacan et Lévi-Strauss ou le retour à Freud (1951–1957).* Paris: Presses universitaires de France, 2003.

Zaoui, Pierre. "L'ordre symbolique, au fondement de quelle autorité?" *Esprit,* March–April (2005): 223–41.

Žižek, Slavoj. *Enjoy Your Symptom! Jacques Lacan in Hollywood and Out.* New York: Routledge, 1992.

———. *Organs without Bodies: Deleuze and Consequences.* New York: Routledge, 2004.

———. *The Sublime Object of Ideology.* London: Verso, 1989.

INDEX

Bold page numbers refer to figures and images.

abortion, 46–47, 59, 153–54, 233
   condemned by *natalistes*, 30, 42, 45
   Manifesto of the, 204, 343
Adler, Karen H., 46, 146n11
adoption, 1, 243, 250, 260
   in Civil Code, 24–25
   Dolto on, 134–35, 137–38, 230–31
   laws governing, 6, 155–56, 159–60, 214,
      248
Agacinski, Sylviane, 252
AIDES, 241–42
Alby, Nicole, 136n124
Alliance nationale pour l'accroissement de
     la population française (Alliance
     nationale contre la dépopulation), 37,
     119, 123, 241
   fighting depopulation, 30–33
   links with other groups, 45, 51–52,
     106–7
Althusser, Louis, 102, 172, 179
Anatrella, Tony, 245
anthropology, 64, 83, 103, 234
   anthropological function of the law, 1–2,
     161n9, 216, 220, 226, 234
   assisted reproduction debates and, 223,
     227–29, 236–37
   Deleuze and Guattari on, 183, 186
   disciplinarity and, 66, 102
   Foucault on, 171
   French, American, and British
     anthropology, 63–66
   Irigaray on, 195
   kinship in, 61, 262
   Lacan on, 92
   Lévi-Strauss on, 81
   PACS debates and, 251, 255–56
   transcendental anthroposociology, 11,
     215
   use in French politics, 1–3, 6, 263

See also Boas, Franz; Borneman, John;
   Héritier, Françoise; Kroeber, Alfred;
   Leach, Edmund; Lévi-Strauss, Claude
anti-Semitism, 45–46, 56, 65, 105, 146
Arcadie, 203–4, 208
Aron, Robert, 51
assisted reproduction, 1–2, 6, 139, 213–38,
   241–43, 248, 260–64
Association nationale de l'insémination
   artificielle par substitution (ANIAS),
   217
Autexier, Jean-Yves, 240

Babeuf, Gracchus, 65
Baby M, 6, 214
Badinter, Elisabeth, 241
Badinter, Robert, 139, 236, 254
   on assisted reproduction, 221–23,
     225–28, 241
Badiou, Alain, 185
Basaglia, Franco, 175
Bataille, George, 62, 86, 208
Baudry, André, 203
Beauvoir, Simone de, 62, 192, 202n119,
   204, 210
Benedict, Ruth, 63
Benjamin, Walter, 104n6
Benveniste, Émile, 83
Berge, André, 106, 107n17, 110, 125–26
   as bridge figure, 11, 104, 139
   at Centre Claude Bernard, 118–22
   role in government, 134, 136
   use of radio, 124
Bernard, Jean, 218
Bersani, Leo, 8–9, 209n146
Bertier, Georges, 119
Bertillon, Jacques, 30–32
Bidault, Georges, 34n53
Bigot de Préameneu, Félix-Julien-Jean, 23

287

288 **INDEX**

Billé, Louis-Marie, 244
bioethics laws, 1–2, 213–23, 229–38, 249, 261–62
    Dolto on, 134–35, 139
    upholding heterosexual nuclear family, 216, 238, 248
    See also assisted reproduction
biopolitics, 36n62, 46
Bioulac, Bernard, 238
birth control. *See* contraception
Blankenhorn, David, 263
Blocq-Mascart, Maxime, 56
Blum, Léon, 246
Boas, Franz, 63
Bonaparte, Marie, 89, 106
Borie, General, 119
Borneman, John, 261
Bourdieu, Pierre, 172, 242
Boutin, Christine, 233, 236–38, 244
Boverat, Fernand, 32, 44–45, 51, 56, 106, 107n16
Breton, Jules-Louis, 42
Briand, Henri, 64
bridge figures, 6, 10–11, 104–5, 128, 214, 253
    See also Berge, André; Dolto, Françoise; Mauco, Georges
Broca, Pierre, 63
Bureau, Paul, 31n43, 39
Burnel, Roger, 58, 220
Butler, Judith, 8–9, 76, 191n71, 253n117

Caillois, Roger, 86
Caisse nationale des allocations familiales (CNAF), 34, 59, 149–50
Camiscioli, Elisa, 46
Camus, Jean, 119
capitalism, 36, 236, 250
    critiques of, 48, 168, 173, 188–89, 206–7
    See also globalization; inheritance; neoliberalism; property
Carbonnier, Jean, 19, 22, 155–65, 220–21
Carrel, Alexis, 50n114
Cassirer, Ernst, 79
Castel, Robert, 172–73
castration, 2, 9, 62, 137, 232, 234
    Deleuze and Guattari on, 181, 187–88
    Deleuze on, 185
    Dolto on, 126, 128–29, 132, 135
    Lacan on, 97–99
Centre Claude Bernard, 114–27, **115**, **116**, **117**, **118**, 130

Centre démocrate (CD), 148
Centre démocratie et progrès (CDP), 148
Centre d'études, de recherches et de formation institutionnelle (CERFI), 177
Centre national de coordination des activités familiales, 52, 56
Centres d'étude et de conservation des œufs et du sperme humains (CECOS), 216, 231
Certeau, Michel de, 190
Chaban-Delmas, Jacques, 144, 151–52
Chalandon, Albin, 108
Chandernagor, André, 165
Chatel, Marie-Magdeleine, 232
Châtelet, François, 232
Chauvière, Michel, 58n136
Cheysson, Émile, 32
Chirac, Jacques, 241, 254
citizenship, 60, 240, 247, 256
    family and, 21, 24, 42, 46, 51
    gender and, 41
    in PACS debates, 262–65
    See also nationalism; republicanism
Civil Code, 158, 231, 241, 261
    construction of family, 4, 11–12, 19–25, 160–61, 166, 217
    reforms to, 144, 154–55, 163
    targeted by familialists, 28, 40
Civil Pact of Solidarity (PACS), 4, 7, 233, 236
    debates over, 213–16, 239–64
civil unions, 3, 7, 214, 240–41, 247, 255
    See also domestic partnerships
Clavreul, Jean, 190
Clot, Yves, 231
Collectif pour le contrat d'union civile, 240–41, 246
Collet, Simone, 56
colonialism, 30, 107, 162–63, 204n123
    critiques of, 173, 178
    Deleuze and Guattari on, 184, 189
    See also Front de libération nationale (FLN); postcolonialism; race; racism
Comité consultatif national d'éthique pour les sciences de la vie et de la santé (CCNE), 218–21
Comité d'action pédérastique révolutionnaire (CAPR), 203
Comité d'études du problème des étrangers, 106
Comité français de la Libération nationale (CFLN), 55

Comité interministériel de la population et de la famille, 56
Comité pour le relèvement de la natalité, 31n43
Commaille, Jacques, 136n124
Commissariat général aux questions juives, 64
Commission de la consommation et de la modernisation sociale, 57
Committee for the Study of the Problems of the Family, 152
communism, 43, 56, 179, 205
  contrasted with republicanism, 8, 48, 215, 235–36, 254
Communist Party, 59, 148, 178
communitarianism, 7–8, 242, 247, 254, 257
Comte, August, 25–26
concubinage, 24, 239, 246, 256
Conedera, Jean, 155
Confédération française des travailleurs chrétiens (CFTC), 150
Confédération générale des familles, 52
Confédération générale du travail-force ouvrière (CGT-FO), 56
Congrès de la natalité, 42, 44
Conseil économique et social, 143, 223n24
Conseil national de la résistance (CNR), 54–55
Conseil national des familles, 52
Conseil supérieur de la famille, 50, 56, 105
Conseil supérieur de la natalité, 50
Constant, Benjamin, 24
contraception, 30, 123, 151, 153–54, 198
Contrat de partenariat civil, 239
Contrat de vie sociale (CVS), 242
Contrat d'union civile (CUC), 240–43, 260
Contrat d'union sociale (CUS), 242–43, 253, 255–57, 260
Cooper, David, 175
Copjec, Joan, 9
Coq, Guy, 249–50, 253

Daladier, Édouard, 44
Danchin, Antoine, 226–28
Dean, Carolyn, 46n96
Dean, Tim, 9, 185, 209n146, 264
Debaene, Vincent, 65n15
Debesse, Maurice, 118
Debré, Michel, 108, 144, 154n37
Debré, Robert, 55–57, 147
Defert, Daniel, 241

de Gaulle, Charles, 58, 105–8
  views on immigration, 146–48
  views on natalism, 55–56, 143–45
De Grazia, Victoria, 19
Delabit, Jeanne Marcelle, 56
Delaisi de Parseval, Geneviève, 231
Délégués régionaux à la famille (DRF), 50
Deleuze, Gilles, 12, 195, 205–6, 263
  Anti-Oedipus, 174–89, 191, 209
  critiques of structuralism, 169, 173, 200
Delors, Jacques, 150–51
De Mun, Albert, 34
Deneuve, Catherine, 204
dépopulation, 45, 57–58, 60, 145–49, 166
  family as solution, 11, 48
  fears of, 19–20, 29–33, 38, 42, 105–6
  See also Alliance nationale pour l'accroissement de la population française (Alliance nationale contre la depopulation); eugenics; Haut comité consultatif de la famille française; Haut comité de la population (1939); Haut comité de la population et de la famille (1945–70)
Derrida, Jacques, 79–80, 85, 169–70, 193n81, 242
Desan, Suzanne, 22
Dinechin, Olivier de, 228
disability, 151, 153
disciplinarity, 61–66, 102–3, 157, 170, 190, 234
  See also individual disciplines
divorce, 12, 151, 153, 222, 263
  in Civil Code, 23, 28
  Dolto on, 134–37
  legalization of, 154
  legal reforms, 164–66
  Théry on, 253, 260
Dolto, Françoise, 90, 119, 125–39
  analysis with Laforgue, 106, 121
  in assisted reproduction debates, 220, 230–31
  as bridge figure, 11, 104
domestic partnerships, 239–40, 247
  See also Civil Pact of Solidarity (PACS); civil unions
Donnez, Georges, 165
Dord, Dominique, 247–48
Doublet, Jacques, 45, 50–51, 107n16
Durkheim, Émile, 26n22, 64–66, 70, 74–75, 77–78, 156
Dutreil, Renaud, 2
Dutton, Paul, 54

290 **INDEX**

École d'anthropologie, 63–64
École des hautes études en sciences sociales
    (EHESS), 223n24
École des parents et des éducateurs,
    119–21, 123, 126–27, 135
École freudienne de Paris (EFP), 102, 125,
    173, 178, 189–91, 209n146
École nationale d'administration (ENA),
    149, 257
École normale supérieure (ENS), 103, 172,
    205
Edelman, Lee, 9, 264
Elbow, Matthew, 59n140
Ellis, Havelock, 69–70
Eribon, Didier, 10n16, 185–86, 242
ethics, 121, 140, 169, 227, 262
    anti-Oedipal ethics, 209–10
    Dolto on, 134
    ethics of sexual difference, 209–10, 238
    Lacan on, 98–101
    Vacquin on, 233
    See also bioethics laws
ethnology, 3, 64–65, 78, 83, 231
    Deleuze and Guattari on, 184
    Foucault on, 170
eugenics, 50n114, 64, 69, 235
    See also Briand, Henri; Carrel,
        Alexis; depopulation; Malthusianism;
        Marin, Louis; Montandon, Georges;
        Neo-Malthusianism; race
European Union, 7, 13, 240, 248
exchange of women, 73–74
    Irigaray on, 169, 192, 195–98
    Rubin on, 8, 76

Fabius, Laurent, 254
familialism, 59, 123, 143–45, 150–53,
    189
    definition, 2–3
    early familialists, 29–38
    family vote and, 38–41
    Haute comité and, 42–27
    as ideology, 18–19
    in interwar period, 55–56
    loss of prestige, 147–49
    structuralism and, 4, 7, 10–11, 61–62,
        102–3, 214–15
    under Vichy government, 47–53
familiaux, 32, 34–35, 42, 151
family, 3, 119, 216, 244, 263
    as answer to the social question, 18–19
    as basis for the social, 11, 48–49, 102–3,
        121–22, 252

critiques of, 168–69, 189, 237
Dolto on, 127–37
Durkheim on, 74
Foucault on, 179–81
gendered and raced, 7
Haut comité on, 42–47
Hocquenghem on, 205–7
immigration and, 262
Irigaray on, 196
Lacan on, 61–62, 86–98
Lemire on, 37
Le Play on, 25–29
Lévi-Strauss on, 61–62, 75, 83, 85
Mauco on, 113
media and, 123
normative heterosexual family, 2, 4, 8,
    12–13
propaganda about, 51–52
See also assisted reproduction; Civil
    Code: construction of family; Civil
    Pact of Solidarity (PACS); civil
    unions; concubinage; domestic
    partnerships; familialism; familiaux;
    family allowances; Family Code
    (1939); family law; family vote;
    kinship
family allowances, 18–20, 34–36, 38,
    42–43, 51
    postwar changes to, 59–60
    as social welfare, 55
    under Vichy, 57–58
    See also Caisse nationale des allocations
        familiales (CNAF); social security
Family Code (1939), 49, 107, 145–46, 155,
    159–60
    linking family to the social, 11, 19–20
    origin of, 44
    passage of, 46–47
    in postwar period, 55, 59
    solution to depopulation, 4
    in Vichy government, 51
family law, 19–25
    bridge figures and, 104–5
    quiet revolution in, 144
    reforms, 11–12, 22, 154–67, 213–14
    structuralism and, 4–6, 10, 215
    See also Carbonnier, Jean; loi Gounot
        (Charte de la famille)
family vote, 38–42, 51, 143
Fanon, Frantz, 176
Fassin, Éric, 7n10, 242n88, 252
Faure, Edgar, 108–9, 160, 174
Fauroux, Roger, 253

Favez-Boutonier, Juliette, 90, 110, 118–19, 121, 125
Fédération des familles nombreuses de France, 52
Fédération des groupes d'études et de recherches institutionnelles (FGERI), 177
Fédération nationale des associations de familles nombreuses, 52
Feher, Michel, 252
femininity, 3, 233n59, 255–56, 260
    Irigaray on, 189–202, 263
    in Oedipus complex, 112–13, 122
feminism, 41, 153–54, 162–64, 203
    Berge on, 122
    exchange of women and, 74n49
    Iacub on, 161n69
    Irigaray on, 197–99
    materialist feminism, 201
    as "problem," 11–12, 30
    radical feminism, 168–69, 204
    Rubin on, 8
    See also Beauvoir, Simone de; Butler, Judith; Firestone, Shulamith; Fouque, Antoinette; Friedan, Betty; gender; Irigaray, Luce; Mouvement de libération des femmes (MLF); Psychanalyse et politique (Psych et Po); Rubin, Gayle; Scott, Joan; Wittig, Monique; woman question; women's rights
filiation, 12, 249, 252, 256
    in assisted reproduction debates, 216–18, 221, 224, 228, 231, 236–37
    in Civil Code, 22–24
    Deleuze and Guattari on, 183
    in family law, 159–62, 165
    Lacan on, 93
    in PACS debates, 246, 259, 262
    See also maternity; paternity
Finkielkraut, Alain, 254
Firestone, Shulamith, 169
Flacelière, Robert, 103
Flis-Trèves, Muriel, 232
Fondation Carrel, 50–51, 56–57
Fondation des œuvres du moulin vert, 37
Fondation française pour l'étude des problèmes humains. See Fondation Carrel
Fondation Saint-Simon, 253–54
Fontaine, Jean, 165
Fontanet, Joseph, 108

Foucault, Michel, 9, 12, 174, 177, 205, 241
    on Anti-Oedipus, 209–10
    critique of structuralism, 170–71
    on neoliberalism, 36n62
Fouque, Antoinette, 12, 201–3, 210
Foyer, Jean, 155, 160–62, 165
Frazer, James, 70
Freud, Sigmund, 99, 106, 110, 117, 128n94, 175–77
    Althusser on, 172
    Dean on, 209n146
    Deleuze and Guattari on, 181, 183
    Deleuze on, 185
    Dolto on, 125
    Foucault on, 171
    Hocquenghem on, 206, 208
    Irigaray on, 191–94
    Lacan on, 89–97
    on sexual difference, 9
    See also castration; Oedipus complex; sexual difference
Friedan, Betty, 168
Front de libération nationale (FLN), 178
Front homosexuel d'action révolutionnaire (FHAR), 12, 154, 173, 201–5
Furet, François, 253–54

Galichon, Georges, 108
Gauchet, Marcel, 11, 215, 223
gay and lesbian rights, 2, 214, 239–41, 242, 245, 247n105
    See also AIDES; Front homosexuel d'action révolutionnaire (FHAR); gay liberation movement; human rights; rights
gay and lesbian studies, 254
    See also sexuality studies
gay liberation movement, 178, 203–4
    See also gay and lesbian rights
Geller, Sacha, 217–18, 220
gender, 6–7, 42, 139, 168–69, 264
    Berge on, 122
    Butler on, 8, 76
    Dolto on, 132–34
    gender deviance, 46n96
    human rights and, 223
    Labrusse-Riou on, 228
    Lacan on, 112
    Marxism and, 203
    Mauco on, 113
    as public, 12–13
    Rubin on, 8

292   **INDEX**

gender (*continued*)
  sexual difference contrasted with, 9
  Théry on, 255–56
  See also exchange of women; femininity;
    feminism; masculinity; misogyny;
    parité law; patriarchy; sexual difference;
    transsexuality; woman question;
    women's rights
Germany, 19, 25, 45, 54n124, 168, 208
gift economy, 72–74, 92, 209n146, 217
Giscard d'Estaing, Valéry, 135, 164
globalization, 8, 13, 264
Glorieux, Achille, 33n48
Grailly, Michel de, 164
Great Britain, 40, 63, 130n101, 216
Grégoire, Ménie, 130n101, 203
Groupe de la famille et de la natalité, 43
Guattari, Félix, 263
  Anti-Oedipus, 12, 169, 174–89, 191,
    209–10
  Deleuze and, 173–74, 194–95, 200,
    205–6
  Oury and, 175
  on transversality, 177
  See also Centre d'études, de recherches
    et de formation institutionnelle
    (CERFI); Fédération des groupes
    d'études et de recherches institution-
    nelles (FGERI); La Borde clinic
Guigou, Elisabeth, 3, 246–47, 253
Gurvitch, Georges, 77

Halimi, Gisèle, 204
Harmel, Léon, 35
Hauser, Jean, 260–61
Haut comité consultatif de la famille
    française, 50–51, 55–56, 105, 143
Haut comité de la population (1939),
    44–47, 49–50, 53, 55–57
Haut comité de la population et de la
    famille (1945–70), 114, 123, 149,
    223n24, 262
  during Liberation years, 104–8, 143–46
Hegel, Georg Wilhelm Friedrich, 86, 111,
    180, 209, 262
Henry, Louis, 145–46
Héritier, Françoise, 255–56
  in assisted reproduction debates, 139,
    220, 223–28, 235
  in PACS debates, 251–53
Hesnard, Angelo, 106, 110
heteronormativity, 5–6, 98, 104
  See also homophobia

heterosexuality, 11–13, 100–101, 260–61
  in assisted reproduction debates, 217–18,
    222–25, 238
  Butler on, 8
  Copjec on, 9
  critiques of, 168–69, 213–15
  Dolto on, 131–37
  Hocquenghem on, 207
  Irigaray on, 196
  Lacan on, 96–98
  Lévi-Strauss and Lacan on, 4, 61–62
  in PACS debates, 1–3, 239–55
  Rubin on, 76
  See also exchange of women; heteronor-
    mativity; incest prohibition (or
    taboo); Oedipus complex; patriarchy;
    sexual difference
Heuer, Jennifer Ngaire, 46
Heuyer, Georges, 117n53, 125
history, 104, 152, 213, 263–64
  in assisted reproduction debates, 231–32
  Berge on, 123
  Deleuze and Guattari on, 180–86
  Dolto on, 137
  Freud on, 83
  historical materialism, 172
  historicism, 9
  history of familialism, 37, 43
  history of sexuality, 9, 170–71, 254
  intellectual history, 3, 10, 103
  Irigaray on, 194, 196, 198
  Lacan on, 62, 94–95
  legal history, 3–4, 10, 155–67
  Le Play on, 27
  Lévi-Strauss on, 62, 68, 71–72, 82, 85
  in PACS debates, 143
  Psych et Po on, 202–3
  Rousseau on, 79
  structuralism and, 3–6, 102, 139–40, 261
  tide of history, 12, 145, 163n77, 229
Hocquenghem, Guy, 12, 201, 204–10, 263
homophile movement, 203
  See also Arcadie
homophobia, 3, 10, 203, 243, 244n93, 250
  See also heteronormativity
homosexuality, 46n96, 113, 177, 203–4,
    222, 265
  in assisted reproduction debates, 214,
    217, 238
  Butler on, 76
  Dolto on, 133
  Hocquenghem on, 205–6, 208–9
  Irigaray on, 195–97

in PACS debates, 2, 239–61
republicanism and, 7
Rubin on, 76
Théry on, 3
Honnorat, André, 31
human rights, 41, 221–23, 225–26,
    228–29, 236, 241
    Declaration of Human Rights, 256
    droits de l'homme, 12, 215
    European Convention on Human
        Rights, 222
    in Revolution, 21, 34n53
Hurstel, Françoise, 231

Iacub, Marcela, 160–61, 238
imago, 87–90, 112, 126–27
immigration, 105
    Haute comité and, 44–45, 107, 145
    as "problem," 146–47, 264–65
    solution to depopulation, 57, 101
    See also Office national d'immigration
        (ONI)
incest prohibition (or taboo), 1–2, 9, **72**,
    84, **93**, 190, 232
    in assisted reproduction debates, 217
    Butler on, 8
    Deleuze and Guattari on, 183
    Dolto on, 129, 131–35, 137–39
    Foucault on, 170–71
    Héritier on, 223n24
    Irigaray on, 195–96
    Lacan on, 92–94, 99–100, 129
    Lévi-Strauss on, 62, 67–72, 75–85, 99,
        170, 234–35
    Mauco on, 111–14
    in PACS debates, 259
    Rubin on, 74n49, 76
    sexual difference and, 4, 62
    See also Oedipus complex; patriarchy;
        sexual difference; state of nature
inheritance, 31, 75, 160
    adoption and, 159
    in Civil Code, 24, 28, 47
    in PACS debates, 2, 241, 260
    partage égal, 24
Institut d'ethnologie, 64
Institut d'étude des questions juives et
    ethno-raciales, 64
institutional psychotherapy, 175–77
    See also La Borde clinic; Saint-Alban
        hospital
International Psychoanalytic Association
    (IPA), 90

Irigaray, Luce, 173, 189–203, 206, 210, 263
    reframing social contract, 12, 169
Isaac, Auguste, 42
Islamic fundamentalism, 8, 215, 254,
    259–60

Jakobson, Roman, 83
Javal, Émile, 30
Jeanneney, Jean-Marcel, 108, **109**, 123
Jervis, Giovanni, 175
Jeunesse ouvrière chrétienne (JOC),
    72–73, 150
Jospin, Lionel, 242, 245, 248, 252
Jouvenel, Baron de, 38
Jouvenel, Henri de, 105–6
Joxe, Louis, 106
Julliot de la Morandière, Léon, 155

Kant, Immanuel, 81n74, 86, 174, 182, 194
kinship, **84**, **93**, 101, 210, 215, 257
    Althusser on, 172
    assisted reproduction and, 226–27
    Butler on, 8, 191n71
    Deleuze and Guattari on, 183–84, 189
    Dolto on, 127–35
    economics and, 217
    ethics and, 99–100
    Foucault on, 170–71
    Héritier on, 223n24, 224–25, 252
    Irigaray on, 203
    Labrusse-Riou on, 221, 236
    Lacan on, 5, 11, 92, 258
    Lévi-Strauss on, 5, 11, 259
    PACS debates and, 262–63
    politics and, 6, 13
    Rubin on, 8
    structuralism and, 4, 61–62, 102–4, 200,
        220
    symbolic nature of, 1–2
    See also adoption; assisted reproduction;
        Civil Pact of Solidarity (PACS); civil
        unions; domestic partnerships; family;
        incest prohibition (or taboo); inheri-
        tance; filiation; Lévi-Strauss, Claude:
        The Elementary Structures of Kinship;
        marriage; maternity; Oedipus
        complex; parenting; paternity;
        structuralist social contract
Klossowski, Pierre, 86
Koeppel, Beatrice, 232
Kojève, Alexandre, 86
Kossowski, Jacques, 3
Kroeber, Alfred, 63

294   INDEX

Laboratoire d'anthropologie sociale, 102,
   223n24
La Borde clinic, 175, 177, 188
   See also institutional psychotherapy
Labrusse-Riou, Catherine, 157–58, 220–21,
   228–29, 236–37
Lacan, Jacques, 85–101, 104, 209n146, 234,
   257–58
   ahistoricism of, 9–10
   Althusser on, 172
   Berge on, 121
   bridge figures and, 104, 110–13, 125–30,
     132, 134, 139–40
   Butler on, 8
   career, 102–103, 190
   Deleuze and Guattari on, 180–81,
     184–87, 189
   Foucault on, 171n7
   Fouque on, 201
   Guattari on, 178
   Hocquenghem on, 206, 208
   institutional psychotherapy and, 176–77
   Irigaray on, 191–94, 199
   Mannoni and, 173
   Oury and, 175
   reconfiguration of kinship, 61
   role in French politics, 1–6, 214–15
   Rubin on, 8
   structuralist social contract and, 11–12,
     62, 169, 264
   See also castration; imago; incest
     prohibition (or taboo); Oedipus
     complex; sexual difference; state of
     nature; symbolic order
LaCapra, Dominick, 10n17
Laforgue, René, 89, 106, 110, 121, 125,
   130n101
Lagache, Daniel, 90, 110, 125
Laing, Ronald, 175
Lamartine, Alphonse de, 38
Lamirand, Georges, 119
Landry, Adolphe, 45, 56, 106, 107n16
La plus grande famille, 33, 56
Laroque, Pierre, 54, 57, 152, 220
Latour, Bruno, 220
La Tour du Pin, René, 34–35
law, 27, 49, 61, 79, 95n125, 137, 191n71
   abortion laws, 46–47, 153
   adoption laws, 24–25, 155–56, 159–61,
     214, 248
   anthropological function of the law, 1–2,
     161n9, 216, 220, 223, 226–27, 234
   citizenship laws, 147

civil laws, 21, 156–57, 220
contraception laws, 153
divorce laws, 23, 28, 154, 164–67
education laws, 174
electoral laws, 39–40
ethics and, 99–100
familialism and, 11–12, 18–19, 42, 44, 102
family's role in, 2–7, 18–19
fascist laws, 19
filiation laws, 31, 138, 164, 168, 218,
   221, 231–32
immigration law, 147
labor laws, 37, 43
laïcité, 31, 40, 243, 244, 248, 256, 264
language and, 90n105, 92, 128–29
legal formalism, 228
legal history, 3–4, 10, 155–67
legal individualism, 49, 220
legal pluralism, 157, 164
legal positivism, 215, 229, 263
marriage laws, 12, 22–24, 46, 155,
   161–67
natural law, 22, 234, 245n97
Oedipus complex and, 81, 88, 92–93,
   96, 185
parité law, 7, 252
pleasure and, 202, 206–207
psychoanalysis and, 171
racial laws, 65
Roman law, 24
sexual difference and, 112–13, 127, 194,
   196–98, 225
sodomy laws, 263
See also bioethics laws; citizenship; Civil
   Code; Civil Pact of Solidarity (PACS);
   family allowances; Family Code (1939);
   family law; human rights; Law
   (technical term); *Lawrence v. Texas*;
   liberalism; loi Gounot (Charte de la
   famille); Name-of-the-Father; *partage
   égal*; rights; social security; sociology:
   juridical sociology
Law (technical term), 170, 172n8, 235
Lawrence v. Texas, 263
Leach, Edmund, 183
Lebovici, Serge, 90, 115
Lecanuet, Jean, 165–66
Leclaire, Serge, 190–91
Ledoux, Michel, 129
Lefebvre, Henri, 162n77
Lefort, Claude, 61
Legendre, Pierre, 234, 257
Lellouche, Pierre, 244n93

Lemire, abbé, 37, 39–40
Lenoir, Rémi, 47, 119n59, 148–49
Le Play, Frédéric, 25–34, 39, 49, 74
Le Roy-Ladurie, Emmanuel, 253
Lestienne, Pierre, 33n48
Lévi-Strauss, Claude, 101–4, 111, 132, 134,
    223, 234
  Butler on, 8
  Deleuze and Guattari on, 183
  Derrida on, 79, 169–70
  Dolto on, 139
  The Elementary Structures of Kinship,
    62–63, 65–78, 80–85, 87–88
  Foucault on, 171n6
  Héritier and, 251
  history and, 9–10
  Hocquenghem on, 206, 208
  Irigaray on, 195
  Lacan on, 90–91, 93–96, 99
  reconfiguration of kinship, 61
  role in French politics, 1–6, 214–15, 259
  Rubin on, 8
  Schneider on, 257–58
  structuralist social contract and, 11–12,
    62, 169, 264
  See also incest prohibition (or taboo);
    sexual difference; state of nature;
    symbolic order
Lévy-Bruhl, Lucien, 64, 156
liberalism, 17, 24, 165–66, 235
  contrasted with republicanism, 8, 37, 48,
    215, 253–54, 257
  human rights and, 223, 228, 236
  law and, 25, 147n13, 161n69, 226, 263
  Le Play on, 26
  Œuvre des cercles on, 34
  in PACS debates, 236, 243
  See also neoliberalism; rights
Ligue des fonctionnaires pères de familles
    nombreuses, 32–33
Ligue française du coin de terre et du
    foyer, 37
Ligue ouvrière chrétienne (LOC), 57
Ligue populaire des pères et mères de
    familles nombreuses, 32
Linton, Ralph, 63
loi Gounot (Charte de la famille), 52–53, 58
Lowie, Robert, 63
Lubbock, John, 70
Lyotard, Jean-François, 189, 205

Maguin, Jacqueline, 136n124
Maine, Henry, 69

Maire, Simon, 32–33
Maison de la famille, 52
Malinowski, Bronislaw, 73, 89, 92
Malthusianism, 46, 123
Mannoni, Maud, 116
Mannoni, Octave, 173
Marcus, Sharon, 76
Marin, Louis, 63
marriage, 151, 184, 225, 249
  as economic system, 72–73
  familialists on, 31, 37
  Foucault on, 170–71
  gay marriage, 1–2, 7, 214–15
  Lacan on, 92–93
  Lévi-Strauss on, 68–69, 75–80
  marriage counseling, 119
  marriage laws, 12, 22–24, 46, 155, 161–67
  republican marriage, 243–44, 246,
    255–56
  Rubin on, 8
  See also Civil Pact of Solidarity (PACS);
    civil unions; domestic partnerships;
    Pacte d'intérêt commun (PIC);
    patriarchy
Martel, Frédéric, 254
Marxism, 25, 28, 65, 176
  Deleuze and Guattari on, 188
  feminism and, 201, 203
  Hocquenghem on, 207
masculinity, 3, 10, 122, 255–56
  Irigaray on, 192–95, 197, 199–200
maternity, 6, 59, 163, 224, 237, 245,
    252–53
  Althusser on, 172
  Berge on, 122, 124
  citizenship and, 41
  in Civil Code, 24, 217
  Deleuze and Guattari on, 180
  Dolto on, 126–28, 130–33, 136–37, 139
  incest prohibition and, 72, 82, 259
  familialism and, 43, 58
  family allowances and, 46, 59, 153
  Héritier on, 224
  Irigaray on, 196, 198
  Lacan on, 87–88, 92–94, 96, 98–99
  Mauco on, 112–13
  single mothers, 1, 222, 263
  surrogate mothers, 217–18
  See also adoption; assisted reproduction;
    parenting; surrogacy
Mauco, Georges, 45, 57, 104–26, 139,
    146–47, 149
  as bridge figure, 11, 134, 136

Maurice, Lucien, 130
Maurras, Charles, 34n53
Mauss, Marcel, 64–65, 73–75, 77–78, 92, 95
May 1968, 11, 109, 166, 178, 203
Mayeur, Jean-Marie, 34n53, 38, 40n70, 59n140
Mazeaud, Pierre, 164
McLennan, John, 70
McNulty, Tracy, 9, 264
Mélenchon, Jean-Luc, 239–40
Melman, Charles, 128n94
Mendès-France, Pierre, 108
Merleau-Ponty, Maurice, 85, 100, 110
methodology, 6, 9, 26, 125, 223
    dialogical methodology, 10
    ethnography, 63, 66
    historical materialism, 172
    historicism, 9
    intellectual history, 3, 10, 103
    juridical sociology and, 156
    legal methodology, 155
    Lévi-Strauss and, 68–70, 78, 82–83, 85
    pedagogical methodology, 119n59
Michel, Jean-Pierre, 240, 246
Mijolla, Alain de, 117n52
Miller, Jacques-Alain, 9, 103, 128n94, 171n7, 190
Millerand, Alexandre, 42
Minc, Alain, 253
Ministry of Family and the Condition of Women, 135
Ministry of Population, 44
misogyny, 10, 202
Mitterrand, François, 144n4, 218, 220
Molines, Henri, 136n124
Monsaingeon, Maurice, 58, 107n16
Montandon, Georges, 64
Montrelay, Michèle, 190
Moreau, Jeanne, 204
Moreno, Jacob, 115
Morgan, Henry Louis, 63, 69
Morgenstern, Sophie, 125
Mounier, Emmanuel, 150, 249
Mouvement de la condition paternelle (MCP), 137
Mouvement de libération des femmes (MLF), 153–54, 198–203
Mouvement du 22 mars, 178
Mouvement républicain populaire (MRP), 34n53, 57, 59, 144, 147–48
Muel-Dreyfus, Francine, 48n101

Musée d'ethnographie, 63, 65
Myard, Jacques, 2, 244n93

Nacht, Sacha, 90
Name-of-the-Father, 1, 5, 94, 96–97, 110–11, 127, 185
Napoleon, 17, 20–21, 24, 26
Napoleonic Code. *See* Civil Code
nationalism, 11, 30, 51
Nau, Jean-Yves, 220
Nazism, 8, 50n114, 179, 215, 235–36, 257
neoliberalism, 36n62, 250
Neo-Malthusianism, 30, 42–43
Newton, Huey, 204
Noiriel, Gérard, 36
Nora, Pierre, 253
normativity, 74, 169, 194, 224, 227
    critiques of, 173, 183, 194, 209n146, 214, 245
    heteronormativity, 5–6, 98, 104
    law and, 22, 145, 161, 166
    normative heterosexual family, 2, 13, 216, 225
    Oedipus complex and, 88, 96–98
    sexual difference and, 251
    structuralism and, 4, 215, 230, 234
    symbolic order and, 11, 229, 261, 264
Novack Affair, 159–60
Nunberg, Hermann, 125

Oedipus complex, **93**, 126, 233
    anti-Oedipal lifestyles, 12, 173, 200–210, 263
    Anti-Oedipus, 12, 169, 173–89, 191, 209
    Berge on, 122
    Butler on, 8
    Dolto on, 130
    Foucault on, 12, 209–10
    in French politics, 2–3, 123
    Freud on, 6, 81
    Hocquenghem on, 205–6
    Irigaray on, 173, 191, 196–97, 199
    Lacan on, 88–89, 92–100
    Lévi-Strauss on, 70
    Mauco on, 111–14, 124
    sexual difference and, 4
    See also incest prohibition (or taboo); Law (technical term); patriarchy; sexual difference
Œuvre des cercles catholiques d'ouvriers, 34–35
Office national d'immigration (ONI), 107
Opposition de gauche (OG), 178

INDEX   297

Ortigues, Edmond, 184
Oury, Fernand, 175
Oury, Jean, 175–77, 187
    See also La Borde clinic

Pacte d'intérêt commun (PIC), 243, 260
Palewski, Gaston, 106
parenting, 111, 185, 219, 224, 232–33, 258
    Badinter on, 222
    Berge on, 122, 124
    Deleuze and Guattari on, 180–81
    Dolto on, 127–39
    family size, 31, 34
    Foucault on, 171
    gay parenting, 3, 214, 247, 250–53, 256,
        259–60
    law and, 12, 163–64, 231
    Mauco on, 125
    in PACS debates, 2–3, 246–48, 250–53
    single parents, 1, 151, 153, 214, 221,
        259, 265
    See also adoption; assisted reproduction;
        Centre Claude Bernard; École des
        parents et des éducateurs; family;
        family allowances; filiation; incest
        prohibition (or taboo); maternity;
        Oedipus complex; paternity
parité law, 7, 252
Parodi, Alexandre, 54, 147
partage égal, 24
Parti socialite unifié (PSU), 148
paternity, 172, 217, 233, 245
    Althusser on, 172
    Dolto on, 128, 132
    Lacan on, 87, 97–98
    law and, 23–24, 155, 168, 224, 231
    Mauco on, 112–13
    See also *partage égal*
patriarchy, 10, 25, 55, 173, 202
    patriarchal family, 22, 28, 197
    See also heteronormativity; incest
        prohibition (or taboo); Law (technical
        term); Name-of-the-Father; Oedipus
        complex
Pedersen, Susan, 36, 41n77
Pelabon, André, 147
Pelletier, Monique, 135–36, 220
Pernot, Georges, 43–45, 49–51
Perreau, Bruno, 247n105
Perrot, Michelle, 242
Pétain, Maréchal, 48–49, 64
Peyrefitte, Alain, 135
Pichon, Édouard, 106, 125

Picq, Françoise, 154n37
Pinton, Michel, 243
Pleven, René, 161, 164
Poinso-Chapuis, Germaine, 147
Pollard, Miranda, 52–53
Pompidou, Georges, 148–49, 164
Poniatowski, Michel, 109
Popenoe, David, 263
Popular Front, 65
pornography, 42, 46n96
Portalis, Jean-Étienne-Marie, 20–21, 23
Portelli, Hugues, 257
postcolonialism, 13
Prigent, Robert, 56–57, 59, 152
privacy, 167, 244
    marriage and, 245, 256
    parenting and, 128, 215, 222, 224–25
    private interests, 23, 27
    relation to public, 4, 198, 236
    sexuality and, 12–13, 133, 207–8, 243
pro-natalists (*natalistes*), 30–32, 42
property, 21, 28, 39, 84, 99, 207
    marriage and, 162–63
    See also capitalism; exchange of women;
        gift economy; inheritance
Prost, Antoine, 46
prostitution, 24, 59, 196
Psychanalyse et politique (Psych et Po), 12,
    173, 200–204
psychiatry, 3, 86, 121, 171, 175–77
psychoanalysis, 10n16, 61, 87, 209n146
    Castel on, 172–73
    child psychoanalysis, 116, 125, 149n19
    ethics and, 98–100, 134
    Foucault on, 170–71
    in French politics, 1–6, 236–37, 264
    institutional psychotherapy and, 177
    Lévi-Strauss on, 83
    media and, 123–39, 231
    structuralism in, 89, 93, 103, 229,
        262–63
    training, 90, 114, 118
    See also Anatrella, Tony; Berge,
        André; Bersani, Leo; bridge figures;
        castration; Centre Claude Bernard;
        Certeau, Michel de; Chatel, Marie-
        Magdeleine; Clavreul, Jean; Copjec,
        Joan; Dean, Tim; Delaisi de Parseval,
        Geneviève; Deleuze, Gilles; Dolto,
        Françoise; Edelman, Lee; Fanon,
        Frantz; Favez-Boutonier, Juliette;
        Flis-Trèves, Muriel; Fouque,
        Antoinette; Freud, Sigmund;

psychoanalysis (*continued*)

Guattari, Félix; Heuyer, Georges; Hocquenghem, Guy; incest prohibition (or taboo); International Psychoanalytic Association (IPA); Irigaray, Luce; Lacan, Jacques; Laforgue, René; Leclaire, Serge; Legendre, Pierre; Mannoni, Maud; Mannoni, Octave; Mauco, Georges; McNulty, Tracy; Miller, Jacques-Alain; Montrelay, Michèle; Morgenstern, Sophie; Oedipus complex; Ortigues, Edmond; Pichon, Édouard; Psychanalyse et politique (Psych et Po); psychodramas; Schneider, Michel; sexual difference; Shepherdson, Charles; symbolic order; Winter, Jean-Pierre; Žižek, Slavoj

psychodramas, **115, 116, 117, 118,** 130

queer theory, 9, 209n146, 245n97, 252

See also Bersani, Leo; Butler, Judith; Dean, Tim; Edelman, Lee; Foucault, Michel; Hocquenghem, Guy; Rubin, Gayle

Quéré, France, 219

race, 204n123, 235, 244, 264

anthropology and, 63–64

in Family Code, 46

republicanism and, 7

See also colonialism; eugenics; immigration; racism

racism, 32, 147, 162n77

See also anti-Semitism; colonialism; eugenics; immigration

Rassemblement du peuple français (RPF), 148

religion, 31, 34n53, 194, 218, 238, 263

in assisted reproduction debates, 228

Catholicism, 10n16, 23, 27, 50n114, 110n24, 166n92

Christianity, 40, 128n94, 150, 164, 254

Durkheim on, 64, 75

familialism and, 37, 39

family and, 55, 60, 63

in French politics, 1

Freud on, 81, 88

Islam, 8, 215, 254, 259–60

Lévi-Strauss on, 77, 258

marriage and, 23

in PACS debates, 243–45, 249–51, 256, 258

Protestantism, 158n58, 166n92

See also Jeunesse ouvrière chrétienne (JOC); *laïcité*; La plus grande famille; Œuvre des cercles catholiques d'ouvriers; Social Catholicism

Renaudin, Philippe, 49, 51–52, 57

republicanism, 31, 236, 250, 252, 254, 261

contrasted with liberalism and totalitarianism, 8, 215, 223, 257

definition, 18

family as basis, 13, 40, 47, 60–61, 262

law and, 54, 58, 147, 158

privacy and, 222

race and gender in, 7, 41

republican marriage, 243–44, 246, 255–57

republican morality, 30

social question and, 17

symbolic order and, 215, 249, 260, 264

universalism and, 241

Reynaud, Joseph-Honoré, 25, **108,** 109

Richet, Charles, 30

rights, 32, 68, 222, 261, 265

children's rights, 24, 159, 232, 247n105, 250

civil rights, 198–99, 204

family rights, 48, 55, 145–46

gay and lesbian rights, 2, 214, 239–42, 245, 247n105

individual rights, 21–22, 190, 223, 225, 235, 259

marriage rights, 23, 162, 240

parenting rights, 2, 12, 215–16, 219, 260

rights to indifference, 241–42

suffrage rights, 39–41

women's rights, 29–41, 162–63

workers' rights, 34, 43

See also Civil Pact of Solidarity (PACS); human rights

Rivet, Paul, 64

Rocard, Michel, 254

Romanet, Émile, 35

Rosanvallon, Pierre, 18, 39–40, 44n89, 253–54

Rosental, Paul-André, 38, 53

Ross, Kristin, 154, 162n77

Roudinesco, Elisabeth, 10n16, 81n74, 201n112

Roujou, Frédéric, 45

Rousseau, Jean-Jacques, 17, 27, 78–79, 110

Rousseau-Dujardin, Jacqueline, 173

Roussopolous, Carole, 205n126

Rubellin-Devichi, Jacqueline, 156

Rubin, Gayle, 8, 74n49, 76, 195n90

Saint-Alban hospital, 175–76, 188
Sangnier, Marc, 34n53, 39
Sartre, Jean-Paul, 204
Saussure, Ferdinand de, 83
Sauvage, Pierre, 51
Sauverzac, Jean-François de, 103n3, 129
Sauvy, Alfred, 45, 50, 56–57, 107n16, 147
Schérer, René, 205
Schlumberger, Maurice, 121, 125
Schneider, Michel, 257–60
Schumann, Maurice, 34n53
Scott, Joan, 7n10, 40, 252
Secrétariat général à la famille et à la
    population, 56
Seillier, Bernard, 237
Serre, Philippe, 45
Sérusclat, Franck, 238
Servan-Schreiber, Jean-Louis, 132–34
sex education, 119, 123, 134
sexual difference, 9, 12
    in assisted reproduction debates, 232–33,
        235, 238
    basis for the social/political, 62, 101,
        111, 139–40, 251–52
    Berge on, 122
    Danchin on, 227
    Dolto on, 127–28, 131, 134
    filiation and, 224
    Héritier, 225, 251, 253
    Hocquenghem on, 208
    Irigaray on, 191–95, 200, 210
    in PACS debates, 3, 236, 243–45, 249,
        254
    Psych et Po on, 202
    Schneider on, 258–59
    in structuralist social contract, 4, 6, 123,
        214
    Théry on, 255–56
    See also femininity; gender; heteronor-
        mativity; masculinity
sexuality, 42, 139, 160, 169, 203, 213,
    223
    Butler on, 8
    Dolto on, 127, 130n101, 131, 133–35,
        138
    Freud on, 81
    Héritier on, 225
    history of sexuality, 170–72
    Hocquenghem on, 205–9
    Irigaray on, 192–99
    Lacan on, 88–91, 112
    Lévi-Strauss on, 67
    Mauco on, 114

in PACS debates, 2, 241–42, 248, 252, 255
    Psych et Po on, 202
    as public, 13
    Rubin on, 8, 76
    sexual revolution, 153–54, 168
    structuralism and, 4
    See also abortion; assisted reproduction;
        contraception; gay and lesbian rights;
        gay and lesbian studies; gay liberation
        movement; heterosexuality; homo-
        phile movement; homosexuality;
        incest prohibition (or taboo);
        pornography; prostitution; queer
        theory; sex education; sexual
        difference; sexuality studies
sexuality studies, 9
    See also gay and lesbian studies
Shepard, Todd, 162n77, 204n123
Shepherdson, Charles, 9
Slama, Alain-Gérard, 257
Social Catholicism, 32–39, 56–57, 59n140,
    119, 147, 150
    familialism and, 150–52
socialism, 3, 18, 27, 31, 57, 65, 168, 257
    Catholic Church as alternative to,
        34–35, 37
    Christian socialism, 40
    See also Socialist Party
Socialist Party, 64, 148, 239–40, 242,
    245–46, 248–49
social security, 20, 37, 43, 53–54, 59, 146,
    241
    See also family allowances
Société d'anthropologie, 63
Société de géographie commerciale, 64
Société du logement ouvrier, 36
Société française de psychanalyse (SFP),
    90–91, 102, 110, 128
Société psychanalytique de Paris (SPP), 89,
    90, 102, 106, 110, 125, 128
sociology, 62, 64, 66, 77–78, 223, 255
    Dolto on, 137
    juridical sociology, 156–57, 163, 165–66
    Lévi-Strauss on, 68–69, 71, 73, 83, 85
    sociology of the family, 6, 83
    transcendental anthroposociology, 11, 215
    See also Blankenhorn, David; Castel,
        Robert; Commaille, Jacques;
        Durkheim, Émile; Latour, Bruno;
        Le Play, Frédéric; Mauss, Marcel;
        Popenoe, David; Sullerot, Evelyne;
        Théry, Irène; Waite, Linda
Soukaz, Lionel, 205n126

300   INDEX

Spencer, Herbert, 70
Spire, Alexis, 147
state of nature, 67–68, 72, 78–79, 84, 95,
  234
structuralism, 83, 102–3, 139, 173, 181,
  230
  ahistoricity and, 9
  Althusser on, 172
  critiques of, 12, 181–89, 200, 209n146,
    214
  familialism and, 10, 61, 102
  Foucault on, 170
  in French politics, 1–6, 12
  See also exchange of women; incest
    prohibition (or taboo); Lacan, Jacques;
    Lévi-Strauss, Claude; Oedipus
    complex; structuralist social contract
structuralist social contract, 124, 139–40,
  210, 215, 220
  critiques of, 183, 185, 189
  Dolto on, 129–31
  forced choice, 100
  heterosexual family as basis, 7–8, 62,
    123, 169
  Hocquenghem on, 206
  Irigaray on, 192–96
  as linguistic contract, 84
  in PACS debates, 244, 249, 251, 253
  popularization, 6, 11, 104, 263
  See also structuralism
Sullerot, Evelyne, 246–47
Surkis, Judith, 166n92
surrogacy, 1–2, 6, 213–14, 217–20, 233
symbolic order, 11, 84, 161, 185, 189,
  209n146
  ahistoricism of, 62
  alternatives, 12, 167, 169, 173, 210, 213
  in assisted reproduction debates, 220–21,
    229–32, 234–35
  basis for the social, 22, 67
  Deleuze and Guattari on, 183–84, 187,
    191
  Dolto on, 127, 129, 131–32, 136–37
  Fouque on, 202
  in French politics, 1–4
  heterosexual family as center, 61
  incest prohibition and, 81, 85
  Irigaray on, 192–200, 203
  kinship and, 71–78
  Lacan on, 10n16, 90–98, 101, 112, 215
  Mauco on, 110, 113, 124
  in PACS debates, 244–45, 249–60, 264
  Žižek on, 100

Taittinger, Jean, 164
Tasca, Catherine, 246
Testart, Jacques, 220
Teyssonière, Paul, 231
Théry, Irène, 157, 166–67, 215
  on PACS, 3, 213, 253–57, 260
Thorez, Maurice, 43
Tort, Michel, 10n16
Tosquelles, François, 176–77
totalitarianism, 233
  contrasted with republicanism, 8, 215,
    235–36, 254
Toubon, Jacques, 241, 247, 260
Toulemon, André, 41
transsexuality, 1, 252
Troubetzkoy, Nikolai, 83

Union nationale des associations familiales
    (UNAF), 58–59, 107n17, 143–44,
    149, 220, 223
Union pour un mouvement populaire
    (UMP), 247
United States, 13, 156, 235–36, 242n88,
    257
  anthropology in, 63, 66
  assisted reproduction in, 6, 214, 217
  domestic partnership in, 7, 240
  gay activism in, 204, 254, 263
  gender theory in, 8
  women's rights in, 40, 168–69,
    204
universalism, 53, 104, 123, 143
  Deleuze and Guattari on, 181, 184,
    188
  Derrida on, 193n81
  Dolto on, 128, 139
  Durkheim on, 64
  family and, 11, 18, 38, 102, 263
  Foucault on, 170
  Fouque on, 202n119
  Irigaray on, 194
  Lacan on, 89, 92, **93**, 95–96
  law and, 145, 157, 161
  Lévi-Strauss on, 67–68, 70–71, **72**,
    76, 84–85
  in PACS debates, 241–47, 256, 259,
    261
  in postwar period, 12, 54
  republicanism and, 7–8, 13, 264
  structuralism and, 4, 9, 62, 101, 169
  suffrage and, 39–41
University of Vincennes, 174, 189–91, 205,
    209n146

Vacquin, Monette, 232–36
Vérine, Hélène, 199
Verjus, Anne, 41
Veyne, Paul, 242
Vichy government, 64, 119, 153, 176
    familialism in, 47–53, 123, 143, 144n2
    family policy legacies, 19, 55–59, 105
    immigration policy in, 146–47
    resistance to, 34n53
Vidal-Naquet, Pierre, 242
Vie Nouvelle, 150
Villiers, Phillippe de, 243, 250
Viollet, abbé, 36–37, 39, 50, 119
Vive la révolution (VLR), 204

Waite, Linda, 263
Warner, Michael, 104n5
Weil, Patrick, 147n13
Westermarck, Edward, 69
Winnicott, Donald, 130n101
Winter, Jean-Pierre, 3
Wittig, Monique, 203
woman question, 30, 41
women's rights, 29–40, 162–63
    suffrage, 40–41
    See also feminism; parité law

Žižek, Slavoj, 9, 100
Zola, Émile, 32

Made in the USA
Columbia, SC
15 May 2024

5   Michaéla C. Schippers, Dominique Morisano, Edwin A. Locke, W. A. Scheepers, Gary P. Latham, and Elisabeth M. de Jong, "Writing about Personal Goals and Plans Regardless of Goal Type Boosts Academic Performance," *Contemporary Educational Psychology* 60 (January 2020). Mark Murphy, "Neuroscience Explains Why You Need to Write Down Your Goals If You Actually Want to Achieve Them," Forbes.com, April 2015.

6   Bessel van der Kolk, *The Body Keeps the Score: Brain, Mind and Body in the Healing of Trauma* (Penguin Books, 2014).

7   Role definitions are found in Chapter 3.

8   Sam Norman-Haignere, Nancy G. Kanwisher, and Josh H. McDermott, "Distinct Cortical Pathways for Music and Speech Revealed by Hypothesis-Free Voxel Decomposition," *Neuron* 88, no. 6 (December 16, 2015): 1281–1296.

9   *Frontiers in Psychology*, 5 (May 8, 2014): 392, doi: 10.3389/fpsyg.2014.00392.

10 Jill Suttie, "Four Ways Music Strengthens Social Bonds," *Greater Good Magazine*, January 15, 2015.

11 Ibid.

12 Eugen Wassiliwizky, Stefan Koelsch, Valentin Wagner, Thomas Jacobsen, and Winfried Menninghaus, "The Emotional Power of Poetry: Neural Circuitry, Psychophysiology and Compositional Principles," *Social Cognitive and Affective Neuroscience* 12, no. 8 (August 2017): 1229–1240.

13 Jill Suttie, "What Art Does for Your Brain," *Greater Good Magazine*, April 25, 2023.

14 Ibid.

15 "The Science of Awe," The Greater Good Science Center at UC Berkeley, September 2018.

16 Ibid.

17 http://ccare.stanford.edu/education/applied-compassion-training/.

18 Ashley Ford and Howard L. Forman, "Being Human: An Interview With Daniel J. Siegel, MD," *Psychiatric Times*, September 14, 2017, https://www.psychiatrictimes.com/view/being-human-interview-daniel-j-siegel-md.

19 "How The Meditation Technique, 'Wheel Of Awareness,' Can Improve Your Well-Being," *Forbes*, May 14, 2021.

20 Ibid.

21 Ashley Ford and Howard L. Forman, "Being Human: An Interview With Daniel J. Siegel, MD," *Psychiatric Times*, September 14, 2017, https://www.psychiatrictimes.com/view/being-human-interview-daniel-j-siegel-md.

22 Inanimate things are designed by humans. We interact with them, making them part of our coevolving living system.

23 Jeffrey West, *Scale, The Universal Laws of Life, Growth and Death in Organisms, Cities and Companies* (Penguin Books, 2017).

4   Koike, Tanabe, Okazaki, Nakagawa, Sasaki, Shimada, Sugawara, Takahashi, Yoshihara, Bosch-Bayard, Sadato, "Neural Substrates of Shared Attention as Social Memory: A Hyperscanning Functional Magnetic Resonance Imaging Study," *PubMed*, https://www.ncbi.nlm.nih.gov/pubmed/26514295. Andrea Bartz, "This Is the Amazing Thing That Happens When You Stare into Each Other's Eyes," *Glamour*, December 22, 2015, https://www.glamour.com/story/eye-contact-syncs-brain-activity.
5   Dacher Keltner: "Hands on Research: The Science of Touch," *Greater Good Magazine*, September 29, 2010, https://greatergood.berkeley.edu/article/item/handsonresearch.
6   Nicholas Christakis, "The Hidden Influence of Social Networks," TED Talk, https://www.ted.com/talks/nicholaschristakisthehiddeninfluenceofsocialnetworks/transcript.
7   Vivek Murthy, *Together: The Healing Power of Human Connection in a Sometimes Lonely World* (HarperCollins, 2020).
8   *Scientific Reports* 9, no. 1 (2019).
9   S. C. van Hedger et. al., *Psychonomic Bulletin & Review* 26, no. 2 (2019).
10 *Science Advances* 5, no. 7 (2019).
11 *Journal of Environmental Psychology* 42, no. 1 (2015). R. L. Dopko et al., *Journal of Environmental Psychology* 63, no. 1 (2019).
12 Dan Siegal, MD.
13 September 29, 2022, https://hbr.org/2022/09/what-is-a-good-job?ab=atartart1x4s03.
14 You'll see this visualized and described in detail on the right side of the Connection Continuum, in Chapter 7.

Chapter 12: So…How Do We Live a Show-Up Life? And…a Call to Action

1   Aaron Toumazou, "Neuroscience-Backed Reasons to Start Journaling," *Form Magazine*, November 2020.
2   Karen A. Baikie and Kay Wilhelm, *Emotional and Physical Health Benefits of Expressive Writing* (Cambridge University Press, January 2, 2018). "Longer-term benefits of expressive writing for emotional health outcomes include mood/affect (Pennebaker *et al*, 1988; Páez *et al*, 1999), psychological well-being (Park & Blumberg, 2002), depressive symptoms (Lepore, 1997), post-traumatic intrusion and avoidance symptoms (Klein & Boals, 2001)." https://www.cambridge.org/core/journals/advances-in-psychiatric-treatment/article/emotional-and-physical-health-benefits-of-expressive-writing/ED2976A61F5DE56B46F07A1CE9EA9F9F.
3   J. W. Pennebaker, *Opening Up: The Healing Power of Expressing Emotions* (New York: Guilford Press, 2012).
4   Cinsi May, *A Learning Secret: Don't Take Notes with a Laptop*, Scientific American (June 3, 2014).

11 Alison Alexander, "The Power of Purpose: How Organizations Are Making Work More Meaningful," *Journal of the School of Education and Social Policy*, Northwestern University (2015).

Chapter 10: Situational Readiness

1   Deborah J. Mitchell, Jay Russo, and Nancy Pennington, "Performing a Project Premortem Developed by Gary Kline," *Harvard Business Review,* September 2007.
2   I'm using the old-fashioned separation of mind and body for ease and clarity. That said, the mind and body are very much one.
3   Six Seconds: The Emotional Intelligence Network, "Envisioning Your Way to Success: The Power of Mental Practice," accessed October 17, 2022, https://www.6seconds.org/2018/01/15/envisioning-way-success-incredible-power-mental-practice/.
4   Jim Lohr, "Can Visualizing Your Body Doing Something Help You Learn to Do It Better?" *Scientific American,* May 1, 2015, https://www.scientificamerican.com/article/can-visualizing-your-body-doing-something-help-you-learn-to-do-it-better/.
5   Tara Swart, *The Source: The Secrets of the Universe, The Science of the Brain* (New York: HarperOne, 2019).
6   From Chapter 2, "Why do I choose the word attuning, not awareness, when discussing Showing Up? Because attuning takes the next step past awareness to include responding. Attuning is not just sensing or alert to how we're Showing Up, it is also *attending to it*."
7   I use "brain" here instead of "mind" because mind contains the combination of our intellectual interpretation of sensate and emotional experience. Mind has also been described as including the shared space between and among people when eye to eye.
8   Bessel van der Kolk, in conversation with Krista Tippett, "On Being," November 15, 2021. Bessel van der Kolk is the founder and medical director of the Trauma Research Foundation, in Brookline, Massachusetts, and professor of psychiatry at Boston University Medical School. His books include *Traumatic Stress: The Effects of Overwhelming Experience on the Mind, Body, and Society* and *The Body Keeps the Score: Brain, Mind, and Body in the Healing of Trauma*.
9   Ibid.
10 Ibid.

Chapter 11: Societal Alltelligence

1   Emma Seppälä and Kim Cameron, "The Best Leaders Have a Contagious Positive Energy," *Harvard Business Review,* April 18, 2022.
2   Neuroscientist Dan Siegel, MD, referencing the Connectome Studies by Smith, et. al.
3   This explains some of why I felt the need to create a word for this third skill of Showing Up. Beyond relating to ourselves and our Situation, we need a label for the way of relating to the world that supports us in performing at the level we aspire to.

2 Daniel Siegel and Edwin Rutsch, "Dialogs on How to Build a Culture of Empathy," YouTube video, 2013, https://www.youtube.com/watch?v=XIzTdXdhU0w
3 Examples of Evie's work are on ChooseToShowUp.com.
4 Admiral William McRaven. "2014 Commencement Speech," University of Texas at Austin.
5 Nassim Nicholas Taleb, *Antifragile* (Random House, 2012).
6 Ibid.

Chapter 9: Self-Grounding

1 Dr. Gabor Maté, interviewed by Alex Howard at the Trauma Superconference by Conscious Life. https://trauma.consciouslife.com/video2/. Accessed February 26, 2023. Author of *In the Realm of Hungry Ghosts: Close Encounters with Addiction*; *When the Body Says No: The Cost of Hidden Stress*; and *Scattered Minds: The Origins and Healing of Attention Deficit Disorder*.
2 These physical symptoms can also be caused illness, in addition to psychological sources, such as how well we understand ourselves.
3 Wiesel and Hubel, 1963 and 1965. (For which they won the Nobel Prize.)
4 I know reducing an encounter or person to a score has an air of unfairness, harshness, and judgment. I agree. And I'm feeling the tension. Remember, we're not scoring the person. We're scoring how they chose to Show Up. The goal is for you to have an opinion. Putting a raw, cold number on it triggers as much. Maybe you agree with my assessment. Maybe you don't. Both are worthy. The experience of thinking it through is the point. It's practicing Showing Up.
5 Bessel van der Kolk, *The Body Keeps the Score* (New York: Penguin, 2015).
6 Substantial research has helped us move past the old paradigm of a "rational" and an "emotional" brain. More recent insights show we experience instinct first, followed by our emotional centers (such as the limbic system), then our (likely misnamed) executive systems in the frontal cortex, among other areas.
7 I first encountered this in a session at Stanford University with Dave Evans and Bill Burnett, professors at The Hasso Plattner Institute of Design at Stanford, commonly known as the d.school.
8 Randy Cohen, Chirag Bavishi, and Alan Rozanski, "Purpose in Life and Its Relationship to All-Cause Mortality and Cardiovascular Events," *Psychosomatic Medicine* 78, no. 2 (February/March 2016): 122–133, https://journals.lww.com/psychosomaticmedicine/Abstract/2016/02000/PurposeinLifeandItsRelationshiptoAllCause.2.aspx.
9 Yoona Kang, Danielle Cosme, Rui Pei, Prateekshit Pandey, José Carreras-Tartak, and Emily B. Falk, "Purpose in Life, Loneliness, and Protective Health Behaviors During the COVID-19 Pandemic," *The Gerontologist* 61, no. 6 (September 2021): 878–887, https://doi.org/10.1093/geront/gnab081.
10 Richard Boyatzis, *Transformational Leadership*, accessed October 2022, https://transformleaders.tv/richard-boyatzis/.

10. Over 40 percent of our society are living with the impacts of insecure attachment relationships from not getting what we needed in our earliest years. This translates into relationship challenges across our professional and personal lives. Sources: report published by Sutton Trust, March 2014. Researchers from Princeton University, Columbia University, the London School of Economics and Political Science and the University of Bristol.
11. In the Realm of Hungry Ghosts, drgabormate.com.

Chapter 7: Level 1: Barely There

1. Moving ourselves productively through trauma or grief can certainly be seen as productive and a positive model for the world, as well as worthy of deep respect and support. It can be viewed as a form of Truly Showing Up to the circumstance. That notwithstanding, I'm choosing to locate this positive behavior as actively Barely There since it often makes Showing Up as we'd ideally choose (outside of the extenuating circumstance) impossible. For example, when grieving, we won't be bringing our A-game to work.
2. According to John Gottman, these four emotions "describe communication styles that, according to our research, can predict the end of a relationship." https://www.gottman.com/blog/the-four-horsemen-recognizing-criticism-contempt-defensiveness-and-stonewalling/.
3. This groups mind wandering within Barely There. Level 1 is broader than that, including un-engagement, active disengagement and other forms of being "checked out." Referring to mind wandering exclusively Matt Killingsworth's Track Your Happiness project showed our minds wander 47 percent of the time and in this state are almost always consumed with concerns and ruminations.
4. Tucker and Williamson. 1984. Referenced in McGilchrist, Iain, *The Master and His Emissary: The Divided Brain and the Making of the Western World* (Yale University Press, 2018).
5. Hope Reese, "How a Bit of Awe Can Improve Your Health," *New York Times*, January 3, 2023.
6. Ibid.
7. Daniel Goleman and Richard J. Davidson, *Altered Traits, Science Reveals How Meditation Changes Your Mind, Brain, and Body* (Avery, an imprint of Penguin Random House, 2017).
8. Ibid.
9. Srini Pillay, "Your Brain Can Only Take So Much Focus," *Harvard Business Review*, May 12, 2017.

Chapter 8

1. Thomas Hübl. With Julie Jordan Avritt. 2023. Sounds True. Boulder, Colorado.

4   Dan Siegel, https://drdansiegel.com/interpersonal-neurobiology/, accessed November 27, 2022.
5   John Cacioppo, quoted in *Together: The Healing Power of Human Connection in a Sometimes Lonely World*, by Vivek H. Murthy, MD.
6   Ibid.
7   Vivek Murthy, *Together: The Healing Power of Human Connection in a Sometimes Lonely World*, (HarperCollins, 2020).
8   Ibid.
9   Affecting one in six children, according to the ACE (Adverse Childhood Experiences study), and one in four adults. The ACE study measures the number of adverse experiences someone has had, including abuse, mental illness, divorce, incarceration, or neglect.
10 Rob Cross and Karen Dillon, "The Hidden Toll of Microstress: Small, Difficult Moments Can Zap Your Performance. Here's How to Restore Your Well-Being" *Harvard Business Review* (February 07, 2023).

Chapter 5: The Show-Up Continuum

1   This refers to my research on achievement and Showing Up, which extends back to 1999. That said, endless other common behaviors and patterns demonstrate the same parabolic distribution.
2   Author of *The Productivity Zone*. SmartMoves Coaching (December 18, 2014), https://pennyzenker360.com/.

Chapter 6: Level 2: Just Showing Up

1   These are direct quotes from my national surveys that took place between 2016 and 2019.
2   More on this point in Chapter 9: Groundedness.
3   Detailed statistics for loneliness, anxiety, depression suicide and addiction are listed in Chapter 1.
4   Martha Henriques, "Can the Legacy of Trauma Be Passed Down the Generations?, March 26 2019.
5   Rachel Yehuda, "Holocaust Exposure Induced Intergenerational Effects in FKBP5 Methylation," *Biological Psychiatry* 80, no. 5.
6   Thomas Hübl, presenting about our Ancestral Collective and Individual Trauma at the May 2022 SAND Event – "Opening to Our Humanity and Resilience in a Time of Upheaval."
7   *My Grandmother's Hands*, (Central Recovery Press, 2017. And 2016: 372–380). The conclusions are supported by further studies.
8   https://www.ted.com/talks/marcyaxelrodshowingupisacontactsport.
9   The digesting and processing of emotional, physical and intellectual sensations that comprise an "experience," or even a moment of time.

12. Matthew Killingsworth and Daniel Gilbert, "A Wandering Mind Is an Unhappy One," *Scientific American* 330, no. 6006 (November 12, 2010): 932, DOI: 10.1126/science.1192439.
13. Marcy Axelrod, *On Your Game!: Succeed In a World Designed to Knock You Off Your Game* (Black Rose Writing, 2019).
14. "Habits are response dispositions that are activated automatically by the context cues that co-occurred with responses during past performance." David T. Neal, Wendy Wood, and Jeffrey M. Quinn, "Habits—A Repeat Performance," *Current Directions in Psychological Science* 15, no. 4 (2006).
15. Dan Siegel, *IntraConnected: MWe (Me + We) as the Integration of Self, Identity, and Belonging* (W. W. Norton, 2022).

Chapter 3: The Model of How We Show Up

1. Iain McGilchrist in conversation with Mark Vernon, "The Attack on Life and Understanding Our Times," 2022, Accessed May 8, 2023.
2. Dan Siegel, *IntraConnected: MWe (Me + We) as the Integration of Self, Identity, and Belonging* (W. W. Norton, 2022).
3. Iain McGilchrist, "Understanding The Matter with Things Dialogues: Episode 3: Chapter 3."
4. Adrian Bejan and Peter Zane, *Design in Nature: How the Constructual Law Governs Evolution in Biology, Physics, Technology, and Social Organization* (New York: Anchor Books, 2012).
5. "Our findings point to the fact that finding a direction for life, and setting overarching goals for what you want to achieve can help you actually live longer, regardless of when you find your purpose," says Hill. "So the earlier someone comes to a direction for life, the earlier these protective effects may be able to occur." "Having a Sense of Purpose May Add Years to Your Life," *Association for Psychological Science* (May 12, 2014), https://www.sciencedaily.com/releases/2014/05/140512124308.htm.
6. Nicholas Christakis and James Fowler, *Connected: The Surprising Power of Our Social Networks and How They Shape Our Lives* (New York: Little, Brown & Company, 2009).
7. Aliya Alimujiang, Ashley Wiensch, Jonathan Boss, et al., "Association Between Life Purpose and Mortality Among US Adults Older Than 50 Years," *JAMA* (May 24, 2019).

Chapter 4: How Grounding, Readiness, and Alltelligence become "Showing Up"

1. Chapter 9 on Groundedness explains this concept in further detail.
2. "Differential Pattern of Functional Brain Plasticity after Compassion and Empathy Training," *Social Cognitive and Affective Neuroscience* 9, no. 6 (June 2014): 873–79, doi:10.1093/scan/nst060.
3. Daniel Goleman and Richard Davidson, *Altered Traits: Science Reveals How Meditation Changes Your Mind, Brain, and Body* (Avery).

ENDNOTES

Chapter 2: Defaulting through Life

1. Cigna (2019) found that 61 percent of Americans report feeling lonely. The book *Bowling Alone* (2000), by Robert D. Putnam, explains loneliness is a serious public health issue. Former U.S. Surgeon General Vivek Murthy called loneliness a public-health "epidemic" in 2017. The United Kingdom appointed a "minister for loneliness" in 2018.
2. "Anxiety disorders are the most common mental illness in the U.S.," impacting 40 million adults, or almost 1 in 5 people. https://www.medicalnewstoday.com/articles/322877.
3. 9.7 percent of American youth have severe major depression (2021). In 2017–2018, 19 percent of adults experienced a mental illness, an increase of 1.5 million people over 2020's dataset. https://mhanational.org/issues/state-mental-health-america.
4. Roman Krznaric, *Empathy: Why It Matters, and How to Get It* (TarcherPerigee, November 3, 2015).
5. Our Epidemic of Loneliness and Isolation 2023: The U.S. Surgeon General's Advisory on the Healing Effects of Social Connection and Community.
6. Daniel Kahneman and Amos Tversky, *Thinking Fast and Slow* (Farrar, Strauss and Giroux, 2011).
7. Ibid.
8. The phrase "The map is not the territory" was coined by Polish-American philosopher and engineer Alfred Korzybski, written in *Science and Sanity: An Introduction to Non-Aristotelian Systems and General Semantics*, 1933, republished in 1994 by Institute of General Semantics. It conveys the idea that we abstract and reduce reality to make sense of it, leaving much richness and information behind. This is a predominant function of our left brain hemisphere.
9. Iain McGilchrist, "The Divided Brain," Matter of Fact Media, November 22, 2018.
10. Ibid.
11. https://www.gallup.com/workplace/352949/employee-engagement-holds-steady-first-half-2021.aspx.

Marcy is the executive director of the Show Up Institute, a social enterprise dedicated to creating a more grounded, ready, Alltelligent culture. The institute delivers corporate and social impact projects, training, education, and ongoing research toward creating the society we all want.

When not reading, writing, or speaking, Marcy creates large pieces of abstract expressionist art. She lives in Westchester, New York, with her two daughters.

ABOUT THE AUTHOR

Award-winning author, TV contributor, and two-time TEDx speaker **MARCY AXELROD** has spent the past twenty-five years uncovering nature's model of how humans are designed to thrive. Since 1999, her insights have helped individuals, teams, and some of the world's largest companies succeed.

Marcy started her career at Lehman Brothers on Wall Street before becoming a leader at KPMG Consulting's high-tech strategy practice in Silicon Valley. In partnership with top technology companies across the globe, she tested and refined a mindset and model for how each of us relates to our Selves, Situations, and Society—in other words, how we Show Up.

Marcy's work combines neuroscience, psychology, behavioral economics, and biology with top consulting strategies and twenty years of her own research. Her work has received praise from professors at Harvard, Yale, Columbia, and Cornell. Grounded and practical, the model of how we Show Up is essential insight for anyone seeking meaning, efficacy, and happiness.

ACKNOWLEDGMENTS

SO MANY PEOPLE STRONGLY supported the value of Showing Up and my writing, research, and creation process. To name just a few, editor and inspirist Kristin Clark Taylor; publishing experts Naren Aryal and Nina Spahn; and thought partners Jennifer Lane, Jonathan Rudolph, Jack Genser, Dan Haar, Tamara Thompson, and many more.

—Marcy

> **imbibed by everyone and everything, including the ocean of time.**

We've reached the end of the road. It's up to you to determine how to infuse Showing Up into your life. No one is perfect. Give yourself permission to Just Show Up when appropriate and to bring your best when it matters most. The key is in the *choosing*—it's up to you to choose when, how, and to what degree you commit to Showing Up in each moment.

> **Human to human, I hope you'll accept my invitation to Show Up just a little bit better. Only as individuals—and accomplices in our collective—can we steer the world into a healthier, happier place.**
>
> **The choice and power are yours. I can't wait to see what you do with them.**

> **in a culture of being "good to go" and just walk in. Then, amid the flow of our days, we bounce off our emotions, not fully feeling them, or defend ourselves from them, living in separateness more than unity.**

As we think about our responsibilities to Society and those we love, we recognize it is incumbent on us to overcome this. JSUPing and Barely There are low-performance zones that leave us and society unfulfilled and sick. We can—and must—live in them less often since we're actively weaving our insights, brilliance, and pain into today's dynamic world. Our pasts and current patterns become our parenting, technology, fashion, economics, innovation, design, education, and legal systems, as well as the spread of disease and prevention and all animate and inanimate life.[22]

In this way, Showing Up is the performance medium of all individuals—hopefully now understood to be alldividuals—Situations, and the world. It is our systemic contribution to this moment, to all days, and years and to the ongoings of the universe. It's the infinite process we're contributing and responding to.

This explains how our lives are expansive. We recur, predictably, at every scale.[23] Despite this, we never truly see the completeness of who and what we are. After all, the puzzle box and site map demystifying our behavioral causes and impacts remains ungifted, amid a coevolving world. One thing is clear, however: our three roles merge into one, creating a collective Self, also called Society.

> **In this way, Showing Up is how we fertilize, infect, and perpetuate our poison...and our remedy, our crack, and our enterprisingly unique elixir. All are**

- - Review notes of how I want to interact.
  - Envision myself Showing Up as I choose.
- G: Review the type of mother I aim to be (supportive, deeply attuned, raising an independent, capable, compassionate, grounded adult).
- Review before walking in and afterward to reground myself in my goals and to see how I did.

ALL OF US

I'm hoping by now I have effectively communicated that Showing Up is not esoterica. It is not mere reframing of presence, mindfulness or basic self-improvement. It is an organic, relational, unifying, and powerful way of seeing ourselves, the world, and how we fit into it as accountable cocreators of all there is.

The concepts in this book are about our human condition. Being cognizant of how we're Showing Up unmasks this, revealing that we often live without sufficiently contemplating, or intentfully choosing. We default into circling behavioral eddies. We relive past generations' Show-Up choices. We instill behaviors into our children, and into following generations that we launch into iterative swirls of their own.

> **We see the world as WE ARE, not as IT IS. How can it be any other way? This is why it's so important to consider how we Show Up. To what extent are we with and for others in addition to our Selves?**
>
> **My research illustrates that we think we're more Self-aware than we are. We know we're often Just Showing Up, leading us to slip into patterns that disconnect us and leave us uninspired. Yet we live**

on being more grounded, ready, and Alltelligent. These folks are well on their way practicing Showing Up.

Others needed one thing to focus on to get started. They chose a target Situation in which they want to Show Up better and prepared a high-level roadmap. If this is you, here are five steps you may find to be helpful:

1. Choose a Situation in which you'd like to Show Up a certain way.
2. Choose the behaviors and tools that feel like a fit.
3. Test them by trying them out in another, perhaps lower stakes, Situation.
4. Learn and revise.
5. Reliably integrate them into your day.

Reviewing the Show-Up Matrix on page 308 may help.

Example Show-Up Roadmap v. 1.0

- Target Situation: Speaking to my teen daughter after school

TOOLS

- Show-Up Levels and Target:
  - Chosen Show-Up Level: 3, Truly Show Up
  - Plot desired G/R/A levels:
- Grounding: 8
- Alltelligence: 8
- Readiness: 8
- Review my G/R/A setup and behaviors:
  - R and A:
    - In Advance: Complete the Readiness Guide
    - Right beforehand: Quick compassion meditation to reground and reconnect myself with my daughter and the bigger (human) picture, to avoid getting caught up in her behavior.

> **and "us," reinforcing our Alltelligence. Research findings[21] explain this exercise strengthens our regulatory skills to monitor and modulate our behavior, stabilizing us. And the more rooted we are, the less threatening the world is, so we can be open, accepting of, maybe even curious about others' behavior and views. Beyond this, we start to perceive others' energy and information flow with enhanced discernment and penetration. Life becomes more engaging.**

Since our experience of the world is gated by our ability to sense our own body, reintegrating ourselves is a powerful step to vitalize how we're Showing Up. As Dr. Siegel states, this "integrated identity" is how we "bring more well-being into our individual and collective lives." Further exploring of the Wheel of Awareness is at your fingertips at DrDanSiegel.com.

SUMMARY

Practicing the ideas in this chapter as well as those throughout the book will help us Show Up closer to how we choose, more often. There's no need to be hard on ourselves or negative if we fall off our practice or don't perform as well as we'd like. Simply noticing how we're doing shows we're making progress.

NEED A PLACE TO START?

Some people tell me after a few chapters they started asking themselves the main Show-Up question. They consider their roles and skills often through the day. People also mention regularly noticing how others Show Up. Some people tell me they use the roles and skills in discussion with their teammates, family, and friends. And they work

2. We then focus on our interior perception of the body's muscles, bones, lungs, heart, and other organs.
3. Next, we turn to mental activities like thoughts, feelings, and memories.
4. Then we turn to our relations with other people, feeling our sense of them and their reality.
5. Finally we turn to nature, and to open awareness of what's going on around us.
6. In a powerful closing exercise, we visualize the spoke of attention bending back toward us as we absorb others' care and nature's energy into us.

This experience helps us feel felt, when we sense 'our objective experience known by another.'"[18] It is a root of integration and belonging. Paying attention to these areas in succession wires neural connections across them. It steps us closer to feeling whole. This includes a broad oneness with others, helping alleviate issues including burnout, disengagement, loneliness, judgment, bias, anxiety, depression, and related challenges. The result? "You find yourself becoming patient, understanding, compassionate, and more whole as a person."[19]

After we bend the world's attention back into us, we're asked to be aware of our awareness, consciously experiencing what our mind is doing. "It is becoming the observer to your thoughts and experience, as well as the experiencer."[20] This is the dual awareness I mentioned we're practicing as we choose how we Show Up. This is recognizing the mind as both our subjective experience of thoughts and sensations and also an objectively observable process, as if we're watching our interactions from outside ourselves. It is explained more in Chapter 8, Truly Showing Up.

> **Attuning to how our mind, body, and relations Show Up Readies us, deepens our Grounding, and makes tangible how we exist beyond "I," into "we"**

Research[17] to be a deep resource. You can access their articles, videos, interviews, and other assets online. It also offers a community of people working to deepen their compassion, and with it, their Alltelligence.

I find that many exercises direct compassion toward our Selves, instead of toward others. This may seem like a reasonable starting place if we're unhappy with our Selves. Our Grounding, which includes our ability to fully meet, receive, and love our Selves for who we are, becomes the limit and boundary of our ability to connect with others. That said, I find focusing outward on others, bearing witness, affirming them, and supporting their journeys offers a significant source of meaning, helping us feel whole.

Wheel of Awareness

Exercises that connect our brain, body, and society are powerful tools supporting how we Show Up. They build muscle across all three roles and skills. One approach called the Wheel of Awareness is proven to add structural connections within our brains and to expand our compassion for others. This makes it a top recommendation.

Developed by Dr. Dan Siegel, clinical professor of psychiatry at UCLA's School of Medicine and director of its Mindful Awareness Research Center, the Wheel of Awareness is an exercise that can be completed in as little as twenty minutes or less with practice. It directs our attention toward four core experiences in succession. Aiming focus at one target after another creates linkages between them since neurons that fire together wire together.

We begin the exercise by imagining our awareness resting at the center of a circle or wheel. Now we send out spokes of attention to points on the rim.

1. First, we focus attention on our five senses (hearing, touch, taste, scent, and sight). They tell us what the outer world is doing. We spend from a few seconds to a minute feeling what each sense is perceiving.

Remembering Feeling Felt

As Maya Angelou reminds us, people remember not what we said, but how we made them feel. Think back to when you last experienced Alltelligence from others.

- When did someone deeply listen to us?
- When did we sense being understood? Feeling felt?
- Who did we share close emotional time with recently?
- What tools described above (music, art, literature, dance, sources of awe) are we choosing to engage with?

We're drawn to people who gift this. We support them, invite them, and open opportunities for them. And they, us. Now, consider:

- In what areas of your life would you like to deepen your sense of belonging?
- Do you feel disconnected in a particular place, such as at your office, at home, or with certain friends?
- Consider the people you care about in these spaces. What habits or energy do you value in them? How can you impact their growth and success?

These insight prepare you to step into Situations more Alltelligently.

Compassion Training

As mentioned in Chapter 11, Alltelligence, sending positive wishes to people is proven to deepen our sense of togetherness, evoking trusting, caring behavior. The exercises to do this take mere seconds, making them a high-return addition to our days. The typical practice instructs us to think of someone, hold their image in mind, and recite, "May you feel happy. May you feel healthy. May you feel peaceful."

In addition to the myriad books on compassion, I've found my time training at Stanford University's Center for Compassion and Altruism

Awe

In Chapter 7 describing Level 1, Barely There, I briefly explained how Awe sparks sustained attention. Compelling new insights show it also prompts a sense of unity and leads us to be more helpful and kind. These meaningful shifts benefit us as individuals and as a collective.

Psychologists Dacher Keltner and Jonathan Haidt explain that awe experiences are Self-transcendent. They turn our "Self-mirror" outward, linking us with "something greater than ourselves, and make us more generous toward others." This goodness is linked with two phenomena prompted by awe experiences: "perceived vastness" and a "need for accommodation."[15] "Need for accommodation" is prompted when experiences stretch our minds, requiring we cognitively realign our mental structure of how we see the world for us to comprehend them. In moments of awe, our expectations and normal thought structures are insufficient. They've been violated by what we're now perceiving. "Perceived vastness" is experienced in the presence of something physically large or from "a more theoretical perceptual sense of vastness—such as being in the presence of someone with immense prestige or being presented with a complex idea like the theory of relativity."

"Awe is often accompanied by feelings of self-diminishment and increased connectedness with other people. Experiencing awe often puts people in a self-transcendent state where they focus less on themselves and feel more like a part of a larger whole."[16] It diminishes the individualistic Self, described in Chapter 3. Consistent with this, it also decreases materialism, puts us in a better mood and gives us a sense of having more time. Awe boosts critical thinking, skepticism, and feelings of social bonding. Art of all kinds can be sources of awe, including music, sculpture, dance, literature, poetry, acts of creativity, and imagination. These are sincere, often emotional expressions of our humanness. And they bond us through our individual bodies, regardless of skin shade, and economic, educational, social, and sexual identities.

well-proven sources. They include music, dance, many kinds of art, time in nature, poetry, literature, and feeling awe. Practicing compassion and gratitude also support living into our Societal role. They are mentioned in Chapter 11, Alltelligence.

Finally, I'll help us evoke memories of times we felt seen and heard and will close this chapter with a description of a very powerful tool supporting Alltelligence, Dr. Dan Siegel's Wheel of Awareness.

Music and Art

Many of us have experienced the social glue of swaying together to music, whether at a concert or at home. Evolution created a brain circuit specifically for it.[8] Music's brain circuit also engages neural areas for empathy, trust, and cooperation. Listening together fosters social cohesion within families and between peer groups[9] by raising oxytocin, a neuropeptide that spurs bonding and trust.[10] "In 2009, archeologists unearthed a flute carved from bone and ivory that was over 35,000 years old. This proved that even during the hunting/gathering stage of human evolution, music was present and important to society. Why else take time away from survival tasks to create a musical instrument?"[11]

Considering art more generally, in their recent book, *Your Brain on Art*, Susan Magsamen and Ivy Ross Reading explain reading poetry,[12] fiction, moving our bodies in dance, and other forms of art biologically create a neurochemical change in us, releasing feelings of connectedness within our Selves and among others.[13] Many studies show music and art reduce stress and physical pain while increasing happiness, health, and well-being. Activities known to create these benefits are wide reaching, including cooking, painting, coloring, composing, watching a play, or sitting inside a cathedral. These activities "cultivate our curiosity" and help us "stay open to our emotions, experience surprise or novelty, think differently about life, embrace ambiguity, engage the senses, [and] feel awe."[14]

- Is the busy season at work (or our partner's work) predictable, and we'd like to be in a better mental space this year before it gets really wild?

Once we stop to consider the predictable activities and seasons of our lives, we can prepare our mind, energy, calendar, and cadence to Show Up better. I find medium-term planning every quarter/season works well. About every three months, I take an hour or so to list the new challenges, changes, or circumstances coming my way. Inevitably, I gain clarity about hopes and concerns that point me to the preparing I need to smooth the way.

It often feels satisfying and even soothing. For example, if I identify my daughters' restarting school in the fall as the event to ready for, I might write, "Provide an organized, supportive, stress-free environment for my girls to come home to after school, honoring their growth and happiness." Recognizing the words I used—organized, supportive, stress-free, growth, happiness—gave me ideas. We need a better place for their school supplies and backpacks. I need to greet them after school in a low-key manner (not my typical overenthusiasm). Perhaps I'll play their favorite music as they walk in the door. These are easy things that would not have come to mind without dedicating myself to sit for a few minutes to plan. Even if my kids just laugh with me about the music, it'll be a memorable moment helping to connect us (which, since they're teens, we desperately need).

While basic, these planning steps achieve what my research shows is widely needed—dedicating more time to ready ourselves.

Now let's look at how to live with greater Alltelligence, supporting our role as members of Society, nature, and all systems outside the individualistic definition of Self.[7]

ALLTELLIGENCE

Everything that helps us feel unity with others or with something beyond our Selves fosters Alltelligence. I'll briefly touch on a few

THE SHOW-UP MATRIX

SELF

1. With what thoughts, emotions, and actions do we want to Show Up?

- What in the Situation may prompt behaviors to avoid? What are these behaviors?
- Which behaviors (thoughts, emotions) are we choosing to experience?

SITUATION

How are we choosing to Show Up?

SOCIETY

1. How are we choosing to impact those involved?
2. How deeply are we choosing to attune to others, to be there with and for them?

Longer-Term Planning

While planning may sound basic, my research shows a majority of Americans feel a huge cost from not doing enough of it. When we fail to step outside of the rapid cadence of our workdays, children's activities, and social gatherings that encircle us, it's virtually impossible to Show Up as we choose as often as we'd like. Reviewing a few common scenarios may prompt us to set aside planning time:

- Do certain people or events (family visits? doctor's appointments? a certain person? etc.) make us feel tense, telling us we should better ready ourselves?
- Do we often feel behind the eight ball each fall when school starts and want to take steps this summer to set up for a lower-stress school year?

move through the Situation more favorably.

People share how this plays out. Before a Situation they stop to intentfully envision what they expect and what they'd like to see happen. Perhaps a few of the goals people express to me will be familiar to you. They say, "I want to":

- Feel confident (Grounding)
- Manage emotions such as fear and anger (Grounding)
- Help others feel heard and felt (Alltelligence)
- Deeply engage and be productive (Readiness)
- Infuse positivity or creativity into the situation (All Show-Up skills)
- Share ideas more readily (Grounding and Readiness)

Write down your goals for the next situation you want to Truly Show Up for.

Now, what will help you to accomplish this?

If your goal is to confidently share your ideas, write your ideas down to bring them front and center in mind. Envision people hearing them and liking what they hear. How does it feel to be well received? What will you and others be doing in this instant? Take note of these details. Now you're closer to enacting these behaviors, bringing the successful situation about.

We can also practice coping mechanisms in advance. For example, if we're trying to maintain composure, decide now, before entering the situation, that if triggered, we'll take five deep breaths and count to fifteen before speaking. Prime your ability to do this by taking the breaths and counting to fifteen twice right now. This practice makes it easier and more likely that we'll do it in the spur of the moment. A simple matrix can help.

As mentioned before, people have had good results from putting Post-it notes on their phone, laptop, bathroom mirror, coffee cup, or another place they see often.

Which of these suggestions do you want to try?

Acting on these prompts is also becoming more ready, which we'll explore next.

READINESS

We just reviewed how the main Show-Up question is valuable to ground us. Here we'll get into how it works to Situationally prepare us by prompting us to use our right-brained attention system. Then we'll apply Show-Up techniques to longer-term planning.

Short-Term Planning and Preparing: "How Am I Choosing to Show Up?"

Often, we don't have weeks, days, or even minutes to prepare for Situations. And that's okay. Considering an experience for as little as a few moments can be sufficient to help surface implicit emotions and expectations, changing how we Show Up. The key is to bring ourselves into the future moments so we see and feel the Situation playing out. It's similar to asking, "How do I expect the Situation to Show Up?" And it opens our hearts to attune to the Situation and participants more deeply.

As we envision the Situation, our expectations or fears readily rise in our minds and bodies. Valuable details emerge the more closely we see the participants and look around the room (park, restaurant, school, field, etc.), experiencing the interaction. We're aiming to be in it as deeply as we can, while being in a safe space, separate from the actual Situation, with emotional distance and time to surface expectations, fears, hopes, excitement, and interests. These insights are exposing our truth. Are they emotions we've been pushing away? From our protected, unpressured space, we can explore them and find ways to

Identity Development. Mostly done over video, selected participants are chosen from a small group to attune to different parts of our experience, and reflect it back to us in a supportive environment. This practice of structured resonating has been used in Norway for twenty years, and has been known to create breakthroughs in a single session. I highly recommend it. (IdentityDevelopmentInstitute.com)

Our In-the-Moment Check-In: "How Am I Showing Up?" and "How Am I choosing to Show Up?"

Asking this question is a powerful check-in. We're aiming our minds at how we are behaving right now. And we're prompting, "How do we want to be?" This check-in brings choice. It reveals who we are in this moment. This is our truth. It confronts us, and as such, it informs us of how we want to change. Alternatively, if we're Showing Up as we chose, our check-in fills us with contentment for being who we want to be. In both cases, we're more in touch with our behavior, enabling us to be here for our Selves and our influence beyond. This deepens our Grounding and all Show-Up skills.

Some of us have already started asking ourselves the Show-Up question. Others need a prompt until it becomes a habit. People tell me they prompt the question by doing the following:

- Adding the question to their calendar right before meetings, activities, or in open space when they have time to reflect
- Affiliating a common activity with the question so it acts as a prompt. Driving does this for me. As I pull out of my driveway, I hear, "How am I choosing to Show Up?" Then I envision the situation, including my behavior, others involved, the environment, how I want to feel, and things to keep in mind. As I do this, I notice my body shifting into a more relaxed, planful state. You can choose any activity—pouring coffee, making dinner, walking into a meeting or appointment, seeing family members. Take a moment to write what you think will work for you.

known grows, we're more able and likely to bring it to our Selves and to others. This includes creating more Grounded, Ready, and Alltelligent family and work cultures in which people feel they belong, encouraging them to Truly Show Up.

Like Showing Up, generally, the therapeutic relationship is one in which there is no failing, just testing and learning. We're bringing our current level of skill…our raw Selves. As I learned years ago and am retaught by life often, the relationship is the therapy.

My personal experience is that it's valuable to have a friend in my corner. I've used my therapist for basic tactical advice, "What do I do now?" for "How do I move through this sadness effectively and efficiently?" and for "Help me think through what may happen next so I can be ready." We're all transgenerational beings carrying what our parents and grandparents taught us and ideally desiring to bring our best into today and the lives of those we encounter. A therapeutic relationship helps us to do this.

We can design our sessions with specific goals to deepen each Show-Up skill, as I do. After all, every challenge and experience of life evokes and crafts how we Show Up. Why not invest in ourselves based on these skills? Resources include qualified practitioners with degrees in psychology, psychiatry, social work, and related foci. Therapeutically minded groups such as the ManKind Project and Woman Within can also offer significant value.

When I couldn't find an available therapist due to the COVID-19 pandemic, I resorted to crisis-management services. Experts were available and helped my family. Sometimes we don't utilize this level of provider, thinking our Situation is not so extreme. That's what I did. I waited longer than perhaps I should have. Sometimes achieving our desired level of performance requires more urgent action than we realize.

Identity Development Institute

I recently discovered a fast, inexpensive path to process unmet needs below the surface of daily life that may be challenging us. It's called

- Confirm it in your calendar. Make it a ritual.

Gratitude Journaling

This is the simple practice of listing or describing things we feel grateful for. Such savoring is a proven happiness practice. Consistent with the research, I find I am happier when my practice is consistent, at least a few times each week. When I let it lapse, I find I'm less happy. This is HUGE bang for the buck. I simply answer, "What am I grateful for right now?" It's simple, easy, and takes nothing to start.

Now let's look at a more formal type of reflecting—with a trained practitioner.

Working with a Professional Psychologist, Psychiatrist, Psychoanalyst, Social Worker, or Other Therapeutically Focused Practitioner or Group

Too often, what we feel and need is lost, as is how to effectively interact with it. When we are sensing our reality in the moment, we're often doing so outside of language. Being safe with someone and discovering what we feel, need, and the words to make sense of it can be a transformative experience. Yoga, dance, and other embodied, movement-based approaches can be a helpful addition to talk therapy. Exploring our Selves in a safe therapeutic relationship moves the Situation from our nonverbal brain centers, and often specific body parts, to our verbal centers. This is a big step in metabolizing difficult emotions and healing. It helps us communicate authentically. This is connecting with our Selves and others. It is healing, the opposite of trauma.[6] And it is Showing Up.

The therapeutic relationship is designed to create this safe, accepting, open space for us to explore in words and through embodied exercises who we are and why, deepening our Grounding. The unconditional positive regard of the relationship allows us to experience Alltelligence. As our lived experience of feeling accepted, approved of, cared for, and

2. What did I notice that was unusual, pleasing, or unsettling? Why?
3. What has been repeatedly coming to mind lately? Why?
4. What has been challenging me? Why?

Feel free to try them or see how it feels to start writing whatever is top of mind for you. The goal is to make a practice of actively exploring our experiences. Issues repeatedly confronting us reveal what we need to explore to better understand ourselves. They're the ones that stay with us until we sufficiently process them. They're all windows telling us something important about ourselves that we may not appreciate. A saying I like about this is, "What we resist is our path." When we don't take the time to understand it, we feel ungrounded. When we think it through, especially in the focused process of writing, we're creating a sense of order.

A Few Important Tactical Guidelines

I suggest you choose a specific place to journal and do so at least three days a week. Keep it consistent. Set time aside. Have a specific book handy with a pencil or pen of choice, sufficient light, and distance from distractions. I do not look at text or email when I journal and recommend you either silence notifications or keep your devices far away. The most important part is to start. Then do it again. And again. Here's the summary of how to get started.

- Set aside fifteen to twenty minutes. Have your journal and pencil/pen (or device) ready.
- Sit in a private, personalized place, free from distractions.
- Write at a regular time and place.
- Know it's private, just for you. Grammar, spelling, and phrasing are unimportant. So don't get stuck on any of this. No one is judging you. Draw pictures, designs, anything that helps express the situation and your feelings about it.

and had better physical health than those who excluded their feelings. They visited the student health center half as often as those writing just about facts of the situation but excluding feelings.[3] Journaling also releases working memory by helping us develop coherent narratives about events. This reorganizes and structures our memories, resulting in more adaptive, flexible, and supportive views.

When we physically write with pen and paper, our brain processes the information more thoroughly. It's a heavier mental lift than typing, talking to a friend, or being in our heads, so we understand and retain more. Writing is slow. There are no racing thoughts at a pace of one word every two to three seconds. Slowing our thoughts relaxes us.

College students learned more when writing notes than when typing them. The writers "had a stronger conceptual understanding and were more successful in applying and integrating material."[4] Beyond this, written goals are 20–40 percent more likely to be achieved than unwritten ones, even if we put the paper in a drawer and never read it again.[5] All this supports how and why journaling offers a significant opportunity to better ground ourselves in who we are and how we choose to Show Up.

Wondering What to Write?

Journaling can start with documenting what comes to mind (stream-of-consciousness journaling) or experiences of the day (daily-events journaling), or you can dive into something that pops up for you often, such as a troubling situation or relationship. Gratitude journaling focuses on what we appreciate and is proven to boost feelings of well-being. A few prompts are below to help you get started.

Journaling Prompts

1. What did I appreciate about today (or the past few days)?

to draw conclusions and choose actions. Getting our experiences out of our heads and bodies and being with them as we write is a highly effective tool to deepen our Grounding. It slows us. It heals feelings of busyness, distance, and estrangement. It creates safety. And it makes us naturally patient and compassionate with our experience. This reconnects us as we explore and recreate our lived experiences at a safe distance within our Selves.

Journaling links our past, present, and future Selves. This helps us get out of our own way. It reestablishes us as the agent of own journeys. It's us being there for our Selves, without social pressure or an audience. It's why people tell me their inner critic and imposter syndrome fade when they journal.

The written word also challenges us to clarify our lived experience, making it concrete. Sitting to write pulls us into a focused state, prompting mindfulness with the benefit of perspective. It can be cathartic, fortifying our identity. It also helps us regulate emotions, evoking confidence.

Significant medical and neurobiological research supports the dramatic physical and emotional benefits of journaling. It literally changes our brain and is known to impact more than a dozen tangible components of well-being including the following:[1]

- Health: reducing stress, blood pressure, depressive symptoms, post-traumatic intrusion and avoidance symptoms; improving immune system, lung, and liver functioning; and reducing work absenteeism
- Overall: improved mood, working memory, sporting performance, grade point averages, reemployment after job loss, and feelings of well-being[2]

One of the earliest systematic tests of journaling was conducted by James Pennebaker at the University of Texas, Austin. He found that students who wrote about the details of a deeply personal experience, including the facts and their feelings, felt happier and more optimistic

- **Leadership:** The concept of Showing Up itself boosts the magnetism people feel for us by leading us to relate more human to human. It orients us to "feel with" and to relate with unconditional positive regard. These experiences are reinforcing and contagious. We can infuse them into our business cultures, customer acquisition strategies, and societal impacts.

TOOLS TO DEEPEN OUR SKILLS

The three Show-Up skills are well tested as sources of achieving and flourishing. This has led to a depth of research and proven approaches, helping us become better at each and at Showing Up in general. The methods I've reserved for this chapter are among of the best I've come across through my thirty-plus years of research, interviews, and putting the exercises to work. And they're heavy hitting. They are not whispers. They are scientifically proven ways to fortify, extend, and strengthen our skills. They help us utilize our more integrative attention system of the right hemisphere that connects us with a bigger picture and reads our social world. I hope you find them to be good additions to your arsenal, or a starting place for Showing Up as you choose, more often.

For clarity I've loosely categorized the recommended practices by skill, although they each fortify all skills and roles in which we Show Up.

GROUNDING

Three ways to deepen our inner strength, solidness, and clarity are journaling, working with a therapeutically focused practitioner, and the in-the-moment check-in, "How am I Showing Up?" We'll start with journaling since it's familiar, powerful, and quick to start.

Journaling

We can't process all our emotions in the moment, let alone metabolize them. We need to break down impactful Situations and do so with space

What else are you doing?
What else do you want to be doing?

Now it's time to congratulate yourself for practicing Showing Up! Let's zero in on the gains.

- How are these practices helping you be more of who you want to be and to achieve your goals?
- What would support you in sustaining them?

SHOWING UP IN BUSINESS

Ways to apply Show-Up thinking in business and leadership are provided throughout the book. Here's a quick list of a few for reference.

- **Sales:** Eddy in Chapter 4 shows how to use Grounding, Readiness, and Alltelligence to boost sales and business development of all kinds.
- **Negotiation:** Toward the end of Chapter 5 is an example of "Winning a Contract with Help of Showing Up," explaining how a negotiating team strategized by plotting the other team's Show-Up skills on the target, helping them anticipate roadblocks and craft an insightful approach.
- **Managing, Collaboration, and Communication:** Chapter 5 also explains how the continuum naturally prompts us to safely communicate our and others' Show-Up levels any day or over time. To collaborate more effectively, team members can plot themselves on a single continuum on the wall, amid a busy, burn-out-risking project. Knowing everyone is pushed toward limits, it's valuable to know where each other stands, and who needs relief. This approach creates emotional safety by supporting authentic communication.

- Feeling generally kinder, more worthy, accepting of your self and others?

- Do you want to keep it going? If so, what would help you do this?

Here is a list of Show-Up practices. Circle the ones you're using, starting with our example above. Are you doing the following:

1. Asking yourself, "How am I Showing Up?" (right now) or "How am I choosing to Show Up?" (to that future event)?
2. Noticing how you're Showing Up?
3. Using the continuums? Perhaps they're in your mind, reminding you to choose how you Show Up. Perhaps you're writing them in a notebook or on a whiteboard to remind you.
4. Considering what pulls you toward Level 2 or Level 1, and what Show-Up practices will help you avoid it?
5. Prioritizing activities and people to Truly Show Up for?
6. Identifying when and with whom Just Showing Up is a good way to go?
7. Noticing your choice (intent) for upcoming activities?
8. Noticing how others Show Up?
9. Choosing the priority of your Self and Societal roles for a current or upcoming Situation?
10. Recognizing levels of Grounding, Alltelligence, and Readiness in other people's behaviors?
11. Recognizing levels of Grounding, Alltelligence, and Readiness in your own behavior?
12. Planning your level of skill for an upcoming Situation?
13. Doing things to be more Ready, more Grounded, or more Alltelligent?
14. Using the model to help you recognize and move past personal challenges, such as feeling judged, unworthy, afraid, inauthentic, overly driven or too socially conscious?

6. **Through these choices we create our personal and collective legacy. We create our happiness and sense of meaning. And we create our culture, companies, and all systems in which we're living.**
7. **Embracing nature's model of how humans are designed to Show Up orients us in service of others and Society, elevating our sense of belonging, meaning, and purpose. In doing so, we're creating the Society we want.**

This is the big picture. Keeping it in mind helps us naturally put it to work.

Now here's the rest of the closing chapter.

BUILDING ON WHAT WE'RE ALREADY DOING

Our next step is to identify what we're already doing. I'll prompt you with a set of questions below. Then we'll explore other proven tools and approaches. Have a pen or pencil handy. Answering the questions is practicing Showing Up and will help you create a toolkit or roadmap that works for you. We're designing our way forward, testing and revising as we go. There's no wrong answer. There's no risk. There's just test and learn, like Showing Up itself.

You're probably practicing Showing Up at least a little bit. Let's capture this valuable progress before we go further. For example, people tell me, "The moment I learned the concept, I couldn't get it out of my head. Now the question pops up throughout the day: 'How am I choosing to Show Up?' It makes me feel different, more relaxed and open, and I know the question has done it's work." If this is you, let's take note of it.

- What benefits have you experienced?
  - Feeling more connected to others, less alone, more supported?

We Are:

1. **Designed to live interconnected lives.**
2. **Always Choosing**—consciously and not.
3. **At a Level of Showing Up**—either Barely There (Level 1), Just Showing Up (Level 2), or Truly Showing Up (Level 3). We dynamically move across these levels all day and across years and seasons of our lives.

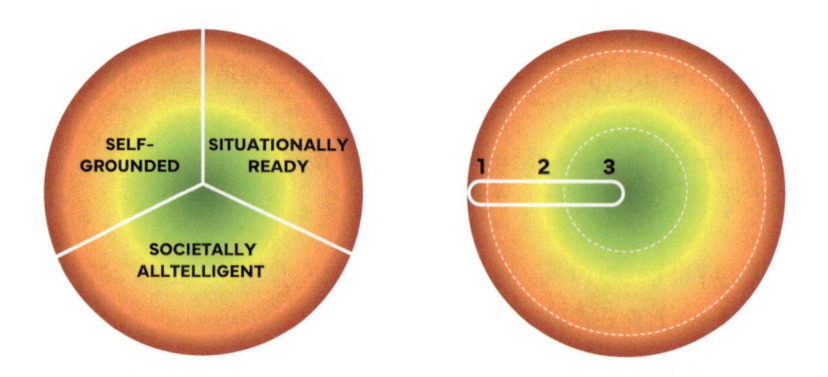

BARELY THERE	JUST SHOWING UP	TRULY SHOWING UP
SELF-FOCUS	NOTICING ▶ TUNING-IN	FEELING WITH ▶ ENACTING CARE
SELF	SELF + SITUATION MEMBER	SELF + SITUATION + SOCIETY MEMBER

Lower:
- GROUNDING
- READINESS
- ALLTELLIGENCE

Higher:
- GROUNDING
- READINESS
- ALLTELLIGENCE

4. **Always Prioritizing Our Three Roles**—How Self-focused, Situationally focused, and Societally focused are we choosing to be?
5. **And Depth of Skill in Each**—Self-Grounding, Situational Readiness, and Societal Alltelligence.

when achieving feels hard, just as I did. Focusing on the concept of Showing Up, or the continuum, can keep things simple and useful. I hear things like, "Marcy, just knowing I have a choice makes such a difference!" Others point to the three roles and relate personal patterns that trip them up at work and home. A common one is, "Knowing our three roles helped me see I struggle with Alltelligence at work, struggle in staying open to colleagues, and get tripped up with low Grounding at home. I can be tired and impatient with my kids and spouse. It's helpful insight." Both these readers used Showing Up to step back and see a bigger picture. This is a huge step forward.

When it comes to specific recommendations, much of how to practice Showing Up has already been described in the flow of past chapters. I hope you have been testing the ideas and practices along the way. Showing Up is a way of being at least as much as a set of tactical tools to help us get there. As much as I'd like to offer you a pill or quick fix to help you Show Up more as you choose, in reality, I cannot.

> **Our progress in Showing Up, like all meaningful endeavors, comes from reflecting. The simple act of sitting with these concepts, reviewing them in your mind, is a perfect start. Sharing them with your journal, family members, or friends is also progress. The idea is to sense how they may help you step back, relax, and see situations more broadly, bringing you into closer contact with people and experiences, adding meaning to your life, and adding meaning to the lives of those around you.**

Reviewing Showing Up is easy. The core concepts are right up front in Chapters 2 and 3. If you want the minimal, CliffsNotes version, here it is.

I didn't write a thing. I couldn't. Now, months later, I realize why. It's an ugly truth. I didn't like what I saw. I Just Showed Up.

Here's my reality. I often Truly Show Up for work activities but too often JSUP with family. It's something I heard often from people I spoke with. But I wasn't admitting I do it too. This made me deeply sad. My parents are elderly. Moments with them, always precious, are requiring ever-more acceptance of their senior predispositions. Additionally, my daughters and I are early in a process of reconnecting following the divorce of their father and I. Both are priority areas in my life. How can something be both a priority and a default space?

To curtail the sadness, I jumped off it and didn't write. Protecting myself from feeling disappointed, I simply resolved to do better tomorrow and start my Show-Up log then. It was a classic example of separating from my Self to avoid painful emotions. Needless to say, the month went by. Had I stayed with the sadness a few moments longer, granting myself the gift of connecting with the feeling, perhaps I would have learned. But I didn't. (Low Grounding)

Now I realize the log didn't start because I didn't want it to. I wasn't Ready to confront myself with dropping the ball like this, despite all my work to the contrary. But that's exactly what I did.

Months later I see that simply knowing I was defaulting is a huge insight. It has given me the power to practice Showing Up more effectively. I learned that keeping the levels in mind can be enough. I'm maintaining dual awareness more often. And I'm far more accepting of the natural flow up and down the levels all day.

I started a new Show-Up log recently. It's going well.

YOUR OWN "HOW TO"

Many readers have told me they relate to my mistake. They, too, try to achieve too much too fast. And they're guilty of putting goals aside

confession. It's a classic case of trying to do too much at once and losing sight of the big picture. Sound familiar? It led to temporary failure—helping me succeed. Here's how I Showed Up.

MY CONFESSION— THE UNWRITTEN CHAPTER

To come clean, right here, right now (boy this feels vulnerable), I'll admit there was supposed to be a chapter titled "One Woman's Show-Up Journal." It was going to be excerpts from my nightly log on how I Showed Up that day. The idea was for us to all live "a day in the life" of someone working diligently to truly Show Up, someone with decades of practice and deep intent to get it right in real life, not just on paper.

It proved to be an incredibly humbling experience. How could I not have known? I scheduled it to be December 1–31, 2021. I was all set. My journal was by the bed. My calendar read "Thirty-Day Show-Up Journal" at 9 p.m. nightly. Reflecting in bed is a common practice for me, so I thought it was a dependable plan. And if it didn't work that day due to mothering responsibilities (I have two school-age daughters in the house), I had a strong backup plan. A few times a week I review my endless do-list and catch up on over-due activities, or at least start to. So the plan felt relatively safe.

How'd it go? Well, if you've checked the table of contents, you've noticed that the chapter doesn't exist. Sigh. December 1 came and went. Then the second, then third. I reoriented my effort to be three weeks of Show-Up journal. Then two. Then one. Yes, I know this is akin to "moving the goal posts," but I was determined to get it done. "And sometimes setting a smaller goal, like one push-up, is all we need to get started," I optimistically told myself. How naive I was.

Finally, as the end of the month approached, I stepped back. Time to register reality. This is hard. But what, *exactly*, is so hard? And why? I realized that each night I was doing a quick mental check-in about how I showed up. I actually did it! I did what I set out to do—reflect on how I Showed Up that day. But it stopped there…five seconds in.

CHAPTER 12

SO...HOW DO WE LIVE A SHOW-UP LIFE? AND...A CALL TO ACTION

This chapter leads you through the following ideas:
- My confession: the unwritten chapter
- Your own "How To"
- The finished puzzle
- Building on what we're already doing
- Proven practices
- A targeted way to get started
- Our clarion call

I'VE DESIGNED THIS CHAPTER to be an on-ramp to help you put Showing Up to work in the ways most effective for you. It's part confession, part workbook, and part proven recommendations. The idea is for you to use these pieces to you build your own toolkit, making Showing Up as you choose easy and successful.

To help you avoid my mistake and to keep it real, I'll start with a

MAKING IT EASIER TO SHOW UP AS WE CHOOSE

12 SO...HOW DO WE LIVE A SHOW-UP LIFE? AND...A CALL TO ACTION

PART IV

CHOOSING How We Show Up

This is where the rubber meets the road. Be ready.

1. What choices are you making right now about your future level of Alltelligence? (What do you want it to be?)

2. How will you live into these choices? (What will you do?)

REFLECTING QUESTIONS—ALLTELLIGENCE

Individually Showing Up

1. In what ways do you demonstrate higher Alltelligence?

2. In what ways do you demonstrate lower Alltelligence?

3. How well does your Alltelligence Show Up for you? (Rate it one to ten. 1=low, 10=high)

4. How does your Alltelligence Show Up?
    a. In what thoughts and emotions?
    b. In what behaviors?
    c. In what situations?
    d. With which people?
    e. With what preparation?

5. What could you do to be more Alltelligent?

Societally Showing Up

1. How would the world be different if people showed up more Alltelligent?

2. How big an impact would it make?

3. Who, specifically, do you want to see deepen their Alltelligence?

4. What systems (e.g., educational, corporate cultures, governmental policies, etc.) would you want to become more Alltelligent?

5. What do you plan to do about this?

LOW	HIGH
EMOTIONAL	
Often feels disconnected from others and the broader community.	**Feels a sense of belonging** and connectedness with others and the broader community. Attunes to others' emotions.
Can be equally negative or abrasive as neutral or positive.	**Is more likely to be positive** or neutral than negative.
INTELLECTUAL	
Thoughts are mainly individualistic, Self-centered, and dismissive of others' interests.	**Tending toward broadmindedness** and systems thinking.
The world is **fundamentally competitive**. Win/lose mentality. Zero-sum game thinking.	**Thoughts are naturally inclusive,** cooperative, and supportive of others' interests.
SOCIAL	
Not driven to work with others.	**Driven to support others.**
Episodically engaged/average performance (e.g., "The company doesn't care about me, so why should I care?").	**Typically highly engaged. Personally dedicated and attuned within social situations.**

7. When we fail to attune to others, or to our beliefs about the world, we cannot show up as we choose.

SUMMARY OF LOW AND HIGH ALLTELLIGENCE

This table lists the extremes of low and high Alltelligence. They apply to every aspect of our lives and can be applied to organizational processes and systems across Society.

LOW	HIGH
BEHAVIORAL	
Behaves with little or inconsistent positive regard, compassion, and shared responsibility for others and more broadly.	**Behaves with unconditional positive regard,** compassion, and shared responsibility for others.
Does not naturally reach out to engage, support, or to care for others.	**Actively reaches out** to engage, support, and care for others.
Lives with a generalized mistrust, assuming others are Self-centered (e.g., "Cover your back." "You gotta do what you gotta do." "It's a dog-eat-dog world").	**Generally trusting,** assuming others are on their team and people can be counted on (e.g., "People are generally good.").

CHAPTER 11 SUMMARY— ALLTELLIGENCE

1. Alltelligence is our reciprocal, symbiotic connectedness within Society and natural systems beyond our Selves. It's the skill native to our role of Societal member.

2. Alltelligent behavior and beliefs are rooted in the innate interdependence of human beings, including that we create and bear responsibility for each other's well-being. Alltelligence is founded on scientific, medical, biological, and evolutionary realities that our survival and thriving is a communal process.

3. These beliefs lead us to trust and care for each other, creating mutual positive regard, and making Alltelligence a fundamental leadership skill as well as asset for a healthy, successful life.

4. Low Alltelligence is an outcome of the separateness and individuality inherent in today's culture. It is a source of America's social biases, injustice, mental-health epidemics of loneliness, anxiety, depression, among others, as well as workforce disengagement.

5. Most leadership and personal improvement approaches underrate the significance of the systems view of Self and Societal interconnectedness. Our lives presence to others, across all our Situations. They exist within and outside of us as individuals.

6. Together with Grounding and Readiness, Alltelligence is a core part of our behavioral infrastructure. It's part of our cognitive and psychological skeleton. It scaffolds our experience. We bring it into the room with us always.

As a majority of us live with more Alltelligence, the result will be nothing short of a more peaceful, supportive, healthy, happy, and sustainable world. This makes Alltelligence a worthy pursuit not just for individuals, but for communities, companies, governments, and countries.

little about the rest of who he is as a person. This suggested he was not identifying with his deeper Self and the breadth of who he is, at least not during the duration of our visit.

Readiness: Low

Despite a first date being a very other-centered activity, Chad did not show any signs he readied himself for the Situation beyond being dressed acceptably, getting there on time, and knowing my name.

He didn't prepare questions or specific thinking for our time together. It's hard to identify any forethought, planning, or preparation that Chad may have done. His mind game seemed to be completely missing. You'd think he would have tried to put his best foot forward. Sure, it's possible he wasn't all that interested in me from the get-go, but our Zoom visit the previous week suggested otherwise.

Like Self-Grounding and Situational-Readiness, Alltelligence is a core part of our behavioral infrastructure. It's part of our cognitive and psychological skeleton. It scaffolds our experience. We bring it into the room with us always. When we fail to attune to our beliefs about the world, we cannot Show Up as we choose. A closed mind, bias and judgment can quickly take hold of us. This is how the structural role of Alltelligence fortifies our Showing Up. It vitalizes our grounding in who we are. And it supports positive interaction, making us more ready.

This makes Alltelligence an essential skill for us to perform at our best and a cardinal component of every effective leadership and performance system.

CHAD'S SHOW-UP SCORE: 2

BARELY THERE   **JUST SHOWING UP**   **TRULY SHOWING UP**

Alltelligence: Low

In this situation, Chad Showed Up significantly Self-absorbed. His world was sad, small, and closed. He was disconnected from me, and likely most others, from the beginning. He allowed one topic and his sadness about it to dominate our experience together. The impact on me seemed to be far from his mind. This suggested no effective forethought about how he might influence me, despite our meeting being a first date. And he was neither emotionally nor intellectually open to getting to know me, while sharing little about himself beyond that one topic.

Had Chad explained his Situation and then tried to relate with me about it, perhaps with a question—"Where does your family live?" "Have you been far from them for an extended period?" "How did you manage to stay present in each other's lives?"—this would have demonstrated higher Alltelligence. I did indeed live for twenty years in Silicon Valley, in addition to living in Shanghai, Geneva, and Munich while my family was in New York. All fertile ground for mutually relating. But for the duration of our time together, Chad felt like a closed, inwardly facing, solitary soul unable to break free from the tethers of his chosen theme. His performance meandered between Just Showing Up and Barely There.

Grounding: Low

Chad was protecting himself from the pain of not living the life he ideally wanted, near his family and friends. While he seemed to recognize his challenge and was interested in being happier, he shared a self-defeating narrative of his own design. It's his handiwork, fabricated in sorrow and helplessness. It not his truth. Yet he created a seemingly pervasive, permanent, and deeply personal hole for himself. But he's not stuck. His defeating victim-world is a story, not a fact. Just like all our stories.

Why did he choose this Barely There state for himself, and Just Showing Up situation for us? Because, I rationalized, that night he wasn't ready to choose anything else. It was who he was, right there, right then, absent of forethought. Options of more sanguine Selves and stories had yet to ascend.

His diamonds remained in the ground.

Perhaps I could have helped. Perchance a worthy question could have tripped his emotions into a new space and time, a more joyful matter around which to converse. Surely, I could have animated him anew with a little focus and fortitude. Did I fail us as well?

Of course I did. It takes two.

I could have stepped into a sniper's mind, keenly targeting a favorable topic, part of a well-practiced plot to engage my suitor. But how to hit a target in the fatigued, emotionally drained darkness?

For Chad, formerly Mr. Particularly Promising, I chose to give up. No need, amid our tired track, to dig for his glory. I'll let myself off the hook. I'll slink out the back door. After all, if he chose, however consciously, to present this mind-numbingly lackluster sliver of himself, it was clearly time to make a polite escape.

"Soccer practice is over soon," I told him. "I need to get going. Thank you so much for coming to meet me," I said. "I feel your sadness and hope you feel better. Good night." Then I jogged away.

Later I realized Chad's initial physical presence had chemistry written all over it...even more of a loss. My learning? Next time be ready and more assertive in keeping dialogue on a promising track. Be perched and ready to insert levity, laughter, and joy, my chosen Alltelligence. If guys aren't going to bring a prepared, nimble mind, I will. (Readiness and Grounding)

Sigh, given how fatigued I felt, it was 8:15 p.m. by then, I started emotionally heading for the door. Mr. PP, my Dapper Date masquerading as Ample Prospect, finally left Chicago wistfulness behind. But it was too late. And his go-to new topics were, well... I'll let you judge: ...kids' tech addition, school from bed in Covid-times, irksome driving patterns, favored drinks, a messy home and car and generally disorganized mind, all expressed in stunning monotone with wanton abandon. I call this "droning on about simplicities." It's not a prized pastime, especially when dispensed via a mutter and paced with minimal pauses.

Even his body was strangely still, except for his mouth. It was Grammy-caliber nonengagement. Even more so, it was the opposite of engagement. A-engagement? Un-engagement? Intra-engagement? (That's engaging with oneself, I think...and not the good kind.) What transpired between us was less one-on-one and more one-on-nothingness. His presence was inert. This was Date-as-Persona. I felt I was more with culture or context than with the unique contribution we each make to it. Was I supposed to relate? Was he hoping to be affirmed?

Oh wait! He's leaning forward a bit! Is he about to remember he's not alone? I felt oddly concerned. Might he ask my opinion about something? Stress and surprise overcame me. I'm woefully unprepared to mask my astonishment about the past ninety minutes. He shifted his position, then leaned back. Silent. Whoa! That was a close one.

What an experience! Ninety minutes of rapt attention, and we didn't get to know each other. The night was a track and a closed door in my face. My compassion was exhausted. It morphed into disbelief, then subtle anger. Dismissed! That's how I felt. Irked, unappreciated, and dismissed.

He had so many choices that night. A bit of conscious choice could have changed everything. How about, "Marcy, I need to sprint a lap to reset my mind. I'll be back!" Or before we met, he could have explained he was missing his family, and preferred to have our first date another time. Guess he lacked this skill. My post-compassion thinking continues...I feel for you, Chad, but at the same time, how self-absorbed?

His mind was a collective echo chamber, generously reverberating

I paused too and wished we knew each other well enough for a hug to feel appropriate. Since we met just twenty minutes before, I was limited. My expression, frozen body, and attention was all I had to give.

He said again, "It's okay. I like New York and am fine here."

Ummm, really? Is this proclamation your way of convincing yourself of this not-quite-trueness? I wondered.

LAP 3

We switched to clockwise and commenced another four laps. This was the pivot point of the night, our chance to fan the dwindling embers of a potentially promising first date. Back to my narrow lens, brimming with predefined hopes and unjust appraisal. And this is despite pre-date meditation and music, my predetermined Readiness plan.

So, I switched the topic, wanted to learn something new. I asked about his work. Anything in finance interests me. My time on Wall Street created a lattice of experience on which to hang new knowledge. This speeds learning, making the topic rewarding. No such luck. I got meager responses. Mere snippets. He just couldn't get there with me. His mind and heart and family and friends were, are, and will remain in Chicago.

Roots in Chicago became the Broadway show of the night. All songs, dances, plotlines, minor characters, and exultant scenery aggregated into a final number called "Date with Chad Goin' South."

Absent was the classic first-date chatty ping-pong of reciprocal get-to-know-you stats. Kids, work stuff, current-life topics, and goals were all omitted, deprioritized by one dominating Just-Show-Up reality. Or should I say one *un-chosen* reality? He practically spent the night trying to talk himself into something untrue.

If there are three primary ways in which humans interact, conversations, transactions, and collaborations, he invented a noninteractive fourth space. Wow! Perhaps I wasn't giving him credit. He just invented the two-way soliloquy! Indeed, learning lurks around every corner... or curve, in the case of our track.

"But with my ex in a good job nearby and son in high school, it doesn't appear a Chicago move is in the cards."

He seemed to be telling me he was deeply unhappy, didn't want to be here, and doesn't plan to change his outlook. Well, that's a shame. And it came out within minutes of the start of our date. *Quite the decision!* I thought, or nondecision. *Such classic Just Showin' Up*, I thought. Why would he do that? Let's just shut the door before it opens. Why bother meet people when you want to be somewhere else?

Either truly work to accept what is or hatch a transition plan…or both! Doesn't seem like rocket science my suave, curly-haired friend. In thirty-six months your son will be in college, and you're free to go. Why not experience the northeast to the fullest between now and then while having friends and family keep their eye out for the perfect new home in Chicago? Seems clear enough to me.

Perhaps he was Barely There, so unhappy he couldn't see past his nose, and that's why he was presenting himself as being devoid of thought in terms of what came out of his mouth. It's perfectly reasonable to look for women open to living in Chicago or, even better, who would prefer it! Why not? Either way, it wasn't me. I had just gotten to New York. My family is here, and I didn't welcome a relationship with someone shortsighted, sad, and wistful about how to spend their, and my, time.

Putting my instinctual, Just Showing Up judgment aside, perhaps he was simply being authentic and forthright with me. Perhaps I created an accepting space that he felt safe stepping into with his truth? I decided to expand my lens past our date, and into an image of two souls sharing our truth on a beautiful evening. It felt kinder, and more human. I glanced at Chad again. No harm done.

This family-in-Chicago topic, however finite and bounded it may seem, became the gift that kept on giving. He explained how his best friends of all time are out there. But he maintains close contact with them nonetheless, and it's really okay that he's here. Chad stopped walking. The whole track seemed to freeze. Sad, gloomy red rubber morphing to blue. It seemed a bit softer then, more caring.

LAP 1

"What? You got your teenage son to sweep the garage? And he does other chores? I'm so impressed! How do you do it?" I asked.

"He lied. That's how. It was not a bad lie, just that he had showered when he hadn't one night. He's a really good kid...was just tired that night."

"How did you address it?"

"I just asked a few questions that uncovered what happened. He admitted it. And I told him lying is one of those things we just don't do, so he was being punished, a rarity in our home. We rely on natural consequences, not punishment. When he heard punishment, he felt terrible, knew he had disappointed me."

"Well done, Chad. It shows the depth and quality of your relationship."

We paused to appreciate the moment, switching from looking ahead at the track toward each other. *What a friendly face,* I thought. Smiling eyes. Interested. Kind. Energized discussion. Common interests. Pertinent topics, all punctuated with pauses for eye contact and appreciation. All sounds pretty good so far, I know.

Then, with the next topic, the tone shifted. Good thing the end of soccer practice hovered just ahead. We're lookin' at an 8:30 p.m. wind-up, like it or not, complete with swift "time to go!" or, truer to my perspective, "your time is up!"

Along the way, however, was a taxing and torrid tale. Here's the summary.

LAP 2

As we meandered around counterclockwise, pausing to be with each other instead of the track, Mr. PP (Particularly Promising) explained, "My family lives in Chicago. My folks, sister, brother, each with two kids, other relatives, all my college buddies...they ask all the time when I'm moving back..." His tone was somber and turned a bit ironic with the "when I'm moving back" part.

Subjective Indicators of Our Alltelligence:

1. How often do you feel alone or lonely?
2. How connected do you feel with people in general, for example, to your mother, father, siblings, children, partner, friends, or colleagues?
3. How open to others do you feel in general? For example, how often do you hear what people say without applying judgment? The more open we are, the more nonjudgmental we are, allowing us to let people in, feeling them and allowing them to feel us.
4. How unified do you feel with nature?

Here's a fun first-date story that exemplifies how Alltelligence can play out.

READINESS ENCOUNTER— MY DATE WITH CHAD

The Person: There he was. Prompt. Wearing a smile, dark curls, stylish jacket, well-fitting jeans, running shoes. Suave. Reserved. Well-proportioned. And, from a previous call, I learned successful in business. Good start. (They all seem to start well...)

The Purpose: This is a first date. Need I say more?

The Experience: We met at a high school track at 7 p.m. near my daughter's soccer practice, both pleased to swap cocktails for burning calories. I had done enough cocktailing last night with Mr. Right Now and suffered a crappy night's sleep to pay for it. So the track was my dear, caring friend that night. Chad and I were set up well.

Then he led me up the mountain, and just as I was anticipating the vista, dense clouds blew in. Was he tired? Medicated? Insecure? Determined to come across as an unassuming coat rack? All of the above? Here's what happened.

3. Which Situations and people bring it out?
4. How can we do more of it?

> As we review the depth of our interrelatedness, its direct impact on our thoughts, feelings, and actions becomes apparent. We feel its impact in our business meetings, during walks in the park and friendly chats. Our depth of Alltelligence guides whether we get off the couch at all. Ultimately, if deep down we're alone, making achieving hollow, why bother?
>
> In contrast, are you someone who naturally keeps up with old friends, easily connects with people, and enjoys the spirited nature of life? The belief system underlying these favorable experiences is Alltelligent. The more top of mind it is, the more we'll naturally live into it.

MEASURING IT

Concrete indicators of our and others' Alltelligence include things such as:

Objective Indicators of Our Alltelligence:
1. Do people say you're a good listener?
2. Do people come to you when in need of an ear or advice?
3. Do you find yourself participating in community events or doing kind things for people?
4. Professionally, do you prioritize people over tactical business needs?

consistent with what we experience in the observable world, which is that "-telligence," knowingness and capability, doesn't exist anywhere exclusively. It's not derived solely from the inside out or outside in. And it doesn't derive singularly from any one place or person. Human and societal "-telligence" is not a finite, dead, square box. It's not capable of being somewhere in particular while nowhere else, all the while stingy and scarce. This is just not the way the world works. And we all know it. The truth is closer to "-telligence" as a living quality. The world's skill and knowledge are a facet and feature of nature and the world itself. This means it's an ever-evolving process. And it's in all of us and everything. That's why Alltelligence feels more honest, integrous, and accurate as the skill native to our role as Societal members.

EVER-PRESENT CHALLENGES TO ALLTELLIGENCE

All our encounters—with media, ideas, people, workspaces, and places—travel through our choice level of Alltelligence. And they influence it endlessly. One could argue these ever-present forces challenge it more than bolster it. What sense of oneness for a mutually reinforcing, symbiotic humanity can we really maintain when our movies and daily news feeds numb us to violence, war, biases, and generalized disregard? How well do we maintain, marinate, or mature a semblance of Alltelligence when compelled to compare, compete, and consume? All this opposes the warm contentment and fun we experience from relating deeply with each other.

TAKING STOCK

It's worth pausing to consider the following:

1. How consistently do we demonstrate the natural trust, care, and feelings at the core of Alltelligence?
2. Which of our behaviors show it?

> According to one reader, Alltelligence is the "harmony of being self-aware and standing in your truth while also recognizing the state and value of those around you."

The years of downplaying our Alltelligent nature happened innocently enough. Across centuries our community tribes have broken down. The evolution of modern business erected emotional and physical walls between workers and management. Modern work and living within high-rise buildings, reliant on abstracted AI-based processes and efficiency-focused mentalities shelter us from nature and divorce us from the wholistic and unifying perspective of our right-brained attentional system. Our needs are served through products and services as much as (or instead of) fellow humans. And who among us doesn't love our privacy, video-streaming services, phones, and work-from-home flexibility that keep us on our couches at home instead of physically together? Among its value, these benefits also divide us. They distort, darken, and shroud where and how Alltelligence lives within us and our interconnected world. When we lift the cloak—and rinse the mud—we start to recall that it is our unity that sustains us. And it is how we perform best.

WHY "ALLTELLIGENCE"?

You may ask, Why create a word to explain this? Because we need something specific to bring the core ideas together. Starting "telligence" with "all" avoids the connotations and assumptions that accompany the prefix "in." Intelligence implies skills and knowledge originate from and reside in *us*. It's what we all grew up with. But when we step back to consider this, does it make sense? Surely, we as individuals are not the almighty keepers of skill and knowledge.

OUTelligence or extelligence imply the opposite, that skill and knowledge originate and exist outside of us, perhaps in books, media, education systems, and other people. Neither feels particularly

> **Demonstrating Alltelligence**
>
> *I'm in the relationship business. Clients know I'm vested in their success. They see me as a trusted advisor.*
>
> —Michael Silver, executive coach specializing in the financial services industry and cofounder of Focus Partners

Leaders who embrace this reality are the ones we instinctually follow. These are the people we stay late for, focus better for, and live into our best Selves with. They're the teams we don't quit and the ones we refer our friends into. These leaders become the limits of America's mass resignation and quiet quitting. And it's because these Alltelligent leaders are the ones who truly care. They help us be more of who we want to be. They help us respond with creativity and resourcefulness to those unanticipated customer needs that arise in the moment.

This outlook sits us on the same side of the table with others as opposed to against or independent of them. We're now one team.

Vitally, living as one team transcends behavior. It can persist even when others disagree with us or we them. **This perspective is a crucial step toward empathy and action.**[14] **Living this interlocked reality improves how we treat people and our planet. It is integral to performing well. And it is integral to achieving all goals that transcend us as individuals to benefit the greater whole. Climate change is a good example.**

Imagine if employee handbooks and corporate culture statements included Alltelligence. They could say something like, "Company X recognizes our mutual impact on, and accountability for, each other's well-being and success, considering the broad ecosystem of customers, employees, and society in which we all function. At the corporate level we act on this through... At the division level we act on this through... At the individual level we act on this through..."

Despite the substantial evidence supporting Alltelligence as a core success skill, it isn't yet the center of many well-known self-improvement, leadership, and business-growth paradigms. Even well-deserving books that are timeless favorites like *First Things First*, *Strengths Finder* and *Atomic Habits* approach achieving with primarily an individual focus. Their suggested actions and approaches treat us more as individual actors than as nodes in a global, interwoven, Show-Up network. While valuable, relating to our behavior in this classically individualist way omits our essential nature—that our purpose and energy stems from shared wiring on a common, living planet. **Our interrelationships create us. They motivate us. They fund our loyalty, engagement, and performance. Our relationships are the seat of our learning. This means personal-improvement approaches, business cultures, and leadership systems are well served to recognize and utilize this wellspring of achieving far more prominently.**

ALLTELLIGENCE IS LEADERSHIP AND ENGAGEMENT

Our depth of Alltelligence fundamentally frames how we walk into our 9 a.m. Monday meeting and greet our teams, boss, family, and friends. How would you walk in if you believed we're each other's makers and product? I bet we'd be more interested. We'd listen better. We'd be more open to each other's ideas. We'd ask more questions. We'd seek to truly understand. We'd feel secure to be authentic and clear within our and others boundaries. It's the opposite of mistrust, disengagement, quiet quitting, and absence of meaning.

In his *Harvard Business Review* article titled, "What Is a Good Job?" Marcus Buckingham recognizes Alltelligence as a key part of it.[13] He explains a good job is one in which "you sense that your colleagues have your back; you don't experience discrimination...and you have confidence that you'll get help navigating constant changes in the working world." The trust, symbiosis, and mutual care of Alltelligence are present in each of these job characteristics.

> **Watts, "In much of Western culture, the definition of self has been too narrowly circumscribed." We don't stop with the firm boundaries of people we see. We transpire through our energy, emotion, behavior and intent—into each other and the natural world.**

ALLTELLIGENCE COUNTERS BIAS

Accountability and other-centeredness heighten caretaking. We become more patient, tolerant, and open minded. We feel less out-group bias, that subtle sense of being against people different from us. This bias explains so much of our racism, sexism, political divide, and "not like us" mentality. It is measured in children as young as fourteen months old. As mentioned in Chapter 4, explaining the connectivity continuum at the core of Showing Up, fourteen-month-old infants defaulted to an us-and-them state from something as simple as seeing other babies prefer a different cereal from the one they prefer.[12]

> **This is critical to maintain in the forefront of our minds. Human beings, under a state of even minor threat (insomnia? multitasking? micromanaging boss? teenagers at home? in-laws around?) immediately defend ourselves. Now we're in an us-and-them mode, creating in-group out-group distinctions of people we do and don't identify with. And we dislike people we don't identify with. As our bloody history of war proves, we're capable of unkindness, murder, and genocide once we label someone in our minds as "not like us." What if we could wake each day with a bit more Alltelligence, assuming the best of each other, feeling humans' inherent kinship, symbiosis, and reciprocity?**

and other necessities. Rotating leadership daily made all survivors needed, respected, and valuable. Sixteen of nineteen people survived.

Nature

Alltelligence recognizes that humans are facets of our natural world. Flourishing requires we behave in a manner consistent with this. For example, as little as two hours in nature across a week measurably increases feelings of calmness. It raises endorphin levels and dopamine production and boosts happiness. It deepens concentration and attention while simultaneously reducing anxiety, depression, loneliness, irritability, blood pressure, and cortisol (our stress hormone).[8] Wow! Need anyone hear more? Beyond this, even mere "contact" with nature, such as hearing it,[9] is associated with positive social interactions, a sense of meaning and purpose and decreased mental distress.[10] Time in nature is also shown to make us nicer, more cooperative, and generous.[11]

The concept of Alltelligence has existed for centuries in many traditions. Desmond Tutu, the late South African Anglican bishop and theologian, discusses the concept of *ubuntu*. The word is translated as "I am because of you." This mutual, cocreating aspect of Alltelligence dramatically affects how we choose to Show Up by priming partnering through shared responsibility. It even changes how we JSUP by rewiring our default. It doesn't get any more powerful than this.

> Our thoughts, feelings, and actions exist on the same plane as nature itself. We're part of something much larger than us, which many of us innately believe and feel ourselves to be. This belonging within nature's "-telligence" places us in a coevolving system, one we shape and are correspondingly shaped by. It means we are not just "in" the world; we are "of" the world. And, going a step further, we are with and for the world. In the words of philosopher Alan

This goes for becoming rich or poor, sustaining our marriage, drinking alcohol, school grades, whether we vote, smoke, and even our level of altruism and happiness, among many other behaviors, emotions, and conditions specifically tested.

Wow. These examples show how much of our health, success, happiness, and meaning in life is due to the influence we have on each other. Neuroscientists John Cacioppo and Gary Berntson, founders of the field of social neuroscience, describe the human need for social connection as "a biological and social imperative rooted in thousands of years of human evolution."[7] Psychologist Bill von Hippel, author of *The Social Leap*, explains that "we're the only animal on the planet that goes out of its way to share the contents of our minds with others, even when there's no immediate gain."

Doesn't it make sense for performance systems to recognize this and encourage us to live in a way that benefits from this outstanding power? Now, with Alltelligence, we have a word for it and a clear description, making it far easier to measure and implement, helping us Show Up and perform closer to how we choose.

Shipwrecks—Interconnectedness with Communities

Beyond this support for individual interconnectedness is a fascinating example of community interdependence. It comes through the experience of two shipwrecks occurring off the coast of Auckland, Australia, in 1856. Survival was determined by social structure, one Alltelligent, one not. The less lucky twenty-five-person crew of a ship named *Invercauld* was led by Captain George Dalgarno. He created a competitive, "every man for himself" environment. All but five men died. The second ship, the *Grafton*, hit the south side of the same island under the capable leadership of cocaptains Musgrave and Renault. They built an Alltelligent "we need each other" culture. Among other things, they implemented a school where people took turns teaching each other what they could—languages, how to make concrete, shoes,

Here are a few proof points.

- Physically, we bond right through our skin and skulls. In eye-to-eye conversations, our brain waves synchronize in a process called "resonance," leading two people to function as one physical unit. In Japan, one study paired ninety-six strangers who maintained eye contact while MRIs examined their brain activity. The scans showed two brains functioning as a "singular connected system." One brain section called the *inferior frontal gyrus* was active, showing "inter-individual neural synchronization."[4]
- Emotionally, with a one-second touch to a stranger's forearm, we accurately feel what they're feeling about 50 to 60 percent of the time. Yes, you read that right—in one second, and that's when we can't see the person. They were behind a curtain. In the mere blink of an eye, we can absorb someone else's fear, anger, love, gratitude, or compassion. The likelihood of guessing right in this study—done by Dacher Keltner at the Greater Good Science Center at the University of California, Berkeley—was a mere 8 percent. So these weren't guesses. We simply feel what others feel, instantly. And we know, "thanks to neuroscientist Edmund Rolls, that touch activates the brain's orbitofrontal cortex, which is linked to feelings of reward and compassion."[5] This drives us to help each other and demonstrates the primacy and inescapable nature of humanity's bond.
- Socially, we mimic others' behaviors, motivations, and goals. One concrete example is Nicholas Christakis's findings, originally referenced in Chapter 2. We're a whopping 45 percent more likely to be obese if our friends are. We're 25 percent more likely if it's our friends' friends, and are 10 percent more likely to be obese if our friends' friends' friends are.[6] As Dr. Christakis tells us, "It's only when you get to your friend's friends' friends' friends that there's no longer a relationship between that person's body size and your own body size."

> Humans are designed to raise our young, sustain ourselves, and thrive in community. It has always been this way, as many Indigenous peoples and religions well know. Alltelligence is living through this evolution-aware lens. It primes our behavior for success and fills our lives with meaning as we dynamically cocreate our and others' achievement, health, and happiness.

WE REVEAL OUR ALLTELLIGENCE EACH MOMENT

A friend in a corporate middle-management job recently explained to me, "Alltelligence leads me to be more vulnerable and authentic, something I'm working on. I engage more with everyone in the room. It's like I'm living with a generosity of spirit, believing in people's basic goodness."

Alltelligence compels us to see another's perspective and to listen empathically. It makes our behavior expansive and our lives engaging by priming us to be open, curious, collaborative, and motivated. All this makes it far easier to Show Up as we choose.[3]

LIVING BEYOND INDIVIDUALITY

> While we live as individuals with names and personalities, outside of this Self-focused Grounding we also relate within Situations, with the ideas, purpose, structure, and environment of those experiences (Readiness). Going the next step beyond ourselves and our Situations, we relate within and across networks of people and environments in one integrated system. Alltelligence recognizes and honors this.

integrated reality is good for employee and corporate performance.

As Angelica describes, her current team's high Alltelligence leads them to feel safe and supported. They bring their best and encourage it in others. They ask, speak up, learn, and try out ideas. It's naturally engaging and uplifting. With moderate to high Alltelligence, we feel accountable for the impact of our behavior on others. This mutual care imbues our interactions with symbiosis and reciprocity. It naturally motivates us today and fortifies us when times are hard.

Beyond the positive relational energy described as a source of success in so many leadership studies, Alltelligence recognizes the roots of how leadership works. It is based on emotional contagion that naturally links us with others and the natural world. **This cohesive worldview extends our experience from Self-Grounding, through Situational Readiness, into Societal Alltelligence. How we live into our native roles and skills designs how we Show Up to each day, activity, and moment of our lives.**

GENERAL DESCRIPTION AND ORIGINS

Alltelligence—connectedness within Society—extends from the experience-dependent way in which humans developed. The physical structures of our brains and nervous systems are crafted through our early interactions with primary caregivers. It's dramatic and obvious in infants but continues throughout our lives. As infants, whether our neurons grow, connect, or wither is a result of the sufficiency of safety and care we receive. When sufficient, our brains become deeply integrated, providing resilience throughout life. It's why "the number one predictor of every measure of well-being is how interconnected our brains are."[2] And it clearly indicates humans are meant to live interdependent lives. Our individualistic, us-them oriented Society reframes our natural bias away from our evolutionary, tribal, collective nature to a more protective, privacy-seeking, lonely world. It's infused with fear and Self-doubt and it isn't healthy because it's not our natural state.

modern culture of discrete individuals explains why Alltelligence is an essential skill helping us reclaim the sense of meaning and happiness many of us are searching for.

A LOW ALLTELLIGENCE CORPORATE CULTURE

"In my last role, I used to second-guess myself endlessly," Angelica explained, "fearing I'd be harshly judged. It was the culture. We were all afraid and sat on our work, searching for a sense that it was adequate, which never came. I would sit on my completed deliverables for days before sending them in. Now I trust my judgment. I'm asking far more questions and feel in touch with what's right. It's so clear and easy now! I get things done much faster!"

She finished with, "Marcy, we're not wasting time. We're not second-guessing. I hadn't realized, in my twenty years of successful career, how many people, including myself, are working within fear and anxieties. I used to think it was smart business to position my work to be supported by the loud voices on the executive team. Now I realize it was a low-Alltelligence leadership team creating fear. And it should have been addressed from the top."

In her past, working in a predominantly competitive culture of individuals (as opposed to a team mentality of "alldividuals") impeded Angelica's confidence, creativity, and even sense of self. The culture was far more "us and them" than integrated, high-performing team. Her work and happiness suffered, along with corporate performance. She explains, "Had Alltelligence been higher, the judgmental leaders would have recognized our deep impact on each other. They would have been encouraged to Show Up more compassionately and supportively." These leadership qualities of compassion and support create positive relational energy. They're affiliated with "substantially higher levels of engagement, lower turnover, and superior shareholder returns exceeding industry averages in profitability and productivity by a factor of four or more."[1] Clearly, living in a manner consistent with our

place of us and them. We feel less emotionally safe. And once unsafe, we defend. The stress of our body's triggered alert systems nudge us to help less, mistrust, disengage, demotivate, and sour on our possibilities. We structure our companies, management hierarchies, roles, incentives, and lives around partial trust, and a divided way of being. But it's neither natural nor healthy to live with sustained vigilance. It's exhausting. And it further challenges our ability to connect with our Selves, our work, our friends, family, Situations, and Society. Ultimately, our modern culture of left-brain-dominated systems and priorities work to detach us from our shared humanness. This leads us to deprioritize our role as members of something beyond our Selves.

> One interviewee describes it this way: "Alltelligence brings us all into the middle, not too Self-focused or too other-focused.
>
> It's so useful to live purposefully in the healthy middle, neither emotionally blind nor overwhelmed by others' stress or the violence in our culture."

When we're upset, we simply shut down our feeling brain, limiting how we experience our body's raw sensations. As Dr. Bessel van der Kolk explains it, people "have very cut off relationships to their bodies" and "may not register what goes on with them...we needed to help people for them to feel safe feeling the sensations in their bodies, to start having a relationship with the life of their organism...we turn these things into these chin-up experiences. We separated ourselves. We divided ourselves." This Shows Up in our choices to busy ourselves, multitask, partially engage, and, of course, Just Show Up. In the absence of trust and care, we're seeking succor and security far more than we're pursuing passions and spreading nourishment.

This works against our naturally Alltelligent, prosocial mindset and behavior. **The conflict between our essential nature and our**

> always existed as members of families, teams, communities, and humanity. This reality designed us, making us inherently interdependent custodians of each other's well-being.
>
> Alltelligence is founded on scientific, biological, psychological, and evolutionary realities that we exist beyond our skin, making each other's health, safety, and happiness a communal process. It functions at the level of humanness, well above race, ethnicity, education, ability, social strata, gender identity—all categories that may be used to divide us. This is why underweighting our Societal role, and perhaps overweighting our Self role, is a source of unhappiness, anxiety, illness, unkindness, and Societal divisiveness.

Like Self-Grounding and Situational Readiness, Societal Alltelligence is a fundamental and formidable creator of our experiences and of our choices, successes, and challenges. It shapes our behavior every moment. Do we feel isolated and separate from others? Are we likely to defend or to unnecessarily compete? Or are we supported and symbiotic? Our answers design how we choose to Show Up and therefore how our culture and Society Show Up.

Humans evolved to survive as one team. Trust and care are in our DNA. It's what naturally arises when people feel safe, supported, and valued. As Angelica described, when we're in it together, belonging creates a wellspring of accountability and generativity. This is Alltelligence.

While Alltelligence is inherent, we need to consciously choose to behave this way today since our culture, language, and systems promote disunity and individuality over unity. The result? We feel alone. Instead of being supported and cared for within an extended tribe, we tend to turn inward toward our Selves and our families. Society becomes a

CHAPTER 11
SOCIETAL ALLTELLIGENCE

This chapter leads you through the following ideas:
- Not competing and not afraid
- Interconnected to survive
- Designed by evolution
- Counteracts separateness and prejudice

HOW ALLTELLIGENCE SHOWS UP

"No one's competing. And we're not afraid," Angelica told me, shortly after starting an executive-level role at a well-known hospitality company. "We're collaborating at a height I've never seen. New ideas are commonly bantered about. There's no judgment, no imposter syndrome. Everyone feels valued. I've never experienced such pure effectiveness." Then she added, "We're here because we want to be, not because we have to. I've even had people call in to meetings from the customs line at the airport when they were still on vacation! Now that's dedication! It's like working in a chorus line of all-stars."

> This is the power of Alltelligence. It is the skill native to our role as members of Society, something larger than our Selves. It is our evolutionary truth. We've

The conflict between our essential nature of interconnectedness and our modern culture of individualism explains why Alltelligence is an essential skill for us to reclaim the sense of meaning and happiness many of us are searching for.

5. What do you do today to support your Readiness?

6. What could you do to be more ready?

Societally Showing Up

7. How would Society be different if people Showed Up more ready?

8. How big an impact would it make?

9. Who, specifically, do you want to see deepen their Readiness?

10. What systems (e.g., educational, corporate cultures, governmental policies, etc.) would you want to see become more ready?

11. What do you plan to do about this?

Choosing How We Show Up

This is where the rubber meets the road. Be ready.

12. What choices are you making right now about your future level of Readiness?

13. How will you live into these choices? (What will you do?)

LOW	HIGH
SOCIAL	
May be nonchalant, aloof, or nervous. May unconsciously push people away or signal something is wrong, potentially instilling fear or concern in others.	**Comfortable. Often socially adept and well liked.** People are drawn to those who are well prepared due to their confidence, ease, and strong showing.
	Attuned to others. Perceptive of behaviors and implicit realities differing from what was expected.

REFLECTING QUESTIONS—READINESS

Individually Showing Up

As you think about an important Situation you routinely engage in, ask yourself the following:

1. In what ways do you feel ready?

2. In what ways are you less ready?

3. How well does your Readiness show up for you? (Rate it one to ten: 1=low, 10=high)

4. How does your Readiness Show Up?
    a. In what behaviors?
    b. In what situations?
    c. With which people?
    d. With what preparation?

	LOW	**HIGH**
INTELLECTUAL	**Often walk in with minimal forethought, preplanning, or direct preparation.** Partial or episodic planning and preparing.	**Regular practice of forethought, planning, and direct preparation**, including cognitive and sensate components. Systematic, dependable planning and preparing.
EMOTIONAL	**Regular unease from not knowing what to expect.** Easily destabilized from situations playing out in unexpected ways due to insufficient consideration.	**Tending toward a sense of ease, confidence, and heightened perceptiveness** within a situation from considering the situations' content, participants as well as emotional, social, functional and spiritual aspects.
BEHAVIORAL	**May be mildly concerned, agitated, or turbulent.** Tending toward inconsistent behavior due to limited forethought.	**Calm, comfortable behavior, seemingly familiar with the situation,** its topics, participants, requirements, and other aspects of the experience. Tending toward dependable behavior.

CHAPTER 10 SUMMARY—READINESSS

1. Readiness is a big idea. It asserts that we can Show Up more prepared for each moment.

2. Readiness is our degree of Situation-specific setup helping us Show Up as we choose. Like a pregame plan, it has a short-term preparing component and a longer-term planning component.

3. Of the three roles and skills, Readiness can be the fastest route to Showing Up better, given its tactical surface layer.

4. Together with Grounding and Alltelligence, Readiness is a core part of our behavioral infrastructure. It's part of our cognitive and psychological skeleton. It scaffolds our experience. We bring it into the room with us always.

5. Practicing Readiness can be as simple as asking the question, "How am I choosing to Show Up right now?" Or it can be strategic, longer-term planning: "How do I want to Show Up?" and "How will I make it happen?"

6. Both preparing and planning have mental and physical components.

7. Readiness is an expiring asset. Once the activity or Situation is upon us, we lose the option to re-prepare. We Just Showed Up, but we can still attune to how we're Showing Up in the moment and adjust as we choose.

SUMMARY OF LOW AND HIGH READINESS

The table on the following page lists the extremes of low and high Readiness. They apply to every aspect of our lives and can be applied to organizational processes and systems across Society.

term. Her current phase of months, if not years, however, is more aligned with Level 2.

> Instead of being owners who manage a team, they were closer to shopkeepers.
>
> Sophie could have a sophisticated career as an attorney but instead is straddling both worlds. This is a perfect setup for her to be overstretched like her parents and her childhood. To maintain equilibrium within her family, she needs to be at their level of success, just like them, and not exceed them. Being more successful would create jealousy or a subtle sense of "I'm better than them," disconnecting her from them. The first step to overcoming this is strong boundaries.
>
> Becoming a lawyer was hedging her bets. She wanted out from the suffering she was taught but isn't fully able to accept it. The framed law degree on the floor is part of it. She can't really enjoy her success while also maintaining her dutiful relationship with her mom and dad.
>
> Sophie's Readiness and Alltelligence are limited by her Grounding. If she understood how she's mimicking the limits of her parents, she'd be more open to trusting employees in the plastics business.

Sophie described the law firm as being unsupportive. It's a place where she can't ask questions and has to rely on herself. While that's likely an accurate description of the culture, she isn't approaching it with a sense of curiosity or openness. She didn't describe working to foster relationships or caring for coworkers inherent in Societal Alltelligence. Her approach to building a team to support the acrylic sign business shows the same "I'm all alone out here" perspective of how people interrelate.

Note: This is a singular Show-Up experience. Like all of us, Sophie Shows Up at different levels at different times in each aspect of her life. She may live in Level 3 more often than not across the longer

While Sophie clearly suffered the costs of her parents' choices, requiring she work when she needed to study and causing her miss out on social life, she had yet to recognize she was treating herself today as they did. She became them. Sophie became her own task master. She was doing her parents' work for them, even as a well-educated, skilled adult.

Stuck in their scarcity narrative, she was its prey, not its predator or governess. Sophie needed to grant herself permission to slow down and make changes, including delegating work misaligned with her chosen career. Until she acts on these insights, she will live at the base of an insurmountable wall sustained by her parents' mindset. When she stops carrying their life's boulders, their feelings of insufficiency, she'll be able to make choices better aligned with her personal goals and interests.

Here we have a clear example of low Grounding limiting our Readiness and Alltelligence. Through her work situation, Sophie is living a Self-focused life. She seems disconnected from her role as Societal member and the potential collaborative solutions to overworking that it likely offers.

Alltelligence: Low

> **Psychoanalyst Comments—Alltelligence**
>
> This is where her fear of success plays out. The power of Alltelligence—it's trust and oneness—is strongest when supported by well-defined boundaries. Sophie doesn't have strong boundaries.
>
> She's deeply and ambivalently connected to her parents, so she can't redefine success as a smooth experience. Doing so would be going against her connection with them. Doing right by them is being really busy, overstretched, and never quite getting there. If she succeeded, she'd create a disconnection with her parents.

direct our discussion to what seems helpful. Yet, no such forethought of her mind, body, thinking or options, seemed to have occurred.

Sophie was clear that she seeks to be "happy and calm." These are specific, measurable targets. That said, neither she nor I raised explicit ways to accomplish either and she didn't ask. Contrary to achieving happiness and tranquility, Sophie didn't seem open to change. She more described challenges than sought a path forward. Readying herself to make our discussion productive would logically include opening herself to consider options, yet I didn't sense such openness. And there was no apparent prewritten or structured thinking which would have focused and prioritized our time together.

If Sophie's needs were to be heard and considered, one could argue she was more ready. But even then, her readiness was through default, not preplanning. She Just Showed Up.

Grounding: Low

Psychoanalyst Comments—Grounding

Sophie's Grounding is impacted by the unconscious belief that life is suffering, and if you're not, you're doing something wrong. Her martyrdom is passed down from her parents. They didn't grow the business enough to hire people, so the family was overtaxed, and she was pressured into both physical labor and emotional discord. Her school priorities and social needs conflicted with her parents' needs. Her mode of operating is to suffer, making it familiar and comfortable for Sophie to live that way. Sophie neither sees this pattern nor allows herself to step out of it.

To theorize what's behind this, we'd need to uncover the family's intergenerational traumatic narrative. Where did the scarcity narrative come from? Even then, insight into the source of an issue is often insufficient to help someone change.

"I feel heard," Sophie said. This was music to my ears. I could tell she felt a with-ness in my presence. We were eye to eye, attuned to each other for the hour, sharing her challenges and suffering. This resonance, our shared Alltelligence, is healing. As we parted, she asked if we could meet again. "Of course!" I responded. The exchange had been a gift for both of us.

SOPHIE'S SHOW-UP SCORE (1-10): 4

BARELY THERE — **JUST SHOWING UP** — **TRULY SHOWING UP**

SOPHIE'S SHOW-UP TARGET

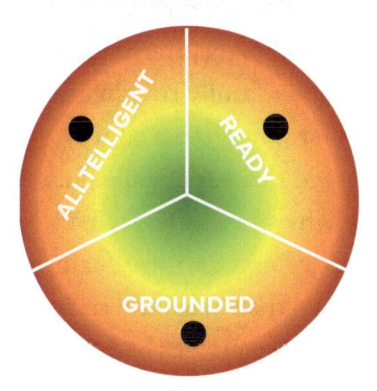

(ALLTELLIGENT / READY / GROUNDED)

Readiness: Low

Sophie Showed Up late, physically disheveled, and breathless. This may have been a subconscious choice since it directly expressed how she was functioning.

Higher Readiness could Show Up a number of ways. For example, as being on time or early, with questions prepared, a calm, focused mind and body, and perhaps some ideas to toss around. She also could have accessed some of my articles, podcasts or other content as a way to

"Guess I have it all. I just can't handle it. Too much of a good thing, as my mother says. Reality is that I think I see it clearly. I just can't get out of it. And I'm miserable, totally drowning. And I'm twenty-seven! I want to meet someone!"

"Sounds like you understand the decisions you've made and a few of their roots. You're playing out exactly what your parents taught you. Take it all on yourself. Just keep pushing…"

"I have to!" Sophie dramatically yelled. It was too loud, even for the café. A few heads looked over. She just told me so much.

"What about stepping back to get perspective and see broader options?"

"What are you taking about???" The irate response stabbed me. *Wow, this feels dangerous*, my body jabbed. *Did I just mess up?* That would be bad. Friendship with Heather suddenly hung in the balance, fragile.

But at the same time, *There we go*, my mind realized. Even pausing to review the situation and recuperate is forbidden fruit and feels irresponsibly indulgent. She's been suffering with overwork and feeling insufficient for so long. Her family couldn't afford a break then. How could she now? She's just not wired that way.

Sophie and I discussed this for a while. She slowly settled, understanding more clearly why she was triggered.

We also talked about timing for introducing a few new people into her business, how to scope their roles and compensate them to create a win-win. Plenty of similar businesses had sprung up on Etsy. It seems she could find experienced people, maybe even some who could teach her a few things. That way she could step back from fulfilling orders. It was something she hadn't permitted herself to consider.

The business wasn't her passion. It was a means to an end and should be developed as such. Sophie seemed open to this perspective. It felt right to her. Law felt more aligned with her interests.

We ended the discussion feeling warm and pleased with our journey together. She was better grounded and more conscious of her choices. Sophie realizes she's been imprisoning herself in a world of time scarcity and Self-depletion while subjugating personal interests. Now she knows better who she was and why.

"I don't care anymore that I don't make it. The bed, I mean. I leave the sheets each morning the way I found them. I feel they understand me. We're both a mess."

"In what ways are you a mess?"

"I just can't do it all. There aren't enough hours in the day."

"Is that what it is? Time?"

"Yes. I have two full-time jobs."

"Which is more fun?"

"Right now? Neither. They both suck."

I sat silently, sensing the suckiness.

"The law firm is everything you hear about. Endless pressure. Everyone is drained. Even after two years, so much is new. I'm always finding my way, needing to ask many more questions than I'm comfortable with. I push the research and discovery as far as I can, then give up and call the partner for help. It feels bad every time.

"I wish asking for help felt better. It's just not how the system is designed. We bill hours, need to make each one count. Training isn't client billable, but there's one partner who seems to sense my dedication, so I go to her."

"That sounds promising," I encourage. "Tell me about the business." I hesitated to leave the topic of needing training but preferred to get the big picture across both jobs before going deeper into one.

"It's a custom plastic-sign business. Basically, the family bought an acrylic cutting machine many years ago. I was in college. I made custom signs at fairs over the summer. They sold well and are high margin. So I kind of took over the website, made signs nights and weekends, and shipped them out. Now the whole business is basically mine.

"About a year ago I rented out a warehouse and bought two more machines to satisfy demand. Thought I'd hire people to run it. But that hasn't happened. Every order is different, needs design help. Plus, I'm using new software to keep up with demand. Someone new would be lost. I'm barely figuring it out. I lay in bed at night wondering when I can get orders made and shipped. All have deadlines… birthdays, events…

The background I had from her mom was that in addition to her role as a litigator in progress, she runs a business that consumes any remaining time and energy. It's a source of significant stress. Endless trial by fire, and she can't—or won't—hire people to help. The pattern perpetuates the one she was raised with, a family business run by Heather and Joe, her parents, ever on the verge of extinction.

Explaining those days, she said, "There was too much work and too few people to do it. And it never stopped. I worked every weekend. Important school projects didn't matter to my parents," she explained. "We were often at the fairs past midnight. I missed out on high school social life to move heavy boxes, assemble and disassemble rides, and fulfill my parents' expectations instead of studying for tomorrow's test.

"But grades were my priority. Fighting with my folks was endless, daily, and deep. They'd say, 'Just do what's needed. Just make it work.' I was miserable and still am."

This all happened before I met her family last year after moving to New York from Silicon Valley. But her mother had described it to me. She was thankful to have had her daughter's help all those years, thought the business would go bust without it. Both she and Sophie's dad significantly relied on their daughter's labor year-round. My sense is that they missed the toll it took. She needed a way out of being their indentured help.

Amid Sophie's sense of duty, she learned to subdue, maybe even dishonor, her own needs. Now she couldn't access them. And she couldn't respond.

"I really want a man in my life. I thirst for someone to be there for me, to support me. I picture a big cushion I can crash into when I open the door each night. Something or someone soft and caring to prop me up as I swap the emotionally cold office desk for the home office. It's still a mess of endless folders and piles I drown in. My law degree is framed on the floor next to my desk. Oof, the stress of it all. I can never catch up. But, at least by 9 p.m., when I'm home, it's mine. And it's a few exhausting steps from the bed.

The Experience: Sophie dashed in seven minutes late, breathless, disheveled, apologizing all the while. Her momentum slung three heavy totes on the chair and simultaneously looked right at me. What gushed was a heartfelt, "Thank you so much for agreeing to meet me!" It was quite a declaration. But it didn't end there. "Somehow, I'm always late and can't get my act together!"

At that moment I felt my nervous system get jerked out of alignment. My heartrate jumped beyond anything befitting a low-burn-café-sit. Now, as in her, aortic zaps of stress filled me. *Cortisol poison,* I heard my mind proclaim. *And such a misfit for the location, a placid cafe. Perhaps we should have met for a hill walk,* my noticing blurted into my skull. Nodding, my neck seemed to agree. But it was too late. She sat…but didn't settle.

There we were. *Oh my,* I felt. *What to do here?* My forehead muscles tried to tenderly grab my brows and settle them down, to no avail. *Fine, let them rise,* the failed muscles conceded. *She'll sense the tension in my body anyway. Nothing left to do. I can give words to it later if needed. After all, she chose to Show Up this way for a reason. A dramatic call for help. This just emblazons it through my body. Point taken.*

With that I let the thought-events go and looked right at her, signaling my Readiness to engage. In that moment I fastened my Truly-Show-Up black belt, the one I'm endlessly seeking. It lives over the mountain, just out of reach. Nonetheless, I queued my resources: calm mind, serene body, intent to deeply connect, notes on hand. In the middle of my internal pep talk I heard, "You always seem happy and calm. I've been jealous for years. Since I first met you, to be honest. It escapes me. Never in my whole life…I just can't seem to get there."

This was quite something for me to take in, my silent, agitated stillness absorbing her sadness. Thank goodness she continued. I was seeking relief from processing the weighty comment.

"Can I tell you what I'm up against? Maybe you can help me see something I'm missing."

"Of course, Sophie."

instead of empathic listening. There are a few ways to move into this thoughtful space. Forms of meditation are one (described more in Chapter 12). Music and time in nature are others.

It can be helpful to gauge how ready we generally are. So let's ask the following:

- On a scale of one to ten, across your daily experience, how ready would you say you are most of the time? Circle your answer.

  1   2   3   4   5   6   7   8   9   10

- What are your most effective Readiness activities?
- If you were to choose one activity to Show Up more ready for, what would it be?

Here's an example of how low Readiness can Show Up.

READINESS ENCOUNTER— MENTORING SOPHIE

The Person: Sophie is the twenty-seven-year-old daughter of my friend Heather. She was having a hard time. Life was late nights at the law firm with no one to help and endless figure-it-out-as-you-go moments. Weekends were similarly pressured by a fast-growth side business. She was desperate for a break or any semblance of perspective, neither of which she had nor gifted herself.

The Purpose: We met for coffee on a Thursday. It was an advisory session in which she intended to tap my supposed wisdom. The desired outcome was to help her feel more on top of it all. Her mother pointed out that Sophie doesn't ready herself and requested a bit of coaching in this core Show-Up skill. I felt her hopes and wanted to be up to the task.

someone. This is often in my car. My mind spontaneously jumps to the person I'm about to meet and places me into their day. What are they dealing with? What might be on their mind? This helps me connect with them. I feel some of what they may be feeling and realize the behaviors, questions, depth of listening, or other modes of interacting that feel right to honor the Situation and people involved. I also think of specific actions to ready myself, such as looking up information, reviewing notes, bringing an item with me, or thinking something through.

This spontaneous preparing helps me relax and feel happy. I like that it happens. It creates a sense of preparedness. It focuses and grounds me. One example is when I'm on the short drive to my parents' house for our weekly dinners. They like to meet early, as in 5 p.m. This requires I prematurely end a busy workday, leaving me urgently writing or practicing a speech until a few minutes after "the last minute." Then I finally grab my purse, jump in the car, and, after a minute or two, my brain clicks into "Mom-and-Dad mode." It asks, *What have they been doing all day? Are they tired? Should I have brought dinner to them? (YES!)*

Clearly this is a last-minute Readiness routine. Even when I don't bring dinner, it leaves me Showing Up calmer and with far more perceptive of their feelings and needs than I would have been. Most of the time I feel okay about how I Showed Up, not thrilled, but okay.

SETTLING OUR MIND AND BODY ARE READINESS ROUTINES

Settling our minds and bodies helps us experience life more deeply and naturally, readying us and contributing to our Grounding and Alltelligence. I behave differently after my (mostly) daily twenty-four-minute meditation than I do beforehand. Afterward, I feel braided into the world. My presence expands softly into others and nature. It Shows Up as I ask open-ended questions and reflect on what I hear. I am more "with" people. I consider more. In this mind-space, novel thoughts arise, something far more common after I meditate than at day's end, when knee-jerk responses, silly jokes, and quips burst forth

This disharmony may be our bodies telling us we're not ready. There's more thinking and attuning needed. Once we've invested time to consider our feelings more, disharmony often gives way to greater peace and comfort. This tells us we're more ready. We may also move into an energized state of positively anticipating the upcoming experience and good outcomes.

"Western culture is astoundingly disembodied, and uniquely so," Dr. van der Kolk goes on to explain. "The way I like to say it is that we basically come from a post-alcoholic culture. If you feel bad, just take a swig or take a pill. And the notion that you can do things to change the harmony inside of yourself [without alcohol or pills] is just not something that we teach in schools and in our culture, in our churches, in our religious practices. And, of course, if you look at religions around the world, they always start with dancing, moving, singing...physical experiences. And then the more respectable people become, the stiffer they become, somehow."[10]

We each live with differing degrees of access to this embodied information. Many of us are more cut off than we realize. Our upbringing and culture have taught us to be. Beyond our external conditioning, we may have partially disengaged from our somatic knowledge channels for other reasons as well, to protect ourselves. This means our sensate experience of Readiness may be hazy and our intellectual interpretation downplayed or inaccurate. Practice brings it back into focus.

HOW I PRACTICE READINESS

This is admitting a lot since I may not be the ideal role model. But here goes: I feel I've been failing at Readiness my whole life. It's probably a key reason I'm writing this book.

Readiness is a tripwire that catches me way too often...once I'm already in the middle of a discussion or racing out the door. Can you say, "Just Showing Up"?! By default, I practice Readiness in two ways and at two different times. In informal Situations I find myself checking-in about how I want to Show Up once I'm already on my way to meet

> **is a somatic experience and that the function of the brain is to take care of the body."[8] Our sentient awareness can be viewed as the core of our intellect. It lives in the combined functioning of our brains, emotions, and bodies, despite what our schooling and culture may lead us to believe.**

Much of what we know occurs through senses below the brain that exist outside of access to language. We can perceive these somatic insights—such as emotional warmth, unexpected fear, "something's not right," and other perceptions—but not think them. We must sit with the physical experience of the information at least a few seconds, long enough to recognize what it means within the Situation. Then we can consider how to respond. Everyday life is full of examples of people not doing this.

> **As Dr. van der Kolk explains, "When you look at the political discourse, everybody can rationalize what they believe in and talk endlessly about why what they believe is the right thing to do, while your emotional responses are totally at variance with seemingly rational behaviors."[9] He's pointing to people Just Showing Up. By disregarding how they feel, they're behaving inauthentically. They're consciously or unconsciously turning down—or denying—their somatic dial. This often creates stress that Shows Up across a range of symptoms—generalized tension, fatigue, headaches, stomachaches, or other gut problems, irritability, short temperedness, and other more severe diseases.**

SITUATIONAL READINESS 239

these three sources of consciousness—our bodily senses, emotions, and cognitive thinking—readies us more thoroughly than utilizing fewer sources.

Our brain-based intellect (as opposed to our embodied intellect) works in all sorts of clandestine ways to protect us, sometimes obscuring our truth. We doubt, deny, defend, and shut out what we don't like. We can also create what's not there as we see the moment through a wary, fear-captured mind. Similarly, confidence and positive expectations emanate from us into the Situation and others involved as well. They go a long way to create openness and success.

Knowing the world can scare, disappoint, and hurt us, our bodies become trusted advisors of unadulterated truth. They can express what our unconscious minds may be managing for us—that is, pushing away, sugarcoating, disbelieving, or amplifying—in attempts to make the world a safe place. Our minds want our world and experience to be copacetic. The shortcuts and tricks our brain[7] plays as it interprets reality makes it unreliable as our sole arbiter of truth. Tuning in to our sensate experience is a critical component that enables us to Show Up as we choose more often.

Our body's knowledge includes present experience as well as past experience, all of which remains alive in us. This lifetime of embodied learning is often underappreciated. As described in Chapter 9, Grounding, past experience silently directs thoughts and actions, often without our knowing, even right now. Much of recent history ignores the sensate dimension of human experience, reducing us to thinking beings instead of more-integrated thinking-feeling beings. This denies us crucial insights.

> **As Bessel van der Kolk explains, medical professionals, including "psychiatrists, just don't pay much attention to sensate experience at all. Antonio Damasio, in his book, *The Feeling of What Happens*, discusses how our core experience of ourselves**

judgment, and Self-knowledge (Grounding), considering our impact on others (Alltelligence), and imagining possibilities.

Preparing puts our planning into action. It closes the gap between what's required to achieve our goals and the foundation our Grounding and Alltelligence provide.

PREPARE

Closer to the event, we ready ourselves by getting our mind and body in position to Show Up as we choose. It is imminent preparing. This can be a few days before or night before. But it's also right beforehand and as we walk in or commence the activity. I experience this as getting my head in the game, clearing my mind of remnants, and settling my body.

Getting my head in the game is reviewing and practicing the desired behaviors, physically, intellectually, and emotionally. It's giving the keynote speech over and over in front of the mirror in the clothes I'm going to wear with full enthusiasm, gestures, and intent. It is asking questions of my envisioned audience, hearing answers and interacting with them. It is being asked things I'm not prepared for, things that seem out of left field, and getting used to flowing productively with it. This is testing how our chosen behavior feels and how effective it may be. In doing so, we can add nuance and precision. We'll also sense if it doesn't feel good. Recognizing this, we can change course.

READINESS IS A FULL-BODY EXPERIENCE

Beyond our "rational," top-down thinking, Showing Up requires that we attune ourselves to what our body and emotions tell us. This sensate experience includes the degree and location of muscle tension, the depth, speed, and quality of our breath, our facial expressions, posture, behavior and gut sense, among other things. These sensations, combined with our emotions and our brain's interpretation, communicate how we authentically feel. Checking in with these physical and emotional experiences reveals our unfiltered truth. Utilizing

PLAN

We can plan at any level, from across our lifetime down to our next moment. Planning starts when we clarify, "What do I want to have happen in that future activity or span of time?" It is crystalizing and choosing how we want the Situation to Show Up for us and us for the experience, others, and ourselves. How do we relate to the upcoming activity? It starts with our level of sturdiness as a person, our Grounding. It helps us answer, *Why does the activity matter? What broader goals does it support?* If others are involved, what are their answers to these questions? How might they, the topics, timing, location, and broader environment of the Situation Show Up? How may this impact the quality of our performance?

We're invoking what *could* take place as opposed to predicting what *will*. We're planning for a range of outcomes, not forecasting one. This suggests all plans are wrong (at least a little bit). But they're helpful. The process of planning reveals for us a set of next steps toward outcomes. In planning, it's also helpful to assume things went horribly wrong, then ask, *Why?* This is a premortem. It can be more effective than asking, *What can go wrong?* or *How do we minimize risk?* because in a premortem we're putting ourselves into a state in which the failures have already occurred, freeing us and others from reluctance to share concerns. Jumping into failure evokes emotions. They may point us to unseen sources of negative or positive outcomes, furthering our Readiness.

Planning also recognizes and honors that we naturally have needs, hopes, and expectations. Many are deeply personal and meaningful. They identify our destinations as people. As Winston Churchill said, "He who fails to plan is planning to fail"…in Showing Up as we choose to ourselves, Society, and our lives.

Given the breadth of things we plan for—kids' birthday parties, marathons, losing weight, financial independence, repairing our car, regaining health, and tonight's dinner—the process can include endless activities. In all cases we're organizing ideas into actionable steps. Doing this well requires mental time travel. We're envisioning the end state, intervening stages, and steps to get there. We're also engaging focus,

I'm doing this right now in a new romantic relationship. After eight months, we love each other, but physical distance means we see each other only one night a week. For me, it's not enough. I'm in a stage of life with challenging family members and prefer to have a supportive partner physically around more often. But I'm afraid to raise the topic. It seems I have needs he doesn't. I fear pushing him away. By keeping this to myself, he doesn't even have an opportunity to meet my needs more fully. My fear is holding our relationship hostage.

Knowing I can't leave us where we are, my Readiness plan is to brainstorm ways to be together more. Maybe it'll give me the confidence to discuss it. Then I'll envision a lighthearted chat, with laughter, silliness, and a sense of unity, moving us toward a few ideas.

As this example demonstrates, Readiness, achieving, and all of Showing Up happen in the context of a Situation. It can be planned or impromptu. In both cases, Readiness happens in two ways, through planning and preparing. It's what transitions DefaultWorld and ImprovLife into ShowUpLife. Without it, choice is like awareness. It shines a light on where we are but offers few tools for stepping inside.[6] Let's take a closer look at planning and preparing.

PLANNING AND PREPARING

The main distinction is that planning often has a longer-term, strategic aspect, while preparing is more imminently targeted. We plan for holiday break next year. We prepare for rain this afternoon. It may seem that planning is more comprehensive, including identifying goals and the set of actions required to achieve them, while preparing is acting on our planning. This implies preparing is more of an implementation step once our intent is clear. When put it into action, however, they often mix, causing definitions to become fluid. Regardless of where the lines of planning and preparing are drawn, both longer-term strategic thinking and more imminent preparing are important components of readying ourselves.

VISUALIZING

Evidence proves the mental practice of keenly visualizing how we want to Show Up is effective in bringing our chosen behaviors to life. It puts our brain into the future activity, causing us to experience it. The following are a few points on this: Mental practice has the power to strengthen and even heal our bodies. "Guang Yue, an exercise psychologist at the Cleveland Clinic Foundation in Ohio, discovered that people who went to the gym increased their muscle strength by 30 percent, [while] those who did mental visualizations of weight training increased their muscle strength by as much as 13.5 percent."[3] That's almost half the benefit from imagining ourselves at the gym. Looking at mental-Readiness practices in MRI brain scanners shows, in real time, the regions activated by our activities. "Visualizing something and actually doing something look remarkably similar in terms of brain activation...visualization activates the same motor pathways as actually doing it."

Visualizing by watching others also readies us. It activates our mirror neurons, so we experience it.[4] Both watching others and visualizing ourselves in an experience, such as playing piano, confidently presenting to senior staff, or winning a race, prime our bodies and brains to achieve it. According to Dr. Tara Swart, a neuroscientist and medical doctor, "When you imagine your success, you'll be more attuned to opportunities that can help you get there. You'll be able to anticipate and plan for setbacks, and you'll also have a constant reminder of why you chose to pursue those goals in the first place."[5]

READINESS GRANTS SPACE TO SHOW UP AS WE CHOOSE

When apprehensiveness or other concerns appear in our vision, preparing grants us the space to notice and act on the fears. What a gift! We can explore. Why has it Shown Up? What is it teaching us about this Situation, person, and ourselves? If we notice fear and don't prepare to avoid the unwanted outcomes, however, we may be making the negative experience more likely.

What is this real-time research telling us about the sufficiency of our Readiness practices? Our answers are likely telling us the natural flow of our days doesn't currently include all the preparing and planning we need, highlighting a huge opportunity. Since our activities are repeated patterns, improving our Readiness for a common Situation can yield daily gains, making a huge difference in our lives. Readiness is a huge opportunity for me, as you'll read below.

LOW-HANGING FRUIT?

People tell me Readiness feels like the easiest of the three skills to improve. It's readily accessible, more tactical than Grounding, and can be done in the moment. I feel there's truth to this. Prepping can be bite-sized. It is as simple as, *What do I need or want to do for this next activity or that activity tomorrow morning?* It can also be, *How do I want to feel during the activity? How sincere, unguarded, and supportive do I choose to be?* (Alltelligence). Then we've already stepped into the process of getting there. Our minds are envisioning the upcoming experience, location, people. Our bodies are experiencing the emotions. And we naturally live into the future moment, practicing what we want to happen, familiarizing ourselves with our preferred behavior. This is Readiness working for us.

HOW TO DEEPEN OUR READINESS

As my research shows, our challenge is not how to plan and prepare; it's investing time and effort to sufficiently do it. Sometimes becoming aware of a different approach—one with compelling proof behind its efficacy—is just the nudge we need. I'll introduce visualizing as a Readiness tactic here and will expand upon it more in Chapter 12.

> **This demonstrates how readying our Selves for one moment is also choosing how we're Showing Up for the next and all that follow. It makes attuning and choosing what we do determinative because we're setting up for success—or something else—every moment. The goal is to avoid excess default behavior. Readiness—internal and external, mind and body, long-term and short—achieves this.**

Taking Stock of Our Readiness Behaviors

We evolve in an experience-dependent way. Readiness helps us design our experience and, therefore, how we evolve. I think of it as becoming the sculptor of our stunningly beautiful statues. There we are on pedestals in Rome for all to see. But how much care do we invest?

LET'S TAKE A LOOK

1. How often do we feel "I should have been better prepared"?
2. How often do we plan or prepare for our next moment? That activity tomorrow? Or next week?
3. How rewarding or challenging do we find this experience?
4. Just before walking in, to what extent do we remind ourselves of our Show-Up choices? How often do we jot down a few notes, mentally or physically?
5. How often do we think about how others feel or what they may need?
6. How often do we notice our degree of openness to connect, trust, and care (or our biases, negativity, or fear) in advance?
7. How often do we focus on our breath for a few minutes to settle ourselves, open our minds, and attune to what our bodies are telling us?

> **autopiloting? Considering or just moving through? When are we readying ourselves to Show Up as we choose? As always, the question becomes, "How conscious a choice are we making?"**

This fleeting nature of time to ready ourselves is a great motivator. It defines urgency. As Yoda says in Star Wars, "Do, or do not. There is no try." Sure, we can be partially ready. In fact, we always are. That's the root of Just Showing Up. But default Readiness not what we're talkin' 'bout here. Leading a Show-Up life means we're assigning our JSUP experiences to chosen parts of our day, or to chosen activities and people, while intentfully preparing to truly Show Up when it matters most. Readiness is the gateway bringing us there.

We Reveal Our Readiness Each Moment

We experience life as a flow. We're always bringing our mood, energy, thought pattern, and intent into each incremental moment. It's how each experience primes our next, making everything we do a Readiness activity for our subsequent moment and our subsequent level of performing. We may not often think of it this way. But it's exactly what happens. Each action is the on-ramp for what we do next.

> One interviewee explained this natural linking effect: *"The first feeling I have when I get out of bed sets the tone for the day. That's the Show-Up moment that matters most to me. It pulls through everything else. How I greet my kids, what I wear, the food I pack for lunch, all result from that first daily experience. I used to accept the negativity and stress I woke up with. Now I see its impact, and far more often ask as I push the covers off, 'How am I choosing to Show Up to this day?' It changes everything that follows."*

HOW READINESS RELATES TO GROUNDING AND ALLTELLIGENCE

As the Situational component of Showing Up, Readiness is where our depth of Grounding and Alltelligence reveal themselves. The latter two create our foundation of sturdiness and integrity that we greet all experiences with. Contrasting this, Readiness is contextual to a specific Situation and everything happening in those moments. We can ready ourselves for any and all of them, making Readiness as expansive or as limited as we choose.

Readiness—Our Expiring Asset

Let's ground ourselves in the urgency of Readiness. Our experiences are arriving, then passing. We have only so long until each is upon us. Now we're in it, and our opportunity to prepare for success is gone. Like airplane seats and hotel rooms, Readiness is an expiring asset. When we haven't done it sufficiently, we're stuck. And we know immediately. It's that, "Darn it! I should have known this would happen!" that we're too familiar with. People and events can be predictable. We often know what preparation is needed. But once the plane doors close, no one else is getting on. And come midnight, that empty hotel room won't be booked. Now that Situation, empty hotel room, and plane seat are an expense, not an asset. They're also a potential future liability…as are all experiences we don't sufficiently ready ourselves for.

How we prepare for the moments of our lives reveals to us, and confronts us with, what we truly value. It comes through in how Grounded and Alltelligent we are. Such insight is invaluable. Are we preparing or

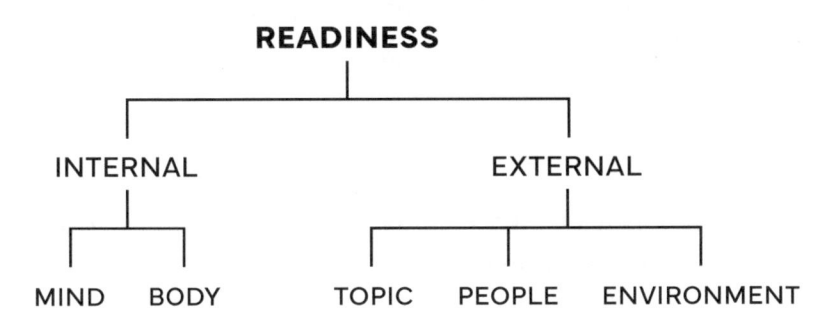

```
                    READINESS
          ┌────────────┴────────────┐
       INTERNAL                  EXTERNAL
       ┌──┴──┐              ┌──────┼──────┐
      MIND  BODY          TOPIC  PEOPLE  ENVIRONMENT
```

Reviewing the internal/external perspective on readying ourselves can help us see options we may regularly miss. A common example is how most business meetings favor external, cognitive factors over internal, emotional factors. In my experience with large companies, topics are often tactical or about growth targets, sales approaches, and market dynamics. Human factors are largely omitted.

Rapid discussion and rational thinking move quickly. We may miss or dismiss sensate experience (body-focused preparing). Simple questions can change this, such as, "How do we feel about this set of options?" or "Who is sensing we may be missing important topics?" Then give time and space for people to tap into their visceral knowledge base of experiences. This could go a long way toward expanding the quality of work.

Tapping into sensate experience to ready ourselves can focus on ourselves or others. Internally it may Show Up as muscle tension or ease, excitement, fear, rigidity, or stress. From others it may Show Up as positivity, openness, support, and creativity or as negativity, opposition, or mistrust. When these internal states are recognized, we can use the information to communicate clearly with ourselves and others, preparing better and creating value for everyone involved. We need it all—internal and external Readiness across what, when, and how.

and the near-term efforts "preparing." Both are critical for Showing Up as we choose. And both are expiring assets.

HOW TO READY

At a high level, we're either doing longer-term planning or shorter-term preparing. Both can be mental and physical.

- Longer-term planning = typically strategic and less immediate, mental and physical
- Shorter-term preparing = typically tactical and imminent, mental and physical

Categories like these are valuable because they encourage us to consider how we relate to and ready ourselves for each situation:

- Are we generally more internally focused or externally?
- Toward which process—longer-term planning or imminent preparing?
- Toward which time frame—as we "walk in," hours or days beforehand, or weeks or months in advance?
- How is this serving us? What should we consider adjusting?

In the example of Jordan's visit to his in-laws, applying the Readiness Guide is planful. Putting it into effect soon requires preparing. Jordan can put his planning into practice by putting a note in his calendar, packing notes in his suitcase so he finds them when unpacking upon arrival, wearing a shirt they gave him as a reminder, or many other prompts, including asking himself as he walks in, "How am I choosing to Show Up?"

Jordan told me his experience this year was substantially more enjoyable than past trips to his in-laws. He felt different going into it and thinks his Readiness-guide process impacted not just his immediate family but also his in-laws. The guide can easily be applied to business meetings, projects, and other activities. Choose the elements (e.g., purpose, context, participants, physicality, emotions, etc.) that seem valuable to explore. You can add others and push your Readiness as far as needed to attain insight and the sense of preparedness you seek.

Jordan could have included social impacts on the family as a whole, and even on his community and our broader culture. For example, what energy might his kids return to school with after a more positive, emotionally warm visit with their grandparents? How might deeper appreciation and compassion for elders translate into their classroom participation, behavior with friends, or on the soccer field?

WHEN TO READY

The timing of our Readiness activities determines how well we can prepare and how effective the process is. Up to a point, more time is typically better. It's the opposite of winging it or Just Showing Up. That said, at least some of our Readiness has to take place relatively close to the target activity. Even if weeks or months of planning have ensued, we still need to reground ourselves right beforehand in our choice behaviors. Both have mind and body components. The timing of our preparation can be organized in three buckets:

- Imminently as we "walk in"
- Hours or days beforehand
- Longer term, such as weeks or months in advance

We can plan long term for when our kids go to college, medium term for our daughter's birthday party next week, and right now for the appointment in two minutes. I call the longer-term focus "planning"

- Comment: I can offer to bring or buy them an air mattress to give us more flexibility as the kids get older. Spending more time in the study surrounded by books would be good. Better than being in the kitchen all day or in front of the TV. I can also buy them a lamp to make the lazy chairs in the corners more useful for relaxed reading at night.

- <u>Emotional</u>: We definitely have nice times but also have peaks of frustration around the same old topics—how insufficiently strict my parenting is, for one.
    - Comment: I expect my genuine interest in getting to know them better will create more positive emotional space for us. It'll also likely diminish how critical my mother-in-law can be.

- <u>Social</u>: Our shared time together happens only twice a year. There's mutual interest in being together so they have a role in my children's lives and we share a sense of family.

- <u>Functional</u>: Visiting my in-laws gives my kids a sense of their lineage, of people they descend from, and our family's culture, rituals, and practices. It's also a time when we get away and take a break from school, work, and daily patterns, something I often need but don't get.

- <u>Spiritual aspects</u>: I do think I rejuvenate somewhat on these family visits. I slow down, carry my phone less, and do feel I recharge.
    - Comment: It's great to recognize this value. I'm looking forward to the trip much more now that I realize this benefit and the actions I'll take to bring us closer. And I feel grateful that they take care of so much (food, activities for the kids) so I have the time and space to relax.

- Comment: As I write this, I'm realizing how limited our topics are. There's only two or three times across fifteen years that my father-in-law has opened up about his life. I'm just now recognizing that I don't know my in-laws particularly well. What makes them who they are? How do they feel about their lives? Perhaps this trip I'll ask about their past. What was it like? It'll be healthy for my kids to appreciate this as well.

- Broader context: It feels repetitive. Same topics and frustrations. I expect more of the same, with a few age-related issues built in. It dissuades me from suggesting we visit more often.
  - Comment: Hmmm. I'm recognizing an interest in shifting our pattern and including new topics. I know we need to invest in keeping the family close. I'll ask a few of my favorite questions and jot down a few new subjects to ask about. We can start with the following:
    - What is your most treasured memory?
    - If you were asked to tell your life story in five minutes, what would you say?
    - If you could change anything about the way you were raised, what would it be?

- Participants: Typically only my in-laws, wife, and two kids. It was fun one year when a friend joined us for an evening.
  - Comment: I'll ask about including friends more often, recalling how enjoyable it was to infuse new people, energy, and ideas.

- Physical environment: A small but cozy, clean home. My kids sleep on the couches in the family room. Their mom and I sleep in the guest room. It's physically comfortable, but we do feel cooped up by day three of five.

- What aspects of our Grounding are at play in this Situation, and how are we choosing to Show Up to them? For example, if we've recognized we seek to impress or to avoid the spotlight, to seek leadership roles, to say yes to burdensome amounts of work, to avoid being put on the spot, how are we choosing to rely on or manage these tendencies?

External Readiness directs our focus into a Situation's purpose, content, broader context (what came before and what follows) participants, physical environment, and its emotional, social, functional, and even spiritual aspects across groups, community, and culture. Applying these categories to an upcoming Situation can help us discover relevant details. Notably, this also makes us more responsible to and for our impacts on each other (Alltelligence).

My friend Jordan was telling me about an upcoming visit with his in-laws that he wasn't looking forward to. He commonly experiences raw, uncomfortable behavior on these visits. Below is what he jotted down based on the Situational Readiness elements listed above.

Situational Readiness Guide: Jordan's Family Visit

- Purpose: To help my wife, kids, and Self reconnect with my mother- and father-in-law. To feel close and supported.
  - Comment: This is something I often lose sight of.

- Content: We'll likely hear about the typical stuff: football, health issues, issues with Jay (my wife's brother), and, of course, how our kids are doing according to them, including their judgment that I'm not a strict enough parent.

SELF	SITUATION	SOCIETY
INTERNAL READINESS	EXTERNAL READINESS	
Cognitive and physical (mind/body[2]), across time	Reciprocal and reverberative flow of information Purpose, topic/content, plus the broader context of participants, environment, including emotional, functional, social, spiritual aspects	Reciprocal and custodial impacts on groups, community, culture, and nature, across time

Internal Readiness starts with settling our minds and bodies from extraneous thoughts and sensations. Directing attention to our breath for a few minutes or longer, stretching, taking a short walk, dancing, or other movement-based activities are typically effective in achieving this. Laughing and being in or focusing on nature are also helpful.

Once our mind has made space for discovery, we focus it on how we want to arrive in the future circumstance, physically and emotionally. For example, we can ask ourselves questions such as:

- What degree of openness and connectedness with people and the experience do we seek? This is asking, "How Alltelligent am I (my family, team, company) choosing to be?"
- What behaviors and emotions feel on point? Which are to be avoided (calmness, attentiveness, conscientiousness, openness, optimism, subtle judgment, bias, fear)?

Foreboding is the feeling we get when we haven't sufficiently prepared for something important. It's that apprehensive intuition, that tension, informing us there's risk. Now we're in DefaultWorld and about to JSUP. Amid our hardworking day, foreboding (Madam F.) arrives innocently. We'll get to that task-responsibility-thing we're procrastinating about...later. L-a-t-e-r. We may interpret foreboding as mere nerves before an event. "It'll be okay," we tell ourselves. "Just nerves. No prep needed." After all, casting Madam F. away is our habit. But then, things go only so well. We end the activity disappointed or mad. We could and should have done better. The remedy to this low-performing pattern starts with asking ourselves, "How am I choosing to Show Up?" As we ask we're already starting to ready ourselves.

So what is it, really? Let's dive into the *what*, *when*, and *how* of Situational Readiness through a Show-Up lens. Then we'll explore its two parts, planning and preparing.

WHAT TO READY

Our lived experience has an internal component and an external component. We Show Up at a level of Readiness for each, whether consciously or not.

the before, during, and after, helping you remain relaxed and flexible. This is Readiness.

Readiness is a big idea. It asserts that we can Show Up more prepared—and higher performing—for the Situations we choose. This directly confronts the reality of our often-reactive, Just-Showing-Up lives. But we know it to be true. Research from a team at Cornell, Wharton, and the University of Colorado found that prospective hindsight, when we imagine a Situation already occurred, makes us 30 percent more capable in piecing together reasons for future outcomes.[1] Now we can shift our behavior to achieve more of the desired outcomes.

Yet a majority of survey respondents tell me, "I rarely feel truly ready" or "I need more time to plan," making Readiness a huge opportunity for many, if not most, of us. How can we perform as we'd ideally choose when we're Just Showing Up with minimal forethought a good amount of the time? We can't. Readiness offers a priceless option for lifting us up, and out, of typical patterns. It confers tangible advantage over Just Showing Up and is materially absent when we're Barely There.

> **Readiness, when practiced through a Show-Up lens, turns our "To-Do" list into a "To-Be" list. It makes tactical preparing meaningful by focusing us on how we're choosing to be in a Situation.**

HOW UNREADINESS SHOWS UP

Nervous. Sloppy. Strained. Unprepared. Unhappy. And—unforgiving. Unready feels like a flashing red neon sign in our body. It reads "Stress… Consequence Hovers Ahead." By neglecting these visceral gauges, our unpreparedness becomes a dark visitor. Her name is *foreboding*. Like procrastination, she's menacing. She predicts, prophesizes, and portends loss if we don't heed her call: "Get Ready!"

when we feel threatened by uncertainty. Such stressors close us to opportunity.

The prework of Readiness opens us, unlocking our sincerity and care. As Gavin explained, he knew he'd be handed alcohol in the future, with no harm intended. He planned and prepared by pre-living in that moment, and "saying 'no, thank you' with my arms down over and over." This demonstrates how Readiness exists within situations, the context in which we come alive. They're the vessels and vehicles of our lived experiences, and the containers through which our Self and Societal roles interact.

THE INTENSITY OF READINESS

> **You may think of Readiness as a preparing process. It's also a felt state. An expiring asset. A priceless option. And a required input to Showing Up as we choose. It's worth pausing to appreciate the intensity of Readiness. It hoists agency on us. It gives us power. It's the boundary and the cusp upon which our Show-Up choices become reality. Before the boundary we're preparing. Once we cross it, we're Showing Up with whatever level of Readiness we chose. Either we're prepared or we're not. And we know it in both cases.**

Fortune favors the Ready. We know who these people are. If it's you, you're the one whose phone rings with offers of the next gig before you need it. You're able to pivot toward open doors others don't see and walk past. Your life flows with a directedness, an interest, a drive because you naturally do your homework to plan, learn, organize, arrange, and prime your chosen outcomes. In the moment you maintain perspective because you've thought things through, considering

outstretched, mindlessly prompting Gavin to take it. Gavin looked away from me toward the host and waved his hand as he said, "No, thanks." The moment passed. Tension diffused. Commitments kept. Not just all night. All weekend.

Wow! How does a twenty-year-old in such an environment do that? Later he told me, "Marcy, I've been preparing for this moment for six months. I knew it would happen. And it'll happen again. I've practiced that 'no, thank you' with my arms down over and over. The situation used to be filled with fear and stress, even longing. Now it makes me feel great! I love the power I have." (Readiness)

Then he explained, "The capable feeling extends into everything I do. (Grounding) I don't blame people. Very few know I don't drink. I trust their intentions and can still be close with them, even when they repeatedly encourage me to have a beer or two." (Alltelligence)

Gavin shared how being out of control in one area of life made a mess of it all. Now he can Show Up as he chooses to alcohol and, in doing so, is choosing the rest of his life too. For him it comes down to how ready he is for trials like this. It's one more example of how Showing Up exists in each moment and across all Situations. It demonstrates the integrated, reinforcing nature of our Readiness, Grounding, and Alltelligence. Said another way, it demonstrates how we Show Up as Selves within Situations and Society at all times. Skill in one role extends into and feeds the others.

This is the power of Readiness.

HOW READINESS SHOWS UP

Confident. Composed. Engaging. Present. Familiar. Readiness acquaints us with situations in advance. We're visiting the anticipated experience, topics, people, environment, and emotions. "Hello" we say. "How do you do?" This reduces uncertainty, making the encounter feel more relaxed. Readiness gifts access to our creativity, playfulness, and a manner of interacting more likely to bring people toward us. It primes Alltelligence by reducing the us/them distinction prompted

CHAPTER 10
SITUATIONAL READINESS

This chapter leads you through the following ideas:
- Handing a drink to a recovering alcoholic
- Situational connectedness
- The boundary and cusp
- Our expiring asset and invaluable option
- The fastest route to Showing Up better
- Taking stock
- Ask the question

ONE SATURDAY NIGHT LAST August, a stunning example of Readiness Showed Up. It was at a weekend-long college-guys party... resembling classic 1960s sex, drugs, and rock 'n' roll. I was one of two adults bearing witness—and providing some version of light supervision—to a full house of twenty-year-olds imbibing and celebrating. Chatting with a fit young man we'll call "Gavin," I learned he was six months out of an alcohol rehabilitation program. Everyone knew. But just then an outstretched arm handed him a glass of wine. It all happened quite innocently among toasting and enjoying the barbecue.

As the glass came, my body tensed. We were eye to eye. About three seconds passed as he recognized what was happening. I think I was holding my breath. The host kept his chardonnay-bearing arm

*Readiness attunes us to others.
It opens our hearts so we
feel with them, supporting
AIltelligence and Grounding.*

Societally Showing Up

1. How would Society be different if more of us showed up more deeply grounded?

2. How big an impact would it make?

3. Who, or what groups of people specifically, do you want to see deepen their Grounding (e.g., politicians, first responders, educators, corporate leaders, specific friends, family members, others)?

4. What systems (e.g., educational, corporate cultures, governmental policies, etc.) would you want to see become more grounded?

5. What do you plan to do about this?

Choosing How We Show Up

This is where the rubber meets the road. Be ready.

1. **What choices are you making right now about your future level of Grounding?**

2. **How will you live into these choices? (What will you do?)**

3. **How will they impact you?**

Recognize how you answer these final questions; you are illuminating how your integrity is Showing Up right here, right now. "What will you do?" is a commitment to yourself. I encourage you to write from your place of Level 3, Truly Showing Up. You'll be happy you did.

I don't mean to come across as confrontational. I'm just living into my calling on this planet of supporting people in Truly Showing Up.

And…I know you can do it!

LOW	HIGH
SOCIAL	
Not often attuned to how calm or agitated our and others' nervous systems are or why.	**Often attuned** to how calm or agitated our and others' nervous systems are and why.
Rarely able to make decisions based on this.	Able to make decisions based on these reflections.

REFLECTING QUESTIONS—GROUNDING

Answering these questions deepens our Grounding.

Individually Showing Up

1. In what ways are you well grounded?

2. In what ways are you less well grounded?

3. How well does your Grounding show up for you? (Rate it one to ten. 1=low, 10=high)

4. How does your Grounding Show Up?
    a. In what behaviors? (Positive and negative)
    b. In what situations?
    c. With which people?
    d. With what preparation?

5. What do you do today to support your Grounding?

6. What could you do to be more grounded?

LOW	HIGH

BEHAVIORAL

Shows minimal or ad hoc reflective practices such as journaling, meditation, therapy, or informal therapeutic friendships.	**Shows dependable reflective practices** such as journaling, meditation, therapy, or informal therapeutic friendships.

INTELLECTUAL

Inconsistent about what matters most and why.	**Consistency about what matters most and why.**
Wavering sense of identity.	Strong sense of identity.
Unsettled sense of past and purpose.	Clarity of past and purpose.
Shifts in interests, potentially also in professional pursuits, friends, and meaningful relationships.	**Consistency of interests** across years, potentially also in professional pursuits, friends, and meaningful relationships.

EMOTIONAL

Often controlled by the emotions of the moment.	**Rarely controlled by the emotions of the moment.** Often able to reset as needed.
Behavior can be inconsistent, not well reasoned, or moderated by choice.	Mainly levelheaded, self-assured, and dependable.
May show sudden shifts in behavior: potential bouts of aggression, sadness, or unpredictability.	Solid. Stable. Secure. Genuine.

CHAPTER 9 SUMMARY— GROUNDING IN OUR SELVES

1. Grounding is the skill native to our role as Selves. It is the degree to which we understand who we are and why. It's our depth of connectedness with our true nature.

2. Together with Readiness and Alltelligence, Grounding is a core part of our behavioral infrastructure. It's part of our cognitive and psychological skeleton. It scaffolds our experience. We bring it into the room with us always.

3. It creates safety from inside our Selves, making us solid, clear thinking, and dependable.

4. The better we understand ourselves the more able we are to interact with others as we choose.

5. Deepening our Grounding requires we explore our physical, emotional, and cognitive experiences.

6. Knowing ourselves is an ongoing growth practice, as is Showing Up.

SUMMARY OF LOW AND HIGH GROUNDING

The table below lists the extremes of low and high Grounding. They apply to every aspect of our lives and can be applied to organizational processes and systems across Society.

however, your relationship with your Self, a family member, or a specific event is an ever-present source of unhappiness, it's likely indicating more reflecting on this topic is needed.

TAKING STOCK

To identify our degree of Grounding, consider the following:

1. How often do we stop to notice what we're feeling and what it may be telling us?
2. How often do we journal about, consider, or speak with friends about meaningful experiences?
3. How often do we take time to align our activities with what's most meaningful?
4. How often do we meditate, or do related activities such as yoga or martial arts?
5. How grounded (solid, clear) do we typically feel?

almost twice as many new products (56 percent compared with 33 percent), and succeeded far more often in major transformation efforts (52 percent compared with 16 percent) according to a study in *Harvard Business Review*. Finally, purpose-driven leaders are found to have happier, more productive employees, according to research from Northwestern's School of Education and Social Policy.[11] In sum, a sense of purpose makes a big difference in helping us Truly Show Up.

It need not be grandiose. Purpose can be as simple as being a kind person who does our best each day for our families and community. Purpose can be domestic or global, family-focused or professional, spiritual or social. That said, *Purpose* can also be a tough word. Many of us do not know "our purpose." In life we've often worked to earn money and done more of what's needed than what truly drives our soul. Eighty percent of us are searching for a clear sense of purpose and passion, one that we can articulate simply and rely on to ground and steer daily activities. Only 20 percent of us, according to Bill Damon, director of Stanford's Center on Adolescence, live with such clarity. For the other 80 percent, practicality and earning a living dominate.

Even if we're not completely living our dream, we can foster a sense of purpose around our families, aspects of our jobs, and our humanness. As described in the first three chapters, we're united within a universal Show-Up network. We're designed very much as integrated aspects of each other and the natural world. Chapter 11, Alltelligence, describes this in detail. This knowledge creates a sense of purpose because we're responsible for each other. And it's a core tenet of Showing Up. It also supports us in being good people, healthy people, and happy people.

Reflecting Cycles for Grounding (e.g., Knowing Our Selves, Our Past, and Our Purpose)

At its most basic, Grounding comes from reflecting calmly and openly about things that happened and how they impact us, others, and society. There's no hard-and-fast rule as to how often we should stop to think about what just happened or what happened long ago. If,

This coherence, meaning, and purpose function as a compass. We feel it when we pause. In this space purpose grabs our attention. It spotlights what's important, guiding us toward what we want to achieve. This reinforces our identity. It's our distinctiveness and character. As described in Chapter 1, purpose seized my attention when I was twelve and at the rehabilitation hospital, where I was supposedly learning to speak. I watched elders coached in how to walk, sit, stand, and feed themselves independently. They knew how they wanted to Show Up—as capable, independent people. At that moment I realized the world lacked a simple model for what it means to Show Up, making it hard for us to do so. I was determined to answer this clarion call.

Imagine the three components of who we are, what we believe, and what we do as a Venn diagram, with three evenly sized circles. If our three components are not much overlapping in the center, our lives do not feel imbued with a clear throughline of Grounding, coherence, or connectedness. We may still derive meaning from isolated aspects, our children, extended family, friendships, work, sports, and other areas, but they compete for our attention, time, and energy, instead of supporting each other.

Connecting to our purpose, or a universal or spiritual purpose, is so central to our lives that our health depends on it. A meta-analysis designed to "assess the net impact of purpose in life" found that people possessing a high sense of purpose have reduced risk of cardiovascular events and all-cause mortality.[8] This means that living with and nurturing our sense of purpose does more than make us feel fulfilled; it also keeps us well and, literally, alive. We also feel less lonely and make better choices to protect our health when imbued with purpose.[9] Other research shows purpose relaxes and motivates us.[10] It lowers stress, supporting creativity, innovativeness, and adaptability. This clarifies what's important. Now we're more solid and grounded. We're more integrated within our Selves.

Companies with a clearly articulated and widely understood purpose achieved stronger growth (52 percent versus 42 percent), launched

These unmetabolized or partially processed encounters deaden our ability to connect with our Selves, everyday experiences, and people. They challenge our memory, processing capability, focus, curiosity, dedication, compassion, and performance. It's hard to live fully today and be grounded in a solid sense of Self when past stressors dim or strip even basic connections from our world. As Brené Brown, Marianne Williamson, and many others express, we cannot give others what we don't give ourselves. So we must work to understand ourselves as a first step to creating goodness with and for others.

I'm not suggesting we all need years of therapy. I am saying taking the time to reflect on past events enables us to process them at least a bit more deeply and to uncover new perspectives. Our interpretations of what happened, as well as the effects on us, can mature. We can assign new meaning, one that supports our chosen path. Then we bring these matured insights into today and Show Up more connected and capable.

What, specifically, should we explore? Ripe topics often include how safe, accepted, supported, and loved we felt across our childhood.

- How thoroughly did we belong?
- What were we taught about whether our basic needs would be met and our boundaries respected?
- What were we taught about our capabilities, opportunities, value, deservingness, and place in the world?

These are often topics that hold wisdom for us, should we choose to explore them.

PURPOSE

When we see a throughline connecting who we are, what we believe, and what we do, we feel coherence in our lives. This supports a sense of purpose.[7] We feel we matter. Our work matters. Our time matters. Our choices matter. We Show Up engaged. All are part of a heightened state of Grounding.

received? Am I able to receive it? What habits involved with supporting a partner's eighty-hour workweek should I extinguish? And finally, *Can I actually do it?*

OUR PAST AND PRESENT EXIST IN OUR BODIES

> "America is a particularly disembodied culture," according to Bessel van der Kolk, MD, head of Harvard's trauma center and author of a bestselling book, *The Body Keeps the Score*.[5] "Many [people] are completely detached from both their sense of self and their physical bodies." He explains that our experiences are not just the lens through which we see the world; they're also the emotional and visceral reactions of our bodies. Experiences live in our muscle memory, our gut, and our nervous system. We may not understand why we flinch or pull away when someone approaches us with a hug, but our body does. We may feel disproportionate anxiety about a Situation and struggle to reset because our rational thoughts can't quite make sense of it. This happens when our (supposedly) rational brain[6] doesn't have access to what our body knows.

When painful, traumatic, or defining moments of our past are only casually considered, they remain—at least in part—in our present lives. This happens when we can't create an integrated story about an event, one that makes sense of the experience in context of our lives today. This leaves it, and our response, frozen in time, unchanged inside us. We live ever alert to the past experience. It's in our ongoing reality. We're recreating the events and our reaction endlessly.

> **ourselves through intentful reflecting can help to pinpoint their sources so we can regain control and Show Up closer to how we choose.**

MY PERSONAL EXAMPLE

Examples of this Showed Up as I started dating after divorcing my husband in 2018. I met men who had worked to understand at least some aspects of themselves. They told me things like, "I realized I seek women who need help. My mother was depressed. I grew up helping her. So I click with women who have health issues." Then they'd usually tell me they'd been divorced twice, and their children are repeating the pattern of Showing Up primarily as helper, instead of partner. Recognizing the pattern is an essential first step. It means they can choose to Show Up differently. Many other manifestations of low Grounding were encountered on these early dates. I heard about parents addicted to their jobs, dogged beliefs, painkillers, spending, angry outbursts, or emotional distance. My story also shows perpetual negative childhood patterns. It's scary. My kids may uphold its legacy. Here's what happened.

My physician parents prioritized work over me, or so it seemed. This led me to be most "at home" with a partner working very long hours, limiting our time together. I feel unattracted to wonderful partners with more flexible schedules who want to love me more fully. If I were unaware of this, I would still be searching for Mr. Eighty-Hour Workweek. My soul says he's in high demand and is contributing and doing important things. I like him! Our calls get his last embers of energy for the day and are a brief reprieve before he gets back to work at 10:00 p.m. Yep, he's my match.

Stopping to consider this led me to redefine my path. Now I'm questioning my own reasons for turning potential partners away. *Why does having flexible time for me make him unappealing, unimportant, and noncontributing? Is he offering the sought-after attention I've never quite*

GROUNDING REQUIRES UNDERSTANDING OUR PAST

Knowing our past means taking time to recognize our and our family's patterns, including their lessons and gifts. My friend Alyssa told me, "We didn't discuss emotions in my home. I always felt a bit marginalized, as if the fullness of me was not quite welcome. To cope, I became overly self-reliant. I learned to take care of my own emotional needs by pushing them aside. The unspoken message was that my parents aren't responding to these feelings, so I shouldn't either. It became automatic." Over time we normalized to such responses, even though the underlying craving to be known and understood remains.

Alyssa went on to explain, "Now my relationships show a repetitious, volatile, push-pull pattern. I want to feel close to people but clash with my own tendencies to keep emotions to myself and not seem needy. So, people can't get close to me. They want more, but it's unsafe for me. I can't get at what I really feel, let alone express it. I know it's a source of my loneliness. Partners fit my automatic behavior, but it's not my full, or true, self. It's like I'm destined to forever sabotage myself." Like Anthony, Alyssa needs to keep herself busy to distract from sustained sadness and dissatisfaction. It dances in the background of her days, breeding loneliness.

> **Sometimes we tango with these patterns across decades, with fresh scenery, addresses, and names. If we're not looking, the patterns can remain invisible. We're like fish not knowing we're in water. Unseen coping mechanisms sabotage us in many forms. They're little "a" addictions such as false charisma or confidence, overworking, unnecessary spending, eating, binge watching, overexercising, or other behaviors that we can't quite control. Many emerge as adaptations of early experiences that we haven't yet understood. Working to Ground**

our degree of belonging within Society. These priorities, extending from our past and purpose, are where our motivation, mind, and body naturally flow.

Reflecting on these stories enables us to question them and even rewrite false beliefs that may be causing problems. As we choose narratives that serve who we are today, they become wind at our back, not old anvils holding us down.

> Here's what a professional photographer named Brad told me. It shows he's Grounded in his subject's experience, enabling him to apply his gifts.
>
> *As an image-maker, I find clients feel uncomfortable being photographed. It stops them from revealing themselves, veiling what I need to capture. And it gets worse. When a client is in fear, not power, it is projected into me. I lose clarity of my own instincts and fall into the trap of doing what I assume the client expects, all because my subject is not comfortable with themselves.*
>
> *I had to feel it myself, so I had someone photograph me. The experience felt naked, raw, exposed. I even felt weak. It was such an intrusive yet instructive way to learn. I uncovered the unspoken question, "Is he here to take something from me? Or to do something with me?"*
>
> *It grounded me. Hard. Now people respond to how I bring myself, verbally, visually. I fail if they feel "taken from." We can succeed only if we are "with" each other. I act on my visual instincts first, then a more subconscious instinct seeking the soul of my subject. It lives in the uncertainty, on the edge of risk...not knowing how the images will turn out. Will I get the crème de la crème? The magic that turns all heads, that no one forgets?*

be particularly insightful. Is it meandering or more consciously structured? How intentful and purposeful is his approach to a given issue or to problems in general? And to what extent does he recognize and consider these tendencies? Perhaps he would have exposed a bit more sensitivity, a regard for others, outside of reflections about himself.

After terminating a long marriage and needing to put the pieces of our lives together, as most divorcees need to do, you'd think the table would be set for a robust discussion about challenges and Self-learning, with no need to touch on specifics. This makes it even more startling that all this was conspicuously absent.

Parting thoughts: It is possible Anthony is not as blind to his ways or as overbearing as this singular meeting portrays. Forty-five minutes reveals only so much. But it's how he Showed Up to me.

It's also quite possible a strong, firmly empowered woman can partner with him effectively, benefiting from his tendencies while still owning her choices and being true to herself. It's simply a point of sensitivity for me, having learned I lack such skill or, at least, used to.

Finally, there's a reason Anthony is this way. He's playing out what his parents taught him or did *to him*. That's what we all do. He's doing his best, as we all are, for who we are in this moment.

PAST AND PURPOSE

As Anthony demonstrated, our past is our cognitive and emotional inheritance. How we interpret it flows into today and tomorrow. These interpreted stories are the context through which we're experiencing life right now. We assign meaning, significance, and purpose based on these stories we tell our Selves about our past.

They become a reinforcing system directing our choices, which then feed back into our Grounding of who we are and why. Our past becomes our purpose. It informs our priorities—things like hard work, integrity, caretaking, generosity, connection with others, and

> more homework. In this case, it's clear Anthony is Just Showing Up. Perhaps he's even Barely There.

Alltelligence: Low

> **Psychoanalyst Comments**
>
> Anthony shows low Alltelligence by thinking he knows what Marcy wants. Her preferences are either dismissed or assumed, maybe both. They show he is disconnected. He's not open to new experiences, not open to who the other person actually is.
>
> In treating Marcy in such a controlling manner, Anthony clearly doesn't feel part of a greater whole. His behavior is more indicative of someone feeling isolated, alone, and scared.
>
> Had he felt something beyond his individual world, he'd have come across less lost and would have behaved more flexibly, showing openness to exploring with her. Instead, he did the opposite. He controlled her, both physically and verbally.

In contrast to partnering, caring, and sharing connection, Anthony came across as controlling, almost competitive. Asserting myself would have threatened him. This contrasts the inherent trust, mutual care, and collaborative nature of Alltelligence.

A few ways he could have shown higher Grounding, Readiness, and Alltelligence would be to Show Up more human, to share challenges he faced or is facing, and how he approached moving forward. What did he have to work through recently? How did it go? What types and shapes of issues and learnings did he contend with, and is he still contending with them? Understanding his process of dealing with challenges would

Unfortunately, it seems to be more Self-centered and domineering than ideal. He comes across blind to the possibility that he can do what he was taught with direct input from—and respectful consideration of—others.

This would be Showing Up with more equal balance across our roles as Selves in Situations and Society.

Anthony's behavior didn't reveal a broader purpose guiding his actions. We don't have insight into the endgame of his drive beyond succeeding with his clients in selling real estate. Perhaps money is viewed as an important tool enabling him to "get it done," whatever the need of the moment or across the years may be.

Readiness: Moderate

It's likely safe to assume taking me out is part of a longer-term plan to meet a future partner. However important that may sound, his preparation was clearly superficial—checking his hair and walking out. No intellectual set up took place. I asked. No questions were prepared, no checking my LinkedIn, and no watching any of the readily available videos, talks, and so on. He had no knowledge of me beyond my online dating profile and our short initial conversation, which told me a lot.

Psychoanalyst Comments

Perhaps there was no higher Readiness needed, no further thought or other preparing called for, and it is appropriate to Just Show Up.

I'm struggling with this. The answer lies in what we're preparing for. How important and impactful is it?

Really, it's a question for Anthony. Why is he Showing Up? If he's trying to meet a long-term companion, it makes sense to do

ANTHONY'S SHOW-UP TARGET

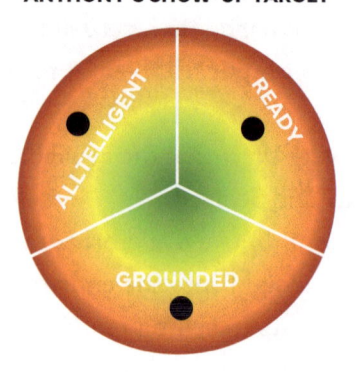

Grounding: Low

> ### Psychoanalyst Comments
>
> I agree with the low rating of Anthony's Grounding. What matters here is the difference between taking care of things in a thoughtful, responsible way versus a patriarchal, controlling manner. As described here, Anthony is showing male-dominant, patriarchal behaviors. And he's doing so without recognizing it.
>
> His *I'll take care of everything. I don't care what you want. I'll tell you what you want* lacks empathy and dismisses the needs and wants of others. Anthony is assuming he knows what's right for another mature adult and is claiming ownership over delivering on her needs. Priding himself on this shows distorted thinking.

While Anthony mentioned the roots of his behavior in his father's modeling, he seemed not to have a sense of how he Shows Up, or the larger purpose his father's guidance may have created. Seeking his father's approval and earning it by "taking charge" and "getting things done" seems to have happened with limited consideration of others.

who need not prepare internally for life's opportunities, preferring to control all he encounters. He's a man who sees not the beauty and honor of supporting others in their individuality or self-expression.

Why not ask his dates where they're comfortable meeting? Or his family how they want things to work out? Or what would be fun for them? Has he turned his kids into robots? Or are they stronger than that, having managed to push back in some way, desperately exerting their need to be recognized and approved for who they actually are, not who he wants them to be?

Motherfucker, my mind faintly whispers. It's a word my brain has never, in my life, evoked. *Wow.* Anthony has truly brought me to a new place. *Don't overreach,* my internal coach advises. Just because he doesn't think before a date doesn't mean he overcontrols his children.

Hmmm...well, perhaps my profanity is more justified than that, I realize. Within forty-five minutes I've learned his friends think he's overcontrolling, he dictates location for dates, physically controls women's bodies, encourages them to drink, hyper-manages interactions with his clients, makes sure "things work out" according to his definition in his family and work life, all while thinking he knows "everything he needs to know" and viewing his performance as immensely successful.

Stay neutral, my coaching mind reminded me. *Neither encourage nor dissuade.* Just say, *Thank you, Anthony. I need to get home now.*

And so, I did—tossing a twenty-dollar bill on the table in my wake. He failed to earn the privilege.

ANTHONY'S SHOW-UP SCORE:[4] 3

BARELY THERE   **JUST SHOWING UP**   **TRULY SHOWING UP**

his smirk, self-satisfaction, and conceit. It was insipidly sweet...rancidness. It moved in my mouth, burning. My tongue searched to somehow find a better taste, as I followed with an important question, "Did you think about anything in particular to be ready for our date? Or have you with other women?"

In my mind the options are endless. What type of day are they likely coming from? What type of transition into our evening of getting acquainted may be helpful, such as walking a bit, stopping to watch the river that runs right by our wine bar, stepping into the art gallery a few doors down, or looking at the library's new releases shelf? In general, what would she/he enjoy? Might she be fatigued or have a parenting challenge on her mind that we both relate to? The list goes on.

"Think? Do I think? No..." His words trailed off, seeming to have heard their ridiculousness and simultaneously embark on a desperate search to justify and vindicate themselves. Quaint. *Time to double down*, I think, faintly wishing him luck and barely tolerating the fiery tang on my tongue.

"I'm a great conversationalist," he comes back with, desperately hoping to redeem himself. "So I just show up, and things flow. No prep needed."

The trend lines in my data were strong now. His overconfidence, likely masking insecurity, was impeding on both his Grounding and his Readiness. Why prepare when you "know everything you need to know," are a "great conversationalist," and know how to make things "work out"? No interpretation needed. No data outliers to clean. He had reinforced the pattern many times. *This is great!* I thought. *Clarity!* But my tongue still stung. A gap existed in the experience he and I were having. And what a strange date. Glancing to the table, I search wildly for my gin and tonic. Quickly raising the drenched glass and thankful for a straw to suck, I forcefully imbibed.

It was a long swig. Savoring the drink, my tongue danced, a bit happier now. The sucking was soothing. Primal, it notably relaxed me. Finally, I swallow. *Can I go now?* my mind asks. I'd be pleased to rid myself of this self-congratulatory, non-thinking being. Someone

I tried to keep my expression in check. No need for him to be privy to my disenchantment. And well I did. He was sufficiently encouraged to ask a dreaded question.

"How's your date going? You having fun?"

Brows up! Mouth agape. Searching for words...it was quite the curveball. Finally, I tipped my head unconsciously and heard subtle but urgent diplomacy. "It's good to get to know you, Anthony."

Nice work! I congratulated myself. Don't know where it came from but glad it came out.

Honesty is central to my being, so direct questions with no good answer can be tricky. I needed to sidestep self-sabotage. Relaxing, he showed acceptance of my emotionally vacuous platitude. I sighed in relief while judging him harshly for failing to wince at my blank cliché. Amid the fun of my racing internal insults, I realized I'd better get out of there before he tried to take my hand or offered another premature and presumptuous physical overture. My body hinted at the presence of subtle dread hovering ahead. Just then a thought barged in—I didn't ask!

What came out in a tepid, sweet tone, was, "Anthony, I'm wondering, how did you prepare for this date?"

Not skipping a beat, he said, "I got my hands wet and ran them through my hair. You know, check the quaff. Then I walked out and saw you!" His smiling tone, flush with confidence, said it all. Everything was as it needed to be. His preparation was pure perfection.

After a momentary pause, he continued, "I know everything I need to know. Like with my clients, I react in the moment. I tell them what's needed, and they do it. That's how it works. I'm good once conversation gets going. I get things done."

I'm not surprised! my brain puked up. Luckily it got trapped in the density of my skull and failed to ooze. Not even a whisper escaped. *That's all a high-potential date is worth?* I thought. *Check your hair and all is ready? Tell us what's needed, and we do it?* Nausea, which had abated, was re-cued. It waited patiently in the staging area, sensing its special guest performance was suddenly necessitated.

Anthony rested back, an elephant of smugness. My tongue tasted

make leaving your kids be for naught tonight…you've got only thirty-five more minutes.

Luckily, he continued with a doozy.

"I was upset for a few years, then my friends asked, 'Are you still mad because she filed and you weren't in control? Because, you know, you like to manage things.'"

This is his friend's perspective! He's telling me he has control issues and has no idea! Could it get any better?

"I'm not overcontrolling," he assured me, once again showing sensitivity to the topic. "I just like to arrange things…you know, so they work out. It's how I was raised. Know what you want and get it done. Take charge. It's what my dad did. He made his expectations clear, and I rose to the occasion."

Brilliant reframe, my friend! I never could have thought of it! Arranging things so they work out? Take charge? That's what he thinks he's doing!?

I quickly asked, "Does anyone else have a say in what is 'arranged'? Or what it means for them to 'work out'?"

"Nah, I just take care of it. Make things smooth. I like to get it all done…don't need help. It's better that way."

His tone and body reeked of pride. *Boy, does he think he's successful, a glowing, ever-giving treasure on this planet. Every woman should flock to him for the privilege of his all-encompassing care and devotion. Perhaps he thinks he's doing great favors for his family, taking brilliant and comprehensive care of them. What a great dad (and former husband) he must be.*

Encouraging him, I repeated, "I see, you like things to work out… you take care of it all, arranging things well so they're smooth." *How great it all sounds!*

"Yes!" he glommed on. Getting animated now. Eyes wide. Arms outstretched. Clearly encouraged. "I make things happen. That's why I'm so good at my job. It's all about MY effort. I'm the boss. No one tells me what to do. I put in the time, and I create results."

Anthony settled into himself, clearly sensing our date was going swimmingly. He felt affirmed, understood, perhaps even appreciated.

and we've barely sat down. This feels hard. I didn't want to pilot the night too much. *I want to create an environment where he comes alive and I get to experience his true colors. That's the whole point.*

"Okay, I'll have a gin and tonic, please. Water, too, when you have a chance." *That'll solve this*, I thought, pleased with my resolution and gifting myself a shiny gold star for having made it this far.

A gold star, I thought. *Wow*. I shouldn't be earning those on a date. This is the moment it switched from a date to a book interview. If it's this hard in the first few minutes, no future do we have. I got my head back into the game and asked, "What do you do when a woman wants to meet somewhere other than Tina's Wine Bar?"

"They don't," he said, then followed with, "I don't meet anywhere else. If they don't want to meet at the bar where I'm comfortable, we don't meet."

Quite the confession! It *IS* his way or the highway! And he seems not to realize this. I sensed I was dealing with an epiphenomenon, the top-level manifestation of so much of his life. *How had his ex-wife and children survived? How do they continue to survive?* I felt a rush of compassion for the two children he mentioned on our first call. *How are they coping? Are they able to access their true needs and interests, what I lost in exchange for sustaining my marriage?*

Straining to stay focused, I asked, "Does it happen often?"

"Sure! Lots of women ask to meet other places. A restaurant or coffee shop or for a hike or activity. But I say no. Then they agree to the bar. I know how to get women to come around. The few who don't aren't for me," he replied.

Nausea. *Welcome to the party*, my mind greets my sick stomach and repugnance. My awareness of a subtle smirk tells me I'm on my game. I ask, "What led to your divorce, if you don't mind my asking?"

"We realized we wanted different things. Where to live, how to live, how to raise the kids."

How surprising! I try to hide my sustained smirk. Sounds like his wife realized she was always saying yes to his dictates and finally stood up for herself. *Listen well*, I coach myself. *You're here for a reason. Don't*

know them? Is he making a point? My body felt tight. His governing arm, unwelcome. Never had I felt this before. He was steering me. It started the moment he saw me. The message was, "I'm his." This was all new...and bizarrely alarming.

Still, I can see how some women might love it. Feeling totally cared for in the protective cocoon of a strong man's grasp. No need to think. Enjoy the ride. It's spectator life. Not a concern in the world.

As we approached the table, I smiled in expectant compliance. My body slowly sat. I removed my coat, revealing a slim waistline and unintentionally chest-defining bright white sweater. His well-attuned eyes met my subtle cleavage. They landed on my bust a little heavy. It felt like an unwanted hand batting away a fly and hitting a bit too hard. *Yuck. You're not welcome here*, my chest responded. His face didn't seem to receive the message.

Why does this feel oddly invasive? I asked myself. *Is he taking care of me or conducting me?* I forced myself to inhale deeply, hoping to relax my body. The breath was hard. My upper chest muscles clenched, unhappy. *Well, this is certainly new and something to be avoided.*

Before we had fully settled in, Anthony called a waiter and summonsed a bourbon like an old friend. The alcohol seemed to be his deep breath, his oxygen, his requirement for normal functioning. The few seconds I needed to consider my drink order were clearly a nuisance to him, an uninvited guest to our party, delaying his preferred pace of affairs. *Guess I'm not supposed to hesitate in ordering.* But at that moment, my brain remained hazy from being steered like a robot to our table and my bust being swatted. I didn't want alcohol to interfere, especially now, with what I had just discovered about Anthony.

After a second to reclaim cognitive functioning amid the series of emotional slaps, "Tonic water, please," is what came out. I wanted to remain sharp. No room for alcohol with Anthony.

"Tonic water? Surely you want a drink!" he commanded.

I do? I questioned, considering his suggestion.

No, I don't, my mind silently affirmed. Sigh. Too many challenges,

Anthony: *No.*

Me: *Why?* I felt my attention zero in on his response, my night and future with Anthony hanging in the balance, even at this early stage.

Anthony: *It's just what I'm comfortable with. After the first date, I'm flexible.*

Wow. Important insight. Could it be right? Feels rigid. It's his way or the highway. He did use the word "flexible." After resetting from this unwelcome discovery, I decided to prioritize getting to know Anthony over a beach walk, however desperately needed. *Perhaps I can fit it in before we meet*, I told myself unrealistically.

Fine, I responded. *I'll be there.*

After two decades with (what felt to me like) an overcontrolling husband, my antennae are up when it comes to inflexible, manipulative partners. I became hyper-accommodating. Had to be. Sustaining the marriage required it. The toll is vast. My preferences, my authenticity, and much more got lost. It's hard to even know when I'm capitulating. Which answer is true to myself? There's a point when accommodators like me cease to be our Selves at all—or to be anyone. Life becomes about enabling the dominant person…just to get by.

That evening, I headed to Anthony's spot. Had he not said an immediate *Hi!* as I approached along the sidewalk, I wouldn't have recognized him…he looked nothing like his photos. Older, short hair, thirty-plus pounds of unexpected girth. Made me wonder why he seemed so confident. Another mystery.

After securing an assumptive hug, which I'm not sure I would have granted had I seen a way out, he proceeded to guide me down the sidewalk. Approaching the wine-bar door, he pulled it open and propelled me in. Then, somehow, he managed to maintain his arm securely around my shoulders as we walked past fellow bar goers. He maneuvered me around the tables. It was subtle but commanding, a few choice fingertips steering my upper body with keen precision, as if skirting cones on a racetrack.

As we passed people, a few heads turned. I wondered why, starting to feel possessed by this strange man I had agreed to meet. *Does he*

GROUNDING ENCOUNTER— MY DATE WITH ANTHONY

The Person: His online dating profile and photos were appealing. Longish hair, confident, stylish clothes, works in a white-collar sales role with lots of upside, suggesting plentiful ambition and drive. Seemed extroverted with a good personality. A positive, fun guy. (Spoiler alert: How wrong I was!)

The Purpose: Despite high hopes, my date soon became a nondate or what I skillfully repurpose as a "book interview"—when the date goes south and I shift my focus from romantic interest to assessing how he chose to Show Up.

The Experience: A few days before we met, we had a predate call. He came on strong. Ten minutes into the call I hear, *I really want to meet you! We're going to hit it off. I can tell. We already have. Meet me for a drink at Tina's Wine Bar Tuesday night!*

Unmoved by his gushing, I responded, *That night actually works. How fortuitous. See you there. 6:30.*

The morning of our date, I texted him. *Good morning, Anthony. What an exquisitely warm day! Want to start at the beach five minutes from the wine bar?* I had visions of strolling in calm waves at our feet. My sandals hung loosely in my fingers, cool sand contouring to my bare feet with each step. Silly conversation and giggles bubbling between us.

His response put that to rest. *That's not really my style for first dates. I like to meet at Tina's and have a drink. It's comfortable. Come meet me there.*

Bleh. Inside? I thought. *Hard surfaces and dim lights on a day like today?* We had endured a cold, long winter. That day's warm glory and sun were my wish for months. Six-thirty would be the day's last hours of light. How could I let it go? It pulled on me. *Invest me well,* it advised.

Me: *Inside? On a day like today?* I asked, concerned and disenchanted.

Anthony: *Yep. Meet me there!* he playfully(?) demanded.

Clearly, we didn't share this fundamental sensibility. *Noted,* my brain remarked with a thud. Then curiosity struck.

Me: *Do you ever meet somewhere other than a bar?*

and reasonable, so, yes, of course I'll do it! We're copacetic. You're with "Miss It's-all-good. No worries." Now I realize that really this is "Ms. No Boundaries." Time to slip into a new outfit called, "Ms. Show-Up-for-Myself-and-BE-REAL!" This also means being in touch with what I'm feeling. I need to access the part of myself that wants to say, "Isn't that better done yourself?," not bury it, jump off it, or rationalize it. No more detaching from my feelings or burying my true tiny voice in the brisk wind of the moment.

What we're discussing here—living in echoes of old patterns that are a misfit for our lives today—is what Brené Brown is talking about when she recommends *rumbling*. "A rumble is a discussion, conversation, or meeting defined by a commitment to lean into vulnerability, to stay curious and generous." Rumbles are needed when we are not copacetic and we need to express something we fear someone else won't like.

A dear old friend (read: man who broke my heart) told me, "I can see you go up. You feel something, then immediately jump into your head, not fully experiencing the emotion." He's describing how I leave the embodied sensation, defaulting to thought instead. What priceless insight! It's one way we protect ourselves from pain. I've been practicing feeling emotions in my body and addressing them ever since.

Contrasting this is an entertaining date experience illustrating one man's challenge to know himself. Yes, this actually happened.

within all of us. How can we possibly keep up with the microstressors of daily life? We can't. And it's okay.

How to Deepen Our Grounding

In addition to interviewing different parts of ourselves, reviewing our experience through writing is known to deepen our grounding. It opens space for us to recognize more fully what we feel and why. In Chapter 12 I detail ways to do this, such as journaling, working with a trained therapist, and a targeted reflecting process called "Wheel of Awareness." All three approaches have been well studied and proven to better connect us with our Selves.

In the absence of such reflecting we're moving through Situations with a degree of blindness. Lived experiences, be they notable shocks, sways, or invisible nudges, all change us. We evolve in an experience-dependent way.[3] This means we carry both bold and silent impacts into all that comes next. The only way to choose who we are and how we Show Up is to bring more consciousness, time, and intent to considering the events of our lives and how to productively interpret them.

These are big aspirations. And they're ongoing pursuits. The work can be fun and hard and rewarding. It doesn't mean we all need therapy nor does it mean we must probe our dusty emotional corners. And it certainly doesn't mean we're inadequate or failing. On the contrary, it is vital work enabling us to live more aligned with our true nature. And it does just this with each nugget we recognize about our Selves.

> **My Personal Case Study**
>
> Working to deepen my Grounding led to recognizing that I can be a people pleaser. It Shows Up when I'm overly flexible, eagerly yielding to others' whims. I rarely say no and have minimal boundaries. When people ask things of me or have certain expectations, I see their perspective as completely valid

> **It's how one person's emotional work is all our work. Society, with its splendor and squalor, is the synthesis of all of us. And we individually are slices of Society. We're in a collective and made of the collective. This makes us simultaneously INdividuals and ALLdividuals. It explains how and why we're affected by how we each Show Up.**

Our Internal Family System

One common challenge to our Grounding is the competing interests and priorities we all wrestle with. This plays out daily as wanting nice things versus keeping money in the bank and getting to bed early versus watching that next episode or going out late. Longer-term competing interests may be keeping the job versus pursuing what we love. These inconsistencies are like a personal family inside each of us. Some parts we like, others we don't. Some get along. Some don't. We're constantly negotiating among and between them since some parts exist to solve for, or work against, others. Dick Schwartz is the creator of this concept called *internal family systems.*

To honor our various internal factions, it's helpful to interview them. This way we can understand the distinct aspects of each, and we can thank them for their service. After all, even our coping behaviors that challenge us today originally developed to help us. Interviewing the parts of us aids our Grounding, Readiness, and Alltelligence by helping us make sense of our conflicting needs and interests. All are expressions of honest needs developed in response to past experiences. One conflict I feel, for example, is to protect myself from a judgmental family member while also wanting his friendship and support. Questions I can ask include: Why is this person important to me? How can I enjoy the good this person offers while maintaining safe boundaries against their judgments? What will I do when I feel fearful of their criticism? Realistically, limited Self-knowledge lives

> They are actually yours. They are…designed specifically for you by a part of you that loves you more than anything else….The part of you that loves you more than anything else has created roadblocks to lead you to yourself. You are not going in the right direction unless there is something pricking you in the side, telling you, 'Look here! This way!' That part of you loves you so much that it doesn't want you to lose the chance. It will go to extreme measures to wake you up. It will make you suffer greatly if you don't listen. What else can it do? That is its purpose."

It's setting a high bar to be well grounded. Our native sense of belonging, overlapping Me and We, feels unnatural. (See chart and description of Me-We on page 42.) And, like Truly Showing Up, it's an endless pursuit since life keeps flowing. This is why, even with a consistent Situation of years in the same job, in the same hometown, with a dependable partner and family situation, taking time to reflect on what happens and to learn about our Selves is an important contributor to our health and happiness. Reviewing how we Showed Up in specific Situations helps us codify and claim our learning. While a reflecting process can be hard to sustain, chances are the more Grounded among us do more of it.

> Grounding, like all Show-Up skills, cascades through Society. One person's depth of Grounding is absorbed by their children, partner, colleagues, and friends. It becomes the safety and authenticity (or disengaged disregard) of our workplaces. It fertilizes the school playground, classroom, and soccer team.

Such emotions may Show Up as a general tension or dissatisfaction. We may not know what it is or what to do about it. Or we may know full well what it is we're feeling yet permit fear to steer us instead of courage, or lethargy instead of discipline. This is incredibly common. It can be hard to notice our feelings or what our body is telling us, let alone pause to honor it. This is challenged further by the fast flow of our days, especially if we lack a regular reflecting process and have yet to identify the roots of our core behaviors and drive. We may be doing a few things at once, functioning more as human doings than human beings. We may be trained to jump off our emotions (avoidance) or be quick to tell ourselves a different, more convenient narrative (JSUPing). "It'll be okay. No need to discuss that issue right now" (denial or procrastinating).

Physical sensations of being partially disconnected from our Selves play out as symptoms of stress and anxiety—headaches, stomachaches, back pain, bowel issues, muscle tension, gnawing in our bellies, feeling caved in or hollow, and so much more.[2] These symptoms are natural responses to life's realities. And they are more intense and stick around longer when we're less grounded. When poorly grounded, we're also less able to recognize these symptoms as indicating we need to stop, think, and reconnect with our deeper, truer Selves.

We may drift, unsure of what will fulfill us, at least for the moment. Or we may have clear conviction based on chasing an unmet craving for acceptance, worthiness, importance, or other basic need. This clouded view into who, what, and why we are means answers may keep changing. Goals become harder to reach or are unfulfilling once reached. Dissatisfaction may lead frustration, anger, or ineffectiveness to creep in. Intrinsic gratification becomes scarce. Basically, our ability to Show Up as we choose is hindered. Low Grounding, like low Readiness and Alltelligence, may swirl into a reinforcing spiral.

> **As described so eloquently by A. H. Almaas, "Your conflicts, all the difficult things, the problematic situations in your life are not chance or haphazard.**

> these needs. If our tendencies are long lived, we've been rewarded by Society for our compensating behaviors for just as long. It can be scary to recognize significant relationships may exist in service of compensating roles that are not our true Selves. Now it's risky to dismantle them. Working to deepen our Grounding gets under our compensating behaviors to access and heal our vulnerable places. This reconnects us as a more stable, intrinsically satisfied Self. It fortifies the underlying wholeness within each of us. It was always there. Now more of our genuine Self can Show Up.

This is novel insight for many of us. It explains a striking feature of our minds and how we Show Up, how limited our understanding of our Selves may be. Said eloquently by Alain de Botton's company, The School of Life, "Although we inhabit ourselves, we seldom manage to make sense of more than a fraction of who we are." Yet the patterns shaping us are often common and understandable, offering significant gateways to happiness, fulfillment, and effectiveness. By observing and considering these tendencies, we deepen our Grounding and sense of Self. The process often requires pausing, perhaps with pen and paper or a laptop, to reflect on how we're Showing Up and why.

Low to moderate Grounding manifests in myriad forms. We may feel ill at ease because our drive is fueled by needy striving more than a purposeful calling. We may behave inconsistently because we're unclear which way is our true north. Emotionally, we may not be clear what we're feeling or why. Unexpected emotions may startle us or throw us off. And we may be overly sensitive. We may feel like imposters in a room of better thinkers, the one who doesn't deserve to be there, sabotaging potentially earned opportunities. This makes us magnetic for other porous Selves, reinforcing our status quo, potentially bringing each other down.

through, make repairs, and grow into new perspectives. But some of these compensating behaviors are less sustainable. Those involving external gratification can become runaway addictive. They keep us busy, and our companies in business, but never quite meet our needs.

> **Even when hard won, if we're driven by unmet needs, the promotion, title, award, and attention don't satisfy us for long. The external world will never like us enough, tell us we're attractive enough, nice enough, or successful enough. Our Self-doubt festers. Do people like me for me or for what I do for them? Is my attention or success, because I'm worthy, or because I'm presenting an attractive package? Inner doubts can't be satisfied from the outside. No spa treatment, cruise, fast car, or fabulous night on the town can make us feel whole. But our modern-day salves are often the drug that works almost well enough, keeping us addicted and needing more. Alas, only understanding and accepting our true Selves can make us feel whole. This truth is one reason I'm writing this book. I want everyone to feel whole, satisfied, and peaceful. And I'm hoping learning about Showing Up moves us toward this worthy goal.**
>
> **We're all living along the continuum of low to high Grounding. Our friends, romantic partners, careers, spending habits, and fashion choices all relate to either our true Self, if we're well grounded, or to our performance Self, the part developed in response to partially unmet needs in the world we grew up in. It can be challenging to see how we've constructed our relationships, home life, and work life to meet**

of value, our daily life may still include striving to compensate. Do we overprioritize being attractive to others? Need we earn accolades to prove our worthiness? Such grasping for wholeness orients our Self disproportionately toward I, me, and mine than toward us, we, and ours.

Nuances of unmet and partially met childhood needs extend well beyond worthiness. If we didn't get sufficient approval, we may be consumed by winning approval, Showing Up with a winning personality, even if it's more an act of performance than being true to our Selves. Dr. Maté explains more of the nuanced ways our early years Show Up as "our personality" today. For example, "if we didn't feel valued for who we are, we need to measure up to feel valued. If we were not made to feel special, we may be demanding, perhaps going into politics or other leadership roles that give us authority. If we weren't honored for who we are, we may need to impress people with our fabulous attributes. If not made to feel important for who we are, we may seek to help others and be needed, perhaps through becoming a physician or first responder. If not liked for who we are, we may become so very nice that people will like us. Never can our real emotions be revealed because that's not nice. If we didn't feel loved, we'll adapt by becoming charming. And if we weren't sufficiently recognized, we may live a life of seeking status."[1]

Our response to work situations, illness, accidents, and other life events shapes us as well. Collectively, these external influences craft not just our behavior, but the behavior of everyone we know. Over time our actions and tendencies are interpreted as attributes. But they're false attributes. To one extent or another, we're all striving and grasping to address unmet needs extending from our past. We also cover up and compensate for painful feelings. Our culture, economy, and society are created this way. Many of our industries, businesses, products, and services are tending drives and cravings emanating from unresolved past experiences that continue to guide us every day.

In many cases it's fine to process challenging experiences over time. Compensating behaviors of being a bit stressed, less happy, motivated, or engaged may be okay for a while. They gift us time to think things

Each moment we reveal the depth of our Self-knowledge, our internal connectedness. People sense it in the calm or disquiet of our presence. They see it in our tendencies, biases, patterns, and preferences. It can be as simple as whether we're happy with ourselves. My friend Joe Pastore, chief HR officer at RNN TV, shared just this: "I know myself well enough to be happy with who I am." Many of us strive to achieve this, yet it remains partially outside our grasp.

Like Readiness and Alltelligence, Grounding exists along a continuum. Level 3 Grounding best supports Showing Up as we choose. People with this level of skill can often trace their emotional and psychological DNA back to seminal experiences, those decisive moments that sculpt our current way of living.

These memorable moments mold our work ethic, ambition, integrity, how trusting we are, and much more. Knowing these decisive moments, such as the three seminal experiences I describe in the first few pages of this book that lead me to focus on Showing Up, helps us feel at home inside ourselves.

Without at least a moderate degree of Grounding, we may seek saviors outside of ourselves. Unhealthy saviors include living in performance mode, relationships existing primarily to validate ourselves, overworking, hollow busyness, eating, or drinking as emotional relief, and other compensating behaviors. Fundamentally, we all need to feel good about ourselves. Achieving this from the inside by being grounded is the way to get there.

Low Grounding

Judging from today's elevated degrees of divisiveness, racism, bullying, microaggressions, antisemitism, and extremism, low to moderate Grounding is widespread. It can be hard to understand our Selves. Roots of our behavior may be hidden. Often they extend from our earliest years when we weren't conscious of how sufficiently caregivers responded to our basic needs. Dr. Gabor Maté explains that if our young Selves didn't get the attention needed to develop an inherent sense

WE REVEAL OUR GROUNDING EACH MOMENT

Deepening Grounding through Screenwriting

Dan Pulick is an adjunct professor at one of America's premier film schools. He explains:

True development in the arts is a difficult process, especially early on. We must have an intact, robust ego and sense of self to even try to write, in the first place, and yet, that very ego will be the single biggest obstacle to our work finally realizing its honest depths.

It takes an entire semester to even begin to understand how big that mountain is for us to climb, and for how long—well past our college years—we'll be climbing it.

The role I find myself in is one of a tight-rope walker, providing the balance of positive support with honest and often times painful critique. What's most painful for the students is that the critique reflects back at them the gap between what the piece needs to be, organically of its own insistence, and what they want it to be.

By default, then, this is a confrontation of their ego and identity. But that's my job, to help them see that gap, and be comfortable with it, and accept it and start to close it.

As painful as that may be, I have to be willing to risk the relationship, to a degree, and the feel-good/everything's-fine euphoria that comes with first-draft creation, in the service of their long-term development.

Showed Up for me in spades that difficult day.

To be real, I did walk out. I didn't push back when Karen commanded me to leave. I fell into little Marcy's pattern of compliance, people-pleasing, lacking boundaries and spine. My daughter saw me abandon her. I could say this was a failure. But I'm not. With the security guard at my hip and my purse in Karen's hand, my instinct told me to go with the flow, trusting I'd turn the situation around quickly enough. That's exactly what happened.

HOW GROUNDED SHOWS UP

Solid. Stable. Secure. Durable. Enduring. Genuine. Calm. You know who these people are. And if it's you, you'll relate to the phrase "feeling in touch with ourselves." I like the physicality of it. It's tactile, describing being able to "touch" who we are. It gets at our essence, character, and sustaining traits. This concreteness also implies grounded people are predictable. We know how they are going to respond and we know their boundaries. When this is us, we're steady for others as we safely depend on and belong to ourselves.

More grounded people often have rituals supporting their Self-understanding. These rituals include things like formal reflecting practices, journaling, meditating or working with a coach or therapist. Regular exercise, sleep, and nutrition practices are common as well. Examples of grounded people include my friend Mark. He's the parent who remains a go-to sounding board for his teen children…and their friends! It's his house they flock to on weekends to hang out. He's the boss, colleague, and friend many in the office and neighborhood confide in. He's the person who is equally contented alone and with others. Wow. The power. This is being grounded.

why I believe it. This knowledge makes me solid. It guided me through a triggered moment, providing the support I needed. Without such insight into who I am, volatile emotions driven by fear and urgency would have ruled the day. My Grounding saved me…and my daughter. After Karen shared her story and a long hug, she walked me back to my daughter's bedside. Then, with a caring smile, left.

> **Beyond Self-awareness, in which the Self becomes the focus of attention, deep Grounding orients us outward. It is the source of our mature, connected Self described in Chapter 3. It enables us to flexibly receive others because we have assimilated our own experiences. Grounding creates space to sense, gather and accept the implicit nuances arising in our Situations. And it enables us to be still. We're close friends with quiet and solitude because our inner world is coherent. Even when with others, Grounding affords us shelter from within. We're clear about our core nature and relate positively to it. This helps us be true to ourselves, further validating who we are. And it creates a sense of belonging to our Selves as part of a larger whole, flowing within our relational world.**

Deeper Grounding makes us confident in our judgment. It helps us be focused, capable, and productive. We experience less fear, imposter syndrome, and second-guessing of our Selves, exchanging it for precise thought and conviction. We're genuine, less likely to put on an act, or to perform. When in performance mode, behaving a certain way to earn others' favor, we're Showing Up more as persona than person. Deep grounding renders these common patterns irrelevant. It is our infrastructure of poise, levelheadedness, and self-assuredness. And it

people with genuine care, believing deep down we're wired to help each other. These are core aspects of my identity. They guide me always. But I couldn't leave my daughter alone. She shouldn't see her mother turn and walk away without calmly framing the situation for her and creating at least a bit of emotional safety.

Overwhelmed, I felt tears cascading down my cheeks. I closed my eyes, feeling their cool wetness, and found a few calm words. "Karen, I need thirty seconds to reset and speak with my daughter." As I took my first deep breath and met my daughter's eyes, Karen handed my purse to the security guard. I felt trapped. I looked for two long seconds into my daughter's eyes, showing her strength and care as Karen, the guard, and I turned and walked out, leaving my daughter in the ER bed alone.

Pausing in the lobby, defeated and angry, I stared Karen in the eyes, my enemy. No, a professional needing to keep the ER at a low simmer so desperate people like my daughter and I can get help. "Look at us," I said. "Two strong women. Good at what we do. In other circumstances, we'd be friends." Her body shifted. Mine settled. "I have a question. Need your expertise." Pointing to my still river-soaked face, I asked, "How do I stop the tears? It's been happening a lot." Within a few seconds Karen said in a far softer voice, "The same thing happened to me. My son is dealing with a similar mental health issue, and just a year ago I was crying uncontrollably, not sleeping…" And in that moment we transitioned from adversaries into something closer to sisters.

This is the power of Grounding. It is the degree to which we know our Selves, and the skill native to our role as individuals. This internal connectedness supports us in accessing judgment and skill, even in unsettling situations. When well developed, it supplies safety from within. And in that safety lies strength and our genuine nature. This opens us to feeling others more deeply. People sense this "with-ness." It leads them to open to us, trust us, and help us. In befriending Karen, I lived into a core belief that grounds me. It's that we're all driven by the same fundamental fears and needs and therefore share similar experiences. It led me to relate to her at the level of our shared humanness (Alltelligence). I know where this skill and belief come from and

CHAPTER 9
SELF-GROUNDING

This chapter leads you through the following ideas:
- Source of power
- Past and purpose
- Doomed to perpetuate patterns?
- Living in our body
- Ongoing growth

GROUNDING— CONNECTED WITHIN OUR SELF

I was kicked out of the emergency room at Greenwich Hospital yesterday. I had brought my twelve-year-old daughter in for an acute mental health need. After keeping us there for close to thirty hours, a head nurse we'll call Karen said my family was creating too much commotion. Security was at my left hip initiating our exodus, leaving my young daughter in the hospital bed, alone. I hadn't been told patients can have only one visitor, so my mother and father had come. Standing sternly at my daughter's bedside, Karen got right in my face: "You need to leave! Security and I are escorting you out. Is this your purse?" she asked as she picked it up.

My brain and body crackled. I was triggered, pressured, and violated all at once. I noticed. But there was no time. In situations like this, our default behavior rules. Somehow my mind clicked in reminding me that I play by the rules and make it work. I cooperate while disarming

The legacy of how we Show Up

lives well beyond us

and well beyond what we realize.

A DEEPER DIVE INTO THE THREE SHOW-UP ROLES AND SKILLS

Self-Grounding, Situational Readiness, Societal Alltelligence

9 SELF-GROUNDING

10 SITUATIONAL READINESS

11 SOCIETAL ALLTELLIGENCE

PART III

Longer Term

4. Place an X on the continuum where you've been living recently.

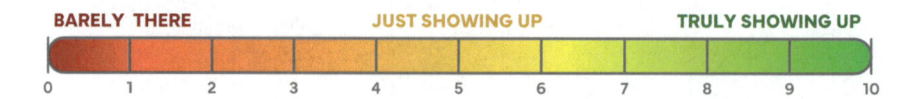

BARELY THERE — **JUST SHOWING UP** — **TRULY SHOWING UP**
0 1 2 3 4 5 6 7 8 9 10

Now mark a few Show-Up scores for goals you want to achieve, such as being promoted and improving a relationship. What Show-Up level is needed to achieve them?

- What does it look like?
- How does it feel?
- What will you do differently to achieve it?

6. Showing Up is a growth process. Not asking, "How am I choosing to Show Up?" is letting ourselves off the hook of our own learning. Over time it degrades us, entrenching us in a cycle of below-potential performance. This absence of growth and learning is not treading water; it's sinking. It degrades our lives and our Society.

REFLECTING QUESTIONS

Right Now

Applying a one-to-ten scale, at what level are you performing? (For example, I'm Showing Up at six right this morning, the high side of Just Showing Up.)

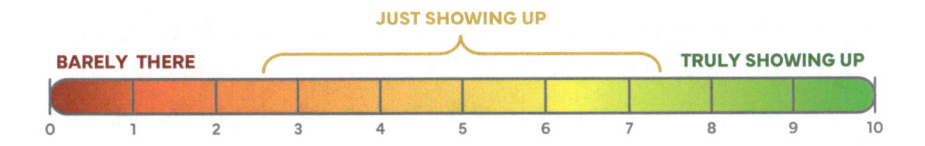

1. How satisfied are you with this? Why?

2. Where would you like to be? Why?

3. What is one small next step you can take to move toward your chosen performance?

CHAPTER 8 SUMMARY— TRULY SHOWING UP

1. Truly Showing Up is our highest level of performance, identified as Level 3 on the Show-Up continuum. It means we're keeping our three roles in mind, intentfully choosing the degree of each skill to Show Up with. It also means we're attuning to how we're Showing Up sufficiently often to improve or deliver the interaction we seek.

2. The word "attuning" is more on target for checking in on how we're Showing Up than "awareness, noticing, or presence" since it contains active qualities of being viscerally with another or a situation, of adjusting, movement, and progress.

3. Choosing our preferred behavior happens in one of two ways: either we planned in advance how we want to Show Up or we realize it in the moment. In both cases, attuning to our behavior immediately enables us to behave differently, moving us closer to interacting as we choose.

4. The steps can be simplified to attune-choose-Show Up or simply, notice-decide-act. It often happens simultaneously. It's how Showing Up works.

5. Level 3 is not an aspirational place. *It's a real place.* One many of us can and do live in, at least for a short while, during many, if not most, days. Like many peak-performance states, living in TSU 30–50 percent of the time is a solid goal. Above that is beyond a stretch for most of us.

practicing Showing Up is adventuresome. It's journeying through life with curiosity. Checking in and shifting toward our choice behavior roots us in our values, imbuing consistency, quality, and honor into our interactions. We're more dependable, less volatile. More purposeful, less adrift.

I believe the right side of the Show-Up continuum can be a common home to us all. This is the truth about Showing Up. And the whole point of this book. We can live more on the right side, perhaps even defaulting to the low end of Truly Showing Up, and we can make the conscious choice of where we live on the continuum more often.

> **With a bit of reflecting, Level 3 can be the place we regularly reside after a good night of sleep or quality family time. We can check in with each coffee break, walk, or other simple recharge practice. And we can sustain it by asking our simple question, "How am I choosing to Show Up?"**
>
> **Feeling satisfied is our reward. Like all Show-Up levels, it's contagious. Unlike the others, Truly Showing Up is the only responsible choice. It honors our interconnectedness, our resonance, with others and the world. This is why I believe it is incumbent on us to follow a systematic approach to practice Showing Up as individuals, organizations, and societies, to the greatest extent we can.**

> **degrades us. Absence of learning is not treading water. It's cracking without healing. Eventually, we die. Luckily, non-learning goes against our design.**

We're part of nature's learning system. Incremental adjustments are built into "our biological apparatus."[5] Adaptations are "a ubiquitous property of every system that has survived," Nassim Taleb explains.[6] And mother nature is one of our greatest examples. Where do we find other long-standing systems as "aggressive in destroying and replacing, in selecting and reshuffling" what doesn't serve it? In the long run, "everything with even the most minute vulnerability breaks, given the ruthlessness of time," yet Earth and systems that endlessly adapt and improve themselves survive. They gain from stressors by shifting how they Show Up.

And we need these minor stressors—new ideas, work projects, different people, new places, and self-improvement challenges—to keep us engaged. Otherwise, life feels stale. We need to attune, to test and learn, to grow. And most of the time, this is exactly what life offers. It's how Showing Up is the better fit for us, and the antidote to Just Showing Up. It challenges us to rise above the opt-out false luxury of "doesn't matter-ness," even during life's grind of Groundhog Day moments, unpleasantries, or disproportionate challenges. Complacency doesn't feel good in any circumstance because we're designed to engage, shift, and adapt. **We're designed to actively practice Showing Up. It's human nature. And it's our evolutionary inheritance.**

JSUPing is the opposite. It disregards learning. It shelters fragile and unpleasant emotions like, "That didn't go so well" or other versions of, "Awww shit" and often follows them with a masked or direct, "Whatever." Quotes from survey respondents of, "It is what it is," and, "I'm okay the way I am" are serious cop-outs. They perpetuate the downside. They're less Showing Up and more Showing Down. JSUPing means we're not realizing the risk to our Selves and Society we're creating by deciding it's okay to live DefaultLife. On the contrary,

> example demonstrates low Alltelligence at a minimum, if not also low Readiness and Grounding.

Dr. Klein's awareness of wanting to Truly Show Up 50 percent of the time focuses his mind on how he's interacting, helping him Show Up as he chooses.

NATURE'S LEARNING SYSTEM

> **It's important to pause here to be clear. We're aiming to instantiate—to bring to life—a ritual. It's a practice, not a destination. We're creating something deeply meaningful and core to our lives. It starts when we begin to regularly ask ourselves a simple question: "How am I choosing to Show Up?" After all, how we Show Up IS our life.**

I'm not promising nirvana here. I am, however, standing firmly on the mountain of data proving the power of small steps as an effective path to achieve goals. As Admiral William McRaven stated in his speech about Navy Seal training, "One step leads to another and another."[4] Then we begin noticing positive changes in the quality of our experience. And people notice a difference in us. There are only two paths. Either we decide to start checking in on how we're Showing Up, making small improvements, or we don't.

> **Not checking in on our behavior is letting ourselves off the hook as responsible for our own learning. And it likely sustains us in a cycle of performing below our potential. Over time, Just Showing Up**

peak-performance states, living in TSU 30–50 percent of the time is a solid goal. Above that is beyond a stretch for most of us. What we actually achieve matters far less than whether we make progress in bringing intent to our behavior more often. Practicing Showing Up is achieving.

Research for my last book, *On Your Game*, explains that on average, people achieve TSU-level performance only intermittently. Some of us don't focus on our behavior much. People report interacting as they'd choose as little as a few hours each month. And let's face it, most of us don't attune to our behavior with the frequency or consistency we'd like. This doesn't have to be the case. Practicing Showing Up shifts our baseline, our average performance, toward our chosen state.

> Dr. Arthur Klein, former president of the Mount Sinai Health Network, told me he aspires to Truly Show Up a minimum of 50 percent of the time. He explains that when meeting people, his first focus is AllTelligence. *"I start by relating personally. I'm a partner person, a collaborator. I want to meet at the time and in the environment that makes the person comfortable to reduce hierarchy."*
>
> Then he leans on Readiness. *"I like an agenda. Many people Show Up for meetings not knowing why it was called or what they're doing there. They Show Up with passivity as opposed to an attitude of, 'I'm going to actively participate.' You can be passive in lots of ways, like Showing Up without anything active to contribute."*
>
> Another behavior Dr. Klein notices is Showing Up passive-aggressively. *"In this case you've already decided you don't agree with what is promulgated, or you're being protective and don't want to put time into this particular agenda."* This final

A poignant example comes from a talented makeup artist and hair stylist I had the privilege of working with recently, Evie Selaty. She explained that doing makeup was the only time she felt connected with her mother. Their ritual was to rise at 5:00 a.m. each morning to do each other's makeup, gifting themselves a full hour of quality togetherness and fun before school and work. When not doing makeup, her mother could be hard to connect with. She was self-medicating with alcohol to cope with her own childhood challenges, leaving her less able to care for Evie and her siblings.

"Now," Evie explained, "I spend my life doing makeup and hair for others in an ongoing effort to re-feel that closeness with my mother and to give the feeling of being cared for to my clients. When I check in with, 'How am I Showing Up?,' my attention to detail is what I notice. It's in the makeup process but also in my preparation, timeliness, the questions I ask, and the emotional openness I create before walking into the venue or film set. It tells me I'm fully Showing Up for them and for myself, and I know it."

Evie paused, then shared, "My mom finally came to visit me last spring, after ten years in Texas. I try hard to accept who she is and what she has to offer. I don't want to be angry any longer. I want to accept her and move forward with my life." Evie loves her craft and is well rewarded for her dedication and skill. Knowing why she chose it, the deeper significance, helps her Truly Show Up with Readiness, Grounding, and Alltelligence to her professional world. She sure did with me.[3]

HOW OFTEN CAN WE DO IT?

Level 3 is not an aspirational place. *It's a real place,* one many of us can experience most days. People tell me they feel successful aiming for Level 3 approximately 30–50 percent of the time. Like many

A friend who works in publishing explained, "I review my calendar every Sunday evening. I take a full thirty minutes, typically just before dinner, to identify the important meetings and activities of the week. For each I ask myself, 'How do I want to Show Up?' I consider the people, purpose of the event, what I want to accomplish, and what success looks and feels like. I envision myself acting just the way I want. I know my weak points and what I need to change. This weekly practice has made it much easier to be mindful of how I act. I'm so much closer to my ideal than I was even three weeks ago."

Showing Up as a Court Officer in a Small Long Island Town

A uniformed court officer taking a lunch break at a local café started talking to me. (Maybe it was the cowboy hat.) He asked what I do. When I responded, *I help people choose to Show Up. What does the phrase mean to you?* I heard:

It is being mentally and physically prepared to present yourself in certain situations.

You bring who you are and what you need to know, and that's how you present yourself. People sense who you are instantly.

You always need to emphasize your strengths and downplay your weakness. We all know what we're good at and not good at. It all plays in to how we present ourselves.

As in hundreds of chats I've had like this one, the court officer listed Readiness, Grounding, and Alltelligence clearly in his definition of Showing Up.

1. Grounding in who we are and why
2. Readiness from planning and preparing
3. Alltelligence, from living prosocially with trust, care, and knowledge of our reciprocal impacts on each other

Given the trifecta of moderate to high Grounding, Readiness, and Alltelligence, we've set ourselves up for success in the moment and long term, however we're defining success and whatever the moment is. This helps us stave off, at least for a while, defaulting into judgment, bias, fear, or distraction. They'll come visit soon enough.

A NATURALLY CUMULATIVE GROWTH PRACTICE

> **Showing Up is naturally cumulative. What we do first creates what we do next. Then we infuse our choices with feedback from others and the environment. It's how we learn. It's how we Show Up better each moment, creating our future, whether it's DefaultLife (JSUPing) or learning and adjusting (Truly Showing Up).**

Ways to apply "How am I choosing to Show Up?" include the following:

1. Before a Situation: engaging forethought to identify <u>how we want</u> to Show Up
2. Right now: attuning ourselves to how we're Showing Up <u>in the moment</u>
3. After a Situation: considering our behavior without excuses or justifying it

A SUFFICIENT DEGREE

What's "a sufficient degree"? Any amount that creates progress. While this may sound vague, it's not. We know what progress feels like. And we know when we're on a good path. We also have a clear sense of when checking in on how we're Showing Up matters. It's often when the activity feels important. We may have goals around it or feel compelled to do well. We intuitively know when and where to focus on Showing Up. And if we don't, part of our life will be nudged further and further out of line until something breaks or we get to the point of "this has to change!" Then we know. Something has become out of whack to "a sufficient degree" that it prods-triggers-inspires us to ask, "How am I choosing to Show Up…to this relationship, job, project, health issue, emotion, situation?" This is why I think and feel "a sufficient degree" is quite clear.

HOW IT FEELS TO TRULY SHOW UP

> **At a deeper level, Truly Showing Up is delivering on our vision for our lives. By checking in we're progressively linking our current behavior with our desired vision for our lives. This brings us in line with our chosen legacy. This fortifies our confidence. We feel strong. Our mind, heart, and body are ready, calm, engaged. We emanate leadership. We invest not just skin in the game. We invest soul. And those around us know. They feel it and connect with us more deeply by absorbing our positive relational energy into their own body and behaviors.**

Achieving Level 3 happens most regularly when we're moderately to well developed in three areas:

an expanse of time, such as football season, year-end, or retirement. And since we do it most often and most purposefully in Level 3, our lives have an active quality when we Truly Show Up. Life feels dynamic. It has momentum as we attune to our actions and choose how we behave. We feel more of life is in our hands and that we exist in a space of opportunity. This makes Level 3 a positive state that brings us closer to who we want to be. It reinforces our Grounding and promotes Readiness and Alltelligence as we check in more often on how we're Showing Up.

> Taking the positive momentum of Truly Showing Up a step further, in psychology, attuning is used to describe a deeper state of connecting and caring for someone. In his book *Attuned: Practicing Interdependence to Heal Our Trauma—and Our World*,[1] Thomas Hübl defines the concept as "coming into resonance by listening mindfully to the inner sensations, feelings, images, and information that arise." Dr. Dan Siegel, an author and neuroscientist says, "When we attune with others, we allow our own internal state to shift, to come to resonate with the inner world of another. This resonance is at the heart of 'feeling felt,' the meaningful sense that emerges in close relationships. Children need attunement to feel secure, and throughout our lives we need attunement to feel close and connected."[2] As I've described, Truly Showing Up happens with, to, and for our Selves, others, Society, and the world.

Finally, let's explain (in more real and vulnerable terms, let's justify) the use of "a sufficient degree" in my two-step explanation of Truly Showing Up.

ATTUNE-CHOOSE-SHOW UP: A BEHAVIOR CHAIN

Recognizing "I'm being defensive" implies "let's let it go and be open minded." A familiar example, "I'm not paying attention," immediately helps us refocus and be present. It's often clear what our choice demeanor is and what to do about it. This is a behavior chain. It's when attuning to how we're Showing Up immediately creates a positive shift. The process is as follows: attune-choose-Show Up.

Notice in point two above, I say *"shifting toward"* our choice behavior. We often can't implement 100 percent right away. Sometimes our chosen behaviors are a series of actions or a long-term plan. Attuning may not get us all the way there, but it's the crucial starting point. We take one small step at a time.

The process, attune-choose-Show Up, is basically notice-decide-act. Unless we're in planning mode, it often happens simultaneously. Our thought-feeling-action cycle is inherently integrated. This is how Showing Up works. Simply noticing our behavior steps us into it. It's why living a Show-Up life—one in which we regularly ask ourselves, "How am I choosing to Show Up?"—becomes natural. It's also why I choose the word *attuning* (not awareness) to describe it. So let's dive into what attuning means and why it is the more accurate word for Showing Up than awareness, noticing, or presence.

ATTUNING

As I briefly mentioned in Chapter 2, "attuning," while less commonly used than "awareness," "noticing," or "presence," more accurately describes Showing Up since it contains active qualities of adapting, adjusting, movement, and progress. Tuning is actively becoming harmonious with something. When we harmonize, we're congruent. There's a compatibility, congeniality, and a "being with-ness" that arises. It can be with our Selves, our behavior, emotions, sensations, or thoughts. Or it can be with another person, activity, or state. Attuning ourselves can focus us on now, a future activity, or across

When we're feeling good about how we're Showing Up and like the outcomes we're getting, we know we've settled into a helpful cycle and should keep it going.

Many people have shared that they naturally check in each morning as they wake. "How am I choosing to Show Up today?" Some do it as they start a new activity. Others tell me they check in around certain people, their boss, kids, or partners. For example, "How am I choosing to Show Up for Jennifer (or Jose) when she (he) walks in?"

We can also target our check-ins around important events of the day. How often we actually attune to our behavior is influenced by our goals, what we're doing, and how important and challenging the activity is, in addition to our general state of alertness, drive, hunger, and so on. It's also influenced by our depth of Grounding, Readiness, and Alltelligence, the subject of part III. The better we're Showing Up, the more often we're likely checking in. The two go hand in hand as cause and effect.

> **The process is testing and learning what works for us. We become more accepting and compassionate with ourselves as we discover, adjust, and improve. There's no failing. Life is one step, one choice, one chance at a time. This gives Show-Up living inherent grit and perseverance. Even when we forget for a while and don't check in, at some point a flare of emotion shoots up. It notifies us with, "Look how I'm Showing Up!" And we know right away. We either like it, or we don't. And we choose to Show Up differently. This is learning. It's growth. And it's a moment of calling.**

Up but lose focus on our behavior soon thereafter. Then the positive behavior we shifted into dissipates as well. This intermittent approach is our natural starting place.

When Truly Showing Up, we're noticing and checking in again and again, reclaiming the improvement, whether listening more openheartedly, feeling someone else's perspective, calming ourselves, managing fear, or something else.

Sustaining Level 3 is a systematic practice of reflecting. It's not controlling things or people nor is it grasping or over-striving. It's intent with acceptance. We're setting ourselves up for success, priming flexibility, and making ourselves capable of bringing our best while honoring nature's course.

Truly Showing Up Means We're Doing Two Things to a Sufficient Degree

1. **Attuning to our behavior (how we're Showing Up)**
2. **Shifting toward our choice behavior**

This is a natural process, one we experience often. Why? It's part of a behavior chain since the moment we notice our behavior, we've already changed it. Let's dive in further. Then we'll see what it means to do things "to a sufficient degree."

Note: It's important to realize this definition doesn't say what our choice behaviors are or should be. Instead, we're focused on the process of bringing intent to how we're Showing Up.

HOW OFTEN NEED I CHECK IN: HOW AM I CHOOSING TO SHOW UP?

People ask, "How often need I check in on how I'm Showing Up?" There's no specific frequency. If we want to Show Up differently, we should check in more often to keep ourselves on our desired path.

> stepped into an informative separateness. It's a distance at which we make novel connections, recognize things we would have missed had we been only in the moment, without perspective of how it Shows Up across space and time, and we are Showing Up within it.
>
> The experience of JSUPing, being partially engaged, multitasking, rushed, pressured, or stressed, makes it very hard to access this dual awareness or to Truly Show Up. Stressors handcuff us within our fixed field of attention and alerted nervous system. As described in Chapter 2, Defaulting through Life, and Chapter 6, Level 1, Barely There, attending to the world this way re-presents to us predefined experiences. We hear and see what we expect, what happened before. We miss much of what's happening right now.
>
> As we work to Truly Show Up, we're opening our Selves to the wonders and joys within our imminent moments. This "zooming out" lets us recontextualize our common moments, restoring them, through right-brained attention, to the profound.

Dual awareness is mindful. It aids us in thoughtfully responding instead of reacting. It gifts us more control over how we behave. With practice we attune for longer periods and more often. I'm told this ability to remain subtly attuned to our behavior across minutes or longer begins soon after we start asking ourselves the question, "How am I choosing to Showing Up?" It helps us sustain dual awareness.

At first, it's common for our attuning to function like intermittent windshield wipers. We check in every so often on how we're Showing

> In Level 3 we're turning our mirror outward. We're resonating with the emotions and intent of others. We're presencing within the live situation, morphing within it. Correspondingly, it is presencing and interacting with and within us. We're engaging our unifying attention system. Now we see possibility. Now we're not stuck. Now we have options. We have choice. We're empowered.
>
> "How am I choosing to Show Up?" becomes "How is the Situation Showing Up, with, to, and for me? And for others, Society, our planet, and our futures?" It's how Showing Up goes beyond resetting ourselves, to changing how we attend to the world.

SHOWING UP DUALLY AWARE

I've mentioned a few times that practicing Showing Up is also practicing a powerful dual awareness in which we're both in our Situation and also stepping back from it. We're part of what's going on while intermittently checking in on our behavior. It's helpful to understand how our attention systems make this happen.

> This stepping back engages our global attention system. It senses what's new, integrated across space and time. It's what keeps us alive, noticing the predator that our left-brained constricted attention system misses in its drive to pick the small blueberry off the bush.
>
> Now we're perceiving broader patterns, sensing nuance and the implicit, within the situation. We've

3
TRULY SHOWING UP

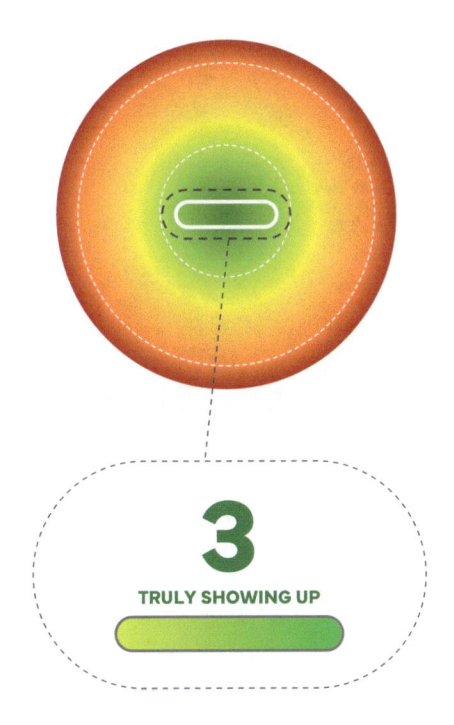

> **We're in Level 3 naturally when we attune with sufficient frequency to how we're Showing Up. Noticing our behavior changes it. We're no longer mindlessly reacting or just going through the motions.**

People tell me things like, "How I was Showing Up popped into mind and something clicked. I recognized I was feeling attacked and defensive and wasn't listening. Right then I heard her words differently. They felt less attacking and became something I could work with. I asked to understand more." This is how attuning to how we're Showing Up naturally shifts us toward our preferred behavior.

Unlike Barely There, when we're negative or dominated by Self-focused emotions, Truly Showing Up is positively engaging with our Selves and others. We're all in. We care—about people, decisions, ideas, and actions. We want to keep our perceptions open to the new and the nuance. And we experience more playful, connected flow.

CHAPTER 8
LEVEL 3: TRULY SHOWING UP

This chapter leads you through the following ideas:
- Real, not aspirational
- Dual awareness—the situation and our behavior within it
- A growth practice
- Attune-Choose-Show Up
- What's sufficient?
- Lower risk and feeling good
- The responsible choice

TRULY SHOWING UP IS what we aspire to achieve more often. It means we're performing at our chosen level enough of the time to feel good about ourselves. We like who and how we are. And we're satisfied with the direction our lives are taking.

Showing Up is a dual process

of being in the moment

while also being

an observer of it.

3. What were some of the impacts? (For example, feeling disconnected, unmotivated, deeply challenged to engage? Feeling minimally effective or productive?)

4. What helped you recognize you were Barely There? (For example, the situation became too extreme/desperate? Friends, colleagues, or other supportive sources helped you see and move forward?)

5. Recognizing you feel/felt this way, what are you choosing to do? (For example, accept it/change nothing? Defend it as fine/change nothing? Engage differently with the activity and people involved by stepping up more or stepping away?)

CHAPTER 7 SUMMARY—
BARELY THERE

1. Barely There is the lowest level of Showing Up, represented by Level 1 on the Show-Up continuum. It is a sad, lonely, and sometimes even desperate place. It describes a low level of performance.

2. We can be Barely There knowingly, unknowingly, and negatively.

3. We can get stuck there since the state often orients our thinking and resources inward, leading us to pull away and diminish our interest, engagement, and healthy outreach.

4. Causes include sustained overwork, stressful family situations, loneliness, illness, unmetabolized trauma, addiction, or other entrenched challenges. It can also happen when we've plummeted into profound negativity, blame, anger, or despondency.

5. Breaking out of Level 1 can be extremely difficult. It requires us to attune to how we're Showing Up and deepen our Grounding, Readiness, and Alltelligence, enabling us to interact more intentfully.

REFLECTING QUESTIONS

1. When have you experienced feeling disinterested or apathetic about aspects of your life, an activity, or just more generally? List a few examples.

2. How long were you Barely There before you recognized it?

Just Showing Up. And we may not even know we're in Level 1. We're either not choosing how we're Showing Up, or we can't.

RISK—THE TIRELESS GIFT OF SHOWING UP BARELY THERE

Risk is heightened on the left side of the continuum. Our behavior may be erratic, volatile, or irresponsible. Compensating behaviors of drinking, unnecessary spending, oversleeping, and many others may arise. Over time, even our most dedicated support structures of family, friends, colleagues, and jobs become weary and wear thin as we bring others down with us. Ongoing efforts to deepen our Grounding, Readiness, and Alltelligence invest in our well-being and the well-being of the people, processes, and systems around us.

Now let's dive into what it means to live more often on the right side of the Show-Up continuum in Level 3, Truly Showing Up.

about current or future events. These are the weighty artifacts of an unfocused—yet still busy—mind.

> **Another noteworthy aspect of unguided attention and rumination is that the thoughts it provokes are most often "I/me/mine" focused. One description of the default mode written by Ritchie Davidson and Daniel Goleman, psychologists and neuroscientists, reads, "The default mode makes each of us the center of the universe as we know it. Those reveries knit together our sense of 'self'...and continuously rescript a movie where each of us stars, replaying particularly favorite or upsetting scenes over and over."[8] Not a great contributor to feeling grounded, ready, or Alltelligent, eh?**

This is the small "s" self. It's the separate, modern self described in Chapter 3 as "the smallest unit of consideration in which we Show Up." I explain it's our most limited role, predominantly driven by our left hemisphere's attentional system. In this state we feel the most isolated. We are severed from context. We are often not calm since separateness amps the dial on our alert systems. And we are not deeply Grounded. Life appears to be distinct and evident, and distinctly unimpressive. The implicit is lost. Experiences feel thin. Situations, items and, dare I say, people, around us are to be acted on, more than with and for. It often Just Shows Up, but may become our long term home when we're Barely There.

In Barely There, this mind wandering is less of a coffee-break creativity restorer, which it can sometimes be,[9] and more numbness. **In Level 1, how we're Showing Up is too well practiced, becoming sustained mental absence and generalized disregard.** This goes well beyond the intermittent (and sometimes implicit) jadedness of

does this by "deactivating the default mode network, the part of our brain's cortex involved in how we perceive ourselves."[5] These Self-critiques come alive in moments of unguided attention, which we'll dive into next. Just before we do, know that accessing the restorative attention of wonder can be as simple as "witnessing the goodness of others."[6] To notice the small kind acts surrounding us requires we choose to look around. It means we're choosing not to stare at our phones or succumb to the commonly distracted state of Just Showing Up. Intentfully arriving in our moments with interest and curiosity is aided by varying our daily routine. Walking and driving different routes, choosing different books and conversation topics all help us productively guide attention, and succumb less often to being Barely There.

Unguided Attention and Ruminating

The latter two attention states, unguided attention and ruminating, are default-world tangos, laden with tension, uncertainty, fear, remembrances of unfinished tasks, and sundry unpleasantries. When in these attention states, we're at the whim of a specific brain region called the *default mode network*.

Our default mode is surprisingly active when we're doing nothing. In fact, it may be even more active than brain regions tackling the spreadsheets, and complicated "what's best?" questions we come across daily.[7] It's one of the fascinating discoveries of modern neuroscience. Our gray matter is equally busy whether we're modeling stock-market patterns or zoning out.

When our minds are wandering or we're ruminating, our neurons are still firing, creating random thought-events. These thoughts may masquerade as meaningful ideas, feelings, and beliefs, yet more often they are untruths conjured by deeper fears. And they're unpleasant. Common concerns in this category include imposter syndrome, when we fear that everyone is smarter than us or that we don't deserve to be in the room, insecurity about how others perceive us, or unease

> and recharge. Such attention may be significantly challenged when we're Barely There. In Level 1 our sad, absent, or negative state often challenges us in purposely steering and sustaining attention.
>
> Contrasting this, in moments of wonder, enchantment, or fascination we may experience extended periods of rapt attention, with scant fatigue. It's what we experience when we stare at our newborn child, the vastness of the Grand Canyon, and thunderous roar of our planet's great waterfalls. In moments like this we naturally access the wholeness that is primary within the world and dominant across both of our attention systems. It extends from our right hemisphere, and rules over both, left and right. Practicing Showing Up, with its unifying view of the world, primes us to experience more of it.

The boost these moments of wonder elicit lasts longer and feels more profound than the quick dopamine hits we get from shopping, tech-based entertainment, dessert, risky behaviors, social conquests, or nicotine. The quality of attention we experience as wonder is affiliated with noradrenaline. It is less prone to quickly fatigue. These noradrenergic neurons remain "excited," "so exploratory attention is held open across a expanse of both space and time."[4] Unfortunately, we experience it as exception, especially when we're Barely There.

Eliciting wonder can have a positive impact wherever we are along the Show-Up continuum. Such emotions calm our turbulent minds, stimulate creativity and connectedness. In his book *Awe: The New Science of Everyday Wonder and How It Can Transform Your Life*, UC Berkeley psychologist Dacher Keltner explains how awe seems to quiet the negative self-talk many of us hear in our heads telling us we're not good enough, smart enough, wealthy enough or worthy. It

WHEN WE'RE CHECKED OUT, BARELY THERE, WHERE ARE WE?

Let us ask, Where do we go when we're unable to implement our choices or to choose how we're Showing Up? And where does low Grounding, Readiness, and Alltelligence leave us? In all Show-Up levels we're experiencing different qualities of attention, including:

- **Guided attention,** when we steer what our minds and body attend to
- **Unguided attention,**[3] when we're allowing our mind to float, often away from what we're doing
- **Ruminating,** when our attention is hijacked, often by swirls of concern

Let's take a look at each.

GUIDED ATTENTION

> We guide our attention by aiming it on purpose. We're choosing to attach it to an item, person, topic, emotion, bodily sense, process, or scene. The active center of our experience is in our control. It is an active state, filled with motion. It moves us toward something that we select, a stimulus to process. In doing so we're deselecting other options. They recede from context. It's how we choose and design our situations, as described in Chapter 3. And like consciousness itself, all attention has a direction. When guiding our attention, we're choosing the direction. It's what we're doing when we check our behavior, and when we plan, prepare, organize, and decide. Guiding our mind feels rewarding, but we can only do it for so long before needing to rest

to end his angry efforts. The thought of it eases our aching head while also making our gut clench. Ugh.

Perhaps you've had a similar experience. Were John more Grounded, he'd recognize why he's hanging on, in such a personal way, to dogged beliefs. He'd have at least a bit of curiosity about why he lost trust in the leadership team, one he's been part of for fifteen years. But for now, no such luck. John is actively, negatively Barely There. My head still hurts. How is yours?

Just as positivity opens relationships, creativity, and opportunity, negativity closes them. It's uncollaborative, hijacks attention, drains us, and inhibits choice. It's a low quality of performing, one that breeds hurt, loss, regret, and even shame. Fits of defensiveness, criticism, contempt, even stonewalling, may all sustain negative Level-1 performance. These four negative behavior patterns are known as "The Four Horseman," according to relationship scientist John Gottman.[2] They destroy relationships. We simply can't Truly Show Up while carrying them with us. They're as far across the continuum as we can get from the naturally positive, prosocial, engaging, collaborative, flexible, and productive state of Truly Showing Up.

> **Negativity is not just small; it's actively constricting. It's the opposite of play. While fun creates a generative, imaginative, invitational energy, negativity is a fiery place. It's often combative and destructive. Even if we're raised to be critical, suspicious, or negative, making it part of our Grounding and true to our family culture, negativity opposes Alltelligence. It closes our brains off to listening, let alone considering. It shuts us down, creating reluctance and even refusal to receive someone's basic human energy. It cuts off the resonance of Alltelligence. This is how negativity, even when consciously chosen, can leave us Barely There.**

This moves us back into a space of choice. We're investing in our Grounding, reflecting on who we are, what matters most in the Situation, and why. Now we feel more solid. We're sensing confidence in a chosen next step. We're Readying our Selves, anticipating options and what may come next. And we're feeling responsible for our shared impacts in each other, Alltelligence.

Practicing our Show-Up skills, we'll be hard-pressed to be stuck in Barely There for long. Instead, we'll have perspective, a sense of where we are with the issue today, and its transient nature. Challenges will seem less pervasive, permanent, and personal. It's how the three Show-Up skills naturally lead us to step up—and step out—of Barely There.

How Actively Negative Barely There Shows Up

In addition to the active and passive forms of Barely There-ness, there's one more behavior state that's also Level 1: negativity. To keep it simple, I'm describing it in the context of a colleague at a business meeting, but it could just as easily be a partner, other family member, or friend.

Join me. The meeting is about to start. Look, that's John walking in now. We all know how combative he is. No fun, but here we go! Ugh. There's that telltale stress above our left brow. His scowling face cranks the dial on our headache with no time to take Tylenol. We inhale, trying to breathe through it. Our team has made its decisions about which customer segments to focus on and what functionality the product line will have, yet he just keeps insisting that we're wrong. John just won't get on the bandwagon. And he won't step out of the way. He's been wasting resources, directing his thirty-person team to prove us wrong and work against what was decided.

"You know it's a mistake, potentially too big to dig our way out of!" he spews with judgment, disapproval, and dismay. He takes out the latest reports his team created, working in crisis mode to convince us. Yet another attempt to change our minds. So unproductive! We give him the respect of listening, cutting short our discussion time to vet next steps. It's time to have a heart-to-heart chat with John. We need

Then we get frustrated. Or sad. Or even nasty. We may scream at ourselves. We may harm ourselves in attempts to become effective. Yet for some period, we remain unable. We want to be the better partner, parent, athlete, leader, worker, musician, creator, and person. But something is in the way. When we're unable to Show Up as we choose in a particular area of life for a sustained time, we're Barely Showing Up for that need and goal…and for ourselves…and for all Society.

Last week my neighbor Victor told me, "I overwork. I do it to avoid talking to my wife. We don't have much of a marriage anymore. It's been a while. My guess is she knows too since I stay away, and when I'm home, I busy myself with things to keep us apart."

"What's in the way of discussing it?" I asked.

"Fear," he plainly said. "I just can't imagine it going well. She's generally agitated and screams. Why would I walk into that? So my choice seems to be to keep going like this. It's been twenty years." This is actively Barely There.

Victor is unhappy and is knowingly choosing to sustain it. Imprisoned by fear, he sees no options. Were the challenge less deep, he'd have a few ideas. Victor could write a note or engage a mediator, therapist, or coach to create a safer space for discussion. He could share a book with passages highlighted that are relevant to their challenges and potential repairs. Perhaps he has. For now, at least, he's choosing to remain spinning.

As a Society we self-medicate, buy things we don't need, pursue extreme sports, overwork, opt out, or engage in other paths to escape the unhappiness of Situations in which we feel stuck. When others are involved, as in Victor's case, we expect the person to respond poorly. Without this fear we'd be better able to express something like, "I'm afraid you'll be angry (or hurt or violent), so I've hesitated to share that I'd like us to be a better team. Currently, when you do x I feel…" That said, there are plenty of cases when our hesitancy is warranted. When others involved have proven they'll respond poorly, even to vulnerable, well-intended gestures, it may be advisable to simply step away as best we can, at least for a while.

and I couldn't snap out of it. I knew exactly what was going on but was powerless. I'll never forget it. The words 'Actively Barely There' describe it well, however much I hate it. Looking back, that episode lasted three years. I'll never get that time with my son back." Recognizing his need to Show Up differently, Jacob focused on his Grounding and Alltelligence. With the help of medication and a therapist, he was gradually able to be there more for his son.

More ordinary examples are all around us. How many of us want to slim down? We're both attuned and even intentful in our choices to be more physically active and switch to healthier foods. But when more indulgent options are on the table, we gobble down more than planned. As our pounds remain or grow (grrr…) we're angry, sad, frustrated, perhaps even fearful for the long-term repercussions. We want those pants to fit! How did we just Show Up for ourselves? Actively Barely There. We're aware and attuned to our choice yet remain unable to effectively act on it.

> My friend Chris, a somewhat amiable yet pensive barista at my local Westchester Starbucks, explains, "I saw your talk, Marcy," referring to "Showing Up Is a Contact Sport" on TED.com.
>
> "It kind of missed the point for me. How to Show Up feels irrelevant. For me it's 'Why Show Up?' None of it seems to matter."
>
> Surprise and sadness flashed through me. I wouldn't have known. I felt an urge to help Chris, perhaps starting with a hug, but the register between us (and long line of eager caffeine addicts behind) shut it down.
>
> Chris is consciously Barely There, invisible. And perhaps he's the only one who knows.

to scan the LinkedIn profiles of the customer team members she was about to meet (low Readiness). Doing so would have exuded interest and care. But she was not in touch with the reciprocity of how people impact each other or how the interaction may support shared interests (low Alltelligence). Instead, low levels of the three Show-Up skills left her passively Barely There. She was holding on to her job by a thread because she dependably turned in what's needed with adequate quality.

Like many of us making similar choices, Maria was defending herself against pain. She self-anesthetized by not caring, surrounding herself with an emotional concrete wall. The wall shelters her. It was how she, daily, was euthanizing her dreams…for now, at least.

Active examples of Barely There abound too.

How Active (Conscious) Barely There Shows Up

Active reasons for being Barely There—when we know we're performing in Level 1 but remain stuck—often include unfortunate events largely out of our control such as illness, loss, divorce, or trauma, all of which may linger, pulling us into a persistent, prevailing ditch. Ideally, we're processing and metabolizing the situation's emotional and physical charge as the days go by. This deepens our Grounding so we can dispense with it and emerge whole. It's our healing process and is described more in Chapter 9, Grounding in Our Selves. As we practice attuning to how we're Showing Up and act on it, we'll be stuck for shorter periods, supporting shallower lows as depicted in the chart on page 30, "How Showing Up Improves Performance."

My friend Jacob who lives with depression told to me just this morning of a time he was unable to act, even while keenly aware of it and desperately wanting to. "My son was in the pool with a friend," Jacob explained. "The friend's father was there too, playing and having a great time. I wanted to be in the pool with my son, not just because it would be fun but because I wanted my son to have me there. But I just couldn't get my body to move. I was in a deep depressive episode,

> **or unconsciously Barely There and what we do with the experience is our responsibility and our choice.**

MARIA'S YEARS— PASSIVELY BARELY THERE

My client Maria told me of a time she felt she had no choice. She entered a meeting and absently plopped herself into a chair at the far side of the room. Her team lead had explained just the day before how important this client kick-off meeting was. But after smiling and greeting the three new client team members, she sat and soon drifted off. Not caring about this project or any other in the past year wasn't an active choice she made. It was simply what she did. Her whole life felt like a prison. The dead-end job was just a paycheck. New learning was scarce. She was selling time for money—it had been years by this point. And she saw her life passing by. Pushing aside anger at life's busy schedule and burdens, she detached from work, friends, and family, resigning herself to be merely on time and get through.

She was hanging on but always just about to lose her grip. Sometimes she missed commitments entirely, entering the danger zone of being cut off by her employer and loved ones. Checking out felt safer than enacting change. Kids, rent, health care…no new job. Too scary and destabilizing, her body announced. This was years ago. Now she's going through the motions, numb.

At the meeting, Maria looked up every so often, acknowledging others were there, only to mentally depart again, experiencing a removed "not-there-ness." The meeting passed without her contributing or noticing the work she was assigned. No new relationships were forged. The client noticed.

This, unfortunately, is a common example of passive Barely Thereness. Maria hadn't noticed she was Barely There. She was not linking her sense of Self or any purpose beyond the paycheck with the activity (low Grounding). She didn't find it important to prepare, not even

this happens for too long, our bodies may normalize to the stressors and stop consciously detecting them. Dr. Stephen Porges calls this subconsciously sensed danger in our environment "neuroception." It happens when challenges persist for so long that we no longer perceive them or feel a need to address them.

Common sources include not feeling completely safe in our childhood homes, perhaps from not being held or comforted in a way that taught us to self-regulate. Another example is if we carry intense shame or anger for long periods. Over time the intensity of the emotions is felt less. We detach from them. But we're left with a numbness, emptiness, or a disengaged way living. It's our nervous system dialed down from prolonged overexertion. And it can be insidious when there's no specific event, no adrenaline rush to capture our attention and demand a response. We're left unmotivated and listless, with a vague sense of unhappiness, wondering what's wrong. For a while we remain passive and stuck.

> **This maladaptive state may cause us to push the world away. We're likely to misread social cues because we're seeing through a dysregulated lens. We see neutral faces as dangerous. They appear angry and untrustworthy when they're not. Relationships feel unsafe. Reciprocally, people experience unsafe cues from us. And Society interacts with us in suspicious ways, confirming our interpretations. People are less friendly not because they truly are but because they perceive threat from us. Therapist Alex Howard, CEO of the Optimum Health Clinic, explains that seeing people and environments as threats, even when we're no longer in danger, is an example of earlier experiences echoing in our lives today. Ultimately, how long we remain consciously**

> **is natural and necessary,[1] the cost is high. We're not happy. And we're losing our choice impact on our Selves, Situations, and the world every moment.**

In some cases Barely There is an issue of distance. We're too close to the cause. We can't see the scope or edges of the issue. And we can't see how it may evolve across time. It's as if our book is two inches from our eyes. There's no way to see what it says. So we're stuck. Another helpful metaphor people relate to is being in a nightclub. The darkness, flashing lights, and deadening music shut out all else.

Effectiveness requires a necessary distance from a situation. Stepping back reveals its boundaries and how it relates across a broader context of people, space, and time. Barely There often obscures this. It mires us in a quicksand of left-brained grab-and-get thinking. We're triggered and stuck.

How Passive Barely There Shows Up

When we're passively Barely There, we're unaware we're in Level 1. Our state is too pervasive to choose something better, and we don't have the perspective to see it. This can be the case when we're profoundly angry, desperate, or hopeless, in the depths of severe burnout, illness, accidents, or other trauma. In these depths we often don't feel a sense of agency to effect change.

Like Just Showing Up, we're defaulting. But instead of being intermittently absent or floating through life without active intent, as when we JSUP, Level 1 describes being more deeply "checked out." We can't see the forest through the miserable, sick, desperate trees. Outside the exceptional events of divorce or trauma, we're sometimes pushed to the depths of being Barely There from relentless pressures of daily life. Over time, unfulfilling jobs and adverse relationships impair our sleep, nutrition, focus, and energy. They aggregate ever-present stressors that we could otherwise manage more effectively. When

is absent. Stress has overtaken my sleep and food choices. While I see the hole I'm in and can describe it, I remain stuck.

In addition to being knowingly Barely There, Level 1 can Show Up in two more ways, passively and actively negative. Here's the summary:

1. Passively—When we're <u>unable to see</u> how we're Showing Up
2. Actively—When we notice how we're Showing Up but <u>can't readily change it</u> (my example above)
3. Actively negative—When we're knowingly Showing Up <u>negatively</u>

In these cases we're in a deep or extended period of being tapped out or trapped in performance-depleting patterns of emotions, thoughts, and behaviors. Like Just Showing Up, we may be conscious or unconscious of the state we're in. It's natural to feel versions of hopelessness, apathy, defensiveness, anxiety, depression, and combinations or derivatives thereof. It's a bleaker state than Level 2, Just Showing Up. In Level 2 we're temporarily distracted, indifferent, or lethargic. Being Barely There is more prominent, pervasive, and persistent. It happens when we demonstrate low levels of Grounding, Readiness, and Alltelligence. Once our skills return to moderate levels or higher, we're able to Show Up as we choose more often. It's important to note that even in illness, grief, or trauma, we can Truly Show Up sufficiently Grounded, Ready, and Alltelligent.

> **Barely There is not a fun place. And it can be irresponsible, a sentiment you read in the description of Level 2, Just Showing Up. Moreover, it can be a sad, angry, fearful, or even desperate place. Whatever the cause and however difficult, over time we're answerable to ourselves and to the world. We're responsible to move through and lift ourselves up as smoothly and quickly as we can. While being Barely There at times**

1

BARELY THERE

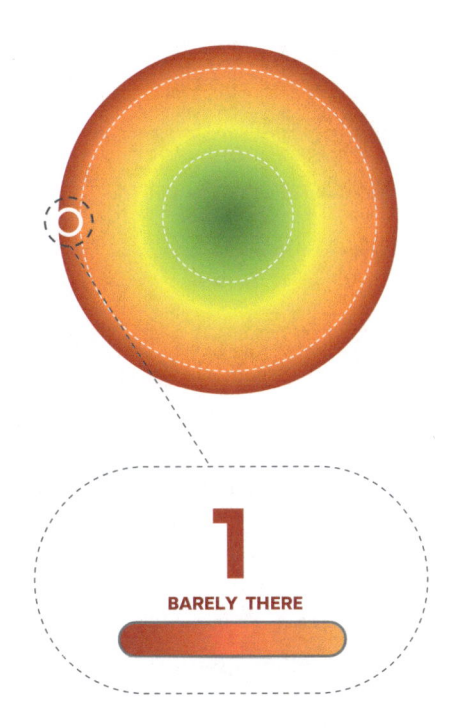

I'm in this state right now, self-isolating as I write this chapter. A family member's mental health situation has overtaken my world. While I see it clear as day, it is creating tunnel vision, narrowing life to one immediate issue. Now the simplest things are hard. I can't even answer a simple question.

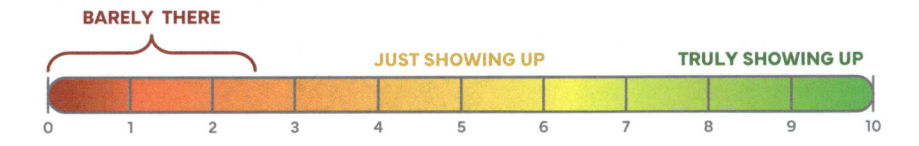

BARELY THERE   **JUST SHOWING UP**   **TRULY SHOWING UP**

0   1   2   3   4   5   6   7   8   9   10

When I stepped out for a walk this morning, an unsuspecting neighbor asked, "How are you?" I froze. How can I be honest but not too revealing or negative? I want to say, "I'm in the greatest struggle of my life." Luckily, the words got hung up in my often-undependable filter. By the tenth episode, I've learned to respond with, "It's a trying time. How are you?" This simple act becomes my victory for the day. Friends and interests feel scarce. Flexible thinking to find solutions

CHAPTER 7

LEVEL 1: BARELY THERE

This chapter leads you through the following ideas:
- Unable to choose
- Passive and active
- Let's be negative
- Breaking out and stepping up

"THAT'S THE HARDEST PART, MARCY," my therapist tells me. "Showing Up when you don't want to."

We've all been there. It's Level 1, Barely There. It describes our performance when we're well below our best and can't or won't shift out of it. And it can happen quite innocently, bit by bit.

*Showing Up transcends
common Self-improvement
and performance approaches.*

*It exists at the level of our souls,
connecting us
through the roles in which we live*

*—as Selves within
Situations and Society.*

3. Think of a time when you were engaging in a discussion and noticed your mind wandered.
    a. What was the impact of your attention drifting?
    b. How often does this happen?
    c. How would your life be improved if you noticed how you were Showing Up more often?

4. How important is it to you to feel inspired by, and dedicated to, your daily responsibilities?
    a. How would Showing Up as you choose change this?

3. In itself, Level 2, Just Showing Up, is not bad. It just needs to be used—and dosed—appropriately.

4. Just Showing Up stems from internal and external sources. Internal causes include the quality of our primary attachment relationships and our ability to metabolize mental health challenges. External sources include cultural influences and basic daily stressors that we don't have time to sufficiently process.

5. Not choosing how we're Showing Up can be viewed as a form of Self-harm. It's us fighting against ourselves. And it's not what healthy souls do. Just Showing Up isn't mere stasis. It's decay. It's a path of reduction. It makes us incrementally less of who we want to be. It's also bigger than us. Collectively, when we Just Show Up too often, we're infusing discontent and ill health throughout Society.

6. Attuning to how we're Showing Up honors our individual and collective Selves by investing in our sense of meaning, contributions, happiness, and survival. Not doing so is the threat hidden in plain sight. It limits connectedness with our Selves, others, and the daily situations of our lives, promoting unhappiness, superficial relationships, and diminished health.

CHAPTER REFLECTION

1. Overall, what portion of your time do you think you Just Show Up? How would you like to adjust this?

2. As you think through daily activities, when do you find yourself:
   a. Moving through things without sufficiently preparing?
   b. Considering why the activity matters?
   c. Considering others involved?

> **our past, present, and future. And they wear all shades of nuance and disguise. This is why to be effective, we must work to know ourselves better (Grounding), Situationally prepare (Readiness), and remember the reciprocal impact we have on each other (Alltelligence).**

JUST SHOWING UP— IT MAY BE THE GREATEST LOSS

Over time, as we Just Show Up partially absent to our Situations' potential, we risk losing our most precious gift: a well-lived life. However we define it, well-lived means we haven't settled. We haven't lessened, dipped, or descended into less than who we know we can be.

This is why Just Showing Up needs to be a temporary resting place, not our primary home.

CHAPTER 6 SUMMARY—JUST SHOWING UP

1. Just Showing Up is moving through the moments of our lives without consciously noticing or choosing how we are behaving. Doing so too often means we're losing the opportunity to meaningfully connect with each other, and to steer our interactions and lives (families, companies, and culture) in ways that are consequential and fulfilling.

2. National research reveals we're Just Showing Up a majority of the time. This is supported by low to moderate levels of Readiness, Alltelligence, and Grounding. "Going with the flow," "hanging out," and "workforce disengagement" describe Just Showing up. It is represented by Level 2 on the continuum.

away the surface behavior, revealing its underlying motivators, he explains unconscious stressors prevented him from feeling successful and satisfied. This is in spite of his very real contributions and successes.

Dr. Maté explains that his overstressed mother trying to care for an infant in such tumultuous times left him feeling insufficiently loved. This drove him to select a demanding, highly respected career, one that elicited external validation and praise. Dr. Maté was driven to work endless hours, in an impossible attempt to meet the needs for maternal love and acceptance he didn't feel as a baby. This unmet craving caused him to be absent for his own three children, passing down a version of the same challenges to them. While Dr. Maté's work superficially met his requirements, it failed to satisfy his deeper longing for love, validation, and worthiness extending from infancy.

From an observer or colleague's perspective, he's dedicated, productive, and Shows Up as he chooses, with intensity and purpose. All good things. What they don't see is his deep dissatisfaction, insecurity, volatile emotions, and choice of excessive work over family time. These realities reveal he's living in Levels 2 and 1 much of the time.

What's important to note with this example is that while Dr. Maté earned external accolades, he was not Showing Up well to life. He describes himself during those years (before recognizing the connection between his childhood experiences and his professional life,) as depressed, volatile, shopping addicted, and unable to make values-based decisions about working less and investing in family more. Once he understood the root of his needs, becoming more grounded in who he is and why, he regained the ability to choose how he Shows Up. In doing so, his relationships significantly improved as did his emotional and physical health. Even the attention deficit disorder (ADD) he had been struggling with abated.

> **We may never be able to shine a light on all roots of our performance. Divers of Showing Up are vast. They appear in all ways and forms, existing across**

flatfooted, having missed the majority of the points. Right there she admitted, "I need you to review the high points again. Something pulled my attention away." No apologies. Just facts and needs but uncomfortable, nonetheless.

And this is not like Ellen. Her company grants her particularly high bonuses, broad freedom to expand her role as she sees fit, and more team members upon request. So why is Ellen Just Showing Up? "I'm pulling away," she tells me. "And I'm not enjoying my children, my marriage, anything. It's really upsetting. The big picture is fine, but I'm unmotivated, which feels miserable. I can't focus like I used to." After more discussion, Ellen and I realized it may be burnout. She had worked so hard for so long without regularly rejuvenating. It's a common cause of JSUPing. We've all been there to differing degrees. Needing a recharge means we're low on Grounding, Readiness, and Alltelligence. How can we Show Up as we choose when our success dials are below zero?

Ongoing stresses from today or early childhood: More insidiously, drivers of Just Showing Up may be echoes of insecure attachment relationships from childhood.[10] This happens when basic needs for safety, love, acceptance, and belonging are not fully met. These early experiences shaped our nervous system as our brains and bodies adjusted to our early environments. How we evolved may have been helpful then, perhaps even lifesaving. It's the process that created our personalities. But the behaviors that proved helpful back then may be a poor fit for our experiences today, such as when they lead us to feel insecure or unduly threatened or angry.

One fascinating example is seen in some people exhibiting insatiable drive. It may appear they Truly Show Up, but their success may be due, at least in part, to an addictive need to prove themselves worthy. They're driven to overcome unmet childhood needs carved into their sense of Self. These and similar experiences design the structure and functioning of our brain's nervous systems, creating how we interact today. Dr. Gabor Maté, a physician and leading trauma expert, explains just this about his own childhood. He was an infant in Hungary during the Holocaust.[11] He appears to be Truly Showing Up, but once we peel

people, poor sleep, money issues, health concerns, and stretched emotional intelligence (EQ). They're all around. They live within our four walls, body, and brain every day. They test and diffuse our Level 3 efforts. They're the friends in our sandbox with whom we're supposed to share our toys, whether we want to or not, and they're troublesome. Bit by bit, these daily challenges insidiously pull us, in the long term, toward lower levels of Showing Up.

Partially processed emotions: Our moments are an onslaught of rich experiences. We feel the vitality of our moments in our bodies, emotionally and intellectually. But we often can't fully process or resolve our experiences before needing to move on. So these experiences—with their emotions, physical sensations, and implications—linger and accrue throughout the day. For example, didn't it seem like Mikela was holding something back in that meeting? Alex didn't seem happy with the team's decision. And at home this morning, Jonah needed more attention before school than either his dad or I could give him. But we're often pushed along by our schedules. So these emotional moments are left lingering, holding hostage bits of our attention and energy. Until we can reflect on them and metabolize their impacts[9]—which can take seconds or years—they pull on us. They command us in conscious and unconscious ways, taxing our focus, motivation, creativity, and sense of purpose. This reality fundamentally challenges all our Show-Up skills.

Not knowing what's challenging us: In some cases, we're aware of a specific event that yanks our attention away from the seventy-five-mile-per-hour road we're traveling. Knowing what it is lets us choose to refocus. In other circumstances, what's challenging us to Show Up as we choose may be rooted in less-apparent soil. It may be simple hunger, tiredness, or the opaque apathy in which it is sometimes frosted.

My friend Ellen, typically a top performer, tells me she's been tuned out since last summer. Now she forgets to call people back, drops the ball on things she said she'd do, and spaces out in meetings. Just last week Ellen described how an executive was framing an important decision, then asked her opinion as the leader of the group. She was

gently infer that we may have an issue here. Are you sensing I'm letting loose that opinion I mentioned just a bit ago? How do I really feel?

In my second TEDx talk, "Showing Up Is a Contact Sport," there's a line people often tell me is a highlight: "We have a national Just-Showing-Up crisis!" It comes after I list statistics detailing America's rates of disengagement, loneliness, anxiety, and depression.[8] It's not a fun list to share, but it's the truth, and it's both the cause and effect of our Just-Show-Up choices. I'm not saying these serious health challenges are a choice. I am saying systems were designed and built that support what exists, one decision at a time. And we're all part of the system. We're its creator, its product, and its supplicant. Its donor and suitor. Lobbyist and client.

It's time to look at the choices we're making, especially when they're sidestepping the effort of doing our best—the only responsible option, however good our best may be. And please don't let me misguide you. The responsibility isn't simply to choose our behavior. It's to value our moments and interactions enough to engage with them more wholeheartedly. This means we need to attune to them.

> **Doing so honors our individual and collective Selves, our sense of meaning, contributions, happiness, and survival. Not choosing how we want to Show Up is a form of Self-harm. It's us fighting against our Selves. And it's not what healthy souls do. You see, Just Showing Up too much isn't mere stasis. It's decay. It's a path of reduction. It makes us incrementally less of who we want to be.**

Daily Drivers of Just Showing Up

These are common inhibitors of Truly Showing Up beyond our culture and genes. It's the sundry basket of stressors—too much to do, grumpy

get passed down from mother to child."[7] The point is, reasons for our behavior may be clear or invisible, with roots in generations past. The lost context of the trauma erodes not just meaning but also understanding. Without knowing why we behave as we do, we may be left with "Who knows?" We start to think certain tendencies are "just the way we are." This makes it harder to Show Up as we choose.

Collectively, these stimuli tire us. They disconnect us. They misdirect us. Once depleted, we JSUP. And it happens—a lot. At times we're not tired or disheartened and can call upon discipline. But discipline is a quickly expiring asset. The COVID-19 pandemic accelerated trends of loneliness, anxiety, depression, alcohol use, drug use, and so many other detrimental, JSUP-promoting behaviors. It prompted mass resignations and quiet quitting—defined as doing the minimum while not quitting. Sound like Just Showing Up? But let's not get mired down by it. Let's simply muster, or prompt or rouse, conscious choice about our behaviors more often.

Now that we're clear on at least some reasons for *why*, let's get back to the *how* of Level 2 performance.

HOW TO SUCCESSFULLY JSUP

Remember, JSUPing isn't bad, unless we live in it too often for too long. That's when it becomes the vast, blurred, no man's land between performing well, Level 3, and some version of hollow vibing in the ring called Level 1.

If JSUPing is our rejuvenating time after stepping up as often as we can, that's great! We've earned a hearty "CONGRATULATIONS!" and can brazenly saunter into a well-deserved night of Netflix and pizza. But if our JSUPing is closer to the full-time, cop-out way of living, no mercy do I grant.

There's a huge difference between these two scenarios. In one case, Level 2 is the *yin* to Level 3's *yang*. It's the devoted partner and supporter. In the other, it's irresponsible living, pulling down the lot of us, our society, economy, educational system, and planet, just to ever so

Evolutionary and Epigenetic Support for Just Showing Up

Epigenetics explains how we pass down generations of physical memories embedded in our genes. Understanding how it takes place and its specific outcomes are coming to light. According to the BBC, a growing number of studies support that "the effects of trauma can reverberate down the generations" through gene expression. Example studies include those showing higher rates of mortality in the grandchildren of prisoners of war from the American Civil War in the 1860s[4] and in a small study of grandchildren of Holocaust survivors showing increased likelihood of stress disorders.[5] "The gene changes in the children could only be attributed to Holocaust exposure in the parents," said Rachel Yehuda, who conducted the study and is a pioneer of work on post-traumatic stress disorder (PTSD).

These examples demonstrate how today's stress and trauma extend in part from our parents' and grandparents' experiences, and specifically from their partial processing of their own suffering. Collective wounds from the past remain in us. One could say we're born into a "pre-traumatized society." But we don't directly see it. We've normalized to it since it's in the water we drink. Yet, we're conditioned by it. Our response is society's collective numbness. Racism, abuse, social inequality, insufficient empathy, and unkindness of all sorts are living within it. This unconscious numbness may Show Up as generalized unhappiness, feeling fragmented or stressed, making it hard for us to heal, or to respond as a collective.

Dr. Thomas Hübl explains this using a metaphor. "Snowflakes falling into a river become water. But when snowflakes fall into an iced-over river (from incomplete healing after personal and global events such as emotional neglect, abuse, accidents, illness, the Covid pandemic, storms, wars, etc.), the snow piles up…so, we can't digest experiences. Our nervous system is blocked."[6] Now we're less able to connect with others.

According to trauma specialist Resmaa Menakem, who works to reduce racialized behavior, "Memories connected to painful events

HOW AND WHY WE JUST SHOW UP

In Chapter 2 and above I describe causes of Just Showing Up, including our culture of separateness, overliving in our left hemispheric attention that turns right now into explicit, re-displays of a static environment, missing the implicit, emotional richness of our experience. In Chapter 4, when describing how Grounding, Readiness, and Alltelligence fuse to create how we Show Up, I described inhibitors to connectedness. They contribute to our overdosing on Just Showing Up. At least some of our excess time in Level 2 extends from obvious sources, such as the momentum of our days. JSUPing fits the pace and stressors of our nine-to-five. It's built into our culture and systems. Outside of such obvious contributors are myriad hidden sources, far harder to identify.

Hidden Sources of Just Showing Up

Contributors in this category include insecure attachment relationships we may have developed during our infancy (described further in Chapter 9, Grounding). These early, pre-conscious interactions with primary caregivers design the relational template through which we see the world today. Innocent responses in our young nervous systems that were helpful back then may be leading us to feel vulnerable, anxious, needy, or overly protective of ourselves in our current relationships. I'll take it one step further to include behavioral predispositions marinated into our genes from past generations that are now playing out, as explained through epigenetics. Given the epidemic-level state of mental health in our nation,[3] these disturbances, surfacing in our trauma-aware society, contribute to living predominantly in Level 2. Then we mix the ingredients and bake at 350°F. There's a point at which drivers of Just Showing Up are so pervasive they don't warrant explaining. But, if you would, indulge me for another page or two to add detail to the causes mentioned above. These challenges are ringleaders and coconspirators crafting how we Show Up.

> **Who we are shows up most when the chips are down...but it's who we are always.**
>
> A friend out on Long Island told me what his father used to say,
>
> *You show up one way in life, and it's how you show up when the chips are down.*
>
> *No matter how much you think you turn it on when "it matters," you don't really. You are who you are in those moments of challenge, and you show up in all places that way.*

Overdosing on Just Showing Up feels disappointing. Over time the feeling can morph into despondence, eventually deadening care, relationships, professional and personal achievements, and our health, not to mention leaching into corporate, economic, and societal culture. This potential of JSUPing to be a slick downward slope is the risk that comes with hanging out there too much. It explains why JSUPing needs to be an intermittent resting place. Ideally, it's a space of intentfully stepping in for a purposeful, predefined period, then pivoting off. When we utilize it this way, Level 2 becomes less about forgetting ourselves and more about productive investment. Examples abound.

The quintessential Sunday football ritual, relaxed family time, and casual drink with friends after work are often Just-Show-Up affairs. Most relaxing transition, wind down, or other non-taxing periods such as walking the dog, strolling to refill our coffee, chatting with friends, really anything not steeped with intentful choice or focus can do the trick to restore us, supporting future Level 3 time. Longer expanses of time in Level 2 may be fine too, if they're serving us well. Not being attuned to "if they're serving us well" is the challenge. The data shows we're doing too much of it, and for too long. How did this come to be America's common resting place? And why do we let it happen?

I fully recognize the data is not exhaustive and that asking different questions often leads to different conclusions. That said, I don't think choosing to raise our level of performance should rest on any data I or others bring forth. Such choices are best derived from intrinsic, and I believe in primal drives to do and be our best.

Putting the details aside, the big picture of how we behave and feel is directly related to partial Grounding, Readiness, and Alltelligence. It can be no other way. One key reality, however, is that our natural Just-Show-Up tendencies don't spawn enough of the fulfilling experiences we seek. It's a crime. We've journeyed well past Barely There but stopped short of our goal. Now here's the kicker: we're losing the precious learning, growth, and satisfaction Truly Showing Up creates. If this weren't the case, we'd be Showing Up better day by day. But this improvement is not what the data shows. Instead, people tell me they're not taking the time to reflect and be intentful. They're not living their choice behavior more and more.

It's About the Dosage

Don't get me wrong. In itself, Level 2, Just Showing Up, is not bad. It's essential a good bit of the time. It just needs to be used—and dosed—appropriately. Like so many things in life—chocolate cake, sleep, work, vodka tonics, family time, and yoga—it's about the dosage. Too little, not good. Too much, not good. Wrong time, not good. You get the idea. The benefits of Just Showing Up are that it's easy to go with the flow. It can be restorative. And it's our point of departure from which we choose to be intentful and achieve more. What is undesirable, however, is living JSUP-life. Too big a dose is complacency. It's an overallocation of our portfolio, and the stock market of life won't treat us well. It will pass us by.

It also implies we're not feeling connected to others we're interacting with. With the exception of trained professionals in medicine, social work, psychology, and related fields, it can be challenging for the rest of us to instantly feel a sense of "with-ness." Bonding isn't a switch. It's a process and an evolving space we nourish together. "Being with"—including the trust, goodwill, and productive collaboration it brings—needs time. Our culture's fast-paced, get-it-done mode often doesn't default-Show Up this way. Across and within any given situation, we need to intently choose to care.

Grounding

Data on Grounding (how well we know ourselves) starts with an optimistic finding that most of us believe we're highly self-aware. Fifty percent of us give ourselves scores of eight out of ten or higher, and another 20 percent rate our self-awareness a seven. Beyond this, my research and interviews show the mixed bag you'd expect. In some cases, people readily and unknowingly reveal their blindness in terms of why they Show Up as they do. You'll read an entertaining example of this in my date with Anthony at Tina's Wine Bar in Chapter 9 on Grounding. What a night that was! Other data reveal how people don't recognize multigenerational patterns, leading them to pass down limiting behaviors. Sophie, profiled in Chapter 10 on Readiness, victimizes herself with her parents' mentality of scarcity and deservingness. Examples are sprinkled throughout future chapters. In other cases, people have shown significant points of insight. Their Grounding functions as a deep well of meaning and success in their lives.

Two of my therapist partners helping with this book—one an MD trained psychoanalyst and another a PhD psychologist—tell me most people don't know themselves particularly well. "Most of us see our challenges but miss the antecedents that create them," Dr. Oren Messeri explained. This leaves us prey to repeating patterns we'd prefer to leave behind[2]—all part of Just Showing Up.

But this may be where it stops. It was unclear what type of planning people are actually doing.

What the majority of us (60 percent) don't do—as indicated by not selecting these survey options—is consider in advance the topics or agenda related to our upcoming activities, even when they're identified as "important." This surprised me since the structured, agenda-driven work meetings so many of us are used to seem to prompt at least some intellectual setup. And work activities were explicitly included in the survey questions. Yet people indicated that in both preplanned and impromptu situations, across work and nonwork settings, the majority of us aren't choosing to Show Up with much content-related or emotional forethought. This is basic preparing and reflecting. It need not be particularly time-consuming, but based on these findings, we're moving through our daily activities without a whole lot of it. Instead, we set up for success by choosing our outfits, checking the weather and time, and heading out (60 percent).

Collectively, I read these findings as indicating low situational Readiness. They point to a few possible conclusions. Perhaps we think we already know what we need to perform at the desired level. We think we're ready. Or perhaps we're moving from one thing to the next and simply not reflecting, regardless of how planful we consider ourselves to be.

Alltelligence

Beyond situational Readiness, most respondents also indicated they don't often give forethought to the feelings of others involved in upcoming situations. We're not asking things like, "What may be on their mind? What sensitivities might they may have?" This happens across situations, including work meetings and informal discussions, in person or by email and text. Less than 30 percent of respondents indicated they consider how they want people to feel in their presence. This suggests we're not thinking about how we're impacting people, let alone how they're impacting us, a core tenet of Alltelligence.

we need a break, or we're on the go, multitasking, stressed, or tired. It happens a lot. And it's totally natural. We may experience it as being unable to focus, or ruminating. Any type of busy mind, what is called "monkey mind" in mindfulness, leaves us missing much of what's new, and experiencing what's expected. And we really believe it's the fullness of what happened. It's what presences for us, so it's our truth, and we have no reason to doubt it. It's how we tend to recreate the past, over and over. It's a common reality when we're Just Showing Up. When we're able to slow down, stop striving, and relax our minds, we start to open our perception to new things and to learn new skills.

Given this, letting our Selves JSUP is also letting ourselves off the hook of being our best. And I just don't get it. I'm going to hold my opinions back, though, and will first define this vast midperformance zone between Truly Showing Up and Barely There. I'll start with the high-level reality from the data and will explain why JSUPing is both essential and beneficial a good portion of the time. What's not good is when we decide it's okay all the time. This is when I'll let her rip.

THE RESEARCH—SUMMARY FINDINGS

My formal research to create the model of how we Show Up began in 1999. Global studies including over ten thousand people across the world explored how they achieve, what gets in their way, and what would enable them to perform better. I continue to conduct interviews and surveys investigating how we Show Up and why. Here are highlights from the findings.

Readiness

Let's start with good news. A majority of survey respondents consider themselves to be planners, with an impressive 60 percent of us rating ourselves eight or higher on a ten-point scale when asked, "To what extent do you consider yourself to be a planful person?" This is great!

be significant in our personal and professional success, relationships, and health. So let's dive in.

HOW JUST SHOWING UP RECREATES OUR PAST

To know something we need to already have a sense of it. A hint of what it is needs to be previously grasped or understood, in some capacity. If something is completely outside the bounds of our previous experience, we have no way of "processing it," making sense of it, no way to ground our knowledge of it. To learn something new, we must attach it to the existing lattice of what we already know. This means some version of the experience needs to be recognized. Our brains search for qualities of the experience that we are familiar with, so we can categorize it within a set of things we've experienced before. These existing categories come with feelings, beliefs, and values. They're filled with subconscious, instinctual reactions.

> All this happens automatically. It means we're not experiencing what's happening as much as we're experiencing a re-presentation of what's happening. And the re-presentation is a creation of our minds. It's a mix of what we already know that functions as an anchor for right now, and, depending on how we're Showing Up, a thin layer of what's going on outside of our Selves. We are left to integrate the soupy mixture of what we've brought into being in any experience.

With fractured attention we have a very hard time perceiving of what's new in the Situation, as opposed to what confirms our expectations, fears, and predictions of what's going on. This happens when

THE MIDDLE OF THE SHOW-UP target and continuum is a common home for us all. Approximately 80 percent of survey respondents say it's their habitat—complete with hanging plants—the majority of the time. As a group, we're content to just walk in. "Winging it" is often the way we live. And it's okay, right? People tell me, "It gets the job done." And, "I go with the flow." We feel, "It got me where I am. So it's fine, right?" Besides, "I don't like to overthink things."[1]

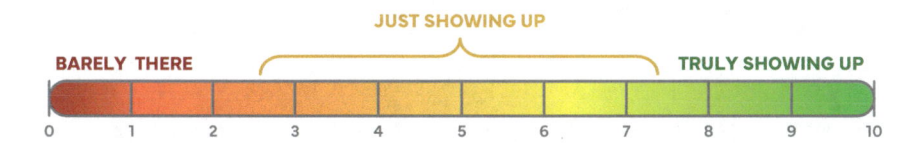

	JUST SHOWING UP	
BARELY THERE		TRULY SHOWING UP

0 1 2 3 4 5 6 7 8 9 10

Can you relate? Okay, here's a better question: How does it sound to you? To me, it sounds like there's conviction around this way of living. Our friends and countrymen like the low effort and ease of it all. Just Showing Up is convenient. Time to order the pizza and wings and get the party started! I'm game. And make it a double. Why dwell exquisitely when we can just hang out? Whose abode need be so fancy?

But here's the rub: When we JSUP too much for too long, we don't like the outcome. The majority of Americans lie in bed each night feeling we're not reaching our potential. It's defeating. Who wants to feel this way? It smells. (Pardon me for pointing it out so plainly.)

And this is where things get personal. Deeply personal. Because I do my share of JSUPing. Not because I'm opting out—I instinctively ask myself, "How am I Showing Up?" multiple times a day—but because it's tricky. The flow of activities pulls us in. Attuning ourselves to our behavior while still being in the moment takes effort. We generally know how we want to act. We just don't get it done as often as we'd like. This challenge of choosing and implementing our chosen behavior dominates our lives. That's why I think it's important to bring this reality to light. **If we can Show Up closer to how we choose even once more each day, for however long it lasts, the benefit can**

CHAPTER 6

LEVEL 2: JUST SHOWING UP

This chapter leads you through the following ideas:
- Going with the flow and hangin' out
- How we recreate the past
- Improv—life or choice?
- Enemy in plain sight
- Dosage

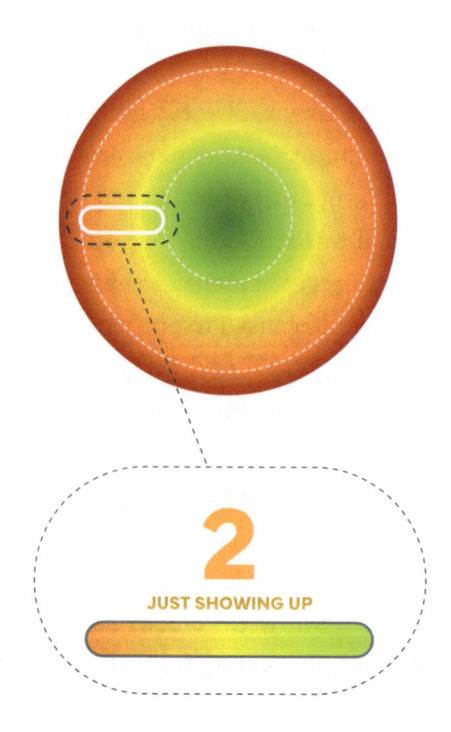

2
JUST SHOWING UP

Just Showing Up too often isn't stasis.

It's decay.

It makes us less of who we want to be,

*degrading us and the
world we all inhabit.*

3. In what areas of your life do you feel you have a firm handle, but could probably improve? Which Show-Up skill do you think pertains most to this?

4. In what area(s) of your life are you feeling energized and inspired? Which Show-Up skill most supports this?

6. The Show-Up target and continuum enable us to evaluate, track, and manage performance. They can also be used as communication, planning, and assessment tools, uncovering insights about how to productively engage with people and situations. They can be used proactively, as a strategy and planning tool, or reactively to evaluate the past. This makes the target and continuum valuable leadership tools helping us evaluate, track, manage, and improve performance.

CHAPTER REFLECTION

1. How would you plot your Grounding, your Readiness, your Alltelligence? Add dots to the target. Draw other Show-Up targets as needed to plot family members, colleagues, or others.

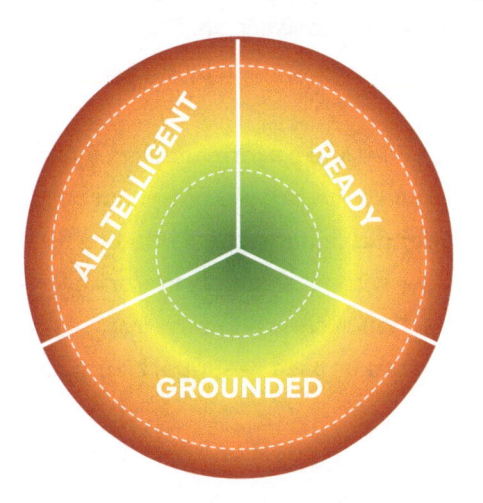

2. In what areas of your life do you feel regularly exhausted, frustrated, or bogged down? Which Show-Up skill do you think pertains most to this?

CHAPTER 5 SUMMARY

The Show-Up Continuum

1. Showing Up is the invisible performance system existing in and around us. When unseen, neglected, or dismissed, we're prone to:
   a. Just Show Up
   b. Disappoint ourselves
   c. Repeat the unsatisfying pattern of behavior

2. Familiarity with the three levels enables us to relate to them with greater ease, flexibility, and acceptance. Level 1 is Barely There. Level 2 is Just Showing Up. Level 3 is Truly Showing Up.

3. The continuum naturally prompts us to plot our performance as an observer in our situation. It gives us the distance needed to see it without being ruled by the emotions of the moment.

4. Viewing behavior and performance as a dynamic flow across our native roles and levels helps us accept our behavior. It provides us perspective and acceptance. By reminding us we can choose how we Show Up—without shame, blame or anger—the tools compel us to take action. Across a family, team, or nation the tools of Showing Up can be used to support connection and kindness.

5. Using the Show-Up target and continuum to discuss behavior creates emotional safety by depersonalizing and abstracting how someone, or a team, is Showing Up. Applying a (left-brained) model shifts thought and communication into an explicit, objective process, supporting open discussion among colleagues, teams, families, and friends. With this benefit we are prompted to step back, to plan and think inventively. This is the valuable process utilizing both ways of seeing the world (objectively and wholistically) that nature designed humans to utilize.

refrigerator. Another person told me it was on his desk. The idea is simply to have it where we'll see it often, prompting us to behave as we choose.

> **In summary, the Show-Up target and continuum are tools helping us attune to our lives and choose how we interact. They help us be accepting of ourselves and others and to create emotional safety, minimizing fear as we relate to our performance flowing across natural peaks and valleys. This mindset supports us in being open, vulnerable, and compassionate with our Selves, and in communicating among colleagues, teams, family members, and friends. And it makes the continuum a valuable leadership tool helping us evaluate, track, and manage performance of people, systems, and organizations.**

In the next chapter, let's explore what it means to be in each of the three Show-Up levels. I'll start with Just Showing Up.

Applying the Show-Up target this way proved fruitful. They recognized new ways to discuss two key topics anticipated as sticking points. In one hour of smooth negotiation, the contract terms were agreed. No one felt pressed because each person's role and disposition were understood and accepted. The two teams finished the negotiations feeling a deeper partnership and more fluid, trusting communication.

This use of the continuum and framework—as a communication, planning, and assessment tool—uncovered insights for productively engaging partners and team members. It's one example of how the continuum and targets function as collaboration, evaluation, tracking, and performance tools.

When thinking about one important person in your life, where would you plot their Grounding, Readiness, and Alltelligence overall? How about related to a common situation?

What about the G/R/A of other important people in your life?

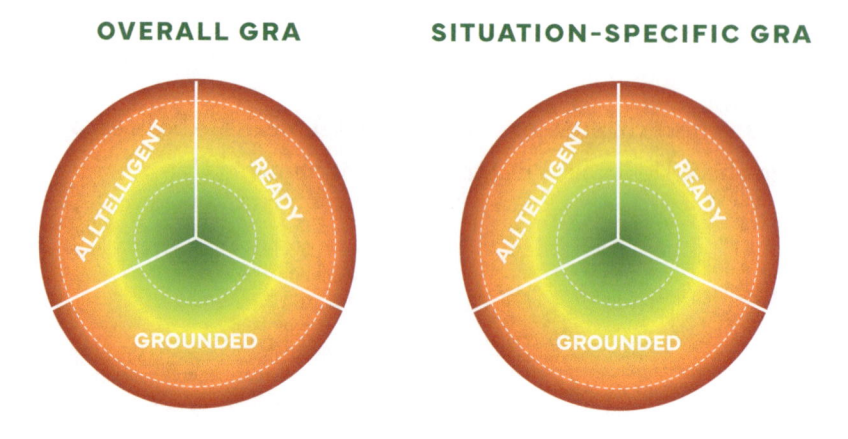

OVERALL GRA

SITUATION-SPECIFIC GRA

STRATEGIES TO USE THE CONTINUUM

I've heard of a number of people printing the continuum and Show-Up target or drawing their own and taping it to the back of their phones or computer screen. Over the summer I saw it taped to someone's

the Show-Up target for each. How would each of VendorCo's team members Show Up? What allocation across their roles, and what depth of Grounding, Readiness, and Alltelligence need my client prepare for? And how could this smooth their negotiation?

ShowUpCo realized that Maya, VendorCo's sales lead, was always looking to say yes. She consistently spoke up about ways her company could help ShowUpCo, such as adding support team members, training, adding levels of security sensing, and additional cloud and server storage. She was also quick to enlist her team members to brainstorm novel approaches to meet my client's needs. Recognizing Maya's high level of Grounding, Readiness, and Alltelligence (left chart), they reached out before the formal negotiation in the hopes of agreeing in advance on a few important points. Together they mapped out who was likely to be Barely There, to JSUP, or to Truly Show Up for which aspects of the negotiation, and how deep they were in each skill.

For example, the vendor's finance leader was often negative, seeming to prioritize financial gain for his company over client needs. As seen in the middle chart, they rated his Alltelligence Barely There, Grounding in the low JSUP range, and Readiness on the cusp of JSUPing and Truly Showing Up. In contrast, the technology integration leader was friendly, showing care and trust after months of on-site client work at ShowUpCo's five largest locations (high Alltelligence). He was always ready but could also be a bit unpredictable in his moods, as shown by the lower Grounding score on the edge-of Barely There.

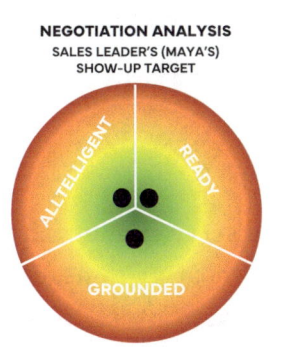

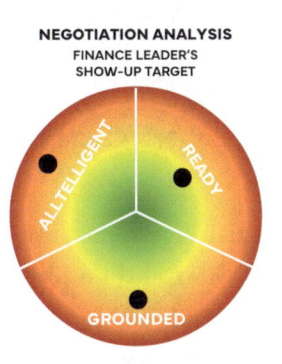

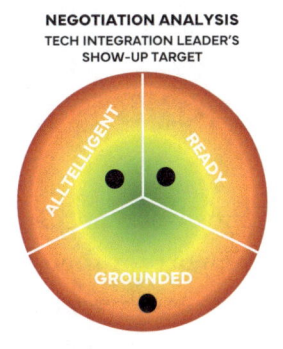

NEGOTIATION ANALYSIS
SALES LEADER'S (MAYA'S) SHOW-UP TARGET

NEGOTIATION ANALYSIS
FINANCE LEADER'S SHOW-UP TARGET

NEGOTIATION ANALYSIS
TECH INTEGRATION LEADER'S SHOW-UP TARGET

doesn't go far enough. We also need to welcome them in and play well in the sandbox. We must choose, "Let's just get started and see what happens," Level 2, Just Showing Up, at least some of the time. Not all moments warrant—or can be given—marathon-level preparedness or the fierce, open receptivity of Alltelligence. We can never be perfectly Grounded nor can we apply our fabulous oneness with the world, team, cohort, or damn exercise routine every day. Doing really well some of the time means we admit, allow—and even choose—something short of it at other times, ideally with grace and gratitude.

It's why training runs for marathons alternate long runs, short runs, and days off—sixteen miles one day, followed by six or eight the next, with a rest day every three, depending on the race. Long-term success requires varying levels of preparing, knowing our Selves, and interrelating with others. It means we need to be flexible and open to how we, and others, choose to Show Up.

EVALUATE, TRACK, AND MANAGE PERFORMANCE

Other ways to apply the continuum are to set targets to measure and track our performance. Expanding our view, we can apply the Show-Up continuum to many things: the performance of team members, family members, ideas, technology, clothing, music, countries, companies, and the world. This lets us relate in a shared language, acting as a common denominator across all spheres helping us interact effectively.

Here's what happened with a top client of mine we'll call ShowUpCo.

WINNING A CONTRACT WITH THE HELP OF SHOWING UP

ShowUpCo needed to revise a contract for cloud services and tech support for their twenty thousand employees. Preparing to negotiate effectively with the vendor (we'll call them VendorCo) and their three team members, my client went to the white board and drew

have the parts without the whole. Similarly, all spaces and moments on the continuum potentiate and effectuate the others. This insight helps us be compassionate about our and others' behavior.

Another crucial understanding is that the more we work to avoid one end of the continuum, at the extreme, the closer we move toward it. This is how consistent striving can turn into burnout and disappointment. And it's how stepping away can show us the solution. I find a magnet example particularly compelling. The south pole, desiring to avoid the north pole, cuts itself in half. Not only did the south pole not succeed in avoiding its other half, the poles are now half the distance they used to be. The idea is to accept all levels in which we naturally Show Up as our needs, capabilities and seasons of life progress, especially versions of Just Showing Up.

WELCOMING ALL SHOW-UP LEVELS

The work to Truly Show Up feels good. It's reinforcing, but it takes energy. And, depending on what we're doing, the energy we expend as we focus, produce, and discipline ourselves toward an outcome gets drained fast. Our muscles fatigue during a hard workout. Succeeding requires that we recharge before utilizing further strength and sweat. This means we must choose to Just Show Up and even occasionally be Barely There out of biological necessity.

Level 2, Just Showing Up, is our home after a busy workday. We need sleep, nutrition, and time with meaningful friends and family. And after we've fought our way out of a two-week flu, Truly Showing Up may still feel like we're Barely There (Level 1) for a while as we dig through missed emails and get back to our schedules while supporting continued healing. This is a healthy mindset. It's the opposite of perfectionism. And it inoculates us against other forms of extremism that cause burnout or volatile emotions and behaviors such as anxiety, depression, excessive drinking, or unwarranted shopping, all of which demonstrate an unhealthy mix of our three Show-Up levels.

Accepting that our lives must include all levels of performance

> our Selves. And let's communicate with the model to help Society move away from unnecessary judgment of good and bad toward acceptance and support.
>
> Once familiar with the target and continuum (roles, skills, and levels in which everyone and everything Shows Up), we start to see how Showing Up is the invisible system existing in and around us. When unseen, neglected, or dismissed, we're prone to Just Show Up, disappoint ourselves, and repeat the unsatisfying pattern of behavior. When we consciously apply and honor the model of how we Show Up, we're connecting with our Selves, our Situations, and broader Society. Whatever we decide, the components of Showing Up are always there, ours to invest in—or to waste—as we choose.

HOW THE LEVELS DEFINE AND SUPPORT EACH OTHER—YIN AND YANG

The continuums and three skills—while they may, at first, seem linear—don't relate according to a plus-minus model or along one dimension. Instead, each level of Showing Up is defined by the other. Level 3 exists because it's neither Level 2 nor Level 1. And it exists because of Level 2 and Level 1. Each is needed. Like freedom and responsibility, they exist in service of each other.

    It's the same with soft and hard, up and down, separateness and togetherness, stressed and contented, emotionally receptive and emotionally clogged. We see the distinction but also recognize how they partner. The defining way they relate is the same as with our disengaged moments in Barely There and our flourishing moments Truly Showing Up. They coincide. The levels are less opposites than they are teammates. They shine bright lights on each other. We simply can't

RELATING FLEXIBLY TO OUR BEHAVIOR

There are significant benefits to relating flexibly to our behavior and performance. Good and bad become stepping stones, not definitive realities. There's no need to judge, criticize, or dwell. We can now be accepting and feel safe, knowing a larger process is at work. And powerfully, feeling safe in our Selves supports a playful mindset. Now we're primed to be more of who we want to be.

This easygoing, fun aspect of Showing Up is not often found in improvement, leadership, or success-focused approaches. Common pursuits (such as communicating clearly, good habits, principle-based decision-making, strengths-based leadership, avoiding biases, creating engaged cultures, willpower, mindfulness, etc.) all encapsulate a version of *better versus worse*. They discuss how some behaviors, thoughts, and feelings move us closer to our goals while others stand in the way. This orients thinking within a plus-minus relationship and along a single plane. Over the short-term, life may seem to work this way. Over the longer term, however, we start to see other, perhaps favorable effects, of what at first seemed negative, and vice versa.

Showing Up doesn't see behavior or Situations as predictable, linear processes. Life is relational. Our actions can only be understood in terms of another's actions. It's how opposites, instead of opposing each other, as we're taught, actually define each other. They need each other to exist. They respond to each other, just as we and our Situations design and respond to each other. This means our behavior Shows Up as aspects of what's around us. Now we start to see our momentary actions, or our partner's, child's, or boss's angry tantrum differently. It meets us in a larger, freer, less judgmental way. What used to cause frustration, sadness, or feeling stuck approaches us with new subtlety. We can sense its implicit realities now and move forward more smoothly and thoughtfully.

> The four benefits of the continuum, awareness, perspective, acceptance, and action, are integrated into the natural way we Show Up. Let's re-instill them in

are turned, we can be there more knowingly for them.

In times of illness or family, financial, and other challenges, when we can't Show Up as we'd ideally choose for days, weeks, or longer, it's okay. It's kind to grant ourselves grace by accepting where and how we're Showing Up right now. When in need, we can allow ourselves to remain there as long as is helpful. Then we can consider moving right on the continuum at a pace that works for us and our loved ones. Easily communicating about it using the continuum can be helpful. It reminds us we're human. And it reminds us we're essentially interconnected.

Beyond periods of challenge, we need transition and recharge time every day. My kids create a much smoother night when they say, "Mom, I'm tired, Just Showing Up. Need time to reset. Can we wait until 7:30 p.m. to eat?" When this is their truth, and they don't tell me, the evening may become a landmine of hormonal teen angst. **The moment they share how they're Showing Up, everything changes. I'm overjoyed and impressed (perhaps overly so) that they had the skill to check in on their Show-Up state and express it. I immediately feel tuned-in to them. I switch into compassion mode. It changes the whole night. And it brings us closer.**

Another benefit people express about using the continuum is that it helps us accept our daily peaks and valleys. We have ups and downs. Our behavior is adaptable. Talking about the three levels makes it easy and acceptable to be anywhere on the continuum. It unleashes choice, ours, and that of those we're with, helping us be kind.

The more we check in—"How am I choosing to Show Up?"—the more spontaneously we'll notice how we're interacting, and adjust. Soon it becomes a habit. We'll choose, far more often, how we're Showing Up. To prompt ourselves we can set reminders on our phone, agree to regularly check in with friends, or use other tactics. I've been told, "My routine of asking in the middle of the day, 'How am I choosing to Show Up right now?' gives me the energy needed to get through. I used to be spent by 5 p.m. and had nothing left when my shift finally ended. Now I meet people after work and feel good."

Sample response:

BARELY THERE — **JUST SHOWING UP** — **TRULY SHOWING UP**

PARTNER PARENTING ME WORK

Use the below continuum to plot your levels.

BARELY THERE — **JUST SHOWING UP** — **TRULY SHOWING UP**

Relating to our behavior and feelings through a framework, such as the model of How We Show Up, switches it from an emotional to a cognitive process. Our behavior is less personal. It's now analytical, abstract, structured, and safe. It's simplified, static, and decontextualized. We're back to employing our left hemisphere's attentional system, in addition to our right. Telling our team, boss, family member, or friend where our dot is on the continuum feels easier than explaining it in a less explicit, more personal way. We're removing stigma that may be related to lower levels of Showing Up. Human Resource teams find it valuable to provide employees safe ways to share how they're doing. Telling your boss, "Hi Anara, I'm having a hard time with my son. I'm on the left edge of Just Showing Up for a while," lets bosses and teams know what to expect about our creativity and contributions until our Show-Up level shifts again. They can choose to lighten the load, to pair us with top performers to help us out, or to walk in with a patient, caring tone, "How are you doing?"

Pointing to a dot on the continuum indicating that we need space to regroup, or are ready for a big assignment, lets us be real. Quick, clear communication helps us exhale. It provides relief if needed. And if we're explaining we're at Level 3, others can also align with us more directly. Our boss may take a chance, giving us that coveted assignment. Or they may be more empathic, patient, and supportive. When tables

to low and around again. Identifying how we're Showing Up (or Showed Up in a past Situation) on a continuum confronts us with our choice and makes it more concrete. It forces us to reckon with our reality. This can be jarring but also healthy and valuable. The three effectiveness levels of high, medium, and low have always been with us, though they are not always appreciated or well defined. Regardless, we've experienced them in our and everyone's behavior every day of our lives through our performance peaks and valleys, all part of nature's dynamic Show-Up system.

How often do you feel challenged to authentically and openly consider how well you're Showing Up?

Admitting to ourselves that we're in the middle of the continuum can feel unwelcome. We try hard. We want to succeed. But we're also human. We need to recognize, and honor, that the human condition is both rich and variable. Life's barrage of media and fast pace can lead us to dim our sensitivity and our emotions. We turn our dials down to be able to keep going, literally to get out of bed and Show Up to our jobs, parenting, and other responsibilities. We also encounter health issues, lose loved ones, or endure other significant life events that leave us on the lower end of the continuum for days or longer. These experiences are part of life. Realizing we're on the left side or middle of the continuum, while difficult, can be helpful when viewed as stepping stones toward healing and toward happiness.

At what level do you feel you're Showing Up right now:

- To yourself?
- With your partner?
- In your parenting?
- At work?

as if circumstances are opportunities to exert our already existing will, need, or desire for something. It leads us to be partially prepared, grounded, and connected. We lose sight of the broader role we play in society, and its reciprocal impact on us.

JSUPing is more commonly our default state. We can certainly refocus and rejuvenate, often jumping into Truly Showing Up at will, but for most of us, as the day passes, we exhaust our intent, perspective, and energy, and with it, we exhaust the sharpness of our Show-Up skills. With practice we can experience a depth of belonging, and live in the more mature, implicit-rich version of Self, naturally interwoven within situations and society. This version of us Shows Up more Ready, Grounded, and Alltelligent.

OBJECTIVITY REMOVES STIGMA

> Friends have told me things like, "Marcy, I taped a photo of the continuum to my coffee maker, and it makes me feel more positive about my day. I choose how I Show Up!" Friends have also mentioned taping the continuum to their bathroom mirror, desk, and phone. "It reminds me to accept myself," my neighbor told me. "I'm still okay, even when I mess up. We move up and down the continuum all day. And it's okay."

Our behavior is impacted by mental, emotional, physical, social, and spiritual aspects. This means daily Situations naturally lead us to traverse many points on the continuum. Ideally, we can call upon each level when needed. But even the most woke, present, intentful, well-prepped, and emotionally intelligent among us live through distracted, tired, and hungry moments, in addition to times when we're pissed, peeved, or impatient. This goes for practitioners of Showing Up as well.

These Situations and performance levels tell us our Grounding, Readiness, and Alltelligence are skipping across a spectrum from high

TARGET DISTIBUTION OF SHOW-UP LEVELS

1 BARELY THERE — <10%
2 JUST SHOWING UP — 30-50%
3 TRULY SHOWING UP — 30-50%

The truth is, even 30 percent Truly Showing Up (TSU) is a stretch. I've been testing this for decades now, and it's been far harder to live in the 30 percent than I thought. Across our population (though not for any specific individual) we find something like this.

COMMON DISTRIBUTION OF SHOW-UP LEVELS IN SOCIETY TODAY

1 BARELY THERE
2 JUST SHOWING UP — CLOSE TO 80%
3 TRULY SHOWING UP

AMERICA'S CONTINUUM: THE MAJORITY OF US, MORE OFTEN THAN NOT, JSUP

From my surveys, formal interviews, and discussions, we Level 3, Truly Show Up approximately 10 to 25 percent of the time. To do this we need to be at least moderately grounded, ready, and Alltelligent across a quarter of our situations and life phases. But most of the time we're not so attuned or intentful. We're often challenged to be Situationally and Societally focused as much as we are Self-focused. And our Self-prioritizing behaviors are likely to reflect the limited, explicit, get-stuff-done orientation of Self. This is us when we interact

Knowing everyone is moving along the continuum all day makes it a safe, objective, and less personal way to view our behavior. We're dialing down the emotional charge since the continuum reminds us our choices are dynamic. They can be shifted in an instant. This supports open discussion among colleagues, teams, families, and friends. Telling Bobby he dipped into Barely There (red) this morning when he got angry at Serena, and that he can move up into green with a single choice, feels less threatening and more accepting and supportive than addressing the behavior outside the context of Showing Up.

Using the continuum turns the subject, our behavior, into an object, data that can be plotted on a line. Others' behavior can now be added, aggregated and analyzed with ours. The continuum acts as a common denominator, reducing and applying human choices to simple, explicit categories. This is exquisitely common across society. All analytic models, business statistics, marketing trends, and assessment systems do this to one degree or another. It's handy to add a bit of it to the practice of Showing Up. And it's utilizing both ways of seeing the world that nature designed humans to benefit from.

MORE TIME IN TRULY SHOWING UP

The continuum may appear to have three equal levels, but it is not ideal to spend a third of our time in each. Existing in Barely There to that extent means we're significantly challenged, likely misinvesting our potential. Ideally, we want Truly Showing Up to be 30 to 50 percent of each day, decade, and our lives, with varying levels of Just Showing Up most of the remainder. This means we're Barely There less than 10 percent of our time.

This is what it looks like when we achieve this.

USING BOTH ATTENTION SYSTEMS

The simple act of stepping back from our imminent Situations, with their emotions, goals, and urgencies, has the power to reset us. Our nervous system has space to relax. We regain access to patience, openness, nuance, and receptivity. These qualities of being naturally refine our thinking and behavior. This is immensely powerful, so powerful it's among the defining features of the human condition. We have the "ability to stand back from the world, from our selves, and from the immediacy of our experience," as psychiatrist Iain McGilchrist explains. "This enables us to plan, to think flexibly and inventively," and to actively respond to the world.

The Show-Up continuum helps us rise above the moment to do this. In short, it stimulates the process we're designed to follow of global attention, followed by local (analytical) attention, which is then returned to global attention. It happens when we notice how we're Showing Up (global, right-brained attention), assess it along the continuum (with narrow, left-brained analysis), and return it to broader thinking right-brained system as we choose how we want to Show Up. Now we're perceiving the Situation more openly and deeply. We're living more human-to-human.

CREATING SAFETY

The continuum helps us separate what we do from who we are. It depersonalizes and abstracts how someone, or a team, Shows Up.

continuum all day, every day, and across the seasons of our lives. This reminds us that it's okay. When we notice we're too far left, as we often will, we can choose and quickly change how we're behaving. Simply remembering the continuum exists—as it always has—reminds us we're choosing how we're Showing Up right now, and that we can shift our behavior immediately.

My friend Penny Zenker[2] describes this acceptance "as part of a 'reset mindset.' It includes letting go of the past, which doesn't only feel good; it's also a critical enabler of growth." In the past we may have been less mindful of our behavior. We may be in the typical pattern of getting mad with ourselves for Showing Up poorly occasionally, but then justify it or tell ourselves we'll do better next time, without making real change. The continuum helps us relate to our behavior and emotions differently. It helps us recognize that everyone is dancing up and down the same Show-Up levels all day. Now we can better accept ourselves and others. And we can start Showing Up closer to how we choose right now.

Even when we are mindful, our focus is likely on a specific aspect of our behavior, such as being patient, listening well, or managing difficult emotions. Such narrow focus is helpful, but we can sometimes be more effective with less effort when we step back to consider behavior at a higher level, such as on the endless flow of behavior across the continuum.

How One Person Uses the Model

One friend told me she took a photo of the Show-Up continuum and put it in her purse.

"I think I'm nicer," she told me. "And in general, I feel better."

After pausing she added, "When I read about it, I didn't think I'd actually use the continuum, but it's in my mind all the time. I think about choice and how we impact each other. It changes how I act."

lays itself out along a parabola, with a hefty dose of life in the middle performance zone and two smaller edges of our "best" and "worst" performance. This is what we'd expect. It follows the general 80/20 rule, or the Pareto principle, explaining that 80 percent of consequences come from 20 percent of the causes.

In our case, it's not consequences and causes. It's Just Showing Up as our dominant, default pattern, with highs and lows of intentionality, Grounding, Readiness, and Alltelligence at the margins. It's how our pattern of Showing Up naturally distributes itself. My research specifically finds that approximately 80 percent of us Just Show Up about 80 percent of the time. And in casual conversations people commonly shake their heads in agreement, or add things like, "80 percent? I think it's 100 percent. All we do is Just Show Up."

The chart below shows a goal of reducing our time Just Showing Up to 50–70 percent. The change from JSUPing 80 percent of the time to 70 percent might seem small, but it can make a world of difference, especially if we focus our choice behavior where it matters most. Even if we don't, we're practicing the fine art of choosing how we Show Up.

TARGET TIME ALLOCATION

1	2	3
BARELY THERE	JUST SHOWING UP	TRULY SHOWING UP
<20%	50-70%	30-50%

PERSPECTIVE AND ACCEPTANCE

The continuum helps us internalize a core power of Show-Up thinking, accepting ourselves. We accept ourselves by recognizing and tolerating that our—and everyone's—behavior naturally flows across the

A simple visual, such as a continuum, prompts us to identify our Show-Up level at any moment. It summarizes our performance across our roles and skills into a single level.

The continuum is a slice of the Show-Up target. It lays out levels of Showing Up that we see around us all the time. I added intuitive names to each level and summarized some of my research in the descriptions to help us create a shared understanding of life at each level.

TARGET TIME ALLOCATION

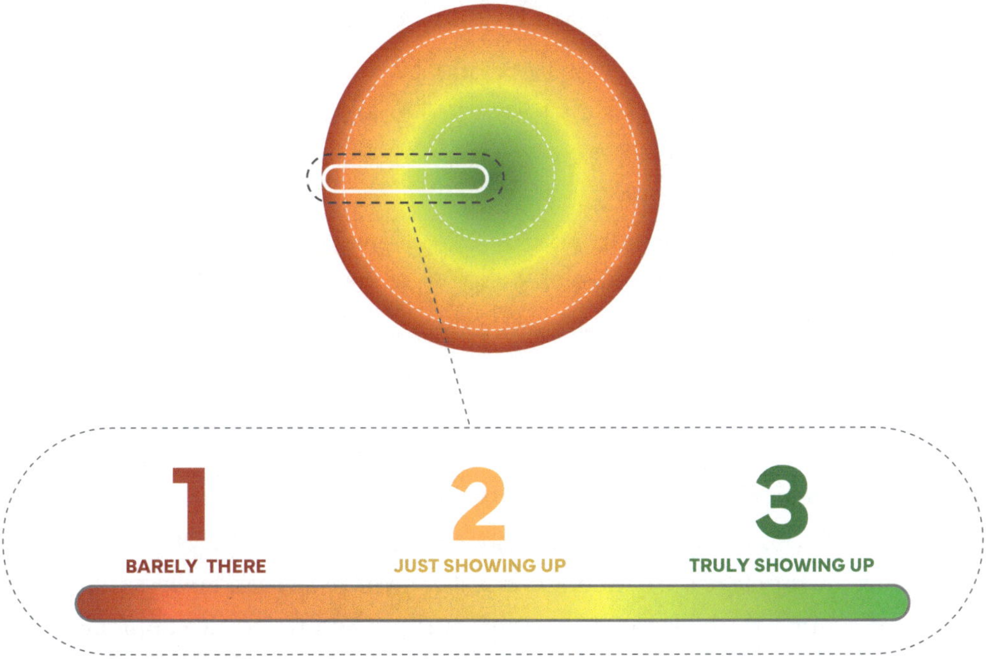

1 BARELY THERE

2 JUST SHOWING UP

3 TRULY SHOWING UP

THE SHOW-UP CONTINUUM

Creating Awareness, Perspective, Acceptance, and Action

The continuum is an easy way to attune ourselves to our behavior choices. Why three levels? Because research on human performance[1]

CHAPTER 5
THE SHOW-UP CONTINUUM

This chapter leads you through the following ideas:
- Three levels of behavior quality
- Right now are you Barely There, Just Showing Up, or Truly Showing Up?
- Dynamic flow
- Acceptance and action
- No more fear. Now we can connect.

YOU'VE PROBABLY NOTICED THE quality of your behavior shifts throughout the day. Our focus, openness, patience, and energy rise and fall. Our ideal performance comes and goes with it. This is natural. Such quality levels are inherent in nature. We've all seen flowers that are symmetrical, bright, and in their prime. And we've also appreciated buds prebloom and the final embers of a sunset before darkness. Seasons of vigor, maturity, stepping back, and stepping up are all around. The quality of our behavior moves with these seasons. And our attentiveness to how we're Showing Up also shifts within our day and with each moment. Whether we pay attention to and exert influence over it is the question.

Show-Up thinking

catalyzes choice.

And we can't stop it.

We're always Showing Up.

THE MODEL OF HOW WE SHOW UP

The Target, Continuum, and Three Levels

5   THE SHOW-UP CONTINUUM

6   LEVEL 2: JUST SHOWING UP

7   LEVEL 1: BARELY THERE

8   LEVEL 3: TRULY SHOWING UP

PART II

2. In what ways do you see your Readiness Show Up in Situations?
   a. How is it helping you perform as you choose?
   b. How is it hindering you?

3. In what ways do you see your Alltelligence Show Up?
   a. How is it helping you perform as you choose?
   b. How is it hindering you?

4. What do the above answers suggest you can do to Show Up closer to how you choose?

CHAPTER 4 SUMMARY— HOW GROUNDING, READINESS, AND ALLTELLIGENCE BECOME "SHOWING UP"

1. Our degree of each skill interacts with Situations, others, and Society to naturally create how we Show Up.

2. Identifying our levels of Grounding, Readiness, and Alltelligence as separate skills playing out in our behavior helps us pinpoint areas to improve.

3. Highly valued behaviors and emotions such as creativity, fun, and many leadership qualities live at the intersection of the three skills and require at least moderate levels of each.

4. Connectedness is at the core of how we Show Up. It drives us to act, to feel with, and to care for, a critical step toward living in a kinder, healthier, happier Society.

5. Both internal and external factors challenge our ability to connect with our Selves, Situations, others, and Society, leading us to Just Show Up, or be Barely There, interacting with less intent than we otherwise could.

CHAPTER REFLECTION

Choose a single daily situation as you reflect on these questions.

1. In what ways do you see your Grounding Show Up?
    a. How is it helping you perform as you choose?
    b. How is it hindering you?

Up the way I want to—prepared, self-assured, and emotionally open for my own kids and colleagues.

What we don't give ourselves time or permission to feel and reflect on, we subtly disconnect from. Prioritizing "rational" responses (e.g., not emotional), as many scientific, educational, corporate and family cultures do, may diminish the quality of our lived experiences. Hopefully we're ready to move past this. Neuroscience has proven instinct and emotion precede reason. We should be tapping into our reservoirs of insight and emotion, not discouraging or discounting them.

All these sources limiting connectivity also limit our Grounding, Readiness, and Alltelligence. The result is less genuine—and less heartfelt—caring. It shifts us toward Level 2, Just Showing Up, and the "Self-focused" left side of the continuum, toward Level 1, Barely There.

There are times when we need to disconnect to protect ourselves. And there are times when we just do it. Tuning out and distractedness are common forms of disconnecting. They lessen our depth of associating with people, information, and Situations. In painful situations disconnecting can be an adaptive and developmental reaction. It has its place. Managing our dosage is the key.

But when we're tired, stressed, or distracted, it's what we automatically do. This is why asking ourselves, "How am I choosing to Show Up?" can be a significant and valuable tool in helping us live more connected, healthy, and fulfilling lives.

a trusting, positive relationship with ourselves and others? Perhaps insufficient care matured us into being overly independent. Now we take good care of ourselves and don't let others completely in. Internal inhibitors of connectedness take many forms. They Show Up in nuanced ways, making them hard to see. Ultimately, not feeling fully emotionally safe and accepted, consciously or not, leads us to feel isolated, priming us to live in an "us and them" reality. But often we don't see our behavior as such. Instead, we view it as just the way the world is, not recognizing that our developmental coping mechanisms built a barrier for us in an unsafe world, leaving us less open to connecting than we're naturally designed to be.

Stressors of all kinds[9]—even microstressors,[10] those quick moments of strain that appear to be manageable—if not processed effectively, can lead us to subconsciously suppress or detach from our feelings. We often remain unaware of this. Pushing emotions away from our attention—social discomfort, fear, or even joy—happens often in the course of our days as our schedules keep us moving.

A Son Not Allowed to Fail

"They built a safety net two feet below me," a friend explained about his parents and the cause of his insecurities today.

They rescued me when I didn't need it. All sorts of consequences, disappointing grades, social rejection, poor performance on my soccer and baseball teams, were softened. I didn't get to experience falling down and needing to pick myself back up. It created dependency and insecurity. It limits my ability to connect with people, even today.

Now I'm fifty-three years old and still need reassurance in more relationships than I should. It limits my ability to connect and Show

> **signals to those around us, making our family or work culture one in which we all protect ourselves.**

This hypervigilance subtly preoccupies us. We seem relentlessly Self-focused. We're far less attractive for others to reach out to, trapping us in a "vicious cycle of suspicion, jealousy, and resentment."[7] Then the fracture deepens. Unconsciously, we're pulling others down around us. We're now primed for racial bias, stereotyping, and other prejudicial behaviors as misperceived situations lead to outsized reactions. Our physiology is simply not engineered to support the degree of disconnectedness in which many of us are living.

> **"Our ancestors' default setting was togetherness."[8] Its absence within today's "tribes" creates sustained stressors that raise our risk of heart disease, cause inflammation, and reduce our immunity to viruses. Social fragmentation also depletes our resources needed to roll with the daily challenges and difficult relationships in our lives. All this primes us to react disproportionately in the moment.**

Other internal inhibitors of connectedness get wired in us from birth and shortly thereafter through insecure or avoidant attachment relationships. Such relationships are created when our primary caregivers were unable to create a sufficient sense of safety, of being loved and accepted, or when our basic needs for food, warmth, and care weren't met. Our body responded to the sufficiency of attention we got by setting a baseline level of calm or stress that, unless rewired, we carry to this day. (More on this in Chapter 9, Grounding.)

It's visible to those around us. Are we vigilant? Prone to worry? Or can we stay levelheaded and grounded most of the time, maintaining

of us reside in urban areas, away from nature and family. Within these urban environments, we value privacy, and peace. But both privacy and peace require physical, auditory, and emotional walls, closing us off from others. In addition to where we live, how we live may be tethered to fixed schedules that fit transactional interactions, creating a misfit when meaningful connecting requires a more fluid relationship with time. It's inconvenient and stressful when our calendars pressure us to finish up and move on, shortchanging or precluding heartfelt interactions and space to savor emotions, rainbows, sunsets, and each other.

Competitiveness is another external force pushing us apart. It's built into our market economy, corporate cultures, educational system, social media, and Society at large. While not inherently bad, how competitions are structured can wire us to experience "us and them," to fight to get ahead instead of supporting each other and feeling abundant.

These cultural realities are far from the tribal, trusted, community-based environment from which we evolved and in which we were designed to thrive. Said another way, we no longer feel like the interconnected "Alldividuals" we used to be. Now we experience ourselves and others as Individuals. We're less members of a collective integral to our survival. Feeling separate creates loneliness. We start to feel an emptiness leading to symptoms such as agitation, fear, listlessness, and turning inward. Separateness makes us more sensitive to threat. We start to "push people away and see risk or intimidation in benign social opportunities."[5]

> **In fact, neuroscientist Dr. Stephanie Cacioppo "found that lonely brains detect social threats twice as fast as non-lonely brains." She goes on to explain that even subtle "hypervigilance causes us to misread harmless or even welcoming people and situations as threats. Fleeing into self-preservation mode, we'll avoid people and distrust even those who reach out to help us."[6] Then we send out threat**

in the description of Self, we've moved from exclusively "me," on the left side of the continuum, to embrace more "we."

Alltelligence fosters integration and connectivity. And vice versa. Dan Siegel explains that "integrated linkages (in the brain and body) enable more intricate functions to emerge—such as insight, empathy, intuition, and morality. A result of integration is kindness, resilience, and health."[4] This is why connectedness is a core mechanism for cultivating well-being. It is described further in Chapter 11, Alltelligence.

The deeper our native skills within our Selves, Situations, and Society, the easier it is to Show Up as we choose. Supporting this, I have added the bulleted lists explaining less depth of all three Show-Up skills on the left side, as we're self-focused, and more depth on the right side, as our belongingness supports Societal Alltelligence, Situational Readiness, and Self-Grounding.

BARELY THERE	JUST SHOWING UP	TRULY SHOWING UP
SELF-FOCUS	NOTICING ▶ TUNING-IN	FEELING WITH ▶ ENACTING CARE
SELF	SELF + SITUATION MEMBER	SELF + SITUATION + SOCIETY MEMBER

Lower:
- GROUNDING
- READINESS
- ALLTELLIGENCE

Higher:
- GROUNDING
- READINESS
- ALLTELLIGENCE

SOURCES INHIBITING CONNECTING SURROUND US

Now that we've reviewed how central connectivity is to being happy, healthy, and performing our best, it's helpful to review its inhibitors. Assaults on feeling connected within our selves, situations, and society are both externally and internally generated. They gnaw at all three Show-Up skills at once. And most, if not all, are unintended. You'll notice they are related to the causes of Just Showing Up described in Chapter 2.

External sources include common aspects of modern Society. Beyond the over-dominant usage of our left-brained attention system, many

much as we expect. Unless we step back to reset our nervous systems at least a little bit, these influences significantly restrict our noticing and tuning-in.

We often haven't readied our Show-Up choices for this specific moment. Our Grounding, Readiness, and Alltelligence skills may be depleted, diffused, or simply absent. The result? We only superficially perceive and embrace others. And they notice it! It's our role as limited, individualistic Selves playing out more strongly than our role of Societal members. Think back to Peter's example of corporate politics. In this Self-as-island state people feel less care as we interact. They feel less heard, less felt and less cared for, emotionally, intellectually, socially, and functionally. This is dissatisfying. It leaves us sad. Yet, this form of Just Showing Up is active among us. Some of us have always lived this way. I sure used to. Often we don't notice it. Does a fish know it's in water?

But living interconnected lives is integral to our humanness. It's a primal need, wired into our physiological structure, chemical flows, perception systems and even breath. Specific research on giving behavior from Olga Klimecki et al.[2] found people double their giving after classic compassion training. This practice is an act as simple as thinking of someone and reciting, "May you feel happy. May you feel healthy. May you feel peaceful." Her research states, "Their brains showed increased activation in circuits for attention, perspective taking, and positive feelings; the more of this activation, the more altruistic."[3] Sending these wishes to others is an easy way to move right on the continuum, and raise our compassion and connection. Unfortunately, if we're not careful, the natural flow of our days pushes against it, keeping us in Level 2, Just Showing Up. It's the reality of low to moderate Alltelligence in the moment. And it's the reality of our partial disconnectedness from our selves and others that's prevalent in society.

As we move into the right half of the continuum, into higher levels of JSUPing (Just Showing Up) and then into Truly Showing Up, we're more likely to feel compassion and be driven to act. We're compelled by a belongingness. It's a "with-ness" connecting us to something larger than our Selves. This is our Alltelligence coming through. As referenced

and "living into" an experience, idea, or person. They Show Up in our third role, that of Societal member. The higher states of other-focus (on the right side of the continuum) of "feeling with" and "enacting care" correspond to Truly Showing Up. They're also aligned with our right brain's way of attending to the world, including its primacy of "wholeness."

BARELY THERE	JUST SHOWING UP	TRULY SHOWING UP
SELF-FOCUS	NOTICING ▶ TUNING-IN	FEELING WITH ▶ ENACTING CARE
SELF	SELF + SITUATION MEMBER	SELF + SITUATION + SOCIETY MEMBER

Lower levels of Showing Up, such as being Barely There and Just Showing Up, correspond to Self-focus and partial or intermittent tuning-in to what's happening within and around us. They may also make us unhappy if we're in our default mode, focused unintentfully on "I, me, mine." These lower levels of connectedness are described in more detail in Chapter 7, Barely There, which is Level 1 on the Show-Up continuum. Lower levels leave us barely caring, helping, or "feeling with" others. After all, we need to notice others to even have the opportunity to "tune in" or "feel with." When we're preoccupied, multitasking, self-focused, or rushing, we're far more likely to walk past others, physically, emotionally, and spiritually.

Narrow Self-focus often happens in work meetings and other informal exchanges with friends and family. We may intentionally be with people or in the meeting, but we don't quite hear, see, or feel what each other needs or is communicating. It's daily life. Interactions are typically rapid. During a workday we may prioritize getting stuff done, which may sidestep how people feel. It can bound thinking at customers and suppliers, leaving out everything else. What we intend or need to transmit is often muddied by pressures of the moment, limiting our word choice, openness, clarity, and amiability. Fixed assumptions, and abstracted metrics (which measure some things while making the rest disappear), together with predetermined "knowledge" of "how things work," reproduce common situations for us. They may Just Show Up,

performance system. Our invisible perspectives, opinions, and attitudes don't just come with us; they predict us by imbuing...or infecting... how we interact with others, and they, us.

Consciously or not, our views (principles, politics, and dogmas) do more than color our experiences. They govern them. What we see and hear each moment, in each activity, work assignment, family discussion, and solo event reflects our core beliefs about the world (our Alltelligence). They mix with our Grounding, a stew of (often projected and/or protected) fears and needs.[1] This is the personal code that we use to decipher the world. Feeling judged or insecure anyone? Expect what we see to reinforce it.

These common unpleasantries are based on beliefs about our Selves, our capabilities, and where and how we fit in (Grounding). Over time we nudge and design our environment to cocreate our expected reality. We choose our friends, work environment, what we read and think. Then, over time, the external world starts to validate what we always knew to be true. This explains how our level of the three Show-Up skills precedes us. Knowing the model helps us choose whether our skills amplify or impede our success.

HOW SHOWING UP DRIVES ACTION— CONNECTIVITY AND THE SHOW-UP CONTINUUM

In addition to preceding us, Showing Up drives action. From there, magic happens. We're driven to act and to care, to be in service of others. This is why "feeling felt" and "feeling with" is critical for living in a healthier, happier Society. And it's what we and the planet are ultimately evolving toward because it's how we started, and it's what we must move toward if we are to thrive.

I have laid out degrees of connectivity within the Show-Up continuum. Below we see Self-focus, the lowest level of connectivity, on the left, and higher levels of connectivity, where compassion lives, on the right. These higher connectivity levels are degrees of "being with"

> are—someone skilled in potentiating serendipity, attracting opportunities, and making ourselves magnetic for the goodness lurking silently around. Readiness preserves and stores our skill. It soaks in richness. In this way, it morphs into a personal quality, approaching the level of character trait.
>
> Importantly, this state of ripened, cured Readiness is constrained by the depth of our Grounding and our Alltelligence. If we're intrinsically or Situationally ungrounded, anxious, distracted, or in a sour mood, even from something as common as checking our phone, hunger or fatigue, our serendipity flees.

HOW WE SHOW UP PRECEDES US AND DESIGNS OUR LIVES

How we Show Up is also projected into our futures. Others expect from us what we did before. They interact based on it, as do we. This dramatically colors what we—and they—think and notice and how we interpret and respond to the world. Does the boss think we're fabulous? This positivity brings out our best. It emboldens us to interact more confidently, bolstering the goodness. And we know the opposite plays out as well. It's hard to pry ourselves out from others' negative judgment or expectations of us. When Just Showing Up, their left-brained attention system re-presents our behavior in their minds no matter what we do. And it's equally daunting to reign in our own judgmental perceptions of our selves and others.

As mentioned in the description of Situations in Chapter 3, how we see the world creates how it Shows Up for us. It's the way our past Show-Up choices precede us. They create our future experiences as much as what's going on right now. These examples demonstrate how our predispositions and beliefs are a critical foundation for any

know ourselves. Seeing behavior through the components of Showing Up and how they relate enables us to understand ourselves and others more deeply.

CULTIVATING SERENDIPITY

Think back to Eddy's story at the beginning of this chapter. Eddy's Readiness is rooted in his sense of Self. If he didn't believe in himself as a skilled individual, he wouldn't have made the favorable impression he did on John. And had Eddy's Alltelligence been low, he wouldn't have anticipated a positive exchange with a stranger when John struck up a conversation. So while Eddy describes it as Readiness, it was the interplay of his Grounding and Alltelligence with his Readiness that prepared him, just as much as his elevator pitch.

Eddy's story describes an opportunity that had been hovering around but hadn't come to fruition. These opportunities often wait for just the right mix of people, timing, and Situation to come together. Eddy's comfort with his skillset (Grounding), practiced sales pitch, interest in securing new clients (Readiness), general trust, and, importantly, desire to use his skill to help people (Alltelligence) cultivated serendipitous opportunity. He expected this moment would arise.

> **Now we're priming luck. It comes together with fortune and chance when preparedness marinates in the background. This skill to initiate, identify, and respond to opportunity where none apparently existed becomes a nourishing resource, like a soup simmering on the stove, ready to be served the moment the family gathers. We're more aware. Is that them now? Our minds are alert, subtly seeking glimmers of opportunity. We've become prone and predisposed to deliver our skill, wherever and whenever chances arise. It becomes part of who we**

the most tactical and quick for us to put to work. Checking in with "How am I choosing to Show Up?" is a Readiness activity. This makes it the easiest investment to boost how we're performing. Like the tip of the iceberg visible above the water, our Readiness is visible to all. It can be enormously impactful. And it can be superficial. An important point about Readiness is that it is naturally limited by our degree of Grounding and Alltelligence. We can ready ourselves up to, but not beyond, our level of those skills.
- **Alltelligence** is infused in, and relies on, our Grounding and Readiness. As our orientation of interconnectedness, this skill also lives on two planes, that of our Situation right now and our ever-present foundation (our Grounding) that we carry into all Situations. We can Ready our Alltelligence by choosing to see others as part of our shared humanity, to be open to their views and to feel compassion with and for them.

These descriptions touch the surface of how elements of our behavior relate to and support each other. Building on them, here are a few more.

- Grounding spurs confidence, openness, and interest (Alltelligence). These emotions encourage us to actively engage with people and to participate in activities (Readiness).
- Positive interactions support trust and care, advancing our Alltelligence.
- Understanding ourselves gives us tools to understand others (Alltelligence).

This makes the depth of our Grounding, like expertise in any area, both the extent and limit of insight we can reach with another. There's a familiar adage that says, "We need to meet people where they are." It means people can't perform beyond their level of understanding. This is true for us all. We can only know others to the extent that we

sentence or two about his services and their value on the tip of his tongue. And they had to be delivered with confidence (Grounding). Then he must draw out his listeners' needs and show genuine care (Alltelligence). All are essential to opening the door to a new client relationship. They merge, becoming our actions, when we consciously choose and when we don't.

> **The synergy of Grounding, Readiness, and Alltelligence is unmistakable. Like ingredients in an exquisite culinary creation, the whole is distinct from, and exceeds, the sum of its parts.**

Many things influence how our skills Show Up. Each environment, including our bedroom, kitchen, office, desk, or a favorite restaurant, mixes our Grounding, Readiness, and Alltelligence into a behavioral cocktail of its own, as does what precedes and follows each Situation.

While some may believe it's ideal to design the Show-Up skills to be mutually exclusive and comprehensively exhaustive, I'm not sure any model of human performance would be accurate if it did so. Here are a few more ways our Show-Up skills compare and interrelate.

- **Grounding** is potentially the most powerful of the three. It's our foundation, Showing Up across all Situations, planned and impromptu. As a result, it is always there, underlying our Situational Readiness and Societal Alltelligence.
- **Readiness** lives on two planes, our foundation of Grounding, and the surface activities of daily life. It is at once our week of solid sleep enabling us to feel curious, patient, and alert (foundation) and the homework we just completed for today's class (surface activity). Readiness is perhaps the most accessible,

MEET EDDY

Just yesterday, a wise neighbor we're calling Eddy told me about a conversation he had on the 7:36 a.m. train to Manhattan. It was with a fellow commuter named John who also rode in daily from our Westchester suburb. They had seen each other over the years but had never spoken or even acknowledged each other. Until one day, they did.

It turns out John needed Eddy's help to complete a real estate transaction. He had noticed Eddy working on real estate projects for years. When John's firm was ready to buy a new property, he immediately thought of the man he saw on the train. The next morning John said hi.

Over time John turned into one of Eddy's biggest clients. Reflecting on the experience, Eddy told me in a definitive tone, "I was ready for that moment long before it happened. I had prepared for years, specifically for opportunities like this. I didn't know when it would happen. But that time, and every time, I'm ready." Here's how I'd rate his performance on the Show-Up continuum, and his skill on the Show-Up Target.

BARELY THERE — **JUST SHOWING UP** — **TRULY SHOWING UP**

EDDY'S SHOW-UP TARGET

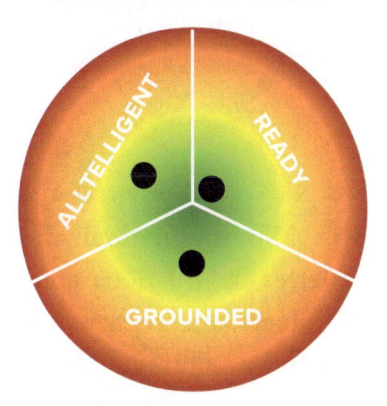

ALLTELLIGENT / READY / GROUNDED

When Eddy used the word *ready,* he was referring to the full set of skills he brought to the table. Being prepared to meet business prospects anywhere and everywhere meant he had to have a succinct

CHAPTER 4

HOW GROUNDING, READINESS, AND ALLTELLIGENCE BECOME "SHOWING UP"

This chapter leads you through the following ideas:
- G/R/A: Organically fusing into how we Show Up
- How we Show Up precedes us
- Priming serendipity!
- Action through connectivity

WHILE GROUNDING, READINESS, AND ALLTELLIGENCE offer benefits as independent skills, they naturally fuse into how we Show Up across our roles as Selves, in Situations, and in Society. Emergent properties such as playfulness and creativity live at the fertile intersection of all three. Creativity requires at least minimum comfort in our own skin, safety, and belonging (Grounding), Readiness to engage with the Situation, and a level of trust (Alltelligence). Collectively, the skills prime our minds to make novel connections, bringing us somewhere new. It feels good. It's validating and fulfilling.

Ease, playfulness, and creativity emerge from the fertile intersection of our Show-Up skills.

4. **Readiness**:
    a. How often do you notice how you're Showing Up?
    b. How often do you choose, in advance, how you'd like to Show Up?
    c. In what areas of your life do you prepare well?
    d. What aspects of your life could use more planning or preparing?
    e. What positive behaviors could you transfer to the areas you struggle with?

5. **Alltelligence**:
    a. To what extent do you sense your impact on others?
    b. What individualized preferences or predetermined mindsets might you be holding that promote or limit your empathizing with other people, ideas, or responsibilities?

REFLECTING QUESTIONS

Consider one area of your life in which you're thriving and one in which you're struggling as you reflect on the following.

Area of thriving: _____

Area of struggling: _____

1. How often are you Showing Up as you choose?

2. What weighting of Self, Situation member, and Societal member are you Showing Up with in your area of thriving? What weighting do you sense in your area of struggle?

Weighting in Area of Thriving

_____ + _____ + _____ = 100%
SELF   SITUATION   SOCIETY

Weighting in Area of Struggle

_____ + _____ + _____ = 100%
SELF   SITUATION   SOCIETY

3. **Grounding**:
   a. What aspects of your Self are prominent when you're thriving (i.e., Feeling Self-assured, organized, at ease, focused, planful, connected with others)?
   b. Which parts of you Show Up when you're struggling (i.e., feeling stuck, experiencing limiting beliefs or distracting emotions)?

6. **Showing Up offers a practical, relational model of how we behave and perform. It provides a dynamic, systemic view of our lives and the world.** In doing so, Showing Up makes it easier to consider a broad set of influences in relation to our behavior, supporting us in Showing Up closer to how we choose.

5. How we Show Up reveals how connected we are within and across the three roles in which we live: as Selves (Grounding), within Situations (Readiness), and within Society (Alltelligence). Fundamentally, this is what we're choosing at every moment. It creates our interactions, sense of meaning, and health, which we infuse into others, and all things we create in the world.

- **Self:** We Show Up between two extremes of Self. One mainly separate, closed and Self-serving, seeing the world as a static, abstracted object to be acted on. The other mainly integrated, emotionally sensing, and actively part of a dynamic world.
- **Grounding** is the native skill of our Self. It is our interconnectedness within. It measures how in touch we are with our inborn nature, the drivers of day-to-day behavior.

- **Situation:** Situations are the instruments and intervals through which we come alive. They're the vehicles of our lived experience as our Self and Societal roles interact with the world. They include the people, their Show-Up choices, content, ideas, goals, and environment of the moment.
- **Readiness** is how deeply we connect within the dynamic dances that are our Situations. It includes our preparatory activities for the content, and to viscerally open our Selves to the shared experience happening around us.

- **Society:** Our Societal role encompasses everything beyond the individualized Self. It's how we interact in groups of people, with ideas, culture, nature, and humanity. It is the largest unit of consideration in which we Show Up. And it is our most expansive role.
- **Alltelligence** describes our degree of interconnectedness with Society and the natural world. High Alltelligence is experienced as a sense of wholeness.

If you're committed to continuously improving yourself, your leadership, family, team, or business, the mental model of Showing Up is an essential part of it.

SUMMARY POINTS—CHAPTERS 1, 2, AND 3

1. Many of us Just Show Up too often, reducing our fulfillment, health, and happiness, and those of Society.

2. A key reason for Just Showing Up is defaulting to the thin, separate, will-driven version of Self, one seeing the world as an object to be acted on, not one we're dynamically integrated within.

3. Just Showing Up is prioritizing our role as Selves, underweighting our roles as enlivening members of Situations and Society.

4. Actively choosing how we Show Up helps us perform closer to our potential. We do it through the following:
   a. <u>Recognizing</u> we're always Showing Up and how it works
   b. <u>Asking</u>: *How am I choosing to Show Up?*
      i. Barely, Just, or Truly?
      ii. How Grounded, Ready, Alltelligent?
      iii. Mostly Self, Situationally, or Societally oriented?
   c. <u>Shifting</u> toward our chosen behavior more often

Alltelligent, or a mixture of them. Showing Up functions across all these. It's overarching. It's inclusive.

All books focused on behavior and performance discuss how we relate within society, although many do so from the individual outward. In this thinking we're attempting to exert control over something outside of us by interacting a certain way. Yet, the Situations that comprise our moments are not ours to utilize. They flow into us, as well as outward from us. All moments and Situations are a blend of our Selves and Society, closer to hearty vegetable soup than pure, individualized broth. And Situations, like us, are in motion. We evolved in, and are designed by, a coevolving system. Structured by this natural system, Showing Up is organically in and part of it, while also functioning across it, over time.

It's why this book is titled **How We** Choose to Show Up, not Choose to Show Up. "How We" is process based, inclusive and wholistic, all core to the relational underpinnings of our behavior. This is vital.

> **These are some of the ways Showing Up functions as an overarching system and mental model into which other performance ideologies fit. Importantly, Showing Up also transcends them. It exists at the level of our souls, human to human, connecting our minds and behavior within Society and nature. It's the way we function, across time.**

This creates a synergistic relationship among approaches you may be using and the natural model of how we Show Up. So fear not. There's nothing competitive or discrediting. If anything, Showing Up functions as connective tissue across business and self-improvement practices. It will amplify your results from other ideologies by helping you live with greater Self-knowledge, preparedness, and connectedness across the three roles in which we and all things Show Up.

HOW SHOWING UP RELATES TO OTHER POPULAR PERFORMANCE APPROACHES

I think it's clear by now that nature's model of how we Show Up is far more than a performance system. It's a way of living. That said, on the chance it's helpful to relate it to popular performance approaches, I have highlighted a few points below.

There are many ways to think about daily behavior, performance and growth. Over the past fifty years, many approaches have been popularized. Each has a lot to offer. Given how familiar many of us are with such approaches, I thought it would be helpful to explain how Showing Up fits among them.

At the highest level, we can loosely group performance thinking into three categories:

- Effective thinking and prioritizing: Ray Dalio's *Principles*, Stephen Covey's *First Things First*, Gary Keller and Jay Papasan's *The ONE Thing*, and many others
- Effective doing, including: habit-based approaches (Tom Cleary's *Atomic Habits* and Charles Duhigg's *The Power of Habit*), productivity (David Allen's *Getting Things Done*), leadership and management (Jerry Porras and Jim Collins's *Built to Last* and Dan Pink's *Drive*), time management (Ken Blanchard's *The One Minute Manager* and Tim Ferriss's *The 4-Hour Workweek*) among many others
- Mindfulness and focus: Mihaly Csikszentmihalyi's *Flow* and many other mindfulness and meditation books and tools

Showing Up is designed to be comprehensive, to the degree this is possible. Most of the above categories target one or a few aspects of performance, such as how we think, feel, decide, or organize ourselves. You can think of it as helping us be more Grounded, Ready, or

THE LEVELS OF SHOWING UP

Our Show-Up Continuum

The quality of our performance can be measured along a simple continuum from low to high. It's a slice from the Show-Up target and an intuitive visual helping us keep our dynamic performance—and choice—in mind. The outer rim is Level 1, indicating lower performance. The middle ring is Level 2, Just Showing Up, what my research indicates most of us do 80 percent of the time. The target's center is Level 3, indicating our highest quality of interacting.

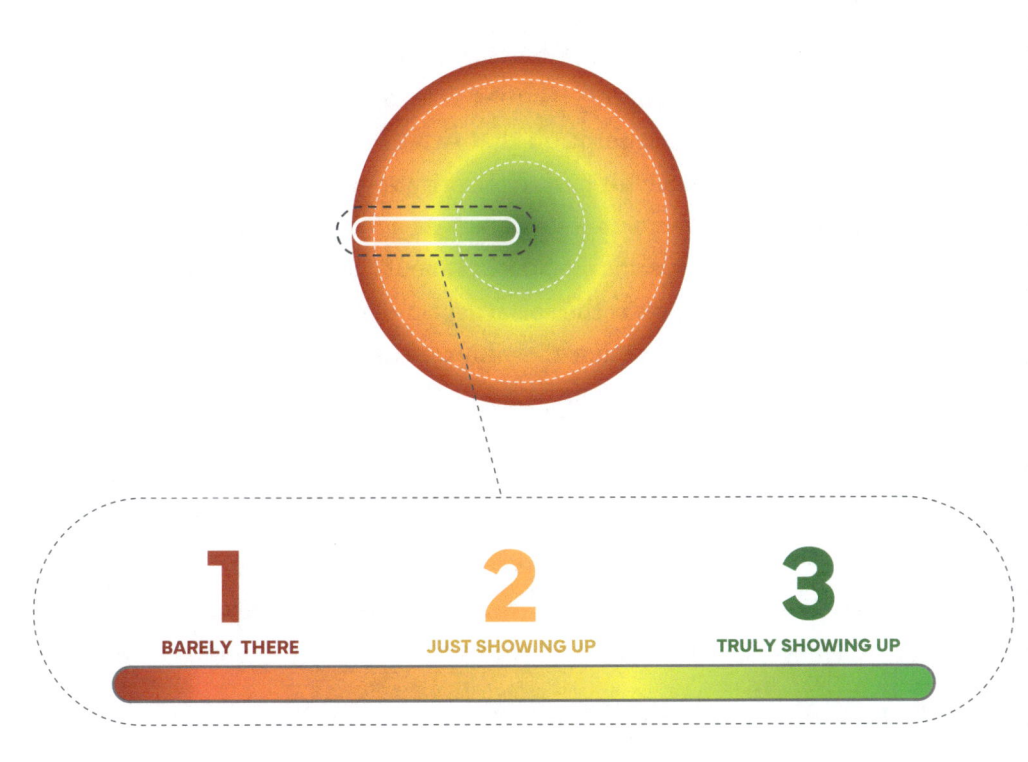

1 BARELY THERE
2 JUST SHOWING UP
3 TRULY SHOWING UP

Described further in Chapter 5, keeping the Show-Up continuum in mind spurs Self-acceptance and action by reminding us we can revise our behavior as we go. There's no reason to be harsh with ourselves. We're always flowing across the continuum and can, and should, attune and reset often.

bleed into her Grounding and Alltelligence. It demonstrates how a high achiever known to Truly Show Up may temporarily Just Show Up when circumstances are challenging.

In the Wall Street example, Rachel's Self-understanding (Grounding) and connected, trust-based orientation (Alltelligence) are the heart of her competence. She describes "technical" Readiness as less important due to her years of experience, a common evolution as our skills mature, but she's highly ready to judge the risk level of the deal, her primary responsibility. She is Truly Showing Up, demonstrating high levels of the three Show-Up skills as they pertain to this Situation.

In the Amazon Web Services example, Lucas's challenge, and therefore focus, is to feel Grounded. This is the lynchpin for him to achieve what is needed at the meeting. His reference to finding himself "falling back on a ridiculous assumption that what I do doesn't matter" is likely long standing from his past. His clarity about this insecurity and intentful effort to overcome it demonstrate a focus on deepening his Grounding. Content-specific preparation about the agenda is described with ease (Readiness), as is the social aspect of collaborating productively (Alltelligence). Together they indicate he is Truly Showing Up.

> **Supporting our natural roles as Selves within Situations and Society, the three Show-Up skills each establish unique aspects of our success. They're essential both individually and collectively, constructing the quality of our experience and performance.**

Internalizing the mutuality and reciprocity at the core of Alltelligence naturally engages us in life. It motivates us to Show Up better, with more care, orienting us in service of others. And it's why Alltelligence is the crucial third skill we must internalize, corresponding to our role as social beings.

IMPLICATIONS OF SHOWING UP

The above descriptions reveal notable implications of how we Show Up. They include:

1. A deep sense that "we matter." This engages us in life, infusing us with meaning and purpose.
2. A sense of responsibility motivating us to do our best—with, to and for others.
3. A broadmindedness that sees our moments within a larger context, well beyond ourselves.
4. A feeling of connectedness, of being integrated into the word, fostering belonging and well-being.

These implications are tied to longer, happier lives.[7] We're more likely to experience openness, curiosity, compassion, partnering, and positivity, all states known to support engagement, success, and meaning.

WHAT THESE QUICK EXAMPLES REVEAL

These examples demonstrate how each of the three Show-Up skills exist in all of us. Trevor, in the consulting example, demonstrates limits in all three Show-Up skills, knowing himself (Grounding), being Situationally prepared (Readiness), and not trusting, collaborating with, or caring for others (Alltelligence). He also seems to not be attuned to his Show-Up choices. He's passively Barely There, Level 1 Showing Up. Lucy, the recent college grad, shows how challenges in one skill, Readiness,

> *If I sense they're trying to distort the company's situation, we're done. I can always tell. It's my Alltelligence and my Grounding. Being relaxed in who I am gives me the intuition I rely on.*
>
> *Technical Readiness with the numbers is the easy part.*

It's important to note that the impact of how we Show Up goes both ways, outward from us and inward from others, culture, media, social systems, etc. We can share positivity or concern, high regard for others or indifference, energy or lethargy, busyness or availability. All are contagious. All flow three degrees of separation deep, to and from our friends of friends of friends.

> **When we forget the mutual impact we have on each other, it's easy for short-term influences—being rushed, tired, hungry, or frustrated—to take hold of our behavior. They, by default, cause us to treat ourselves and others with less compassion, support, and generosity of spirit. This hinders our happiness, engagement, and motivation, as it does theirs. This negative pattern of Showing Up then becomes what news reporters investigate and write about. That night it's what we read on our phones on the way home and watch on TV. Now it's in our mind. It's what we think and feel. Over time our products and services are tailored to address these patterns and needs. What and how we strive to achieve is shaped by them. And the impacts go on, ever designing how we, and Society, Show Up.**

Alltelligent Companies

We can create Alltelligent systems, policies, and companies. These are the prosocial organizations that genuinely want to be helpful and care for employees, customers, the full ecosystem of stakeholders, and the environment long term. Such organizations know this is best done with deeply diverse teams and leadership, including differences across cognitive and behavioral styles, as well as ethnic, social, and economic variation.

The description that I have for an Alltelligent world view in one of my TEDx talks, "Showing Up Is a Contact Sport," is, "Beyond us as individuals, we exist as a collective, neither distinct nor discrete. Like leaves on a tree, humans are interlocked with the emotions, thoughts, and actions of others. Peoples' behaviors are silently adjusting, guiding, and even presiding over what we do and who we are. **This means we're not just defined by, but we're designed by, everyone and everything around us.**"

I go on to describe that "behavior is contagious. People absorb how we Show Up and infuse it into others. It goes three layers deep—I'll explain. Our closest friends and colleagues are 45 percent more likely to do what we do. Their friends are 25 percent, and that third layer, those friends of friends of friends'—someone such as our colleagues' daughter's classmate—are 10 percent more likely to do what we do. This is the work of Dr. Nicholas Christakis, professor at Yale.[6] His work explains scientifically how Showing Up is a contact sport." And it means Alltelligence, the skill based on this reality, is an essential component for us to perform at the highest level we're capable of.

MEET RACHEL
A senior leader at a prestigious Wall Street firm.

For me, it starts with Alltelligence. My degree of connection and trust for those on the opposing team are how I decide whether we should underwrite the deal. Are they approaching the [debt] previsions in a collaborative way?

- **What degree of reciprocity naturally exists among and around us?**

Our answers design our behavior and all we create. They source and fund our expectations, making Alltelligence a fundamental and formidable creator of how we experience our Situations, and of our choices, successes, and challenges.

Alltelligence grounds us in something larger than us as discrete individuals. We need each other to flourish. And we share a duty to be a positive force. This feeling viscerally engages us. We care; we're curious. We feel pulled to be of value to others and our environment. Even when our jobs aren't our perfect fit, Alltelligence supports us in Showing Up positively by rooting us in a bigger picture of how the world works and how our roles fit within it.

Alltelligence grants us the patience to continue doing the work, all the while opening us to options to apply our unique skills and preferences. High Alltelligence draws people to our team-based attitude and behavior. We seek to understand more than to be heard. We ask questions. People feel our interest. We become magnetic for them. Do these sound like high-performance behaviors to you? They have "leader" written all over them.

Alltelligence doesn't say no one will hurt us, negative competition doesn't exist, or that bad things won't happen. It also doesn't suggest good people, when opportunity arises, won't make poor choices. **It does, however, posit that there's an essential asymmetry toward goodness, symbiosis, and mutuality built into our humanness. We can choose to support it—thereby attracting it—or to exist against it.**

> *role and responsibilities serve them. It reminds me of how much my work matters.*
>
> *When I don't do this, I sometimes find myself falling back on a ridiculous assumption that what I do doesn't matter. I'm not sure where it's from, but it creeps in.* [Grounding]
>
> *Then I do the standard prep for meetings, especially taking notes, talking points, and so on based on the agenda and objectives.* [Readiness]
>
> *Then I stitch together the two above to have that meaningful conversation with all involved, knowing we're in it to help each other.* [Alltelligence]

Alltelligence is the crucial third skill we Show Up with. It is native within our role of Societal member.

Highly Alltelligent people recognize we're intra- and inter-woven within society and nature. We live in a manner consistent with our reciprocal, system-level impact on others and the natural world. We know our health, happiness, and success are more mutually derived and communal than singularly won. Alltelligence leads us to share responsibility for each other's well-being, and that of our planet.

> **This model for how the world works shapes our behavior every moment. For example:**
>
> - **Are we fundamentally distinct, wary, and competitive? Or are we compassionate, supported, and symbiotic?**

This explains how Readiness requires keeping in mind how situations organically unfold as we respond and react to (with and for) what others say and do, and they to us, and we to them, in an endless spiral. They reverberate to and fro and back again, like waves of the ocean. Waves come and go, reshaping the shore. And the shore, in turn, determines how and where the water crests and flows. This makes Readiness a state and a flowing process, opening us to deeply engaging in what's happening right now.

It goes beyond what's explicit. Our body and mind are instinctually in tune with the implicit signals of someone's tone, movements, depth of eye contact, speech pacing, intonation, and energy. All these ingredients are mixing in real time.

> **This is what we're Readying our Selves for. It's rich. And it's priceless. As I explain in more detail in Chapter 10 on Readiness, it's the boundary and cusp of how we actually Show Up. When we Just Show Up, we speed past, or are dim to, much of it.**

These questions help us be Ready to Show Up as we choose. They also help us create the experience we're looking for, even if it's just hanging out.

ALLTELLIGENCE

MEET LUCAS
A senior product manager at Amazon Web Services.

I try to understand myself prior to engaging with my stakeholders. Realizing my value to them is key. I need to see how my specific

The two parts of Readiness—planning and preparing—are like a behavioral test drive. They bring us a few steps closer to Showing Up as we choose, be it in our 9:00 a.m. meeting, an impromptu chat with our partner, finding a new job, or retirement. Readiness can include obvious tactical activities, such as homework, or choosing to be curious, well rested, considerate, and be limber before the race, whatever our race may be.

Physical sensations of Readiness include ease, flow, comfort, a quiet mind, ability to deeply listen, subtle confidence, and openness to others' perspectives. It primes creativity and ripens our potential to experience empathy and joy. It's hard to access such feelings when we're underprepared. Comfort and creativity can coexist. The stress of low Readiness and creativity rarely do.

Think of an upcoming situation.

- How consciously have you identified and considered your expectations? How about recognizing their impact? A few pages up in the description of Situations I explained how Situations are active. They're responsive encounters. And they're reciprocal. "Situations are alive." This explains our expectations matter—a lot.
- What emotions are your expectations eliciting? (This is a window into our Grounding.)
- How deeply have you recognized the activity's purpose and import? (Also from our Grounding)
- How in touch are you with the aspirations of others involved? (Alltelligence)
- How can you empathize with and support them? (Alltelligence) A version of this is, to what extent are you interacting "human to human"? This is the expansive view that connects us and creates meaning.
- What presence and impact are you choosing to have on others involved? (Alltelligence)

MEET LUCY

A twenty-something professional who went to a prestigious university and found a high-paying job at a digital agency right out of school. She explained:

Life used to be smooth. What happened? My strong relationships with my mom and best friends... AND EVEN my promising career, are suddenly going south!

I'm tired, strained, and even yelled at my roommate, McKenzie. Not good. I'm always stressed about that Friday morning meeting. The boss asks me unexpected questions and I'm left flatfooted, unprepared, every time.

The insecurity is awful! I can't shake it. Now no one is happy with me, and I may lose my job. I feel like I'm recreating the same mess over and over.

To be more Ready, Lucy can start with the impact of her insecurity. Knowing it infects all her situations makes it key to investigate. (Grounding)

She can check her underlying assumptions. Are they true? How do we know? Who would she be without that thought? Then she can work on the right things. (Readiness)

If she's not ready to go to the boss directly, she can ask colleagues how to anticipate the boss's questions, and maybe even ask their help in answering them. (Alltelligence)

Lucy should also gather information to understand the boss's role. How does she succeed? What are her challenges and needs? And how can Lucy help her? (Alltelligence)

emotions known to improve health and to lengthen our lives.[5] The result? We've primed ourselves to Just Show Up. And we're likely living closer to the separate, limited version of Self than the cohesive, expansive Self flowing as part of our larger world.

READINESS

While Grounding is our connectedness with our Selves, Readiness is our connectedness within the dynamic dances that are our Situations. Readiness deepens how we presence within them, and how they presence within us. It includes our preparatory activities for the content, and to viscerally open our Selves to the shared experience happening around us. It guides our attention as we Show Up with context-specific preparedness, granting familiarity, confidence, and acumen. Readiness is pre-achieving.

Readying starts when we make conscious what we're anticipating. Anticipating primes our behavior, emotions, and thoughts. It makes us more likely to behave in a way we've already envisioned. Now our actions are less prone to whim (Just Showing Up). Readying ourselves also makes us more perceptive since it highlights disparities between what we anticipated and what actually happens. Noticing such moments aids our dual awareness of the present experience and how we're Showing Up within it.

This brings us into the moment more deeply. We're more discerning. Now we've opened possibilities. We can be thoughtful, more true to our Selves, and considerate of others. These are gifts of Readiness. They often reinforce our Grounding (Self-knowledge) and Alltelligence (social connectedness).

readily able to control. Our behavior, to protect our Selves, limit our Selves, dislike our Selves, can become so natural and normalized that we identify with ways of being that were Situationally derived but are not our true nature. They become us. But they misdirect us. Such adaptive behaviors from our past and our culture can lead us into a life of striving for things our core Self doesn't value. We may be seeking hollow successes. And often, we don't know exactly why.

Recognizing the events and Situations that create our relational template enables us to choose how we interact with our Selves, Situations, and Society. The deeper our Grounding, the more agility we have to Show Up as we choose.

Higher Grounding links our lives with purpose. It helps us live more genuinely, in touch with what truly matters to us. Deeper Grounding leads our responses to be pure and wholesome. This helps us manage stress, supporting homeostatic balance. When balanced we're less likely to be triggered or to react in fear. This reduces in-group, out-group bias, the state priming unkind, potentially aggressive behavior against people superficially identified as not belonging to "our group." Grounding also makes us solid by bolstering clear personal boundaries. These borders of where we start and stop scaffold us, creating inner safety. They enable us to feel deeply while also remaining stable.

Even among life's challenges, we can cultivate our own healing. We deepen Grounding by being open to experience our feelings, granting them space, and reflecting on them. As we gain clarity, we're more steady, accountable, and integrous. This anchoring to our true north helps us feel safe opening to and connecting with others (Alltelligence), imbuing our lives with meaning. It draws people to us and opens opportunity. We also deepen our Grounding by practicing our ability to utilize, and switch between, our broad and narrow systems of attention.

Low levels of Grounding may indicate we're not yet in touch with roots of our behavior. It may also suggest we have insufficiently metabolized challenges or trauma, making it hard to Show Up as we'd ideally choose. We may feel life is happening more to us than by, with, or for us. Now we're far from feeling a sense of purpose and fulfillment,

> In meetings he was there, but my sense was things didn't get considered too deeply. Trevor rarely asked questions, even when new topics and important decisions were on the table. [Readiness]
>
> To Show Up better, Trevor could work to recognize where his defensiveness is coming from. He could also be open to noticing that others regularly discuss upcoming projects, client needs, and the team skills required to fulfill them. He could take a small step to interact similarly, recognize it feels safe, and even encouraged.

GROUNDING

Grounding describes how well we know our Selves, specifically our inborn nature. It accesses what's underneath the performance art we've all become, at least somewhat, to succeed in our daily world. How deeply do we probe, accept, and live who we truly are? How much of what we've become is actually for, or because of, someone or something outside us, such as a parent, partner, or significant event that misaligns our daily lives with our essential nature?

Recognizing our truth Grounds us. It connects us with our Self, maturing us, opening us for greater peace, happiness, and healthy, enduring relationships. This gives us strength and focus, impacting how directed, motivated, and disciplined we are. In short, our depth of Self-knowledge, together with acceptance, sculpts how fulfilling a life we lead.

This concept of knowing our Self may sound straightforward. But it's not easy to fully live. Even if we cognitively understand a pattern, compensating behaviors that served us when we were young often hang around. These behaviors can be adaptive and beneficial responses to the environment of our childhood homes, such as independence, for example. Compensating behaviors also arise as effects of illness, accidents, danger, and other charged Situations. These experiences build habits, reactions, and preferences we may not be aware of or

Connectivity functions as a singular root system within and across our roles and skills. It provides the model inner strength, coherence, and integrity. It also makes sense given the inherent and inextricable unity of all systems within nature and the universe.

Showing Up explains how Self-Grounding, Situational Readiness, and Societal Alltelligence form our behavioral infrastructure. They're our cognitive and psychological skeleton. They scaffold our experience. We bring them into the room with us—always. They are viewed by others, simply, as how we Show Up.

MEET TREVOR
A senior manager at a "Big 4"
global consulting firm.

Trevor Showed Up impatient and angry in almost every meeting. Whether the purpose of the meeting was to plan project staffing, forecast staff utilization, or troubleshoot a live client issue, Trevor showed up arrogant and Self-absorbed. [Grounding]

He didn't care much about being a team player and acted as if he were independent. Trevor never requested additional team members or expertise, even for unusually large projects delivered against condensed timelines. This is the type of Situation that burns the team out, and everybody knows it. [Alltelligence]

The three roles in which we naturally show up were originally lived more equally than not.

SELF / SITUATION / SOCIETY

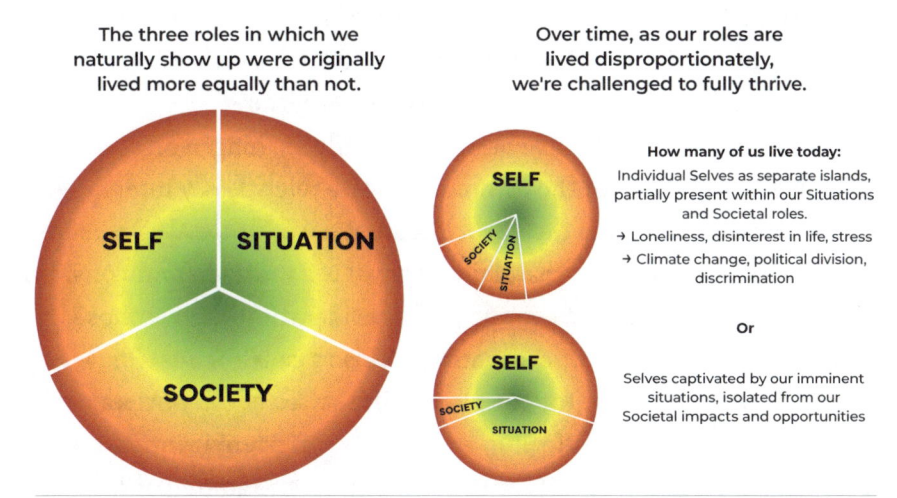

Over time, as our roles are lived disproportionately, we're challenged to fully thrive.

How many of us live today:
Individual Selves as separate islands, partially present within our Situations and Societal roles.
→ Loneliness, disinterest in life, stress
→ Climate change, political division, discrimination

Or

Selves captivated by our imminent situations, isolated from our Societal impacts and opportunities

How are we allocating our attention across our Selves, Situations, and broader Society, i.e., the world outside of our immediate experience? How fully are we living the three roles in which we are designed to thrive? Over time, the more equally we live across our three native roles, the happier and healthier we'll be.

Are we actually separate? It's a profound question. Perhaps the "Situation" of each moment encompasses all as a cohesive whole. This would be defining us as the big circle around the model. We're Showing Up as one, with Self, Situation, and Society within us. Now imagine our circles are water droplets composing Earth's ocean. We're a single, everything-inside instance of the whole. Might this idea help us be kinder, happier, and healthier?

OUR NATIVE SKILLS

Now let's dive into high-level definitions of the skills native to each role.

1. **Self-Grounding**—Knowing who we are and why. Connectivity within our **Selves**.
2. **Situational Readiness**—Being **Situationally** prepared. Connectivity within the moments through which we come alive.
3. **Societal Alltelligence**—Being connected reciprocally and symbiotically, with each other, **Society**, and the natural world.

life's easy flow is aided by living in our three roles somewhat equally. It would mean we're considering group and system-level impacts as deeply as Self-interests across more of our Situations.

Thinking back to our tribal beginnings, daily life hinged on survival. Our needs and those of the community were relentlessly integrated. Early humans likely lived their Self, Situational, and Societal roles more equally than we do. Now that daily survival is a more-distant consideration for many of us, elevating Self considerations above those of Society seems natural. Unfortunately, it's also a cause of Just Showing Up, both for people and for our planet. The states of our Societal and personal systems are suffering, to which our sick environment and scant stillness can attest. (Is anyone feeling serene among us?)

> **Perhaps allocating our focus more evenly across Societal and personal needs could help us. We'd feel a greater sense of belonging, meaning, and fulfillment. Perhaps it could be more of our default, leading us to Show Up better.**
>
> **As you finish this book, considering the interwoven nature of roles in which we natively Show Up, this just may be the case. Perhaps it's a path toward making dark bodies, light bodies, nature's body, and our Societal body healthier.**

> *They walk in, in a rush, wanting their bacon, egg, and cheese. Once they know there's a wait, half the time they get pissed and walk out. Everyone is in a rush. They're grouchy with my staff right in front of their young kids. It's hard to watch it. And on a Sunday morning?*
>
> *During the week people are okay. But when we're busy on the weekend, the energy is more negative. They're really not nice.*
>
> When I shared this with a few friends, their heads nodded. Comments came back such as, "Yup, I can see how that happens. We Just Show Up."

PRIORITIZING THE ROLES IN WHICH WE SHOW UP

In any situation, how should we allocate our priorities between Self, Situation and Society? Self-focus is our original default. It's every child's world. In youth our brains comprehend none other. Everything is personal. Even as adults, Self-focus often remains our guiding principle. It's our natural default in moments of stress, pain, fear, hunger, tiredness, and many other categories of human needs, unmet.

Our modern Self feeds our piggy bank. It supplies our comfort. It's our promotion that matters. Yes, the most important projects belong to *our* team, not to that other group. And my share of the company budget and bonus pool must be tops or pretty darn close. Unfortunately, in too big a dose, this thinking isolates us. It makes us sad and sick. It also doesn't respect how we're designed to Show Up.

A PATH TOWARD PEACE

The model shows an even distribution of our roles. Personal needs (Self), social impacts (Society), and Situational aspects are equally weighted. The shape is reminiscent of a peace symbol. This implies

drawings, tapestries, music, and art of our ancestral humanity continue to Show Up. They may be fading embers in history books and occasional exhibits, or searing sparks igniting our thoughts, words, and deeds right now.

> **Whether beneficial or tragic, our personal stories, social posts and algorithms Show Up in Society for generations, well past our individual lives. It's how through Society we're living our ancestors' Show-Up choices, and those after us will live ours.**
>
> **This makes Society both our collective, social role and an emergent instance of everyone's Show-Up choices across time. Society is wonderful and wild, delightful and despicable, all at once. It is adaptive, Self-organizing and, if we add a bit more choice to how we're Showing Up, Self-healing.**

The more often we choose how we Show Up, the more chance we have to nudge society and each of us toward kindness, peace, and togetherness. We live our Societal role well when we view our Selves as extending into and through others and the world. This is the flowing process through which we cocreate each other. It explains our collective intimacy. And it urgently implies (and applies) a custodianship, a shared responsibility with, to, and for each other. This is the definition of Alltelligence, described in Chapter 11. It is the skill through which our Societal role comes to life.

> One morning last week, I was chatting with David, a manager of a general store and deli at one of the beach towns on Long Island. "How are things?" I asked.

of the moment while also sensing how we're Showing Up in the Situation. By checking in—"How am I choosing to Show Up?"—we're stepping back from the immediacy of the moment. We're choosing our degree of separateness and togetherness, our distinctness from and participation within the Situation. Now we're starting from somewhere new. The Situation Shows Up differently with, to and for us now. We start to perceive each moment as novel. This is the richness of our Situation-member role. Understanding it has the power to immediately change how we engage.

Readiness, the skill native to our role as members of Situations is described in Chapter 10, Situational Readiness.

Society

In the model of how we Show Up, Society encompasses everything beyond the individualized Self. This includes groups of people, ideas, culture, religion and spirituality, nature, and humanity. It is the largest unit of consideration in which we Show Up. And it is our most expansive role. It contextualizes our experiences, placing them within the broader flows of time, impacts, and systems. It's the label we give to the "bigger picture." It's the greater good of any Situation. It's the stepping back to consider implications beyond our Selves (or our immediate family, team, department, company, or social group). Our Societal role is predominantly served by our right hemisphere's attentional system.

Our Societal role is outwardly oriented. It turns our mirror away from us, contrasting the inwardly focused Self common in modern culture. Living in our Societal role can Show Up as considering the family unit over the interests of children or parents separately, corporate priorities over the interests of a department or team, and country or globe over its constituent parts.

Society is also our collective nervous system. It's the ocean of our droplet-Selves, resulting from every decision, purchase, vote, product review, triggered reaction, and tweet. As with each of us individually, today's Society embodies the past far more than the present. The cave

> **Thus, Situations are active encounters. They're not passive. And they're not simple, re-presentations of what happened before. They're reverberating, responsive processes. They present to, with, and for us. And they Show Up with, to, and for us. Quite plainly, what any given Situation is depends on who is attending to it, and how. Every past experience, expectation, value, bias, prejudice, hope, fear, and belief about how the world works Shows Up in our Situations, as does our ability to leave such baggage behind. These factors are our wardrobe, and our lenses for seeing the world. We travel with them. And the world responds to them. Over time the reverberative dance that is our Situations creates who we, and everyone, and everything is. And it creates how we, others and Society Show Up.**

This is how two people in the same conversation can have very different experiences, memories, and conclusions. Meaning does not originate with the interpreter. It's how the very same outcome may be a success for one and a failure for another. A common joke about a shoe business seeking a new market is a fun example. ShoeCo sends two scouts to a potential new territory. They both see people not wearing shoes. One explains, "There's no potential. No one wears shoes." The other excitedly proclaims, "Awesome opportunity! No one has shoes!" This is hugely consequential. It determines what happens next. It also challenges ideas of subjective and objective reality since what we attend to comes into being. What we don't attend to diminishes and may even disappear. "Was Joe there with us? I don't recall." Once again, this demonstrates the intersubjectivity of our Situational experience, what we call our "reality."

Finally, we experience Situations with our full body. Stimuli come from outside and inside. Ideally, we are able to experience the aliveness

Crucial to achieving this is understanding the nature of attention. Situations are defined by, and created by, the attention we pay, consciously and not. This includes what we attend to, and how. Our attentional "payments" (investments) create what we find, and vice versa. For example, is that beautiful meadow across the street a place we stroll each evening and cherish nature? Or is it an empty lot baiting us to build a house and make money? How we attend creates what happens next, and after that, and after that.

Is that person a potential friend, or an irrelevant thing we walk past? This shows there's a reciprocity in how we and our Situations Show Up. They respond to us and we to them. There's an exchange, and a mutuality. This means situations are alive. And, importantly, they have a natural direction. They're flowing systems of behaviors. And, as Duke University professor Adrian Bejan explains in his book with Peter Zane, *Design in Nature*,[4] the direction is to reduce friction, that is, to make things easier and faster. It's nature's and humans' inherent urge. And it designs how we and our situations Show Up.

Situations are created as we interact with others and all influences outside of our Selves.

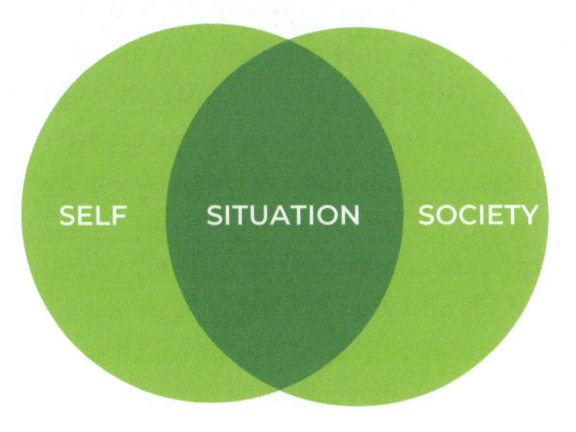

SELF SITUATION SOCIETY

> with what's outside of us. Our Selves and Society come together in these sacred moments. "Situation" is the word we use to describe these experiences. It recontextualizes our experiences as the shared spaces, times, and environments in which our Self and Societal roles come together. How we Show Up to our Situations defines and creates our Selves and our Society.

When we Just Show Up, our experiences can become transactional. We're either passive or have a subtle stance of needing to exert power over something or someone. The Situation is perceived as a vehicle for our gain, and instrument to be acted on. We are there to manipulate it toward a predetermined outcome. Situations become moments of Self-focused striving more than crucibles of trust, care, shared achieving and enjoying. They include the people, their Show-Up choices, content, ideas, goals, environment of the moment, and our experience of them.

Situations can be defined tightly or generously. Narrow views—which happen naturally when we Just Show Up—may hide others' perspectives from us. The mere glaze of presence we commonly see on others' faces may be cutting off opportunities. We miss points of common ground, or clarity into downstream impacts of our and others' behavior. Such limited experiences are often fertile ground for expectation-driven realities. They may breed bias or discrimination, as they predispose us or others toward projecting, or a closed attitude.

This is unfortunate since others sense it and respond. It's how our experience, and the Situation's meaning, is intersubjective. We each create our and the others' "reality." Narrow or strict attention divides us, as in Peter's example above. Peter's job requires aligning interests. This means helping his team more generously define the Situation and how their roles fit among others', the company's mission and the role in Society. This Societally Alltelligent view puts us in a more expansive, shared, dynamic and meaningful sphere, supporting the greater good.

and uniformity. Such economic, cost-effective systems of today call for measurement, control, and surveillance. They maximize utility, classify, catalogue, compile, and live in code. None of it honors our instinctual humanness.

Yet, the routines of today's Society, our white-collar factory, have become our own. We've welcomed them into our relationships with our children, into our beds, and into the health of our bodies. And they have become our Selves. They—and we—work to pull us from our natively grounded Selves, and from each other. This leaves us Showing Up more superficially to our Situations. It distorts and dissuades us from the attuned, satisfied Self we were designed to be. Our ancestral, more innately integrated Self is the one we experience when we live more evenly across our roles, with at least moderate degrees of Grounding, Readiness, and Alltelligence. This Truly-Showing-Up Self suffers far less from today's epidemics of anxiety, depression, diabetes, disengagement, and other ailments of modernity.

Grounding, the skill native to our role as Selves is described in Chapter 9, Grounding in Our Selves.

Situation

> **Situations are the context through which we, and everything, Show Up. Nothing exists in isolation, making our Situation-member role the one in which everything exists and takes place. It's our experiential vessel, the one through which our Self and Societal roles interact. This makes Situations dynamic dances. They're the creative instruments and intervals through which we and all things come alive. They're the vehicles of our lived experiences, animating the world around us, even if we're reading a book.**
>
> **It's the place in which we presence. Mindfully, it's the space, the pause, and the time, when we merge**

infusing others with goodwill, generosity, and generativity. We live deeply with and for all three roles in which we innately exist—far from separate or slave to them.

As Einstein states, "A human being is a part of the whole." Sensing our "thoughts and feelings as something separate from the rest [is] a kind of optical delusion." This means to understand our Selves as the living systems we are, we need to expand our definition of Self to include the dynamic systems around us. This flow of our Selves relating within shifting environments has no boundary. Nora Bateson, author, filmmaker, and educator, calls information about these unbounded interrelationships "warm data." It's a helpful term encouraging us to breathe life and relationality back into the oversimplified, disconnected categories we find our Selves living in (e.g., teacher, analyst, parent). Mirror neurons in our brain create direct expressions inside us of those we're with. We feel what they feel, even from a photo.

This expansive reality of our senses going well beyond the permeable membranes of our skin and skull is also commonly experienced, Ready, in nature. Nature fills us with awe. It soothes us. This interconnectedness with our world "outside" is a key aspect of our Grounded Self. It's more relational than individual. This more mature Self lives in empathic contact with the world. When living this version of Self, we function less as "single, explicit drive, and more as area of active receptivity, responding to the world as a complex whole."[3] We're not necessarily manipulating or directing it, but belonging to, with, and for it.

This is the Self Indigenous peoples, Eastern contemplatives, and many religions have known for thousands of years. It's a more expansive, happy, healthy, and fulfilled Self than the fragmented, stressed, Just-Showing-Up Selves modern Society has taught us to be. It diminishes our ego. The further we wander from this understanding of Self, the more agitated, impatient, unkind and ill we—our Society and planet—become.

Briefly described in Chapter 1, today our schedules, habits, thoughts, and emotions must squeeze into a rule-based, mechanistic, data-driven world. They favor left-brained efficiency, backed by standardization

The Self Practicing Showing Up
More Grounded, Ready, and Connected
Our daily lives emphasize "We" over separate "Me" and "You," supporting connectedness, readiness, and Alltelligence.

The Self Before Practicing Showing Up
Less Grounded, Ready, and Connected
Our daily lives emphasize separate "Me" and "You" over "We," hindering connectedness, readiness, and Alltelligence.

comfortably resting in the middle more than at either extreme. This is being intraconnected[2] within our Selves while also being knitted within larger systems. It's the point from which we collaborate, create, and connect. When Grounded within our Selves, we're powerfully and compassionately solo, not alone. We naturally experience a depth of belonging across the roles in which we Show Up. With a robust root system Ground, Readying us, we function as a sturdy, integrated whole,

Grounded. We need things to be distinct and evident. The implicit is lost. Experiences feel thin. Situations, items and, dare I say, people, around us are to be acted on, more than with and for. Circumstances are mere opportunities to exert our already existing will, need or desire for something. Like an animal foraging for food, experiences are prospects to fulfill "I need this," or "I'm going to get that." This is the Self of corporate politics that Peter described (and of seeking hollow fame, money, or impressive possessions). It often Just Shows Up.

This ego-driven Self is the one we're born into. We're near this extreme role of Self when we experience situations attending to what's best for us to an extent that closes us to much beyond that. We're not choosing to open our Selves to the nuanced happenings alive around us. Instead, we attend to a shallow, dilute, surface layer of the situation created by our Self-referring left hemisphere. In doing so, we're quick to categorize and reduce what's there to what we saw before. So, little new applies. Little is learned. Life can become dull. We may question, "What attention do my repetitive daily affairs actually need?" We become disinterested and simply don't perceive most of what the person in front of us is saying. And sadly, we're also set up to be inert to the opportunities and wonder of the world around us.

As psychiatrist Iain McGilchrist explains, "When the context changes from the one you're thinking [or expecting], then something new applies."[1] But our modern Self, inclined to be sleep-deprived, distracted, anxious and busy, is prone to miss "when the context changes." In doing so we also miss the new that applies. These novel experiences, like diamonds embedded within our days, remain invisible, left behind on the floor. This furthers the dissatisfaction and remoteness many of us feel. (More of this is discussed in Chapter 7, Barely There.) It's fine, and perhaps necessary at times, for us to Show Up in this thin version of our Self. Success lies in intentfully choosing when, and at what dose, to be in each variety of Self.

The more deeply Grounded Self is expansive. Utilizing our right-brained attentional system, we are interwoven within others, society, and nature. We seesaw naturally within "Me" and "We," often

> actively contributing to and flowing within our relational world. It senses the collective intimacy in which we exist.
>
> Our culture defines our "Self" as much as we do. Society's norms craft our choices of how to behave and what identities we claim. Are we a data analyst, physician, hot head, top performer or loser? Explained by Stanford professor Brian Lowery, our identity is far more defined by Society, from the outside in, than from the inside out. Similarly, how we Show Up is defined by the collective culture and environment. We are expressed and created "by those with whom we interact." They educate us about consequences for how we look, behave, think and live. This dramatically expands who we—our Self—can be. And it explains our vital role in creating and permitting who others are. How we choose to experience others is also choosing who our Self is. This choice can be medicinal, or injurious. Nourishing or deadly.

This idea is paralleled in the foundations of communication. In Lance Strade's 2022 book *Concerning Communication,* he writes, "It is the Message that causes or creates the Sender," since one couldn't exist without the other.

The other extreme of this relational Self is the separate, modern Self. It is the smallest unit of consideration in which we Show Up. It is our most limited role, predominantly driven by our left hemisphere's attentional system. At the extreme it is reduced to the "I," "Me," "Mine" moments we all experience. In this state we feel the most isolated. We are severed from context. We are often not calm, since separateness amps the dial on, readiness, our alert systems. And we are not deeply

these roles in ourselves, others and Society. Broadening our lens, our experience is also designed by how well others Show Up across their roles. The same goes for the systems in which we live.

> **Before diving into our three native skills, I'd like to emphasize the systems view inherent within the model. Showing Up recognizes our lives extend past the typically defined boundary of our body and skin. We extend through our social, emotional, and functional environment as its creators and product. This makes our behavior, deliberate or not, a function and feature of the very environment we create. Familiarizing ourselves with the roles through which we—and all things—Show Up helps us be responsible for the experience of others, our environment, and our collective well-being.**

I'll summarize each role and skill here and go into more detail in part III. Just before we dive in, I've included the model in the form of an equation, on the chance it's helpful.

$$\text{SHOWING UP} = \text{SELF GROUNDING} + \text{SITUATIONAL READINESS} + \text{SOCIETAL ALLTELLIGENCE}$$

THE THREE NATIVE ROLES IN WHICH WE SHOW UP

Self

> **We Show Up between two extremes of Self. One is mainly separate, closed and self-serving. Its world is to be utilized for gain. The other is interwoven,**

The natural world created humans in three roles. These are the native roles in which we Show Up.

1. We are Selves within Situations and Society.
2. Each role has a corresponding skill: Grounding in our Selves, Readiness for our Situations, and Alltelligence (connectedness) within Society.
3. Our skill level varies from low to high every moment and across time. Level 1, the lowest quality of Showing Up, is called Barely There. Level 2, the midlevel, is called Just Showing Up. And Level 3, the highest, is called Truly Showing Up.

THE MODEL OF HOW WE SHOW UP

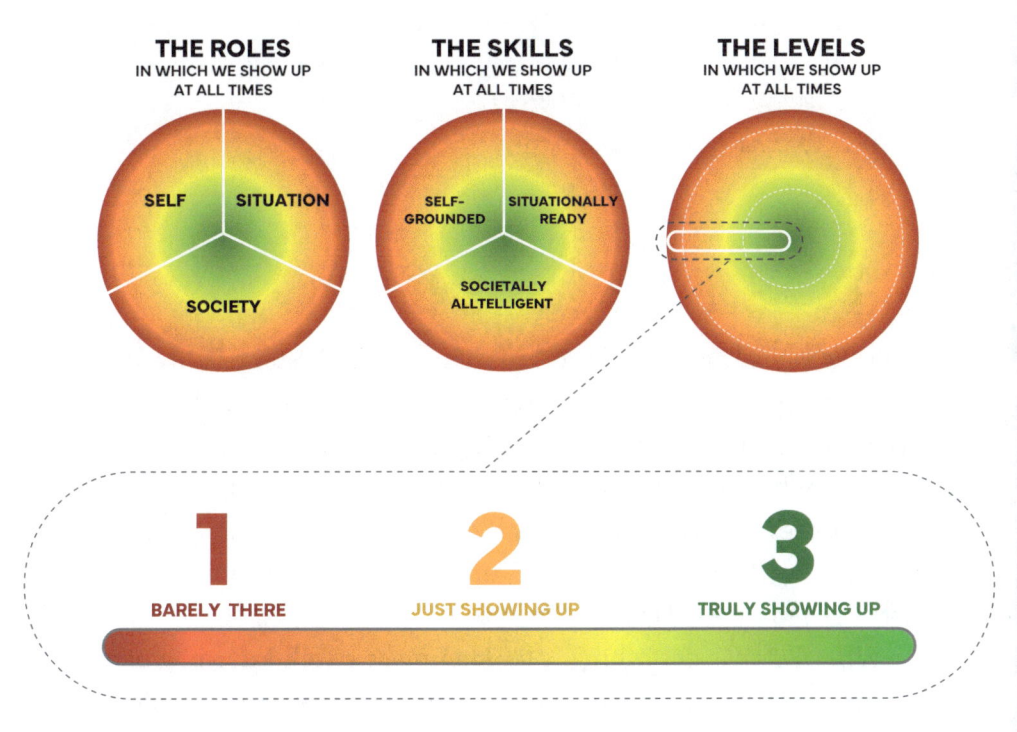

THE ROLES
IN WHICH WE SHOW UP AT ALL TIMES

SELF | SITUATION
SOCIETY

THE SKILLS
IN WHICH WE SHOW UP AT ALL TIMES

SELF-GROUNDED | SITUATIONALLY READY
SOCIETALLY ALLTELLIGENT

THE LEVELS
IN WHICH WE SHOW UP AT ALL TIMES

1 BARELY THERE
2 JUST SHOWING UP
3 TRULY SHOWING UP

Our behavior and achievement—fulfillment, health, and happiness—are the synthesis of how well we Show Up with, to, and for

CHAPTER 3
THE MODEL OF HOW WE SHOW UP

This chapter leads you through the following ideas:
- The natural model of how we Show Up
- Three roles: Selves within Situations and Society
- Native skills: Self-Grounding, Situational Readiness, Societal Alltelligence
- A continuum of performance
- Our singular root system

THE MODEL OF HOW WE SHOW UP

"There's a small fight brewing on one of my teams," Peter tells me. "It's classic corporate politics. People are putting personal gains ahead of what's best for the company. Running global analytics, I care about what benefits the company and all clients, not one person, team, or specific client. I must have three meetings a day to cut through stuff like this. It's like climate change. Everyone sees the problems but still acts like separate kids in the sandbox."

What Peter is describing is happening at a well-known, global accounting firm. But it's common all over. "How do we get people to step back and see the bigger picture?"

Let's review the full model. Then we'll return to Peter and how he used Showing Up to manage his team.

Showing Up is the core practice of our lives.

How deliberate we make it is the choice.

OUR UNIVERSAL SHOW-UP NETWORK

Beyond Society, we exist as nodes in a universal Show-Up network. Humanity absorbs and rebirths our decisions. They root in others' minds and play out at someone else's kitchen table. They're recreated, endlessly. We systematize our Show-Up choices into the sports we watch and play, the music we listen to, the entrepreneurial ventures we fund, the products and services we make and buy, and the degree of compassion or discrimination we live within. How we Show Up becomes our children's sense of Self, how we heal transgenerational trauma, and so much more. It's how this book goes beyond choosing who we are to choosing what Society we want.

This is what we're telling the world when we Show Up.

What is your choice?

other effectiveness strategies are oriented primarily around one role, the Self. They're far less direct in recognizing the collective nature and custodianship inherent in our performance...and our pain. Our traumas and our triumphs.

Phrases such as self-awareness, self-regulation, self-compassion, self-acceptance, and self-care encourage us to relate to our Selves as individuals, distinct from others. While supporting us as solo practitioners is a fine starting place, it's far from where we, as humans, stop.

Models of performance and corporate culture that don't explicitly recognize and elevate the "IntraConnectedness" through which we thrive, as Dan Siegel explains it, are limited in their ability to click into place the "how to succeed" puzzle we're spending our lives completing.[15]

> **Effective performance models must recognize that how we Show Up is an emergent property of all roles in which we exist. This means embracing our lives as the synthesis of Self-Grounding, Situational Readiness, and Societal Alltelligence is essential.**
>
> **Absorbing this reality prompts us to behave with intent and compassion. And it's a crucial insight if we, as individuals and a collective, are to perform at our highest level. Moderate or higher levels of all three skills are required components for people, policies, systems, and organizations to effectively, responsibly—and, I believe, morally—Show Up.**
>
> **Attention, itself, is a moral act. How we choose to attend, that is, to Show Up, can be nothing less.**

> **These realities plant seeds in us, and we in them. We incubate the wealth. Our behavior simply exposes how these influences come together within us, and are rebirthed back into our bedrooms, Spotify lists, and absentee ballots. All are created by, and infuse, how we Show Up.**

TEACHING SHOWING UP TO KIDS

A client and busy mother who works in the sustainability group at a well-known university in Manhattan said to me:

We're not taught to think like this. We're taught math, science, literature. But who is teaching us the impact of how we Show Up, that we influence each other every moment, and that we have a responsibility to Show Up with our best?

What we tell our kids, "be kind," is too much about them. It reinforces that each child is separate. It misses our unity. How can we start teaching kids about Showing Up?

Imagine kids growing up with this knowledge: "Be grounded. Be ready. And be responsible for—in fact, OWN, your impact on others and society." THIS is what we need to teach!

This book is about this truth. Despite this, separateness and individualism remain the epicenter of our economy, steering common leadership, management and self-improvement approaches. Even emotional intelligence, mindfulness, good habits, willpower, and many

and social circles start to feel more like a unified team when we truly Show Up. We create a "with-ness," a "because of-ness," a "for-ness," and a togetherness. This is Alltelligence. It is native to our societal role. Alltelligence is also the crucial—often missing—skill explaining how our innate connectivity works. Low levels of Alltelligence Show Up as volatile relationships, loneliness, disengagement, quiet quitting, employee retention issues, customer churn, and poor corporate performance. High Alltelligence is a leadership skill, a parenting skill, a community building skill, and an essentially human skill.

SYSTEMS AND LEADERSHIP

As described above, **Showing Up isn't limited to one person interacting with intentful choice. It naturally functions at the system level—in strategy, in corporate leadership approaches, in social justice norms, in how trusting a populace we are, and in the ways our families function. How we Show Up establishes how interlocked our behaviors, feelings, health, and performance are. It vitalizes our responsibility for, to, and with each other.**

> The systems level of Showing Up is particularly expansive. It explicitly substantiates our custodianship and accountability for cocreating a flourishing world. We're responsible because our choices become how the systems, people, and structures around us Show Up.

- **What security and care are fostered at our tables?**
- **What curiosity and embodied learning are instilled in our schools?**
- **What loyalty defines our work cultures?**

HOW SHOWING UP IMPROVES PERFORMANCE

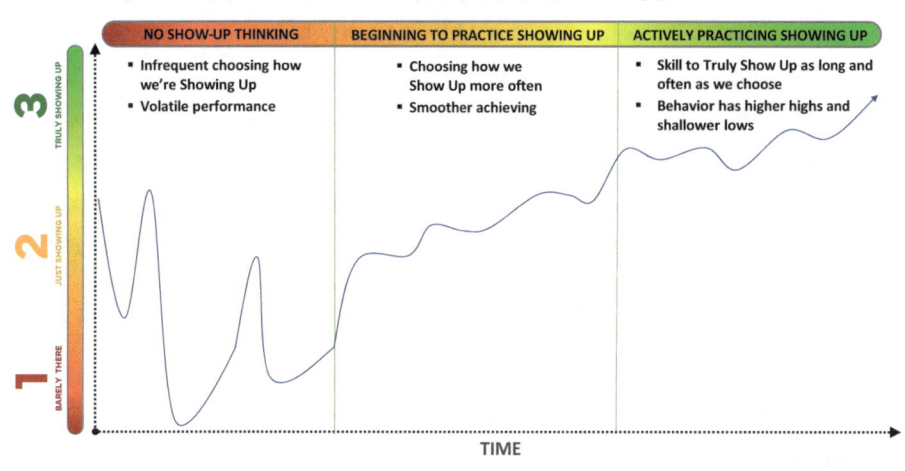

NO SHOW-UP THINKING	BEGINNING TO PRACTICE SHOWING UP	ACTIVELY PRACTICING SHOWING UP
• Infrequent choosing how we're Showing Up • Volatile performance	• Choosing how we Show Up more often • Smoother achieving	• Skill to Truly Show Up as long and often as we choose • Behavior has higher highs and shallower lows

3 TRULY SHOWING UP
2 JUST SHOWING UP
1 BARELY THERE

TIME

Practicing is exercising choice. Over time we'll dip less often into subpar behavior, what I label "Barely There" on the bottom of the chart. It's the lowest level of Showing Up, and is more prone to happen when we're not checking in, or bringing a contextual lens to our behavior. This is depicted on the left side of the chart, labeled "No Show-Up Thinking." Here we see volatile interactions, and the most Barely There experiences.

Practicing Showing Up sounds a lot like the common process of "returning to the breath" in mindfulness meditation. As with that experience, each bit of practice strengthens our skill, creating a habit. It untethers us from common, negative habitual patterns impacting today's performance, personality, limits, and legacy.

Another parallel to practicing Showing Up is the design phase of a product or service, bridge, building, or other project. It creates and even dictates everything that follows. Trained as a strategist at one of the "Big 4" global management consulting firms, this up-front planning phase of a project looms large for me. After thirty years of practicing my craft, I can tell you, Phase 1, what we call strategy or design, is worthy of investment.

When practicing Showing Up, the design phase illuminates our intent. "Who and how do we want to be?" We're alert. More definitive, ready, resolved. It's contagious. People are drawn to us. Our professional

ATTUNING, NOT AWARENESS

The practice of Showing Up attunes us to our behavior. Why use the word *attuning* and not *awareness* or *presence*, when discussing Showing Up? Because attuning takes the next step, past awareness and presence, to include responding. Showing Up leads us to utilize both systems of attention, the narrow, grab-and-get mode, and the wholistic, sensing mode. It brings us into a dual awareness "in and with" the experience. We're now sensing our and others' behavior while also responding to the situation.

Attuning also means making things harmonious. Once noticed, we can accept our behavior as it is, or we can adjust. Either way, we've checked in. We've felt what our roles and actions mean. Now we're responding to a different experience. Unlike awareness and presence, we're not left at the door. Attuning unlocks it, bids us entry, and grants us choice.

WHAT HAPPENS AS WE PRACTICE SHOWING UP

We're seeking to Show Up as we choose as often and for as long as we want. As we understand the model, its evolutionary roots and implications, we start to attune to our behavior more frequently. This is shown in the middle of the chart below, labeled "Beginning to Practice Showing Up." With more frequent attuning, we catch subpar performance faster, such as being caught up in self-limiting, me-centric thinking, assuming or judging. Over time we experience higher highs and shallower lows, as seen on the right side of the chart, labeled "Actively Practicing Showing Up."

reflexes and habits. When Just Showing Up, our automated beliefs, emotions, triggers and impulses automatically arise. Our minds are narrowly categorizing our experience as something we "know" and have experienced before. This slings the old stories, assumptions, and pain of the past into right now.

In contrast, the moment we ask, "How am I choosing to Show Up?" we're stepping above the immediate Situation. Our attention shifts toward openness. We can attend more to the implicit. We perceive emotional content more deeply. We pick up on nuance. There's more that's distinct because we've engaged a mode of attending to the world attuned to newness and difference. This attentional system, our Societally Alltelligent system, also imbues our experiences with kinship, the coveted "with-ness" many of us experience as an absence today. Now we're more likely to respond with curiosity, with questions, with care. Our mind sees more broadly and makes connections, accesses creativity, and senses options. Life feels more symbiotic.

My research explains that when we don't quite Show Up as we'd choose, we commonly justify it. After all, "It was fine, not a big deal." Right? "We'll prepare better next time." But we often don't. Then we feel disappointed with ourselves. "How could we let this happen, again?" To avoid the pain we protect our Selves. We subtly disconnect from the bad feelings. In doing so, we're also disconnecting from part of our Selves, leaving us less Grounded, and less able to feel emotionally felt by others. As described more in Chapter 9 on Grounding, over time, relationships don't seem as deep, meaningful or supportive. A subtle aloneness may creep in, diverting our motivation, focus and joy. This reinforces our default of Just Showing Up. Breaking the pattern[14] starts the moment we grasp the truth about Showing Up. Our essence is intimately collective. Practicing Showing Up moves us closer to who and how we want to be. This is growth—and a big step toward fulfillment, health, and happiness—for our selves, others, our businesses, nations, and all we create.

> *I appreciate how Showing Up gets me to focus where it matters and get it right.*

WHAT PEOPLE TELL ME

Throughout decades of surveys and interviews, people tell me, "Everyone Just Shows Up," "I rarely feel truly ready," "I need more time to plan," and, "I know I can be so much more." We feel it. It tugs on us. Beyond the tactical, I'm told, "I never get to step back. I yearn to think more strategically and creatively about my life." And, "I'm lonely. I need to be part of something bigger." This hurdle to reflecting, to expanding our lens, isolates us. It creates a thirst, a yearning to feel more grounded, and to sense a "with-ness" and a "within-ness" beyond our selves.

PROMPTING WHOLISTIC ATTENTION

Practicing Showing Up addresses this. It prompts us to intentionally choose the breadth of our lens. Is it Self-focused, oriented toward control? Is it Situationally and Societally focused, viewing what's going on as part of a responsive, ever-shifting system of influences?

While we're applying a "model," utilizing left-brained attention, we're also embracing context. We're living our Situational and Societal roles more prominently, welcoming belongingness into our daily lives. We start perceiving life more wholistically, with greater Alltelligence, that is, more through a right-brained attentional system. Instead of experiencing our teenagers' irresponsible spending, or boss's demands, as unchanging and therefore threatening, the experience Shows Up within a stream of happenings. It is adaptive. It is flexible. This lowers our stress. It opens us to nuance, fellowship, and with it, a new way of relating to our challenges. It brings a layer of freedom and acceptance.

We're less bound by expectation and judgment which re-present the past world back to us. It's how Just Showing Up triggers our default

Better to resolve our Show-Up choice before the verdict than to regret. It parallels what I heard during my days on Wall Street: "the win is in the buy." This means the initial decision of whether and when to own a security determines the outcome. Yes, when we sell is important. But it's irrelevant if we didn't choose how and when to buy, that is, how to Show Up.

PRIORITIZING A SITUATION TO TRULY SHOW UP

One dedicated father and successful entrepreneur explained it this way:

I chose time with my kids as my target situation. It happens first thing in the morning before school and right when I pick them up. What does a child need? A grounded, ready, connected parent. This is where the focus should be. It's really helpful.

Does your spouse need all three? No. There's no need to be prepared. It's more unprepared, letting go, and just being.

Knowing the three parts of Showing Up is a cheat sheet for achieving. We can never Truly Show Up 100 percent of the time. Children and some work meetings get Level 3 effort. Friends, free time, and all else get whatever Shows Up.

When I look at all my hours in the week, parenting time is probably 30 percent. This is plenty. I can't work at it anymore. And I know this. I'm good at doing a few things very well. I'm not good at doing lots of things well.

DUAL AWARENESS

Sound easy enough? These steps are practicing being dually aware of the situation and of how we and others are Showing Up within it. I'm not saying let's achieve nirvana. We can't and don't need to choose or to Truly Show Up all the time. We simply need to bring a bit more choice to our behavior when we decide it matters most.

Living more aligned with how nature designed us to Show Up is something I believe we're all responsible for. This is why explaining Showing Up is the goal of this book, my TEDx talks, TV roles, radio interviews, keynotes, corporate projects, and of all my work.

Whether we choose to or not, we're living our behavior choices—our investments—right now. This moment is the result of yesterday's, last year's, and our younger Selves' Show-Up choices. It's also the result of our parents', teachers', coaches', colleagues', employers', the media's, and politicians' Show-Up choices. What have we gifted ourselves? What have our choices gifted others?

> **This is why Showing Up is not only a Self-project. It exists in the collective.**
>
> **It's how authentically our families relate. It's how effectively our schools and workplaces function, how nations come together toward peace, and how our environment heals. It's living more aligned with the evolutionary roles that shaped us and through which we're designed to flourish.**
>
> **And it demands forethought. This moment's Show-Up choices—in a second—become conclusions. When we've Just Shown Up, the moment rarely returns as a redo. It returns as a "what now?"**

> **through the Situations in which we Show Up. How well we function depends on how aligned we live in this reality.**

From a low of one to a high of ten: **Score:**

How often do we choose how we're Showing Up?   _____

How often do we recognize that we're not
simply individuals, but belong and function
within something beyond our Selves?   _____

How Grounded are we in our Selves?   _____

How Ready are we for upcoming Situations?   _____

How Connected do we feel with
others, nature, and Society?   _____

If we rate ourselves with midlevel scores (4–6), we may be Just Showing Up more often than we realize. With higher scores (7–10), we're more often able to Show Up as we choose. Rating lower on these questions (0–3), we may be Showing Up Barely There.

Choosing how we Show Up grants the satisfaction people told me they're searching for.[13] How do we do it? In three simple steps.

1. Recognizing we're always Showing Up and how it works
2. Choosing: *How am I choosing to Show Up?* (At what level? Depth of skill? And allocation of roles?)
3. Shifting toward our chosen behavior

Then we repeat as needed to Show Up more as we choose.

up to the mostly safe, comfortable, well-fed, well-educated, pampered, and often indulgent reality many of us are living. So the swarm of default behavior continues to pilot us. We're like marionettes tethered to evolution's slow, staccatoed progress.

> **However natural it may be, Just Showing Up, with limited choice and intent, is failing to take possession of our own minds. It means we're forgoing agency over our lives, our results, our legacy.**

The loss? Nothing less than a meaningful, fulfilling life.

How Showing Up Works

> **It starts with recognizing that we're designed to live more integrated, wholistic lives. Within this context, we choose our behavior. We're responsible, even when our choices are unconscious. This is a big idea, bigger than I realized when I started researching Showing Up two decades ago. Even globally recognized people who have achieved the height of their field have told me this point shook their world. It was a huge "aha!" for far more people than I had anticipated.**

> **After recognizing that our behavior is our choice and responsibility, we consider the three roles we Show Up in every moment. Humans are not solitary, self-contained entities existing only in our personal space and time. We're naturally interconnected beings (Selves) existing within a living system (Society). We experience our Self and Societal roles**

least in part, from the unnatural degree of left-brained, self-focused, dominance in today's world. This is why the naturally relational Self defined through how we Show Up offers a healthier view.

Its evolutionary roots clarify we're linked more as leaves on a tree, nodes in our universal Show-Up network, and water droplets in the ocean, than the resource-depleted islands too many of us feel like today. Clearly, a healthier flow across our two ways of experiencing the world is called for. This is what Showing Up offers, a practical, yet flexible framework, within an expansive, relational view of the world. It helps us flow across both modes of attention, as nature designed us to do.

Picking up on our need to reconnect with our relational Selves, business, leadership and teaching processes emphasize emotional intelligence today. Wise practitioners, such as Marc Brackett, founder of Yale's Center for Emotional Intelligence, are giving the world Permission to Feel, the title of his last book. And thousands of K-12 schools around the world have implemented RULER, the evidence-based approach to social and emotional learning that he founded. In business, incentive systems are starting to show care through flexible schedules, less formality, mindfulness and mental health programs. Our culture is trying, in bits and pieces, to help us be more whole. For now, however, our default is often to Just Show Up.

Just Showing Up remains a consequence of our modern world. It's also an enabler and perpetuator. It contributes to partial engagement, superficial care, and fragile connections. It causes unhappiness, ill-health and hinders performance. At work, labels of unengagement and active disengagement are seen in up to 70 percent of us much of the time, costing corporate America over $4 billion each year.[11] And wandering minds, whether at work or elsewhere, are seen in 47 percent of Americans at all times.[12] We see these minds walking by. It's a classic symptom of Just Showing Up and its collective sources, described above.

Choosing how we Show Up can slow us down, grating against the fast current of our days. It encourages us to step out of life's Class 4 rapids. How common does that sound? Our brains haven't yet caught

its primacy. Once perceived, "processing" Situations moves them into our analytical left side. Later attention returns to our right-brained system as we realize implications across Situations, context, space, and time. Shifting back and forth, right-left-right, is our natural pattern. This is what's happening as we practice Showing Up. And it's what we're designed to do.

As Dr. McGilchrist explains in the documentary *The Divided Brain*, "Our right side reads body language, facial expressions, and implicit meaning. It engages with life, understands jokes, movement, story, and metaphor. It is the brain's true master."[9] It's the home of Monet, Beethoven, and experiencing life across larger systems. It tunes in to natural flow and implications across time. And it is where unity, harmony, acceptance, and sustained prosperity are produced.

Crucially, it's our predominant source of caring, satisfaction, and fulfillment. Our right brain hemisphere processes the interconnectedness inherent in the social roles in which we Show Up, as members of Situations and Society. I call this unifying social perception Alltelligence. It functions as a required counterbalance and companion to the left-brain driven, "target it, get it, and get it done," activities prominent in our daily lives.

Let's face it. Our nine-to-five is conducted according to schedule. This inclines our attention system toward efficiency. We innately simplify, decontextualize, and quantify. We desire, even fetishize data,[10] regardless of how it reduces people to statistics. These learned habits push us to perceive the world as a set of disconnected parts. Over time we start to feel emotionally distant, living more as severed Selves than as Alltelligent Societal members. Requirements for productivity and precision pull us away from "broader patterns of judgement, taste and discernment," as Rowson warns. After all, the quality and artistry of our humanness aren't well captured in analytics. Digits can't define, prototype, or promote passion.

Luckily, science and medicine are catching up. They're demonstrating how physical and psychological illness, elevated levels of stress, aggression, autism, loneliness, reduced empathy, and other issues stem, at

for an iPhone, but it fails to reassemble the magic of friendship, and it sure doesn't get the joke. In society today we succeed by reducing complexity, categorizing, modularizing, objectifying, and controlling. Fixity rules over flexibility and flow. How natural does that sound? And how kind?

Over the last hundred years, the creation of our transportation, education and health care systems, financial markets, management structures, urban grid-like layouts, and so much more has relied disproportionately on the narrowly focused, "grab and get it" attention system of our left hemisphere. Our efficient world has now molded our morning routines and family schedules. Much about our lives, jobs, priorities, how we see the world and interact is set up to succeed within, and in service of, these mostly transactional, left-brained systems.

But this perspective of the world sees parts, not wholes. It isolates us as individual actors. It divorces us from Society. And it lives in the map, not the territory.[8] Sadly, since the map is fixed and definitive, nothing is new. No wonder we feel flat and disengaged. In our world of explicit right and wrong, no consideration is needed. Our left attentional system sees only either/or. It cannot work with both/and. It sees black or white, when much of life, and its meaning, is a dynamically flowing shade of gray.

One example of the dominance of left-brained preference today is how we measure the health of our economy. We measure, report and make decisions based on GDP, gross domestic product. It's supposed to reflect how well the people of our fine nation are doing, including opportunities for work and wealth. But how well does America's output, the monetary value of goods and services we produce, measure the degree of meaning we feel in our lives? It doesn't understand, let alone honor, precious human competencies of the right hemisphere—tenderness, humor, and empathy. No wonder we're Just Showing Up.

Experiences rooted in the right hemisphere are core features of our humanness. They're foundational to how we're designed to Show Up. And they're the reason the model of Showing Up is structured the way it is. All new experiences start in our right hemisphere. This explains

To feed us, our left hemisphere has a narrow focus. It targets food, grabs and gets it, exactly what was needed to survive back in the savannah. It manipulates things. And it perceives Situations as trials to be acted upon. Surviving back then required exerting our power, controlling what we needed, and being sure of ourselves. We had to immediately categorize and simplify what we saw. Is that plant poisonous, medicinal or nutritious? Is that noise in the brush indicating danger? We simply had to know. There's no room for nuance. And no value of doubt.

Attending to the world this way cleaves it from its natural context. The broader Situation recedes as it necessarily aims tight attention at bits, not wholes. Within that slim world we perceive truth. All is explicit. What we know we know. And what we don't doesn't matter. We're always right, even in the face of irrefutable, contradictory evidence. When attending to the world this way, we can't take another's perspective. We connect with no one. Our logical, analytic Selves are alone.

Our sense of belonging, a cherished source of meaning and health, is offered by our brain's right hemisphere. It interprets context and safety. It is relational. It returns us back home, restoring our wholistic experience of the world. Instead of what's known, it attends to what's new. It senses the flow of time, how things transition, evolve and correspond. This is the world of the nuanced, the emotional, social, and meaningful. It's how we experience the interdependent realities in which we live. As such, it understands poetry, art, feels love and the rich, implicit aspects of life. In perceiving the big picture, it registers choice, including how we Show Up.

As Iain McGilchrist, a Scottish psychiatrist, explains, with the Industrial Revolution, we began a period significantly dominated by left brain thinking. Our world of economics, robotics, artificial intelligence, and efficient production favors explicit thinking, analysis, and code. We create models of the world to help us decide and dominate. We break things into parts to understand them, thinking their essence can be grasped as we reassemble them. This may be true

How Modernity Reinforces Just Showing Up— Low Alltelligence

Advancements of the industrial revolution have led us to live in a manner vastly different than the life we were designed for. Our nervous system, body, and brain are now responding to unnatural environments and to new threats. Like any product or process configured for one environment but deployed into a vastly different one, we're likely to experience problems. This is what we're feeling today.

Dr. Robert Sapolsky, evolutionary biologist at Stanford University, explains that our nervous system is structured for quick, extreme stressors—think lion in the savanna. Our stressors are supposed to Show Up and either kill us or give up. We're designed to strongly react, then resent. But we're dealing far more with pleasing bosses, being slim, and driving a car as nice as our neighbor's. These stresses simmer. They sit there with us all day, making them misfits for our biology. Our nervous system doesn't do well on simmer. Anxiety, diabetes, depression, heart disease, and many other illnesses are advanced from years of our system's misuse.

There has never been as great a distance between the life we were designed for and the one we're living. Most of us identify more with being "in nature" than "of nature." Dr. Jonathan Rowson, chess grandmaster and director of the Social Brain Centre at the Royal Society of Arts in London, states that "the implicit understanding that we're part of nature is no longer a default position." Together, our façade of separateness and overworked nervous systems trigger our natural threat response. This primes in-group, out-group bias, a core of discrimination, social injustice, and violence. It's clearly not a choice way to Show Up.

The two-part structure of our brain is another design aspect that worked well in our distant past but challenges us to Show Up as we choose today. The structure offers two attentional systems. Both are essential. And they're designed to work in complementary ways. One feeds us. The other helps us thrive. Flowing back and forth is the way to go.

Neuroscience Contributors to Just Showing Up

Pointing to our brains' biological processes, Nobel Laureate Daniel Kahneman and Amos Tversky tell us that our brains rely on a fast, intuitive mode of thinking. They call it System 1.[6] It applies assumptions and past lessons to what's happening right now. It detects people, patterns and Situations as familiar, quickly resurfacing our beliefs and feelings about them. We're recognizing (re-cognizing) what's already "known." It's been pre-categorized, labeled and judged. This makes System 1 quite handy. It simplifies life. Not only do we feel a sense of "knowingness," supplying confidence, we're also reassured our judgments are accurate, since they re-create much of what we experience, and conveniently omit much of what's new.

Our intuitive System 1 conferred survival benefit when we lived in the savannah. But it's so automatic that we don't recognize the seemingly real, re-presentation of what's happening from the "real thing." This makes it hard to be present now since we're at least partially living in virtual recreations of past experiences. While saving us precious time and mental effort, System 1 also makes it our default to Just Show Up.

Careful interpreting slows us down. It relies on what Kahneman and Tversky call System 2,[7] the effortful thinking that taxes our brain and creates fatigue. Such effort is a misfit for life's rapid flow. Our days run at a fast clip, favoring instinct and assumption. And our quick System 1 feels right, becoming—quite innocently—what we do and who we are most of the time.

Unfortunately, living in AssumptionWorld is hollow. It mixes our past and present far too equally. Perhaps you've noticed how predictable people, positions and patterns have become. This is what happens when we live more in a re-presentation of what is, projected by our expectations, than what truly is. In System 1 we can become imprisoned within patterns of sadness, anger, bias and judgment, many of which we'd be well served to break.

first time in human history…no matter how far away, we can witness and react to what's happening in active conflict zones or disaster scenes a world away." We're not designed for this. How can we not be overwhelmed, desensitized or numb? Moving from one thing to the next helps us cope. Pausing to reflect, to be in touch with ourselves, creates space for difficult feelings to arise. It starts to feel dangerous.

Our response is a deadly duo. We're coping by not reflecting and by dimming our emotional dial, both sources of Just Showing Up. But these coping behaviors feed a sense of separateness. Our social disconnection causes health issues so dire that Vivek Murthy, America's 19th and 21st Surgeon General, created "a national strategy to advance social connection."[5] Our grasping for solace has evolved into a dangerous culture of self-focus. It has become the water we drink. And it's been swelling for decades. Back in August of 1997 a new, trendy magazine called *Fast Company* came out with a flashy cover emblazoned with "The Brand Called You!" It describes, "Today, in the Age of the Individual, you have to be your own brand. Here's what it takes to be the CEO of Me Inc."

Now, over twenty years later, *Harvard Business Review* is still beating this drum. The cover of its May–June 2023 issue says, "Build Your Personal Brand: How to Communicate Your Value to The World." What's not great about this? Well, do you prefer people who care and cherish? Or compete and self-congratulate? Besides, who needs to feel healthy and whole? What if instead of brands, we worked to be human beings? Might we Show Up a bit more compassionately?

What's that, you feel compassion fatigue? It's not just you. Society is showing collective burnout. We're taught to anesthetize ourselves against unfettered, global spectacles of struggle and suffering streaming through our screens every moment. Many of us feel a secondhand or vicarious traumatization. It's for good reason. We care. We seek connectedness. And we strive to feel integrated into something bigger than ourselves. The struggle perpetuates our culture of Just Showing Up.

how modern society uses our brains' biological processes and structure. These powerful drivers of Just Showing Up have little to counteract them. But what if we had a simple model explaining how Showing Up naturally works? An "easy button" of sorts, presenting the parts and how they become our behavior? Would such a model help us? At a minimum, might it remind us we have a choice in how we Show Up? And in how our companies and the world Shows Up?

How did we get to this point? Let's take a look at a few of the evolutionary, cultural, and biological forces that have led us into today's Just-Show-Up world. I'll start with how we evolved and how it plays out today.

Does Human Nature Work against Us?

Evolution designed us for action. Back in the savannah, the lion ate the thinker but may have spared the runner. To survive we became better at doing than thinking. It's why we default to instinct and improv. Just Showing Up was naturally selected. "DefaultWorld" became "The World." Now it's in our dense schedules, activities, and even colloquial phrases. Why pause to ponder when we can hit the ground running? Today, living as Selves in Situations and Society—the components of Showing Up—does certainly occur, but the weight is far more on individualized Self than on Societal member. Our sense of membership in the tribe of humanity has been filtered to a trickle. Deep belonging exists as exception. It's wedged between meetings, outings, binge watching, and kid care. It's hard to stop and think—let alone feel one with others and nature—when our continuous partial attention is urgently making the most of fractured focus, deadlines, dates, and deliverables.

Cultural Contributors to Just Showing Up

Just Showing Up is an adaptive response to the constant flow of media sensationalism, violence, danger and disease threatening to drown our drive to care. In his book, *Attuned*, Dr. Thomas Hübl writes, "For the

occasions get solid forethought. So, what's the problem?

For starters, research for my last book, *On Your Game!*, showed that over 80 percent of us believe we're underachieving our potential. Hmmm. Might there be a link here? The key isn't whether we do or don't underachieve—it's the dissatisfaction Just Showing Up creates across our lives. It quarterbacks a huddle of related challenges, including loneliness,[1] disengagement, anxiety,[2] depression,[3] and reduced empathy.[4] Their emotional residue plays out as physical symptoms and behaviors in our business meetings, schools, supermarkets, and family dinners. Just Showing Up pilots our choices about the products we buy and food we ingest. It limits how deeply we know ourselves, connect with others, and prepare for what's next. Just Showing Up becomes our attitude and bedfellow. And it's rampant.

What we're identifying is that a good portion of our lives isn't getting the consideration it deserves. Over time, our vision for our life diverges from the life we're living. We start feeling unsettled. We're unhappy, edgy, stressed, and strained. Yet we passively accept our dissatisfaction amid the momentum of our days. It's a choice no one would consciously choose. And it's simply *not okay*. We want to feel satisfied, to be, to belong, and to become.

Why do so many of us feel dissatisfied? Years of interviews, surveys, and analysis illuminate an important aspect of this discontent and its surrounding challenges. It's obvious but subtle: we've accepted a norm of Just Showing Up. In doing so we're relinquishing results—too often—to luck and whim. Research shows a familiar pattern: we feel stressed or underprepared yet often do too little or nothing about it. We're leaving preferred performance and meaning behind. And we know it! But our culture reinforces an "I'm good to go" default state. We've normalized to it. "Just Showing Up is simply the way it is," I'm told. But this is an excuse. It placates feelings of ungroundedness, unreadiness, and disconnection. Yet for many of us, it's our daily breakfast on the go.

There are many contributors to our default state of Just Showing Up. Some are evolutionary. Some are cultural. Others are built into

CHAPTER 2
DEFAULTING THROUGH LIFE

This chapter leads you through the following ideas:
- Life as improv
- Why does it matter?
- Showing Up as Selves, and members of Situations and Society
- Disconnects everywhere...attuning reconnects us
- A few causes: cultural, biological, neurological
- Life as universal Show-Up network

HOW WE'RE SHOWING UP

What if a solution to our stress and unhappiness was lurking in plain sight but too nuanced to be clear—until someone points it out? Simply put, daily life pushes us to Just Show Up. Here's how it plays out.

"I check my look, the time, weather, and I head on out!" Anthony tells me. And did he ever! As you'll read in Chapter 9, Anthony didn't choose how he Showed Up. It's a bit surprising for a first date, I agree. As you can guess, he hasn't seen me since.

What's so bad about this? In Anthony's defense, much of life is made up on the go. We chat, do, and decide. It's life's natural flow, often impromptu, unplanned, and unrehearsed. Viewing it this way, we're living a Just-Show-Up party. Sure, important meetings and formal

Showing Up isn't a peripheral feature of our operating system.

It's our defining characteristic.

Let us fortify

and profit from it.

LIFE TODAY AND A BETTER WAY

2   DEFAULTING THROUGH LIFE

3   THE MODEL OF HOW WE SHOW UP

4   HOW GROUNDING, READINESS, AND ALLTELLIGENCE BECOME "SHOWING UP"

PART 1

be hard to accept limitations and boundaries. It is my wish that one day we all are supported in Showing Up as we choose.

> **Finally, this is not simply individuals tuning our Show-Up dials toward choice. As more of us practice Showing Up, we shift social norms of behavior, acceptance, and justice. We shift media, music, fashion, and fame. We shift business strategies and incentive plans. We make interactions with our Selves and each other healthier. Showing Up becomes a movement and a way of life. We all must act to achieve this worthy goal.**

Real-world examples and the "how to" are integrated throughout. This way you can see it in action and start practicing Showing Up right away. Experiment with what works for you. Since Showing Up is a growth process, this test-and-learn approach is the way to go.

NEW WORDS

Languages, like all living systems, Show Up. They also sometimes need to catch up. They are designed by the past yet shape—and bound and expand—our thinking and behavior today. Some new concepts I describe are well served by stretching existing words or by introducing new ones. I do this to be clear and to break free from explicit confines of today's language that limit thinking, mislead, and even harm us. Alltelligence™, living with intentful interconnectedness with others and Society, is one example. It is described in detail in Chapter 11.

WHY ORANGE AND GREEN?

Orange indicates our common behavior of "Just Showing Up." It's the midpoint of the circle on the cover, and our typical way of being. Green represents our preferred behavior, when we choose more consciously how we're Showing Up, creating a happier, higher achieving life and Society. This book explains what this choice is, and how we make it.

REFLECTING

Each chapter ends with a set of questions designed to help us excel in the fine art of Showing Up. Taking time to answer these questions is practicing these competencies. I highly recommend it.

INCLUDING ALL OF US

We all can Show Up more as we choose. All of us. That said, I recognize many of us face disproportionate hurdles beyond our control. It can

HOW I SHOWED UP

Like so many of us, my personal Show-Up story is one of inner wiring working against me. My nervous system isn't calm. It paces, like an intensity dial set to HIGH. "You're trying too hard," I'm told, all the while captivated by people who flow with ease, as I'm so challenged to do.

Multiple times a day I notice my behavior, choose to Show Up poised and thoughtful. But then something grips me. I wind up not interacting as I choose. It's hard to stay aware of our behavior and be in the Situation simultaneously. This skill of dual awareness is one I actively track. It indicates meaningful growth. But how do we rewire our natural state?

A childhood of desperately fighting against locked vocal cords—I stuttered—molded me into a perpetual state of over-alertness and over-exertion. Brows endlessly raised, I needed to brilliantly contribute to prove my worthiness, to no avail. I labored daily to feel a solid sense of self, ready for the moment and open to connecting with people.

Years of mellowing, meditating, and finally distilling and testing the simple model of how we Show Up gave me better tools. These are the tools, with years of refining and testing, that I'm laying out for you. I hope my research and this book will help you in your worthy and perpetual endeavor to Show Up as you choose.

HOW THIS BOOK SHOWS UP

The ideas are organized in four parts:

PART I—LIFE TODAY AND A BETTER WAY

PART II—THE MODEL OF HOW WE SHOW UP

PART III—A DEEPER DIVE INTO THE THREE SHOW-UP ROLES AND SKILLS

PART IV—MAKING IT EASIER TO SHOW UP AS WE CHOOSE

3. **We Need a Roadmap:** Then, at age twelve, at a rehabilitation hospital where I spent my summer, supposedly learning to speak, I witnessed elders struggling to Show Up as they chose. Given their advanced age, I assumed they had wisdom and experience supporting their efforts to relearn to walk and feed themselves. Yet, even with solid effort and caring helpers moving them through customized plans, they still couldn't Show Up as they chose. "Why is it so hard?" I asked myself. Even eighty years into our lives, our roadmaps for achieving are insufficient. How to Show Up as we choose—across Situations and life stages—remains unclear. It stayed with me.

These seminal experiences taught me three things:

1. Our lives have purpose.
2. Many who can choose how they Show Up, don't.
3. There's no instruction book or framework that helps us Show Up as we choose. We need a flexible, comprehensive model, yet we don't even have a definition. What does it mean to truly Show Up?

Today, forty years after these experiences, my life has been defined—and designed—by them. I started devouring psychology at age twelve and led my first global study of personal effectiveness, with over ten thousand participants, in my late twenties. What prevents us from behaving as we choose has remained remarkably consistent.

The data exposes a simple three-part model that has always been with us but has yet to be documented. Once known, it becomes an intuitive and powerful toolkit helping us live more integrated lives, ones that dissipate our loneliness, separateness, biases, and discriminations. We'll lead lives that bring us together, helping us and our Society be happier, healthier, and more sustainable.

> **is to use this insight to create a happier, healthier, kinder, more just, and higher-performing world.**

WHY I AM WRITING THIS BOOK

When people ask, "Marcy, what led you to study Showing Up?," I explain, "I saw many people struggling to be who they wanted to be. Some seemed not to recognize they have a choice in how they Show Up. Others knew their goal but not how to get there." I realized we need a simple roadmap to help us. We need to see the basic structure of how people and Society are designed to thrive. Then we can guide our Selves and systems toward happiness or at least satisfaction. Three moments in my childhood showed me parts of this roadmap. Now I'm consistently told, "Marcy, knowing what it means to Show Up has changed my life." Here's where it started.

1. **Our Lives Have Purpose:** At age eight I was on "driveway duty," meaning I shoveled the snow so Mom, a pediatrician, could race to the hospital in the middle of the night when an emergency call came. One night I was suddenly woken. It must have been 3 a.m. "I have to go in," Mom said and rushed out of my room. I shoveled that dark snow as if my life depended on it, with the family of the baby who needed help firmly in mind. "I matter," my mind told me. That deep sense of purpose stayed with me.

2. **We Can Choose How We Behave:** It was in the four-square line on the blacktop behind my third-grade class. I had been stuttering for two years already, unable to Show Up as I chose. Yet I saw the same kids Showing Up either as bully dominators in the A square, slamming the ball at people, or as victim scaredy-cats waiting to be slammed out. They all have a choice, I thought, but they're throwing it away. How could they, when here I am, unable to Show Up as I choose? I was angry and confused. It stayed with me.

most? What distribution across them aligns with our success? And how do we naturally equalize them?

My twenty years of research codified what most of us innately know. Most of us "Just Show Up" most of the time. I'm using the phrase "Just Show Up" to describe how we live on the go, often reacting more than reflecting, preparing, or connecting. We're winging it too often, not quite grasping the success, closeness, and meaning we seek. Marcus, a busy realtor in Westchester, New York, puts it this way: "Marcy, each morning I'm just happy to get the kids and myself out of the house on time. If I have half my wits about me at 10 a.m., I consider it a success." But is it?

The state of the world's physical health, mental health, grasping for mindfulness and peace, tells us something big is amiss. We've taken a wrong turn somewhere, living more inertia than agency, more momentum than meaning. I think how we're choosing to Show Up has a lot to do with it. In short, we're not choosing—we're Just Showing Up. And we're doing it far too often, prompting our dreams to escape and our contentment to wander.

> **Decades of research have surfaced a model of how we're naturally designed to Show Up. Once we're aware of it, we immediately shift how we interact. I lay it out and explain how our native roles and their corresponding skills come together to create our reality. The model shows the building blocks of our culture and systems. It explains how our family, friends, companies, economies, innovations, systems of education and social justice, voting patterns, and governments Show Up. And it offers a practical path to improve them.**
>
> **Knowing the model makes it easier to not only choose our behavior, but to implement it. The goal**

your couch and going where you're supposed to be." And "Showing Up is walking into a room." I get a kick out of those last two. They keep expectations low. No "presence," "engaging," or "best" needed. Just get off your couch and walk in. Is that really all we're responsible for?

None of these answers are explicitly wrong. But they're woefully incomplete…perhaps gravely so. **A more precise, conclusive and wholistic understanding of what it means to Show Up is critically needed. One that connects us, that draws upon our instincts to care and to serve. One that uses the two attentional systems of our brain more equally and collaboratively, as they were intended. One that steers our political, economic, and business systems toward good.**

> There is such a model. One rooted in our evolutionary self, situated in nature, belonging to a tribe. Like back then, we are today Selves in Situations, belonging to Society. These three roles are inescapable. They're ever present. And they placed humans, even then, at some level of Grounding in themselves, Readiness for Situations and Connectedness with nature and the broader world. It remains this way today—although we don't often live as if it does.

Also now as then, we're choosing how we Show Up each moment. Sometimes we choose consciously. Sometimes not. Knowing we're exerting choice as we enter a room, family dinner, sporting event, or company meeting—gifts us the ability to intentionally Show Up. It grants agency, power, and fulfillment. These are things we all seek. And they are more likely to remain fleeting until we put into practice the truth about Showing Up. Which of our roles, individualized Selves, members of Situations or members of Society, are guiding our behavior

CHAPTER 1
HOW WE'RE SHOWING UP

THIS BOOK IS ABOUT a choice we all have but don't often make.

It's a choice so valuable our lives and legacies depend on it.

What am I describing?

How we choose to Show Up.

...Or whether we're choosing at all.

We're living in unprecedented times of anxiety, loneliness, disconnection, and depression. They're causing epidemic levels of apathy, substance abuse, and searching for solace. These troubles are telling us something big is going wrong. There's urgency to cut through the crises and understand. Why are we Showing Up this way?

I've asked thousands of people these and related questions. What does Showing Up mean to you? Perhaps more importantly, what would the impact be if you had a more scientific and complete understanding of how it works?

"Showing Up is presence," some say. "It's actively engaging." "It's doing your best." Others set a lower bar. "Showing Up is getting off

"I don't think anybody thinks about how they're Showing Up.

When I have something to put in front of the Board of Directors, do I think about it? Of course.

On a day-to-day basis? No. Who does?"

Joe Pastore, former HR executive, Nestlé and Gerber Foods

Showing Up serves as a roadmap for fulfilling lives,

a connected, prospering Society,

and a sustainable planet.

Showing Up unites us as humans, transcending race, ethnicity, education, ability, social strata, gender identity— categories too often used to divide us.

PART III
A DEEPER DIVE INTO THE THREE SHOW-UP ROLES AND SKILLS

9. SELF-GROUNDING 179
10. SITUATIONAL READINESS 219
11. SOCIETAL ALLTELLIGENCE 259

PART IV
MAKING IT EASIER TO SHOW UP AS WE CHOOSE

12. SO...HOW DO WE LIVE A SHOW-UP LIFE? AND...A CALL TO ACTION 291

ACKNOWLEDGMENTS 321
ABOUT THE AUTHOR 323
ENDNOTES 325

CONTENTS

1. HOW WE'RE SHOWING UP 1

PART I
LIFE TODAY AND A BETTER WAY

2. DEFAULTING THROUGH LIFE 13
3. THE MODEL OF HOW WE SHOW UP 37
4. HOW GROUNDING, READINESS, AND ALLTELLIGENCE BECOME "SHOWING UP" 75

PART II
THE MODEL OF HOW WE SHOW UP

5. THE SHOW-UP CONTINUUM 95
6. LEVEL 2: JUST SHOWING UP 117
7. LEVEL 1: BARELY THERE 137
8. LEVEL 3: TRULY SHOWING UP 157

Showing Up is a big idea.

It asserts that:
There's a natural model for
how humans are designed to Show Up,

and that we choose our
behavior each moment,

making us responsible for our impacts
on each other and the world.

How We Choose to Show Up

Nature's Playbook for Creating a Meaningful Life and the World We Want

Marcy Axelrod

To everyone on the planet working to truly Show Up each moment—we're all doing the best we can with who we are right now.

And to:

- My parents, Judie and Bill, who modeled Showing Up intentfully for our Selves, our Situations, and Society every day.
- To my daughters, Zoe and Victoria, who will infuse their own calling into the world.

How We Choose to Show Up: Nature's Playbook for Creating a Meaningful Life and the World We Want

©2024 Marcy Axelrod. All Rights Reserved. No part of this publication may be reproduced, stored in a retrieval system or transmitted in any form by any means electronic, mechanical, or photocopying, recording or otherwise without the permission of the author.

ISBN-13: 978-1-63755-429-6

Printed in the United States

"This book is an essential guide to making the best decisions possible from moment to moment. An exploration into what makes us tick, this is an eye-opening must-read that will transform your life from a defensive standstill to an offensive power play."

Paul Epstein, former NFL and NBA executive, award-winning speaker, and bestselling author of *Better Decisions Faster* and *The Power of Playing Offense*

"Marcy has written the ultimate blueprint for what it means to Show Up well for our Selves, Situations, and Society. This must-read book is a guide to making the world a kinder, healthier, and more peaceful place."

Urs Koenig, UN Peacekeeper and author of *Radical Humility: Be a Badass Leader AND a Good Human*

"Marcy Axelrod shows that too often we don't think about how we 'choose to Show Up,' and that we can lead better lives if we are better prepared. She introduces three stages of Showing Up and discusses how we move between them. Her concepts are valuable. This is an important book."

Cheryl Einhorn, adjunct professor, Cornell, and author of *Problem Solver, Maximizing Your Strengths to Make Better Decisions,* among others

"I had to yield to this 'force field' of positive energy, because it was speaking directly to me. It was whispering in my ear—no, it was shouting to my heart—'*you cannot walk away from this.*'"

Kristin Clark Taylor, author, editor, journalist, and former White House communications strategist

"The way each of us Shows Up becomes our reputation and creates the culture that we all want (or don't want!) for our organizations. In *How We Choose to Show Up*, Marcy doesn't just expand on theories—she actually outlines how we can all Show Up with intent. An insightful read!"

Marc Brackett, PhD, director, Yale Center for Emotional Intelligence

"*How We Choose to Show Up* includes the wisdom we need to break the burnout cycle, start living human-to-human, and foster the healthy society we crave. In a culture that all too often prioritizes the singular over the collective, Marcy deftly charts a path to living a high-achieving, balanced, harmonious life that's in service of the greater good."

Josh Linkner, five-time tech entrepreneur, *New York Times* bestselling author, and venture capitalist

How We Choose to Show Up

"You and I have a choice every day about how we make our mark on the world. Marcy Axelrod is making it easier. Using her expertise in neuroscience, she reveals the roadmap you need to live a purpose-driven life."

Mel Robbins, bestselling author and host of the award-winning *Mel Robbins Podcast*

"A landmark book! With Showing Up, Marcy crafts a blueprint and vehicle for fulfillment. It's a narrative spark launching us toward a more grounded, connected, healthy way of living. This must-read book distills mainspring ideas that carry us long after we've turned the last page."

Dan Haar, senior editor and columnist, Hearst Media

"This book is about life. In *How We Choose to Show Up*, Marcy describes a straightforward yet effective mindset that helps you get the most out of each day. It is well worth learning from an expert."

H. William Strauss, professor emeritus: Harvard, Cornell, and Stanford medical schools

Printed in Great Britain
by Amazon